Imperial Cities in the Tsarist, the Habsburg, and the Ottoman Empires

This book explores the various ways imperial rule constituted and shaped the cities of Eastern Europe until World War I in the Tsarist, Habsburg, and Ottoman Empires.

In these three empires, the cities served as hubs of imperial rule: their institutions and infrastructures enabled the diffusion of power within the empires while they also served as the stages where the empire was displayed in monumental architecture and public rituals. To this day, many cities possess a distinctively imperial legacy in the form of material remnants, groups of inhabitants, or memories that shape the perceptions of in- and outsiders. The contributions to this volume address in detail the imperial entanglements of a dozen cities from a long-term perspective reaching back to the eighteenth century. They analyze the imperial capitals as well as smaller cities in the periphery. All of them are "imperial cities" in the sense that they possess traces of imperial rule. By comparing the three empires of Eastern Europe this volume seeks to establish commonalities in this particular geography and highlight trans-imperial exchanges and entanglements.

This volume is essential reading to students and scholars alike interested in imperial and colonial history, urban history, and European history.

Ulrich Hofmeister is a historian at the Ludwig Maximilian University of Munich, where he leads a research project on Russian city planning during the eighteenth century. His research interests include the imperial history of the Russian Empire and the Soviet Union as well as Russian urban history. He has published a monograph on Russian notions of an imperial civilizing mission in Central Asia (*Die Bürde des Weißen Zaren,* 2019).

Florian Riedler is the scientific coordinator of the research network Transottomanica at the University of Leipzig, Germany. His research interests include Ottoman urban history, migration and mobility studies, and the history of infrastructure in the Ottoman Balkans. Among his latest publications is the co-edited volume *The Balkan Route: Historical Transformations from Via Militaris to Autoput,* 2021.

Routledge Advances in Urban History

Series Editors: Bert De Munck (Centre for Urban History, University of Antwerp) and Simon Gunn (Centre for Urban History, University of Leicester)

This series showcases original and exciting new work in urban history. It publishes books that challenge existing assumptions about the history of cities, apply new theoretical frames to the urban past, and open up new avenues of historical enquiry. The scope of the series is global, and it covers all time periods from the ancient to the modern worlds.

For more information about this series, please visit: https://www.routledge.com/Routledge-Advances-in-Urban-History/book-series/RAUH

Imperial Cities in the Tsarist, the Habsburg, and the Ottoman Empires

Edited by
Ulrich Hofmeister and Florian Riedler

Routledge
Taylor & Francis Group
NEW YORK AND LONDON

First published 2024
by Routledge
605 Third Avenue, New York, NY 10158

and by Routledge
4 Park Square, Milton Park, Abingdon, Oxon, OX14 4RN

Routledge is an imprint of the Taylor & Francis Group, an informa business

© 2024 selection and editorial matter, Ulrich Hofmeister and Florian Riedler; individual chapters, the contributors

The right of Ulrich Hofmeister and Florian Riedler to be identified as the authors of the editorial material, and of the authors for their individual chapters, has been asserted in accordance with sections 77 and 78 of the Copyright, Designs and Patents Act 1988.

The Open Access version of this book, available at www.taylorfrancis.com, has been made available under a Creative Commons Attribution-Non Commercial-No Derivatives (CC-BY-NC-ND) 4.0 license.

Funded by Konsortium der sächsischen Hochschulbibliotheken.

We acknowledge support for the Open Access publication by the Saxon State Digitization Program for Science and Culture.

Trademark notice: Product or corporate names may be trademarks or registered trademarks, and are used only for identification and explanation without intent to infringe.

ISBN: 978-0-367-65544-0 (hbk)
ISBN: 978-0-367-65547-1 (pbk)
ISBN: 978-1-003-13003-1 (ebk)

DOI: 10.4324/9781003130031

Typeset in Sabon
by codeMantra

Contents

Figures and Maps

Figures

Maps

Contributors

Michel Abesser is a Lecturer for Russian Studies at the University of Freiburg, Germany. He studied the history of Eastern Europe and sociology at the University of Jena and the European University at St. Petersburg. His dissertation explored cultural change and the economics of Soviet culture after 1953 through the lens of jazz and was published in 2018. He is currently working on a book project on Russian, Cossack, and Armenian economic entanglement in the lower Don region in late Imperial Russia.

Robert Born is a Research Fellow at the Federal Institute for Culture and History of the Germans in Eastern Europe (BKGE) in Oldenburg, Germany. He studied art history, classical archaeology, and the history of Eastern Europe in Basel and Berlin. His research activities focus on the cultural exchange between the Ottoman Empire and East Central Europe in the Early Modern Period, Baroque art and architecture in East Central Europe, and the historiography of art in this region.

Elisabeth Haid-Lener studied history and Russian language in Vienna. She was a fellow in a doctoral program and research assistant at the University of Vienna. Her dissertation on Galicia as a subject of Austrian and Russian propaganda in World War I was published in 2019. Currently she is a post-doc researcher in an ERC project at the Institute of Political History in Budapest, Hungary, on post-World War I transitions.

Elke Hartmann is the Director of the Institute for Ottoman Studies and Turcology at Freie Universität Berlin, Germany. She obtained a PhD at FU Berlin for her book *Die Reichweite des Staates. Wehrpflicht und moderne Staatlichkeit im Osmanischen Reich 1869–1910*, which was published in 2016, and her habilitation at Péter Pázmány Catholic University Budapest for her studies on Armenian life and autobiographical writing in the Ottoman Empire. Her research areas focus on modern Ottoman history, especially on the military, political, administrative, social, ideological, and cultural transformations during modernization processes, contextualizing micro-historical case studies in a global context.

Ulrich Hofmeister is a historian at the Ludwig Maximilian University of Munich, where he leads a research project on Russian city planning during the eighteenth century. He holds a doctoral degree from the University of Vienna, Austria, in history. His research interests include the imperial history of the Russian Empire and the Soviet Union as well as Russian urban history. He has published a monograph on Russian notions of an imperial civilizing mission in Central Asia (*Die Bürde des Weißen Zaren,* Stuttgart: Steiner, 2019).

Aida Murtić is an architect and doctoral candidate in art history at Heidelberg University, Germany. She is a member of the Heidelberg Centre for Transcultural Studies (earlier Cluster of Excellence "Asia and Europe in a Global Context"). She was a doctoral fellow at the Leibniz Institute of European History in Mainz. Her research interests include history of architecture, planning history, and heritage studies with a special focus on Southeastern Europe.

Gulchachak Nugmanova is an architect and leading researcher at the Scientific Research Institute of Theory and History of Architecture and Urban Planning, Moscow, Russia. In 2000, she defended her dissertation "The Tatar Estate in Kazan' From the Middle of the Nineteenth to the Beginning of the Twentieth Century" at the State Institute for Art Studies, Moscow. She is a specialist in nineteenth-century Russian provincial architecture focusing on the Middle Volga region. Her current research centers on architecture and imperial power in the relation between imperial center and provincial society in nineteenth-century Russia.

Julia Obertreis holds the chair of Modern and East European History at the University of Erlangen-Nuremberg, Germany. Her research interests include the imperial history of Russia and the Soviet Union, urban history, environmental history, oral history, and the relation between global history and East European history. Her dissertation on housing and everyday life in Petrograd/Leningrad in the 1920s and 1930s was published in German in 2004. The habilitation thesis, *Imperial Desert Dreams: Cotton Growing and Irrigation in Central Asia, 1860–1991,* was published in 2017.

Nilay Özlü is an Associate Professor of Architectural and Cultural History at Istanbul Technical University, Turkey. Her research focuses on late Ottoman architecture and urban landscapes, court studies, and museum studies. Özlü was the Barakat postdoctoral fellow at the University of

Oxford (2019–2020) and the Chevening visiting fellow at the Oxford Centre for Islamic Studies (2021). She co-edited *The City in the Muslim World* (Routledge, 2015) and *Spectacle, Entertainment, and Recreation* (Intellect, 2023), and her research and publications have received awards from the Society of Architectural Historians, Barakat Trust, University of Oxford, Getty Foundation, and Istanbul Research Institute.

Florian Riedler studied history and obtained a PhD from SOAS, London, for a thesis on Ottoman political history. He was a research fellow at the German Orient Institute in Istanbul and at ZMO in Berlin. Currently, he is the scientific coordinator of the research network Transottomanica at the University of Leipzig, Germany. His research interests include Ottoman urban history, migration and mobility studies, and the history of infrastructure in the Ottoman Balkans. Among his latest publications is the co-edited volume *The Balkan Route: Historical Transformations from Via Militaris to Autoput* (2021).

Olga Zabalueva holds an MA in Museology from the Russian State University for the Humanities, Moscow, and an MA in Cultural Analysis from Lund University, Sweden. As a museum professional, she has worked in different cultural institutions in Russia and in Sweden at research and collection departments. Olga is currently doing her PhD in Culture and Society (Tema Q) at Linköping University, Sweden. Her research focuses on cultural policies and cultural memories in Russian and Swedish contexts, with special emphasis on the institutionalization of contested memories and "difficult heritage" in different political regimes.

Acknowledgments

Figure 0.1 Eszter Gantner (1971–2019). Photo by Michel Abesser, 2018.

This book is dedicated to the memory of Eszter Gantner. Her life was cut short by illness long before this book was finished, but without her, work for this volume would have never started at all. The Imperial Cities project began as a collective endeavor of Eszter and me, and her share in this project is immense. Eszter was an urban historian with a focus on East Central Europe. Her innovative and very diverse research covered questions of Jewish history, intellectual history, urban anthropology, and much more. When we were invited to jointly organize a conference on the three Eastern European empires at the German Historical Institute in Moscow, we quickly agreed that it should be dedicated to the relationship between urban and imperial structures. It was our common idea to subsume this research under the label of the Imperial City, and from the very beginning we planned to publish the outcome of the conference as an edited volume. We developed the framework of the book together, discussed different topical approaches and suitable cities, and selected conference participants and other potential authors. While outlining the structure and the content of the book, however, we did not pay enough attention to the bureaucratic necessities of such a project. It was only after Eszter passed away that I learned that without a signed contract with the publisher, Eszter cannot be officially named among the editors of the volume. But even without formal acknowledgment we would like to emphasize: Eszter is a co-author of the Imperial Cities concept, and this book is also hers. It is inexpressibly sad that she cannot see this volume finished. My colleague and friend Florian Riedler stepped in as co-editor after Eszter passed away, and we finalized this book together. It is our hope that Eszter would have also been satisfied with this volume.

* * *

From the first plans to organize a conference until the last steps of the editing process, the editors have received the assistance of many helping hands. Support for funding and organizing the conference and for publishing the volume was provided by the German Historical Institute in Moscow, the German Association for East European Studies, the Association of Historians of Eastern Europe, the Herder Institute for Historical Research on East Central Europe, the Department of Eastern European History of the University of Vienna, and the Department of History of the LMU Munich.

For their help in organizing the conference and in preparing the volume and for their contributions to our discussions, the editors are deeply grateful to Christoph Augustynowicz, Elena Bragina, Peter Clayson, Sandra Dahlke, Edhem Eldem, Gabriele Freitag, Ilya Gerasimov, Kerstin S. Jobst, Birte Kohtz, Max Novick, Julia Obertreis, Heidemarie Uhl, and Jeremy F. Walton.

As the starting point for her chapter on Kars, Elke Hartman took a text she had initially written in German for a collective volume on Russian cities in Asia, which is being edited by Helena Holzberger, Andreas Renner, and Sören Urbansky. We are obliged to the editors of that book for the permission to include in our volume a chapter which is based on a text for their book. We are looking forward to that volume, which will contribute to the relationship between cities and empires from a different angle.

It was a long journey from the planning of the conference to the publishing of this volume, but our authors stayed the course. We therefore want to express our gratitude to them for their readiness to review their chapters time after time, for their patience, and for their ongoing commitment to this project. We hope that this book will further stoke the discussion on the relationship between cities and empires.

On behalf of the editors
Ulrich Hofmeister

1 Introduction

Ulrich Hofmeister and Florian Riedler

As in all empires, imperial rule also constituted and shaped the cities of the three empires that dominated Eastern Europe until the First World War – the Tsarist, Habsburg, and Ottoman Empires. Cities served as hubs of imperial rule: their institutions and infrastructures enabled the diffusion of power within the empires while they also served as the stages where the empire was displayed in monumental architecture and public rituals. To this day, many cities possess a distinctively imperial legacy in the form of material remnants, groups of inhabitants, or memories that shape the perceptions of in- and outsiders.

This book explores the various ways imperial rule manifested itself in cities and how cities shaped the three empires under consideration. The contributions to this volume address in detail the imperial entanglements of eleven cities from a long-term perspective reaching back to the eighteenth century. The focus is not only on the imperial capitals but also on smaller cities in the periphery that had important functions as trade or border cities (Map 1.1). We call all of these cities "imperial cities," but it is important to note that we do not postulate the imperial city as a new city type. Rather, we understand the term as a research perspective that can be applied to all cities within an empire where traces of imperial rule can be found. While there is probably a general relationship between political power and cities, by comparing the three empires of Eastern Europe this volume seeks to establish commonalities in this particular geography and highlight transimperial exchanges and entanglements.

The first chapter of this volume, "Cities, Empires, and Eastern Europe: Imperial Cities in the Tsarist, the Habsburg, and the Ottoman Empires" by Ulrich Hofmeister, explains the conceptual framework of the volume in greater detail. After addressing the history of the term "imperial city," which was never employed in a consistent manner, it proposes a new usage for this expression. In the framework of postcolonial research focusing on colonial overseas empires, the term "imperial city" has been employed to highlight transfers and influences from the colonies back to urban Europe,

DOI: 10.4324/9781003130031-1

Map 1.1 The three Eastern European empires in 1815 with the cities portrayed in
this volume. For the sake of simplicity, the modern city names have been
used. Cartography by Florian Riedler, 2022.

which have long been methodologically sidelined by a focus on colonial
cities. However, the author questions the sharp distinction between colonial and imperial cities by identifying many cases in which these categories
overlapped or shared common characteristics. This overlap is even more
apparent in the case of continental empires, where geographical boundaries between center and periphery were harder to draw and where the legal distinction of homeland and colony in many cases did not exist. As
a consequence, the author proposes using "imperial city" as an encompassing term for examining cities in the center as well as the borderlands
of the Habsburg, Tsarist, and Ottoman Empires, whose urban development increasingly converged from the eighteenth century onward. Cities
in all three empires had structural similarities such as population groups
who traditionally brokered contact with the imperial center; they had to
position themselves vis-à-vis Western European urban modernity, and,
in the nineteenth century, they had to answer to the challenges of rising

nationalism. Used as an umbrella term for cities both in the imperial core regions and the peripheries, the concept of "imperial city" offers a vantage point from which to determine the role of a given city for an empire and, at the same time, examine the presence of the empire in that city in an attempt to bring imperial and urban history together.

The second part of the book, "Manifestations of the Imperial in Urban Space," offers different examples of how empires were present in cities ranging from palaces and churches to settlement patterns and urban infrastructures. The section starts with the chapter by Nilay Özlü, "The Imperial Palaces in Comparative Perspective: Topkapı, Kremlin, and Hofburg." The author examines the ideological messages that were encapsulated in the palaces in the (former) capitals of Istanbul, Moscow, and Vienna and how these messages changed during the nineteenth century. All three palaces formed the symbolic centers of the respective imperial capitals and therefore played a key role in processions, accession festivities, etc. Particularly the dynasties' collections that were housed in palace armories and treasuries became important places to display imperial power, first to aristocratic circles and later to the public at large. Often these collections were given to museums, or the palaces themselves were musealized, a process that started in the Habsburg Empire in the eighteenth century and continued in Russia. Finally, in the second half of the nineteenth century, the Ottomans, directly influenced by the other courts, began to show their collections, but only to foreign visitors. Only after 1908 was the Ottoman public allowed to visit Topkapı Palace in Istanbul. Overall, the chapter demonstrates how the three traditional palaces became sites of transition and modernization in a period when the power of all three dynasties was at stake. This process was particularly visible in the shared goal of popularizing the dynasties by opening the palaces and repurposing them as museums.

The next chapter by Robert Born, "Temeswar as an Imperial City in the First Half of the Eighteenth Century," focuses on the reorganization of the city by the Habsburg Monarchy after the conquest from the Ottomans. This reorganization began immediately after 1716 when Temeswar and the province it belonged to were awarded a special status and were ruled directly by Vienna (and not as part of Hungary to which it was added only in 1778). Thus the city was rebuilt according to a plan that mainly reflected the military, fiscal, and representational considerations of the center and the dynasty. This was also expressed in a richly illustrated publication praising the contributions and construction activities of the Habsburg rulers, in particular Charles VI. Among the first measures, a number of new churches run by Jesuit and Franciscan missionaries were built and furnished to support Catholic settlers in the city. Another urgent task was the construction of new fortifications and barracks, which both also had representative functions through inscriptions and the naming of gates and bastions after members of the dynasty. Hydraulic works such as the redirection of rivers and the digging of canals, as well as the development of the province's transport infrastructure, served military, and economic purposes. In the city itself, utilities such as street lighting, pavement, and water fountains were installed. The Habsburg dynasty's influence on the urban development of Temeswar was felt most strongly in the religious field through the promotion of Catholicism in the otherwise multi-ethnic and multi-confessional city. The ruling family sponsored the first public monument and a church dedicated to St. John of Nepomuk, who was the family's patron saint. At the same time, Emperor Charles VI acted as the patron of the Catholic cathedral that was, however, not completed until well into the second half of the century, long after the emperor's death. Two votive columns on the city's main squares completed the sacralization of urban space in the name of the dynasty.

Gulchachak Nugmanova's chapter, "Imperial Power, Imperial Identity, and Kazan Architecture: Visualizing the Empire in a Nineteenth-Century Russian Province," examines the creation and evolution of imperial architecture from the eighteenth to the nineteenth century. It focuses on the transformation of the provincial city of Kazan, the important Tatar city conquered by Russia in the mid-sixteenth century. The author analyzes the construction and renovation of several prominent buildings during the nineteenth century. She shows that in Kazan the neoclassical style, which was perceived as the embodiment of imperial rule, was replaced by the so-called "Russian style" much later than in most other cities of the Tsarist Empire. This can be explained by the significance of the conquest of Kazan for Russia's identity as an empire, which is also underlined by a range of mutual interactions between prominent buildings in Kazan and the capitals of St. Petersburg and Moscow. The chapter thus shows not only the impact of architectural models of the center on cities in the province but also the significance of Kazan for Russia's self-representation as an empire. Moreover, the chapter analyzes controversies about the appearance of non-Christian prayer houses during the late nineteenth and the early twentieth centuries. In these debates, Russia's claims as a protector of the Orthodox faith collided with the need to accommodate the needs of minority confessions. In conclusion, Kazan can be understood as an example of an imperial project of internal colonization with a feedback loop between center and periphery.

Michel Abesser's chapter, "Bound by Difference: The Merger of Rostov and Nakhichevan-on-Don into an Imperial Metropolis during the Nineteenth Century," offers the case study of twin cities that embody some typical features of a Russian imperial city in the periphery. Nakhichevan was founded by the empire in the late eighteenth century to settle Armenian traders and craftsmen from Crimea and soon established itself as an important trading hub. In direct proximity, and drawing on Nakhichevan's resources, the town of Rostov grew in a rather uncontrolled process from a small fortress to an important commercial center, which overshadowed its neighbor in the second half of the nineteenth century. The success of Rostov was built on the close cooperation of trade networks from both cities in the booming Black Sea region. The chapter examines the conflicts over land, cooperation over infrastructure development, and the gradual merger of both cities into one metropolis in the late nineteenth century. In contrast to many other case studies in this volume, the key factors that expressed the imperial character of the two cities were ethnic diversity and migration rather than imperial representation.

The third part of the book, "The City as a Palimpsest of Empires," focuses on case studies of cities whose imperial character was defined by more than one empire. Florian Riedler's chapter, "Guarding the Imperial Border: The Fortress City of Niš between the Habsburgs and the Ottomans, 1690–1740," examines how the geopolitical competition between two empires that resulted in the formation of a new border at the end of the seventeenth century fundamentally changed a city. At the center of attention is the fortress that was designed by the Habsburgs when they conquered Niš for a short time in 1690 and that was kept by the Ottomans when they repossessed the city. In the restoration that the Ottomans initiated in the 1720s, the fortress became the prime location to represent the empire architecturally in a number of ornamented gates. In addition, the frequent wars between the imperial contenders also affected Ottoman urban governance of the multi-ethnic city that had a large minority of Christian inhabitants. Ottoman policy oscillated between suspicion vis-à-vis the Christian population of the city for alleged acts of treason and the will to reintegrate them into urban life. Overall, the chapter shows that imperial politics shaping the urban environment in this border zone were always relational: they have to be conceived as mutual reactions to the imperial competitor beyond the border.

In the next chapter, "Empire after Empire: Austro-Hungarian Recalibration of the Ottoman Čaršija of Sarajevo," Aida Murtić examines the restructuring of the market area of the city in a time of imperial transition. Čaršija, the traditional economic hub of Sarajevo, had been designed according to the rules of Ottoman urbanism in the sixteenth century as a place where different urban groups interacted. It was destroyed to a large extent by a fire in 1879 at the beginning of Austrian rule, and thus the rebuilding that went along with new planning procedures and architectural practices became a test case for the efficiency and modernity of Austrian rule. Pragmatic considerations resulted in a reformed Čaršija where many of the old structures were preserved. Especially the conservation of the central mosque and its transformation into a historical monument was a way to integrate the Muslims symbolically into the new order. This happened in a wider framework of a new discourse on monument protection, new techniques of preservation, and the propagation of a new Orientalizing style for public buildings. The example shows how one empire used material elements from its predecessor in its imperial representation and self-conception, which evolved over time from a modernizing project to one of inclusion of different elements of urban heritage.

Elisabeth Haid-Lener's chapter, "Lemberg or L'vov: The Symbolic Significance of a City at the Crossroads of the Austrian and the Russian Empires," examines the situation of a city with a religiously and ethnically diverse population in a border region between two empires. Lviv became part of the Habsburg Monarchy as the capital of Galicia in the end of the eighteenth century and thrived because of investments in infrastructure and education. The city developed as a cultural and educational center of the imperial German culture and the local Polish nobility's culture, the latter becoming dominant in the second half of the nineteenth century. This was challenged by the Ruthenian/Ukrainian national movement, which could act much more freely in Lviv than in neighboring Russia. During the First World War, when Galicia became a battleground between Austria-Hungary and Russia, Habsburg propagandists presented Lviv as a center of European culture in the East within the Austrian concept of a state composed of different nationalities. In contrast, Russian propaganda described the city as an outpost of Russian culture that needed to be liberated and fully Russified. However, the heavy-handed Habsburg military administration and the short Russian occupation of the city were instrumental in destroying the established model of an imperial city that was characterized by the peaceful cohabitation of different groups.

In a similar manner, Elke Hartmann's chapter, "Kars: Bridgehead of Empires," focuses on a border town between two empires. She analyzes the East Anatolian city of Kars between the Ottoman and the Tsarist Empires. Located in Russia's Trans-Caucasian zone of expansion, Kars was under Tsarist rule between 1878 and 1918 and flourished due to Russian investments in infrastructure and agriculture. Especially the Armenian population profited economically and culturally from Tsarist rule, while many Muslims fled to Ottoman territory. Armenians became the majority population in the city and the region, where other communities such as Russians, Greeks, Germans, and Orthodox religious sects also settled. When Kars became part of the Turkish Republic after the First World War, the Russian and Armenian heritage of the city was largely left to decay. The location at the Iron Curtain and the recent hostility between the Turkish Republic and the Republic of Armenia exacerbated the situation so that to this day this heritage can be appreciated only on a local level. Apart from the Armenian traders, the chapter highlights the military element as another important feature of Kars as an imperial city: the fortress, barracks, and other military installations characterized the city materially and symbolically. At the same time, the territorialization of the Russian Empire also heightened the effect of the imperial border as a defining element for Kars.

The contribution by Olga Zabalueva, "(De)constructing Imperial Heritage: Moscow Zaryadye in Times of Transition," offers an imaginary archaeology of Moscow's central district of Zaryadye located close to the Kremlin. The chapter examines how three consecutive regimes – Tsarist Russia, the Soviet Union, and the present-day Russian state – used this site for their own history politics. In the nineteenth century, the imperial legacy of the district was rediscovered by the restoration of a historical palace of the founder of the Romanov dynasty. Because of the proximity to the Kremlin, the Soviet Union used the main part of the quarter as a construction site for buildings representing the new regime. Several projects from the 1920s to the 1940s failed, but in the 1960s a hotel complex was realized. After the demolition of the hotel in 2006, in a last step, the empty space was turned into a park that was to bring Moscow in line with other world cities. With each step, the original district turned from a residential area with an individual character into a non-place, which serves only passers-by. The chapter shows how imperial cities such as Moscow are being transformed in a long-term process, which is responsible for the palimpsestic nature of their heritage.

In the concluding part of the volume, the contribution by Julia Obertreis, "Imperial Cities and Recent Research Trends: Nostalgia, Water Infrastructure, and Segregation," offers a résumé and outlines three further fields of research that could profit from a focus on imperial cities. The first field is memory of empire and its transformation at historical turning points, such as the inter-war period and the year 1989. The history of renaming streets or entire cities, the destruction or repurposing of buildings such as churches, and especially the public discussions about monuments can give valuable insight into how memories of empire are contested in an urban environment and can result in a specific form of nostalgia. Second, environmental and infrastructural history could gain new insights by directing their attention to imperial cities. All empires tried to gain legitimacy through their policies toward nature and especially water, sometimes sustaining costly infrastructures to harness or overcome natural forces. In cities, this created a special relationship to nature, as in the case of rivers that could threaten cities by flooding but also act as conduits of transport. Third, in the field of urban history proper, segregation and diversity as one central feature of imperial cities should be addressed more directly. In Eastern Europe, especially the Jewish ghetto and quarters of other ethnic minorities are cases in point. Segregation was often tied to larger processes such as industrialization or migration and was thus intricately entwined with economic processes on the housing and job market. This can be observed on the microscale of yards and even inside apartments, which need more attention.

Through its case studies, the present volume hopes to inspire more research that brings together the sources and concepts of urban and imperial history in and beyond Eastern Europe. The imperial city approach can meaningfully connect the urban microscale with the macroscale of empire, highlight imperial borderlands as zones of heightened interactions and transfers, and help to locate the cities of Eastern Europe in a common historical time and space that makes comparisons a fruitful enterprise.

Part I

Conceptual Opening

2 Cities, Empires, and Eastern Europe

Imperial Cities in the Tsarist, the Habsburg, and the Ottoman Empires

Ulrich Hofmeister

The term "imperial cities" is often used but so far rarely conceptualized. In tourist marketing, it is a popular designation for cities as diverse as Marrakesh, Budapest, or New Delhi, all of which are somehow associated with splendor and monarchic grandeur. Among historians, the term is also widespread, but with rather different meanings. Only historians of the Holy Roman Empire have been using the term "imperial city" (*Reichsstadt*) for a long time in a well-defined way: for them, imperial cities are cities like Frankfurt or Nuremberg, which were under the direct authority of the Emperor, not being subordinate to a territorial prince. In the context of the nineteenth and twentieth centuries, however, the term "imperial city" usually lacks such a clear definition, even though it seems to be very popular among historians. Often, it refers to European metropolises of global empires like Paris or London, but sometimes it also denotes major port cities such as Hamburg and Rotterdam, or it relates to capital cities of non-European empires.[1]

This volume is devoted to the Habsburg, the Tsarist, and the Ottoman Empire during the long eighteenth and nineteenth centuries. In this context, the term "imperial cities" also frequently appears, characterizing cities as different from each other as Istanbul and Minsk. The lack of conceptual clarity regarding this term in Eastern Europe was already criticized a decade ago,[2] but in spite of the wealth of literature on both urban history and imperial history, so far there has been no systematic attempt to clarify the relationship between cities and contiguous empires such as Russia, the Habsburg, and the Ottoman Empires during the last two centuries of their existence.

In this volume, we would like to propose a new usage for the term "imperial city." We contend that the current use as a type of city is too unspecific and has little analytical value, most significantly in the context of the land-based empires of Eastern Europe where the conventional distinction between "imperial" and "colonial" cities does not apply. We, therefore, suggest a new convention that understands the imperial city rather as a

DOI: 10.4324/9781003130031-3

research perspective that can be applied to all cities which are shaped by the imperial character of the state or which contribute to the latter's imperial form – regardless of their size and location. This approach explores the imperial dimensions of a given city by asking how empire manifested itself in this urban formation on the one hand, and what role the city played in the functioning of the empire on the other hand. Integrating research on cities and empires in this way first contributes to a better understanding of the structures of the empire, which became manifest primarily in their cities, and second it enables deeper insights into the functioning of many cities, whose political, economic, and social dynamics were conditioned by the imperial character of the state. This chapter will expound on this suggestion by first offering some thoughts about the relationship between cities and empires in general. It gives an overview of how historiography has hitherto treated this relationship and argues that the current usage of terms like "colonial city" or "imperial city" is not convincing as it overstates the differences between cities on the periphery and in the center of an empire. This chapter then turns more specifically to the empires of Eastern Europe and their cities. After a short characterization of these empires and their cities, it demonstrates how our proposed perspective can help to unveil neglected aspects of the relationship between Eastern Europe's empires and their cities.

Cities Colonial and Imperial

In all empires, cities played a leading role as the sites of power and legitimacy and as the transmitters of imperial ideas – it was always the city where the power structures of the empire became most tangible.[3] Institutions of the imperial state were concentrated in the cities: the governor's residence, law courts, police stations, and the customs houses provided the infrastructure for the administration of people, goods, and ideas. In the cities, imperial authority was performed in festivities, processions, concerts, and balls. Museums, cathedrals, mosques, cemeteries, and monuments served as manifestations of imperial ideologies and imaginations. Along with private establishments such as bank offices, they made the empire, its institutions, and principles evident for imperial subjects and foreign visitors as well as for today's scholars. As points of intersection in empire-wide trading networks, cities were sites of exchange of goods, peoples, and ideas. Their markets, warehouses, and harborages brought together peoples and goods from all parts of the empire and even beyond. While empire-wide exchange contributed to processes of differentiation on a local level, it also promoted the homogenization of the empire in its entirety. Buildings and landmarks of the capital inspired the shaping of minor cities as well. Bound together by economic networks, infrastructures for transport and communication, and a growing imperial bureaucracy, the cities of an empire often developed a specific style. Characteristics of urban planning and architecture, building types, and even colors – e.g., Vienna's famous "Schönbrunn Yellow" – spread throughout the empire and thus gave the empire's cities a common appearance.

Given the importance of urban centers for all empires, it is surprising how little attention they have been given by historians of empire. Historiographic works on empire often engage with cities only in passing, and rarely do cities form the structuring element of the account.[4] Even though both Urban and Imperial History have experienced a boom during the last three decades, it seems that these two research approaches mainly co-existed side by side, with little points of contact. It is one aim of this volume to bring them closer together.

The one type of city in the overlapping of imperial and urban history that has so far attracted the most attention is the so-called colonial city. Even though this term has firmly established itself both in academic and popular literature, no consensus has been reached on the meaning of the concept. There is only one feature of the colonial city that all historians agree on: its location in a colony. When the term "colonial city" was first coined in the 1950s by Robert Redfield and Milton B. Singer, they used it for cities in colonial societies with a mixed population and ethnically segregated quarters.[5] During the following decades, the designation "colonial city" was occasionally taken up, albeit with an inconsistent usage: Janet Abu-Lughod used it in 1965 to describe just the western part of Cairo, which was built under European influence. She called the eastern part of Cairo the "old" or "native city," while for Cairo as a whole, she proposed the term "dual city."[6] Anthony D. King returned to Redfield and Milton's more encompassing understanding of the term "colonial city" in his 1976 book, where he turned this term for the first time into a category of analysis on its own and proposed a refined matrix for analyzing a colonial city. His analysis was based on a clear distinction between two components of the colonial city, which he labeled as the "indigenous city" and the "colonial settlement."[7] King's works certainly contributed to the popularity of the term during the following decades;[8] however, the success of the designation "colonial city" came at the expense of its analytical value, as it became a widespread expression for all kinds of cities in the colonies. In this sense, in a 2013 overview article for the *Oxford Handbook of Cities*, Thomas R. Metcalf draws a long line from early modern Spanish town foundations like Veracruz and Manila (Filip. Maynila) with their cosmopolitan populations to British town projects like Singapore, where separated quarters were provided for the different population groups, to the French *nouvelle ville* in Morocco, where European settlements were built right beside ancient Islamic towns, and to settler cities like Sydney and

Melbourne, which had no indigenous traditions and were built exclusively for settlers of European origin.[9]

The extraordinary variety among so-called colonial cities was emphasized in 2001 by Franz-Joseph Post. He expressed some unease with treating the colonial city as a type of city on its own, arguing that most criteria that are usually assigned to colonial cities apply just for some of them: while in some cities spatial segregation prevailed, others were characterized by the mixing of the different population groups; some colonial cities were exclusively ruled by "Europeans," while in other cities, locals were also involved in city administration; and while some colonial cities served primarily the economic need of the metropolis, others had hardly any connection to long-distance trade.[10] It is along these lines that most newer research does not attempt to find a precise definition of colonial cities and rather tends to work with lists of criteria without postulating that all colonial cities need to conform to all proposed features.[11] Others have sought to avoid the term "colonial city" altogether, suggesting such alternative designations as "colonized metropolis" or "frontier city."[12]

Generally, research on colonial cities has focused on the impact of European rule on cities in Africa, Asia, and the Americas. However, in the wake of the rise of postcolonial studies, scholarly attention was turned to European cities as well. In his 1990 book on the global urban system, King argued that developments in the colonized periphery affected cities in the core as well. He contended that if the fate of Kingston (Jamaica) or Bombay (today Mumbai) could not be understood without reference to Europe, it was equally true that the modern history of London or Manchester similarly could not be understood without reference to India, Africa, and Latin America.[13] This call was backed by Edward Said, who argued in 1994 that it was impossible "to draw a clear circle around British London or French Paris that would exclude the impact of India and Algeria upon those two imperial cities."[14] This suggestion to include European cities into the analysis of empire was taken up in 1999 by geographers Felix Driver and David Gilbert, who for the first time introduced the term "imperial cities" as a distinct category of analysis for modern empires. In their edited volume *Imperial Cities: Landscape, Display, and Identity* they asked how the imperial past and present shaped the urban outlook of several European cities, among them metropolises like Paris, London, and Vienna, but also second-rank cities such as Glasgow, Seville, and Marseille.[15] This volume for the first time systematically collected essays on the imprint of empire in European metropolises, even if the editors refrained from an explicit discussion of their understanding of the term imperial city and how it related to a modern European city more generally. Since then, studies have investigated traces of empire not only in Europe's capital cities like London, Paris, Brussels, or Berlin,[16] but also in "second imperial cities," as European port cities like Antwerp, Hamburg, Liverpool, or Marseille have been labeled.[17] Building on the growing literature on empire in European cities, Jürgen Osterhammel described the imperial city in 2009 as "a political command center, a collection point for information, an economically parasitic beneficiary of asymmetrical relations with its various peripheries, and a showplace for emblems of the dominant ideology." In contrast to Driver and Gilbert, who focused on visual representation of empire in the cityscape, Osterhammel emphasized the economic dimension as well. For him, an imperial city was characterized not only by the monumental staging of imperial power but also by its parasitic dependence on the exploitation of the empire.[18]

Colonial cities are often described as being fundamentally different from European metropolitan cities.[19] The distinction between cities in the colonies and their counterparts in Europe is, however, not always as sharp as it might seem. Certainly, political participation was generally much more limited in colonial cities than in the cities of the metropolis, but nevertheless one should not overlook the structural similarities between "colonial" and "imperial" cities, especially when they served similar functions for the empire. The flourishing field of research on port cities, for example, has shown that they have much in common, regardless of their geographical location. Their role as junctions for the global movement of goods, people, and ideas shaped their architecture and their socioeconomic and cultural development, no matter if they are located in Europe or in a (former) colony. They thus undermine the all-too clear-cut distinction between colonial and imperial cities.[20] It is symptomatic that Osterhammel's description of the imperial city could also apply to colonial capitals such as Hanoi (today Hà Nội) or Calcutta (today Kolkata) around 1900, both of which were dressed up as showcases of imperial splendor at the expense of their hinterlands.[21] At the same time, conventional features of the colonial city can also be traced in major European port cities like Marseille and Seville. Both colonial and imperial cities housed buildings of the imperial administration, both were important hubs of colonial trading networks, and both possessed an ethnically and culturally diverse population. This means that the differences between colonial and imperial cities are not as striking as it is often assumed, and there is instead a certain overlap between the presumed two types of cities.

In addition, the distinction between "colonial" and "imperial" cities blurs even more when we look at capital cities of non-European empires which later became seats of a colonial administration. When New Delhi was founded by the British in 1911 as the new capital of British India, it deliberately drew on Delhi's nimbus as the ancient capital of the Moghul Empire. The restoration of the old capital was intended to give the Raj the air of an empire of its own and should thus mitigate Indian demands for independence.[22] Another example for the overlapping of imperial and colonial structures is Mexico City. This city was founded on the ruins of Aztec Tenochtitlan, which had been the capital of a vast tributary empire that controlled a large part of central Mesoamerica. Despite the physical destruction of the Aztec city, newly founded Mexico City took over the general layout of its imperial predecessor, and in large parts of the urban space pre-colonial political, social, and economic practices and arrangements persisted. Moreover, being the capital of the Viceroyalty of New Spain, the city emerged as the center of a new, highly hierarchized domain reaching from the Caribbean to the Philippines. Colonial Mexico City thus not only inherited part of Tenochtitlan's functioning but also became the capital of a new sub-empire that encompassed territories on three continents. Its imperial status thus prevailed at least partly also under colonial rule.[23] Cairo is another example of the complex relationship between non-European imperial and European colonial structures. Once one of the predominant economic and cultural centers of the Islamic world, Cairo came under colonial rule when the British took control of Egypt in 1882. However, its bisection into an "old" and a "European" city, generally regarded as being typical for colonial cities, predated formal colonization. It originated when Khedive Ismail Pasha, the viceroy of Egypt, which was still formally part of the Ottoman Empire, commissioned in 1867 the building of a new quarter of the city on its western end, modeled on Paris.[24] Although Egypt had already come under European economic domination by that time, it pursued its own imperial ambitions in Sudan, making Cairo a colonial and imperial city at the same time. Moreover, even in cases where there was no formal colonization such as in nineteenth-century Istanbul, an imperial capital could become "peripheralized."[25] In such cases, certain parts of the respective city were often ascribed a "colonial" character and function as, for example, Istanbul's European quarter Pera (today Beyoğlu) in the second half of the nineteenth century.[26]

These examples reveal that a clear analytical distinction between colonial and imperial cities is not possible. All cities that were engaged with empire shared central features, no matter if they were located in the metropolis or in the colony. Moreover, autochthonous empires and European colonial structures overlapped, and colonies functioned as sub-empires of their own, so that colonial capitals assumed imperial features as well. Even if the colonial city as an ideal type is a useful tool for analysis, overstating the distinction between imperial and colonial cities threatens to obscure

structural commonalities between cities in empires in general and to reproduce an inadequately binary understanding of center and periphery.

If the dichotomy of "colonial" and "imperial" cities does not fully function in seaborne empires, it is even less suited for the continental empires of
Eastern Europe. However, this is not because concepts of colonial rule could
not generally be applied to them. Especially during the last two decades,
concepts developed in the context of western colonial history have been
adopted by many historians of the Tsarist, the Habsburg, and the Ottoman
Empires.[27] Among the regions most often investigated with the tools of
colonial history are Central Asia, Yemen, Bosnia, and Galicia.[28] Moreover,
a colonial lens has also been proposed for the investigation of Russia's core
regions, as the relationship between the Tsarist Empire's educated elite and
the rural masses also bore colonial traits.[29] The concept of the colonial city,
however, has only rarely been taken up in the context of Eastern Europe's
empires. Even studies that explicitly identify Tsarist or Habsburg rule in
the periphery as colonial usually refrain from using the term "colonial
city."[30] In the context of the Ottoman Empire, historians in general also
do not use the term "colonial city" for peripheral cities such as Baghdad,
Sana'a, or Hudayda in Yemen, even if they identify colonial perceptions
or spatial structures that were implemented by the Ottoman rulers during
the nineteenth century.[31] Quite the contrary – in Ottoman studies the term
"colonial city" is rather used to discuss the presence of Europeans in cities
of the Ottoman heartland like Izmir.[32]

While cities of the Tsarist, the Habsburg, and the Ottoman Empires
were rarely described as colonial cities, the concept of an imperial city,
as proposed by Driver and Gilbert, has already been applied to cities of
these empires, namely to Vienna and Moscow.[33] These works have demonstrated the significance of empire for the study of Eastern Europe's cities.
Still, a harsh division between "imperial" and "colonial" cities does not
seem appropriate for contiguous empires, where, in the absence of a maritime boundary, a clear distinction between "colony" and "motherland"
cannot be drawn. Analyzing nineteenth-century Kyiv (Russ. Kiev), Serhiy
Bilenky has shown that the way Russian nationalists claimed this city as
Russia's spiritual capital bore distinct colonialist overtones.[34] Thus from
Budapest to Sarajevo, from Kiev to Tashkent (today Toshkent), and from
Adrianople (today Edirne) to Sana'a, the cities of these empires incorporated both "imperial" and "colonial" elements at the same time, and metropolitan discourses and structures intermingled with colonial ones. These
cities defy an unequivocal categorization and allocation to one of the two
sides of the colonial divide, as neither geography nor power relations, neither their economic structures nor their ethnic composition favor a clear
label for them.

Empires of Eastern Europe

In the framework of the Tsarist, the Habsburg, and the Ottoman Empires, making sharp distinctions is difficult for various reasons – even their designation as "Eastern European empires" is problematic. The definition of Eastern Europe is a matter not only of geography but has cultural and ideological dimensions as well.[35] This is clearly shown by the fact that cities like Prague or Zagreb, which are often associated with Eastern Europe, lie further to the West than Vienna. Political, cultural, and linguistic criteria influence our understanding of Eastern Europe more profoundly than geography does. Apart from that, of the three empires under consideration, it was the Habsburg Monarchy alone that confined itself to European territory (if we overlook several short-lived overseas colonization attempts), and much of its lands were located in Central or even Western Europe, but not in Eastern Europe. The Ottoman Empire, which had its roots in Anatolia, held possessions in Europe, Asia, and Africa until the very last years of its existence, and the Russian Empire stretched from Europe to Asia and extended to the American continent until the Alaska sale in 1867. For lack of a better term, this book still designates all three empires as "Eastern European." This seems legitimate, as all three empires had their core in the eastern part of Europe, and all cities covered by the chapters of this volume are geographically located in and around Eastern Europe. Still, we are aware that this term covers only part of the historical and geographical reality.

Equally ambivalent is the designation "empire," a term that generations of historians have been struggling with.[36] Some stricter definitions tie empires to pretension of world domination and thus propose the existence of only one or two empires in their "worlds" at the same time.[37] Others are more generous and propose a composite and multilingual nature of the state, which opens the field for many middle-size states to be called empires as well.[38] Often, empire is understood as an antonym to nation states.[39] Jane Burbank and Frederick Cooper, however, pointed to the manifold overlaps between empires and nation-states, and thus emphasized that especially in Eastern Europe, empire and nation cannot be treated as antagonistic and mutually exclusive categories.[40] Burbank and Cooper have suggested an elementary definition of empire that seems particularly useful for research on Imperial Cities. They describe empires as "large political units, expansionist or with a memory of power extended over space, polities that maintain distinction and hierarchy as they incorporate new people."[41] This characterization includes the dominions of the Ottomans, the Habsburgs, and the Romanovs during most of their existence. Together, these three empires determined the historical development of Eastern Europe from the early modern period until the beginning of the twentieth century.[42]

The Ottoman state developed from an Anatolian frontier principality into a mighty centralized empire encompassing Anatolia and the Balkans by the fifteenth century. With the conquest of Constantinople in 1453, it incorporated the last remnants of the Byzantine Empire. Its maximal geographic extent was reached in the second half of the seventeenth century, when the Ottomans ruled over Baghdad in the East, controlled Algiers in the West, and threatened Vienna in the Northwest and Kyiv in the Northeast. Having inherited the title of Caliph, the Ottoman Sultans saw themselves as leaders of the entire Muslim world. Until the eighteenth century, they claimed a superior position over the other powers also in the European context.[43]

A Russian imperial polity came into being during the fourteenth and fifteenth centuries, when the Grand Duchy of Muscovy, still a vassal of the Tatar-Mongolian Golden Horde, assembled many of the components of the decayed Kievan Rus'. Parallel to the disintegration of the Golden Horde, and reinforced by the fall of Constantinople in 1453, Moscow rulers started to claim imperial accessories. The annexation of the Tatar Khanate of Kazan in 1552 affirmed Russia's imperial character, and the conquest of Siberia during the sixteenth and seventeenth centuries made it the world's most extensive state. The final claim for imperiality was made by Tsar Peter I in 1721, when he adopted the title of "Imperator."[44]

In the case of the Habsburg dynasty, determining the imperiality of their dominions is the most difficult. In the course of more than six hundred years, they presided – simultaneously or subsequently – over three different imperial conglomerates. The Holy Roman Empire lent the Habsburgs for the first time the title of Emperor in 1273, and even though this position was dependent on election, from the middle of the fifteenth century onward the imperial crown remained nearly uninterrupted in the possession of this dynasty. Moreover, the House of Habsburg assembled extensive domains in hereditary possessions as well, which were divided between the Spanish and the Austrian branch of the dynasty in the middle of the sixteenth century. The Spanish line ruled over Spain with its colonial possessions in Africa, America, and Asia until 1700. The Austrian line, on the other hand, kept the title of Holy Roman Emperor and received a conglomerate of lands encompassing the Austrian hereditary possessions, the Bohemian Lands, and the Western parts of Hungary and Croatia. Together with later acquisitions, these lands developed into a Central European empire of its own – the Habsburg Empire in the narrower sense. Yet, while the Tsars and to a lesser extent the Ottomans succeeded in establishing centralized rule over most of their possessions and applied more flexible forms of domination for a long time only in the peripheries, the Habsburg Empire remained a composite monarchy, an array of diverse and scattered lands.[45]

All three empires under consideration adorned themselves with impressive imperial genealogies that reached back to the ancient Roman Empire. While the Habsburgs positioned themselves as the successors of the Western Roman Emperors, the Tsars and the Ottomans claimed the Byzantine Heritage for themselves. At the same time, the Tsars and the Ottomans, the dominions of which had emerged out of the remnants of the Mongolian Empire, also saw themselves as the successors of the Khans. The Ottoman Sultan, moreover, also gave his rule a religious slant by claiming the title of Caliph. This sense of a religious mission was shared by the two other empires: since the fall of Constantinople, Russia was the last remaining stronghold of Orthodoxy, while the Habsburgs saw themselves as the defenders of Catholicism.

For the histories of all three empires, the turn of the eighteenth century marked the beginning of a new era. Since 1686, when the Tsarist Empire joined the Holy League against the Ottoman Empire, all three empires were united in a system of direct diplomatic and military interaction. While Russia rose to great power status during the first quarter of the eighteenth century, and the territories of the Austrian Habsburgs reached their greatest extent between 1717 and 1739, the Ottoman Empire was forced to start its slow retreat from Central and Eastern Europe. As the eighteenth and nineteenth centuries proceeded, borders constantly shifted due to the rivalries and changing alliances of the three empires and the rise of national movements which increasingly challenged the empires' territorial integrity. In all three empires, continuous reform of administrative structures contributed to temporary consolidation of state power. It could not, however, preclude the three empires' simultaneous collapse during the First World War.

Cities in the Tsarist, Ottoman, and Habsburg Empires

In all three empires, the eighteenth and nineteenth centuries were a period of decisive importance for their cities. During this period, the political, economic, and representative significance of the cities grew remarkably, and all three empires became more and more visible in their cities. For the urban landscape of the Tsarist Empire, the eighteenth century brought especially pervasive transformations. The foundation of the new capital St. Petersburg in 1703 already upset the established urban system of the empire, but several consecutive reforms of town administration and the empire's gradual expansion into the steppe had even more far-reaching consequences. Under the rule of Catherine II (r. 1762–1796) alone, more than two hundred towns were newly founded. One important area of town foundations was the vast and sparsely populated steppe region north of the

Black Sea, but many more new towns were built in central regions of the state. These new towns, which were typically founded upon already exist-ing settlements, often did not follow economic or demographic necessities but were intended solely to serve as administrative centers.[46] At the same time, a series of municipal reforms set the towns to an increasing degree legally apart from the countryside and for the first time provided the towns with limited autonomy. Even if this did not free urban communities from dependence on the state, the reforms contributed to the emergence of an urban middle class in the long term.[47] Moreover, the outlook of nearly all Russian cities underwent profound changes from the last third of the eigh-teenth century onward. Fostering a "regular" and "European" outlook of the towns, Catherine's administration provided them with buildings in a classical style and with a geometrical street grid.[48] Toward the end of the eighteenth century, about eight percent of the empire's population lived in towns and cities, which was not much below the European average of ten percent.[49] At that time, by far the largest cities of the Tsarist Empire were the two capitals Moscow and St. Petersburg with 350,000 and 220,000 inhabitants, respectively. The other towns lagged far behind and had no more than 35,000 residents.[50] All towns served as administrative seats, but until the first decades of the nineteenth century, the majority of the active population in most towns was engaged in agriculture.[51] In Russia, the industrial revolution commenced later than in Western Europe, and only after the emancipation of the peasants in 1861 did the pace of ur-ban growth quicken significantly, driven mainly by migration from the countryside.[52] In 1916, the share of Russia's urban population had reached 17.4 percent.[53] However, urbanization affected the regions of the empire very unevenly. By far the largest cities at the turn of the century were St. Petersburg and Moscow with 1.26 million and 1 million inhabitants, respectively.[54] These two metropolises shared many features with other European metropolises like Vienna, Berlin, or Paris. They faced compara-ble social problems, tried to solve infrastructural problems in similar ways, and built their buildings in a related style.[55] On the other hand, most pro-vincial towns and even the smaller provincial capitals had no paved streets, no water lines, and no street lighting, and only a very narrow segment of the population involved itself in communal affairs.[56] Apart from the two capitals, there were seventeen more cities with more than 100,000 inhabit-ants at that time, the biggest of which was Warsaw with a population of around 683,000. It is striking that hardly any of these cities were located in the Russian heartland. Bigger than most "traditional" Russian cities were those which had been either annexed since the sixteenth century, like Kazan, Riga, or Lodz, or which had been built from scratch in the steppes to the South or East, like Odessa (Ukr. Odesa) or Rostov-on-Don. Most of the Empire's biggest cities had a clear East Slavic majority, non-Russians dominated numerically only in the Baltics (Vilna [today Vilnius] and Riga) and in the cities most recently annexed in the West (Warsaw, Kishinev [today Chişinău], and Lodz), the Caucasus (Tiflis [today Georg. Tbilisi], Baku [Azer. Bakı]), and Central Asia (Tashkent).[57]

The urban landscape of Central and Southeastern Europe also experienced profound changes in the course of the eighteenth century, mainly caused by Ottoman retreat from and Habsburg advance into Hungary. While only a few towns were newly founded after the change of the rulers, existing fortresses and towns were restored and enlarged. As Muslims had to leave the region together with Ottoman troops, they were replaced by German-speaking immigrants, among others, which from now on formed the majority in the towns of the region.[58] At the same time, the German element gained importance during the eighteenth century across the Habsburg Monarchy. Due to immigration and assimilation processes also underway in Bohemian and Moravian towns, German established itself as the means of communication between the different parts of the Habsburg Monarchy. In 1780, the most populous city of the empire was Vienna with 200,000 residents. Prague followed with a population of 70,000, and Hungary's largest city was Pozsony (Germ. Preßburg, today Bratislava) with 30,000.[59] With only five percent of the population living in towns and cities, urbanization in the Habsburg Empire was comparatively low.[60] Apart from that, toward the end of the eighteenth century, most town-dwellers were primarily engaged in agriculture, especially in the towns of the Hungarian plain. Still, unlike in the Tsarist Empire, the towns already served as centers of education and culture during the eighteenth century.[61] In the aftermath of the Napoleonic Wars, the towns and cities of the Habsburg Monarchy experienced enormous growth rates. Vienna's population increased to 357,000 in 1848, but even more impressive was the growth of those provincial towns where Austria's economic development was mainly located: Pest (today part of Budapest) grew from about 35,000 inhabitants in 1810 to over 100,000 in the late 1840s; the port city of Trieste (Germ. Triest, Slov. Trst) transformed from an eighteenth-century fishing village into a world-class port with a population of more than 80,000 in 1840; and Brno (Germ. Brünn), the most industrialized town of that time, approached 30,000 in 1830 and 45,000 a decade later. The economic boom of these cities rested on the settlement of merchants and manufacturers who employed increasing numbers of workers in their shops, factories, warehouses, and, in the case of Trieste, on their docks.[62] In the second half of the nineteenth century, such growth rates were seen in more and more provincial towns: by 1910, nine cities already had more than 100,000 inhabitants, with the two capitals Vienna (2,100,000) and Budapest (880,371) being the biggest cities.

The enormous growth of most provincial towns came mainly from their direct hinterlands, the villages, and smaller towns of their surrounding areas. This meant that earlier Germanizing tendencies were now quickly reversed. Most towns lost their German majority and character and aligned themselves linguistically with their non-German provinces.[63] The growing share of non-Germans demanded representation and participation in urban life, which met with resistance from the established German-speaking burghers. This led to growing disputes along national lines on an urban level and often to parallel institutions for each population group.[64] But even if national pride was sometimes expressed in "national" styles in architecture,[65] a homogenization of the urban space gained momentum all over the Habsburg Empire.[66] Following the example of Vienna, many towns tore down their medieval walls and replaced them with public parks and boulevards. Upon communal initiative, water lines were established, roads were paved, and representative public buildings were erected. Their historicist design became the dominant style of the Habsburg Monarchy. Train stations, administrative buildings, and cultural institutions shared a uniform neo-baroque or neo-renaissance appearance.[67] Notwithstanding the profound transformation of many Habsburg towns and cities around the turn of the twentieth century, the overall urbanization rate of the Habsburg Empire remained comparatively low. Except for several industrial enclaves, the country retained a mainly agricultural character: in 1913, more than half of the population of the Cisleithanian part of the empire lived in localities of less than 2,000 inhabitants, and nearly two-thirds in villages or even smaller settlements.[68]

Until the middle of the nineteenth century, the Ottoman Empire was distinctly more urbanized than the Tsarist and Habsburg Empires, and also most of Europe. We don't have any numbers for the eighteenth century, but in the 1830s and 1840s, 17 percent of the Ottoman population lived in towns of more than 20,000 inhabitants.[69] Apart from that, Ottoman cities were much larger than the ones in the Habsburg and the Tsarist Empires. Toward the end of the eighteenth century, Istanbul, together with its suburbs, had a population of about 600,000; Cairo followed with 210,000–260,000 inhabitants, and Saloniki (today Thessaloniki), Izmir, Aleppo, and Edirne had about 100,000 inhabitants.[70] Even though Ottoman towns generally had no charters, they enjoyed a kind of unofficial autonomy. In most provincial towns, urban elites gathered in informal councils that often included Christians and Jews. These councils represented the town to the central government and had considerable room for political maneuvering.[71] During the eighteenth century, when the central bureaucracy yielded much of its power to local rulers, the scope of local forces became even larger. Contested issues – for example, the rights of non-Muslims and foreigners in the urban space – were therefore treated very differently in the different cities of the empire, which contributed to the highly divergent development of Ottoman cities.[72] It was only during the Tanzimat period (1839–1876), when the government initiated a series of constitutional reforms, that local self-administration became codified. The formerly unofficial councils were now formalized, and their rights and duties systematized.[73] The Tanzimat reforms greatly enhanced the significance of the cities for the empire, as they became the main sites for the central government's attempts to regain control over the provinces.[74] The transformative impetus of the middle of the nineteenth century became especially visible in the cityscapes. The capital Istanbul was to be the first to undergo a far-reaching reconstruction. Oriented on contemporary European cities and based on projects of mainly French architects and town planners, the network of streets was partly regularized, new building codes and regulations fostered a uniform residential fabric, and modern transportation systems were introduced.[75] Even if in the end the transformation of Istanbul's urban fabric was not as radically implemented as initially proposed, it influenced similar projects in provincial towns as well.[76] Newly erected barracks embodied the state's attempt to exercise more control over the cities. They were often located in the vicinity of new roads or railways in order to improve the mobility of the troops. Governor's palaces, schools, and judicial courts became new landmarks in old city centers.[77] Tramways and other communal infrastructure were established, often financed by foreign investors.[78] Government initiative, however, was only one factor in the great transformation of Ottoman cities during the nineteenth century. Another was the increase in population, both natural and due to migration. Since the Ottoman Empire had opened its markets in the 1838 Treaty of Balta Liman, foreign contractors settled in Ottoman towns and opened factories, which in turn attracted workers from the countryside. Port cities were first and foremost affected by migration and population growth and became a gateway for European influence, even if the adaptations to a European way of life were modified according to local needs.[79] Istanbul's number of inhabitants grew to 1,125,000 in 1912, Izmir grew from 110,000 to 300,000 inhabitants between 1840 and 1913, and Beirut climbed from less than 10,000 in 1800 to around 150,000 in 1914, measuring up to Salonica and Baghdad, which had themselves doubled during the same period. The general share of urban dwellers rose from 17 to 22 percent between 1840 and 1913.[80] At the same time, the share of Muslims among the empire's population steadily grew, as Muslims from lost provinces resettled to remaining Ottoman territory. Between the middle of the nineteenth century and 1906, their proportion rose from 60 to 74 percent.[81] On an urban level, there was generally no strict segregation according to national or religious lines, and the different communities interacted intensively with each other. Still, the significance of national and class affiliation grew during the nineteenth century.[82]

Common Dimensions of the Cities of Eastern Europe

Even though each of the three empires shaped its towns and cities in a distinct way, they had several crucial traits in common. A significant moment was their ambiguous relation to modernity.[83] In Eastern Europe industrialization occurred comparatively late and unevenly, so that the three empires were not able to fully keep pace with the technological and economic development of Western Europe. They were thus often labeled as backward,[84] and it was the shape of their cities that became the main yardstick for this assessment. The general verdict of backwardness, however, conflicts with historical evidence; it is sufficient to mention that the honor of having built the first undergrounds on the entire continent is claimed by Budapest and Istanbul. Moreover, historians of architecture and urbanism have rediscovered a particular adaptation of urban modernity in the Habsburg Empire. It thrived on the diversity of Central European cities and the productive tension between an overarching imperial style and local adaptations that were to reflect the diversity of the empire. The Viennese model of urban development won international acclaim and was copied not only inside the Habsburg Empire.[85] Still, the assessment of backwardness did play a role in the contemporary perception of the cities both by their own inhabitants and their visitors, and the theme of catching up with Western Europe left its imprint in the urban fabric. To this day, the map of St. Petersburg reflects the orientation of its builders to Amsterdam and Paris – cities which never felt a need to explain themselves.[86] Similarly, the urban modernization of Istanbul in the nineteenth century was planned according to European models, most notably Paris, and involved foreign experts. However, this also shows that despite the backward image, the empire was actively adopting innovations in urban planning and governance.[87] To a certain extent, these efforts can be read as a reaction on the allegations of being backward: the cities were intended to prove these claims wrong.

The development of the cities of all three empires under consideration was to a certain extent influenced by the continental character of their states. Still, the contrast between contiguous and overseas empires should not be overstated.[88] Oceanic empires were not necessarily more difficult to integrate, because in the pre-railway age territorial distances were easier to overcome on water than on land.[89] For example, after the opening of the Suez Canal in 1869 and before the completion of the first railway line in Central Asia in 1888, a journey from St. Petersburg to Tashkent took much longer than the passage from London to Calcutta.[90]

But even if the dichotomy of overseas and continental empires should not be absolutized, the lack of a sea barrier did have consequences that in some regards distinguished the cities of the different types of empires. While the emergence of the Western European colonial empires was conditioned by technological innovations that enabled transoceanic shipping, the continental empires of Eastern Europe often rested on much older structures and incorporated territories that had maintained ties for a long time already. They were thus able to rely on trading points, transportation routes, and mediator groups that had been previously established. Cultural differences between the center and the peripheries of these empires were thus often moderated by historical connections or linguistic kinship. The population of a borderland town often had longstanding ties if not with the population of the core itself, then at least with some other established group of the empire. In the Tsarist Empire, Tatars regularly served as mediators between central agencies and their religious and linguistic kinsmen in Central Asia,[91] and in Habsburg Bosnia, Serbs and Croatians took over a similar role as mediators between Vienna, Budapest, and Sarajevo.[92] In the Ottoman Empire, it was the common adherence of the elites to Islam that connected the borderlands with the center in Istanbul. This meant that even in the most distant towns, the cultural gap between locals and representatives of the center was partly bridged by shared cultural references and by mediators which found a common language with all groups concerned. Continental ties between periphery and center also inhibited the establishment of a clear legal distinction between colonial and metropolitan populations. The Tsarist Empire introduced the category of *inorodtsy* (literarily "of different descent") in 1822s, but as this label was soon extended also to the empire's Jews, it was not equivalent to the category of African *sujets* of the French colonial empire.[93] In the Ottoman Empire, the main societal dividing line also did not correspond to geographic, ethnic, or cultural criteria, but rather passed between the *askeri*, who performed military or administrative duties, and the tax-paying *reaya*, both Muslim and Christian.[94] The Habsburg Empire, lastly, declared in 1867 the equality of all citizens before the law. This provision, which principally rejected a systematic differentiation between purported colonizers and the colonized, was later also included in the Constitution of Bosnia and Hercegovina.[95] So while urban life in the western overseas empires was marked by the legal distinction between colonial and metropolitan populations, such hierarchies were less pronounced in the cities of the continental empires, although they also often exhibited segregated ethnic or religious quarters.

While the elites of the Western empires were inspired by one core nation, the empires of Eastern Europe were dominated by multi-ethnic elites, the loyalty of which was generally more often directed toward the sovereign than toward a particular national project.[96] This precluded an excessive orientation toward the metropolitan nation, characteristic, for instance, of French colonialism. On the other hand, when nationalism gained momentum in the course of the nineteenth century, the perspective of a national homogenization of the entire empire – perceived either as a goal or as a threat – could seem more realistic in a contiguous empire than in an empire whose diverse possessions were scattered all over the globe. Discourses and practices of Russification, Germanization, Magyarization, or – in the Ottoman case in the very last phase of the empire after 1908 – Turkification were therefore much more politically sensitive than the merely theoretical *assimilation* doctrine of the French colonial empire.[97] On an urban level, this led to fierce disputes about schools, churches, and other representative buildings of imperial power. A telling example is the disputes around Warsaw's Russian Orthodox Alexander Nevskii Cathedral, which was completed by the Russian administration in 1912 and torn down by the Polish authorities less than 15 years later.[98]

At the same time, the closer ties between center and periphery sometimes also evoked a more pronounced discourse of differentiation, which highlighted religious or alleged civilizational and racial distinctions between different population groups and raised calls for apartheid regimes on a local level.[99] The question of differentiation became especially urgent in the second half of the nineteenth century, when constitutional arrangements spread. In contiguous empires, it was more difficult to exclude the population of the periphery from political rights than in empires with a clear separation between colony and motherland. In the cities of Eastern Europe, this led to increased struggles over political participation, representation in elective bodies, and, more generally, resources. Some of the chapters of this volume show in more detail how the national aspirations of competing ethnic groups shaped the development and the outlook of the cities.

Imperial Cities of Eastern Europe: A Research Program

In this volume, we suggest using the term "imperial city" in the context of Eastern Europe not as a counterpart of "colonial city" but rather as an umbrella term that can encompass cities in the core of the empire as well as in its borderlands. For us, an imperial city is a city where the empire manifests itself and which is marked by the imperial form of the state. This understanding of the relationship between city and empire is heavily indebted to the work of other scholars. We follow Driver and Gilbert in their approach of tracing empire in the urban landscape,[100] but we expand their approach by overcoming the traditional division between "colonial" and "imperial" cities and by analyzing them together, as Tristam Hunt has done for the British Empire.[101] This enables us to draw on the findings of research on colonial cities as well as on metropolises of colonial empires and to deploy them for the investigation of the cities of Eastern Europe's contiguous empires. We are convinced that research on continental empires will profit from the historiography on maritime empires and their cities, even if the specificities of a continental empire need to be considered. It is therefore one aim of this volume to explore to what extent the specificities of continental empires shaped the outlook and the functioning of their cities and the daily life of their inhabitants.

It is important to note that we do not propose the imperial city as a new type of city on the same lines as, say, a garrison town or a residential city. Instead, we suggest the imperial city as a point of view for analysis. Investigating an imperial city means for us examining the significance of a given city for the empire and exploring marks of empire in its urban structure. In accordance with the most basic features of empire, the latter include, among others, the ostentatious display of power, the ethnocultural heterogeneity of the population, and a hierarchical arrangement of the empire's regions and population groups. These features can be found in very different kinds of towns and cities, irrespective of their size or their location. There are, however, three main groups of cities that are especially well suited to be investigated as imperial cities. First, there are cities in which the highest organs of the imperial state have a particularly strong presence – for example, capitals, former capitals, and residential or coronation cities. Such cities are the most important sites for the expression of the power and the ideological foundations of the empire. In this volume, the contribution of Nilay Özlü on the ancient imperial palaces of Kremlin, Topkapı and Hofburg follow this path, but also that of Olga Zabalueva, who investigates the fate of a Moscow quarter in the direct vicinity of the Kremlin. An imperial city in this sense is not necessarily a metropolis. Smaller towns are often equally shaped by the imperial character of the state: provincial or district capitals also housed institutions of the imperial administration, and fortress cities accommodated garrisons of the imperial army. The chapter on Temeswar (Rom. Timişoara) by Robert Born shows how architecture in a provincial city was shaped by the capital and by references to the ruling dynasty. Border towns served as gates into the empire and therefore were particularly equipped with imperial accessories. Florian Riedler uses the example of Niš, a town that changed hands between the Ottoman and the Habsburg Empires several times, to show how imperial ideologies were expressed in the city's fortress. Formerly Ottoman Kars, discussed by Elke Hartmann, acquired under Tsarist rule a "European" cityscape, but in terms of demography and economics, it was dominated by Armenians. Second, towns that serve as trading centers of imperial significance are also particularly shaped by the empire, even if their success often rested on a relatively loose administrative integration into the structures of the empire. As port cities or railway junctions, they brought people and goods from different corners of the empire together, as Michel Abesser shows in the case of Rostov-on-Don. Research on cities of this group can particularly profit from research on colonial cities, as many of the classical colonial cities are port cities. The third group of cities that we propose to investigate as imperial cities are those with a significant share of inhabitants of a non-dominant population group of the empire. Being sites for the negotiation of the rights and the status of different ethnocultural groups, they mirror the uneven treatment given by the imperial state to its diverse population. Yet, specific requirements of imperial rule mean that this does not necessarily coincide with the discrimination of minority groups, who are sometimes even given priority over otherwise dominant groups. In the Tsarist Empire, several towns were founded for specific non-Russians – for example, Nakhichevan on Don, where Armenian merchants enjoyed large privileges, as described in the chapter by Michel Abesser. Another case is foreign cities that were incorporated into an empire. Here, the new authorities together with autochthonous inhabitants transformed the cityscape according to the new requirements and expectations, a process that included elements of dismantling, preserving, and adapting the architectural and social heritage of the city, as shown by Aida Murtić in the case of Čaršija, Sarajevo's old commercial district, and by Robert Born with Temeswar. Other towns had a special significance for non-dominant groups, such as Kazan for the Tatars of the Tsarist Empire. Gulchachak Nugmanova shows that much of Kazan's relevance for both Russians and Tatars derived from its history as the capital of the Kazan Khanate. Other cities were home to an ethnoculturally mixed population and thus were claimed by different groups as "their" own, and sometimes also by rival empires, as Elisabeth Haid-Lener shows with regard to the multinational city of Lviv (Ukr. L'viv, Pol. Lwów, Germ. Lemberg, Russ. L'vov).

All such cities have been profoundly shaped by their respective empire(s). Their urban morphology with representative buildings and often segregated ethnic quarters mirrored the ideological ambitions and the heterogeneity of the empire itself. Each of the three empires under consideration in this volume developed its specific architectural, societal, and performative solutions for representing the imperial state in the urban space. The imperial character of a city emerged from the often contradictory dynamics of imperial rule on a local level, where factions of the established population, representatives of the political power center, and various other incoming groups collaborated and competed with each other, each one striving to enforce its own economic goals, political ideas, and ideological agenda.

At the same time, it needs to be kept in mind that urban imperiality is not an objective, given feature, but the result of societal attributions. There is no universal answer to the question which elements of the urban landscapes can be regarded as specifically "imperial." This differs from region to region, and it might change over time. In Sarajevo, the historicist façade of Hotel Europe served as an embodiment of imperial rule, as Aida Murtić shows in her chapter; in the Styrian city of Graz, however, an identical building would not have evoked any imperial connotations. A similar case can be made regarding Ottoman central domed mosques, which acquired a particular meaning in the Arab provinces that had their own architectural traditions.[102] Finally, the gilded cupolas of Warsaw's Russian Orthodox Alexander Nevskii Cathedral, mentioned above, acquired a specific imperial connotation in the Polish capital they would have lacked in the Russian cities of Tver or Tula. However, it was not only "metropolitan" architectural conventions and styles that were transferred to the periphery and thus became charged as markers of empire. The same mechanism also worked the other way around: when the St. Petersburg Mosque was erected from 1910 on, it was patterned after the grand mausoleums and madrasahs of Samarkand (Uzb. Samarqand). In the foreign setting of St. Petersburg, this style was used to celebrate the conquest of Central Asia and thus acquired a specific imperial meaning it lacked in Samarkand.

Moreover, the assessment of what is "imperial" and what not is subject to changes in the course of history. Such a re-configuration of codes and symbols is especially apparent after regime changes.[103] In Southeastern Europe, the alternation of Habsburg and Ottoman rule often led to a re-interpretation of religious buildings as markers of imperial power. Consequently, after a town changed hands, churches and mosques were regularly subject to destruction or conversion, as Florian Riedler discusses in his chapter on Niš. All these cases indicate that it cannot be universally defined which elements of the urban space can be regarded as "imperial." It depends on the specific historical and cultural circumstances and can change over time.

After such an enumeration of imperial cities, one might ask if there are non-imperial cities at all, and if there are any cities that are not suited for investigation as an imperial city. This would be an ethnoculturally homogenous settlement without direct access to the main trading routes, and where the state does not appear to be an "alien" power. At first glance, all empires appear to have numerous sleepy towns in the province seemingly unaffected by the empire and its dynamics. If we look closer, however, we assume that hardly any provincial town remained completely independent of the structures of the imperial state. Even in remote settlements, administrative buildings were designed according to imposing models in the capital, monuments remembered historical deeds and figures of empire-wide significance, and products and groceries found their way from distant corners of the state. To some extent, it is left to the creativity of the researcher to locate the traces of empire. We are confident that most Eastern European cities and towns will turn out to be fruitful sites for the investigation of empire in the urban space.

Acknowledgment

I want to express my gratitude to Michel Abesser, Eszter Gantner, Börries Kuzmany, Julia Obertreis, Florian Riedler, and Alexandra Wachter for their help in developing this chapter.

Notes

1 See Andrew Lees and Lynn Hollen Lees, *Cities and the Making of Modern Europe, 1750–1914* (Cambridge: Cambridge University Press, 2007), 244–80, notwithstanding the attempt of a typology on p. 246.
2 Guido Hausmann, "Osteuropäische Stadt oder Stadt in Osteuropa?" in *Urbanisierung und Stadtentwicklung in Südosteuropa vom 19. bis zum 21. Jahrhundert*, ed. Thomas M. Bohn and Marie-Janine Calic (München: Sager, 2010), 41.
3 Derek Keene, "Cities and Empires," *Journal of Urban History* 32, no. 1 (2005): 9, 13–14.
4 One of the rare exceptions is Tristram Hunt, *Ten Cities That Made an Empire* (London: Penguin, 2015).
5 Robert Redfield and Milton B. Singer, "The Cultural Role of Cities," *Economic Development and Cultural Change* 3, no. 1 (1954): 62.
6 Janet Abu-Lughod, "Tale of Two Cities: The Origins of Modern Cairo," *Comparative Studies in Society and History* 7, no. 4 (1965), 429–30.
7 Anthony D. King, *Colonial Urban Development: Culture, Social Power and Environment* (London: Routledge, 1976), 17–18, 22–40.
8 See, for example, Robert J. Ross and Gerard J. Telkamp, eds., *Colonial Cities* (Dordrecht: Nijhoff, 1985).
9 Thomas R. Metcalf, "Colonial Cities," in *The Oxford Handbook of Cities in World History*, ed. Peter Clark (Oxford: Oxford University Press, 2013), 735–69.
10 Franz-Joseph Post, "Europäische Kolonialstädte in vergleichender Perspektive," in *Kolonialstädte: Europäische Enklaven oder Schmelztiegel der Kulturen?*, ed. Horst Gründer and Peter Johanek (Münster: Lit, 2001).
11 Jürgen Osterhammel, *The Transformation of the World: A Global History of the Nineteenth Century* (Princeton, NJ: Princeton University Press, 2014), 285.
12 Arbeitskreis für außereuropäische Geschichte, "Kolonisierte Metropolen," special issue, *Periplus: Jahrbuch für außereuropäische Geschichte* 6 (1996); Jay Gitlin, Barbara Berglund, and Adam Arenson, eds., *Frontier Cities: Encounters at the Crossroads of Empire* (Philadelphia: University of Pennsylvania Press, 2013).
13 Anthony D. King, *Urbanism, Colonialism and the World Economy: Cultural and Spatial Foundations of the World Urban System* (London: Routledge, 1990), 78.

14 Edward W. Said, *Culture and Imperialism* (London: Vintage, 1994), 15.

15 Felix Driver and David Gilbert, eds., *Imperial Cities: Landscape, Display and Identity* (Manchester: Manchester University Press, 1999).

16 Jonathan Schneer, *London 1900: The Imperial Metropolis* (New Haven, CT: Yale University Press, 1999); Michael Goebel, *Anti-Imperial Metropolis: Interwar Paris and the Seeds of Third World Nationalism* (Cambridge: Cambridge University Press, 2015); Amandine Lauro, "Bruxelles et le Congo," special issue, *Les Cahiers de la Fonderie* 28 (2008); Ulrich van der Heyden, *Kolonialmetropole Berlin: Eine Spurensuche* (Berlin: Berlin-Edition, 2002).

17 Daniel Tödt, "Making Second Imperial Cities: Modern Ports, Colonial Connectivity and Maritime Globalization," *Moderne Stadtgeschichte*, no. 2 (2019): 115–39. Sheryllynne Haggerty, Anthony Webster, and Nicholas J. White, eds., *The Empire in One City? Liverpool's Inconvenient Imperial Past* (Manchester: Manchester University Press, 2008).

18 Osterhammel, *The Transformation of the World*, 295–96.

19 Metcalf, "Colonial Cities," 753.

20 Carola Hein, "Port Cities," in *The Oxford Handbook of Cities in World History*, ed. Peter Clark (Oxford: Oxford University Press, 2013), 809–27; Lasse Heerten and Daniel Tödt, "Some Reflections on Imperial Port Cities in the Age of Steam," *Global Urban History* (blog), October 10, 2016. https://globalurbanhistory.com/2016/10/29/some-reflections-on-imperial-port-cities-in-the-age-of-steam/ (Accessed October 20, 2022); Lars Amenda and Malte Fuhrmann, "Hafenstädte: Mobilität, Migration, Globalisierung," special issue, *Comparativ* 17, no. 2 (2007); Carola Hein, ed., *Port Cities: Dynamic Landscapes and Global Networks* (London: Routledge, 2011).

21 Ranjit Sen, *Calcutta in Colonial Transition* (London: Routledge, 2019); William S. Logan, *Hanoi: Biography of a City* (Seattle: University of Washington Press, 2000).

22 Swapna Liddle, *Connaught Place and the Making of New Delhi* (New Delhi: Speaking Tiger, 2018), 1–12.

23 Barbara E. Mundy, *The Death of Aztec Tenochtitlan, the Life of Mexico City* (Austin: University of Texas Press, 2018).

24 Abu-Lughod, "Tale of Two Cities."

25 Edhem Eldem, "Istanbul: From Imperial to Peripheralized Capital," in *The Ottoman City between East and West: Aleppo, Izmir, and Istanbul*, ed. Edhem Eldem, Bruce Masters, and Daniel Goffman (Cambridge: Cambridge University Press, 1999), 135–206.

26 Steven T. Rosenthal, *The Politics of Dependency: Urban Reform in Istanbul* (Westport: Greenwood Press, 1980); for a revision of this "colonial" approach, see Christoph K. Neumann, "Modernitäten im Konflikt: Der sechste Munizipal-Bezirk von Istanbul, 1857–1912," in *Istanbul: Vom Imperialen Herrschersitz zur Megapolis: Historiographische Betrachtungen zu Gesellschaft, Institutionen und Räumen*, ed. Yavuz Köse (München: Meidenbauer, 2006), 351–75; Zeynep Çelik, *The Remaking of Istanbul: Portrait of an Ottoman City in the Nineteenth Century* (Berkeley: University of California Press, 1993).

27 For the Habsburg Monarchy, a fulminant starting point was Johannes Feichtinger, Ursula Prutsch, and Moritz Csáky, eds., *Habsburg postcolonial: Machtstrukturen und kollektives Gedächtnis* (Innsbruck: Studien Verlag, 2003). For an overview of the historiography of empire in the three continental empires, see the following literature reviews: Laurence Cole, "Visions and Revisions of Empire: Reflections on a New History of the Habsburg Monarchy,"

Austrian History Yearbook 49 (2018): 261–63; Kerstin S. Jobst, Julia Obertreis, and Ricarda Vulpius, "Neuere Imperiumsforschung in der Osteuropäischen Geschichte: Die Habsburgermonarchie, das Russländische Reich und die Sowjetunion," *Comparativ* 18, no. 2 (2008): 27–56; Theodore R. Weeks, "Nationality, Empire, and Politics in the Russian Empire and USSR: An Overview of Recent Publications," *H-Soz-u-Kult* (2012). https://www.hsozkult.de/literaturereview/id/forschungsberichte-1134 (Accessed October 20, 2022); Virginia Aksan, "What's Up in Ottoman Studies?," *Journal of the Ottoman and Turkish Studies Association* 1, no. 1–2 (2014): 3–21.

28 Just to mention a few examples: Ussama Makdisi, "Ottoman Orientalism," *The American Historical Review* 107, no. 3 (2002), 768–96; Thomas Kühn, "Shaping and Reshaping Colonial Ottomanism: Contesting Boundaries of Difference and Integration in Ottoman Yemen," *Comparative Studies of South Asia, Africa and the Middle East* 27, no. 2 (2007), 315–31; Birgit Schäbler, "Globale Moderne und die Geburt der Zivilisationsmission an der kulturellen Binnengrenze: Die mission civilisatrice ottomane," *Periplus: Jahrbuch für außereuropäische Geschichte* 13 (2003): 9–29; Michael David-Fox, Peter Holquist, and Alexander Martin, eds., *Orientalism and Empire in Russia* (Bloomington: Slavica, 2006); Clemens Ruthner, "Habsburg's Little Orient: A Post/Colonial Reading of Austrian and German Cultural Narratives on Bosnia-Herzegovina, 1878–1918," *Kakanien Revisited*, May 22, 2008. http://www.kakanien.ac.at/beitr/fallstudie/CRuthner5.pdf (Accessed June 20, 2023); Klemens Kaps and Jan Surman, "Postcolonial or Post-colonial? Post(-)colonial Perspectives on Habsburg Galicia," *Historyka: Studia metodologiczne* XLII (2012); Alexander Kratochvil et al., eds., *Kulturgrenzen in postimperialen Räumen: Bosnien und Westukraine als transkulturelle Regionen* (Bielefeld: Transcript, 2013).

29 Alexander Etkind, *Internal Colonization: Russia's Imperial Experience* (Cambridge: Polity, 2011).

30 Piro Rexhepi, "The Politics of Postcolonial Erasure in Sarajevo," *Interventions* 20, no. 6 (2018): 930–45; Robert D. Crews, "Civilization in the City: Architecture, Urbanism, and the Colonization of Tashkent," in *Architectures of Russian Identity, 1500 to the Present*, ed. James Cracraft and Daniel Rowland (Ithaca, NY: Cornell University Press, 2003); Alexander Morrison, "Na Dunganskoi ulitse: Gorod Vernyi kak 'pliural'noe obshchestvo'," *Istoriia – Elektronnyi nauchno-obrazovatel'nyi zhurnal* 10 (75), no. 1 (2019): 1–22. https://history.jes.su/s207987840002553-7-1/ (Accessed June 20, 2023); Victor Zatsepine, "Russia, Railways, and Urban Development in Manchuria, 1896–1930," in *Harbin to Hanoi: The Colonial Built Environment in Asia, 1840 to 1940*, ed. Laura Victoir and Victor Zatsepine (Hong Kong: Hong Kong University Press, 2013), 17–35. An important exception is Jeff Sahadeo's barnstorming history of Tashkent under Russian rule, where he explicitly calls Tashkent a colonial city. See Jeff Sahadeo, *Russian Colonial Society in Tashkent, 1865–1923* (Bloomington: Indiana University Press, 2007).

31 Christoph Herzog, "Nineteenth-Century Baghdad through Ottoman Eyes," in *The Empire in the City: Arab Provincial Capitals in the Late Ottoman Empire*, ed. Jens Hanssen, Thomas Philipp, and Stefan Weber (Beirut: Ergon Verlag, 2002), 311–28; Thomas Kühn, "Ordering Urban Space in Ottoman Yemen, 1872–1914," in *The Empire in the City: Arab Provincial Capitals in the Late Ottoman Empire*, ed. Jens Hanssen, Thomas Philipp, and Stefan Weber (Beirut: Ergon Verlag, 2002), 329–47.

32 Daniel Goffman, "Izmir: From Village to Colonial Port City," in *The Ottoman City between East and West: Aleppo, Izmir, and Istanbul*, ed. Edhem Eldem, Bruce Masters, and Daniel Goffman (Cambridge: Cambridge University Press, 1999).

33 Jill Steward, "The Potemkin City: Tourist Images of Late Imperial Vienna," in *Imperial Cities: Landscape, Display and Identity*, ed. Felix Driver and David Gilbert (Manchester: Manchester University Press, 1999), 78–95; Monica Rüthers, "Moskau als imperiale Stadt," *Jahrbücher für Geschichte Osteuropas* 56, no. 4 (2008): 481–506. More often, the term "imperial city" has been used with a much broader meaning, see, for example, John Freely, *Istanbul: The Imperial City* (Harmondsworth: Viking, 1996); Steven Maddox, *Saving Stalin's Imperial City: Historic Preservation in Leningrad, 1930–1950* (Bloomington: Indiana University Press, 2015).

34 Serhiy Bilenky, *Imperial Urbanism in the Borderlands: Kyiv, 1800–1905* (Toronto: University of Toronto Press, 2018), 90.

35 Frithjof Benjamin Schenk, "Mental Maps: The Cognitive Mapping of the Continent as an Object of Research of European History," *European History Online (EGO)*, July 8, 2013. http://www.ieg-ego.eu/schenkf-2013-en (Accessed October 20, 2022). Larry Wolff locates the origins of Eastern Europe as a concept in the age of enlightenment; see Larry Wolff, *Inventing Eastern Europe: The Map of Civilization on the Mind of the Enlightenment* (Stanford, CA: Stanford University Press, 1994).

36 See, for example, the overview in Kathleen Wilson, "Introduction: Histories, Empires, Modernities," in *A New Imperial History: Culture, Identity and Modernity in Britain and the Empire, 1660–1840*, ed. Kathleen Wilson (Cambridge: Cambridge University Press, 2004), 1–26.

37 Herfried Münkler, *Empires: The Logic of World Domination from Ancient Rome to the United States* (Cambridge: Polity, 2007), 9–11.

38 Uffe Østergård, "Nation-Building and Nationalism in the Oldenburg Empire," in *Nationalizing Empires*, ed. Stefan Berger and Alexei Miller (Budapest: Central European University Press, 2015), 461–509.

39 Josep M. Colomer, "Empires versus States," *Oxford Research Encyclopedia of Politics*, June 28, 2017. https://doi.org/10.1093/acrefore/9780190228637.013.608 (Accessed October 20, 2022).

40 Frederick Cooper, *Colonialism in Question* (Berkeley: University of California Press, 2005), 192.

41 Jane Burbank and Frederick Cooper, *Empires in World History: Power and the Politics of Difference* (Princeton, NJ: Princeton University Press, 2010), 8.

42 In analyzing cities of three empires together, this book takes on a transimperial perspective as proposed in Daniel Hedinger and Nadin Heé, "Transimperial History – Connectivity, Cooperation and Competition," *Journal of Modern European History* 16, no. 4 (2018): 429–52.

43 Karen Barkey, *Empire of Difference: The Ottomans in Comparative Perspective* (Cambridge: Cambridge University Press, 2008); Suraiya Faroqhi, *Subjects of the Sultan: Culture and Daily Life in the Ottoman Empire* (London: Tauris, 2005); Halil İnalcik and Donald Quataert, eds., *An Economic and Social History of the Ottoman Empire, 1300–1914* (Cambridge: Cambridge University Press, 1994).

44 Andreas Kappeler, *The Russian Empire: A Multiethnic History* (Harlow: Longman, 2001); Valerie A. Kivelson and Ronald Grigor Suny, *Russia's Empires* (New York: Oxford University Press, 2017); Boris N. Mironov, *The Social History of Imperial Russia, 1700–1917, Vol. 1–2* (Boulder, CO: Westview Press, 2000).

45 John Deak, *Forging a Multinational State: State Making in Imperial Austria from the Enlightenment to the First World War* (Stanford, CA: Stanford University Press, 2015); Pieter M. Judson, *The Habsburg Empire: A New History* (Cambridge, MA: Belknap Press, 2016); Arno Strohmeyer, "Die Habsburgermonarchie in der Frühen Neuzeit – ein Imperium? Ein Problemaufriss," in *Imperien und Reiche in der Weltgeschichte*, ed. Michael Gehler and Robert Rollinger (Wiesbaden: Harrassowitz, 2014). On the concept of composite monarchy, see J. H. Elliot, "A Europe of Composite Monarchies," *Past and Present* 137, no. 1 (1992): 48–71.

46 Robert E. Jones, *Provincial Development in Russia: Catherine II and Jakob Sievers* (New Brunswick: Rutgers University Press, 1984); Robert E. Jones, "Urban Planning and the Development of Provincial Towns in Russia 1762–1786," in *The 18th Century in Russia*, ed. J. G. Garrard (Oxford: Clarendon Press, 1973), 321–44; N. F. Gulianitskii and G. V. Alferova, "Oblastnaia reforma i pereplanirovka russkikh gorodov," in *Russkoe gradostroitel'noe iskusstvo: Moskva i slozhivshiesia russkie goroda XVIII – pervoi poloviny XIX vekov*, ed. N. F. Gulianitskii (Moskva: Stroiizdat, 1998), 22–60.

47 J. Michael Hittle, *The Service City: State and Townsmen in Russia, 1600–1800* (Cambridge, MA: Harvard University Press, 1979).

48 A. S. Shchenkov, "Formirovanie novoi struktury rekonstruiruemykh gorodov," in *Moskva i slozhivshiesia russkie goroda XVIII – pervoi poloviny XIX vekov*, ed. N. F. Gulianitskii (Moskva: Stroiizdat, 1998), 209–21.

49 Gilbert Rozman, "Comparative Approaches to Urbanization: Russia, 1750–1800," in *The City in Russian History*, ed. Michael F. Hamm (Lexington: University Press of Kentucky, 1976), 78; Jan De Vries, *European Urbanization, 1500–1800* (Cambridge, MA: Harvard University Press, 1984), 45.

50 Rozman, "Approaches," 78f; Nancy Shields Kollmann, *The Russian Empire, 1450–1801* (Oxford: Oxford University Press, 2017), 386, 88.

51 Mironov, *The Social History*, 1:443–48.

52 Robert E. Lewis and Richard H. Rowland, "Urbanization in Russia and the USSR, 1897–1970," in *The City in Russian History*, ed. Michael F. Hamm (Lexington: University Press of Kentucky, 1976), 209.

53 Mironov, *The Social History*, 1:467.

54 Henning Bauer, Andreas Kappeler, and Brigitte Roth, eds., *Die Nationalitäten des Russischen Reiches in der Volkszählung von 1897, Vol. B: Ausgewählte Daten zur sozio-ethnischen Struktur des Russischen Reiches* (Stuttgart: Steiner, 1991), 400–2.

55 Manfred Hildermeier, "Die russische Stadt: Subtyp europäischer Entwicklungen?," in *Die europäische Stadt im 20. Jahrhundert*, ed. Friedrich Lenger and Klaus Tenfelde (Wien: Böhlau, 2006), 53.

56 Guido Hausmann, ed., *Gesellschaft als lokale Veranstaltung* (Göttingen: Vandenhoeck & Ruprecht 2002).

57 Bauer, Kappeler, and Roth, *Nationalitäten, Vol. B*, 395–409.

58 Márta Fata, "Einwanderung und Ansiedelung der Deutschen (1686–1790)," in *Deutsche Geschichte im Osten Europas, Bd. 6: Land an der Donau*, ed. Günter Schödl (Berlin: Siedler, 1995).

59 Robin Okey, *The Habsburg Monarchy, c. 1765–1918: From Enlightenment to Eclipse* (Basingstoke: Macmillan Press, 2001), 9–11.

60 De Vries, *Urbanization*, 45. This number does not include Hungary and the other eastern lands of the Habsburg Monarchy.

61 Okey, *The Habsburg Monarchy*, 9–10.

62 Judson, *Habsburg Empire*, 112–13.
63 Renate Banik-Schweitzer, "Der Prozess der Urbanisierung," in *Die Habs-burgermonarchie 1848–1918, Bd. 9: Soziale Strukturen, Teilbd. 1: Von der feudal-agrarischen zur bürgerlich-industriellen Gesellschaft, Teil 2: Von der Stände- zur Klassengesellschaft*, ed. Ulrike Harmat, Helmut Rumpler, and Peter Urbanitsch (Wien: Verlag der Österreichischen Akademie der Wissenschaften, 2010), 194–95.
64 Hannes Stekl and Hans Heiss, "Klein- und mittelstädtische Lebenswelten," in *Die Habsburgermonarchie 1848–1918, Bd. 9: Soziale Strukturen, Teilbd. 1: Von der feudal-agrarischen zur bürgerlich-industriellen Gesellschaft, Teil 2: Von der Stände- zur Klassengesellschaft*, ed. Ulrike Harmat, Helmut Rumpler, and Peter Urbanitsch (Wien: Verlag der Österreichischen Akademie der Wissenschaften, 2010), 569–70; Eve Blau, "The City as Protagonist: Architecture and the Cultures of Central Europe," in *Shaping the Great City: Modern Architecture in Central Europe, 1890–1937*, ed. Eve Blau and Monika Platzer (Munich: Prestel, 1999), 13–14.
65 Harald Heppner, "Wien als Orientierungsmuster städtischer Gestaltung im Karpatenraum." *Transylvanian Review* 14, no. 1 (2005): 76–77.
66 Meinhard v. Engelberg argues that this process had already begun in the early modern era and had been intensified by the centralizing tendencies of the late eighteenth century. See Meinrad v. Engelberg, "Partielle Autonomie und 'Stellvertretende Repräsentation' oder: Gibt es ein 'habsburgisches' Stadtbild?," in *Les villes des Habsbourg du XVe au XIXe Siècle: Communication, art et pouvoir dans les réseaux urbains*, ed. Ludolf Pelizaeus (Reims: ÉPURE, 2021), 135–54.
67 Blau: "City;" Charles S. Maier, "City, Empire, and Imperial Aftermath: Contending Contexts for the Urban Vision," in *Shaping the Great City: Modern Architecture in Central Europe, 1890–1937*, ed. Eve Blau and Monika Platzer (Munich: Prestel 1999), 25–41. For the architecture of Habsburg public buildings, see also the conference "The aesthetics of public service," Vienna, February 13–14, 2020. CfP in ArtHist.net, September 9, 2019. https://arthist.net/archive/21475 (Accessed October 20, 2022).
68 Wolfgang Maderthaner, "Urbane Lebenswelten: Metropolen und Großstädte," in *Die Habsburgermonarchie 1848–1918, Bd. 9: Soziale Strukturen, Teilbd. 1: Von der feudal-agrarischen zur bürgerlich-industriellen Gesellschaft, Teil 2: Von der Stände- zur Klassengesellschaft*, ed. Ulrike Harmat, Helmut Rumpler, and Peter Urbanitsch (Wien: Verlag der Österreichischen Akademie der Wissenschaften, 2010), 499.
69 Charles Issawi, *The Economic History of Turkey, 1800–1914* (Chicago, IL: University of Chicago Press, 1980), 34–35.
70 Bruce McGowan, "The Age of the Ayans, 1699–1812," in *An Economic and Social History of the Ottoman Empire, 1300–1914*, ed. Halil İnalcik and Donald Quataert (Cambridge: Cambridge University Press, 1994), 652–55.
71 Nora Lafi, "Petitions and Accommodating Urban Change in the Ottoman Empire," in *Istanbul Seen from a Distance: Centre and Provinces in the Ottoman Empire*, ed. Elisabeth Özdalga, Sait Özervarlı, and Feryal Tansuğ (Istanbul: Swedish Research Institute, 2011), 73–82; Albert Hourani, "Ottoman Reform and the Politics of Notables," in *Beginnings of Modernization in the Middle*

East: The Nineteenth Century, ed. William R. Polk and Richard L. Chambers (Chicago, IL: University of Chicago Press, 1968), 41–68.

72 Edhem Eldem, Daniel Goffman, and Bruce Masters, *The Ottoman City between East and West: Aleppo, Izmir, and Istanbul* (Cambridge: Cambridge University Press, 1999), 212–13.

73 Nora Lafi and Florian Riedler, "Einleitung: Die osmanische Stadt im Wandel, 1850–1920," in "Die osmanische Stadt," ed. Nora Lafi and Florian Riedler, special issue, *Moderne Stadtgeschichte*, no. 1 (2018): 7–9.

74 Jean-Luc Arnaud, "Modernization of the Cities of the Ottoman Empire (1800–1920)," in *The City in the Islamic World*, ed. Salma K. Jayyusi et al. (Boston, MA: Brill, 2008), 956–57.

75 Çelik, *Remaking*; Neumann, "Modernitäten."

76 Alexandra Yerolympos, *Urban Transformations in the Balkans (1820–1920): Aspects of Balkan Town Planning and the Remaking of Thessaloniki* (Thessaloniki: University Studio Press, 1996); Zeynep Çelik, *Empire, Architecture, and the City: French-Ottoman Encounters, 1830–1914* (Seattle: University of Washington Press, 2008).

77 Tetsuya Sahara, "The Ottoman City Council and the Beginning of the Modernisation of Urban Space in the Balkans," in *The City in the Ottoman Empire*, ed. Ulrike Freitag (London: Routledge, 2010), 26–50; Arnaud, "Modernization," 970.

78 Erol Ülker, "Multinational Capital, Public Utilities, and Urban Change in Late Ottoman Istanbul: Constantinople Tramway and Electric Company," *Moderne Stadtgeschichte*, no. 1 (2018): 68–81.

79 Malte Fuhrmann, *Port Cities of the Eastern Mediterranean: Urban Culture in the Late Ottoman Empire* (Cambridge: Cambridge University Press, 2020).

80 Arnaud, "Modernization"; Donald Quataert, "The Age of Reforms, 1812–1914," in *An Economic and Social History of the Ottoman Empire, 1300–1914*, ed. Halil İnalcik and Donald Quataert (Cambridge: Cambridge University Press, 1994), 781–82; Issawi, *History*, 34–35.

81 Quataert, "Age," 782–83.

82 Florian Riedler, "Segregation oder gemeinschaftliches Zusammenleben? Vom Umgang mit Vielfalt in der osmanischen Stadt," *Moderne Stadtgeschichte*, no. 1 (2018): 39–52; Eva Anne Frantz, *Gewalt und Koexistenz: Muslime und Christen im spätosmanischen Kosovo, 1870–1913* (Berlin: De Gruyter Oldenbourg, 2016), 237–40.

83 Jan C. Behrendts and Martin Kohlrausch, eds., *Races to Modernity: Metropolitan Aspirations in Eastern Europe, 1890–1940* (Budapest: CEU Press, 2014); Eszter Gantner and Heidi Hein-Kircher, eds., "'Emerging Cities': Knowledge and Urbanization in Europe's Borderlands 1880–1945," special issue, *Journal of Urban History* 43, no. 4 (2017).

84 The category of economic backwardness has been most influentially proposed by Alexander Gerschenkron; see Alexander Gerschenkron, *Economic Backwardness in Historical Perspective: A Book of Essays* (Cambridge, MA: Belknap Press, 1962). For the history of the discourse of Eastern Europe's backwardness, see Maria Rhode, "Rückständigkeit und Osteuropa: Zwei Seiten einer Medaille?," in *Die Zukunft der Rückständigkeit: Chancen – Formen – Mehrwert*, ed. David Feest and Lutz Häfner (Köln: Böhlau, 2016), 50–81.

85　Eve Blau and Monika Platzer, eds., *Shaping the Great City: Modern Architecture in Central Europe, 1890–1937* (Munich: Prestel, 1999).

86　James Cracraft, *The Petrine Revolution in Russian Architecture* (Chicago, IL: University of Chicago Press, 1988), 147–241.

87　Çelik, *Remaking*; Arnaud, "Modernization."

88　Jobst, Obertreis, and Vulpius, "Imperiumsforschung."

89　Jürgen Osterhammel, "Russland und der Vergleich zwischen Imperien: Einige Anknüpfungspunkte," *Comparativ* 18, no. 2 (2008): 11–26.

90　Alexander S. Morrison, *Russian Rule in Samarkand, 1868–1910: A Comparison with British India* (Oxford: Oxford University Press, 2008), 3.

91　Edward J. Lazzerini, "Volga Tatars in Central Asia," in *Central Asia in Historical Perspective*, ed. Beatrice Manz (Boulder, CO: 1994), 82–100.

92　Valeria Heuberger, "Politische Institutionen und Verwaltung in Bosnien und der Herzegowina 1878–1918," in *Die Habsburgermonarchie, Vol. 7: Verwaltung und Parlamentarismus, Part 2: Die regionalen Repräsentativkörperschaften*, ed. Helmut Rumpler and Peter Urbanitsch (Wien: Verlag der Österreichischen Akademie der Wissenschaften, 2000), 2405.

93　John W. Slocum, "Who, and When, Were the Inorodtsy? The Evolution of the Category of 'Aliens' in Imperial Russia," *The Russian Review* 57 (1998): 173–90.

94　Halil İnalcik, "The Ottoman State: Economy and Society, 1300–1600," in *An Economic and Social History of the Ottoman Empire, 1300–1914*, ed. Halil İnalcik and Donald Quataert (Cambridge: Cambridge University Press, 1994), 16.

95　Heuberger, "Institutionen," 2416.

96　Andreas Kappeler, "The Center and Peripheral Elites in the Habsburg, Russian and Ottoman Empires, 1700–1918," *Ab Imperio* (2007); Tim Buchen and Malte Rolf, eds., *Eliten im Vielvölkerreich: Imperiale Biographien in Russland und Österreich-Ungarn, 1850–1918* (Berlin: De Gruyter Oldenburg, 2015).

97　Raymond F. Betts, *Assimilation and Association in French Colonial Theory, 1890–1914* (New York: Columbia University Press, 1961), 21–22.

98　Malte Rolf, *Imperiale Herrschaft im Weichselland: Das Königreich Polen im russischen Imperium (1864–1915)* (Berlin: De Gruyter - Oldenbourg, 2015), 169–71.

99　Selim Deringil, "'They Live in a State of Nomadism and Savagery': The Late Ottoman Empire and the Post-Colonial Debate," *Comparative Studies in Society and History*, no. 2 (2003): 311–42; Ulrich Hofmeister, "Civilization and Russification in Tsarist Central Asia, 1860–1917," *Journal of World History* 27, no. 3 (2016): 411–42; Ruthner, "Habsburg's Little Orient."

100　Driver and Gilbert, *Imperial Cities*.

101　Hunt, *Ten Cities*; see also Emma Hart and Mariana Dantas, eds., "Early Modern Global Cities," special issue, *Urban History* 48, no. 3 (2021).

102　Çiğdem Kafescioğlu, "'In the Image of Rūm': Ottoman Architectural Patronage in Sixteenth-Century Aleppo and Damascus," *Muqarnas* 16 (1999), 70–96.

103　For the afterlife of imperial cities, see the publications of the research group "Empires of Memory" at the Max Planck Institute for the Study of Religious and Ethnic Diversity, Goettingen, see https://www.mmg.mpg.de/mprg-walton (Accessed October 20, 2022). See also Caroline Humphrey and Vera Skvirskaja, eds., *Post-Cosmopolitan Cities: Explorations of Urban Coexistence* (New York: Berghahn, 2012).

Bibliography

Abu-Lughod, Janet. "Tale of Two Cities: The Origins of Modern Cairo." *Comparative Studies in Society and History* 7, no. 4 (1965): 429–57.

Aksan, Virginia. "What's Up in Ottoman Studies?" *Journal of the Ottoman and Turkish Studies Association* 1, no. 1–2 (2014): 3–21.

Amenda, Lars, and Malte Fuhrmann, eds. "Hafenstädte: Mobilität, Migration, Globalisierung." Special issue, *Comparativ* 17, no. 2 (2007).

Arbeitskreis für außereuropäische Geschichte, ed. "Kolonisierte Metropolen." Special issue, *Periplus: Jahrbuch für außereuropäische Geschichte* 6 (1996).

Arnaud, Jean-Luc. "Modernization of the Cities of the Ottoman Empire (1800–1920)." In *The City in the Islamic World*, edited by Salma K. Jayyusi, Renata Holod, Antillio Petruccioli, and André Raymond, 953–75. Boston: Brill, 2008.

Banik-Schweitzer, Renate. "Der Prozess der Urbanisierung." In *Die Habsburgermonarchie 1848–1918, Bd. 9: Soziale Strukturen, Teilbd. 1: Von der feudalagrarischen zur bürgerlich-industriellen Gesellschaft, Teil 2: Von der Stände- zur Klassengesellschaft*, edited by Ulrike Harmat, Helmut Rumpler, and Peter Urbanitsch, 185–232. Wien: Verlag der Österreichischen Akademie der Wissenschaften, 2010.

Barkey, Karen. *Empire of Difference: The Ottomans in Comparative Perspective.* Cambridge: Cambridge University Press, 2008.

Bauer, Henning, Andreas Kappeler, and Brigitte Roth, eds. *Die Nationalitäten des Russischen Reiches in der Volkszählung von 1897, Vol. B: Ausgewählte Daten zur sozio-ethnischen Struktur des Russischen Reiches.* Stuttgart: Steiner, 1991.

Behrendts, Jan C., and Martin Kohlrausch, eds. *Races to Modernity: Metropolitan Aspirations in Eastern Europe, 1890–1940.* Budapest: CEU Press, 2014.

Berger, Stefan, and Alexei Miller, eds. *Nationalizing Empires.* Budapest: Central European University Press, 2015.

Betts, Raymond F. *Assimilation and Association in French Colonial Theory, 1890–1914.* New York: Columbia University Press, 1961.

Bilenky, Serhiy. *Imperial Urbanism in the Borderlands: Kyiv, 1800–1905.* Toronto: University of Toronto Press, 2018.

Blau, Eve. "The City as Protagonist: Architecture and the Cultures of Central Europe." In *Shaping the Great City: Modern Architecture in Central Europe, 1890–1937*, edited by Eve Blau and Monika Platzer, 11–24. Munich: Prestel, 1999.

Blau, Eve, and Monika Platzer, eds. *Shaping the Great City: Modern Architecture in Central Europe, 1890–1937.* Munich: Prestel, 1999.

Buchen, Tim, and Malte Rolf, eds. *Eliten im Vielvölkerreich: Imperiale Biographien in Russland und Österreich-Ungarn, 1850–1918.* Berlin: De Gruyter Oldenburg, 2015.

Burbank, Jane, and Frederick Cooper. *Empires in World History: Power and the Politics of Difference.* Princeton, NJ: Princeton University Press, 2010.

Çelik, Zeynep. *The Remaking of Istanbul: Portrait of an Ottoman City in the Nineteenth Century.* Berkeley: University of California Press, 1993.

Çelik, Zeynep. *Empire, Architecture, and the City: French-Ottoman Encounters, 1830–1914.* Seattle: University of Washington Press, 2008.

Cole, Laurence. "Visions and Revisions of Empire: Reflections on a New History of the Habsburg Monarchy." *Austrian History Yearbook* 49 (2018): 261–80.

Colomer, Josep M. "Empires versus States," *Oxford Research Encyclopedia of Politics*, June 28, 2017. Accessed October 20, 2022. https://doi.org/10.1093/acrefore/9780190228637.013.608

Cooper, Frederick. *Colonialism in Question*. Berkeley: University of California Press, 2005.

Cracraft, James. *The Petrine Revolution in Russian Architecture*. Chicago, IL: University of Chicago Press, 1988.

Crews, Robert D. "Civilization in the City: Architecture, Urbanism, and the Colonization of Tashkent." In *Architectures of Russian Identity, 1500 to the Present*, edited by James Cracraft and Daniel Rowland, 117–32. Ithaca, NY: Cornell University Press, 2003.

David-Fox, Michael, Peter Holquist, and Alexander Martin, eds. *Orientalism and Empire in Russia*. Bloomington: Slavica, 2006.

De Vries, Jan. *European Urbanization, 1500–1800*. Cambridge, MA: Harvard University Press, 1984.

Deak, John. *Forging a Multinational State: State Making in Imperial Austria from the Enlightenment to the First World War*. Stanford, CA: Stanford University Press, 2015.

Deringil, Selim. "'They Live in a State of Nomadism and Savagery': The Late Ottoman Empire and the Post-Colonial Debate." *Comparative Studies in Society and History*, no. 2 (2003): 311–42.

Driver, Felix, and David Gilbert, eds. *Imperial Cities: Landscape, Display and Identity*. Manchester: Manchester University Press, 1999.

Eldem, Edhem. "Istanbul: From Imperial to Peripheralized Capital." In *The Ottoman City between East and West: Aleppo, Izmir, and Istanbul*, edited by Edhem Eldem, Bruce Masters, and Daniel Goffman, 135–206. Cambridge: Cambridge University Press, 1999.

Eldem, Edhem, Daniel Goffman, and Bruce Masters. *The Ottoman City between East and West: Aleppo, Izmir, and Istanbul*. Cambridge: Cambridge University Press, 1999.

Elliot, J.H. "A Europe of Composite Monarchies." *Past and Present* 137, no. 1 (1992): 48–71.

Engelberg, Meinrad v. "Partielle Autonomie und 'Stellvertretende Repräsentation' oder Gibt es ein 'habsburgisches' Stadtbild?". In *Les villes des Habsbourg du XVe au XIXe siècle: Communication, art et pouvoir dans les réseaux urbains*, edited by Ludolf Pelizaeus, 135–54. Reims: ÉPURE, 2021.

Etkind, Alexander. *Internal Colonization: Russia's Imperial Experience*. Cambridge: Polity, 2011.

Faroqhi, Suraiya. *Subjects of the Sultan: Culture and Daily Life in the Ottoman Empire*. London: Tauris, 2005.

Fata, Márta. "Einwanderung und Ansiedelung der Deutschen (1686–1790)." In *Deutsche Geschichte im Osten Europas, Bd. 6: Land an der Donau*, edited by Günter Schödl, 90–196. Berlin: Siedler, 1995.

Feichtinger, Johannes, Ursula Prutsch, and Moritz Csáky, eds. *Habsburg Postcolonial: Machtstrukturen und kollektives Gedächtnis*. Innsbruck: Studien Verlag, 2003.

Frantz, Eva Anne. *Gewalt und Koexistenz: Muslime und Christen im spätosmanischen Kosovo, 1870–1913*. Berlin: De Gruyter Oldenbourg, 2016.

Freely, John. *Istanbul: The Imperial City*. Harmondsworth: Viking, 1996.

Fuhrmann, Malte. *Port Cities of the Eastern Mediterranean: Urban Culture in the Late Ottoman Empire*. Cambridge: Cambridge University Press, 2020.

Gantner, Eszter, and Heidi Hein-Kircher, eds. "'Emerging Cities': Knowledge and Urbanization in Europe's Borderlands 1880–1945." Special issue, *Journal of Urban History* 43, no. 4 (2017).

Gerschenkron, Alexander. *Economic Backwardness in Historical Perspective: A Book of Essays*. Cambridge, MA: Belknap Press, 1962.

Gitlin, Jay, Barbara Berglund, and Adam Arenson, eds. *Frontier Cities: Encounters at the Crossroads of Empire*. Philadelphia: University of Pennsylvania Press, 2013.

Goebel, Michael. *Anti-Imperial Metropolis: Interwar Paris and the Seeds of Third World Nationalism*. Cambridge: Cambridge University Press, 2015.

Goffman, Daniel. "Izmir: From Village to Colonial Port City." In *The Ottoman City between East and West: Aleppo, Izmir, and Istanbul*, edited by Edhem Eldem, Bruce Masters, and Daniel Goffman, 79–134. Cambridge: Cambridge University Press, 1999.

Gulianitskii, N.F., and G.V. Alferova. "Oblastnaia reforma i pereplanirovka russkikh gorodov." In *Russkoe gradostroitel'noe iskusstvo: Moskva i slozhivshiesia russkie goroda XVIII - pervoi poloviny XIX vekov*, edited by N.F. Gulianitskii, 209–21. Moskva: Stroiizdat, 1998.

Haggerty, Sheryllynne, Anthony Webster, and Nicholas J. White, eds. *The Empire in One City? Liverpool's Inconvenient Imperial Past*. Manchester: Manchester University Press, 2008.

Hart, Emma, and Mariana Dantas, eds. "Early Modern Global Cities." Special issue, *Urban History* 48, no. 3 (2021).

Hausmann, Guido, ed. *Gesellschaft als lokale Veranstaltung*. Göttingen: Vandenhoeck & Ruprecht 2002.

Hausmann, Guido. "Osteuropäische Stadt oder Stadt in Osteuropa?" In *Urbanisierung und Stadtentwicklung in Südosteuropa vom 19. bis zum 21. Jahrhundert*, edited by Thomas M. Bohn and Marie-Janine Calic, 29–66. München: Sager, 2010.

Hedinger, Daniel and Nadin Heé. "Transimperial History: Connectivity, Cooperation and Competition." *Journal of Modern European History* 16, no. 4 (2018): 429–52.

Heerten, Lasse, and Daniel Tödt. "Some Reflections on Imperial Port Cities in the Age of Steam." *Global Urban History* (blog). October 29, 2016. Accessed October 20, 2022. https://globalurbanhistory.com/2016/10/29/some-reflections-on-imperial-port-cities-in-the-age-of-steam/.

Hein, Carola, ed. *Port Cities: Dynamic Landscapes and Global Networks*. London: Routledge, 2011.

Hein, Carola. "Port Cities." In *The Oxford Handbook of Cities in World History*, edited by Peter Clark. Oxford: Oxford University Press, 2013: 809–27.

Heppner, Harald. "Wien als Orientierungsmuster städtischer Gestaltung im Karpatenraum." *Transylvanian Review* 14, no. 1 (2005): 69–79.

Herzog, Christoph. "Nineteenth-Century Baghdad through Ottoman Eyes." In *The Empire in the City: Arab Provincial Capitals in the Late Ottoman Empire*, edited by Jens Hanssen, Thomas Philipp, and Stefan Weber, 311–28. Beirut: Ergon Verlag, 2002.

Heuberger, Valeria. "Politische Institutionen und Verwaltung in Bosnien und der Herzegowina 1878–1918." In *Die Habsburgermonarchie, Bd. 7: Verwaltung und Parlamentarismus, Teilbd. 2: Die regionalen Repräsentativkörperschaften*, edited by Helmut Rumpler and Peter Urbanitsch, 2383–425. Wien: Verlag der Österreichischen Akademie der Wissenschaften, 2000.

Hildermeier, Manfred. "Die russische Stadt: Subtyp europäischer Entwicklungen?" In *Die europäische Stadt im 20. Jahrhundert*, edited by Friedrich Lenger and Klaus Tenfelde, 45–60. Wien: Böhlau, 2006.

Hittle, J. Michael. *The Service City: State and Townsmen in Russia, 1600–1800*. Cambridge, MA: Harvard University Press, 1979.

Hofmeister, Ulrich. "Civilization and Russification in Tsarist Central Asia, 1860–1917." *Journal of World History* 27, no. 3 (2016): 411–42.

Hourani, Albert. "Ottoman Reform and the Politics of Notables." In *Beginnings of Modernization in the Middle East: The Nineteenth Century*, edited by William R. Polk and Richard L. Chambers, 41–68. Chicago, IL: University of Chicago Press, 1968.

Hunt, Tristram. *Ten Cities That Made an Empire*. London: Penguin, 2015.

İnalcik, Halil. "The Ottoman State: Economy and Society, 1300–1600." In *An Economic and Social History of the Ottoman Empire, 1300–1914*, edited by Halil İnalcik and Donald Quataert, 9–409. Cambridge: Cambridge University Press, 1994.

İnalcik, Halil, and Donald Quataert, eds. *An Economic and Social History of the Ottoman Empire, 1300–1914*. Cambridge: Cambridge University Press, 1994.

Issawi, Charles. *The Economic History of Turkey, 1800–1914*. Chicago, IL: University of Chicago Press, 1980.

Jobst, Kerstin S., Julia Obertreis, and Ricarda Vulpius. "Neuere Imperiumsforschung in der osteuropäischen Geschichte: Die Habsburgermonarchie, das Russländische Reich und die Sowjetunion." *Comparativ* 18, no. 2 (2008): 27–56.

Jones, Robert E. "Urban Planning and the Development of Provincial Towns in Russia 1762–1786." In *The 18th Century in Russia*, edited by J.G. Garrard, 321–44. Oxford: Clarendon Press, 1973.

Jones, Robert E. *Provincial Development in Russia: Catherine II and Jakob Sievers*. New Brunswick: Rutgers University Press, 1984.

Judson, Pieter M. *The Habsburg Empire: A New History*. Cambridge, MA: Belknap Press, 2016.

Kappeler, Andreas. *The Russian Empire: A Multiethnic History*. Harlow: Longman, 2001.

Kappeler, Andreas. "The Center and Peripheral Elites in the Habsburg, Russian and Ottoman Empires, 1700–1918." *Ab Imperio*, no. 2 (2007): 17–58.

Kaps, Klemens, and Jan Surman, "Postcolonial or Post-colonial? Post(-)colonial Perspectives on Habsburg Galicia," *Historyka: Studia metodologiczne* XLII (2012): 7–35.

Keene, Derek. "Cities and Empires." *Journal of Urban History* 32, no. 1 (2005): 8–21.

King, Anthony D. *Colonial Urban Development: Culture, Social Power and Environment.* London: Routledge, 1976.

King, Anthony D. *Urbanism, Colonialism and the World Economy: Cultural and Spatial Foundations of the World Urban System.* London: Routledge, 1990.

Kivelson, Valerie A., and Ronald Grigor Suny. *Russia's Empires.* New York: Oxford University Press, 2017.

Kollmann, Nancy Shields. *The Russian Empire, 1450–1801.* Oxford: Oxford University Press, 2017.

Kratochvil, Alexander, Renata Makarska, Katharina Schwitin, and Annette Werberger, eds. *Kulturgrenzen in postimperialen Räumen: Bosnien und Westukraine als transkulturelle Regionen.* Bielefeld: Transcript, 2013.

Kühn, Thomas. "Ordering Urban Space in Ottoman Yemen, 1872–1914." In *The Empire in the City: Arab Provincial Capitals in the Late Ottoman Empire,* edited by Jens Hanssen, Thomas Philipp, and Stefan Weber, 329–47. Beirut: Ergon Verlag, 2002.

Kühn, Thomas. "Shaping and Reshaping Colonial Ottomanism: Contesting Boundaries of Difference and Integration in Ottoman Yemen." *Comparative Studies of South Asia, Africa and the Middle East* 27, no. 2 (2007): 315–31.

Lafi, Nora. "Petitions and Accommodating Urban Change in the Ottoman Empire." In *Istanbul Seen from a Distance: Centre and Provinces in the Ottoman Empire,* edited by Elisabeth Özdalga, Sait Özervarlı, and Feryal Tansuğ, 73–82. Istanbul: Swedish Research Institute, 2011.

Lafi, Nora, and Florian Riedler. "Einleitung: Die osmanische Stadt im Wandel, 1850–1920." In "Die osmanische Stadt," edited by Nora Lafi and Florian Riedler. Special issue, *Moderne Stadtgeschichte,* no. 1 (2018): 5–15.

Lauro, Amandine, ed. "Bruxelles et le Congo." Special issue, *Les Cahiers de la Fonderie* 28 (2008).

Lazzerini, Edward J. "Volga Tatars in Central Asia." In *Central Asia in Historical Perspective,* edited by Beatrice Manz, 82–100. Boulder, CO: Westview Press, 1994.

Lees, Andrew, and Lynn Hollen Lees. *Cities and the Making of Modern Europe, 1750–1914.* Cambridge: Cambridge University Press, 2007.

Lewis, Robert E., and Richard H. Rowland. "Urbanization in Russia and the USSR, 1897–1970." In *The City in Russian History,* edited by Michael F. Hamm, 205–21. Lexington: University Press of Kentucky, 1976.

Liddle, Swapna. *Connaught Place and the Making of New Delhi.* New Delhi: Speaking Tiger, 2018.

Logan, William S. *Hanoi: Biography of a City.* Seattle: University of Washington Press, 2000.

Maddox, Steven. *Saving Stalin's Imperial City: Historic Preservation in Leningrad, 1930–1950.* Bloomington: Indiana University Press, 2015.

Maderthaner, Wolfgang. "Urbane Lebenswelten: Metropolen und Großstädte." In *Die Habsburgermonarchie 1848–1918, Bd. 9: Soziale Strukturen, Teilbd. 1: Von der feudal-agrarischen zur bürgerlich-industriellen Gesellschaft, Teil 2: Von der*

Stände- zur Klassengesellschaft, edited by Ulrike Harmat, Helmut Rumpler, and Peter Urbanitsch, 493–538. Wien: Verlag der Österreichischen Akademie der Wissenschaften, 2010.

Maier, Charles S. "City, Empire, and Imperial Aftermath: Contending Contexts for the Urban Vision." In *Shaping the Great City: Modern Architecture in Central Europe, 1890–1937*, edited by Eve Blau and Monika Platzer, 25–41. Munich: Prestel, 1999.

Makdisi, Ussama. "Ottoman Orientalism." *The American Historical Review* 107, no. 3 (2002): 768–96.

McGowan, Bruce. "The Age of the Ayans, 1699–1812." In *An Economic and Social History of the Ottoman Empire, 1300–1914*, edited by Halil İnalcik and Donald Quataert, 637–758. Cambridge: Cambridge University Press, 1994.

Metcalf, Thomas R. "Colonial Cities." In *The Oxford Handbook of Cities in World History*, edited by Peter Clark, 753–69. Oxford: Oxford University Press, 2013.

Mironov, Boris N. *The Social History of Imperial Russia, 1700–1917, Vol. 1–2.* Boulder, CO: Westview Press, 2000.

Morrison, Alexander S. *Russian Rule in Samarkand, 1868–1910: A Comparison with British India.* Oxford: Oxford University Press, 2008.

Morrison, Alexander S. "Na Dunganskoi ulitse: Gorod Vernyi kak 'pliural'noe obshchestvo'." *Istoriia – Elektronnyi nauchno-obrazovatel'nyi zhurnal* 10 (75), no. 1 (2019): 1–22. Accessed June 20, 2023. https://history.jes.su/s20798784 0002553-7-1/.

Mundy, Barbara E. *The Death of Aztec Tenochtitlan, the Life of Mexico City.* Austin: University of Texas Press, 2018.

Münkler, Herfried. *Empires: The Logic of World Domination from Ancient Rome to the United States.* Cambridge: Polity, 2007.

Neumann, Christoph K. "Modernitäten im Konflikt: Der sechste Munizipal-Bezirk von Istanbul, 1857–1912." In *Istanbul: Vom imperialen Herrschersitz zur Megapolis: Historiographische Betrachtungen zu Gesellschaft, Institutionen und Räumen*, edited by Yavuz Köse, 351–75. München: Meidenbauer, 2006.

Okey, Robin. *The Habsburg Monarchy, C. 1765–1918: From Enlightenment to Eclipse.* Basingstoke: Macmillan Press, 2001.

Østergård, Uffe. "Nation-Building and Nationalism in the Oldenburg Empire." In *Nationalizing Empires*, edited by Stefan Berger and Alexei Miller, 461–509. Budapest: Central European University Press, 2015.

Osterhammel, Jürgen. "Russland und der Vergleich zwischen Imperien: Einige Anknüpfungspunkte." *Comparativ* 18, no. 2 (2008): 11–26.

Osterhammel, Jürgen. *The Transformation of the World: A Global History of the Nineteenth Century.* Princeton, NJ: Princeton University Press, 2014.

Post, Franz-Joseph. "Europäische Kolonialstädte in vergleichender Perspektive." In *Kolonialstädte: Europäische Enklaven oder Schmelztiegel der Kulturen?*, edited by Horst Gründer and Peter Johanek, 1–25. Münster: Lit, 2001.

Quataert, Donald. "The Age of Reforms, 1812–1914." In *An Economic and Social History of the Ottoman Empire, 1300–1914*, edited by Halil İnalcik and Donald Quataert, 759–943. Cambridge: Cambridge University Press, 1994.

Redfield, Robert, and Milton B. Singer. "The Cultural Role of Cities." *Economic Development and Cultural Change* 3, no. 1 (1954): 53–73.

Rexhepi, Piro. "The Politics of Postcolonial Erasure in Sarajevo." *Interventions* 20, no. 6 (2018): 930–45.

Rhode, Maria. "Rückständigkeit und Osteuropa: Zwei Seiten einer Medaille?" In *Die Zukunft der Rückständigkeit: Chancen – Formen – Mehrwert*, edited by David Feest and Lutz Häfner, 50–81. Köln: Böhlau, 2016.

Riedler, Florian. "Segregation oder gemeinschaftliches Zusammenleben? Vom Umgang mit Vielfalt in der osmanischen Stadt." *Moderne Stadtgeschichte*, no. 1 (2018): 39–52.

Rolf, Malte. *Imperiale Herrschaft im Weichselland: Das Königreich Polen im Russischen Imperium (1864–1915)*. Berlin: De Gruyter - Oldenbourg, 2015.

Rosenthal, Steven T. *The Politics of Dependency: Urban Reform in Istanbul*. Westport: Greenwood Press, 1980.

Ross, Robert J., and Gerard J. Telkamp, eds. *Colonial Cities*. Dordrecht: Nijhoff, 1985.

Rozman, Gilbert. "Comparative Approaches to Urbanization: Russia, 1750–1800." In *The City in Russian History*, edited by Michael F. Hamm, 69–85. Lexington: University Press of Kentucky, 1976.

Rüthers, Monica. "Moskau als imperiale Stadt." *Jahrbücher für Geschichte Osteuropas* 56, no. 4 (2008): 481–506.

Ruthner, Clemens. "Habsburg's Little Orient: A Post/Colonial Reading of Austrian and German Cultural Narratives on Bosnia-Herzegovina, 1878–1918." In *Kakanien Revisited*, May 22, 2008: 1–16. Accessed June 20, 2023. http://www.kakanien.ac.at/beitr/fallstudie/CRuthner5.pdf.

Sahadeo, Jeff. *Russian Colonial Society in Tashkent, 1865–1923*. Bloomington: Indiana University Press, 2007.

Sahara, Tetsuya. "The Ottoman City Council and the Beginning of the Modernisation of Urban Space in the Balkans." In *The City in the Ottoman Empire*, edited by Ulrike Freitag, 26–50. London: Routledge, 2010.

Said, Edward W. *Culture and Imperialism*. London: Vintage, 1994.

Schäbler, Birgit. "Globale Moderne Und Die Geburt Der Zivilisationsmission an Der Kulturellen Binnengrenze: Die Mission Civilisatrice Ottomane." *Periplus: Jahrbuch für außereuropäische Geschichte* 13 (2003): 9–29.

Schenk, Frithjof Benjamin. "Mental Maps: The Cognitive Mapping of the Continent as an Object of Research of European History," *European History Online (EGO)*, July 8, 2013. Accessed October 20, 2022. http://www.ieg-ego.eu/schenkf-2013-en.

Schneer, Jonathan. *London 1900: The Imperial Metropolis*. New Haven, CT: Yale University Press, 1999.

Sen, Ranjit. *Calcutta in Colonial Transition*. London: Routledge, 2019.

Shchenkov, A. S. "Formirovanie novoi struktury rekonstruiruemykh gorodov." In *Moskva i slozhivshiesia russkie goroda XVIII – pervoi poloviny XIX vekov*, edited by N.F. Gulianitskii, 22–60. Moskva: Stroiizdat, 1998.

Slocum, John W. "Who, and When, Were the Inorodtsy? The Evolution of the Category of 'Aliens' in Imperial Russia." *The Russian Review* 57 (1998): 173–90.

Stekl, Hannes, and Hans Heiss. "Klein- und mittelstädtische Lebenswelten." In *Die Habsburgermonarchie 1848–1918, Bd. 9: Soziale Strukturen, Teilbd. 1: Von der feudal-agrarischen zur bürgerlich-industriellen Gesellschaft, Teil 2: Von der Stände- zur Klassengesellschaft*, edited by Ulrike Harmat, Helmut Rumpler, and Peter Urbanitsch, 561–619. Wien: Verlag der Österreichischen Akademie der Wissenschaften, 2010.

Steward, Jill. "The Potemkin City: Tourist Images of Late Imperial Vienna." In *Imperial Cities: Landscape, Display and Identity*, edited by Felix Driver and David Gilbert, 78–95. Manchester: Manchester University Press, 1999.

Strohmeyer, Arno. "Die Habsburgermonarchie in der frühen Neuzeit – ein Imperium? Ein Problemaufriss." In *Imperien und Reiche in der Weltgeschichte*, edited by Michael Gehler and Robert Rollinger, 1027–55. Wiesbaden: Harrassowitz, 2014.

Tödt, Daniel. "Making Second Imperial Cities: Modern Ports, Colonial Connectivity and Maritime Globalization." *Moderne Stadtgeschichte*, no. 2 (2019): 115–39.

Ülker, Erol. "Multinational Capital, Public Utilities, and Urban Change in Late Ottoman Istanbul: Constantinople Tramway and Electric Company." *Moderne Stadtgeschichte*, no. 1 (2018): 68–81.

Van der Heyden, Ulrich. *Kolonialmetropole Berlin: Eine Spurensuche*. Berlin: Berlin-Edition, 2002.

Weeks, Theodore R. "Nationality, Empire, and Politics in the Russian Empire and USSR: An Overview of Recent Publications." *H-Soz-u-Kult.* (2012). Accessed October 20, 2022. https://www.hsozkult.de/literaturereview/id/forschungsberichte-1134.

Wilson, Kathleen. "Introduction: Histories, Empires, Modernities." In *A New Imperial History: Culture, Identity and Modernity in Britain and the Empire, 1660–1840*, edited by Kathleen Wilson, 1–26. Cambridge: Cambridge University Press, 2004.

Wolff, Larry. *Inventing Eastern Europe: The Map of Civilization on the Mind of the Enlightenment*. Stanford, CA: Stanford University Press, 1994.

Yerolympos, Alexandra. *Urban Transformations in the Balkans (1820–1920): Aspects of Balkan Town Planning and the Remaking of Thessaloniki*. Thessaloniki: University Studio Press, 1996.

Zatsepine, Victor. "Russia, Railways, and Urban Development in Manchuria, 1896–1930." In *Harbin to Hanoi: The Colonial Built Environment in Asia, 1840 to 1940*, edited by Laura Victoir and Victor Zatsepine, 17–35. Hong Kong: Hong Kong University Press, 2013.

Part II
Manifestations of the Imperial in Urban Space

3 The Imperial Palaces in Comparative Perspective
Topkapı, Kremlin, and Hofburg

Nilay Özlü

In his book *Around the Kremlin,* George T. Lowth compared the city of Moscow to Constantinople and emphasized the cosmopolitan character of both imperial capitals and their role in bridging the East with the West:

> There is a charm peculiar to Moscow among the cities of the world. It is in itself the centre of the history of a people – a people one day fated to play a great part in the drama of the future. But at present the charm of Moscow is in its past story and in its present life. The interest of the past story of the city arises out of its peculiar position as the connecting link between the East and the West. In this its situation is something analogous to that of Constantinople, standing upon the confines of two divisions of the earth, and thus it has had to bear the discords of different races and to be the scene of the conflicts of opposing peoples.[1]

The concept of the "imperial city" has many layers, nuances, and complexities; and its definition still lacks scholarly consensus in the post-imperial world. Imperial capitals, on the other hand, provide fertile ground for analyzing and studying the imperial city as sites of imperial power and monarchic grandeur, as stages of royal ceremonials and ostentatious processions, and as urban showcases of imperial architecture. Particularly Istanbul, Vienna, and Moscow, the capitals and former capitals of the three continental empires, are prolific centers for a comparative discussion of how imperial ideologies were transmitted and disseminated and how these empires manifested themselves in the urban context. This chapter investigates the architectural, administrative, and ceremonial configurations of the three capitals of the Ottoman, Habsburg, and Tsarist Empires, with a particular focus on their imperial palaces.

Imperial cities, particularly the imperial capitals, are spatially shaped, culturally defined, and architecturally marked by civil and religious monuments, administrative buildings, public works and institutions, and, most remarkably, by imperial palaces. Strategically located and, more often

DOI: 10.4324/9781003130031-5

than not, surrounded by imposing walls, elevated towers, and monumental gates, palaces dominated the urban fabric of the pre-modern city as the epicenters of architectural glory, court culture, and ostentatious ceremonials. As stated by Lawrence Vale, the government centers, capitols, and palaces, apart from fulfilling bureaucratic or official needs, convey ideological messages as symbols of state power and identity.[2] In the pre-modern world, imperial palaces confirmed the continuity of the monarchy, manifested courtly power, and displayed the empire's glory and endurance via court traditions, processions, and rituals. Thus they were accepted as urban imprints marking the longevity, patrimony, and legitimacy of the court. Moreover, imperial palaces – apart from defining and shaping the urban morphology of the city they were built in, with their vast areas, immense number of inhabitants, and parasitical formations – were configured as a city-within-the-city. Therefore, imperial palaces themselves can be scrutinized as an imperial city with certain institutional, architectural, and urban characteristics.

This research discusses the role of palaces, both as architectural monuments and as seats of monarchs, in defining and shaping the imperial city. Particularly focusing on the Tsarist, Ottoman, and Habsburg Empires, this chapter undertakes a comparative analysis of the imperial palaces of these neighboring rival empires. Apart from bearing the utmost political significance as centers of the state and residences of the imperial households, these palaces also played a significant role in shaping the urban landscape of the three imperial cities: Vienna, Istanbul, and Moscow. Therefore, with their unique architectural features and remarkable morphologies, the imperial palaces became distinguishing landmarks of these cities and were positioned as visual and spatial insignias of the empires. The Hofburg, Topkapı, and Kremlin palaces were established during the late medieval era and, being the seats of royal dynasties for several centuries, they responded to the changing sociopolitical and urban contexts. These royal edifices reflected the political and ideological transformations of the state as their architectural, physical, ceremonial, and symbolic configurations changed over time.

Contrary to the illusion of stability and permanence, palaces alter with time, transforming their urban and natural environment with them. As suggested by Donald Preziosi, cities and their architectural components are not "perceived in a vacuum"; rather, their "formal and functional characteristics are understood in relationship to those of other structures."[3] In other words, "cities and its parts engender, reflect, legitimize and sustain the lived realities of social groups."[4] Therefore, within the scope of this research, I do not address imperial palaces as static architectural edifices; on the contrary, I position them as dynamic entities in constant relation with the city, as interactive institutions that responded to the sociopolitical and urban transformations and changing power balances. The ongoing modifications, renovations, and extensions that shaped the morphology of the palaces over centuries reflected the changing self-image and transforming visual ideologies of the empires.

These modifications were most apparent during critical times when the futures of the empires – or the dynasties – were at stake. From this perspective, rather than scrutinizing the early modern period, during which courtly power dominated the political arena, I will focus on the turbulent long nineteenth century, when all three continental empires faced drastic changes in their political, economic, and social structures. Hence, in this study, I aim to highlight the role of the imperial palaces in the urban layout of imperial capitals and touch upon the most significant transformations that took place during the long nineteenth century. Numerous studies have been conducted on imperial courts and palaces, focusing on the medieval and early modern eras when the imperial canons and royal decorum were established.[5] However, the last century of these palaces, as witnesses of turbulent transformations, modernization endeavors, and eventually the collapse of these empires, has been mostly overlooked.

During the modernization of the Eastern European empires, the capitals and the imperial palaces transformed physically and symbolically, adopting new roles, meanings, and functions. Rather than tackling numerous new palaces built by the Ottomans, Habsburgs, and Romanovs during the eighteenth and nineteenth centuries as showcases of modernization, progress, and grandeur, this chapter will focus on the transformation of the "premodern/medieval/traditional" palaces. My discussion revolves around the imperial palaces of the Topkapı in Istanbul, the Kremlin in Moscow, and the Hofburg in Vienna as the historic cores of the three continental empires. I address the transformation of these royal edifices during the modernization of the empires, simultaneous to the decline of the absolute authority of the monarchies. Therefore, this research deals with the strategies of legitimacy developed by the Ottomans, Habsburgs, and Romanovs during the long nineteenth century and discusses their common and diverging features. Such an analysis also sheds light on the cross-imperial interactions and aspirations; offering a transnational perspective, it hopes to open a discussion on the comparative analysis of urban landscapes of "imperial cities."

In this chapter, I focus on the developments and transitions within these three imperial complexes that blur the physical and symbolic boundaries between the ruler and the ruled, between the realms of the imperial and the mundane. In this regard, I discuss the opening of the royal grounds and imperial treasures for public visits. The sacred and secular collections preserved in the imperial palaces for several centuries started being displayed for distinguished guests as symbols of dynastic longevity, imperial prosperity, and religious legitimacy as early as the eighteenth century. Nevertheless, the public display of the imperial regalia and royal treasures became a common practice by the nineteenth century. I analyze the symbolic and museological implications of these displays in the context of the politics of imperial self-fashioning of the Austrian, Russian, and Ottoman Empires.

I also address some of the physical and architectural transformations that took place in imperial precincts, mainly focusing on the urban landscape surrounding the palaces. Apart from the addition of new wings and annexes to the palace proper, modern institutions, particularly museums, were erected within the precincts of the imperial complexes. In a similar manner, reconfiguration of the imperial gardens into public parks during the nineteenth and early twentieth centuries is discussed as a political strategy responding to the changing power structures, as well as social and urban trends of the era. The royal domains opened up for the use of the people, promoting their education and well-being. Therefore, during these turbulent times, the strict spatial and patrician division between the citizens and the monarchy started to fade and became permeable within the imperial city. Under growing pressure to establish constitutional regimes, the monarchs of Eastern Europe had to renounce their ultimate authority and demand popular support from their subjects. In this regard, the inauguration of imperial museums and the conversion of imperial gardens into public parks were not solely urban interventions for modernizing the cityscape but were manifestations of changing political power balances.

Urban Layout

The palace, being the seat of the court and the visual and political epicenter of the empire, defined the urban layout of the imperial capitals and shaped the so-called "imperial style." The imperial palaces of the Kremlin, Topkapı, and Hofburg within the urban fabric of Moscow, Istanbul, and Vienna employ comparable architectural morphologies, particularly for their urban environments. While the palaces defined the cityscape of the capitals, they were also shaped by the urban landscape and the sociopolitical structure. In other words, the imperial palaces were not unchanging and stable elements adorning the city; on the contrary, they were historically active participants in shaping and defining the urban fabric. As administrative and ceremonial centers, the palaces and their environments were positioned as the markers of imperial processions and became places of attraction for the urban elite to inhabit and relate with the main public squares of the cities in question, promoting exuberant urban life and trade. Moreover, the immediate surroundings of the imperial palaces were mostly adorned with various monumental civic, military, and religious structures characterizing the urban morphology.

Before the emergence of the Russian Empire, the timber Kremlin was founded as early as the thirteenth century at a triangular site along the Moskva River as a military base. The medieval citadel established the nucleus of the urban precinct and has remained at the heart of the city of Moscow until this day; the city developed around this historical core peripherally. Kremlin literally means "fortified castle," and its timber walls were replaced with white stone during the fourteenth century. The fortifications were reconstructed with red brick during the reign of Ivan III (the Great) (r. 1462–1505) in the late fifteenth century. Italian architects Pietro Antonio Solario, Marco Ruffo, Antonio Friazin, and Alevisio the Milanese were responsible for the construction of the fortification walls and the nineteen significant towers that characterized and monumentalized the Kremlin. There are five stepped gate towers, three circular towers at the corners of the triangular plot, and eleven watchtowers on the Kremlin's walls. The main gate of the Kremlin opening to Red Square and St. Basil's Cathedral also marked the ceremonial route for imperial processions. This gate was marked with the renowned Savior (*Spasskaia*) Tower, which was built in 1491, and its height was later extended with the addition of the clock tower in 1625. The gate and the tower of the Savior were the loci of royal ceremonies, processions, and triumphal parades, including coronations, funeral corteges, campaign processions, and religious rituals in Tsarist Russia.[6] The imperial complex of the Kremlin encompassed numerous administrative, residential, and religious buildings, including the Palace of Facets, Terem Palace, and the Bell Tower of Ivan the Great. Religious structures were mostly grouped around the Cathedral Square, which housed the renowned Cathedral of Annunciation, Archangel Cathedral, the Cathedral of Assumption, and the Palace of Patriarchs. The Kremlin defined the administrative and religious center of the imperial capital and remained the main seat of the tsars until the eighteenth century.[7]

When Peter the Great moved the court from Moscow to St. Petersburg in 1712, the Kremlin lost its superior position yet kept its symbolic and ceremonial significance as the historical and traditional core of the empire. Being at the heart of the Russian motherland, Moscow and the Kremlin continued to host numerous royal ceremonies, such as coronations and weddings. Architectural modifications to the palace continued even after the relocation of the capital. Especially after the fire of 1737, the royal complex went through comprehensive renovations. In 1787, the monumental Kremlin Senate was constructed by Matvey Kazakov in neoclassical style with the order of Catherine II (the Great) (r. 1762–1796). Following Napoleon I's siege in 1812, the palace complex, which was severely damaged, was renewed by the Commission for Construction in Moscow. Between 1838 and 1848, the Great Kremlin Palace was constructed by Konstantin Ton in Russo-Byzantine style. During the same period, a modern and monumental armory was designed by the same architect and inaugurated in 1851.[8] Being the largest building in the Kremlin, the Great Kremlin Palace redefined the Kremlin's view from the river Moskva, and together with the new armory, these new additions glorified the imperial complex and restored its former prestige. By the turn of the century, a grand monument to Alexander II was commissioned by Alexander III and unveiled in 1898 during the time of Nicholas II. In this imposing monument that contributed to the renowned silhouette of the Kremlin, the bronze statue of the former tsar was centrally placed under a pyramidical canopy and flanked by colonnaded galleries overlooking Moskva River.

Similar to the Kremlin Palace, the Topkapı Palace in Istanbul was constructed along the water, over the Acropolis of Constantinople after its conquest by the Ottomans in 1453. The palace was constructed by Mehmed II (r. 1444–1446, 1451–1481) as his second palace in the city and therefore known as the New Palace (*Saray-ı Cedid-i Amire*). Being located at the tip of the peninsula known as Seraglio (Ital., from *saray* = palace), the royal complex is surrounded by the Sea of Marmara, the Bosphorus Strait, and the Golden Horn. Due to its location at the edge of an already inhabited Byzantine capital and due to the geographical limitations of the peninsula, the city of Istanbul could not expand peripherally around the palace. Thus, the city developed across the Golden Horn toward the north and the east along two shores of the Bosphorus Strait.

The Topkapı Palace was already bordered by Byzantine city walls along the sea, and Mehmed II later added the imperial land walls (*Sur-i Sultani*) in 1478, creating a fortified citadel. There were seven external gates, four on the land walls and three on the sea walls. The palace's main gate called the Imperial Gate (*Bab-ı Hümayun*) marked the ceremonial route toward the main imperial mosque Hagia Sophia and the principal square of the city, the Hippodrome.[9] The palace was composed of successive courtyards, dedicated to different functions, which were positioned from more public to more private. These courtyards, each surrounded with walls, were pierced with majestic imperial gates.[10]

The palace underwent extensive renovations and remodeling during its life as the seat of the Ottoman rulers for almost four centuries. Major interventions took place during the reign of Süleyman I (the Magnificent) (r. 1520–1566), monumentalizing the existing architectural program. By the late sixteenth century, the Harem section of the palace had been expanded and reformulated. During the seventeenth and eighteenth centuries new sultanic pavilions were added to the complex and the timber summer palace was built at the tip of the Seraglio peninsula. Especially following catastrophic fires and earthquakes, the Topkapı Palace underwent intensive renovations, yet its initial architectural and ceremonial composition was preserved. During the course of the nineteenth century, new and modern institutions, such as barracks, military hospitals, ammunition depots, museums, and a school of fine arts, were erected within the precincts of the palace. The walls surrounding the Topkapı Palace were also partially demolished in 1870 during the reign of Abdülaziz (r. 1861–1876) for the construction of the Orient Express railway, which connected Istanbul to European capitals. Thus, the sultan's privy lands were opened for public use and the palace grounds had become a symbol and an agent of modernization by the late nineteenth century.[11]

Geographically speaking, both the Topkapı and the Kremlin were built on hilltops, bordered by water on two sides and surrounded with imposing walls, marked with imperial gates and towers. Thus, the two fortified palaces encompassing vast areas of land were defined as a "city within the city." While the Kremlin constituted an actual walled city, around which the suburbs of Moscow developed, the Topkapı Palace was established at an already inhabited and developed capital of the Eastern Roman Empire. Unlike the Kremlin, which had developed and transformed over centuries, the Ottoman Palace was commissioned by Mehmed II and built in a short period, between 1460 and 1478, and secluded from the rest of the vibrant port city of Constantinople by majestic walls. The imposing walls enclosing the Kremlin and Topkapı – both of which were built during the fifteenth century – have remained mostly intact to this day, and the silhouettes of these imperial palaces shaped the impressive and picturesque panoramas of Istanbul and Moscow.

In contrast, the Hofburg Palace was neither built on a hilltop nor by the water, and it was not surrounded by fortification walls. The medieval Swiss Court (*Schweizerhof*), establishing the core of the palace, was built as a part of the new fortifications of Vienna during the thirteenth century, outside the Roman city that established the historic city center. Even though Vienna had become one of the seats of the Habsburg dynasty by the thirteenth century, the city only flourished after its declaration as the residence of the Holy Roman Emperor during the fifteenth century. The two Ottoman sieges of Vienna in 1529 and 1683, respectively, were crucial turning points in its history. Following the first Ottoman siege, the fortifications of the city were reinforced by state-of-the-art technology, and an empty band of land surrounding the city walls, known as a glacis, was left uninhabited, which became an integral element of Vienna's urban development. As Vienna developed into an imperial city, the Hofburg Palace also expanded and transformed; during the sixteenth century it took the form of a Renaissance palace.[12] As the Hofburg continued to develop at the south-west edge of Vienna, adjacent to the city walls, the palace remained the passage between the city center and the suburbs for many centuries, until the demolition of the city walls in the second half of the nineteenth century.

The Hofburg Palace, located adjacent to the city walls, was historically positioned as the entrance to the city proper, and access to Vienna took place through its royal gates. This route, heading toward St. Stephen's Cathedral, the city's religious center, and its main square, Stephansplatz, was the main itinerary for royal and religious processions. Unlike most of its counterparts, the Hofburg was located at the periphery of the city and positioned as the threshold between the suburbs and the city center. It remained visually and physically accessible for the Viennese and was not segregated from the urban fabric with walls. The medieval morphology of the Hofburg, a quadrangular castle with four corner towers known as the Alte Burg, was almost completely transformed with subsequent additions and extensions. During the sixteenth century, a new wing known as the Amalienburg and a new Renaissance building known as the Stallburg, housing the imperial stables and later the royal art collection, were added to the complex. A new wing was constructed by Leopold I (r. 1658–1705), connecting the old and new sections of the imperial complex. Following the elimination of the Ottoman threat after the second siege of Vienna, the city enjoyed a period of prosperity and political stability during the eighteenth century. The Hofburg Palace underwent significant modifications – its corner towers were removed and the Court Library, the new Imperial Chancellery, and the court stables were constructed. The renewal of the Michaelerplatz façade of the royal complex transformed the architectural morphology of the palace, as well as its relationship with the urban context. The reign of Maria Theresa (r. 1740–1780) also marked a symbolic transformation, when the strict distinction between the sections for men and women was blurred.[13]

Despite these extensions, the Hofburg's integration with the urban fabric of Vienna and its "permeability" remained unchanged.[14] The concept of accessibility and visibility became even more evident when the walls surrounding the inner city that bordered the royal complex were demolished during the mid-nineteenth century. During the reign of Franz Joseph I (r. 1848–1916), under the supervision of the imperial council, the inner city walls of Vienna were demolished, and the area was converted into a ring road that encircled the urban core of the city. The vicinity of the Ringstrasse was adorned with numerous monumental buildings, including the City Hall, the Parliament, the Opera, the University, and the Museums of Art and Natural History. On the empty lot that emerged with the demolition of the city walls, a new ostentatious wing, known as the Neue Burg, was added to the Hofburg Palace. Also, an ambitious project for creating a large ceremonial imperial plaza (*Kaiserforum*) between the palace and the museums was initiated. The project was interrupted due to the outbreak of World War I and it was never entirely completed. Still, the Hofburg Palace remained an integral part of the modernizing city that extended toward the Ringstrasse and positioned itself as a dynastic hub while successfully shaping and integrating with Vienna's urban development.[15]

Politics of Relocation

During the long course of their dynastic rule, the Ottoman, Habsburg, and Romanov rulers built numerous residences and summer palaces at various locations within their capital cities as well as in their imperial domains, while the late medieval palaces of the Topkapı, Hofburg, and Kremlin remained as the main seat of the empires for many centuries. However, by the end of the early modern era, these traditional medieval palaces were being gradually neglected and abandoned in favor of new, modern, and ostentatious residences. The relocation of the imperial family, in this respect, was a clear political message and manifested a break with the past.

The most radical shift took place in Tsarist Russia during the early eighteenth century, when Peter the Great abandoned the traditional capital city, Moscow, in favor of his new capital, St. Petersburg, in 1712. While St. Petersburg represented the modern and Westernized face of Tsarist Russia, Moscow and the Kremlin were associated with traditional values and the historical roots of the empire and were believed to represent the real essence of the country. Even though the most significant pieces of the royal collections were transferred to St. Petersburg together with the royal family, Moscow maintained its prominence as a historical and ceremonial center, and imperial regalia continued to be kept in the Treasury of the Kremlin.[16]

Notably, coronation ceremonies were performed in the Kremlin. These ceremonies were conducted as grand public spectacles, where the entry procession of the emperor or the empress to Moscow, their arrival at the Kremlin through Red Square, and their greeting ceremony through the imperial gate of the Kremlin were celebrated with great pomp and splendor. All coronation ceremonies between 1724 and 1896 were held in the Kremlin, performed to confirm the legitimacy of the ruler and to reinforce the sentimental relation of the tsar and the tsarina to their subjects.[17] Especially during the turbulent nineteenth-century, when the legitimacy of monarchies was at stake, "invented traditions," ruler visibility, and public spectacles gained even more significance as means of assuring imperial power and confirming dynastic continuity.[18] In this context, the historic capital and the old imperial palace of the Kremlin were positioned as the symbol of the Russian imperial past, and coronation ceremonies were promoted with ostentatious processions, photo albums, public spectacles, and press coverage.

The Ottoman case was also similar to that of Russia, even though Istanbul remained as the capital of the empire until the collapse of the Ottoman Empire.[19] By the early eighteenth century, the Topkapı Palace started losing its principal position with the construction of several new summer palaces and pleasure gardens beyond the *intra muros* city of Istanbul, particularly along the Asian and European shores of the Bosphorus and the Golden Horn.[20] The traditional Topkapı Palace was frequented less and less, and, eventually, by the mid-nineteenth century, it was completely abandoned by the imperial family. Sultan Abdülmecid I (r. 1839–1861) relocated the imperial household in 1856 to his newly built Dolmabahçe Palace along the European shores of the Bosphorus. This grand masonry structure designed by the Ottoman-Armenian architects Garabet and Nigoğos Balyan, with its neo-classical and rococo architectural style, 600-meter-long white marble facade, and ostentatious decoration, was accepted as a manifestation of Ottoman Westernization and modernization. During the course of the nineteenth century, the Çırağan, Beylerbeyi, and Yıldız palaces were also erected on the shores and hills of the Bosphorus and served as the main seats of the late Ottoman rulers, shifting the locus of power and the urban development of the city toward the north.

As the function of the Topkapı Palace as an imperial residence came to an end, its ceremonial and symbolic roles were emphasized, and the historic palace continued to be the venue for the ceremonies of utmost importance, such as accession and allegiance ceremonies, sword girding processions,[21] royal funerals, weddings, and *bairam* (religious feast) greetings. Annual visits of the sultan to the Chamber of Sacred Relics, where the Holy Mantle of the Prophet Muhammad was kept, also started being conducted as flamboyant public processions from the new palaces to the traditional Topkapı Palace, representing the religious and political role of the sultanate.[22] It is also notable that a new imperial pavilion, Mecidiye Kiosk, was erected for Abdülmecid I. at the prestigious Fourth Court of the palace after the monarch's move to Dolmabahçe Palace. This was a clear manifestation of the value attributed to the old Topkapı Palace by the Ottoman rulers even after its abandonment, and with its neo-classical and baroque architectural features, Mecidiye Kiosk visually and architecturally linked the traditional Topkapı to the new Dolmabahçe Palace.[23]

Unlike the Russian or Ottoman dynasties, the Habsburgs, as the Holy Roman Emperors, had several seats and residences in various cities of Europe. While Vienna had always kept its prominence, Prague housed the imperial court between 1583 and 1611. After the return of the dynasty to Vienna, the city flourished as the imperial capital, and new residences, such as Favorita, Laxenburg, or Kaiserebersdorf in the vicinity of Vienna, were erected or expanded. Especially following the elimination of the "Turkish

Figure 3.1a Funeral of Sultan Abdülaziz by the Middle Gate of the Topkapı Palace, 1876.

Source: Le Monde Illustré, June 24, 1876, p. 412; Bibliothèque nationale de France, FOL-LC2–2943, ark:/12148/bpt6k63714684.

Figure 3.1b The funeral procession of Emperor Franz Joseph leaving the Hofburg Palace, 1916.

Source: Wikimedia, https://commons.wikimedia.org/wiki/File:Funeral_Franz-Joseph.webm.

Figure 3.1c Coronation procession of Tsar Nicholas II by the Spassky Gate of the Kremlin Palace, 1894.

Source: Russian Historical Library, https://algoritm-centr.ru/en/greece-and-rome/velikii-greh-kak-koronaciya-nikolaya-ii-obernulas-hodynskoi-davkoi.html

Threat" with the defeat of the Ottoman army in 1683, Vienna enjoyed economic prosperity and a growing population, and the city was adorned with impressive baroque monuments. During the eighteenth century, the Hofburg Palace was also expanded with the addition of new wings. Additionally, flamboyant new palaces on a grand scale were also built around Vienna, such as the Belvedere and Schönbrunn palaces. The Schönbrunn Palace and gardens served as the primary summer residence of the royal family until the end of the empire, and especially during the last years of Franz Joseph, this baroque palace became the main residence of the imperial family.[24] Yet the Hofburg Palace retained its political and symbolic prominence and remained as the seat of the government and served as the winter residence of the royal family until the collapse of the Austro-Hungarian Empire.

The Hofburg Palace also continued to serve as the stage for the most significant religious and royal ceremonies, such as coronation ceremonies, funerals, Corpus Christi processions, *Anniversarium* military ceremonies in commemoration of the dead, crowning anniversaries, and birthday celebrations of the rulers. Hence, the imperial palace remained as the chief ceremonial venue, manifesting the historical legitimacy of the ruling elite. Following the death of Charles VI, the House of Lorrain took over the dynastic line in 1740 with the bond of marriage; nevertheless, the daughter of Charles VI, Maria Theresa, continued to rule the hereditary lands herself. Therefore, the Habsburg dynasty and their long hereditary line of succession became more crucial for justifying her rule, as well as the sovereignty of her successors. Especially during the eighteenth and nineteenth centuries, the palace was surrounded by public plazas, which were adorned with monumental statues of national heroes such as Empress Maria Theresa, Archduke Carl, Prince Eugene, and Emperor Joseph II. Thus, the ceremonial role and the architectural configuration of the traditional Hofburg Palace communicated the empire's past, accentuating its link with the Habsburg dynasty.[25]

Hence, during the period of political and social transformations, the traditional imperial palaces of all three empires were utilized as symbols of dynastic continuity and imperial legitimacy. The palaces adopted new roles as stages for ostentatious imperial ceremonies that were conducted for the public visibility and approval of the ruler. Therefore, these royal edifices continued to mark the route for the royal processions and remained significant imperial hubs and urban landmarks in the transforming cityscapes of Istanbul, Moscow, and Vienna (Figures 3.1a–3.1c). In the turbulent sociopolitical context of the nineteenth century, the traditional medieval palaces assumed new roles representing the history of the empire and confirming the hereditary rights of rulers, thus endorsing the legitimacy and durability of dynasties.

The Imperial Collections

The imperial palaces were not only spatial manifestations of power but also the loci of imperial heritage, within which royal treasures and imperial regalia were collected and preserved generation after generation. Royal collections, apart from their material and tangible value, were also considered as symbols of dynastic and religious continuity and legitimacy. The treasures and heirlooms of the dynasty ranged from books and manuscripts to arms and armor, from sacred relics to jewelry, and from artworks to regal garments. These invaluable objects, either produced in royal workshops, brought in as war spoils, or offered as diplomatic gifts, provide insights about the material culture and artistic achievements of the empire. Previously exclusive to the gaze of courtiers, the royal collections became of scholarly interest and intellectual curiosity during the early modern period. Thus, the princely collections, imperial treasuries (*Schatzkammer*), cabinets of curiosities (*Kunstkammer*), and royal collections of arts, armory, and antiquities started being displayed first to aristocratic circles and diplomatic audiences, then to distinguished guests and visitors, and eventually to travelers and to the public at large.[26] The treasuries of the Ottoman, Habsburg, and Romanov dynasties were no exception, with the royal collections being displayed to certain visitors by the eighteenth century.

The Habsburgs were among the earliest to display their royal treasuries. The Habsburg Treasury, which included the imperial crown of the Holy Roman Empire, was comprised of ecclesiastical and secular collections, both of which had been kept at the sacristy of the Hofburg Chapel since the fourteenth century.[27] By the sixteenth century, both collections had been moved to another wing of the Hofburg Palace and placed in spatially connected chambers, known as *Schatzkammer*. The collection, including relics, regalia, royal documents, artworks, curiosities, and jewelry, had an essential role in the Habsburg dynastic tradition and was enriched over time, especially with the incorporation of the insignia and the treasures of the Holy Roman Empire by the end of the eighteenth century. The Treasury Chamber remained in the Swiss Wing, the oldest remaining section of the palatial complex, and underwent several restorations, especially during the seventeenth century. During the eighteenth century, the ecclesiastical and secular collections of the treasury were separated, an inventory of the collections was made, and some pieces were transferred to various other palaces for display.[28]

For instance, the royal art collection was sent to the Upper Belvedere Palace for display, and the Lower Belvedere was designated for the amber and antiquarian collections. Similarly, the imperial arms collection was displayed in the Imperial Arsenal, which was built in 1855 near the

Belvedere Gate and served as a military museum. Following the decree of Emperor Franz Joseph I ordering the demolition of city walls in 1857, several public institutions were established on the Ringstrasse that promoted and enriched artistic and intellectual life in Vienna. Two major museums, the Museum of Art History (*Kunsthistorisches Museum*) and the Museum of Natural History (*Naturhistorisches Museum*), were built across from the Hofburg Palace as a part of the Kaiserforum project. The collections of these two prestigious museums, known as Court Museums (*Hofmuseen*), were partially derived from the royal collections; in 1871 the treasury collection was reorganized and in 1891 selected artworks were moved to the newly completed Museum of Art History. The Court Museums, as their names imply, were strategically positioned across from the Hofburg Palace and planned as a part of the ostentatiously expanded royal complex.[29] The aim was to make the invaluable royal collections accessible to a wider public and to glorify the monarchy via modern and scientific institutions. The Hofburg was positioned as an institution for public education, promoting imperial and national identity to the visiting public.[30]

Apart from the royal collections that were transferred to summer palaces and public museums, a special treasury collection, consisting of the crown jewels and the ecclesiastical treasures belonging to the Holy Roman Emperors and the Habsburgs remained at the Treasury Chamber (*Schatzkammer*) of the Hofburg Palace. The Treasury Chamber at the Hofburg included objects of political and religious value, which were accepted as symbols of dynastic power and legitimacy and therefore guarded in the historic Swiss Wing in line with the court traditions. The most celebrated items of the imperial treasury included insignia and regalia of the Holy Roman Empire and the heirlooms of the House of Habsburg. The Ainkhürn (Unicorn) and the Agate Bowl from the fourth century, which was looted from Constantinople during the Latin invasion of the city in 1204, were considered the most precious possessions of the Habsburg collection, in addition to the Imperial Crown, Coronation Gospels, Imperial Cross, the Sabre of Charlemagne, the St. Maurice Sword (*Reichsschwert*), the Imperial Orb (*Reichsapfel*), and the silk coronation robes belonging to the Holy Roman Emperors.[31]

Maria Theresa, being the last sovereign of the Habsburg line, ordered the opening of the Treasury Chamber for visits, which was enriched with the invaluable jewel collection belonging to her husband Francis Stephen of Lorraine. Walnut display cases with windows were installed in 1747 to create a mesmerizing impact on the visitor.[32] As the Habsburg dynasty came to an end with the reign of Maria Theresa, the public display of the ecclesiastical collection, together with the imperial regalia and insignia, reinforced the legitimacy of her rule and manifested the power and longevity of the House of Habsburg. The public exhibit of the treasury came to a halt during the reign of her son, Joseph II, and the treasury remained closed until the nineteenth century.

By the nineteenth century, the royal collections, including the Imperial Treasury, Minerals Cabinet, Cabinet of Coins and Antiquities, and Zoology Cabinet, together with the imperial apartments, were opened for public visits. As early as 1846, the ceremonial chambers of the Hofburg and the Imperial Treasury collection were opened to the public.[33] The collections were closed in wintertime, could be visited when the imperial family was residing at their summer palace, and were open two days per week during the 1850s. During the 1870s, the number of visiting days was increased to three days per week. Especially before the Vienna World's Fair of 1873, the treasury collection and ceremonial halls of the Hofburg Palace were listed among the major cultural attractions of the city. According to the guidebooks of the era, which provide detailed information about the visiting procedures, the Imperial Treasury was open from May to November, on Tuesdays, Thursdays, and Saturdays from 10:00 a.m. to 1:00 p.m., and a written petition to the Imperial Chancellery had to be made a day in advance.[34]

The Ottoman notable Hayrullah Efendi, who visited Vienna in 1863, wrote in his memoirs that the arms museum, state treasury, emperor's palace, and the library were among the major attractions of the city and open for visits. He proudly added that he even visited the imperial palace. According to his observations, the rooms of the Hofburg Palace, which opened into each other, were adorned with exquisite furnishings and precious tile stoves at each corner. On the invaluable marble tables were numerous priceless antiquities on display. Hayrullah Efendi also noted that the palace walls were covered with paintings depicting old battle scenes between the Ottomans and Austrians.[35]

Hence, the Hofburg Palace and its royal collections laid the foundations of the celebrated museums in Vienna. The imperial palace, with its surrounding vicinity, adopted an educational role and promoted the legitimacy of the Habsburg dynasty by accentuating its longevity and positioning it as the fathers/mothers of the nation. The imperial court, initiating the grand urban project of the Ringstrasse, situated the Hofburg Palace at the cultural and administrative core of the city, as the epicenter of art, civilization, and progress. In this context, opening of the royal regalia, which was kept at the core of the Hofburg Palace, for public visits accentuated their sense of identity and belonging. The visits glorified the rooted history of the empire and its prosperity in the eyes of foreign and local visitors.

Similar to the Hofburg Palace, the Kremlin also included royal ateliers and several treasuries for preserving items of religious, historic, military, and monetary value. Within the royal precincts of the Kremlin, apart from various administrative and religious buildings, there existed the Public Treasury, the Armory Chamber, the Stables Treasury, and the tsar's private treasury. The Armory Chamber (*Oruzheinaia Palata*) in the Kremlin was founded in the sixteenth century as an arsenal for manufacture, purchase, and storage of firearms, jewelry, religious icons, and objects of everyday use for the royal family. Apart from housing ateliers for icon painters, gunsmiths, and jewelry makers, the Armory Chamber functioned as a repository for royal treasures and military spoils.[36] After the relocation of the royal family to St. Petersburg, a remarkable portion of the royal ateliers were transferred to the new capital. Still, the state regalia that were used for coronation ceremonies continued to be kept in the Kremlin.[37]

As the Kremlin Armory lost its industrial importance for housing royal workshops and court artisans, it was incorporated into a single institution and renamed the "Workshop and Armory Chamber" in 1727, becoming a venue for preserving objects of artistic, historical, and ceremonial value. During this era, palace grounds and royal collections were opened for visits during the absence of the royal family. In fact, as early as 1718, the Kremlin's antiquities and jewelry collections were put on display in glass cases and shown to distinguished visitors. During the reign of Catherine II, coronation dresses and ancient state regalia were also placed in the Workshop and Armory Chamber, in addition to historic suits of armor on life-size wooden dummies.

The idea for constructing a new building for the preservation and public display of the collection and for making a scientific inventory of the items was taken up during the mid-eighteenth century. Eventually, on March 22, 1806, the Armory Chamber was officially declared as a museum by the decree of Emperor Alexander I (r. 1801–1825), and construction of a new building to house the unified and expanded collections was commenced. Following its museumification, an inventory of the collection was made in 1807 and the objects that were previously sent to other palaces or departments were brought back. In 1810, again on the order of Alexander I, the St. Petersburg Armory was abolished, and its collections were transferred to the Kremlin, positioning the old palace as the showcase for Russian artistic and military achievements as well as an emblem of Muscovite heritage.

In 1810, the construction of a new Armory Chamber was completed, but right after its inauguration the newly built museum building was damaged by the fire of 1812, during Napoleon I's invasion of Moscow. After Napoleon's withdrawal, the collection that previously had been sent to Nizhnii-Novgorod was partially brought back to the Kremlin.[38] Following the restoration of the Armory Chamber, the collection was opened to visitors in 1814. The exhibition of the collections followed a certain thematic path, which started with ancestral regalia in the Throne Hall, followed by the exhibition of the crowns of conquered kingdoms and diplomatic gifts, and ended with the armament section where ancient military regalia were displayed. Thus, the Armory Chamber became Russia's first national historical museum, where exhibits promoted the idea of dynastic glory, extensive territories, and military power of the motherland in the eyes of its people.[39]

After 1831, a museum director was appointed by imperial edict for scientific museal study and maintenance of the collection, and a catalogue of more than 10,000 objects was compiled.[40] In 1851, as a part of the Grand Kremlin Palace, a new Armory Chamber was constructed by the imperial architect Konstantin Ton at the southwestern corner of the Kremlin. The monumental neoclassical building had two stories and was designed to express the grandeur and prosperity of the Russian tsars. An invaluable collection of ancient state regalia, ceremonial robes, vestments of bishops, gold and silverware by Russian craftsmen, ancient arms and armor, royal carriages, and ceremonial harnesses were pompously displayed in the nine large halls of the new Armory Chamber.

During the nineteenth century, it was possible for tourists and travelers to visit some parts of the Kremlin and the Armory Chamber to see the treasury of the tsars.[41] According to Murray's *Handbook for Russia* from 1865, the Armory at the Kremlin (*Oruzheinaia Palata*) was the "depository of venerated historical objects, and of treasures hereditary in the reigning house," which included the arts of the East and the West. The guidebook also informs its readers that the tickets for visiting the "Kremlin Treasury" could be obtained from the Chamberlain's Office in the Senate building and that the collection was open from Monday to Thursday, from 1:00 to 3:00 p.m.[42]

When the collection was closed to tourists, the students of the Stroganov Art School and artists studied the collections, and the armory became a prominent center for research and methodology.[43] Hence the royal collections, primarily representing the rooted history and glory of the dynasty, were publicly displayed for educational purposes and positioned as prime examples of traditional Russian arts and crafts. The Romanovs, gradually distancing themselves from the idea of Westernization and St. Petersburg during the course of the nineteenth century, deliberately positioned the old capital of the empire and the Kremlin as the ultimate manifestation of Russian identity and national culture.[44] In response to the idea of Russian Renaissance, museums and educational institutions were established in and around the palace with the aim of studying, glorifying, and resurrecting medieval Russian arts.[45]

It is not merely speculation to suggest that the Ottomans were very much influenced and inspired by their most immediate rivals, the Austrian and Russian Empires. The Ottomans closely followed the developments of the Austro-Hungarian Empire during the nineteenth century. The European tour by Sultan Abdülaziz in particular was a turning point in the diplomatic relations and interactions of the Ottoman Empire with European states. Attending the inauguration ceremony of the *Exposition Universelle* in Paris in 1867, Abdülaziz visited London, Koblenz, Vienna, and Budapest, and was hosted by French, English, Belgian, Prussian, Austrian, and Hungarian rulers. During his visit to Vienna, Abdülaziz stayed at Schönbrunn Palace and visited the major monuments and attractions of the city, including museums, palaces, gardens, theaters, and the city's renowned fortifications. Abdülaziz also paid a visit to the art gallery at the Belvedere Palace and the military museum at Ambras Castle, showing a genuine interest in the arms and armor on display.[46]

During the nineteenth century, World's Fairs were among the most important international events that facilitated cross-imperial interactions and cultural exchanges. A couple of years after their royal participation in the Universal Exhibition in Paris, the Ottomans attended the 1873 World's Fair in Vienna. Paying utmost attention to this event, Ottoman pavillons were established at the fairgrounds, as well as a one-to-one scale replica of the Fountain of Ahmed III. In addition to three prestigious academic volumes introducing the cultural richness, sartorial diversity, and architectural eminence of the empire, some 200 pieces from the Imperial Treasury of the Ottoman rulers were sent to Vienna to be displayed publicly.[47] During the assembly of the iron display pavilion, invaluable pieces from the Ottoman Treasury were kept safe at the treasury of the Hofburg Palace.[48] Emperor Franz Joseph I attended the inauguration of the treasury pavilion and, according to Ottoman sources, expressed his appreciation for the "elegance and good taste of the construction."[49] According to Osman Hamdi, who was the exhibition commissioner, "the Emperor seemed really interested in examining the precious objects contained in the windows of the Imperial Treasury, and in particular he was occupied with the fine arms, many of which belonged to our illustrious sovereigns."[50]

In fact, Austrian interest in Ottoman treasuries was not limited to this occasion, as the Topkapı Palace and its Imperial Treasury in Istanbul had been visited several times by Austrian aristocrats and dignitaries during the nineteenth century. In 1855 and 1856, for instance, Austrian aristocrats were given a permit to visit the Imperial Treasury, yet their insistent demand to visit the Chamber of Sacred Relics, in which the Holy Mantle of the Prophet Muhammad was kept, was denied.[51] A number of Habsburg dignitaries subsequently paid official visits to the Topkapı Palace and were shown the Imperial

Treasury, including Crown Prince Rudolf and his wife, Princess Stéphanie, in 1884; the daughter of Emperor Franz Joseph, Princess Gisela, her son Prince Konrad, and her younger relative Prince Heinrich in 1908, and finally Emperor Charles I of Austria-Hungary and Empress Zita in 1918 (Figure 3.2).[52]

In contrast, the diplomatic visits of the Ottoman imperial family to Europe did not continue after the exceptional visit of Abdülaziz. To compensate for his physical absence, Abdülhamid II (r. 1876–1909) exchanged photographic albums with numerous monarchs and sent prestigious ones abroad depicting vast geographies of the Ottoman Empire, including the Topkapı Palace and its treasury.[53] Additionally, the sultan collected prints from all around the world, curating his celebrated photography collection in the Yıldız Palace. There are numerous pictures depicting Vienna and Moscow in his rich collection.[54] The prints of Vienna primarily depicted the ambitious urban transformation project centered on the Ringstrasse. The newly built imperial museums, the Opera, the City Hall, and the boulevards in Vienna were portrayed with captions in German, French, and English, presenting the aspiring modernization of the Austrian capital.

In a similar fashion, there existed numerous prints from the Kremlin in the large photography collection of Abdülhamid II.[55] Photographs depicted

Figure 3.2 The Emperor of Austria-Hungary Charles I and his wife Empress Zita during their visit to the Topkapı Palace in 1918.

Source: Austrian National Library, 212.394-C.

the renewed Armory Chamber of the Kremlin with its wide halls, in which numerous objects belonging to Russian imperial heritage were methodically displayed. The ostentatious and careful display of arms and armor, ceremonial garments, thrones, regalia, portraits, royal carriages, and banners in display cases must have been an inspiration for the Ottomans to display their own imperial heritage. The Ottoman captions underneath the photographs indicate Abdülhamid's interest in the Kremlin Palace museum and verify the physical and symbolic relationship between the two ancient palaces and their collections (Figure 3.3). For instance, a photograph captioned as "*Salle d'Armes*" includes a note written in Ottoman Turkish:

> The picture of the Treasury Chamber of the Russian Tsars in the Kremlin Palace in Moscow (This chamber is very similar to that of the Imperial Treasury in the Topkapı Palace [and] it is believed that a sword belonging to Hazret-i Zeynel Abidin is among the collection).[56]

Figure 3.3 Armory Chamber in the Kremlin displaying the thrones, armor, portraits, and other valuables captioned in Ottoman Turkish.

Source: Istanbul University, Rare Books Library, Abdülhamid II Albums, 91238-0022.

Over the course of the nineteenth century, in line with other dynasties, the Ottomans opened their royal collections to visitors. Historically, there were several treasuries and collections kept in the first, second, and third courts of the Topkapı Palace, which included the collections of antique arms, royal harnesses, books and manuscripts, the Imperial Treasury, and the collection of sacred relics. Among those treasures, the Imperial Treasury, housing the personal treasures of the sultans and located at the Third Courtyard of the Topkapı Palace, was of particular interest for the Europeans and its doors gradually opened for distinguished foreign visitors by the mid-nineteenth century.[57]

It is documented that some sections of the palace and its outer gardens were already being shown to European ambassadors and high-ranking royals from the late eighteenth century. The Russian ambassador, together with the French and English ambassadors, was among the first notables that were granted access to visit the gardens of the Topkapı Palace, as stated in an imperial decree from 1805.[58] In 1846 a double collection of antique arms and antiquities was also established in the atrium of the Imperial Armory, the former Byzantine church (St. Irene) located at the first court of the Topkapı Palace. The double collection was established by the Marshall of the Imperial Armory, Ahmet Fethi Pasha, who was formerly the Ottoman Ambassador to Russia, France, and Austria; he is believed to have visited the collections at Ambras Castle and the Lower Belvedere.[59] In the Imperial Armory, apart from ancient arms and armor, the costumes of the Janissary corps, which had been abolished two decades earlier, were also displayed on life-size mannequins.

While the military collection remained in the Imperial Armory, the antiquities collection was renamed the Imperial Museum (*Müze-i Hmayun*) and in 1875 transferred to a fifteenth-century sultanic kiosk, known as the Tiled Pavilion, in the outer gardens of the Topkapı Palace. Later in the 1890s, the archeological museum flourished under the direction of the renowned Ottoman bureaucrat, painter, and archeologist Osman Hamdi. Between 1891 and 1907, a modern and monumental archeological museum was built (in three phases) in neoclassical style in the outer gardens of the palace by the famous Levantine architect of the time, Alexandre Vallaury, for the display of the expanding archeological collections (Figure 3.4).[60]

During the reign of Abdülmecid I, the inner courts of the palace and the royal pavilions opened to foreign visitors.[61] Only after the sultan's relocation to Dolmabahçe Palace did the Imperial Treasury at the Topkapı Palace open its doors to distinguished visitors, and windowed display cabinets were assembled in the first chamber of the treasury in 1856.[62] Within time, the visits to royal collections and to the inner courts of the Topkapı Palace became more systematic, and the number of visitors increased considerably. The display of some pieces from the Imperial Treasury in the 1873

Figure 3.4 Imperial Treasury at the Topkapı Palace, 1880–1893.
Source: Istanbul University, Rare Books Library, Abdülhamid II Albums, 90838-0011.

Vienna World's Fair must have triggered international attention toward the "exotic and rich" treasury of the Ottoman rulers. By the late nineteenth century, the *Seraglio* (Topkapı Palace) had become one of the most popular tourist destinations of Constantinople. According to a newspaper article from 1886,

> [t]he great museum of Constantinople, though it is not so styled, is of course the Sultan's Treasury in the Seraglio. […] The permission to visit the Seraglio is not so difficult to obtain […] Many people have visited it before […] It is a favor which can only be obtained from the Sultan by the mediation of one's ambassador, and the visitor for whom the *irade* [imperial decree] is made out must be a person of rank or a specialist in art or possess some other qualifications to excuse the trouble he is giving both to the Embassy and to His Majesty.[63]

To visit the Imperial Treasury and the Topkapı Palace, one had to obtain an imperial decree (*irade*) from the palace through diplomatic channels. According to guidebooks of the time, entrance to the Imperial Treasury cost around USD 30 (approximately USD 900 in today's currency) for a tourist group, which could include up to 20 people.[64] During the palatial tour, in addition to the treasury collection, the inner courts and the imperial kiosks of the palace were also shown to visitors with a certain performative ceremonial. The tourists were also hosted at the imperial Mecidiye Kiosk and offered tobacco, Turkish coffee, and sherbet at its terrace. For instance in 1884, during the visit of Austrian Crown Prince Rudolf and his wife, Princess Stéphanie of Belgium, a small-scale political scandal broke out. According to Ottoman archival documents, when the crown prince and his wife arrived at the terrace of the Mecidiye Kiosk, it was recorded that the archduchess admired the beauty of the view, and as a response, the crown prince said that "I assure you that this very point will be your residence with the title Queen of the Orient." According to the document, the King of Belgium, the father of the archduchess, disapproved these comments and reproached her.[65]

The visits to the Topkapı Palace were not exclusive to the members of the royalty. In fact, between 1878 and 1891, during the second quarter of the reign of Abdülhamid II, it is recorded that 531 foreign groups visited the palace and the Imperial Treasury. According to documents from the Topkapı Palace Museum Archives, among those visitors, 64 groups were from Russia and 23 groups were from Austria.[66] However, the doors of the Topkapı Palace remained closed for Ottoman subjects throughout the nineteenth century, up until the end of Abdülhamid II's reign. Unlike its contemporaries, the Ottoman state did not use the imperial collections for domestic propaganda or dynastic legitimacy, but rather utilized the royal collections as tools for promoting the self-image of the empire to the eyes of Westerners. Nineteenth-century Ottoman rulers choose to keep the palace and the heirlooms of their ancestors away from the public gaze, guarding the aura of secrecy and seclusion of the imperial grounds, in line with the traditional Ottoman visual ideologies that promoted the invisibility of the ruler and his locus.[67]

Only after the Young Turk Revolution of 1908, the inner courts and royal collections of the palace became accessible for the Ottoman citizens. Following the declaration of the Second Constitution, in line with the declining prestige and authority of the monarchy, the royal collections at the Topkapı Palace opened for domestic visits.[68] In accordance with their nationalist ideology and aim to debilitate the authority and prestige of the sultanate, the Young Turks started controlling dynastic properties and opening imperial grounds to the public. For instance, the Imperial Armory at St. Irene, which was closed for visits during the Hamidian era, was also reorganized and renamed the Military Museum and opened to the public. The Military Museum aimed at promoting nationalist ideologies and patriotic feelings of Ottoman subjects, especially during the tough years of the Balkan Wars and World War I.[69] Likewise, it is documented that thousands of foreign and local visitors, most of them students, poured into the Imperial Treasury of the Topkapı Palace to visit the world-renowned riches of the Ottoman sultans.[70] Following the museumification of the royal collections, the Imperial Treasury thus attained an educational role, and the heirlooms of the Ottoman dynasty were displayed publicly, creating a sense of national belonging and loyalty.

Over the course of the long nineteenth century, the royal apartments and imperial treasuries of the Ottoman, Romanov, and Habsburg dynasties started being displayed to visitors via parallel strategies of self-display. Dealing with legitimacy crises, monarchies developed various tactics to affirm their sovereignty and popularity, such as increasing the permeability between the imperial and the non-imperial or establishing a symbolic and spatial link between the monarch and his subjects. In this context, the gradual museumification of royal complexes had direct and indirect implications for imperial capitals, rendering novel ways for experiencing and perceiving imperial pasts. Having access to once forbidden quarters of imperial palaces created a sense of privilege, admiration, and belonging for the onlooker, but at the same time broke the spell of mystery and invisibility of the monarchy.

In fact, the imperial palaces displayed themselves not only to the actual visitors – their textual and visual depictions also made them accessible to a wider populace. Travel accounts, guidebooks, newspapers, and illustrated journals of the time depicted the unimaginable wealth of the sovereigns. Apart from increasing the number of travelers – thanks to developments in transportation – postcards and photographs of imperial capitals, historic palaces, royal processions, and dynastic treasures circulated publicly, and some were sent as gift albums to other courts, establishing a visual network among monarchies. Therefore, a shared vocabulary of imperial self-fashioning, based on interaction, emulation, and competition, appeared among the empires of Eastern Europe.

During this period, imperial ceremonies and public processions increased in splendor and visibility, confirming the authority and popularity of sovereigns. Particularly the traffic between the new and old palaces was orchestrated as grandiose urban spectacles. In this context, palaces and their monumental gates marked sublime points of reference in the urban fabric, defining the routes and the ultimate destinations for these royal processions. The ceremonials, therefore, spread beyond the confinements of royal precincts and became public events, shaping the spectators' vision and experience of the city.

Universities, art academies, research institutions, libraries, and modern museums were also founded in and around the imperial palaces, positioning them as centers of academic and artistic knowledge. In a similar fashion, imperial gardens, dedicated to the pleasure of the royal family, were converted into public parks for the benefit of the citizens. For instance, in 1823, the northern part of the imperial gardens of the Hofburg Palace was reconfigured as a public park and renamed Volksgarten. Even though the Hofgarten (Burggarten) remained closed for the public, the imperial domains of the Volksgarten, as suggested by its name, were opened to the populace and, even more so, dedicated to public wellbeing. In a similar manner, following the Napoleonic wars, Tsar Alexander I ordered the conversion of the Kremlin's imperial gardens that were stretching outside its western walls into a public park. The park, known as Kremlin Gardens, was inaugurated for Muscovites in 1823 and later renamed Alexander Gardens.[71] Following their Austrian and Russian rivals almost a century later, the Ottoman ruler Mehmed V Reşad (r. 1909–1918) approved the conversion of the imperial gardens of Gülhane at the Topkapı Palace into a public park. Inaugurated in 1914 with the efforts of the mayor of Istanbul Cemil (Topuzlu) Pasha, the Gülhane Park was dedicated solely to public health and welfare, and any activity that might generate income was strictly prohibited.[72] The project could be interpreted as a political outcome of the constitutional monarchy that was declared in 1908, enforcing control over dynastic properties.

These urban interventions, in fact, could also be considered as the actions of shattering monarchies that were struggling to maintain their rule during the turbulent times before the Great War. The Ottoman, Tsarist, and Habsburg Empires all collapsed following World War I, and their imperial legacies were appropriated and utilized by the subsequent regimes. The Tsarist Empire was the earliest to come to an end after the revolution of 1917. The Bolsheviks brought an end to the monarchy and the Soviet State was founded under the leadership of Vladimir Lenin (1870–1924). Since St. Petersburg was considered too close to the West and vulnerable to external interventions, the capital of the new state was also changed – Moscow was declared the capital in March 1918 and the Kremlin was selected as Lenin's residence. Thus, the Kremlin Palace once again became the seat of the government, and the same year, the memorial monument of Tsar Alexander II was removed, and his statue was demolished. Additionally, several tsarist monuments, including the Church of Konstantin and Elena, the Ascension Convent, and the Small Nicholas Palace were destroyed by the Soviet regime in 1929 and replaced by the Military School of the Central Executive Committee. The modern building of the State

Kremlin Palace (Palace of Congresses) as a grandiose monument of Soviet architecture was erected in 1961 near the Trinity Tower.[73]

In 1924, following the death of Vladimir Lenin, a memorial mausoleum was built at Red Square adjacent to the Kremlin walls. During this period, however, public visits to the Kremlin were not allowed, since the memory of the Tsarist Empire and the massacre of the dynastic family were still fresh in the public memory.[74] The Kremlin reopened for public visits four decades later, and the Kremlin Museums were established as late as 1961. After reopening during the Soviet era, the collections of the Armory Chamber were reorganized, this time not to reflect the dynastic past of the tsars or the glory of the empire, but the merits of Russian fine arts and craftsmanship.

As discussed above, after the relocation of the royal family in 1856, the Topkapı Palace grounds were virtually converted into a museum district even before the collapse of the Ottoman Empire. After World War I, the Ottoman Empire was defeated, and Istanbul was occupied by the Allied powers. Strategic locations within the city – including piers, train stations, and military bases, as well as the outer gardens of the Topkapı Palace – were taken under the control of the occupation forces. In response, Turkish resistance forces, organized in Anatolia under the leadership of Mustafa Kemal, defeated the Greek forces and took control of Istanbul. In October 1923, a year after the abolishment of the monarchy, the Turkish Republic was founded, and Ankara was declared the new capital of the new state. Thus, Istanbul lost its historical position as the imperial capital, and all imperial properties and dynastic collections were appropriated in the name of the nation. The Imperial Treasury and the collection of the Sacred Relics at the Topkapı Palace were sent to Ankara, where these powerful symbols of the sultanate were kept away from the public gaze.[75] In 1926, the first public sculpture of Mustafa Kemal Atatürk was erected within the precincts of the Topkapı Palace, at the tip of Seraglio Point, a spot that is historically and politically significant. The statue, while demonstrating the modern, secular, and Westernized facets of the new republic, manifested the legitimacy and authority of the "founding father of the Turkish nation" over the palace of his ancestors.[76]

In April 1924, approximately six months after the foundation of the Turkish Republic, the Topkapı Palace was officially inaugurated as a state museum by order of Mustafa Kemal and his cabinet of ministers, and the palace-museum was put under the direction of the Museums of Antiquities. The museumification of the imperial palace was a powerful political statement, declaring the end of the Ottoman era and affirming the Turkish nation as the sole inheritor of Ottoman heritage. While the treasury collection and the sacred relics were confined at Ankara for several decades until 1963, the rest of the royal collections were displayed at various halls and kiosks of the Topkapı Palace. The items were catalogued, classified, and displayed as distinct collections, such as silverware, porcelains, paintings and portraits, carriages and harnesses, textiles, manuscripts, and so on. Additionally, various collections of books and manuscripts were unified, registered, and catalogued. Eventually, the Topkapı Palace Museum Library with more than 20,000 manuscripts and books was established at the former palace mosque. Similarly, the archival documents kept in the palace vaults and treasures were classified under the Topkapı Palace Museum Archives. When the treasury and the sacred relics collections were sent back to their original locations in the Topkapı Palace during the 1960s, these items of extreme political and religious significance started being displayed as objects of "national heritage" in a secular museum setting, stripped from their former dynastic, ceremonial, or political connotations. The collection venerated a distant yet glorious past of the Turkish nation.

Like the Ottoman and the Tsarist Empires, the Austro-Hungarian Empire also disintegrated after World War I. In 1918, after the collapse of the empire, Emperor Charles left the country and took the private jewelry of the imperial family with him into exile. The Austrian Republic was founded in 1919 and remained independent until the annexation by Nazi Germany in 1938.[77] Adolf Hitler made his infamous balcony appearance at the Neue Burg wing of the Hofburg Palace in 1938, and the collection of the Holy Roman Empire at the Hofburg Palace was sent to Nuremberg by the Nazis. After World War II, Vienna remained as the state capital of the Republic of Austria and the Hofburg Palace functioned as the presidential residence. The treasury, which was held outside the country for almost a decade, was returned to the Hofburg only after 1946. In 1956, the Hofburg Treasury opened for touristic visits and was organized as a double collection of secular and ecclesiastical treasuries in its original location at the Swiss Court.[78]

The imperial palaces and imperial collections, after the collapse of the empires, conveyed ambiguous messages of history and patrimony. The imperial legacies were instrumentalized, nationalized, and utilized to legitimize the new ideologies, and palaces were reformulated as state museums and/or seats of the new regimes (Figures 3.5a–3.5c). The possession and display of imperial treasuries, objects of extreme political and religious significance, became a contentious issue, and the collections were kept away from the public eye during the aftermath of the empires for several decades. Only after World War II, when the legacy of empires was mostly erased from the public memory, were the imperial collections opened to the public in modern and secularized museum settings.

Figure 3.5a Unveiling of Mustafa Kemal's statue on the grounds of the Topkapı Palace, 1926.

Courtesy of Cengiz Kahraman.

Figure 3.5b Unveiling ceremony of the Prince Eugene monument on Heldenplatz, 1865.

Source: Wien Museum Inv.Nr. 9572/1, https://sammlung.wienmuseum.at/en/object/809826/

Figure 3.5c Demolition of the statue of Tsar Alexander II, 1918.

Source: Kulturologia, https://kulturologia.ru/blogs/260120/45288

To conclude, the traditional imperial palaces of the Russian, Ottoman, and Austrian Empires went through architectural, symbolic, and spatial transformations, especially during the last century of the monarchies. All three modernizing empires, which were considered as bridges between the East and the West, were striving to be a part of the league of European powers, politically and culturally. Architecture, especially of royal residences, was an effective means for manifesting their modernization endeavors. They also developed strategies for sustaining their power and control over their vast territories and multi-ethnic populations. Hence the imperial palaces and royal collections were attributed new meanings as glorious representations of the dynastic past and the heroic history of the empire. While they emulated the "Western" model, the Russian, Ottoman, and Austrian Empires also learned from and competed with each other and developed new politics of representation. The imperial palaces, as embodiments of their imperial history and hereditary rights, were given new functions and positioned as active agents for the modernization of the state and the imperial city, but they also acted as spaces for remembering and forgetting. Post-imperial reconfigurations recontextualized imperial palaces and imperial treasuries as national heritage, as well as agents of public memory. This study aims at raising comparative questions about the parallels and divergences between these continental empires in terms of their strategies for representing and remembering the past and for utilizing imperial spaces as political tools for changing ideologies.

Notes

1 George T. Lowth, *Around the Kremlin; or, Pictures of Life in Moscow* (London: Hurst & Blackett, 1868), 1–2.
2 Lawrence J. Vale, *Architecture, Power, and National Identity* (New Haven, CT: Yale University Press, 1992).
3 Irene A. Bierman, Rifa'at Ali Abou-El-Haj, and Donald Preziosi, *The Ottoman City and Its Parts: Urban Structure and Social Order* (New Rochelle, NY: A.D. Caratzas, 1991), 104.
4 Preziosi, *The Ottoman City and Its Parts*, 4.
5 Gülru Necipoğlu, *Architecture, Ceremonial, and Power: The Topkapı Palace in the Fifteenth and Sixteenth Centuries* (New York: MIT Press, 1991); Herbert Karner, *Die Wiener Hofburg 1521–1705 Baugeschichte, Funktion und Etablierung als Kaiserresidenz* (Wien: Verlag der österreichischen Akademie der Wissenschaften, 2015); Arthur Voyce, *The Moscow Kremlin: Its History, Architecture, and Art Treasures* (Westport, CT: Greenwood Press, 1971); Jeroen Frans Jozef Duindam, *Vienna and Versailles: The Courts of Europe's Major Dynastic Rivals, 1550–1780* (Cambridge: Cambridge University Press, 2003); Jeroen Frans Jozef Duindam, *Dynasties: A Global History of Power, 1300–1800* (Cambridge: Cambridge University Press, 2016).
6 Voyce, *The Moscow Kremlin*; Richard Wortman, *Russian Monarchy: Representation and Rule: Collected Articles* (Brighton, MA: Academic Studies Press, 2013).
7 Voyce, *The Moscow Kremlin*, 32.
8 Vsevolod Vygolov, Alexander Solodkoff, and Bruce Tattersall, "Moscow" Grove Art Online (2003). https://doi.org/10.1093/gao/9781884446054.article.T059795 (Accessed January 22, 2021).

9 Hagia Sophia, built during the sixth century by Byzantine emperor Justinian, was the main cathedral of Constantinople and the seat of Orthodox Christianity. The iconic structure was converted into a mosque and served as the main Friday mosque of Istanbul after the conquest of the city by the Ottomans. In a similar manner, the Byzantine Hippodrome remained as the most significant urban piazza of the city for imperial ceremonials and possessions.

10 Sedad Hakkı Eldem and Feridun Akozan, *Topkapı Sarayı: Bir Mimari Araştırma* (İstanbul: Kültür ve Turizm Bakanlığı, Eski Eserler ve Müzeler Genel Müdürlüğü, 1982); Necipoğlu, *Architecture, Ceremonial, and Power*; Necdet Sakaoğlu, *The Imperial Palace with Its History, Locations, Inscriptions and Memoirs: Topkapı Palace* (İstanbul: Denizbank Publications, 2002).

11 Nilay Özlü, "From Imperial Palace to Museum: The Topkapı Palace during the Long Nineteenth Century" (PhD diss., Boğaziçi University, 2018).

12 Maria Pötzl-Malíková, et al., "Vienna," *Grove Art Online*, (2003). https://doi.org/10.1093/gao/9781884446054.article.T089311 (Accessed January 24, 2021).

13 Karner, *Die Wiener Hofburg 1521–1705*; Hellmut Lorenz, Anna Mader-Kratky, and Christian Benedik, *Die Wiener Hofburg 1705–1835. Die kaiserliche Residenz vom Barock bis zum Klassizismus* (Wien: Verlag der Österreichischen Akademie der Wissenschaften, 2016); Werner Telesko, *Die Wiener Hofburg 1835–1918. Der Ausbau der Residenz vom Vormärz bis zum Ende des 'Kaiserforums'* (Wien: Verlag der Österreichischen Akademie der Wissenschaften, 2012).

14 Werner Telesko, Richard Kurdiovsky, and Dagmar Sachsenhofer, "The Vienna Hofburg between 1835 and 1918 – A Residence in the Conflicting Fields of Art, Politics, and Representation," *Austrian History Yearbook* 44 (2013): 44.

15 Alan Sked, "Franz Joseph and the Creation of the Ringstrasse," *The Court Historian* 11, no. 1 (2006): 29–41.

16 Aleksey Levkin, et al., *Treasures of the Czars: From the State Museums of the Moscow Kremlin* (London: Booth-Clibborn, 1995).

17 Richard S. Wortman, *Scenarios of Power: Myth and Ceremony in Russian Monarchy from Peter the Great to the Abdication of Nicholas II* (Princeton, NJ; Oxford: Princeton University Press, 2006); Wortman, *Russian Monarchy*.

18 Richard Wortman, *Visual Texts, Ceremonial Texts, Texts of Exploration: Collected Essays on the Representation of Russian Monarchy* (Boston, MA: Academic Studies Press, 2014).

19 Darin Stephanov, *Ruler Visibility and Popular Belonging in the Ottoman Empire, 1808–1908* (Edinburgh: Edinburgh University Press, 2018).

20 Shirine Hamadeh, *The City's Pleasures in Istanbul in the Eighteenth Century* (Seattle: University of Washington Press, 2008).

21 Sword Girding ceremonies, which could be interpreted as the Ottoman version of crowning ceremonies, were conducted as public processions from the Topkapı Palace to Eyüp (a sacred area beyond the city walls, dedicated to Abu Ayyub Al Ansari, one of the companions of the Prophet Mohammad) and back to the palace, in which the swords were kept.

22 Selim Deringil, *The Well Protected Domains* (New York: I.B. Tauris & Co., 1999); Hakan T. Karateke and Maurus Reinkowski, *Legitimizing the Order: The Ottoman Rhetoric of State Power* (Leiden; Boston, MA: Brill, 2005).

23 Özlü, "From Imperial Palace to Museum."

24 Jeroen F. J. Duindam, *Vienna and Versailles: The Courts of Europe's Dynastic Rivals, 1550–1780* (Cambridge: Cambridge University Press, 2003); Markus

Jeitler, "Hunt, Amusement and Representation: The Viennese Hofburg and Its 'Satellites' in the Seventeenth Century," in *Looking for Leisure: Court Residences and their Satellites 1400–1700*, eds. Sylva Dobalov and Ivan P. Muchka (Heidelberg: arthistoricum.net, 2018), 274–80.

25 Richard Kurdiovsky et al., "Legitimacy through History and Architecture. The Vienna Hofburg as Dynastic Hub and Seat of Government between Tradition and Innovation," *The Court Historian* 20, no. 2 (2015): 109–36; Telesko, Kurdiovsky, and Sachsenhofer, "The Vienna Hofburg between 1835 and 1918"; Daniel L. Unowsky, *The Pomp and Politics of Patriotism: Imperial Celebrations in Habsburg Austria, 1848–1916* (West Layafette, IN: Purdue University Press, 2005).

26 Tony Bennett, *The Birth of the Museum: History, Theory, Politics* (London; New York: Routledge, 1995); Donald Preziosi and Claire J. Farago, *Grasping the World: The Idea of the Museum* (Aldershot: Ashgate, 2004).

27 Kaiserliche Schatzkammer Wien, https://www.kaiserliche-schatzkammer.at/besuchen/sammlungen/geistliche-schatzkammer/.

28 Rudolf Distelberger and Manfred Leithe-Jasper, *Kunsthistorisches Museum, Vienna: The Imperial and Ecclesiastical Treasury* (Munich: Beck, 2009).

29 Sked, "Franz Joseph and the Creation of the Ringstrasse," 29–41.

30 Telesko, Kurdiovsky, and Sachsenhofer, "The Vienna Hofburg between 1835 and 1918," 37–61.

31 Hermann Fillitz, *Schatzkammer* (Vienna: Kunsthistorisches Museum, 1963), 21; Pötzl-Malíková et al., "Vienna," Grove Art Online (2003).

32 Fillitz, *Schatzkammer*, 4.

33 Werner, *Die Wiener Hofburg 1835–1918*.

34 Constantine William DeBernardy, *The American's Hand-Book to Vienna and the Exhibition* (Philadelphia, PA: Porter & Coates, 1873); The Special Correspondent of "The Graphic", *"The Graphic" guide to Vienna, Containing Illustrations with Map of Vienna* (London, 1873).

35 Hayrullah Efendi and Belkıs Altuniş Gürsoy, trans., *Avrupa Seyahatnamesi* (Ankara: T.C. Kültür Bakanlığı, 2002), 29.

36 Voyce, *The Moscow Kremlin*, 77.

37 Alexei Levykin, "200 Years of Moscow Kremlin Museums," *Tretyakov Gallery Magazine* 2 (2006): 11. https://www.tretyakovgallerymagazine.com/articles/2–2006–11/200-years-moscow-kremlin-museums (Accessed November 30, 2020).

38 Voyce, *The Moscow Kremlin*, 77–78.

39 Levykin, "200 Years of Moscow Kremlin Museums."

40 Voyce, *The Moscow Kremlin*, 79.

41 Alexey Levykin et al., *Treasures of the Czars*; Paul Gilbert, "The Armoury Chamber, Moscow." http://www.tsarnicholas.info/blog/index.blog?topic_id=1069239 (Accessed May 22, 2018).

42 John Murray, *Handbook for Travellers in Russia, Poland, and Finland* (London, 1865), 148.

43 Gilbert, "The Armoury Chamber."

44 Wortman, *Russian Monarchy*, 170–84.

45 Voyce, *The Moscow Kremlin*, 3.

46 Nihat Karaer, "Sultan Abdülaziz'in Avrupa Seyahati ile Osmanlı ve Batı Kamuoyundaki Yankıları" (PhD diss., Ankara Üniversitesi, 2003), 138–39.

47 Ahmet A. Ersoy, *Architecture and the Late Ottoman Historical Imaginary: Reconfiguring the Architectural Past in a Modernizing Empire* (Aldershot: Ashgate,

80   *Nilay Özlü*

2015); Zeynep Çelik, *Displaying the Orient: Architecture of Islam at Nineteenth-Century World's Fairs* (Berkeley: University of California Press, 1992).

48 Ceren Göğüş, "19. yy. Avusturya gazeteleri ışığında Osmanlı İmparatorluğunun 1873 Viyana Dünya Sergisine katılımı" (PhD diss., Istanbul Teknik Üniversitesi, 2006), 179–80.

49 Nilay Özlü, "The Ottomans at World's Fairs: Displaying Imperial Patrimony," in "Papers Presented to István Ormos on His Seventieth Birthday," ed. K. Dévényi and P.T. Nagy, special issue, *The Arabist: Budapest Studies in Arabic* 41 (2020): 121–40; BOA HR.İD.1218.47 (9.7.1873) "Inauguration du Trésor Impérial." Letter to Rachid Pacha from Cabouli Ottoman Ambassador of Vienna: *"L'Empereur m'a également parlé du Kioske ou est enfermié le Trésor Impt. Et a beaucoup apprécié l'elegance et le bon gout de sa construction."*

50 BOA HR.İD.1218.47 (9.7.1873) Report of Osman Hamdi Bey written in French to Cabouli Pasha, Ottoman Ambassador to Vienna: *"L'Emepereur a paru prendre un virai interèt à l'examen des objects précieux contenues dans les vitrines du Pavillion du Trésor Imperial et s'est occupé d'une façon toute particulierè des belles armes qui ont été la propriété de plussieurs de nos illustres souverains."*

51 BOA HR.MKT.125.29 (30.10.1855); HR.SYS.205.8 (31.10.1855).

52 Senem Gönenç, "Prenses Gisela ve Oğullarının İstanbul Seyahati (11 Nisan-4 Mayıs 1908)," *Osmanlı Medeniyeti Araştırmaları Dergisi* 6 (2020): 120–140; Özlü, "From Imperial Palace to Museum."

53 Two identical sets of 50 photographic albums, having 1,800 photographs each and showing various vistas from around the empire, including the Topkapı Palace, the Imperial Treasury, and the Museum of Arms, were sent to the Library of Congress and the British Library by Ottoman sultan Abdülhamid II. Muhammad Isa Waley, "Images of the Ottoman Empire: The Photograph Albums Presented by Sultan Abdülhamid II," *The British Library Journal* 17, no. 2 (1991): 111–27.

54 Abdülhamid II was an ambitious collector of photography; his collection at Yıldız held approximately 33,000 prints. Zeynep Çelik, Edhem Eldem, and Hande Eagle, *Camera Ottomana: Photography and Modernity in the Ottoman Empire, 1840–1914* (Istanbul: Koç University Press, 2015); Ahmet A. Ersoy, "Ottomans and the Kodak Galaxy: Archiving Everyday Life and Historical Space in Ottoman Illustrated Journals," *History of Photography: Photography, Antiquity, Scholarship* 40, no. 3 (2016): 330–57.

55 Nilay Özlü, "'Barbarous Magnificence in Glass Cases': Imperial Treasury and Ottoman Self-Display at the Topkapı Palace," *Muqarnas* 39 (2022): 153–192.

56 The caption of the photograph reads: *"Moskova Kremlin Sarayında Rus Çarları Hazine Dairesinin resmidir [Bu hazine tıbkı Topkapı Sarayındaki Hazine-i Hümayuna muşabih olup havi olduğu asar-ı atika-i mahaller meyanında Hazret-i Zeynel Abidin'in olduğu rivayet edilen bir kılınç mevcud olunuyor]."*

57 Nilay Özlü, "Single P(a)lace, Multiple Narratives: The Topkapı Palace in Western Travel Accounts from the Eighteenth to the Twentieth Century", in *The City in the Muslim World: Depictions by Western Travel Writers*, eds. Mohammad Gharipour and Nilay Özlü (London: Routledge, 2015).

58 BOA HAT.167.7039 (31.3.1805)

59 Belgin Turan Özkaya, "Entangled Geographies, Contested Narratives: The Canning Marbles and the Ottoman Response to Antiquity," *Muqarnas* 39 (2022): 227–54.

60 Ferruh Gerçek, *Türk Müzeciliği* (Ankara: T.C. Kültür Bakanlığı, 1999); Wendy M. K. Shaw, *Possessors and Possessed: Museums, Archeology, and the*

Visualization of History in the Late Ottoman Empire (Berkeley: University of California Press, 2003); Edhem Eldem, "The (Still)Birth of the Ottoman 'Museum': A Critical Reassessment," in *Collecting and Empires: An Historical and Global Perspective*, ed. Maia Gahtan and Eva-Maria Troelenberg (London: Harvey Miller Publisher, 2019), 259–85.

61 Özlü, "From Imperial Palace to Museum."
62 Topkapı Palace Museum Archives, TS.MA.d.4613 (29.01.1856).
63 "The Turks' Art Treasures," The New York Times, February 2, 1887, 14.
64 Noah Brooks, *The Mediterranean Trip: A Short Guide to the Principal Points on the Shores of the Western Mediterranean and the Levant* (New York: C. Scribner's Sons, 1895), 128.
65 BOA Y.PRK.MK.4.81_02 (30.6.1889)
66 TSMA.e.239.3 – TSMA.e.242.108. The data are based on records from the Topkapı Palace Museum Archives from 1878 to 1891. However, the permits to visit the palace between the years 1880 and 1884 were not recorded. Özlü, "From Imperial Palace to Museum," 351.
67 Gülru Necipoğlu, "Framing the Gaze in Ottoman, Safavid, and Mughal Palaces," *Ars Orientalis* 23 (1986): 303–42.
68 Özlü, "From Imperial Palace to Museum," 425–26.
69 Bilge Ar, "Osmanlı Döneminde Aya İrini ve Yakın Çevresi" (PhD diss., İstanbul Teknik Üniversitesi, 2013).
70 Mehmed Raif Bey, *Topkapı Sarayı ve Çevresi* (İstanbul: Okur Kitaplığı, 2010); Özlü, "From Imperial Palace to Museum," 424–50.
71 Lowth, *Around the Kremlin*.
72 Cemil Topuzlu, Hüsrev Hâtemî, and Aykut Kazancıgil, *İstibdat, Meşrutiyet, Cumhuriyet Devirlerinde 80 Yıllık Hatıralarım* (İstanbul: İşaret Yayınları, 2010); Nilay Özlü Karaca, "The Making of Gülhane Park: From Royal Gardens to Public Spaces in Late Ottoman Istanbul," in *Spectacle, Entertainment, and Recreation in Late Ottoman and Early Turkish Republican Cities*, ed. Nilay Özlü Karaca and Seda Kula Say (Bristol: Intellect Books, 2023), 3–27.
73 Paul Gilbert, "Lost Architectural Monuments of the Moscow Kremlin", *Royal Russia*, December 15, 2016. https://orthochristian.com/99637.html (Accessed November 30, 2020); Vygolov, Solodkoff, and Tattersall, "Moscow" *Grove Art Online* (2003).
74 Katerina Clark, *Moscow, the Fourth Rome. Stalinism, Cosmopolitanism, and the Evolution of Soviet Culture, 1931–1941* (Cambridge: Harvard University Press, 2011).
75 Hüseyin Karaduman, *Ulus-devlet bağlamında belgelerle Ankara Etnoğrafya Müzesi'nin kuruluşu ve Milli Müze* (Ankara: Bilgin, 2016).
76 Özlü, "From Imperial Palace to Museum."
77 Eve Blau, *Architecture of Red Vienna, 1919–1934* (Cambridge, MA: MIT Press, 2018).
78 Distelberger and Leithe-Jasper, *Kunsthistorisches Museum*.

Bibliography

Sources

Republic of Turkey Presidential State Archives – Ottoman Archives:
BOA HR.MKT.125.29 (30.10.1855)
BOA HR.SYS.205.8 (31.10.1855)

BOA Y.PRK.MK.4.81_02 (30.6.1889)
BOA HAT.167.7039 (31.3.1805)
BOA HR.İD.1218.47 (9.7.1873)
Topkapı Palace Museum Archives:
TS.MA.d.4613 (29.01.1856)
TSMA.e.239.3 – TSMA.e.242.108

Literature

Ar, Bilge. "Osmanlı Döneminde Aya İrini ve Yakın Çevresi." PhD diss., İstanbul Teknik Üniversitesi, 2013.
Bennett, Tony. *The Birth of the Museum: History, Theory, Politics.* London: Routledge, 1995.
Bierman, Irene A., Rifaʿat Ali Abou-El-Haj, and Donald Preziosi. *The Ottoman City and Its Parts: Urban Structure and Social Order.* New Rochelle, NY: A.D. Caratzas, 1991.
Blau, Eve. *Architecture of Red Vienna, 1919–1934.* Cambridge, MA: MIT Press, 2018.
Brooks, Noah. *The Mediterranean Trip: A Short Guide to the Principal Points on the Shores of the Western Mediterranean and the Levant.* New York: C. Scribner's Sons, 1895.
Çelik, Zeynep. *Displaying the Orient: Architecture of Islam at Nineteenth-Century World's Fairs.* Berkeley: University of California Press, 1992.
Çelik, Zeynep, Edhem Eldem, and Hande Eagle. *Camera Ottomana: Photography and Modernity in the Ottoman Empire, 1840–1914.* Istanbul: Koç University Press, 2015.
Clark, Katerina. *Moscow, the Fourth Rome: Stalinism, Cosmopolitanism, and the Evolution of Soviet Culture, 1931–1941.* Cambridge, MA: Harvard University Press, 2011.
DeBernardy, Constantine William. *The American's Hand-Book to Vienna and the Exhibition*, Philadelphia, PA: Porter & Coates, 1873.
Deringil, Selim. *The Well Protected Domains.* New York: I.B. Tauris, 1999.
Distelberger, Rudolf, Manfred Leithe-Jasper. *Kunsthistorisches Museum, Vienna: The Imperial and Ecclesiastical Treasury.* Munich: Beck, 2009.
Duindam, Jeroen Frans Jozef. *Vienna and Versailles: The Courts of Europe's Dynastic Rivals, 1550–1780.* Cambridge: Cambridge University Press, 2003.
Duindam, Jeroen Frans Jozef. *Dynasties: A Global History of Power, 1300–1800*, Cambridge: Cambridge University Press, 2016.
Eldem, Edhem. "The (Still)Birth of the Ottoman 'Museum': A Critical Reassessment." In *Collecting and Empires: An Historical and Global Perspective*, edited by Maia Gahtan and Eva-Maria Troelenberg, 259–85. London: Harvey Miller Publisher, 2019.
Eldem, Sedad Hakkı, and Feridun Akozan. *Topkapı Sarayı: Bir Mimari Araştırma.* Istanbul: Kültür ve Turizm Bakanlığı, Eski Eserler ve Müzeler Genel Müdürlüğü, 1982.
Ersoy, Ahmet A. *Architecture and the Late Ottoman Historical Imaginary: Reconfiguring the Architectural Past in a Modernizing Empire.* Aldershot: Ashgate, 2015.

Ersoy, Ahmet A. "Ottomans and the Kodak Galaxy: Archiving Everyday Life and Historical Space in Ottoman Illustrated Journals," *History of Photography: Photography, Antiquity, Scholarship* 40, no. 3 (2016): 330–57.

Fantoni, Marcello, ed. *The Court in Europe*. Roma: Bulzoni Editore, 2012.

Gerçek, Ferruh. *Türk Müzeciliği*. Ankara: T.C. Kültür Bakanlığı, 1999.

Gilbert, Paul. "The Armoury Chamber, Moscow." Accessed May 22, 2018. http://www.tsarnicholas.info/blog/index.blog?topic_id=1069239.

Gilbert, Paul. "Lost Architectural Monuments of the Moscow Kremlin." *Royal Russia*, 2016. Accessed October 30, 2020. https://orthochristian.com/99637.html

Göğüş, Ceren. "19. yy. Avusturya gazeteleri ışığında Osmanlı İmparatorluğunun 1873 Viyana Dünya Sergisine katılımı." PhD diss., İstanbul Teknik Üniversitesi, 2006.

Gönenç, Senem. "Prenses Gisela ve Oğullarının İstanbul Seyahati (11 Nisan-4 Mayıs 1908)." *Osmanlı Medeniyeti Araştırmaları Dergisi* 6 (2020): 120–40.

Gordon, David L.A. *Planning Twentieth Century Capital Cities*. London: Routledge, 2010.

Hamadeh, Shirine. *The City's Pleasures in Istanbul in the Eighteenth Century*. Seattle: University of Washington Press, 2008.

Hayrullah, Efendi, and Belkıs Altuniş Gürsoy, trans. *Avrupa Seyahatnamesi*. Ankara: T.C. Kültür Bakanlığı, 2002.

Jeitler, Markus. "Hunt, Amusement and Representation: The Viennese Hofburg and Its 'Satellites' in the Seventeenth Century." In *Looking for Leisure: Court Residences and their Satellites 1400–1700*, edited by Sylva Dobalov and Ivan P. Muchka, 274–80. Heidelberg: arthistoricum.net, 2018.

Karaduman, Hüseyin. *Ulus-devlet bağlamında belgelerle Ankara Etnoğrafya Müzesi'nin kuruluşu ve Milli Müze*. Ankara: Bilgin, 2016.

Karaer, Nihat. "Sultan Abdülaziz'in Avrupa Seyahati ile Osmanlı ve Batı Kamuoyundaki Yankıları." PhD diss., Ankara Üniversitesi, 2003.

Karateke, Hakan T., and Maurus Reinkowski. *Legitimizing the Order: The Ottoman Rhetoric of State Power*. Leiden: Brill, 2005.

Karner, Herbert. *Die Wiener Hofburg 1521–1705. Baugeschichte, Funktion und Etablierung als Kaiserresidenz*. Wien: Verlag der österreichischen Akademie der Wissenschaften, 2015.

Karner, Herbert, Ingrid Ciulisová, and Bernardo José García García. *The Habsburgs and their Courts in Europe, 1400–1700: Between Cosmopolitism and Regionalism*, Palatium e-publication, 2014.

Kurdiovsky, Richard, Günther Buchinger, Renate Holzschuh-Hofer, Markus Jeitler, Herbert Karner, Anna Mader-Kratky, Paul Mitchell, Anna Stuhlpfarrer, and Werner Telesko. "Legitimacy through History and Architecture. The Vienna Hofburg as Dynastic Hub and Seat of Government between Tradition and Innovation." *The Court Historian* 20, no. 2 (2015): 109–36.

Levykin, Alexei. "200 years of Moscow Kremlin Museums." *Tretyakov Gallery Magazine* 2 (2006): 11. https://www.tretyakovgallerymagazine.com/articles/2-2006-11/200-years-moscow-kremlin-museums.

Levykin, Alexey, M.V. Martynova, O.B. Melnikova, I.A. Bobrovnitskaya, I.I. Vishnevskaya, V.M. Nikitina, and T.N. Muntian. *Treasures of the Czars: From the State Museums of the Moscow Kremlin*. London: Booth-Clibborn, 1995.

Lorenz, Hellmut, Anna Mader-Kratky, and Christian Benedik. *Die Wiener Hofburg 1705–1835. Die kaiserliche Residenz vom Barock bis zum Klassizismus.* Wien: Verlag der Österreichischen Akademie der Wissenschaften, 2016.

Lowth, George T. *Around the Kremlin: Or, Pictures of Life in Moscow.* London: Hurst & Blackett, 1868.

Murray, John. *Handbook for Travellers in Russia, Poland, and Finland.* London: John Murray, 1865.

Necipoğlu, Gülru. "Framing the Gaze in Ottoman, Safavid, and Mughal Palaces." *Ars Orientalis* 23 (1986): 303–42.

Necipoğlu, Gülru. *Architecture, Ceremonial, and Power: The Topkapı Palace in the Fifteenth and Sixteenth Centuries.* Cambridge: MIT Press, 1991.

Özlü, Nilay. "Single P(a)lace, Multiple Narratives: The Topkapı Palace in Western Travel Accounts from the Eighteenth to the Twentieth Century." In *The City in the Muslim World: Depictions by Western Travel Writers*, edited by Mohammad Gharipour and Nilay Özlü, 168–188. London: Routledge, 2015.

Özlü, Nilay. "From Imperial Palace to Museum: The Topkapı Palace During the Long Nineteenth Century." PhD diss., Boğaziçi University, 2018.

Özlü, Nilay. "The Ottomans at World's Fairs: Displaying Imperial Patrimony." In *Papers Presented to István Ormos on His Seventieth Birthday*, edited by K. Dévényi and P.T. Nagy. Special issue, *The Arabist: Budapest Studies in Arabic* 41 (2020): 121–40.

Özlü, Nilay. "'Barbarous Magnificence in Glass Cases': Imperial Treasury and Ottoman Self-Display at the Topkapı Palace." *Muqarnas* 39 (2022): 153–192.

Özlü Karaca, Nilay. "The Making of Gülhane Park: From Royal Gardens to Public Spaces in Late Ottoman Istanbul." In *Spectacle, Entertainment, and Recreation in Late-Ottoman and Early Turkish Republican Cities*, edited by Nilay Özlü Karaca and Seda Kula Say, 3–27. Bristol: Intellect Books, 2023.

N.N., *"The Graphic" Guide to Vienna, Containing Illustrations with Map of Vienna.* London, 1873.

Pötzl-Malíková, Maria, Marlene Strauss-Zykan, Eckart Vancsa, Barbara Wild, G. Tobias Natter, Eva B. Ottillinger, Peter Hornsby, Gabriele Ramsauer, S. Träger, Christian Benedik, Jarl Kremeier, and Géza Hajós. "Vienna." *Grove Art Online* (2003). Accessed January 1, 2021. https://doi.org/10.1093/gao/9781884446054.article.T089311.

Preziosi, Donald, and Claire J. Farago. *Grasping the World: The Idea of the Museum.* Aldershot: Ashgate, 2004.

Raif, Mehmed. *Topkapı Sarayı ve Çevresi.* İstanbul: Okur Kitaplığı, 2010.

Sakaoğlu, Necdet. *The Imperial Palace with Its History, Locations, Inscriptions and Memoirs: Topkapı Palace.* İstanbul: Denizbank Publications, 2002.

Shaw, Wendy M. K. *Possessors and Possessed: Museums, Archeology, and the Visualization of History in the Late Ottoman Empire.* Berkeley: University of California Press, 2003.

Sked, Alan. "Franz Joseph and the Creation of the Ringstrasse." *The Court Historian* 11, no. 1 (2006): 29–41.

Stephanov, Darin. *Ruler Visibility and Popular Belonging in the Ottoman Empire, 1808–1908.* Edinburgh: Edinburgh University Press, 2018.

Telesko, Werner. *Die Wiener Hofburg 1835–1918. Der Ausbau der Residenz vom Vormärz bis zum Ende des "Kaiserforums."* Wien: Verlag der Österreichischen Akademie der Wissenschaften, 2012.

Telesko, Werner, Richard Kurdiovsky, and Dagmar Sachsenhofer, "The Vienna Hofburg between 1835 and 1918 – A Residence in the Conflicting Fields of Art, Politics, and Representation," *Austrian History Yearbook 44* (2013): 44.

"The Turks' Art Treasures." *The New York Times*, February 2, 1887, 14.

Thurston, Robert W. *Liberal City, Conservative State: Moscow and Russia's Urban Crisis, 1906–1914.* New York: Oxford University Press, 1987.

Topuzlu, Cemil, Hüsrev Hâtemî, and Aykut Kazancıgil. *İstibdat, Meşrutiyet, Cumhuriyet Devirlerinde 80 Yıllık Hatıralarım.* Istanbul: İşaret Yayınları, 2010.

Turan Özkaya, Belgin. "Entangled Geographies, Contested Narratives: The Canning Marbles and the Ottoman Response to Antiquity." *Muqarnas 39* (2022): 227–54.

Unowsky, Daniel L. *The Pomp and Politics of Patriotism: Imperial Celebrations in Habsburg Austria, 1848–1916.* West Lafayette, IN: Purdue University Press, 2005.

Vale, Lawrence J. *Architecture, Power, and National Identity.* New Haven, CT: Yale University Press, 1992.

Voyce, Arthur. *The Moscow Kremlin: Its History, Architecture, and Art Treasures.* Westport, CT: Greenwood Press, 1971.

Vygolov, Vsevolod, Alexander Solodkoff, and Bruce Tattersall, "Moscow" *Grove Art Online* (2003). Accessed January 22, 2021. https://doi.org/10.1093/gao/9781884446054.article.T059795.

Waley, Muhammad Isa. "Images of The Ottoman Empire: The Photograph Albums Presented by Sultan Abdülhamid II." *The British Library Journal* 17, no. 2 (1991): 111–27.

Wortman, Richard. *Russian Monarchy: Representation and Rule: Collected Articles.* Brighton, MA: Academic Studies Press, 2013.

Wortman, Richard. *Visual Texts, Ceremonial Texts, Texts of Exploration: Collected Essays on the Representation of Russian Monarchy.* Boston, MA: Academic Studies Press, 2014.

Wortman, Richard S. *Scenarios of Power: Myth and Ceremony in Russian Monarchy from Peter the Great to the Abdication of Nicholas II.* Princeton, NJ: Princeton University Press, 2000.

4 Temeswar as an Imperial City in the First Half of the Eighteenth Century

Robert Born

It was with a mixture of admiration and irritation that Nicolae Iorga (1871–1940) described his first impressions after arriving in Temeswar in the autumn of 1905:

> Timişoara is a large, solemn and sombre city, built on orders, according to strict administrative guidelines. It is the utmost artificial and Austrian city I have encountered so far, but at the same time it is the most well-proportioned, the most rational, the most subjected to building and maintenance norms.[1]

The most renowned Romanian historian of the past century visited the Banat capital when the city, under the official name of Temesvár, was an important economic and cultural center on the southern periphery of the eastern (Hungarian) half of the Dual Monarchy.[2] Iorga's visit was part of an extended research trip during which he gathered materials for the two-volume publication on the Romanian population in Hungary. This work was aimed at strengthening the sense of cohesion of the Romanians within the still young nation-state with their co-nationals that lived in the various territories of the Dual Monarchy.

Following the break-up of Austria-Hungary, the Banat was partitioned according to the stipulations laid down in the 1920 Trianon Peace Treaty, and currently, it belongs to Romania, Serbia, and – a small part of the area – to Hungary. Recently, Timişoara was in international headlines when Dominic Fritz, a citizen of the Federal Republic of Germany, was elected mayor of Romania's third largest city in autumn 2020. As an explanation for his spectacular success, the media pointed to the multi-ethnic character of the Banat capital. Similar arguments were also used in Timişoara's application in 2016 to become one of the three European Capitals of Culture in 2021. The slogan of the successful candidacy was "Shine your light – Light up your city!"[3] The metaphor of light recalled the influence of the ideals of the Enlightenment, through which the city has remained a center

DOI: 10.4324/9781003130031-6

for the dissemination of civic cultural values. The application thus took up a three-decade-long debate, centered on whether the multicultural diversity of the Banat capital enabled the emergence of a civil society and a distinct local political consciousness.[4]

This distinctive cultural constellation is reflected on the one hand by the variants of the city's name – the Romanian Timişoara, the German Temeswar, the Hungarian Temesvár, and finally the Serbian Temišvar. Moreover, the reference to the Banat capital as "Little Vienna," which became popular by the mid-nineteenth century at the latest,[5] was presented as an embodiment of the historically forged ties between the Banat and Central Europe.[6] Similar to Lviv (Ukr. L'viv, Pol. Lwów, Ger. Lemberg) and Chernivtsi (Ukr. Černivci, Germ. Czernowitz, Rom. Cernăuţi) in Ukraine or Bielsko-Biała (Ger. Bielitz-Biala, Czech: Bílsko-Bělá) in Poland, which also claim the title "Little Vienna," the Baroque, Historicist and Art Nouveau buildings in Temeswar also function as indicators of a cultural belonging to the Central European (Habsburg-influenced) cultural sphere. Artistic testimonies from the eighteenth century are often linked to the narrative of the Habsburg civilizing mission, which transformed the Banat from a *terra deserta* into a prosperous region. This narrative, which is widespread in the historiography and in numerous literary works, was decisively informed by Francesco Griselini's (1717–1787) description of the country in 1780.[7] This work, penned by an Austrian civil servant, praised the Habsburg rule and also influenced the assessment of the Baroque period. Correspondingly, the bid book of the 2021 Capital of Culture application states: "When European Baroque was exhausted from all perspectives, the Habsburg Banat was building a new world, known as provincial Baroque. Paradoxically, for Timişoara, Baroque is the moment of historical and cultural Enlightenment."[8] This explanatory model for the delayed reception of the Baroque as an Enlightenment impulse represents a striking departure from the widespread perception of the Baroque in East Central Europe until 1989. In the Eastern Bloc, this phenomenon and, consequently, the artistic productions and buildings of the eighteenth century retained an ideologically precarious position due to their association with the church and the aristocracy and were held in low esteem.[9] In alignment with the thematic focus of the volume, some of the previously mentioned views will be critically discussed. The focus lies on the political, economic, and confessional concepts implemented by the new Habsburg sovereigns in Temeswar and the Banat during the eighteenth century. Here, continuities with the preceding Ottoman period, in which the city underwent its first imperial phase, will also be addressed. This complex of questions is also of particular relevance against the background of the just mentioned thesis of a Central European cultural landscape created ex novo by the Habsburgs. Previous studies of the Baroque in the Banat in general and in

Temeswar in particular have often focused on individual structures. When reconstructing the individual layers of Temeswar as an imperial city on the periphery of the Habsburg Empire, the aim is to analyze not only the changes in the texture of the city – buildings, functionaries, and different ethnic groups – but also the media employed in the staging of the dynasty and the institutions associated with it. So far, mainly the buildings associated with the Habsburgs have been studied. This chapter will additionally study previously neglected artifacts such as sacral monuments, inscriptions, and heraldic emblems in greater detail. In this context, the panegyric textual productions from the surroundings of the ruler's court in Vienna form an integral part of the comparative framework. In this way, the question of the existence of an official art policy, which is particularly significant for the thematic complex of imperial cities, will also be discussed. Consequently, this essay is also intended as a contribution to research on the spatial presence of the Habsburgs, as well as on the performativity of power and authority.[10] In the sense of a precise contextualization, the most important stages of the historical development of the city of Temeswar and the Banat region are first outlined.

Medieval Temeswar as a Frontier Stronghold

The growth of Temeswar in the Middle Ages was favored by its topographical location and several special environmental characteristics. These include the location on an important overland route from Central Europe to the Serbian Empire and the Bulgarian Empire, which led through an extensive swamp area in the vicinity. The town itself was surrounded to the east, south, and west by islands of marshland created by the irregular course of the branches of the Bega River, which were referred to by the Romanian population as the Small Temesch (Rom. Timişul Mic), and which are not to be confused with the Temesch (Rom. Timiş) mentioned in the town's name. This natural protection and the link to the trans-regional road network were important incentives for Charles I Robert (Hung. I. Károly/Róbert Károly, 1288–1342) to establish his residence in Temeswar in 1315. While the royal court stayed there, the city was provided with a new stone reinforcement. In addition, the independently fortified royal palace was built as an annex to the south.[11] Outside the city walls, the settlements of the then-called Small Palanka (an area entrenched with palisades, attached to the fortress) south of the castle and the so-called Great Palanka north of the fortified city developed over time, where artisans and merchants resided.[12] After the relocation of the royal court to the residence in Visegrád (Ger. Plintenburg) in 1323, the town did not diminish in reputation by any means, especially in comparison with the neighboring episcopal seat in Csanád. This is indicated by the considerable number of church buildings and chapels in the town known from sources, as well as the regular visits of rulers, above all Sigismund of Luxembourg (Hung. Luxemburgi Zsigmond, 1368–1437), King of Hungary (from 1387), in whose presence the Hungarian Diet met in the city in 1397.[13]

By the end of the fourteenth century at the latest, a city council entitled to use a seal existed.[14] The responsibilities of this body, however, were increasingly reduced in the fifteenth century as the city became the seat of the commanders of the southern defense network of the Hungarian kingdom as Ottoman incursions became more frequent after the defeat of the crusader army at Nicopolis in 1396.[15] This militarization hindered municipal development on the one hand, but it also prevented the city from being captured for almost a century on the other.

In the aftermath of the battle at Mohács in 1526 and the Ottoman occupation of the Hungarian capital Buda (Ger. Ofen; Turk. Budin) in 1541, the area around Temeswar was first controlled by the partisans of John Zápolya (Hung. Szapolyai János, 1490–1540) and, from 1551, by his rival for the Hungarian crown, Archduke Ferdinand I of Habsburg (1503–1564). During these years, the city's fortifications were modernized by Italian specialists, but these measures did not bring the desired long-term outcome. Neither could the fierce resistance of the garrison under the command of István Losonczy avert the seizure of the city by the Ottoman army in the summer of 1552.

Temeswar/Temeşvar as a Political and Military Centre in the Ottoman Empire

The military success of Kara Ahmed Pasha (d. 1555) heralded the first "imperial" phase in the city's history. Temeswar (Turk. Temeşvar) remained part of the Ottoman Empire for 164 years, longer than any other city in historical Hungary.[16] The new sovereigns made the city the center of the Eyâlet (Governorate) of Temeşvar, the second major Ottoman province in Hungary, whose territorial layout repeatedly changed. As the highest representatives of the sultan, the beylerbeys (governors) resided, with few exceptions, in Temeşvar. Jointly with the neighboring Eyâlets of Buda and Bosnia, the Eyâlet of Temeşvar constituted, from the end of the sixteenth century, a cornerstone of the system for safeguarding the border with the Habsburg realm of power and for the control of the Ottoman vassals, especially the Principality of Transylvania.[17]

During the century and a half under Ottoman rule – the first imperial phase of the city's history – both the appearance of the town and its ethnic and confessional structure underwent changes. The extent of these transformations can be reconstructed on the basis of tax registers and chronicles, as well as the reports of Western and Eastern travelers, which occasionally also contain illustrations. Important additions and clarifications of these data were brought by the archaeological investigations carried out over the last two decades.[18]

Immediately after the takeover of the city, two mosques were founded by Sultan Süleyman the Magnificent (r. 1520–1566). These were possibly converted church buildings. Over the years, new mosques were successively built. The increasing number of places of worship reflects the vitality of the settlement at the beginning of Ottoman rule. For instance, eleven mosques are documented in 1569, and a decade later there were 15 places of worship. Further mosques were then built in the seventeenth century, probably including one founded by Sultan Murad IV (r. 1623–1640). Additional buildings were also commissioned by the top echelons of the administration.[19] Around the Islamic places of worship, several quarters (Turk. mahalle) developed.[20] The transformations in the urban fabric have parallels with developments in other regions of Southeastern Europe or in the Hungarian Kingdom following their incorporation into the Ottoman Empire.[21]

The bulk of the non-Muslim population lived in the settlements outside the city walls, where wooden construction dominated. The analysis of the tax records shows that the number of Hungarian-speaking inhabitants had declined by the end of the sixteenth century. An important document from this period is a letter written in 1582 to Pope Gregory XIII (r. 1572–1585), requesting the dispatch of a priest. The letter in Hungarian with a seal also mentions István Herzeg as a head magistrate, thus testifying to the survival of municipal institutions under the Ottomans.[22]

The main part of the non-Muslim population in the Eyâlet belonged to the Greek Orthodox Church. This included Serbs and Vlachs (Eastern Romance speakers), who had progressively arrived from areas south of the Danube. In addition, Wallachians (Romanians) who had immigrated from Transylvania settled in the eastern central areas of the Eyâlet. Serbs, Romanians, and Vlachs were part of the garrisons of the castle and served in the militias responsible for safeguarding the traffic routes.[23]

Considering the inclusion of the Orthodox population in important parts of the security infrastructure, it comes as little surprise that several Greek Orthodox monasteries in the Banat were permitted by the new sovereigns to remain active. In addition, at the beginning of the seventeenth century, the Metropolis of Temeswar came into being, whose layout was orientated on the Ottoman administrative units and was under the control of the Patriarchate of Peć (Turk. İpek).[24] The leaders of the Metropolis presumably resided in the vicinity of the church dedicated to St. George in the Great Palanka. The latter withstood the siege of 1716 and was described in the 1718 fire code of Temeswar as an older structure with a lofty tower.[25]

Lastly, the ethnic and confessional mosaic of the city was rounded off by the Armenians, the Christian and Muslim groups of Roma, and the

Sephardic Jews. Sections of this community had immigrated from Saloniki, as evidenced by the tombstone of the surgeon and rabbi Azriel Assael, who died in 1636.[26]

The changes in urban texture were certainly influenced by the damage in the aftermath of the numerous sieges of the city by imperial troops.[27] And one of the most extensive attacks on the fortress of Temeswar took place in the course of the so-called Great Turkish War, which was ended by the peace agreements reached in Karlowitz (Serb. Sremski Karlovci) in 1699. Through these provisions, about a third of the province (the eastern areas) came under imperial rule. Since Temeswar was the most important remaining political and military center of the Ottoman Empire north of the Danube after the loss of Buda in 1686, the reinforcement of the fortifications was pursued with great vigor. The works included not only the old city walls. In this phase, the Great Palanka was also fortified with palisades and the garrison was staffed. Later, scattered groups of Hungarian rebels, who had fought against the Habsburgs under Francis II Rákóczi (Hung. II Rákóczi Ferenc 1676–1735) after 1703, also settled in the city.[28]

Changing Empires in the Banat of Temeswar

In the course of the Austrian–Ottoman–Venetian War, the imperial troops laid siege to Temeswar, which surrendered after 42 days on October 13, 1716. The capitulation agreement stipulated that the garrison and their families, as well as the Hungarian insurgents, were allowed to leave the fortress with their belongings. The remaining population groups were free to join the departing representatives of the Ottoman state power or to remain in the city under the new sovereigns.[29]

The capture of Temeswar was celebrated with thanksgiving services in all the important cities of the empire. In Vienna, Ignaz Reiffenstuel S.J. (1664–1720) in his celebratory sermon in St. Stephen's in the presence of the imperial family sketched out the vision of an eastward expansion of the Habsburg sphere of power to the eastern rim of the Black Sea.[30] These ambitious goals were not achieved, but with the takeover of Belgrade in August 1717, the Habsburgs secured control of another important center in southeastern Europe. The military successes at Peterwardein (Serb. Petrovaradin), Temeswar, and Belgrade achieved under the command of Prince Eugene of Savoy-Carignan (1663–1736) were extensively staged in a wide variety of media, and their allegorical interpretations became standard themes for the glorification of Emperor Charles VI (r. 1711–1749).[31]

As president of the Court War Council, the main organ responsible for the military security of the empire, Prince Eugene was aware of the strategic importance of Temeswar and the Banat region for securing the border with the Ottoman Empire. The former therefore drafted a comprehensive agenda in a letter to Charles VI immediately after the surrender of the Ottoman garrison in Temeswar, underlining the importance of preparing a holistic program to restructure the Banat, which would encompass political as well as economic and ecclesiastical aspects.[32] In the autumn of 1717, a first project in this direction was commissioned by the cavalry general Count Florimund de Mercy (1666–1734), who was appointed commander of the Banat immediately after the seizure of the fortress of Temeswar.

In the peace treaty concluded with the Ottoman Empire at Passarowitz (Serb. Požarevac) in 1718, Eastern Slavonia, Northern Serbia, the northern part of Bosnia, and Lesser Wallachia were assigned to the Habsburg Empire alongside the Banat as additional territories. They were subsequently organized as three separate special domains of the sovereign and subordinated to the *Commissio Neoacquistica*, newly created in 1719.[33] The latter was made up of representatives of the *Hofkriegsrat* (Court War Council), the *Hofkammer* (the Court Chamber, overseeing finances), and the *Ministerial-Banco-Deputation*, one of the four financial departments of the empire that received customs and toll payments from the various provinces of the empire.[34]

The responsibility for the establishment of the military and administrative structures in the *Neoaquistica* was entrusted to experienced military men who, first, had gained a good insight into the conditions on the ground through their participation in the campaigns and, second, possessed legal, economic, and administrative expertise, such as Count Mercy and the field sergeant general Franz Anton Paul Count Wallis von Karighmain (1678–1737), entrusted with the command of the fortress.

As Josef Wolf has shown, the genesis of the domain state of the Banat of Temeswar represented a classic territorial formation imposed from above. Yet it should be seen not only as the result of rulers, dynasties, and officials but also as the intended outcome of a process of communication in which state organs reacted to complex social problems and the grievances of subjects.[35] In implementing this administrative model, the Habsburg sovereigns pursued both military-strategic and fiscal goals. Simultaneously, efforts were made to hinder a reincorporation of the Banat of Temeswar into the Kingdom of Hungary in order to impede support for a Hungarian uprising through the Sublime Porte, as had been the case during the Rákóczi insurrection.[36] At the same time, the Temeswar base was intended to enable control over Transylvania.[37] In his report of 1734, Mercy's successor in office, Johann Andreas Count Hamilton (1679–1738), described this function as follows: "the Banat of Temeswar and the fortress of Belgrade are not only the bulwarks against the hereditary enemy but also the bridle that keeps the other countries as Transylvania and Hungary in line."[38] In the assignment of this control function for Transylvania, another similarity to the function of the fortress of Temeswar under the Ottomans becomes apparent.

These undertakings were praised as outstanding achievements in contemporary publications, above all in the treatise *Augusta Carolinae Virtutis Monumenta* (1733).[39] In this text, the political measures, as well as the buildings erected on behalf of the emperor, were titled *monumenta* in reference to Roman terminology.[40] For a long time, Antonius Höller SJ (1698–1770), who is mentioned on the title page, was considered the author of this publication. However, he was only the "promoter" of the treatise, which was written by Franz Keller SJ (1699–1762), professor of rhetoric at the University of Vienna.[41] Since the 1980s, Höller/Keller's work has been invoked as an important evidence for the existence of an art policy jointly steered by Emperor Charles VI with a circle of advisors.[42] More recent research, however, sees the treatise as a commentary or reflection on a series of imperial enterprises.[43] Although Höller/Keller mentioned several projects in the *Neoaquistica*, the treatise has only been selectively examined in studies dealing with the early phase of Habsburg rule in the Banat.[44] In the following, therefore, individual areas of imperial activity in the new provincial capital will be contrasted with the accounts in the tract. In view of the strong steering of the Banat authorities by the Viennese institutions, such an approach appears rewarding. Moreover, the planning of the new city layout of Temeswar and its partial implementation took place in parallel with the restructuring of the imperial building system, such as the centralization of the Imperial Construction Office (*Hofbauamt*) between 1716 and 1743 under the director Gundacker Count Althan (1665–1747).[45]

One further measure, the effects of which were particularly noticeable in the Banat from the third decade of the eighteenth century onward, was the systematic build-up of a military engineer corps. After the experiences of the Great Turkish War, during which the imperial army had largely depended on French and Italian specialists, Prince Eugene accelerated the founding of schools for the training of engineers and fortification engineering in Vienna (1717) and one year later in Brussels and Prague.[46] Land surveying and cartography techniques strengthened the spatial grip of the Habsburgs as sovereigns in the territories newly acquired at the beginning of the eighteenth century.

The construction of a belt of fortifications stretching from Transylvania to the middle reaches of the Danube was also largely the initiative of Prince Eugene, who was very familiar with current developments in France, especially the chain of fortifications along the borders of that country planned by Sébastien Le Prestre de Vauban (1633–1707). The central components of the defense system on the Habsburg-Ottoman border were the fortifications in Osijek (Ger. Esseg), Peterwardein, Belgrade, and Temeswar in the south, as well as Weißenburg (Hung. Gyulafehérvár, today Rom. Alba Iulia) in Transylvania. These fortress-towns, the majority of which were situated at communicative nodes, not only provided military protection from outside and enabled control inwards but also functioned as a monumental reminder of the power of the imperial sovereign in the farthest corners of his domain. In this spirit, when the foundation stone was laid for the Weißenburg complex on November 4, 1715, the town was renamed Alba Carolina or Karlsburg. The bastioned structure was completed during the lifetime of the eponymous emperor in 1738.[47]

The Ethnic-Denominational Configuration in Temeswar at the Onset of Habsburg Rule

Following the surrender and the joint withdrawal of the Ottoman garrison and the Hungarian insurgents from Temeswar, the majority of the city's non-Muslim population decided to remain there. These were 466 Rascians (Serbs and Romanians, Ger. Raitzen), 144 Jews, and 35 Armenians.[48] It was with these communities and their institutions that the medieval layer of the city's history lived on.[49]

The new sovereigns reaffirmed the ecclesiastical hierarchy of the Greek Orthodox Church in the Banat in accordance with the "Illyrian Privileges" that Emperor Leopold I (r. 1658–1705) had granted to the Serbs who had fled the Ottoman Empire in 1690. These involved the free practice of religion, exemption from tithe payments to the Catholic clergy, and the freedom to elect their own spiritual leader. The imperial diploma of protection and the national privileges were subsequently renewed on several occasions. The leadership in all the spiritual as well as secular matters of the Rascians was assumed by the top echelons of the Greek Orthodox Church. In addition to the Serbs, the Greek Orthodox Romanians were also placed under this denomination. A special measure was the autocephalous status granted by Emperor Charles VI to the Metropolitan of Belgrade. Furthermore, his jurisdiction was extended to the Banat and Austrian Wallachia.[50]

Although the actual power in the Banat capital was concentrated in the hands of the military, the Court Chamber aimed to maintain remnants of the autonomous municipal administration and to develop it further.[51] The knowledge about the structures that existed at the beginning of the Habsburg rule is rather vague and comes from the city monograph published in 1853 by Johann Nepomuk Preyer (1805–1888). For his work, the then-mayor of Temeswar used several records and chronicles that have not survived. Preyer mentioned Nicola Muncsia, a municipal judge of the Rascians, who traveled between the Temeswar suburbs and the imperial camp as a courier of the Greek Orthodox bishop during the siege of 1716. Muncsia also retained the judge's position in the Magistrate of the Rascians, appointed by the Habsburg provincial administration in 1718. It appears that this magistrate also continued to use the old seal of the

Greek Orthodox community with the depiction of St. George during this transitional phase.[52] Presumably, the seat of the magistrate remained near the bishop's church in the settlement outside the ramparts (Great Palanka), as during the Ottoman period (Figure 4.1).

On January 1, 1718, the German magistrate of Temeswar was formed, headed by the Bavarian-born barber surgeon Tobias Balthasar Holdt (1660–1721) as town judge. Together with the Rascian Magistrate, its task was to enforce measures to maintain public safety and hygiene, collect taxes and, above all, enforce the fire authority's regulations.[53]

The idea of parity between the two large groups of Rascians and the settlers who had migrated from the Holy Roman Empire, which appears in the founding of the two magistrates, is deceptive. In reality, there was an initial attempt to implement spatial segregation, whereby the Catholic settlers from the empire were allowed to live within the enclosed area, while

Figure 4.1 Copper Engraved Plan of Temeswar after Its Takeover by the Habsburg Troops, around 1740.

Source: Matthäus Seutter, Temeswaria Oppidum Superioris Hungariae [Temeswar, Town of Upper Hungary], Augsburg, ca. 1740. State and University Library Bremen, http://gauss. suub.uni-bremen.de/suub/hist/servlet/servlet.hmap?id=247967.

the other ethnic groups and denominations were to live in the suburbs. Similar configurations are also known in Belgrade, where the Catholic settlers lived in the *Wasserstadt* (Water Town) on the banks of the Danube, while the Serbian population lived in the Sava-City.[54] The two settlements in Belgrade also had their own magistrates.[55] The system of spatial segregation of ethnic and confessional groups practiced in Temeswar and Belgrade recalls the practice that prevailed in both cities under the Ottomans. However, this was not a continuation of this custom under the new Habsburg sovereigns. Comparable strategies of segregation are also documented for the aforementioned vast restructuring of Karlsburg in Transylvania, where there were no Ottoman antecedents.[56]

Among the groups settling in the suburbs, the Armenians formed a special community. On the city maps, a cluster of "Armenian houses" were recorded in the north of the Great Palanka until shortly after the middle of the eighteenth century.[57] These were the houses of Armenians who had already settled in Temeswar prior to 1716, as well as members of the community who had moved to the city after the fall of Belgrade in 1739 and from Transylvania and Moldavia. As specialists in textile crafts, specifically leather production, they were purposefully recruited from the Ottoman Empire. At the same time, the Armenians cultivated family and business networks, which turned this community in Temeswar into an influential protagonist in East-West trade.[58]

Finally, another important trans-imperial group were the Jews. The local Sephardim community grew, with new members moving in from the Ottoman Empire and Belgrade, as well as several families of Ashkenazi Jews from Bohemia and Moravia. As in the other Habsburg territories, the Jews in the Banat were under the direct protection of the Habsburg administration and paid a special tax (*Judentax*, later *Toleranztax*) to the Chamber. Through the transfer of licenses to produce beer or brandy, they became important partners of the imperial army. Despite considerable wealth and close relations with the administration, Jews were initially not allowed to settle inside the fortress. However, this provision was repeatedly circumvented by members of the Jewish communities by renting houses inside the fortress.[59]

The Confessional Policy under Emperor Charles VI

From the outset, one of the main focuses of imperial policy was to impose a majority Catholic population structure, or at least ensure the dominance of this denomination – through the controlled influx of Catholic settlers, a confessional counterweight to the predominantly Protestant Transylvania should emerge.[60] Besides the settlers from the German-speaking area and the South Slavic Catholics (Šokcy and Bulgarians), there were also immigrants from the Italian Habsburg Territories and from Spain. The latter had fought on the side of Charles III, later Emperor Charles VI, during the confrontations over the Spanish crown and were forced into exile after its defeat.[61]

Initially, the Jesuits and Franciscans were entrusted with pastoral care. Whereas the Jesuits, who had accompanied the army as field chaplains,[62] were already on the ground, the Franciscans were specifically recruited.[63] In 1718, after the German magistrate had petitioned the provincial administration for the establishment of a parish church as a starting point, the Bosnian Franciscans received permission to move to the interior of the fortress, where they were assigned a mosque building for use as a church. Emperor Charles VI had already endowed a Jesuit mission in the fortress in October 1717. The four priests and one lay brother, who spoke different languages, initially lived in three so-called *Türkenhäuser* (Turkish houses) on the property next to the city's former main mosque, which had been established by the Ottomans in a medieval church.[64] This building has been identified repeatedly as the church of St. George, mentioned in medieval sources.[65] After 1718, the building served as the town parish church with the new patrocinium *Ad Mariam Serenam*.[66] In a very short time, the most important parts of the liturgical furnishings were imported from Vienna. Among them were three bells, which were added to the (probably) still intact medieval tower in 1719, together with a cross.[67] The latter was a bestowal from the South Slavic Catholics, which proves that it was the Catholic confession and not the ethnic affiliation that had been the decisive criterion for the granting of permission to settle inside the fortress.

During the following years, the influence of the state on pastoral care was extended as Charles VI pledged to shoulder the expenses resulting from the endowment of new parishes and the construction of new churches in addition to his patronage rights.[68] This action fueled the conflict with the Bishop of Csanád, to whom the Habsburg authorities had assigned Szeged as a seat. This important center of the Csanád bishopric had already been taken by the imperial troops in 1686/1699. From there, Bishop Ladislaus of Nádasdy (Hung. Nádasdy Lászlo, 1662–1729) presented his first claims to the bishopric territory, which in the meantime had come under Habsburg control, even before the peace treaty in Passarowitz.

His attempt to publicly substantiate these claims through a canonical visitation in the Banat capital met with resistance from the Jesuit mission there, which feared an infringement of its missionary authority. Also, the city commander of Temeswar – Franz Paul Count of Wallis – showed a similarly negative attitude.[69] For the administrations in Vienna and Temeswar it was of utmost importance to prevent the ecclesiastical-canonical affairs of the diocese, whose territory was a domain of the House of Habsburg, from being handled by a Hungarian nobleman as bishop.

The confrontations flared up once again when the succession to the late Nádasdy, who died in 1729, was at stake. The Viennese authorities and the administration in Temeswar were finally able to push through their preferred candidate, Adalbert Freiherr von Falkenstein (1730–1739).[70] In order to compensate for the lost goods and tithes, the bishops and the canons were to be paid from the state treasury.

A further step in the interlocking of the imperial administration and the ecclesiastical hierarchy was the decision to move the seat of the bishop of Csanád to Temeswar.[71] This imperial resolution from November 1733 was possibly also a reaction to the relocation of Metropolitan Mojsije Petrović (1677–1730) from Belgrade to Temeswar. The Greek Orthodox dignitary stayed in the Banat capital for almost a decade from 1721 onward, as he considered it to be considerably more secure than Belgrade.[72]

These measures to bolster the Catholic denomination in the Banat region are featured in the aforementioned tract *Augusta Carolinae Virtutis Monumenta* as radiant models of the piety of Charles VI: "it is the county of Temeswar, where the emperor's exceedingly God-fearing piety becomes most apparent."[73] In coordination with this statement, the illustration of the section presenting the imperial *Aedificia Sacra* shows the personification of the Temeswar region alongside other female personifications of the provinces placed in front of an altar, behind which appears the figure of *Religio*. On this sheet, the restoration of buildings dedicated to religious worship in the former lands of the St. Stephen's Crown and the eastern *Neoaquistica* territories appears on par with prominent imperial foundations, such as the St. Charles Church in Vienna.

Early Initiatives for the Structural Redesign of the Urban Space in Temeswar under Charles VI

According to the records, at the onset of Habsburg rule, there were 227 houses and four mosques within the fortification, 112 houses and one mosque in the Great Palanka, and 62 houses and two mosques in the Small Palanka. Due to practical considerations, the Islamic prayer houses, a powder tower, and the damaged former castle were used as storage facilities during this phase.[74] In addition, repair work was carried out on the buildings inside the fortress that accommodated the soldiers of the garrison as well as members of the administration, along with selective reinforcements of the Ottoman fortifications.[75]

The most pressing measures in this phase included the creation of the infrastructure for the building works and for the maintenance of the garrison and the working staff. Consequently, the erection of a flour mill was considered just as urgent as the construction of brick kilns, lime kilns, and sawmills. The bricks were state monopoly articles with standardized dimensions. For the coordination of construction activities in the Banat, which included not only military structures but also the erection of cameral buildings (office buildings, chancelleries, granaries, and factories) and churches, a building department was founded in Temeswar.[76] This body was also responsible for drafting the plans, which were then sent to the Court War Council, the Court Chamber, or the Imperial Construction Office in Vienna for inspection. Those authorities also made efforts to mobilize skilled artisans. Three hundred "imperial craftsmen" (masons, carpenters, and brickmakers) arrived in the Banat in 1718 alone, many of whom subsequently settled in Temeswar and constituted a large part of the citizenry in the following years.[77]

Successive settlements of different institutions and functionaries in Temeswar impacted the planning of the new fortifications and the new city layout. In addition to the Imperial Administration of the Banat, the General Military Command, the Customs Directorate, the Forestry Office, the Upper Salt Office, the Directorate of Construction, the Provincial Court of Justice (*Landesauditoriat*), and the residence of the Catholic bishop were to be located within the bastioned fortress.[78]

On April 25, 1723, the solemn ceremony of laying the foundation stone for the new fortification, which was to simultaneously define the framework for the urban center, took place. The inscription embedded at the festive ceremony honored the merits of Prince Eugene, who had wrested the province from the Ottomans through the victory at Peterwardein in the name of Emperor Charles VI, and also mentioned Count Mercy as the officiating commander of the province.[79]

However, construction work on the bastioned enclosure did not begin until nearly a decade later (1732).[80] A similar picture emerges regarding the new fortifications in Belgrade. This delay in the start of construction was probably also a consequence of the precarious financing of these large-scale projects. Since Temeswar and Belgrade were deemed to be the "bulwarks of Christendom against the hereditary enemy," a financial contribution from the clergy had been requested in 1720. Initially, this demand was only reluctantly met. Then in 1725 Pope Benedict XIII (r. 1724–1730) sanctioned a five-year levy. The contributions collected during that period from the German Hereditary Lands, the Hungarian lands, and the Habsburg territories in Italy, such as Naples, Sicily, and Milan, eventually amounted to almost two million florins.[81]

Because of the marshy terrain around Temeswar, extensive hydraulic engineering work had to be carried out in the run-up to the construction work. Alongside the excavation of canals to drain swamps, a 16-mile-long canal was built between 1728 and 1732 to direct the course of the Bega along the southern flank of the fortifications. One objective of this was to supply the city with potable water and the manufactories in the neighborhood with industrial water. In addition, the watercourse made it possible to bring in the huge quantities of wood needed for the foundations of the buildings in the swampy underground.[82] Another artificial waterway, the Bega-Canal between Temeswar and Betschkerek (today Zrenjanin in Serbia), was designed to enable the transport of agricultural products and goods manufactured in the Banat across the rivers Tisza and Danube to other regions of the empire and the neighboring Ottoman Empire.[83] One important destination inside the Habsburg Empire was the port of Fiume (today Croat. Rijeka), which handled the export of agricultural products from Hungary and the Banat westwards.[84]

Alongside these economic objectives, the canals functioned as important tools for the self-staging of the state and the ruler in the same way as the network of roads, which was simultaneously being developed.[85] Correspondingly, the hydraulic construction works figure prominently in the *Augusta Carolinae Virtutis Monumenta*. In the sixth vignette of the title page of the chapter dealing with the *Aedificia Oeconomica*, the figure of Heracles, who appears here as the representative of Charles VI, orders the river deity to pour water into a canal; the accompanying quotation from Virgil alludes to the winning of arable land by draining the marshes.[86]

The erection of the bastion-shaped ramparts and the structuring of the inhabited areas inside and outside the fortress did not follow an overall plan. A synopsis of the known plans for the phase 1723–1735 revealed in part significantly diverging concepts regarding the layout of the defensive structures and especially the arrangement of the settlements outside the ramparts. Of these designs, one variant that has survived in copies in Budapest, Dresden, Bern, and Stockholm is worthy of special attention. The Europe-wide distribution of the copies leads to the assumption that it was a design whose realization was planned but later abandoned. The plans illustrate a main fortress with the crown work of St. Catherine situated to the east, in which barracks and other functions were to be located alongside the medieval church of the namesake saint. Further to the east, the "Rascian Town" (the former Small Palanka) were to be built as an outer work in front of the fortress. Both the interior of the fortress and the "Rascian Town" were to be structured as regular square building blocks, interspersed by squares.[87] Judging from a note on the version of the plan for a tripartite fortification preserved in Bern, the project was designed by Nicolas Doxat de Morez (1682–1738),[88] a military engineer with Swiss Calvinist background, who had entered the imperial army in 1712.[89]

It is conceivable that Doxat de Morez was also involved in the planning of the Transylvanian Barracks (*Siebenbürger Kaserne*) in Temeswar. Such an attribution is supported by information in the diary of Metropolitan

Mojsije Petrović, who referred to Doxat's stay in the city.[90] The complex was completed between 1723 and 1728, thus before the work on the bastioned ramparts commenced. With a total length of almost 500 meters, the Transylvanian Barracks were simultaneously one of the earliest monumental representatives of a building type that remained an important medium for visualizing the presence of the state up to the dissolution of the Habsburg monarchy.[91] However, the earliest structures of this type were built at the end of the seventeenth century, immediately after the Great Turkish War in Hungary, and only functioned for a short period.[92] A second wave of larger complexes emerged under Charles VI in Lower Austria, Temeswar, and Belgrade (*Württemberg Kaserne*). In the Hereditary Lands, the erection of these buildings was promoted by the estates in an attempt to lessen the burden of quartering placed on the civilian population.[93] Similar considerations appear to have played a role in Temeswar as well. In the above-mentioned petition of 1718, the new municipal council appealed to the imperial administration to promote the construction of barracks to alleviate the housing situation within the fortress. According to a 1717 survey, more than half of the so-called *Türkenhäuser* were used to house the garrison.[94]

With the installation of the monumental complex of barracks in Temeswar and Belgrade, the provincial administration and the Court War Council were certainly pursuing additional goals, too. Alongside ensuring rapid mobilization and more effective provisioning, the concentration of soldiers in one building enabled extensive control and disciplining.[95] The Württemberg barracks in Belgrade, built at the same time as the facility in Temeswar, also served as the residence of the governor there.[96] Comparable quartering of officials presumably also took place in Temeswar.

It was not only the sheer length of the facade (483 m) that made the Transylvanian Barracks impressive.[97] Its tower, erected above the main entrance, was also the first landmark of the new city layout. The double-headed eagle with the monogram of Emperor Charles VI affixed to the top of the tower at the completion of construction work in 1728 is the earliest-known example of a public display of an imperial emblem in Temeswar.[98] Inscriptions or heraldic references to the Habsburg dynasty were probably positioned in other parts of the city as well. Analogous to the Caroline Fountain in Karlsburg, which was adorned with eagle figures and presented in an illustration in the *Augusta Carolinae Virtutis Monumenta*, corresponding symbolic markings were presumably also found on some of the six public fountains in Temeswar indicated on a city plan of 1734.[99] The panegyric tract mentions these hydraulic devices together with comparable installations and fountains in Vienna and Belgrade. In the case of Temeswar, the transfer of water into a new canal network, made possible by a sophisticated machine, is praised.[100] This is likely to be the city's first water tower, built in 1732, whose designer has not yet been identified.[101]

Besides the military engineers, members of the Jesuit mission, such as Konrad Kerschensteiner SJ (d. 1728), also participated in resolving the tasks related to the water supply, which were essential for urban development, as well as the draining of the marshes. He had moved from Buda to Temeswar at the request of the Banat administration. In Buda, he had coordinated the construction of the Jesuit college and an aqueduct.[102] Furthermore, Augustin Haller von Hallerstein SJ (1703–1774) taught aspiring military officers about matters of fortification and hydraulic engineering at the school opened by the Jesuits in the Banat capital in 1726.[103] In the report of 1734 mentioned at the outset, Johann Andreas Count Hamilton, the second governor of the Banat, emphasized the particular importance of spreading the basic rules of the faith and of "geometry and ethics in the German language." For the implementation of these goals, the Jesuits were to receive the best possible support from the imperial administration.[104]

Further special measures taken by Charles VI mentioned in the chapter on the *Aedificia Civilia* were the paving of streets and the improvement of street lighting in Naples, Temeswar, Vienna, and Prague.[105] The paving of the streets in Temeswar, which began in 1722, was an extremely prestigious project, as the stones needed for it had to be transported over long distances by ship and by the rural population as corvée work. In addition to local prisoners, people who had been sentenced in Vienna to forced labor at the fortress construction site in Temeswar were also used for the laying of the paving stones.[106] Street paving and lighting were considered measures to control disease and ensure hygiene, order, and safety and were cited in political tracts as examples of "Policey." Under the umbrella of the broad term "Policey," regulations for the administration of almost all areas of social life were subsumed.[107] Correspondingly, they also influenced the urban planning concepts developed at the turn of the eighteenth century. France played a leading role in this process.[108]

Unlike in absolutist France and the planned cities in the bordering territories of the Holy Roman Empire, such as Karlsruhe and Mannheim, there were hardly any monuments to the rulers in the towns built or redesigned under the aegis of the Habsburgs.[109] One little-noted exception to this practice is the equestrian statue of Charles VI at the entrance to the fortress in Karlsburg.[110] Already in contemporary panegyric, the widespread abandonment of this classical vehicle of imperial representation had been highlighted as a hallmark of Habsburg virtue. In a series of panegyric texts, the modesty and piety of the Habsburgs were contrasted with the vanity and extravagance of the French king. This was often combined with the praise of the exceptional piety of the Austrian and Spanish lines of the House of Habsburg. In the self-understanding of the Habsburgs, the *Pietas Austriaca* was a hereditary trait of this dynasty, comparable to the imperial office, the very symbol of divine grace (Figure 4.2).[111]

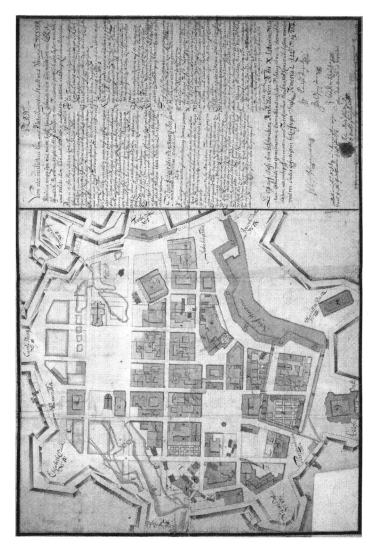

Figure 4.2 The Internal Layout of Temeswar in 1752.

Source: Th. Tröger: Plan von der innerlichen Ein- und Abtheilung der Stadt und Vestung Temesvar... [Plan of the Internal Layout of the City and Fortress of Temeswar], 1752. Budapest, Hadtörténeti Intézet és Múzeum, Sign. G I h 667/7. https://maps.hungaricana.hu/en/HTITerkeptar/36043/?li st=eyJxdWVyeSI6ICJGT1JSShodGkpbn0.

A further way of acknowledging the presence of the sovereign and, at the same time, maintaining the memory of the re-founding of the city was the naming of the bastions.[112] This "patrocinal land seizure" (Karner) or "politicization of the city boundaries" (Kemp), which can also be observed in Temeswar, began as a phenomenon in the seventeenth and eighteenth centuries. In this process, the gates and bastions that had been under the protection of saints in the Middle Ages were re-designated with the names of rulers and military commanders.[113] In Temeswar, the bastions were dedicated to Charles VI and his imperial consort Elisabeth-Christine (1691–1750). Later, the names of the successive rulers Theresa, Francis, and Joseph were added. Three other bastions commemorated significant figures of the early days of the Habsburg city: Prince Eugene, Count Mercy, and Johann Andreas Count Hamilton. Finally, the only bastion without a namesake was the Castle Bastion (Schlossbastei). This center of the medieval and Ottoman fortress was retained in the new fortress but was relegated to the background as a storage facility. Henceforth, the Parade Square (Paradeplatz, today Piața Libertăți) and St. George's Square (Sankt Georgplatz) before the Jesuit Church, whose triangular shape stands out from the otherwise structured grid of the urban space, served as new points of reference in the city.

The Imperial Component of the Sacralization of the Urban Space in Temeswar

Within this special constellation, it appears indicative that the first public monument in Temeswar and the entire Banat province was a statue of St. John of Nepomuk erected on the Parade Square.[114] Starting in the late seventeenth century, the devotion of John of Nepomuk functioned as a connecting bracket for the conglomerate of Habsburg territories.

His veneration in Temeswar had already begun immediately after the handover of the two mosque buildings to the Bosnian Franciscans and Jesuits in 1718. The chronicle of the Jesuit mission referred to John of Nepomuk in those years as a "Bohemian saint."[115] This mention in the sources illustrates that the two religious orders actively promoted the veneration even before the elevation of John of Nepomuk to the honors of the altars. The number of venerators, however, may have been far greater than the Bohemian countrymen groups from the ranks of the administration, the military, and the townspeople. The particular patronages of John of Nepomuk included protection against floods as well as against war, both of which were ubiquitous occurrences in Temeswar and the Banat.[116]

According to a report in the *Viennese Chronicle* (*Wiener Diarium*) on the feast of John of Nepomuk celebrated in Temeswar on May 16, 1721, he is mentioned as the "specially chosen patron saint of this Banat."[117] This is astonishing, however, as the solemn beatification did not take place until

May 31, 1721, by the freshly elected pontiff Innocent XIII (r. 1721–1724). Certainly, the installation of the statue of the Bohemian cleric on the Parade Square in Temeswar in 1722 had been promoted by the representatives of the emperor. Similar initiatives are known from the Habsburg territories in Italy (Messina, Naples, Capua, Pavia) and from Austrian Wallachia.[118] Frequently, the local garrisons were involved in the inauguration ceremonies, thus conferring an official character to these celebrations. That the devotion was supported by the imperial house is also evidenced by the fact that between 1720 and 1721, Charles VI and his spouse Elisabeth-Christine intervened in the process of canonization by submitting petitions to Pope Clement XI (r. 1700–1721).[119] Also at the same time, the first representations appeared, showing John of Nepomuk together with members of the imperial family. In this light, it is hardly surprising that Charles VI and the Bishop of Csanád, Count Nádasdy, designated John of Nepomuk as the "special patron and protector of the entire Banat" in 1726.[120] That decision preceded Nepomuk's official elevation to the honor of the altars by three years. When appointing him as the patron of the Banat, the emperor followed a proposal formulated by the provincial administration in 1724. In the same year, a confraternity of Nepomuk placed under the patronage of the Immaculate Conception was founded on the initiative of the Bosnian Franciscans in Temeswar.[121] Members of this sodality were both the senior officers of the fortress garrison and the president of the civil-military provincial administration.[122] Prototypes for the Temeswar confraternity were the associations in Prague (1696) and Vienna (1709). The latter was joined by the imperial family in 1717.[123]

An additional example of the connection between the imperial agenda and the veneration of John of Nepomuk is the church dedicated to the Bohemian saint, which was the first new sacred building in the fortress. It was erected between 1733 and 1736 by Italian craftsmen with the support of the provincial government.[124] The pediment of the facade was originally surmounted by an imperial double-headed eagle with scepter, crown, and sword.[125] Similar imperial emblems are also found on sacred buildings in the capital, such as the Church of the Servites and the Church of Santa Maria de Mercede of the Spanish Hospital (today *Priesterseminarkirche*), consecrated in 1723. This institution, founded by Charles VI, was intended to accommodate the family members of the sovereign's subjects who had followed the ruler to Vienna from Spain or the former Spanish provinces.[126]

Fortification Construction and the Remodeling of the Urban Space

Facing the church of the Bosnian Franciscans, the seat of the German magistrate was built between 1731 and 1736 over the ruins of an Ottoman bath. In the upper section of the building, also known as the German Town Hall (*Teutsches Rathaus*), the new coat of arms of the town was prominently displayed. Regarding the symbolic politics in the new Banat provincial capital, it seems significant that the Habsburg administration had designed a new seal for the German magistrate. With this paternalistic gesture, the new sovereigns replaced the probably still existing medieval town seal, which showed a figure fighting with a dragon-like creature (probably the symbol of a heresy).[127] The new coat of arms showed a palisade fortification with a gate flanked by two towers in the center, with open door wings.[128] It is highly probable that this was meant as a reference to the Ottoman *Forforos Gate*, through which Prince Eugene had entered the city. This structure, together with the so-called *Lusthaus des Paschas* (Pleasure House of the Pasha) to the north of the Great Palanka, in which the imperial headquarters were located during the siege, was preserved as a place of remembrance.[129]

The inscription placed on either side of the relief presented the new fortifications erected under the guidance of Count Mercy as a counterpart to the Ottoman ramparts. This presentation was combined with wishes for longevity under the wings of the glorious Habsburg eagle and the beneficent scepter of Austria.[130] The final passage of the inscription thus appears as a description of the also newly installed coat of arms of the Banat of Temeswar, on which two eagles protect the central armorial field showing a tower gate. Above the central field is the princely crown, and in front appear the crossed scepter and sword above a banner with the inscription *Providentia Imperatorum*.[131]

The *Providentia Augusti*, the ever-vigilant care for the empire, occupied a prominent position in the catalogue of virtues of the Roman emperors and was closely linked to their initiatives to raise fortifications to guard against external threats. The image of a military camp gate on the reverse of a series of fourth-century A.D. coins commemorating the emperors' leadership in securing the borders probably served as a reference for the motto and the central escutcheon on the coat of arms of the Temeswar Banat.[132] This analogy, which has remained unnoticed until now, will be contextualized through further studies by the author.

However, the fortifications praised in the inscription had not even been completed at that time. As mentioned earlier, the large-scale construction started in 1732 with up to 180 masons and seven military engineers building the ramparts and galleries under the supervision of a building administrator. There were also numerous artisans who worked as independent contractors. At times, the rural population was also forced to corvée works.[133] In 1734, the Charles Bastion in the north and the Eugene Bastion in the west were completed, as can be seen from the inscription plaques placed in those areas, the wording of which has been preserved in transcripts from the nineteenth century. It is likely that similar inscriptions were also originally on the outer sides of the other bastions. Both plaques on the outside of the Eugene Bastion celebrated the namesake. Their chronograms alluded to the completion of the fortress wall over the foundation stone in 1734, the conquest of the city in 1716, and the capture of the city by the Ottomans in 1552.[134] The inscription on the Charles Bastion emphasized the new beginning after 164 years under the "Turkish yoke." The founding of these new bastions by the "Austrian Jupiter" took place in the name of religion and in the service of the "Austrian nation." The emphasis on the firmness and strength of the new fortifications was intended as a reference to Emperor Charles VI's personal motto *constantia et fortitudine*.[135]

The elaborate chronograms and the recurrent topoi of the imperial panegyric suggest a leading role of the local Jesuit mission in the elaboration of these propagandistic statements. Furthermore, the listing of the most recent developments in the Banat capital – in part even projects in the planning stage – in Höller/Keller's tract is indicative of a circulation of information and concepts between Temeswar and the imperial capital, in which Jesuit actors played a leading role not least due to their function as confessors of a series of Habsburg rulers. In addition – not least out of gratitude to Charles VI, the founder of the Temeswar Mission – the Jesuits acted locally as the most important promoters of imperial positions through festive church services and musical and theatrical performances on the anniversaries of the takeover of the city by the imperial troops and the holidays associated with the members of the imperial house (birthdays, festivals of the patron saints).[136]

It appears that around 1733 plans were developed to establish a generously proportioned square in the northern part of the fortress. The new cathedral of the bishopric of Csanád and the episcopal residence were to be built there alongside the new building of the Generalate (Ger. Generalatshaus).[137] In the plans drawn up between 1733 and 1735, these facilities appear as monumental complexes whose elongated façades and block-like structures show clear analogies to buildings such as the Palace of the Invalides (Ger. Invalidenhaus), a hospital and barracks for disabled soldiers in Pest, one of the most ambitious imperial construction undertakings of the time.[138] These conceptual analogies to the complex in Pest, which was designed and realized under the aegis of the Imperial Construction Office, suggest that the planning in Temeswar was modeled on specifications from central institutions in Vienna.[139] A further indication of this is the hierarchical staging of the administrative functions in the cityscape that can be discerned from the plans. The episcopal ensemble was to become a dominant element of the cityscape, but without competing with the facilities of the secular institutions. In this way, the plans for Temeswar differ significantly from episcopal residences that were planned contemporaneously in Hungary, whose marked isolation from the urban area, according to Miklós Mojzer, had its roots in the self-image of the bishops residing there as feudal lords of the respective territories.[140]

The Emergence of a Multi-Confessional and Multi-Ethnic Urban Space

The defeat of the Habsburgs in the Turkish War 1738–1739 and the ensuing plague epidemic in the Banat marked a dramatic rupture in the activities of the Viennese institutions in this region. Even though Temeswar had not been besieged during the conflict, marauding units led by Romanian *harambasas* (senior commanders of hajduk/brigand groups) caused massive damage to the civilian settlements and installations under construction in the Banat. Moreover, a fire destroyed a considerable part of the Great Palanka in 1738, including the wooden building of the old Greek Orthodox bishop's church. The fire had been set intentionally by the Habsburg authorities in an attempt to contain the expansion of the epidemic in the largely depopulated Great Palanka. Altogether, more than one-fifth of the city's residents fell victim to the rampant epidemic.

Upon the return of the territories south of the Danube-Sava line and Lesser Wallachia to Ottoman control, as stipulated in the peace treaty of Belgrade in 1739, Temeswar emerged as an important center for the military security of the empire.[141] As a consequence of the acts of war and the subsequent reorganization of territorial boundaries, the Banat became a destination for migratory movements once again. These were Romanian and Bulgarian groups from Lesser Wallachia, as well as groups of Serbs who fled to the Habsburg territory. Furthermore, in 1739, the commander-in-chief of the Habsburg troops, Georg Olivier Count of Wallis (1673–1744), granted permission to the Sephardic Jews, who had fled Belgrade, to settle in Temeswar.[142]

With the death of Charles VI in 1740, the Banat once again became the subject of Hungarian claims for reincorporation. At the Coronation Diet in Preßburg (Hung. Pozsony today Bratislava in Slovakia) in 1741, Empress Maria Theresa consented in principle to this demand, but pointed out that reincorporation would not be feasible given the prevailing war with Prussia. Along with the peace treaty of Dresden, in which the Habsburg Empire gave up large parts of Silesia, a restructuring of the administration of the Banat was initiated in 1745. The newly created *Commissio Aulica in Banaticis, Transsylvanicis et Illyricis* (The Court Commission for the Banat, Transylvania and the *Illyricum*) under the presidency of Count Ferdinand Kollowrat-Krakowsky (1682–1751) was at first placed under the control of the empress as an advisory body and was then transformed into a court deputation in 1747. The latter was to govern both the territorial units of the Banat and Transylvania as well as the "Illyrian Nation," the contemporary term used for the Serbian Orthodox population irrespective of their concrete settlement area. These were the territories of Banat, Slavonia, and Syrmia, whose Greek Orthodox confessional communities rejected a reincorporation of these territories into the Kingdom of Hungary, as well as the Serbian diaspora in Inner Hungary.[143] In addition, the new administrative institution was intended to counteract the initiatives of Tsarist Russia, which since the early 1750s strove to act as a protector of the Greek Orthodox groups in the region.[144]

This restructuring of the administration, partly influenced by external political developments, impacted the configuration of the interior of the fortress and the suburbs of Temeswar. In order to integrate the Rascians to a greater extent, the area of jurisdiction of their magistrate was redrawn. The jurisdiction of the latter was extended to the area of the settlement Fabrique developed northeast of the fortress, whose name alludes to the manufactures built there before 1739, as well as to the new settlement of Mehalla in the southeast. In addition, Rascian merchants gained the opportunity to purchase real estate within the fortress. Consequently, the Rascian community gained new opportunities to position its image within the urban space.

The primary arena for the staging of this community was the square site under construction in the northern part of the fortification (see Figure 4.2). On the narrow western side of the square, an ensemble of buildings was created in which the leading institutions of the Rascian population were located. The centerpiece of this complex was the new Greek Orthodox cathedral, built from 1740 onward, and the adjacent residence of the eparch. The rapid mobilization of financial resources from the Serbian-Romanian diocesan fund and subsidies from Karlowitz, as well as donations from parishioners, enabled the completion of the congregation's room between 1744 and 1748. The towers, which were originally planned, were not built until 1791. Thus, the Rascian parish managed to complete the main church of their diocese faster than the Roman Catholic Episcopal Church on the opposite narrow side of the square, which had already commenced in 1736.[145] At the end of the western front of the square, the Rascian community's school building was erected (Figure 4.3).

The Rascian complex was completed with the town house of the Rascian magistrate, which was built to the north of the Episcopal Residence between 1758 and 1761 following a design prepared in Vienna.[146] The dimensions of the council building vastly exceeded the requirements, so that from 1771 the council hall was initially rented out for theatre performances. In 1776, the entire building was even turned into a (German) theatre. This transformation took place at a time when corresponding institutions were being built in the major cities of the Kingdom of Hungary, such as Buda, Preßburg, or Hermannstadt (today Rom. Sibiu) in Transylvania. Theatres were considered indicators of urbanity in those years and, according to the ideas of some Cameralist authors, in addition, fulfilled a moral and educational function.[147]

Figure 4.3 Former Complex of Buildings of the Rascian Community in Temeswar with the Bishop's Residence, the Greek Orthodox Bishop's Church, and the Rascian School (from left to right). Photo by Robert Born, 2020.

Along the southern longitudinal sides of the square, the Governor's House and the Palace of the President of the Provincial Administration were erected, while on the narrow eastern side, an additional monumental landmark was built in the form of the Roman Catholic Cathedral Church. The foundation stone for this sacred building, which had been donated by Charles VI, was laid as early as 1736, but the work could not be completed until 1776. This imperial endowment was deemed to be an act of piety and, beyond that, the cultivation of tradition. Such interpretations are supported not only by the aforementioned central illustration of the *Aedificia Sacra* in Höller's treatise but also by the charter of the foundation stone of the new cathedral of the venerable bishopric of Csanád. At the same time, the inscription indicated that the re-establishment of the cathedral was only possible within the secure framework of the new fortification, whose construction was made possible by *constantia et fortitudine*, the virtues mentioned in Charles VI's personal devise.[148] In accordance with the particularly representative aspirations, the elaboration of the design was carried out in the Viennese Imperial Construction Office. Stylistic arguments and above all the analogies to prominent buildings erected under the patronage of Charles VI even speak to a leading role of the head of this institution, Joseph Emanuel Fischer von Erlach (1693–1742) in the design process. Another indication of a relationship with this group of imperial buildings is provided by the sculptural elements of the cathedral church, which were not fully executed but have been preserved in a facade view from 1762. The crowns and double-headed eagle sculptures presented there appear in similar form in the designs for the transformation of the

Abbey in Klosterneuburg into an imperial residence and spiritual center after the model of the Escorial in Spain, a project in which Joseph Emanuel Fischer von Erlach also played a leading role. In Temeswar, only the double-headed eagle on the lower pediment as well as two further counterparts in the interior of the church was realized of the originally planned imperial emblems.[149] Other imperial symbols in the interior are the larger-than-life statues of St. Charles Borromeo and St. Teresa of Avila, the patrons of Charles VI and his successor Maria Theresa (r. 1740–1780), under whose reign the church was completed.[150]

These sculptures seem to be interlocked with other monuments in the city – first and foremost with the Trinity Column on the square in front of the church. The monumental sculptural ensemble, together with the St. Rosalia Chapel, built outside the fortifications but no longer preserved, is one of the most impressive monuments commemorating the menace posed by the plague and Turkish troops to the city's population.

The column was created in 1740 in a Viennese workshop by order of the Administration Councilor Johann Anton de Jean (Deschan) Hannsen (1686–1760) and was subsequently transported by ship to Temeswar. Upon arrival, the column was first installed with the support of professionals of the provincial administration on the square situated between the Transylvanian Barracks, the residence of the Jesuit Mission, and the Administration Council (*Landesadministration*).[151] The surviving written explanations of the program allow for a reconstruction of the original intentions of the founder. According to this, the statues of Saints Francis Xavier, Anthony, and John of God, which were originally placed around the monument, were intended to represent the three religious orders (Jesuits, Franciscans, and Brother Hospitallers) active in the city. The three reliefs placed on the column shaft depict the scourges of plague, famine, and war. On the next level, the figures of Saints Rochus, Sebastian, Charles Borromeo, and the heremit Rosalia, lying in a cave, are grouped together. Somewhat higher up, and thus slightly more prominent, is the Banat patron saint John Nepomuk, together with St. Barbara, the patron saint of miners and of the dying, and King David. A special feature is the emblem of the imperial eagle, which is hidden today and on the chest of which the Temeswar coat of arms was affixed. The uppermost completion is the group of the Holy Trinity, with God the Father and Christ crowning the Blessed Lady.[152] Conspicuously, the crown was designed in close imitation of the Rudolphine (Habsburg) House Crown.[153] The prominent staging of the emblems of imperial highness was intended to show the closeness of the local elites with the ruling house. After the estate was sold by Johann Anton de Jean Hannsen in 1742, the votive column was dismantled. The re-erection on the square between the two Roman Catholic and the Greek Orthodox episcopal churches did not take place until after October 1755.[154]

Almost at the same time, the so-called Marian or Nepomuk Column was erected on the Parade Square. The votive monument was commissioned by the Nepomuk Congregation and replaced the aforementioned statue of the Bohemian saint on the square. In accordance with the patrocinium of the sodality, John of Nepomuk appears here below the statue of the Immaculata. Similar to the Trinity Column, this monument was also manufactured in a Viennese workshop and brought to Temeswar on the waterway.[155]

The erection of the two votive monuments in the city's main squares conforms to a practice whose most prominent antecedent was the imperial-controlled sculptural appropriation of space in the imperial capital in the second half of the seventeenth century. Thereafter, this practice was replicated in almost all the cities of the empire. The propagandistic exaltation of the *Pietas Austriaca* thereby superseded the pillories, which had been installed in the main squares since the Late Middle Ages, and which were among the most significant markers of municipal legal authority. So far, research has primarily interpreted the erection of the two monuments in Temeswar as a form of overcoming the crises triggered by the latest plague and war. In addition, the iconographic program of these financially very lavish monuments served to implement a dynastic model of piety. As shown by the example of the devotion of John of Nepomuk, this *demonstratio catholica* also provided an offer of identification to almost all social classes. Thus, the donors, who belonged to the top echelons of the provincial administration in Temeswar, were able to showcase their confessional identity as well as their loyalty to the imperial house in a tangible way.[156]

We can also observe comparable constellations among the donations of liturgical furnishings for the sacred buildings in Temeswar. Most of these were also ordered by the heads of the Banat administration in Vienna.[157] In their selection of subjects, they also reacted to currents of popular piety and at the same time propagated central components of the post-Tridentine confessional culture. Moreover, the works donated to the churches were linked to the monuments in the public space performatively by way of processions, which brought about a sacralization of the public space. In a similar way as in the imperial capital, where the Corpus Christi procession attained a state-significant note through the participation of the imperial family,[158] the heads of the secular and military administration in Temeswar became important actors in the celebrations on the occasion of this feast. The processions started at the Jesuit church and proceeded to the residences of the fortress commander, the provincial governor, the councilor, and the church of the Bosnian Franciscans. Altars were set up at each of the stations. Prominently involved in the procession were representatives of the military as porters of the canopy and the town magistrates who followed, bearing torches.[159] For a long time, processions remained a constant element of public life. The procession to St. Rosalia's Chapel was an annual event until the onset of the First World War. Not least because of this, the Roman Catholic denomination remained particularly present in the public sphere of the fortress. Similar public events were held by the Greek Orthodox believers in the suburbs. Within the fortress, the complex consisting of the Episcopal Church and the Rascian School and Town Hall was the scene of assemblies of the Serbians, where national demands were increasingly articulated.[160]

In contrast to the Roman Catholic and Greek Orthodox groups, the Jewish communities at first had no official representation. It is likely that both communities settled inside the fortress only after the dramatic events of 1738–1739. The situation of the communities initially deteriorated during the reign of Empress Maria Theresa, who was notorious for her hostile attitude toward Jews. During the War of the Austrian Succession (1740–1748), the city's Jews had been repeatedly summoned to leave, but they were then able to remain in the city after paying a dramatically increased tolerance tax.[161] The empress's negative attitude is documented by a plan presented to the monarch at a meeting with her advisors in 1749. At that time, the two Jewish communities used a vaulted room in the former Ottoman fortress gate, which had been preserved as a commemorative place of the entrance of Prince Eugene as a house of prayer.[162] During the aforementioned meeting, a proposal was made to the Empress to establish a Jewish quarry opposite the Rascian Town Hall.[163] By moving to this area, the section of the former Ottoman city gate was intended to be made available for the construction of a Greek Catholic and Armenian church.[164] The empress rejected the project and personally noted on the plans that she "did not want the Jews in the city." The formation of a Jewish quarter inside the fortress was nonetheless pursued, as can be seen from the city plans drawn up after 1758.[165] Two synagogues were built close to each other after 1760. The construction of these buildings was accompanied by imperial authorities.[166] This episode illustrates that the much-vaunted coexistence of ethnic groups and confessions in Temeswar today is less a result of an enlightened policy of the Habsburg rulers than a reaction to the changed foreign policy constellations and, moreover, the outcome of protracted negotiations at the local level.

The originally planned Greek Catholic and Armenian churches in the neighborhood have not been built. The first Greek Catholic church was presumably constructed only around 1770 in the Fabrique suburb. This was a simple building whose sober design shows significant similarity to the parish churches built at the same time in the other suburbs of the Banat capital and in the newly established rural settlements. The parallels between these areas were not limited to the formal design of the religious buildings. The newly planned Temeswar suburbs after 1744, as well as the rural settlements, were organized according to a regular grid with a central square around which the church and other most important functionaries were grouped. Between 1764 and 1772, 34 villages were built for the colonists who had immigrated to the Banat. Over 9,000 houses were constructed in a similar way to the churches and the buildings for the officials based on normed plans.[167] The typified designs for specific construction tasks – which had been developed under the special preconditions existing in the *Neoaquistica*, where building operations were directly subordinated to the Viennese central administration or the regional commanders – were supposed to meet economic and functional requirements.[168] The standardized building types and settlement models developed in this area were extensively implemented during the colonization of Galicia at the end of the eighteenth century. The uniformly designed buildings, together with the votive columns, remain important visual markers of the former Habsburg Empire in East Central and Southeast Europe to the present day.

With the interventions in the natural environment and the centrally controlled population policy (settlement of colonist groups in coordination with mercantilist policy), the spread of this uniform architecture had a decisive impact on the appearance of the cultural landscape on the middle reaches of the Danube.

These operations and, in particular, the environmental interventions (melioration; introduction of new monocultures) led to a profound transformation in the country's structure, which has clear parallels with the other settlement initiatives of European powers, such as those under Catherine II (r. 1762–1796) in southern Russia and the *poblaciones* established under Carlos IV (r. 1788–1808) in Spain, as well as the settlements established in North America during the eighteenth century.[169] The settlements in the Banat designed on a drawing board and the connected system of land use were already criticized in the eighteenth century. The most prominent disapproving statements came from Emperor Joseph II (r. 1765–1790), who already at the beginning of his co-regency requested a change in the constitutional status of the Cameral Banat and influenced the empress's decision to agree to a reincorporation into the Kingdom of Hungary. With the incorporation in 1778, the Banat was subordinated to the Hungarian county system, thus concluding a period of intensive activities of the Viennese authorities in a peripheral region of the empire.

Concluding Remarks

The genesis of Habsburg Temeswar as an imperial center in Southeastern Europe presented here was, contrary to widespread opinion, not a linear progression. The realization of the new, regularly structured Baroque city complex and the massive fortifications is marked by a multitude of changes in plans, which were at times caused by developments in foreign policy or catastrophes such as the plague epidemic of 1739. Nevertheless, the construction of the new city complex was one of the most elaborate urbanistic projects of the eighteenth century in the Habsburg Empire and at the same time a field of experimentation for planning in which military, economic, and, above all, denominational aspects were the determining factors. The confessional segregation of the inhabitants practiced until the middle of the eighteenth-century stands in striking contrast to today's widespread image of a Baroque city shaped by the Enlightenment. In accordance with the intentions of the Habsburg rulers to establish Temeswar as a military-confessional outpost of the imperial capital Vienna in the border region to the Ottoman Empire, the military facilities and the sacral buildings formed the most important platforms for the visualization of the imperial house. In addition to the few, but lavish, imperial endowments on site, the monuments erected by the top echelons of the administration played an important role in the visualization of the ruling dynasty. The concentration of these elements and their design by leading artists of the time visualizes the rank of Temeswar as an imperial city. In addition, these monuments, closely associated with a post-Tridentine agenda, also function as a visual link between Temeswar and the empire's centers of Vienna, Prague, or Buda.

Acknowledgments

This article has benefited greatly from the generous support of several colleagues. I am indebted to Sandra Hirsch (Cluj-Napoca), Szabolcs Serfőző (Budapest), and Benjamin Landais (Avignon) for providing me with information and unpublished material. I would also like to thank Josef Wolf (Tübingen) for his valuable comments and for providing me with bibliographical material, which was a great help, especially in the difficult working conditions caused by the COVID-19 pandemic. Finally, I would like to thank the two editors for their patience and critical reading of the first drafts of the manuscript.

Notes

1 Nicolae Iorga, "Temeswar," in *Schriften und Briefe*, ed. Michael Kroner (Bucharest: Kriterion, 1978), 304 [passage translated by the author].
2 With 72,555 inhabitants (1910), Temesvár/Temeswar/Timişoara, together with Zagreb/Agram (79,000) and Pozsony/Preßburg/Bratislava (78,000), was one of the medium-sized multi-ethnic cities in the eastern half of the Monarchy. See Catherine Horel, "Temesvár (Timişoara) multiculturelle 1880–1914: 'Klein Wien' et capitale du Banat," *Études Balkaniques* (Paris) 18, no. 1 (2011), 37.

3 Originally, Timişoara, together with Novi Sad (Serbia) and Elefsina (Greece), were to be European Capitals of Culture in 2021. Due to the COVID-19 pandemic, the European Parliament agreed in December 2020 to postpone the Year of Culture for Novi Sad to 2022 and for Timişoara and Elefsina to 2023.

4 Reinhard Leber, *Politische Kultur und Systemtransformation in Rumänien. Lokalstudie zu der Stadt Temeswar* (Frankfurt am Main: Peter Lang, 1996), 31; Victor Neumann, "Timişoara în memoria colectivă contemporană," in *Revoluţia română din decembrie 1989. Istorie şi memorie*, ed. Bogdan Murgescu (Iaşi-Bucharest: Polirom, 2007), 21–45.

5 See György Ambrozy (Baron), *Temesvár im Jahre 1849. Während der Belagerung geschrieben* (Vienna: J.F. Greß, 1850), 36.

6 Victor Neumann, *Identităţi multiple în Europa regiunilor. Interculturalitatea Banatului* (Timişoara: Hestia, 1997). For a critical examination of these positions, see Judy Batt, "Reinventing Banat," in *Region, State and Identity in Central and Eastern Europe*, eds. Judy Batt and Kataryna Wolczuk (London: Frank Cass, 2002), 178–80, as well as Barna Bodó and Alpár Zoltán Szász, "A dekonstruált régió: Bánság," *Romániai magyar évkönyv* (2009–2010): 93–110.

7 Francesco Griselini, *Versuch einer politischen und natürlichen Geschichte des temeswarer Banats in Briefen an Standespersonen und Gelehrte, Erster Theil* (Vienna: Johann Paul Krauß, 1780), http://mdz-nbn-resolving. de/urn:nbn:de:bvb:12-bsb11064187-8. See also László Marjanucz, "Franz Griselini Bánság-képe," *Aetas* 28, no. 3 (2013): 24–43, and Szabolcs János, "Von der 'Strafkolonie' bis zum 'Eldorado': die Neuentdeckung des Banats im 18. Jahrhundert," in *Kulturelle Zirkulation im Habsburgerreich. Der Kommunikationsraum Wien*, eds. Wynfrid Kriegleder and Andrea Seidler (Vienna: Praesens, 2019), 73–97.

8 Timisoara's bid book, *Shine your Light – Light up Your City* (2015), 36, https:// timisoara2023.eu/document/view/43/Bidbook_EN_Timisoara2021.pdf.

9 See the contributions in Michaela Marek and Eva Pluhařová-Grigienė, eds., "Prekäre Vergangenheit? Barockforschung im östlichen Mitteleuropa unter den Bedingungen des Sozialismus," special issue, *RIHA Journal* 11 (2019), https://doi.org/10.11588/riha.2019.1.

10 Herbert Karner, "Der Kaiser und seine Stadt. Identität und stadträumliche Semantik im barocken Wien," in *Städtisches Bürgertum und Hofgesellschaft. Kulturen integrativer und konkurrierender Beziehungen in Residenz- und Hauptstädten vom 14. bis ins 19. Jahrhundert*, eds. Jan Hirschbiegel, Werner Paravicini, and Jörg Wettlaufer (Ostfildern: Jan Thorbecke, 2012), 141–60, 358–61; Frank Rochow, "Die räumliche Erscheinungsform des Neoabsolutismus – Militärarchitektur in Lemberg und Wien in den 1850er Jahren," *Zeitschrift für Ostmitteleuropa-Forschung* 68, no. 2 (2019): 157–59; Szabolcs Serfőző, "'A kétfejű sas szárnyainak oltalmában' A Habsburg uralkodók reprezentációja a kora újkori Sopronban," *Soproni szemle* 74, no. 3 (2020): 294–344. See also the activities and publications of the project "*Visual Culture of Ruler Representation in Cities of the Habsburg Empire – from Ferdinand I to Joseph I (1526–1711)*" funded by the Austrian Academy of Sciences, https://www.oeaw.ac.at/ihb/forschungsbereichekunstgeschichte/ forschung/architektur-repraesentation-und-staedtische-oeffentlichkeit/ herrscherrepraesentation-in-staedten.

11 Paul Niedermaier, "Raportul între factorul politic şi oraşe, cu încadrarea schimbărilor configuraţiei oraşului Timişoara în acest context," *Historia Urbana* 14, no. 2 (2006): 256–58; István Petrovics, "The Fading Glory of a

Former Royal Seat: The Case of Medieval Temesvár," in *The Man of Many Devices, Who Wandered Full Many Ways. Festschrift in Honor of János M. Bak*, eds. Balázs Nagy and Marcell Sebők (Budapest: Central European University Press, 1999), 529–30; Zsuzsanna Kopeczny, "Reşedinţa regală medievală de la Timişoara" [The Medieval Royal Residence of Timişoara], *Analele Banatului, Serie Arheologie-Istorie* 21 (2013): 211–31.

12 Mihai Opriş, *Timişoara: Monografie urbanistică, Vol. 1. Descoperiri recente care au impus corectarea istoriei urbanistice a Timişoarei* (Timişoara: Brumar 2007), 27–31.

13 Georg Bleyer, "Temesvar als Höhepunkt der Baukunst und des Städtebaus der schwäbischen Ansiedlung im 18. Jahrhundert," *Kultureller Wegweiser* 8, no. 1 (1956): 12; Géza Pálffy, "A bécsi katonai vezetés védelmi politikája a Temes–Maros vidékén a 16. század elejétől a 18. század közepéig," in *IV. Honvéd emléknap Makón 1997*, ed. Pál Halmágyi (Makó: József Attila Múzeum 1998), 16–17.

14 Lajos Kakucs, "Temesvár városának régi pecsétjei," *A Móra Ferenc Múzeum Évkönyve: Studia Historica* 13 (2010): 459.

15 Pálffy, "A bécsi katonai vezetés védelmi politikája," 17.

16 See Géza Dávid, "The 'Eyalet' of Temesvár in the Eighteenth Century," *Oriente Moderno* 79, no. 1 (1999): 113–28.

17 Pál Fodor, "Das Wilajet von Temeschwar zur Zeit der osmanischen Eroberung," *Südost-Forschungen* 55 (1996): 29, 31.

18 See Alexandru Szentmiklosi and Dumitru Ţeicu, "Stadtarchäologische Forschungen. Überlegungen zur Stadt Temeswar im 17.–18. Jahrhundert," in *Herrschaftswechsel. Die Befreiung Temeswars im Jahre 1716*, eds. Rudolf Gräf and Sandra Hirsch (Cluj-Napoca: Editura Academia Română, 2016), 24–46.

19 Balázs Sudár, *Dzsámik és mecsetek a hódolt Magyarországon* (Budapest, MTA Történettudományi Intézet, 2014), 88–91, 118, 513–50.

20 Cristina Feneşan, *Cultura otomană a vilayetului Timişoara (1552–1716)* (Timişoara: Editura de Vest, 2004), 58–63.

21 See Győző Gerő, *Turkish Monuments in Hungary* (Budapest: Corvina Press, 1976), 5–7.

22 Kakucs, "Temesvár városának," 463.

23 Fodor, "Das Wilajet von Temeschwar," 38; Klára Hegyi, *A török hódoltság várai és várkatonasága. Vol. III. A temesvári, győri, pápai, egri, kanizsai, váradi és újvári vilájet várainak adattára* (Budapest: MTA Történettudományi Intézet, 2008), 1349–70.

24 Antal Molnár, "Szerb ortodox egyházszervezet a hódolt Magyarországon," in *Szerb székesegyház a Tabánban*, eds. Tamás Csáki and Xénia Golub (Budapest: Történeti Múzeum, 2019), 44–50.

25 Jenő Szentkláray, *Mercy kormányzata a Temesi bánságban. Újabb részletek Délmagyarország XVIII. századi történetéhez* (Budapest: Athenaeum, 1909), 86–87; Ferenc Csortán, "Arhitectura religioasă în Vilaietul Timişoara," *Satu Mare – Studii şi Comunicări (Seria II Istorie-Etnografie-Artă)* 17–21 (2000–2004): 33.

26 Moritz Löwy, *Skizzen zur Geschichte der Juden in Temesvár bis zum Jahre 1865* (Szegedin: Alexander Baba, 1890), 2; Victor Neumann, *Istoria evreilor din Banat* (Bucuresti: Atlas, 1999), 9–10. In addition, immigration from other important Sephardic centers on Ottoman territory, such as Sarajevo and Belgrade, also seems conceivable.

27 Bleyer, "Temesvar als Höhepunkt der Baukunst," 13.

28 Dávid, "The 'Eyalet' of Temesvár," 114 and 126.
29 The terms of the capitulation are listed in Szentkláray, *Mercy kormányzata*, 127–29.
30 Ignaz Reiffenstuel S.J., *Temeswar. Die dem 13.ten Weinmonaths Anno 1716. durch Accord übergegangene Haubt=Festung. In den grossen und starken Baum Nabuchodonosors…* (Wien: Kürner, 1716), 6.
31 See the depiction of the siege on a textile manufactured in Germany, now in the Victoria and Albert Museum, London: https://collections.vam.ac.uk/item/O358580/napkin-unknown/. On the glorification of Charles VI, see Franz Matsche, *Die Kunst im Dienst der Staatsidee Kaiser Karls VI. Ikonographie, Ikonologie und Programmatik des "Kaiserstils"* (Berlin-New York: De Gruyter, 1981), vol. 1, 137–38; Werner Telesko and Friedrich Buchmayr, "Der 'Marmorsaal' im Augustiner-Chorherrenstift St. Florian: Die Verherrlichung des Türkensiegers Kaiser Karl VI. im Lichte schriftlicher und bildlicher Quellen," *Jahrbuch des Oberösterreichischen Musealvereines, Gesellschaft für Landeskunde* 158 (2013): 211–58; Agustí Alcoberro, "From Barcelona to Timişoara and Belgrade – With Stops in Vienna. Exiles from the War of the Spanish Succession (1702–1714) to the Ottoman–Venetian War (1714–1718)," *Acta Historiae* 27, no. 2 (2019): 263–67.
32 Josef Wolf, "Die Genese der Regierungsform des Temeswarer Banats. Mercys 'Einrichtungsprojekt' und die Stellungnahme der zentralen Hofstellen," in *Herrschaftswechsel*, eds. Gräf and Hirsch, 107–108; Sabine Jesner, "Herrschaftswechsel im habsburgischen Banat 1718–1753. Personalmanagement und imperiale Logik," in *Die Personalfrage in neuen Provinzen. Das Banat im regionalen Vergleich*, eds. Sabine Jesner and Harald Heppner (Stuttgart: Franz Steiner, 2020), 27, n. 8.
33 The denomination "Banat of Temeswar" is documented for the first time on a military map prepared in 1685 during the Great Turkish War fought between the Holy League and the Ottoman Empire; see Sorin Forţiu, "Despre prima atestare a denumirii BANATVS TIMISVARIENSIS (1685)," *Analele Banatului, Serie Nouă, Arheologie-Istorie* 14, no. 2 (2006): 67–113.
34 János Kalmár, "Die Commissio Neoacquistica," in *Verwaltungsgeschichte der Habsburgermonarchie in der Frühen Neuzeit, Band 1. Hof und Dynastie, Kaiser und Reich, Zentralverwaltungen, Kriegswesen und landesfürstliches Finanzwesen*, eds. Michael Hochedlinger, Petr Mat'a, and Thomas Winkelbauer (Vienna: Böhlau, 2019), 509–15.
35 See Wolf, "Die Genese der Regierungsform."
36 Josef Kallbrunner, *Das kaiserliche Banat. I. Einrichtung und Entwicklung des Banats bis 1739* (Munich: Verlag des Südostdeutschen Kulturwerks, 1958), 17.
37 A medal created by Georg Wilhelm Vestner (1677–1740) on the occasion of the capture of Temeswar in 1716 was inscribed with *Securitas Transylvaniae Restituta*. See the specimen in the Hungarian National Museum Budapest, inv. no. VI. R.III.114, https://gyujtemenyek.mnm.hu:443/hu/record/-/record/MNMMUSEUM1837861.
38 Johann Andreas Graf von Hamilton, "Chronographia Bannatus Temessiensis sub auspiciis novi gubernatoris edita (1734)," in *Quellen zur Wirtschafts-, Sozial- und Verwaltungsgeschichte des Banats im 18. Jahrhundert*, ed. Josef Wolf (Tübingen: Institut für Donauschwäbische Geschichte und Landeskunde, 1995), 126 [passage translated by the author].
39 Antonius Höller, *Augusta Carolinae Virtutis Monumenta seu Aedificia a Carolo VI. Imp. Max. P. P. per Orbem Austriacum Publico Bono Posita* (Vienae Austriae, typis Joannis Petri de Ghelen 1733), 30. http://mdz-nbn-resolving.de/urn:nbn:de:bvb:12-bsb10844301-8

40 Friedrich Polleroß, "Augusta Carolinae Virtutis Monumenta. Zur Architekturpolitik Kaiser Karls VI. und seiner Programmatik," in *300 Jahre Karl VI. 1711–1740. Spuren der Herrschaft des „letzten" Habsburgers,* eds. Stefan Seitschek et al. (Vienna: Österreichisches Staatsarchiv, 2011), 218–34.

41 Polleroß, "Augusta Carolinae Virtutis Monumenta," 221.

42 Matsche, *Die Kunst im Dienst der Staatsidee.*

43 Werner Telesko, "Zur „Kunstpolitik" Karls VI.," in *Die Wiener Hofburg 1705–1835. Die kaiserliche Residenz vom Barock bis zum Klassizismus,* eds. Hellmut Lorenz and Anna Mader-Kratky (Vienna: Verlag der Österreichischen Akademie der Wissenschaften, 2016), 116–24.

44 Robert Born, "Die Domkirche in Timişoara (Temeswar) im Kontext der habsburgischen Architektur des 18. Jahrhunderts," *Ars Transsilvaniae* 14–15 (2004–2005): 45–46; Ortrun Veichtlbauer, *Zwischen Kolonie und Provinz. Herrschaft und Planung in der Kameralprovinz Temeswarer Banat im 18. Jahrhundert* (Klagenfurt: Alpen-Adria-Universität, Institute of Social Ecology, 2016), 67.

45 Manuel Weinberger, "Konsolidierung des Hofbauamts unter Karl VI," in *Die Wiener Hofburg 1705–1835,* 248–251; Meinrad von Engelberg, "Partielle Autonomie und 'Stellvertretende Repräsentation' oder: Gibt es ein 'habsburgisches' Stadtbild?" in *Les villes des Habsbourg du XVe au XIXe siècle. Communication, art et pouvoir dans les réseaux urbains,* ed. Ludolf Pelizaeus (Reims: Éditions et Presses universitaires de Reims, 2021), 151.

46 István Czigány, "Hadmérnökök és haditérképészet a Magyar Királyságban a 17. század végén és a 18. század első felében," in *A magyar térképészet nagyjai/ Die Großen der ungarischen Kartographie,* eds. Katalin Plihál, Csaba T. Reis, and Enikő Török (Budapest: OSZK–Osiris Kiadó, 2001), 216–17.

47 Gheorghe Anghel, "Alba Iulia în secolul al XVIII-lea. Schimbarea vetrei oraşului medieval," *Historia Urbana* 4, no. 1–2 (1996): 68; Czigány, "Hadmérnökök és haditérképészet," 221–222; Răzvan C. Pop, *PAX URBANA. Impactul administraţiei habsburgice asupra mediului urban din sudul Transilvaniei. Secolele al XVII-lea – al XVIII-lea* (Sibiu/Hermannstadt: Editura ASTRA Museum, 2021), 164–69.

48 Lajos Baróti, "A bánsági legrégibb német települések története," *Történelmi és Régészeti Értesítő* NS 8 (1892): 16.

49 Harald Heppner and Olga Katsiardi-Hering, "Drei Epochen in einer Stadt. Zum Zeitschichtengefüge im südöstlichen Europa des 18. Jahrhunderts," *Das achtzehnte Jahrhundert und Österreich. Jahrbuch der Österreichischen Gesellschaft zur Erforschung des achtzehnten Jahrhunderts* 18–19 (2004), 369.

50 Fabrizio Rudi, "Austrian 'Kingdom of Serbia' (1718–1739). The Infrastructural Innovations Introduced by the Habsburg Domination," in *The 18th Century as Period of Innovation,* eds. Harald Heppner, Sabine Jesner, and Ivan Pârvev (Graz: Grazer Universitätsverlag, 2019), 147.

51 Kallbrunner, *Das kaiserliche Banat,* 26; Sandra Cristina Hirsch, *Timişoara carolină (1716–1740). Geneza oraşului premodern* (Cluj-Napoca: Editura Mega, 2021), 59.

52 Johann N. Preyer, *Monographie der k. Freistadt Temesvár: Mit drei Plänen* (Temesvár: Rösch, 1853), 55, urn:nbn:de:bvb:12-bsb10010930-2; Kakucs,"Temesvár városának régi pecsétjei," 466–67.

53 Preyer, *Monographie,* 55–57; Sonja Jordan, *Die kaiserliche Wirtschaftspolitik im Banat im 18. Jahrhundert* (Munich: Oldenbourg, 1967), 95.

54 Rudi, "Austrian 'Kingdom of Serbia' (1718–1739)," 145–46.

55 Márta Fata, "Karl Alexander von Württemberg. Kaiserlicher General und Statthalter von Serbien," in *Die Türkenkriege des 18. Jahrhunderts.*

Wahrnehmen – Wissen – Erinnern, eds. Wolfgang Zimmermann and Josef Wolf (Regensburg: Schnell & Steiner 2017), 66; Hirsch, *Timişoara carolină*, 67–73.

56 See Anghel, "Alba Iulia în secolul al XVIII-lea" and Pop, *PAX URBANA*, 168.

57 István Berkeszi, *Temesvár szabad királyi város kis monographiája* (Temesvár: Uhrmann, 1900), 43.

58 Anton von Hammer, *Geschichte der Pest, die von 1738 bis 1740 im Temeswarer Banate herrschte: ein aus glaubwürdigen Quellen geschöpfter Beitrag zur Geschichte dieses Landes* (Temeswar: Joseph Reichel, 1839), 111; Sandra Hirsch, "Stadtplanung am östlichen Rand der Habsburgermonarchie im 18. Jahrhundert. Die Umgestaltung Temeswars," in "Planstädte im Zeitalter der Aufklärung," ed. Ulrich Hofmeister, special issue, *Zeitschrift für Weltgeschichte* 20 (2019), 99; Benjamin Landais, *De la ville ottomane à la ville habsbourgeoise: Les diasporas à l'épreuve de la confessionnalisation de l'espace urbain à Timişoara au XVIIIe siècle* (in preparation for print).

59 Hirsch, *Timişoara carolină*, 174–75.

60 Kallbrunner, *Das kaiserliche Banat*, 75.

61 Szentkláray, *Mercy kormányzata*, 50; Alcoberro, "From Barcelona to Timişoara and Belgrade."

62 Koloman Juhász, "Jesuiten im Banat (1718–1773). Ein Beitrag zur Kulturgeschichte des Temesvarer Banats," *Mitteilungen des Österreichischen Staatsarchives* 11 (1958): 157–58.

63 István Iványi, "Adatok a temesvári szent Katalinról czimzett templom és zárda történetéhez 1717–1759," *Történelmi és Régészeti Értesítő* 5 (1879): 71–72.

64 Martin Roos, *Providentia Augustorum. Unter der Obhut des Kaisers: Dokumente zu den Anfängen des Temescher Banats 1716–1739* (Munich: Edition Musik Südost, 2018), 48–49.

65 Szentkláray, *Mercy kormányzata*, 51; Juhász, "Jesuiten im Banat," 163; Kakucs, "Temesvár városának," 467.

66 Höller, *Augusta Carolinae Virtutis*, 12; von Hammer, *Geschichte der Pest*, 95–96; Juhász, "Jesuiten im Banat," 163–64.

67 Juhász, "Jesuiten im Banat," 163–64.

68 Waltraut Sponner, *Kirchenpolitik im Banat von 1717–1778* (PhD diss., University of Vienna, 1941), 40.

69 Szentkláray, *Mercy kormányzata*, 53–54.

70 Kallbrunner, *Das kaiserliche Banat*, 75–78.

71 Joachim Bahlcke, *Ungarischer Episkopat und österreichische Monarchie. Von einer Partnerschaft zur Konfrontation (1686–1790)* (Stuttgart: Franz Steiner, 2005), 192–95.

72 Szentkláray, *Mercy kormányzata*, 83–88.

73 Höller, *Augusta Carolinae Virtutis*, 11 [passage translated by the author]. See also Matsche, *Die Kunst im Dienst der Staatsidee*, vol. 1, 398.

74 Juhász, "Jesuiten im Banat," 162.

75 Jesner, "Herrschaftswechsel," 74.

76 Szentkláray, *Mercy kormányzata*, 119–23; Hans Diplich, *Die Domkirche in Temeswar. Ein Beitrag zu ihrer Baugeschichte* (Munich: Südostdeutsches Kulturwerk, 1972), 86–87; Hirsch, *Timişoara carolină*, 121–23.

77 Baróti, "A bánsági legrégibb német települések," 14; Kallbrunner, *Das kaiserliche Banat*, 31; Jordan, *Die kaiserliche Wirtschaftspolitik*, 46; Lajos Kakucs, *Céhek, manufaktúrák és gyárak a Bánságban 1716 és 1918 között* (Kolozsvár: Kriterion, 2016), 27–28.

78 Hirsch, *Timişoara carolină*, 57, 87–91.

79 von Hammer, *Geschichte der Pest*, 88.

80 Hamilton "Chronographia Bannatus Temessiensis," 108–109; Opriş, *Timişoara Monografie urbanistică*, 70–73.

81 Johann Langer, "Serbien unter kaiserlicher Regierung 1717–1739," *Mitteilungen des k.(u.) k. Kriegsarchivs* NF 3 (1889): 217–18; Sponner, *Kirchenpolitik*, 12–13; Fata, "Karl Alexander von Württemberg," 62.

82 Alexandru Zănescu, "Pagini din istoria alimentării cu apă a oraşului Timişoara," *Tibiscus* 3 (1974): 187.

83 Josef Wolf, "Land unter Wasser. Fließgewässer und Überschwemmungsflächen im spättheresianischen Temeswarer Banat," in *Melioration und Migration. Wasser und Gesellschaft in Ostmitteleuropa vom 17. bis Mitte des 19. Jahrhundert*, ed. Márta Fata (Stuttgart: Franz Steiner, 2021), 154–56.

84 Michal Wanner and Karel Staněk, *Císařsky orel a vábení Orientu. zámořská obchodní expanze habsburské monarchie (1715–1789)* = *The Imperial Eagle and Attraction to the Orient: The Habsburg Monarchy Trade Expansion to Overseas (1715–1789)* (Dolní Břežany: Scriptorium, 2021), 46–53.

85 Andreas Helmedach, *Das Verkehrssystem als Modernisierungsfaktor. Straßen, Post, Fuhrwesen und Reisen nach Triest und Fiume vom Beginn des 18. Jahrhunderts bis zum Eisenbahnzeitalter* (Munich: R. Oldenbourg, 2002), 69–70; Guido Hausmann, "Die Unterwerfung der Natur als imperiale Veranstaltung, Bau und Eröffnung des Ladoga-Kanals in Russland im frühen 18. Jahrhundert," *Frühneuzeit Info* 19, no. 2 (2008): 59–60.

86 Höller, *Augusta Carolinae Virtutis*, 37; Matsche, *Die Kunst im Dienst der Staatsidee*, vol. 1, 414.

87 Johann Georg Maximilian von Fürstenhoff (1686–1753), *Plan von Temeswar Wie Solches von Ihro Röm: Kayserl: Mayst: Carl d: VIten nach der Eroberung Fortificiret worden*, Sächsische Landesbibliothek – Staats- und Universitätsbibliothek Dresden (SLUB), Mscr.Dresd.R.30.m,II, https://www.deutsche-digitale-bibliothek.de/item/JSZ4RVIWFNNFGY3AYD2KL5W2K4JSRTX7; Stockholm, Riksarkivet Krigsarkivet SE/KrA/0406/26/025/001, https://sok.riksarkivet.se/bildvisning/K0008042_00001; *Plan von der Vestung Temeswar*, um 1730, Budapest, Országos Széchenyi Könyvtár, kéziratostérképek TK742, https://maps.hungaricana.hu/hu/OSZKTerkeptar/738/view/?bbox=-1104%2C-5051%2C7836%2C-68.

88 Nicolas Doxat and Emanuel Ryhiner, "Plan des nouvelles fortifications de la ville de Themeswart," projeté de Mr. le general Doxat; fait par Em. Ryhiner le 2.me aoust 1747. Bern Universitätsbibliothek, MUE Ryh 6409: 3 https://biblio.unibe.ch/web-apps/maps/zoomify.php?col=ryh&pic=Ryh_6409_3.

89 Cf. Zlatko Uzelac, "Vrhunac razvitka osječih baroknih fortifikacija, treća projektna faza 1728.–1731. – doprinos Nicolasa Doxata de Demoreta," *Osječki zbornik* 35 (2019): 27–46.

90 On the stays in Temeswar, see Theodor Stefanović-Vilovksy, *Belgrad unter der Regierung Kaiser Karls VI. (1717–1739): Mit Benützung archivalischer und anderer Quellen* (Vienna: Adolf Holzhausen, 1908), 69.

91 Horel, "Temesvár (Timişoara) multiculturelle," 34; Rochow, "Die räumliche Erscheinungsform des Neoabsolutismus," 159.

92 András Oross, "Kaszárnyaépítések a töröktől visszafoglalt várakban a 17–18. század fordulóján," in *Végvár és mentalitás a kora újkori Európában*, eds. Mátyás Berecz, Györgyi Bujdosné Pap, and Tivadar Petercsák (Eger: Dobó I. Vármúzeum 2015), 129–46.

122　*Robert Born*

93　Michael Hochedlinger, *Austria's Wars of Emergence: War, State and Society in the Habsburg Monarchy 1683–1797* (London-New York: Longman, 2003), 315; Oross, "Kaszárnyaépítések," 131.

94　Hirsch, *Timişoara carolină*, 121.

95　Rill, "Der Festungs- und Kasernenbau," 61–62; Oross, "Kaszárnyaépítések," 131–33.

96　Fata, "Karl Alexander von Württemberg," 62.

97　The complex was demolished during the communist period (1961–1965).

98　*Wiener Diarium* of October 27, 1728, 8; see also the façade elevation of the barracks in Opriş, *Timişoara Monografie urbanistică*, Ill. 21 and 22.

99　On the Fons Carolina in Karlsburg, see Matsche, *Die Kunst im Dienst der Staatsidee*, vol. 1, 326, 417; on the situation of the 1734 city plan, see Hirsch, *Timişoara carolină*, 124.

100　Höller, *Augusta Carolinae Virtutis*, 69.

101　Zănescu, "Pagini din istoria," 187; Wolf, "Land unter Wasser," 159.

102　Szentkláray, *Mercy kormányzata*, 125; Juhász, "Jesuiten im Banat," 165.

103　Antal Pfeiffer, *A Kegyes-Tanítórendiek Temesvári társházának és a főgymnásiumnak története* (Temesvár: Csanád-Egyházmegyei Könyvsajtó, 1896), 42. On the Jesuit involvement in the design of fortifications and the order's contribution to the dissemination of models for fortifications and urban designs outside Europe, see Denis De Lucca, *Jesuits and Fortifications: The Contribution of the Jesuits to Military Architecture in the Baroque Age* (Leiden: Brill, 2012).

104　Hamilton, "Chronographia Bannatus Temessiensis," 125.

105　Höller, *Augusta Carolinae Virtutis*, 68–69, 71.

106　Szentkláray, *Mercy kormányzata*, 125; Wolf, "Land unter Wasser," 154, 159.

107　On the impact of these strategies in the Habsburg territories, see Roland Axtmann, "'Police' and the Formation of Modern State. Legal and Ideological Assumptions on State Capacity in the Austrian Lands of the Habsburg Empire, 1500–1800," *German History* 10, no. 1 (January 1992): 39–61.

108　Matsche, *Die Kunst im Dienst der Staatsidee*, 388.

109　Friedrich Polleroß, "Pro deo & pro populo. Die barocke Stadt als 'Gedächtniskunstwerk' am Beispiel Wien und Salzburg," *Barock Berichte* 18–19 (1998): 149; von Engelberg, "Partielle Autonomie," 149–50.

110　Matsche, *Die Kunst im Dienst der Staatsidee*, vol. 1. 61; 308.

111　Matsche, *Die Kunst im Dienst der Staatsidee*, vol. 1, 70–80; Polleroß, "Pro deo & pro populo," 149.

112　Polleroß, "Pro deo & pro populo," 156.

113　Herbert Karner, "Der Kaiser und seine Stadt. Identität und stadträumliche Semantik im barocken Wien," in *Städtisches Bürgertum und Hofgesellschaft. Kulturen integrativer und konkurrierender Beziehungen in Residenz- und Hauptstädten vom 14. bis ins 19. Jahrhundert*, eds. Jan Hirschbiegel, Werner Paravicini, and Jörg Wettlaufer (Ostfildern: Jan Thorbecke, 2012); Wolfgang Kemp, "Die Mauern und Tore von Nancy und Potsdam. Über Stadtgrenzen, vor allem im 17. und 18. Jahrhundert," in *Die Grenze. Begriff und Inszenierung*, eds. Markus Bauer and Thomas Rahn (Berlin, Boston, MA: Akademie Verlag, 1997), 241.

114　In 2013, the statue was re-installed in front of the Millennium Church, which was erected at the end of the nineteenth century.

115　von Hammer, *Geschichte der Pest*, 96; Juhász, "Jesuiten im Banat," 201.

116 Tímea Nemesné Kis, *"Kiben Isten abban az üdőben magát kiváltképpen jelenteni akarta."* Nepomuki Szent János tiszteletének meghonosítása Magyarországon (PhD diss., Budapest, Eötvös Loránd Tudományegyetem Bölcsészettudományi Kar, 2020), 25–26 (Flood), 161 (War).

117 *Wienerisches Diarium* No. 1860 (May, 28–30, 1721), 5.

118 Gerhardt Kapner, *Barocker Heiligenkult in Wien und seine Träger* (Munich: Oldenbourg, 1978), 53; Elisabeth Garms-Cornides, "Pietas Austriaca – Heiligenverehrung und Fronleichnamsprozession," in *300 Jahre Karl VI. 1711–1740. Spuren der Herrschaft des "letzten" Habsburgers*, eds. Stefan Seitschek et al. (Vienna: Österreichisches Staatsarchiv, 2011), 189–90.

119 Elisabeth Kovács, "Die Verehrung des hl. Johannes von Nepomuk am habsburgischen Hof und in der Reichs- und Residenzstadt Wien im 18. Jahrhundert," in *250 Jahre hl. Johannes von Nepomuk*. Catalogue of the Exhibition in the Dommuseum zu Salzburg 1979, ed. Johannes Neuhardt (Salzburg: Dommuseum 1979), 74–77.

120 Szentkláray, *Mercy kormányzata*, 71.

121 von Hammer, *Geschichte der Pest*, 64; Gábor Tüskés and Éva Knapp, "Nepomuki Szent János tisztelete a szabadtéri emlékek tükrében. (Kvantitatív elemzési kísérlet)," Ethnographia 99 (1988), 347; Roos, *Providentia Augustorum*, 157–62.

122 Preyer, *Monographie*, 62.

123 Garms-Cornides, "Pietas Austriaca," 190.

124 von Hammer, *Geschichte der Pest*, 96. Sadly, the church was demolished in 1911.

125 Cf. the drawing of the monastery of the Bosnian Franciscans from 1836 in Zsuzsanna Korhecz Papp and Borbála Fábián, "A Kapisztrán Szent Jánosról nevezett Ferences Rendtartomány barokk művészeti öröksége/ The Baroque Art Heritage of Franciscan Province Dedicated to St. John Capistrano." *Történelem és Muzeológia – Internetes Folyóirat Miskolcon/ History & Museology: Online Journal in Miskolc, Hungary* 3, no. 2 (2016): 79, Ill. 2, http://tortenetitar.hermuz.hu/wp-content/uploads/2020/04/8-Korhecz-Papp-2017.pdf.

126 Cf. the illustration of the *Aedificia civilia* in Höller, *Augusta Carolinae Virtutis* (Nr. VII), Matsche, *Die Kunst im Dienst der Staatsidee*, vol. 1, 420–21.

127 Kakucs, "Temesvár városának régi pecsétjei," 459–60.

128 Preyer, *Monographie*, 56; Roos, *Providentia Augustorum*, 11–12.

129 von Hammer, *Geschichte der Pest*, 87 and 112.

130 von Hammer, *Geschichte der Pest*, 97.

131 See Roos, *Providentia Augustorum*, 8–9.

132 On the Roman coins, see Maria Radnótiné-Alföldi, "Providentia Augusti. To the Question of the Limes Fortifications in the 4th Century," *Acta Antiqua Academiae Scientiarum Hungaricae* 3 (1955): 245–59.

133 Mihai Opriş, *Timişoara. Mică monografie urbanistică* (Bucureşti: Editura Tehnică, 1987), 38–39; Wolf, "Die Genese der Regierungsform," 130; Jesner, "Herrschaftswechsel," 74–75.

134 von Hammer, *Geschichte der Pest*, 90.

135 von Hammer, *Geschichte der Pest*, 88–89: on the motto of Charles VI, see Matsche, *Die Kunst im Dienst der Staatsidee*, vol. 1, 235–36; on the likening of Charles VI to Jupiter against the background of the contemporary victories over the Ottomans, see Werner Telesko and Friedrich Buchmayr, "Der 'Marmorsaal' im Augustiner-Chorherrenstift St. Florian," 213–16.

136 Juhász, "Jesuiten im Banat," 196, 213, 217.
137 Mihai Opriş, *Timişoara. Mică monografie urbanistică*, 36–37, Ill. 33–34.
138 Höller, *Augusta Carolinae Virtutis*, 92; cf. Matsche, *Die Kunst im Dienst der Staatsidee*, vol. 1, 423–24.
139 See Born, "Die Domkirche in Timişoara (Temeswar)," 47–49.
140 Miklós Mojzer, *Werke deutscher Künstler in Ungarn, Teil 1: Architektur* (Baden-Baden: Heitz, 1962), 29.
141 Robert Rill, "Der Festungs- und Kasernenbau in der Habsburgermonarchie," *Das achtzehnte Jahrhundert und Österreich. Jahrbuch der Österreichischen Gesellschaft zur Erforschung des achtzehnten Jahrhunderts* 11 (1996): 56.
142 Gyula Diamant, "A zsidók története Horvátországban az egyenjogusításig," *Az Izraelita Magyar Irodalmi Társulat* Évkönyve 34 (1912): 301; Neumann, *Istoria evreilor*, 16.
143 Philip J. Adler, "Serbs, Magyars, and Staatsinteresse in Eighteenth Century Austria: A Study in the History of Habsburg Administration," *Austrian History Yearbook* 12–13, no. 1 (1976–1977): 128–29; Gottfried Mraz, "Das Banat von Temesvár in der theresianischen Zeit," in *Maria Theresia als Königin von Ungarn*, eds. Gerda Mraz and Gerald Schlag, catalogue of the exhibition in Schloss Halbturn 1980 (Eisenstadt: Amt der Burgenländischen Landesregierung 1980), 140–141.
144 Zsolt Trocsányi, "Reformok előtt: a Ministerialkonferenz in rebus Transylvanicia és a Hofcommission, illetve Hofdeputation in Transylvanicis, Banaticis et Illyricis," *Levéltári Közlemények* 57, no. 2 (1986): 192–93.
145 See von Hammer, *Geschichte der Pest*, 100–01.
146 (Gottfried Mraz), cat. no. 303, in *Maria Theresia als Königin von Ungarn*, 210.
147 Raluca Mureşan, "Theatre Buildings – Proof of Civilisation: Ofen/Buda (1786–7), Hermannstadt (1787–8), Kaschau (1786–90)," in *Entangled Histories, Multiple Geographies: Papers from the International Scientific Thematic Conference EAHN 2015 Belgrade*, eds. Vladan Djokić, Ana Nikezić, and Ana Raković (Belgrade: Belgrade University – Faculty of Architecture, 2017), 79.
148 Preyer, *Monographie*, 69–71 "[...] *Augusta Caroli Austriaci Caesaris Pietas Apostolicorum Praedecessorum zelo Csanadiensem Cathedram, duobus ferme Saeculis partim Mahometano partim propriis antiquitatis ruderibus sepultam, tutiori loco, Temesiensibus videlicet in Moeniis constanti fortitudine restauratis, restaurari voluit [...]*."
149 Born, "Die Domkirche in Timişoara (Temeswar)," 54–56.
150 On this practice of imperial marking in the cities, see also Polleroß, "Pro deo & pro populo," 156.
151 Diplich, *Die Domkirche in Temeswar*, 103–12.
152 Diplich, *Die Domkirche in Temeswar*, 316–17.
153 On other depictions in which the Mother of God appears wearing the Habsburg mitre crown on her head, see Franz Matsche, "Die Pietas Mariana Austriaca: der Marienkult als religiöse Säule des habsburgischen Herrschertums," in *Maria allerorten: die Muttergottes mit dem geneigten Haupt 1699 – 1999; das Gnadenbild der Ursulinen zu Landshut – altbayerische Marienfrömmigkeit im 18. Jahrhundert. Ausstellung der Museen der Stadt Landshut in der Spitalkirche Heiliggeist 1999–2000* (Landshut: Museen der Stadt Landshut, 1999), 38.
154 Diplich, *Die Domkirche in Temeswar*, 109.

155 Ferencz Tóth, "A temesvár-belvárosi Máriaszobor története. Egy temesvári történelmi műemlék," *Történelmi és Régészeti Értesítő* 29, no. 3–4 (1913): 51–72.
156 See Martin Scheutz, "Säulentausch im Stadtzentrum. Vom Pranger als Inszenierung bürgerlicher Gerichtsbarkeit zur Dreifaltigkeitssäule als Ausdruck barocker Frömmigkeit," in *Kommunale Selbstinszenierung. Städtische Konstellationen zwischen Mittelalter und Neuzeit*, eds. Martina Stercken and Christian Hesse (Zürich: Chronos, 2018), 330–41; Robert Born, "Marien- und Dreifaltigkeitssäulen," in *Religiöse Erinnerungsorte in Ostmitteleuropa. Konstitution und Konkurrenz im nationen- und epochenübergreifenden Zugriff*, eds. Joachim Bahlcke, Stefan Rohdewald, and Thomas Wünsch (Berlin: Akademie Verlag, 2013), 396–409.
157 For details on the altar donations to the Church of St. Catherine, administered by the Minorites, in the Great Palanka, see Iványi, "Adatok a temesvári," 72.
158 Regarding the *Pietas Eucharistica* of the Habsburgs, see Matsche, *Die Kunst im Dienst der Staatsidee*, vol. 1, 121.
159 See Juhász, "Jesuiten im Banat," 192–93.
160 See Adler, "Serbs, Magyars, and Staatsinteresse," 144.
161 Landais, *De la ville ottomane à la ville habsbourgeoise.*
162 Löwy, *Skizzen zur Geschichte der Juden*, 69, mentions a use of the gate as a synagogue from 1739. Neumann, *Istoria evreilor*, 37, assumes a use as a prayer space between 1729 and 1754 and from 1755 to 1762.
163 (Gottfried Mraz), cat. no. 304, in *Maria Theresia als Königin von Ungarn*, 210.
164 Landais, *De la ville ottomane à la ville habsbourgeoise.*
165 (Gottfried Mraz), cat. no. 304, in Gerda Mraz and Gerald Schlag, eds., *Maria Theresia als Königin von Ungarn*, 210.
166 Löwy, *Skizzen zur Geschichte der Juden*, 69.
167 Georg Bleyer, "Baukunst und Städtebau der banater-schwäbischen Ansiedlung im 18. Jahrhundert." *Neuer Weg* 30 September, 1955: 4; 7 October, 1955: 4.
168 See Christian Benedik, "Die Bedeutung der Banater Cameral-Domäne für die Reformierung des habsburgischen Bauwesens in der zweiten Hälfte des 18. Jahrhunderts," in *Kuppeln-Korn-Kanonen. Unerkannte und unbekannte Spuren in Südosteuropa von der Aufklärung bis in die Gegenwart*, eds. Ulrike Tischler-Hofer and Renate Zedinger (Innsbruck: StudienVerlag, 2010), 187–213.
169 Bleyer, "Baukunst und Städtebau."

Bibliography

Adler, Philip J. "Serbs, Magyars, and Staatsinteresse in Eighteenth Century Austria: A Study in the History of Habsburg Administration." *Austrian History Yearbook* 12–13, no. 1 (1976–1977): 116–47.
Alcoberro, Agustí. "From Barcelona to Timişoara and Belgrade – With Stops in Vienna: Exiles from the War of the Spanish Succession (1702–1714) to the Ottoman-Venetian War (1714–1718)." *Acta Historiae* 27, no. 2 (2019): 255–78.
Ambrozy, (Baron) György. *Temesvár im Jahre 1849: Während der Belagerung geschrieben*. Vienna: J. F. Greß, 1850.

Anghel, Gheorghe. "Alba Iulia în secolul al XVIII-lea. Schimbarea vetrei oraşului medieval." *Historia Urbana* 4, no. 1–2 (1996): 63–84.

Axtmann, Roland. "'Police' and the Formation of Modern State: Legal and Ideological Assumptions on State Capacity in the Austrian Lands of the Habsburg Empire, 1500–1800." *German History* 10, no. 1 (1992): 39–61.

Bahlcke, Joachim. *Ungarischer Episkopat und österreichische Monarchie: Von einer Partnerschaft zur Konfrontation (1686–1790)*. Stuttgart: Steiner, 2005.

Baróti, Lajos. "A bánsági legrégibb német települések története." *Történelmi és Régészeti Értesítő* NS 8 (1892): 11–27; 53–68.

Batt, Judy. "Reinventing Banat." In *Region, State and Identity in Central and Eastern Europe*, edited by Judy Batt and Kataryna Wolczuk, 178–202. London: Cass, 2002.

Benedik, Christian. "Die Bedeutung der Banater Cameral-Domäne für die Reformierung des habsburgischen Bauwesens in der zweiten Hälfte des 18. Jahrhunderts." In *Kuppeln–Korn–Kanonen: Unerkannte und unbekannte Spuren in Südosteuropa von der Aufklärung bis in die Gegenwart*, edited by Ulrike Tischler-Hofer and Renate Zedinger, 187–213. Innsbruck: StudienVerlag, 2010.

Berkeszi, István. *Temesvár szabad királyi város kis monographiája*. Temesvár: Uhrmann, 1900.

Bleyer, Georg. "Baukunst und Städtebau der banater-schwäbischen Ansiedlung im 18. Jahrhundert." *Neuer Weg*, September 30, 1955; October 7, 1955.

Bleyer, Georg. "Temesvar als Höhepunkt der Baukunst und des Städtebaus der schwäbischen Ansiedlung im 18. Jahrhundert." *Kultureller Wegweiser* 8, no. 1 (1956): 12–17.

Bodó, Barna, and Alpár Zoltán Szász. "A dekonstruált régió: Bánság." *Romániai magyar évkönyv* (2009–2010): 93–110.

Born, Robert. "Die Domkirche in Timişoara (Temeswar) im Kontext der habsburgischen Architektur des 18. Jahrhunderts." *Ars Transsilvaniae* 14–15 (2004–2005): 43–72.

Born, Robert. "Marien- und Dreifaltigkeitssäulen." In *Religiöse Erinnerungsorte in Ostmitteleuropa: Konstitution und Konkurrenz im nationen- und epochenübergreifenden Zugriff*, edited by Joachim Bahlcke, Stefan Rohdewald, and Thomas Wünsch, 396–409. Berlin: Akademie Verlag, 2013.

Csortán, Ferenc. "Arhitectura religioasă în Vilaietul Timişoara." *Satu Mare – Studii şi Communicări (Seria II Istorie-Etnografie-Artă)* 17–21 (2000–2004): 11–38.

Czigány, István. "Hadmérnökök és haditérképészet a Magyar Királyságban a 17. század végén és a 18. század első felében." In *A magyar térképészet nagyjai/ Die Großen der ungarischen Kartographie*, edited by Katalin Plihál, Csaba T. Reis, and Enikő Török, 215–26. Budapest: OSZK–Osiris Kiadó, 2001.

Dávid, Géza. "The 'Eyalet' of Temesvár in the Eighteenth Century." *Oriente Moderno* 79, no. 1 (1999): 113–28.

De Lucca, Denis. *Jesuits and Fortifications: The Contribution of the Jesuits to Military Architecture in the Baroque Age*. Leiden: Brill, 2012.

Diamant, Gyula. "A zsidók története Horvátországban az egyenjogusításig." *Az Izraelita Magyar Irodalmi Társulat Évkönyve* 34 (1912): 293–341.

Diplich, Hans. *Die Domkirche in Temeswar: Ein Beitrag zu ihrer Baugeschichte.* Munich: Südostdeutsches Kulturwerk, 1972.

Engelberg, Meinrad von. "Partielle Autonomie und ‚Stellvertretende Repräsentation' oder: Gibt es ein ‚habsburgisches' Stadtbild?" In *Les villes des Habsbourg du XVe au XIXe siècle: Communication, art et pouvoir dans les réseaux urbains,* edited by Ludolf Pelizaeus, 135–54. Reims: Éditions et Presses universitaires de Reims, 2021.

Fata, Márta. "Karl Alexander von Württemberg: Kaiserlicher General und Statthalter von Serbien." In *Die Türkenkriege des 18. Jahrhunderts. Wahrnehmen – Wissen – Erinnern,* edited by Wolfgang Zimmermann and Josef Wolf, 43–71. Regensburg: Schnell & Steiner 2017.

Feneşan, Cristina. *Cultura otomană a vilayetului Timişoara (1552–1716).* Timişoara: Editura de Vest, 2004.

Fodor, Pál. "Das Wilajet von Temeschwar zur Zeit der osmanischen Eroberung." *Südost-Forschungen* 55 (1996): 25–44.

Forţiu, Sorin. "Despre prima atestare a denumirii BANATVS TIMISVARIENSIS (1685)." *Analele Banatului, Serie Nouă, Arheologie-Istorie* 14, no. 2 (2006): 67–113.

Garms-Cornides, Elisabeth. "Pietas Austriaca – Heiligenverehrung und Fronleichnamsprozession." In *300 Jahre Karl VI. 1711–1740: Spuren der Herrschaft des "letzten" Habsburgers,* edited by Stefan Seitschek et al. 185–97. Vienna: Österreichisches Staatsarchiv, 2011.

Gerő, Győző. *Turkish Monuments in Hungary.* Budapest: Corvina Press, 1976.

Gräf, Rudolf, and Sandra Hirsch, eds. *Herrschaftswechsel: Die Befreiung Temeswars im Jahre 1716.* Cluj-Napoca: Editura Academia Română, 2016.

Griselini, Francesco. *Versuch einer politischen und natürlichen Geschichte des temeswarer Banats in Briefen an Standespersonen und Gelehrte, Erster Theil.* Vienna: Johann Paul Krauß, 1780.

Hamilton, Johann Andreas Graf von. "Chronographia Bannatus Temessiensis sub auspiciis novi gubernatoris edita (1734)." In *Quellen zur Wirtschafts-, Sozial- und Verwaltungsgeschichte des Banats im 18. Jahrhundert,* edited by Josef Wolf, 47–127. Tübingen: Institut für Donauschwäbische Geschichte und Landeskunde, 1995.

Hausmann, Guido. "Die Unterwerfung der Natur als imperiale Veranstaltung, Bau und Eröffnung des Ladoga-Kanals in Russland im frühen 18. Jahrhundert." *Frühneuzeit Info* 19, no. 2 (2008): 59–71.

Hegyi, Klára. *A török hódoltság várai és várkatonasága. Vol. III. A temesvári, győri, pápai, egri, kanizsai, váradi és újvári vilájet várainak adattára.* Budapest: MTA Történettudományi Intézet, 2008.

Helmedach, Andreas. *Das Verkehrssystem als Modernisierungsfaktor: Straßen, Post, Fuhrwesen und Reisen nach Triest und Fiume vom Beginn des 18. Jahrhunderts bis zum Eisenbahnzeitalter.* Munich: Oldenbourg, 2002.

Heppner, Harald, and Sabine Jesner. "Aufklärung mittels 'Aufklärung': Die Rolle des habsburgischen Militärs im Donau-Karpatenraum im 18. Jahrhundert." In *Bildungspraktiken der Aufklärung / Education Practices of the Enlightenment,* edited by Silke Pasewalck and Matthias Weber, 197–212. Berlin: De Gruyter Oldenbourg, 2020.

Heppner, Harald, and Olga Katsiardi-Hering. "Drei Epochen in einer Stadt: Zum Zeitschichtengefüge im südöstlichen Europa des 18. Jahrhunderts." *Das achtzehnte Jahrhundert und Österreich: Jahrbuch der Österreichischen Gesellschaft zur Erforschung des achtzehnten Jahrhunderts* 18–19 (2004): 357–73.

Hirsch, Sandra. "Stadtplanung am östlichen Rand der Habsburgermonarchie im 18. Jahrhundert: Die Umgestaltung Temeswars." In *Planstädte im Zeitalter der Aufklärung*, edited by Ulrich Hofmeister. Special issue, *Zeitschrift für Weltgeschichte* 20 (2019): 83–104.

Hirsch, Sandra Cristina. *Timişoara carolină (1716–1740): Geneza oraşului premodern.* Cluj-Napoca: Editura Mega, 2021.

Hochedlinger, Michael. *Austria's Wars of Emergence: War, State and Society in the Habsburg Monarchy, 1683–1797.* London: Longman, 2003.

Höller, Antonius. *Augusta Carolinae Virtutis Monumenta seu Aedificia a Carolo VI. Imp. Max. P. P. per Orbem Austriacum Publico Bono Posita.* Vienna, Joannis Petri de Ghelen, 1733.

Horel, Catherine. "Temesvár (Timişoara) multiculturelle 1880–1914: 'Klein Wien' et capitale du Banat." *Études Balkaniques* (Paris) 18, no. 1 (2011): 29–50.

Iorga, Nicolae. "Temeswar." In *Schriften und Briefe*, edited by Michael Kroner, 302–5. Bucharest: Kriterion, 1978.

Iványi, István. "Adatok a temesvári szent Katalinról czimzett templom és zárda történetéhez 1717–1759." *Történelmi és Régészeti Értesítő* 5 (1879): 71–78.

János, Szabolcs. "Von der 'Strafkolonie' bis zum 'Eldorado': die Neuentdeckung des Banats im 18. Jahrhundert." In *Kulturelle Zirkulation im Habsburgerreich: Der Kommunikationsraum Wien*, edited by Wynfrid Kriegleder and Andrea Seidler, 73–97. Vienna: Praesens, 2019.

Jesner, Sabine. "Herrschaftswechsel im habsburgischen Banat 1718–1753: Personalmanagement und imperiale Logik." In *Die Personalfrage in neuen Provinzen: Das Banat im regionalen Vergleich*, edited by Sabine Jesner and Harald Heppner, 23–109. Stuttgart: Steiner, 2020.

Jordan, Sonja. *Die kaiserliche Wirtschaftspolitik im Banat im 18. Jahrhundert.* Munich: Oldenbourg, 1967.

Juhász, Koloman. "Jesuiten im Banat (1718–1773): Ein Beitrag zur Kulturgeschichte des Temesvarer Banats." *Mitteilungen des Österreichischen Staatsarchives* 11 (1958): 153–220.

Kakucs, Lajos. *Céhek, manufaktúrák és gyárak a Bánságban 1716 és 1918 között.* Kolozsvár: Kriterion, 2016.

Kakucs, Lajos. "Temesvár városának régi pecsétjei." *A Móra Ferenc Múzeum Évkönyve: Studia Historica* 13 (2010): 459–87.

Kallbrunner, Josef. *Das kaiserliche Banat: I. Einrichtung und Entwicklung des Banats bis 1739.* Munich: Verlag des Südostdeutschen Kulturwerks, 1958.

Kalmár, János. "Die Commissio Neoacquistica." In *Verwaltungsgeschichte der Habsburgermonarchie in der Frühen Neuzeit, Band 1. Hof und Dynastie, Kaiser und Reich, Zentralverwaltungen, Kriegswesen und landesfürstliches Finanzwesen,* edited by Michael Hochedlinger, Petr Mat'a, and Thomas Winkelbauer, 509–15. Vienna: Böhlau, 2019.

Kapner, Gerhardt. *Barocker Heiligenkult in Wien und seine Träger.* Munich: Oldenbourg, 1978.

Karner, Herbert. "Der Kaiser und seine Stadt. Identität und stadträumliche Semantik im barocken Wien." In *Städtisches Bürgertum und Hofgesellschaft. Kulturen integrativer und konkurrierender Beziehungen in Residenz- und Hauptstädten vom 14. bis ins 19. Jahrhundert,* edited by Jan Hirschbiegel, Werner Paravicini, and Jörg Wettlaufer, 141–60, 358–61. Ostfildern: Jan Thorbecke, 2012.

Kemp, Wolfgang. "Die Mauern und Tore von Nancy und Potsdam. Über Stadtgrenzen, vor allem im 17. und 18. Jahrhundert." In *Die Grenze. Begriff und Inszenierung,* edited by Markus Bauer, and Thomas Rahn, 237–54. Berlin: Akademie Verlag, 1997.

Kopeczny, Zsuzsanna. "Reşedinţa regală medievală de la Timişoara (The Medieval Royal Residence from Timişoara)." *Analele Banatului, Serie Arheologie-Istorie* 21 (2013): 211–31.

Korhecz Papp, Zsuzsanna, and Borbála Fábián. "A Kapisztrán Szent Jánosról nevezett Ferences Rendtartomány barokk művészeti öröksége / The Baroque Art Heritage of Franciscan Province Dedicated to St. John Capistrano. *Történelem és Muzeológia – Internetes Folyóirat Miskolcon / History & Museology: Online Journal in Miskolc, Hungary* 3, no. 2 (2016): 75–99. http://tortenetitar.hermuz.hu/wp-content/uploads/2020/04/8-Korhecz-Papp-2017.pdf

Kovács, Elisabeth. "Die Verehrung des hl. Johannes von Nepomuk am habsburgischen Hof und in der Reichs- und Residenzstadt Wien im 18. Jahrhundert." In *250 Jahre hl. Johannes von Nepomuk.* Catalogue of the Exhibition in the Dommuseum zu Salzburg 1979, edited by Johannes Neuhardt, 69–85. Salzburg: Dommuseum, 1979.

Landais, Benjamin. *De la ville ottomane à la ville habsbourgeoise: Les diasporas à l'épreuve de la confessionnalisation de l'espace urbain à Timişoara au XVIIIe siècle* (in preparation for print).

Langer, Johann. "Serbien unter kaiserlicher Regierung 1717–1739." *Mitteilungen des k.(u.) k. Kriegsarchivs* NF 3 (1889): 155–247.

Leber, Reinhard. *Politische Kultur und Systemtransformation in Rumänien. Lokalstudie zu der Stadt Temeswar.* Frankfurt am Main: Peter Lang, 1996.

Lorenz, Hellmut, and Anna Mader-Kratky, eds. *Die Wiener Hofburg 1705–1835. Die kaiserliche Residenz vom Barock bis zum Klassizismus.* Vienna: Verlag der Österreichischen Akademie der Wissenschaften, 2016.

Löwy, Moritz. *Skizzen zur Geschichte der Juden in Temesvár bis zum Jahre 1865.* Szegedin: Alexander Baba, 1890.

Marek, Michaela, and Eva Pluhařová-Grigienė, eds. "Prekäre Vergangenheit? Barockforschung im östlichen Mitteleuropa unter den Bedingungen des Sozialismus." Special issue, *RIHA Journal* 11 (2019).

Marjanucz, László. "Franz Griselini Bánság-képe." *Aetas* 28, no. 3 (2013): 24–43.

Matsche, Franz. *Die Kunst im Dienst der Staatsidee Kaiser Karls VI. Ikonographie, Ikonologie und Programmatik des "Kaiserstils."* 2 vols. Berlin: de Gruyter, 1981.

Matsche, Franz. "Die Pietas Mariana Austriaca: der Marienkult als religiöse Säule des habsburgischen Herrschertums." In *Maria allerorten: die Muttergottes mit dem geneigten Haupt 1699–1999; das Gnadenbild der Ursulinen zu Landshut – altbayerische Marienfrömmigkeit im 18. Jahrhundert*. Catalogue of the exhibition in the Spitalkirche Heiliggeist 1999–2000 in Landshut, 31–41. Landshut: Museen der Stadt Landshut, 1999.

Mojzer, Miklós. *Werke deutscher Künstler in Ungarn, Teil 1: Architektur.* Baden-Baden: Heitz, 1962.

Molnár, Antal. "Szerb ortodox egyházszervezet a hódolt Magyarországon." In *Szerb székesegyház a Tabánban*, edited by Tamás Csáki and Xénia Golub, 32–63. Budapest: Történeti Múzeum, 2019.

Mraz, Gerda, and Gerald Schlag, eds. *Maria Theresia als Königin von Ungarn.* Catalogue of the exhibition in Schloss Halbturn 1980. Eisenstadt: Amt der Burgenländischen Landesregierung 1980.

Mraz, Gottfried. "Das Banat von Temesvár in der theresianischen Zeit." In *Maria Theresia als Königin von Ungarn*, edited by Gerda Mraz and Gerald Schlag, 139–45. Eisenstadt: Amt der Burgenländischen Landesregierung 1980.

Mureşan, Raluca. "Theatre Buildings – Proof of Civilisation: Ofen/Buda (1786–7), Hermannstadt (1787–8), Kaschau (1786–90)." In *Entangled Histories, Multiple Geographies: Papers from the International Scientific Thematic Conference EAHN 2015 Belgrade*, edited by Vladan Djokić, Ana Nikezić, and Ana Raković, 78–85. Belgrade: Belgrade University – Faculty of Architecture, 2017.

Nemesné Kis, Tímea. *"Kiben Isten abban az üdőben magát kiváltképpen jelenteni akarta." Nepomuki Szent János tiszteletének meghonosítása Magyarországon.* PhD diss., Budapest, Eötvös Loránd Tudományegyetem Bölcsészettudományi Kar, 2020.

Neumann, Victor. *Identități multiple în Europa regiunilor. Interculturalitatea Banatului.* Timişoara: Hestia, 1997.

Neumann, Victor. *Istoria evreilor din Banat.* Bucharest: Atlas, 1999.

Neumann, Victor. "Timişoara în memoria colectivă contemporană." In *Revoluţia română din decembrie 1989. Istorie şi memorie*, edited by Bogdan Murgescu, 21–45. Iaşi-Bucharest: Polirom, 2007.

Niedermaier, Paul. "Raportul între factorul politic şi oraşe, cu încadrarea schimbărilor configuraţiei oraşului Timişoara în acest context." *Historia Urbana* 14, no. 2 (2006): 253–61.

Opriş, Mihai. *Timişoara. Mică monografie urbanistică.* Bucharest: Editura Tehnică, 1987.

Opriş, Mihai. *Timişoara: Monografie urbanistică, Vol. 1. Descoperiri recente care au impus corectarea istoriei urbanistice a Timişoarei.* Timişoara: Brumar, 2007.

Oross, András. "Kaszárnyaépítések a töröktől visszafoglalt várakban a 17–18. század fordulóján." In *Végvár és mentalitás a kora újkori Európában*, edited by Mátyás Berecz, Györgyi Bujdosné Pap, and Tivadar Petercsák, 129–46. Eger: Dobó I. Vármúzeum 2015.

Pálffy, Géza. "A bécsi katonai vezetés védelmi politikája a Temes–Maros vidékén a 16. század elejétől a 18. század közepéig." In *IV. Honvéd emléknap Makón 1997*, edited by Pál Halmágyi, 16–28. Makó: József Attila Múzeum, 1998.

Petrovics, István. "The Fading Glory of a Former Royal Seat: The Case of Medieval Temesvár." In *The Man of Many Devices, Who Wandered Full Many Ways. Festschrift in Honor of János M. Bak*, edited by Balázs Nagy and Marcell Sebők, 527–38. Budapest: Central European University Press, 1999.

Pfeiffer, Antal. *A Kegyes-Tanítórendiek Temesvári társházának és a főgymnásiumnak története*. Temesvár: Csanád-Egyházmegyei Könyvsajtó, 1896.

Polleroß, Friedrich. "Pro deo & pro populo. Die barocke Stadt als 'Gedächtniskunstwerk' am Beispiel Wien und Salzburg." *Barock Berichte* 18–19 (1998): 149–68.

Polleroß, Friedrich. "Augusta Carolinae Virtutis Monumenta. Zur Architekturpolitik Kaiser Karls VI. und seiner Programmatik." In *300 Jahre Karl VI. 1711–1740. Spuren der Herrschaft des "letzten" Habsburgers*, edited by Stefan Seitschek et al, 218–34. Vienna: Österreichisches Staatsarchiv, 2011.

Pop, Răzvan C. *PAX URBANA. Impactul administrației habsburgice asupra mediului urban din sudul Transilvaniei. Secolele al XVII-lea – al XVIII-lea*. Sibiu: Editura ASTRA Museum, 2021.

Preyer, Johann N. *Monographie der k. Freistadt Temesvár: Mit drei Plänen*. Temesvár: Rösch, 1853. urn:nbn:de:bvb:12-bsb10010930-2

Radnótiné-Alföldi, Maria. "Providentia Augusti. To the Question of the Limes Fortifications in the 4th Century." *Acta Antiqua Academiae Scientiarum Hungaricae* 3 (1955): 245–59.

Reiffenstuel, Ignaz S.J. *Temeswar. Die dem 13.ten Weinmonaths Anno 1716. durch Accord übergegangene Haubt=Festung. In den grossen und starken Baum Nabuchodonosors*. Vienna: Kürner, 1716.

Rill, Robert. "Der Festungs- und Kasernenbau in der Habsburgermonarchie." *Das achtzehnte Jahrhundert und Österreich. Jahrbuch der Österreichischen Gesellschaft zur Erforschung des achtzehnten Jahrhunderts* 11 (1996): 55–66.

Rochow, Frank. "Die räumliche Erscheinungsform des Neoabsolutismus – Militärarchitektur in Lemberg und Wien in den 1850er Jahren." *Zeitschrift für Ostmitteleuropa-Forschung* 68, no. 2 (2019): 157–188.

Roos, Martin. *Providentia Augustorum. Unter der Obhut des Kaisers: Dokumente zu den Anfängen des Temescher Banats 1716–1739*. Munich: Edition Musik Südost, 2018.

Rudi, Fabrizio. "Austrian 'Kingdom of Serbia' (1718–1739). The Infrastructural Innovations introduced by the Habsburg Domination." In *The 18th Century as Period of Innovation*, edited by Harald Heppner, Sabine Jesner, and Ivan Pārvev, 141–53. Graz: Grazer Universitätsverlag, 2019.

Scheutz, Martin. "Säulentausch im Stadtzentrum. Vom Pranger als Inszenierung bürgerlicher Gerichtsbarkeit zur Dreifaltigkeitssäule als Ausdruck barocker Frömmigkeit." In *Kommunale Selbstinszenierung. Städtische Konstellationen zwischen Mittelalter und Neuzeit*, edited by Martina Stercken and Christian Hesse, 315–53. Zurich: Chronos, 2018.

Serfőző, Szabolcs. "'A kétfejű sas szárnyainak oltalmában': A Habsburg uralkodók reprezentációja a kora újkori Sopronban." *Soproni szemle* 74, no. 3 (2020): 294–344.

Sponner, Waltraut. *Kirchenpolitik im Banat von 1717–1778*. PhD diss., University of Vienna, 1941.

Stefanović-Vilovksy, Theodor. *Belgrad unter der Regierung Kaiser Karls VI. (1717–1739): Mit Benützung archivalischer und anderer Quellen.* Vienna: Adolf Holzhausen, 1908.

Sudár, Balázs. *Dzsámik és mecsetek a hódolt Magyarországon.* Budapest: MTA Történettudományi Intézet, 2014.

Szentkláray, Jenő. *Mercy kormányzata a Temesi bánságban. Újabb részletek Délmagyarország XVIII. századi történetéhez.* Budapest: Athenaeum, 1909.

Szentmiklosi, Alexandru, and Dumitru Țeicu. "Stadtarchäologische Forschungen. Überlegungen zur Stadt Temeswar im 17.–18. Jahrhundert." In *Herrschaftswechsel: Die Befreiung Temeswars im Jahre 1716,* edited by Rudolf Gräf and Sandra Hirsch, 24–46. Cluj-Napoca: Editura Academia Română, 2016.

Telesko, Werner. "Zur 'Kunstpolitik' Karls VI." In *Die Wiener Hofburg 1705– 1835. Die kaiserliche Residenz vom Barock bis zum Klassizismus,* edited by Hellmut Lorenz and Anna Mader-Kratky, 116–29. Vienna: Verlag der Österreichischen Akademie der Wissenschaften, 2016.

Telesko, Werner, and Friedrich Buchmayr. "Der 'Marmorsaal' im Augustiner-Chorherrenstift St. Florian: Die Verherrlichung des Türkensiegers Kaiser Karl VI. im Lichte schriftlicher und bildlicher Quellen." *Jahrbuch des Oberösterreichischen Musealvereines, Gesellschaft für Landeskunde* 158 (2013): 211–58.

Timisoara's bid book. *Shine your Light - Light up Your City.* 2015. https://timisoara2023.eu/document/view/43/Bidbook_EN_Timisoara2021.pdf

Tóth, Ferencz. "A temesvár-belvárosi Máriaszobor története. Egy temesvári történelmi műemlék." *Történelmi és Régészeti Értesítő* 29, no. 3–4 (1913): 51–72.

Trocsányi, Zsolt. "Reformok előtt: a Ministerialkonferenz in rebus Transylvanicia és a Hofcommission, illetve Hofdeputation in Transylvanicis, Banaticis et Illyricis." *Levéltári Közlemények* 57, no. 2 (1986): 189–245.

Tüskés, Gábor, and Éva Knapp. "Nepomuki Szent János tisztelete a szabadtéri emlékek tükrében. (Kvantitatív elemzési kísérlet)." *Ethnographia* 99 (1988): 330–56.

Uzelac, Zlatko. "Vrhunac razvitka osječkih baroknih fortifikacija, treća projektna faza 1728.–1731. - doprinos Nicolasa Doxata de Demoreta." *Osječki zbornik* 35 (2019): 27–46.

Veichtlbauer, Ortrun. *Zwischen Kolonie und Provinz. Herrschaft und Planung in der Kameralprovinz Temeswarer Banat im 18. Jahrhundert.* Klagenfurt: Alpen-Adria-Universität – Institute of Social Ecology, 2016.

von Hammer, Anton. *Geschichte der Pest, die von 1738 bis 1740 im Temeswarer Banate herrschte: ein aus glaubwürdigen Quellen geschöpfter Beitrag zur Geschichte dieses Landes.* Temeswar: Joseph Reichel, 1839.

Wanner, Michal, and Karel Staněk. *Císařsky orel a vábeni Orientu. zámořská obchodní expanze habsburské monarchie (1715–1789) = The Imperial Eagle and Attraction to the Orient: The Habsburg Monarchy Trade Expansion to Overseas (1715–1789).* Dolní Břežany: Scriptorium, 2021.

Weinberger, Manuel. "Konsolidierung des Hofbauamts unter Karl VI." In *Die Wiener Hofburg 1705–1835. Die kaiserliche Residenz vom Barock bis zum Klassizismus,* edited by Hellmut Lorenz and Anna Mader-Kratky, 248–51. Vienna: Verlag der Österreichischen Akademie der Wissenschaften, 2016.

Wolf, Josef. "Die Genese der Regierungsform des Temeswarer Banats. Mercys 'Einrichtungsprojekt' und die Stellungnahme der zentralen Hofstellen." In *Herrschaftswechsel: Die Befreiung Temeswars im Jahre 1716*, edited by Rudolf Gräf and Sandra Hirsch, 103–52. Cluj-Napoca: Editura Academia Română, 2016.

Wolf, Josef. "Land unter Wasser. Fließgewässer und Überschwemmungsflächen im spättheresianischen Temeswarer Banat." In *Melioration und Migration. Wasser und Gesellschaft in Ostmitteleuropa vom 17. bis Mitte des 19. Jahrhundert*, edited by Márta Fata, 135–77. Stuttgart: Franz Steiner, 2021.

Zănescu, Alexandru. "Pagini din istoria alimentării cu apă a oraşului Timişoara." *Tibiscus* 3 (1974): 181–205.

5 Imperial Power, Imperial Identity, and Kazan Architecture

Visualizing the Empire in a Nineteenth-Century Russian Province

Gulchachak Nugmanova

The imperial idea of a great state was a central concept of Russian history beginning at least from Peter I.[1] It was this idea that turned Muscovy into the Russian Empire and that inspired the government of Catherine the Great to start an ambitious project, unprecedented in scale, of transforming the medieval structures of all Russian cities. The architectural model of an imperial city first materialized during the construction of the new capital of St. Petersburg. From the second half of the eighteenth century, it was implemented by the government throughout the vast expanse of the rest of Russia through the strict regulation of building activities, including the artistic styles of the edifices. This project was implemented throughout the long nineteenth century and was filled with new content and demonstrated various forms of visual expressions of the imperial idea on the periphery of the empire.

In this chapter, I explore the creation of an imperial image of the provincial city of Kazan. Kazan was the former capital of the Kazan Khanate, which had separated from the Golden Horde in 1438. The conquest of the Khanate of Kazan by Ivan IV the Terrible in 1552 was a key event in Russian history. It was this event that Muscovites associated with the transformation of Muscovy into a tsardom. Subsequently, the annexation of this ethnically non-Slavic region was interpreted as the beginning of Muscovy's imperial expansion and its transformation into a multinational empire.[2]

The Kazan campaign was seen by contemporaries as a crusade against Islam for the spread of Orthodox Christianity. According to the understanding of the time, the victory could only be won by transforming the former capital of Islam into a Christian city – i.e., by destroying mosques and building Orthodox churches in their place. The first Orthodox churches in the conquered city were erected in two or three days on sites indicated personally by Ivan the Terrible and were sanctified in his presence. The discovery of the icon of the Mother of God of Kazan near the kremlin in 1579 was perceived as an important piece of evidence of the divine blessing of the Kazan conquest. The monastery founded in the same year on this

DOI: 10.4324/9781003130031-7

site enjoyed therefore the special favor of the Russian monarchs, and the icon became the patroness of the Romanov dynasty.

Thus, Kazan evolved from the capital of the Tatar Khanate, which played an important role in trade relations between the West and the East, into the principal town of the Russian administration in the east of European Russia with a multiethnic and multicultural population. At the beginning of the nineteenth century, the population of Kazan numbered 17,000 people, mostly Russians. The second largest group of 5,000 people were Tartars, living compactly and separately from the Russians in the Tatar settlement, a special part of the city.[3] Sergei Solov'ev, Russia's leading historian of the nineteenth century, presented the conquest of Kazan as "an inevitable event of the general course of history in Eastern Europe," conditioned by the aspirations of the Russian state to the "rich countries" of the East. Due to the geographical, historical, and symbolic significance of Kazan, the city was ascribed a special civilizing mission, associated with planting "the fruits of European science and enlightenment in a remote and half-wild land," as Solov'ev put it.[4] The administration of the vast eastern territories required appropriate institutions. Kazan was defined as the center of a huge educational district stretching from the Volga to the Far East, as well as of a military and a judicial district. In the words of Robert Geraci, the city became a true "window to the East" for Russia.[5]

This chapter shows how the state's vision of an imperial city was realized in Kazan in the nineteenth century, which was a time of romanticism, historicism, and national revival. During this period, the idea of the glory and greatness of the country and, at the same time, of the specific place of individual regions in history was formed in the Russian public consciousness. I am interested in what role the region's past and the importance attached to the city in the official ideology of the Russian state played in representation of the empire in the emerging urban landscape of Kazan. New urban accents and local historical and architectural monuments are the focus of my attention, with the kremlin – which was viewed by St. Petersburg as a captured Tatar fortress – at the center.

The growth of national self-awareness engulfed not only the Russians but also the ethnic and religious minorities of the empire. The Muslim Tatars of Kazan with their own architectural traditions and their own sites of historical memory formed a significant part of the population of the city. I analyze how these traditions interacted with state norms and legislation and what tools and approaches were used by the authorities and by the local population.

The inseparable connection of the national idea with the religious one as the main component of the people's self-identification in the nineteenth century requires a special consideration of the construction regulations of religious buildings. The design of prayer houses was based on the romantic idea that the peculiarities of a national culture were determined by its origins. However, the example of Kazan shows that architectural models issued by the government were often at odds with local traditional practices. The preferential treatment of Russian Orthodoxy as the main state religion by the authorities worsened the situation of the non-Christian communities in the country. In Kazan, the emergence of a Jewish community, whose religious claims were perceived as especially painful by the local authorities, exacerbated the situation. In the light of national and confessional movements, I am thus also interested in the fate of Kazan's Tatar settlement, which appeared soon after the conquest of Kazan and which was integrated into a single urban space by the regular plan of 1768. A striking manifestation of these processes was the territorial re-establishment of the Old Tatar settlement around Sennaia Square, which became a symbol of the national revival of the Tatars at the beginning of the twentieth century. In general, the architectural processes in Kazan demonstrate the experience of the empire and the construction of an imperial identity in an annexed non-Russian and non-Orthodox region.

Imperial Images in Urban Space

Catherine II visited Kazan in 1767, and during this trip, which she undertook to "get acquainted with the eastern regions of the state," the Empress discovered the ethnocultural diversity of the empire and realized the need to unite the peoples inhabiting the country around common European values and culture.[6] In a letter to Voltaire, written from Kazan, she called this plan of hers "to sew a dress that would be suitable for everyone."[7] Its implementation acquired a distinct spatial expression through the creation of unified architectural and urban forms for Russia's towns and cities, based on European norms of regularity. All cities were now supposed to be built according to a regular plan, which had to be approved by the Empress and thus acquired the force of law.[8] The city was conceived as a unique architectural ensemble, the appearance of which would correspond to general European artistic norms. The canons of "Europeanness" were determined by the emperor, who personally approved the facades of the buildings.

Kazan became one of the first cities to receive an approved city plan. Catherine signed it in March 1768, less than a year after her trip to Kazan. It radically changed the medieval layout of the city and successively consolidated the historical structure of the city center (Figures 5.1a and 5.1b). The boundaries of the city were significantly expanded by incorporating the suburban settlements into the city limits. The traditional three-part radial-ring structure of Kazan had included the historical core – the kremlin – which was surrounded by a *posad* (suburb), whose wooden walls had already disappeared in the 1730s, and numerous *slobodas* (suburban settlements) further outside.[9] The stone kremlin had been built at the confluence of the Kazanka and Bulak rivers in place of the Tatar fortress during the sixteenth and seventeenth centuries (see Figures 5.1a and 5.1b,C). The market square with the *Gostinyi Dvor* (merchant center, G) and Ioanno-Predtechenskii (John the Baptist) Monastery (H) adjoined the kremlin's Spasskaia (Savior) Tower on the south. Voskresenskaia Street stretched along the crest of the hill from here. The transverse axis embraced the kremlin in an arc and connected the *Gostinyi Dvor* with the Bogoroditskii (Mother of God) Monastery (D) founded shortly after the conquest of Kazan. By the early nineteenth century, the street structure was fully adapted to the principles of regularity. The straightened streets were lined with two-story buildings with flat facades in the early neoclassical style. Thus began the formation of Kazan as an imperial city with a spectacular architectural appearance.

Since the reign of Peter I, architecture in Russia has served as a means of expressing the state's main political and ideological concepts, which allowed Evgenia Kirichenko to count it among the most state-controlled of all types of arts.[10] The central political role of architecture was derived from its perception as the fastest (especially in comparison with the transformation of social institutions) and the most convincing means of demonstrating new values. The regularity that formed the basis for the organization of Russian settlements since the rule of Catherine II was an architectural metaphor for the decisive role of the imperial state in organizing society. The power center and the rest of the empire were embodied in the plans of cities in the form of an urban center and uniform residential quarters. Regular urban development made the sovereign's oversight of the empire visible, which even followed the facades of private houses. Model projects unified the urban environment, turning it into an illustration of equality of all in the eyes of the monarch. The image of the city was associated with its center, as the domain of spiritual and social life, and national and religious landmarks were concentrated here as well.

In architecture, neoclassicism is considered the universal language for expressing imperial ideas. In Russia, this style entered its heyday from the second half of the 1770s, programmatically announced in the project of the Troitskii (Trinity) Church of the Alexander Nevskii Monastery in St. Petersburg by Ivan Starov. In Kazan, new ensembles and buildings were created in key spaces and significant parts of the city. Here, the first building designed in the new style was the Bogoroditskii Monastery just outside the kremlin. This monastery had an enormous ideological significance for the dynasty and the empire, as it had been built at the place where the icon of the Mother of God of Kazan had allegedly been found in 1579, who then became the patroness of the Romanov dynasty. Visiting the monastery may have been one of the goals of Catherine's Kazan visit of 1767, as

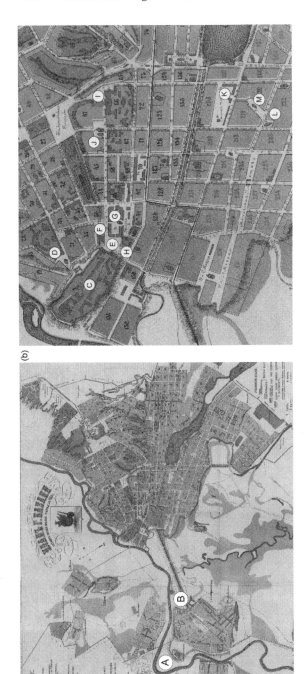

Figure 5.1a Map of Kazan, 1884.

A: Kazan Uspenskii (Assumption) Monastery; B: Memorial Church on the Kazanka River.

Figure 5.1b Map of Kazan, 1884. Detail.

C: Kremlin; D: Bogoroditskii (Mother of God) Monastery; E: Ivanovskaia Square; F: City Duma; G: Gostinyi Dvor (merchant center); H: Ioanno-Predtechenskii (John the Baptist) Monastery; I: Imperial Kazan University; J: Voskresenskaia (Resurrection) Square and Church; K: Sennaia Square and Mosque; L: Usmanovskaia Mosque; M: Orthodox Church of Tikhvin;

Voskresenskaia Street: From Ivanovskii Square (E) to the University (I); Kazanskaia Street: From Gostinyi Dvor (G) to Bogoroditskii Monastery (D).

Source: M. K. Krylov, Plan g. Kazani sostavlen soglasno proekta, utverzhdennogo v 1884 g. [Map of the city of Kazan, according to the project approved in 1884]. Kazan: V. M. Kliuchnikov, 1884.

she was the first Russian monarch to use the ceremonial opportunities of trips to demonstrate her power.[11] In 1790, the year of the consecration of the Troitskii Church in St. Petersburg, Catherine II commissioned Starov to develop a church project for the Kazan Bogoroditskii Monastery, which she remembered from her visit to Kazan.[12] Starov's project was approved by Catherine in 1791, but it owed its implementation to the arrival of Emperor Paul I in the city, in whose presence the first stone of the church was laid in 1798.[13] Paul visited Kazan in connection with the planned construction of the Kazan Cathedral in St. Petersburg, which was conceived by the emperor as a place to store a copy of the icon of the Kazan Mother of God. The copy had been made immediately after the discovery, and in the eighteenth century it was moved from Moscow to the new capital by Peter I. Paul's trip to the place of the icon's discovery, on the eve of the construction of the St. Petersburg Kazan Cathedral, which was designed to become a symbol of Russian statehood, confirmed the special veneration of the icon as the heavenly patroness of the House of Romanov.[14]

During his journey to Kazan, the emperor was accompanied by his eldest sons – Konstantin and Alexander, the heir to the throne. The latter, upon his ascension to the throne as Alexander I, provided annual funding until the church of the Kazan Bogoroditskii Monastery was completed in 1808.[15] It was still under construction when the entire monastic complex was redesigned. Its territory almost doubled by incorporating the adjacent undeveloped areas. The ensemble conceived around the church was a symmetrical composition with an oval square framed by a colonnade and monastic buildings located along its perimeter.[16] The layout obviously mirrored St. Peter's Square in Rome, the most famous monument of the Christian world. However, it was actually based on the Kazan Cathedral in St. Petersburg by Andrei Voronikhin with its famous semicircular colonnade facing Nevskii Prospect (built 1801–1811). The fact that the two churches in Kazan and St. Petersburg were dedicated to the same icon determined the semantic connection between them, which the creator of the monastic ensemble in Kazan visualized through architecture. The first contained the original of the icon of the Mother of God of Kazan, and the other its copy.

Even though Alexander I approved the Bogoroditskii Monastery project in 1810 and allocated funds for its implementation, buildings were erected only along the northern arc of the oval square in the first half of the nineteenth century. Only the visit of the chief prosecutor of the Holy Synod in 1861 provided the impetus to return to what had been intended.[17] The next year the abbess expressed the desire to complete the ensemble. According to Russian building legislation, a project approved by the emperor remained valid for 50 years, and then lost its legal force. More time had passed since Alexander I had approved the Bogoroditskii Monastery project. Nevertheless, it was "in this symmetrical arrangement" that the abbess wanted to complete the monastic complex.[18] The desire to implement the neoclassic project was so strong that it did not succumb to the direct instructions from the metropolitan officials urging the drafting of a project to meet the present needs of the monastery and to disregard the projects of 1810, which had lost their validity after more than 50 years, as the officials argued.[19] Its implementation was timed to coincide with the celebration of the 300th anniversary of the acquisition of the icon of the Mother of God of Kazan in 1879. In 1910–1913, on the initiative of Grand Duchess Elizabeth Feodorovna, and by the design of her favorite architect Alexei Shchusev, a crypt was arranged in the basement of the cathedral at the place where the icon had allegedly been found. The opening ceremony was held in the presence of the princess herself, and the holy place was named "Kazan Caves."[20] The inclusion of the monastery into the program of celebration of the Romanov dynasty's 300th anniversary demonstrated for the last time its significance for the imperial family and for the empire as a whole.

The ensemble of the monastery demonstrated a commitment to classicism unusual for the second half of the nineteenth century. The nineteenth century saw the rejection of the absolutization of antiquity and the classical tradition as an eternal artistic norm and the recognition of the historical significance of one's own national heritage. The new trend primarily affected church construction. In Russia, it was expressed in a targeted state policy aimed at building Orthodox churches exclusively in the Russian style. The idea to revive the Russian style was rooted in the study of ancient structures. Their ancient appearance and the very fact of their preservation acquired an independent value. In Europe, such tendencies first emerged as a result of the upheavals caused by the French Revolution and the Napoleonic Wars. In Russia, they were caused by the Patriotic War of 1812. The victory increased the relevance of the topic of conquest, which was the essence of the representation of Russian imperial power. The places of the glorious victories of Russian soldiers were now supposed to be marked with new architectural structures. In Kazan, the need for an architectural visualization of the conquest of the former capital of the Kazan Khanate was especially felt by the authorities. Thus, they turned their attention to places and structures that were directly related to the conquest of Kazan.

In the midst of a general patriotic upsurge, the abbot of the Kazan Uspenskii (Assumption) Monastery (Figure 5.1a,A), which had been founded in 1552 near the mass grave of Russian soldiers who fell during the capture of Kazan, started an unexpected development with a modest initiative. In 1811, the abbot applied for permission from the authorities to replace the decayed wooden pillar above the burial site with a stone one. However,

Alexander I rejected the idea and suggested building a memorial church on this site to commemorate the Orthodox soldiers killed during the conquest of Kazan. He approved a project developed by architect Nikolai Alferov and arranged for an annual payment from the treasury until the end of the construction. Moreover, an all-Russian public collection to raise funds was announced, which raised more than 100,000 rubles.[21] In 1823, the memorial church was built (Figure 5.1a,B), and in 1832, on the 280th anniversary of the capture of Kazan, it was renewed and decorated with portraits of Tsar Ivan the Terrible and Emperor Nicholas I inside.[22] The emperor visited it in 1836 and prayed in the crypt for a long time.[23] After that, it was this memorial church on the bank of the Kazanka River that embodied the historical events of 1552 instead of the Bogoroditskii Monastery. It became a mandatory place to visit for the members of the imperial family. It is indicative that this nineteenth-century "monument to the conquest of Kazan" was included in the state register of local historical and architectural heritage, which had been created during the implementation of Nicholas I's decree of 1826 concerning the collection of data on ancient buildings and a prohibition against their destruction.[24]

The main architectural and historical monument in Kazan, however, was the kremlin complex, whose buildings were primarily included in the above-mentioned list of local heritage in 1827 (Figure 5.2).[25]

According to archival documents reflecting the implementation of the imperial decree of 1826, the Blagoveshchenskii (Annunciation) Cathedral and the Church of Cyprian and Justina were built on the territory of the kremlin by the order of Tsar Ivan the Terrible right after the conquest of Kazan. Nearby was the chief commandant's complex from the late seventeenth and early eighteenth century, which had been erected from the remains of the khan's abandoned palace. It was in the capacity of a khan's palace that it was declared as an ancient historical and architectural monument. The nearby church was recorded as a "former Tatar mosque turned into a church," and the adjoining "solid stone tower in the form of a pillar" as its minaret.[26] In reality, this tiered structure was a watchtower of Russian origin, which had been built as an entrance to the governor's residence. It nevertheless became known as Suiumbeki Tower, named after Suiumbeki, who was the widow of the last Tatar khan Safa Girei and ruled the Khanate as a regent from 1549 on. The myth of the Tatar origin of Suiumbeki Tower had taken root in the public consciousness and was supported both by Russian authorities and by the faith of the Tatar community. When a tilt in the tower was discovered in 1907, Kazan Muslims, "driven by religious feelings," expressed their readiness to fully cover the costs of its repair.[27]

Figure 5.2 View of the Kazan Fortress by Vasilii Turin.

Source: Perspektivnye vidy gubernskogo goroda Kazani risovanyi s natury, litografirovanyi i izdanyi Vasiliem Turinym [Perspective views of the provinicial city of Kazan, drawn from nature, lithographed and published by Vasilii Turin]. Moskva, 1834.

The stone walls of the kremlin were erected by the Russian government at the end of the sixteenth and during the seventeenth century in place of the Tatar wooden fortress, which had occupied the kremlin's northern part. Nevertheless, at the beginning of the nineteenth century, it was generally considered a conquered Tatar fortress. That was also how Nicholas I perceived it, according to the memoirs of Alexander Benckendorff, who accompanied the emperor in his walk "along the walls of the ancient kremlin once long resisting Moscow's power." According to Benckendorff, that was when the idea came to the emperor "to resume the ancient khan's palace in the taste of that era when the Tatar yoke dominated over Russia."[28] The declared "restoration of the khan's" palace was of course symbolic. The proposed building was intended to be a residence for the governor of Kazan and for the members of the imperial family during their visits to Kazan. The emperor determined that the palace should be constructed near Suiumbeki Tower and ordered that the "plan for this resumption" should be presented to him. The search for an architectural image of the palace started immediately after the emperor's departure with a project by the official architect of Kazan province, Foma Petondi,[29] and took seven years. Nicholas I watched the progress of the case attentively, concerning himself with the details. During the consideration of the project proposals,

Nicholas I formulated a clearer vision for his Kazan residence, which was supposed to be "decent without any luxury." He imagined it in the form of a complex that made up "one whole with the remains of the ancient building near the Suiumbeki tower."[30] Petondi's project was rejected, and the emperor approved a project by the St. Petersburg architect Vasilii Morgan that was designed in late-classicist style.[31] However, in 1843, after construction had already started, changes radically altered the project's architectural appearance. Alterations were made by Konstantin Ton, Russia's leading architect at that time, who was also entrusted with the design of the Grand Kremlin Palace in the Moscow Kremlin. Ton reworked the facade of the governor's palace in Kazan, reproducing a reduced replica of his Moscow palace using the same palette of forms and signs in Russian-Byzantine style, which became the symbol of the reign of Nicholas I.[32] Thus, in the architecture of the Kazan palace, following its Moscow original, the concept of the reign of this emperor was materialized. The assimilation of the images of the two residences in Kazan and Moscow indicated the historical connection between the former capital of the victorious Moscow state and that of the defeated Kazan Khanate. Nicholas I himself did not have a chance to live in his Kazan residence. However, it became a place of official receptions for subsequent members of the imperial family, who were frequent guests in Kazan.

The emperor was categorical about the governor's proposal to build a new church in place of the seventeenth-century church, allegedly built on the ruins of the khan's mosque. According to experts, it could not be restored due to its poor physical condition. However, Nicholas I attached great importance to this restoration and insisted that the old church should be restored to its original form.[33] At this time, an understanding of the value of an ancient structure as a historical monument was formed, which resulted in an appreciation for not only the symbolic but also the physical preservation of ancient monuments.[34]

Great importance was also attached to the renovation of the main regional Blagoveshchenskii (Annunciation) Cathedral, one of the most important buildings inside the kremlin. The development of the first project was prompted by the expected arrival of Nicholas I to Kazan in 1834. The Orthodox citizens of Kazan, according to a common practice in Russia, hoped to hold the ceremony of laying the first stone of the new cathedral in his presence.[35] The new cathedral was planned as a monumental structure in the center of the kremlin.[36] That year, however, the emperor did not reach Kazan as the roads were washed away by rains, which forced him to turn back to the capital from Nizhnii Novgorod. When Nicholas finally arrived in Kazan in 1836, a whole series of new projects emerged. They reflected the radical turn in the field of church building that took place during those years.[37] Created in a transitional period, when the state shifted to the Russian style in church architecture, they were inspired by the Cathedral of Christ the Savior in Moscow by Konstantin Ton, which at that time existed only as a project, approved by the emperor and accepted for construction. Architects used the same set of forms and details borrowed from the practice of the ancient Russian church architecture such as keeled outlines, *zakomaras* (curvilinear finishing of the end of the face of a vault on a church wall), blind arcade belts on the drums of the heads, etc. While all projects implied the demolition of the existing sixteenth-century church, the monarch demonstrated a completely different approach in Kazan. He examined the existing church thoroughly and ordered it to be preserved. It was to be expanded to the west only. The emperor himself even measured the space for this extension. Thus, thanks to the monarch, the church of the sixteenth century, including its three apses built exactly where Tsar Ivan the Terrible had indicated, remained available for public viewing. Old architectural details as a strip of archetypal Pskov ornament encircling the drum of the central dome and running around the top of the middle apse, as well as a belt of blind arcade adorning the apses and drums, recalled that the temple had been built by Pskov masters in the reign of Ivan the Terrible.

The cathedral was located on the supposed site of the Tatar mosque Kul-Sharif. Together with the general-governor's palace that included the alleged khan's building, it formed an ensemble that expressed the state idea of the union of Orthodoxy, Autocracy, and Nationality in its architecture. The "Tatar" Tower of Suiumbeki, finally, represented an indigenous component connected to the Empire's non-Russian people.

Great importance was given to the kremlin's Tainitskaia and Spasskaia Towers. Tainitskaia Tower was built in the sixteenth century on the site of Nur-Ali Tower, which had been blown up during the siege of Kazan. It was from there, on October 4, 1552, two days after the capture of Kazan, that Tsar Ivan the Terrible entered the khan's ruined fortress. Spasskaia Tower marked the place where the tsar's banner had stood during the battle. After the victory, Ivan erected a cross and set up a tent-church with a traveling altar at that site. Tainitskaia Tower was gradually destroyed by annual flooding. Nevertheless, during his visit in Kazan, Nicholas I flatly refused to demolish it, ordering it to be strengthened with buttresses.[38] Moreover, he ordered a military church to be arranged in Spasskaia Tower.[39]

The way the kremlin was rebuilt in the middle of the nineteenth century under Nicholas I visibly expressed the idea of the re-conquest of the Kazan fortress. While restoring the iconic buildings, the emperor symbolically reconstructed the historical events of the mid-sixteenth century, identifying himself with Tsar Ivan the Terrible. It was a period of stylistic changes in the country, characterized by the rejection of the classical heritage and the revival of the national Russian style, which was the style of ancient Orthodox churches.

The memorial church on the Kazanka River and the renewed kremlin – which both related to a key event in local and imperial history, the conquest of Kazan – became an organic part of the city's nineteenth-century image and formed the basis of a new visual identity of Kazan representing its past. The contemporary imperial mission of Kazan, on the other hand, was embodied outside the kremlin by the university and the merchant center *Gostinyi Dvor*, the two architectural ensembles forming major accents on either end of Voskresenskaia Street.

The establishment of the university in 1804 contributed to the formation of Kazan as a center of cultural colonization of the vast region from the Volga to the Far East. It was located in a former gymnasium building (I).[40] Between 1820 and 1825, the architect Petr Piatnitskii, who had arrived from St. Petersburg, united the gymnasium and the neighboring houses into one extended building with a colonnade of Ionic columns.[41] It marked the beginning of the formation of one of the best masterpieces of Russian neoclassicism and the creation of a new image of Kazan as a university city. From 1833 to 1838, it was developed into an ensemble with a library, physical and chemistry laboratories, an anatomical theater, and an observatory, which occupied the entire block. It fully embodied in its architecture the imperial significance of an educational institution of the Enlightenment.[42] The rector Nikolai Lobachevskii directed the construction. The splendor of the university, which met all the requirements of this period, made a great impression on Nicholas I in 1836, who said that the university buildings were the best of any he had ever seen.[43] In the middle of the university block, there was a symmetrical ensemble with a semicircular square surrounded by a colonnade. Upon the emperor's suggestion, a monument to the famous Russian statesman and Kazan native Gavriil Derzhavin was installed in the center of the square to finalize the ensemble.[44]

After years of reconstruction in the neoclassical style, there was a growing tendency from the mid-nineteenth century on to return Russian cities to an allegedly more traditional appearance through the construction of Orthodox churches in the Russian style.[45] This, however, did not concern the central part of Kazan. There, in contrast, the concept of regularity gained a new impetus in the completion of already launched ensembles and the creation of new ones. Thus, in 1878, while constructing the new Voskresenskaia (Resurrection) Church near the university on Voskresenskaia Square in place of the old church (J), the demand to follow neoclassical forms was prescribed in the design assignment from the very beginning, contradicting the general orientation toward the Russian style in church building. Its architect Genrikh Rozen further stressed the project's compliance with the task in the explanatory note assuring that it had been designed in accordance with the given program.[46] A monumental five-headed cathedral with a majestic central dome on a massive drum and facades with classical composition, albeit constructed using an innovative nude brickwork technique, corresponded to the style of the nearby university complex. The square itself became part of the university quarter in 1893 with the celebration of the hundredth birthday of Nikolai Lobachevskii, the famous mathematician and former rector of Kazan University. A bust of the scientist was installed in its center.

The grandiose merchant center *Gostinyi Dvor*, the revenues from which went to the city budget, served as the architectural embodiment of the economically prosperous city under the management of Russian authorities.[47] The early nineteenth-century two-story building, built in place of a seventeenth-century trade complex with funds allocated from the state treasury by the order of Emperor Paul I, encompassed the entire quarter along the perimeter and faced Voskresenskaia Street with a mighty 18-column portico under a triangular pediment. At the end of the nineteenth century, a new square appeared here in front of the western building of the *Gostinyi Dvor* and the building of the City Duma (city council), with a monument to Emperor Alexander II as its main element.

The monument was erected as part of a movement that was encouraged by the state to perpetuate the memory of the author of the Great Reforms, one of which concerned the city governments.[48] In 1889, the City Duma announced an all-Russian competition for a monument to the emperor. The members of the Kazan Duma were in a hurry, since many cities in the country – not only large ones but also district centers – had already seen monuments built. The results were summed up at the beginning of 1890. The democratic selection procedure was consistent with the spirit of the time. An exhibition was organized for the townspeople in the halls of the Duma building, where they could vote for almost a month. The residents of Kazan, the local architectural community, and the Duma members expressed their preference for two projects by Vladimir Shervud, which took the first and second places in the design competition. Presented under the mottos "Slava" ("Glory") and "Velikomu" ("To the Great"), they reflected the pathos of this countrywide activity to glorify the Russian monarchy. They were both intended to convey the idea of royalty and the greatness of state power through the "dear image of the Great Monarch" and his "glorious deeds," expressed in their titles, which combined were "Slava Velikomu," or "Glory to the Great." The first variant was a colossal bust of the emperor; the second one his full-length figure.[49]

The winner of the competition was the only one who took the specifics of Kazan into account. These were most pronounced in the first version. The sculptor embodied the civilizing mission of Kazan for the countries of the East in the seated figure of a sage embracing a youth with his left hand and pointing to an open book with his right. The composition decorated one of the sides of the pyramidal pedestal, the foot of which was trimmed with untreated blocks of stone. According to the artist's idea, the staircase leading upward was supposed to remind the people of Kazan's influence on the local tribes, "still uncultured," which the city led gradually to the Enlightenment.[50] However, it was Shervud's second project that was chosen for implementation, where the full-length figure of the emperor was placed on a pedestal.

All competition projects in Kazan, like all monuments to Alexander II in Russian cities since the end of the nineteenth century, contained symbolic attributes of state authority – i.e., the imperial crown, scepter, orb, and coat of arms, as well as a symbolic representation of the monarch's merits such as the abolition of serfdom, the introduction of a system of local self-government, military and judicial reforms, and the support for the South Slavic peoples under Ottoman rule. Many of these elements were also present in Shervud's project, where the deeds of the emperor were described on boards placed on the sides of the pedestal, at the bottom of which winged snakes, borrowed from the coat of arms of Kazan, hold wreaths of glory, connected by garlands. In considering the project, Emperor Alexander III, who played a vital part in the creation of the imperial monuments to his father in the country, made changes to the Kazan statue.[51]

Two possible dates for the opening of the monument were discussed. October 2 was the day of the capture of Kazan in 1552, the day that determined the fate of Russia as an empire. October 22 was the day of celebration of the icon of the Kazan Mother of God who became the heavenly patroness of the reigning dynasty. However, the 1894 celebration was canceled because of the death of Emperor Alexander III. The following year, the city authorities intended to time the event to the day of the issuance of the decree on the reform of city government in 1870, resulting in the establishment of the Kazan City Duma, but their application was rejected. By the highest will, the opening of the monument was scheduled for August 30, on Emperor Alexander II's Day.[52] The memorialization of the imperial family was the exclusive prerogative of the emperor.

The square was renamed Alexander Square and became an important part of the city center. In its appearance, it embodied both a new vision of the empire, expressed through self-government, a key concept of "Europeanness" of that time, and the ideas of royalty and greatness of state power, transmitted through the "dear image of the Great Monarch."

The monument to the emperor pointed to the significance of the millennial power of the Russian monarchs.

Thus, at the end of the nineteenth century, as before, the concept of the empire was manifested through an expressive public space, indicating its genetic and substantive connection of the visual urban narrative with the ideas of regularity, which was the clearest architectural expression of the imperial idea of state greatness. In Kazan, the relatively early appearance of a regular plan favored the birth of the traditions of classicism, which flourished in the first half of the nineteenth century thanks largely to state support. The sustainability of these traditions in the subsequent period of the second half of the nineteenth and early twentieth centuries can be explained by the relevance of the idea of empire in the conquered region endowed with a special role and by the continuing need to visualize it by means of architecture.

Kazan's identity was based on its past as the former capital of the Kazan Khanate, annexed to the Russian state by conquest. In the eighteenth and nineteenth centuries, the conquest of the region was interpreted as its inclusion not only in a more powerful but also in a more orderly, more civilized, and culturally more advanced state structure. This idea was embodied in Kazan's architecture of the nineteenth century, the expressive image of which was formed by its main structures – the kremlin, the Bogoroditskii Monastery, the ensemble of Voskresenskaia Street with the university and the Gostinyi Dvor, and the memorial church on the Kazanka River. The marked neoclassicist appearance of the central space of Kazan was maintained throughout the century due to the need to visualize the idea of empire in the capital of a conquered region. Russian power appropriated Kazan's historical past and architectural heritage, both Tatar and Russian, using them for representative purposes.

Representing Ethno-Confessional Diversity

It is obvious from the above-mentioned letter of Catherine II to Voltaire that the ethno-confessional diversity seen firsthand in Kazan amazed the empress. The image of a vast multicultural country that appeared before her eyes predetermined the subsequent state policy aimed at smoothing out the differences. One of the best means to unite peoples was, according to the empress, religious tolerance. The architectural embodiment of the religious tolerance declared by Catherine was the construction of two stone mosques with baroque facades in Kazan. Erected in the Old Tatar Sloboda on the personal order of the Empress, they marked not only the revival of the monumental religious architecture of the Kazan Tatars, which had been lost more than 200 years earlier, but also a radical shift in state policy toward Russian Muslims. Catherine II's 1773 decree "On tolerance of all faiths" legislatively consolidated the multi-confessional nature of the Russian Empire. There were already eight mosques in Kazan at the beginning of the nineteenth century. Then, however, the imperial policy of religious tolerance of the Age of Enlightenment was replaced by a policy of direct demonstration of the superiority of the Russian Orthodox Church. This will be illustrated by the practice of constructing non-Orthodox religious buildings in Kazan.

The image of a multi-confessional empire was created by regulating the appearance of religious buildings. The need for state regulation of the style and appearance of religious buildings of different faiths arose during the reign of Nicholas I, when the religious revival, which had started in Europe at the turn of the nineteenth century, affected all confessions. It was implemented through the creation of model projects for religious buildings not only in Russian but also in other ostensibly national styles, bearing visible signs of belonging to a particular religion.[53]

When Catherine II ordered the construction of the stone mosques in Kazan, a type of wooden rectangular mosque with a minaret on a gable roof was developed, which had become traditional in the region since the conquest of Kazan (stone mosques were banned). The mosques allowed by Catherine, although they had baroque facades, corresponded to this tradition, as did all subsequent ones, built in the dominant style of early classicism. The model mosque approved by the emperor in 1829 interrupted this established practice.

The model project for mosques, created in the Building Committee of the Ministry of Internal Affairs in 1829, was inspired by a depiction of a fourteenth-century *türbe* (mausoleum) recently discovered in the Kazan province during the execution of the decree of 1826 concerning the collection of data on ancient buildings and a prohibition against their destruction. The appeal to heritage reflected the romantic ideas of the era that a national culture was determined by its origins. The centric structure in the form of an octagonal prism was approved "as a general model for mosques in Russia."[54] However, it was never implemented in the Kazan province, as it ignored the traditional type of a rectangular building with a gable roof and minaret above. The model project was expensive and did not meet local climatic conditions – the flat roof kept snow from shedding; more importantly, it was difficult to reproduce in wooden structures.

This forced the Muslim communities to appeal to the government in 1843 with a request to develop a new model project in accordance with the custom of the Muslims, and which would replace the model of 1829, the centric composition of which the petitioners associated with a cross. To make it more convincing, they submitted architectural projects with descriptions attached. The mosques they suggested followed the tradition and consisted of two or three halls in a row and had a mihrab and a covered porch in the front, as well as a minaret on the roof.[55] Good proportions and well-drawn details of the minarets, most likely copied from existing mosques, testified to longstanding practice. By adopting the neoclassical style, the Muslim community desired to associate with the imperial idea expressed through it.[56] This, however, meant that the projects did not correspond to the architectural and stylistic concept of the time, according to which religious buildings were supposed to visibly express in their appearance their belonging to a particular confession. Therefore, the projects suggested by Muslims were rejected, and new model mosque projects were developed for them in the Building Committee of the Ministry of Internal Affairs. The new projects took into account the wishes of the Muslims for a specific internal layout. But this time, the idea of a mosque was perceived through the European fascination with the Orient. It prompted government architects to turn to alternative sources and images of Islamic architecture – namely, to the mosques of the Middle East, again forgetting about the traditions of their "own East," the Tatars of the Volga region. Four model projects of wooden mosques met the planning requirements requested by Muslims.[57] However, endowed with domes and up to six free-standing minarets, they again proved to be unsuitable for small rural communities. Only one of them, which was the simplest design with only one minaret adjoining the main building, entered the building practice in Kazan. It turned out to be in demand even after the decree of 1862 abolished the compulsory adherence to model projects. However, mosques built according to this model were mostly located in cities where wealthy philanthropists financed the construction.

The stone Sennaia Mosque on the commercial Sennaia Square in Kazan (K), erected in 1845 by the merchant Ibragim Iunusov, was modeled after the mosque with one minaret. At the merchant's request, rows of shops joined the building. These changes to the model project necessitated reapproval by the emperor. Nicholas I approved the project of a mosque with shops, the income from which the merchant intended to donate to benefit Tatar orphanages in Kazan.[58] Two other cases where this model project was used relate to smaller towns in Kazan province. In 1859, the same sample was chosen by the merchant Khasan Iakupov for the construction of a wooden mosque in Chistopol', a small town in the province of Kazan. A similar wooden mosque was supposed to be erected in Tetiushi in 1854, but the project remained unrealized since the Tetiushi Muslims declared it "inconvenient and burdensome."[59] In 1879, they submitted a project for approval that responded to the tradition, with a rectangular log construction under a gable roof and minaret in its center.[60] Thus, it seems that in the entire province of Kazan, only two mosques were built according to the model project of 1843, and of the four variants of this series, only one was used – the cheapest. The demand to have religious buildings constructed in accordance with plans approved by the emperor forced communities to delay even repairing them for many years.[61] In 1862, Alexander II canceled the decree on the compulsory adherence to model projects in the construction of mosques, authorizing projects "which parishioners would find convenient."[62] This led to a spike in mosque building in Tatar settlements.

The Sennaia Mosque in Kazan reproduced the model project, contrary to its original purpose, in stone rather than wood. It was this composition with one minaret above the entrance that formed the basis of all five-stone mosques built in Kazan after the decree of 1862. Thus, the imperial model project was received by the Kazan Muslim community and initiated a new tradition of monumental architecture of the Kazan Tatars. This model retained its relevance in the late nineteenth and early twentieth centuries during the period of growth of a national identity. It was this composition of the state model project of 1843 with one free-standing minaret that acquired a new decor during this period, when Tatar developers, wishing to express their religious affiliation through architecture, reproduced their own images of the "East" on its basis. Likewise, a few decades earlier, the creators of model mosque projects had fantasized about the "East" using the artistic language of European Orientalism. The standard composition, now with a traditional pitched roof instead of a dome, was "dressed" in a set of "oriental" decorative motifs adopted in Russian stylization practice, such as horseshoe-shaped and pointed openings, geometric arabesques, colored stained-glass windows, stalactite cornices, castellate "Arabian" parapets, motley coloring, portal entrances, glazed multicolor tiles, etc. High multi-tiered minarets were made according to Arab and Turkish models. Local medieval Bulgar-Tatar monuments could also be taken as a basis for the new images. This stylistic approach, coupled with local traditions, formed a distinctive branch of the Muslim cult architecture – the Tatar one.[63]

From the second half of the nineteenth century, a new government policy aimed at creating a Russian Orthodox state, which required the maintenance of the Orthodox Church as the national religion. This policy aggravated the relationship of confessional communities with the authorities, which had to balance satisfying the rights of religious minorities with protecting the main religion of the state. The construction of non-Christian prayer houses caused serious conflicts, the resolution of which required the involvement of the central authorities.

One telling example is Usmanovskaia Mosque (L), which was built in a border quarter between the Russian and Tatar parts of Kazan. Its location near the Orthodox Church of Tikhvin (M) provoked extreme indignation from Kazan Bishop Antonii in 1867. In a complaint to the chief prosecutor of the Synod, he described the building as a "humiliation of the dignity of the Orthodox faith."[64] Such a statement on the part of an official representative of the titular religion became possible only as a result of the government's course of direct demonstration of Russian superiority. The decree of Catherine II on religious tolerance of 1773 prohibited the intervention of the Orthodox clergy in the affairs of other confessions, leaving their decision to the secular authorities. Now the Orthodox clergy became one of the main actors in matters of religious construction.

The distance between mosques and Orthodox churches was regulated by the requirement "that there should be no temptation in faith for Christians and newly baptized Tatars living with the Mohammedans," which allowed everyone to freely interpret the degree of this temptation. Annoyed by the allegedly excessive proliferation of mosques in Kazan, where they were located "one near the other and across one street, obviously unnecessarily," Antonii demanded that the already completed mosque should be demolished or turned into a residential building. However, an inquiry undertaken by order of the minister of internal affairs concluded that the construction was legal. The number of parishioners in the nearest mosque significantly exceeded the norm, so that on holidays the building could not accommodate all worshipers. The place was inhabited by Tatars, and there were no cases of members of the Orthodox flock defecting to Islam in Kazan.[65] Governor Nikolai I. Skariatin personally shared the bishop's views, but, being a state official, he was bound to ensure the peaceful coexistence of all confessional groups in the province and was forced to admit that halting the already authorized construction would be inexpedient, which could only lead to the "irritation of the minds of the Mohammedans."[66]

The law did not dictate the exact distance between mosques and Orthodox churches. However, when the Kazakovskaia Mosque was erected in 1875, the degree of "temptation for the Orthodox Russian people," contrary to the law, was primarily measured by the distance to the Church of the Four Evangelists.[67] The opinion of the local Orthodox authorities in the construction of non-Christian religious buildings played a decisive role in the period under review. Meanwhile, the position of the consistory was at times obviously illegitimate. Thus, it justified the refusal to build a second mosque in aforementioned Chistopol' on the grounds that the Orthodox population, which was significantly larger in number, was quite satisfied with two parish churches. The appearance of a new mosque for Muslims, of whom there were not even a thousand in the city, would be considered "extremely unpleasant." The Muslims of Chistopol' petitioned the Senate, which recognized the petition as legal.[68]

The emergence of another non-Christian community in Kazan in the second half of the nineteenth century – the Jewish one – was a matter of great concern for the local authorities. By the end of the nineteenth century, the Jewish population had grown, and the community needed its own prayer building.[69] Alexander II's decree of 1868 gave Russian Jews the right to establish prayer houses in the cities, with spiritual boards "to manage the internal arrangement and economy," upon recommendation of the governor and permission of the minister of internal affairs.[70] The growth of the Jewish population was caused by the expansion of their permitted area of residence. Certain categories of Jews were now allowed to settle outside the Pale of Settlement, i.e., the territory to which permanent Jewish residency had been restricted since 1791. Russian legislation differentiated between synagogues and prayer houses.[71] While both served for worship for Sabbath and holiday prayers, synagogues were representative buildings that were built in exceptional cases in large cities of the Pale of Settlement, where there were large and wealthy communities. Outside the Pale of Settlement, it was only allowed to open houses of prayer, which, in essence, performed the functions of a synagogue, but did not have the right to be called so.

In Kazan, a small Jewish community had existed for many years in an unregistered form, renting premises for their prayers in the house of the merchant Smolentsev on Malaia Prolomnaia Street opposite the back wall of the university complex. In 1889, the Jewish community began to petition for the official opening of a prayer house, which would not only allow it to build its own building for the performance of religious rites but also to record the acts of the civil status of Jews – births, marriages, deaths. However, Governor Petr Poltoratskii refused on the grounds that, in his opinion, an insignificant number of Jews lived in the city.[72] The next petition in 1895 was left unanswered altogether.[73] A year later, in response to a third petition, the governor acknowledged the growth of the Jewish community, but he still considered their number too insufficient, compared with other faith groups, to open a prayer house. In his letter to the Minister of Internal Affairs, Poltoratskii frankly stated that he was unwilling to allow further "influx of this element into the city."[74]

By the end of the nineteenth century, most cities not only in central Russia but also in the Volga region had acquired government rabbis and houses of worship. Kazan was a rare exception. Meanwhile, this question went far beyond the construction of a prayer house. More significant was the problem of elementary civil rights, which, as it turned out, the Jewish citizens of Kazan were completely deprived of. Due to the lack of a rabbi, more than a hundred Jewish families lived, married, and died without official registration and, therefore, in complete lawlessness. Accordingly, the children descended from these marriages were formally considered illegitimate. In this situation, the Kazan police chief, unlike the governor, found the appointment of a state rabbi and the organization of a prayer house "even desirable."[75] In 1897, the Ministry of Internal Affairs gave permission to set up a prayer house in Kazan.[76]

The question of the location was put on the agenda. The current location of the prayer house in the rented house of Smolentsev on Malaia Prolomnaia Street was a problem for the Kazan authorities because of its central position. Unlike mosques, the location of Jewish prayer houses was clearly regulated by law. They had to be distanced from Orthodox churches by at least 100 *sazhen* (213 m) in case they were located on the same street, and by 50 *sazhen* (a little more than 100 m) if on a different one. The Bogoiavlenskaia (Epiphany) Church was the nearest church to Smolentsev's house. The shortest distance between them was more than 200 *sazhen* through a passage from Malaia Prolomnaia Street to Bol'shaia Prolomnaia, and more than 300 *sazhen* if the long way around was taken. Thus, the distance was completely in line with the building law. Nevertheless, the governor addressed this issue to the spiritual consistory. When making the request, the governor provocatively used the term "synagogue" instead of a prayer house, the former of which was banned in cities like Kazan. Since the construction of synagogues outside the Pale of Settlement was prohibited, the consistory could not and did not have the right to give its consent to the opening of a synagogue in Kazan, and even less so in the city center under any circumstances.[77] During the next four years, the Jewish community proposed several alternative sites for their prayer house. Yet none of the various options that fit into the legal framework satisfied the authorities, who feared that the future prayer house would overshadow the nearby Orthodox churches in size and architecture.[78] The authorities persistently recommended to the Jewish community to give up the idea of constructing a new building and instead to limit itself to buying a finished house on the periphery. Finally, after four years, a site satisfying both sides was found. Purchased from a Tatar owner, it was located not far from the Tatar quarters and, most importantly, outside the central part of the city. However, construction was postponed for another three years due to the disapproval of the project by the authorities (this will be discussed below). When the project was finally approved in 1904, a part of the property had already been sold. The search for a new site took another eight years.[79] A favorable resolution of the problem was facilitated in 1912 by the intention to erect the State bank building on Smolentsev's plot.[80] It was here that the community had been renting the house for many years, and now they were threatened with being left without premises. The authorities were forced to agree to a house on the same Malaia Prolomnaia Street. The place was now acceptable, being the "backs" of Bol'shaia Prolomnaia and Voskresenskaia streets and therefore relatively sparsely populated. Thus, the search for the construction site took 15 years. Construction was permitted on the condition that the praying house did not differ from the surrounding residential buildings, both in size and appearance.[81]

Russian legislation did not regulate the architectural design of synagogues and Jewish prayer houses, which in the Pale of Settlement were simple functional buildings. From the middle of the nineteenth century in Western Europe, the Jewish architecture of Moorish Spain became a stylistic reference point for the construction of synagogues, making them a symbol of Jewish culture. The search for the image of synagogues as a form of expression of confessional affiliation reflected the aspirations of the Jewish people in the context of the national movements of that time. The same hope fed the St. Petersburg Jewish community when, following the example of European co-religionists, it chose for its capital synagogue the "strictly Moorish style" to imitate the Alhambra. Tsar Alexander II, when considering the St. Petersburg project in 1880, ordered it "to keep a more modest size," but he approved the Moorish style of the building. Thus, he officially recorded this style for future Russian synagogues. The Orthodox Church, which strengthened its status under the next emperor, tried to prevent the spread of synagogues throughout the country. In fact, however, the second synagogue in the ancient capital of Moscow had already been built under the guise of a prayer house. In order to avoid the indignation expected from representatives of the Russian Orthodox Church, the oriental style was not even considered for this building. It was designed in a classical style, anachronistic for the 1880s, with a portico and a dome, which, at the request of the central authorities, was demolished shortly after its erection. The oriental style that had taken root in the synagogues of Western Europe did not apply to Jewish prayer houses in nineteenth-century Russia.

The situation changed radically at the beginning of the twentieth century, a time of growing national and religious problems. The social upheaval taking place in the country demanded that the authorities resolve many pressing issues, including national and confessional ones. It led to the so-called First Russian Revolution and the decree of 1905 "On strengthening the principles of religious tolerance." As a consequence, a number of grandiose Jewish prayer houses were erected in the empire in these years, including in Samara in the Volga region. The monumental red-and-white striped brick building with a massive four-sided dome topped with a Star of David and facades rich with oriental details was a great challenge for the Russian authorities, who sought to limit the claims of the non-Russian population to express their national identity.

The design of the Jewish prayer house for Kazan, drawn up in 1901 by the city architect Konstantin Oleshkevich, became the subject of a three-year secret correspondence between the Kazan governor and the Ministry of Internal Affairs. The gaps in construction legislation allowed the authorities to freely interpret its provisions in the interests of the state religion, dealing not only with such technical issues as the location in relation to Orthodox churches but also with the artistic style. The explanation of the deputy minister of internal affairs, given in connection with Oleshkevich's project to Kazan's provincial government, expressed the position of the authorities in this matter. In his interpretation of the law, Jewish prayer houses should be placed in existing ordinary buildings. And in the case of new construction, they should not have the appearance of a Jewish religious building – elements such as domes, towers, emblems, or other similar decorations were to be avoided.[82] The construction of houses of worship outside the Pale of Settlement was a new phenomenon. This interpretation by a high-ranking official was based solely on the existing practice of building houses of worship within the Pale of Settlement at a time when the question of expressing confessional affiliation had not yet arisen. In fact, the law did not say anything about the appearance of houses of worship, requiring only that the projects be approved by the authorities.

Oleshkevich's prayer house did not have the obvious appearance of a Jewish religious building. But it still stood out from the mass of Kazan's buildings, which were unified under the influence of state model projects. In the eclectic façade with small four-sided towers on the sides, an arched entrance marked with a rosette window, and a row of double windows, the governor observed an "Oriental style that gave the building a special character."[83] The governor started a correspondence with the Department of Spiritual Affairs of Foreign Confessions. He also pointed to the building's length, too excessive in his opinion, which actually was only a little more than 12 meters in length along the street. The governor again assured the central authorities that the prayer house was not needed, explaining the Jews' petition exclusively by their commitment to isolate themselves from the local Russian population.[84] The project, which had already been approved by the Kazan construction department, was ordered to be redesigned by simplifying the façade so that it would not have the "characteristic features of a synagogue."[85] Thus, in fact, the real dissatisfaction on the part of the Kazan administration was caused by their unwillingness to acknowledge one more "alien" community in their city, which was already inhabited by a large number of non-Christians, with whom relations were also uneasy at that time.

The new social situation had a beneficial effect on solving the problem of the Kazan Jews. In December 1904, the Department of Spiritual Affairs of Foreign Confessions suddenly recognized that it was possible to approve Oleshkevich's 1901 project, which by this time, however, had lost its relevance due to the loss of part of the site, as mentioned above.[86] It took eight years to develop a new project, as the Orthodox clergy in Kazan continued to obstruct the local Jewish community in their search for a new construction site despite the changes in the country. The Kazan Jewish community did not settle in its three-story building until 1915, almost half a century after the 1868 decree permitted the construction of Jewish prayer houses. Designed by the Kazan province engineer Nikolai Andreev, it had no domes. Yet, highly recognizable details and symbols such as horseshoe-shaped openings, niches-tablets, stylized Torah scrolls, etc., demonstrating the building's confessional affiliation, were included in the fashionable Art Nouveau façade, receptive to the art of the East.[87] Through the new style, Kazan Jews found their own architectural language to express their cultural and religious identity.

The favorable position of the Tatar elite during the Enlightenment contributed to the acceptance of European culture and the formation of new traditions, including the tradition of religious architecture. However, while the Tatars reinterpreted this new culture through imperial architectural practices, the Jewish elite directly borrowed their cultural landmarks from Europe to demonstrate a modernized Russian Jewry.

The highest state power had to balance between the patronage of the Russian nation and the Orthodox religion on the one hand and the protection and patronage of people with a different culture and faith on the other hand. The history of the construction of houses of worship of non-Christian religions in Kazan showed that the authorities clearly realized the need to satisfy the religious needs of the non-Orthodox inhabitants of the empire. On the one hand, attempts at forced baptism had shown their ineffectiveness in relation to Jews and Muslims. On the other hand, starting from the eighteenth century, an orientation toward the European experience of relative religious tolerance arose. However, ancient fears and prejudices continued to determine the mood of the authorities, which seemed averse to any indulgence in relation to the non-Christians. Local Orthodox authorities, both secular and spiritual, found themselves in the position of mediators between the state and the population. In carrying out the laws and regulations of the central authorities, they often created more obstacles than these laws and regulations suggested, thereby joining the xenophobia of a significant part of the Orthodox population and in many ways inspiring it.

Tatar Quarters in the Unified City Space

Until the middle of the eighteenth century, numerous *slobodas* (suburban settlements) surrounded Kazan. In two of these settlements, the Old and the New Tatar *sloboda*, lived the Tatar population of Kazan. The first was founded shortly after the taking of the city by the Russians at the mouth of the Bulak River on the left bank of Lake Kaban, where the Tatars were evicted from Kazan. An extensive Muslim cemetery separated it from the Russian town. The emergence of the New Tatar settlement, located at some distance away from the city, was a result of a large-scale Christianization campaign during the 1740s. After newly baptized Tatars were settled on the territory of the Old Tatar settlement, part of the Tatar population preferred to move to a place newly allocated by the government.

The plan of 1768 drastically changed the urban space of Kazan, covering not only the Russian-Orthodox city inside the walls but also its periphery comprised of ethno-confessional "Others" such as Muslim Tatars and Orthodox minority groups like Old Believers. The regularized Tatar quarters were incorporated into one city space and into a single system of straight and wide streets and squares, one of them having been arranged directly on the place where the Muslim cemetery was. The regulation of the artistic style of mass housing was carried out with the help of model projects created by the state, which were mandatory for urban developers. Thus they solved the problem of the lack of qualified architects in the province and – what was especially important for the authorities – controlled the emerging architectural appearance of the cities. The practice of forced architectural unification came in conflict with local urban planning features and residential traditions. It was resolved by adapting the state norms to the local conditions by using alternative architectural and planning solutions. For example, a consequence of the small size of the properties in Kazan in comparison with the capital led to the use of only fragments of model facades, or their free interpretation. Regulations demanded that houses be built directly on the line of the street. The custom of placing a manor house at the center of a plot, which was best preserved in Tatar dwelling tradition, forced the adherents of this tradition to put auxiliary buildings instead of a residential building on the line of the street.

However, the most striking response to the demands of the state was the mass designing of "individual projects" in Kazan, which required approval from St. Petersburg. The Russian building legislation provided for the possibility, as an exception, to build "not in everything according to exemplary projects."[88] However, such an individual project required the emperor's approval, which significantly complicated the construction process. Nevertheless, developers in Kazan took up the challenge. The main reason for the rejection of the facades published in the capital was that they were developed based on the tastes and economic conditions of the capital's residents. A house designed to occupy the entire front of the site did not correspond to the nature of the development and the way of life of the provincial city, regardless of the ethnocultural affiliation of the owners. A more traditional type of small house was required, as well as a variety of services, shops, and outbuildings, which were an indispensable part of Kazan estates and were not provided for in the capital's albums. If the drawing delivered from Kazan did not pass muster, a new one was developed in the capital. After approval by the emperor, these drawings also acquired the status of a model project and were adopted into widespread practice, used by both Russian and Tatar developers. The houses built according to the Kazan model projects were one- and two-story buildings with three, five, and seven axes of windows on the main facade. Most popular among both the Russian and Tatar populations were three-axis houses.

It should be especially noted that we are not aware of cases where Tatar developers requested individual projects. Legislation, public interest in stylistic diversity, supported by a preference for drawings of buildings of various countries and times, and cultural contacts of Tatar merchants with eastern countries gave the Tatars the opportunity to create images reflecting their ideas in the appearance of their homes. However, they did not seem to have taken advantage of this opportunity. One gets the impression that they were quite satisfied with the available samples, both sent from the capital and developed in Kazan, which they adapted to their ideas, affecting mainly the internal structure of the estate and the house. Kazan facades, rather simple in architecture, contained elements and details of state models. Thus, the European tradition was once again revised, taking into account the tastes and needs of the Kazan dwellers. These projects were the result of the adaptation of state norms to local conditions, reflecting the characteristics of social rather than national ordering, both Russian and Tatar. To a significant extent, it was these local model projects that determined the appearance of Kazan. As a result of the strict legislative and administrative regulation of construction in cities, the state task was fulfilled – the districts of Kazan acquired a unified face. Thanks to the success of imperial integration, the Tatar quarters did not outwardly differ from the Russian part of the city.[89]

From the second half of the nineteenth century, with the growth of national self-awareness, the need arose among Kazan Tatars to emphasize their Tatar identity by external means. A conscious attitude toward "Tatarness" developed at the turn of the twentieth century, when the minds of the Tatar bourgeoisie and the emerging intelligentsia were seized by notions of a national revival. In architecture, this was expressed through national motives, previously alien to the facades of Tatar houses, which until then had reproduced state model projects. New design details included inscriptions in Arabic script on the pediments, as well as bay windows, multi-layered stalactite-like consoles, color glass, and keeled windows and doors. They were drawn from the local traditions, which still existed in Tatar villages.

The driving force behind these transformations was the Tatar-Muslim population, who rallied toward nation-building. It was led by the financially secure and ideologized Tatar national bourgeoisie, which, moreover, now had its own representatives in the local government. The commercial and business life of the Kazan Tatars was concentrated in the vicinity of Sennaia Square, formed in accordance with the regular plan of 1768 and completely renewed between the 1860s and 1910s. Along with its own "Tatar *Gostinyi Dvor*," the so-called Usmanov's building, erected between 1860 and 1888, signs of modernity such as cinemas appeared on the square. In addition to specific goods (Tatar leather shoes, for example), the appearance of the square, similar in architecture to other trade areas in the city, was distinguished by colorful signs mentioning Tatar surnames, local place names, and oriental institutions – merchant Apanaev's hotel "Apanaevskoe Podvorie," hotel rooms "Bulgar," "Caravanserai," etc. However, Sennaia Square is also associated with another phenomenon that goes beyond the framework of the architectural and urban structure and its commercial function. Between 1880 and the 1910s, Sennaia Square became the center of the entire socio-political and cultural life of the Tatars. The need for public buildings appeared in Tatar society for the first time, the absence of which had been satisfied by using the apartment buildings located here. The editorial offices of numerous newspapers and magazines settled in hotel rooms, and the intelligentsia, who thought and talked a lot about the fate of the Tatar nation in those years, lived in these hotels.

The special role of Sennaia Square in the life of the Tatars was related to the implementation of the regular plan of 1768, which radically changed the fate of the Kazan Tatar settlement that appeared in the suburbs soon after the conquest of Kazan.[90] According to this plan, the square was designed on the site of the Muslim cemetery, and the moat separating the city from the suburb was laid right through the territory of the old settlement, dividing it into two parts. The first part included Sennaia Square and was to be inhabited by Russians. Tatars were ordered to move to the re-planned outer part of the old settlement in a suburb on the other side of the moat. However, from the very beginning, the eastern side of Sennaia Square was built up with the shops of Tatar merchants, since, contrary to the 1768 plan, the Tatar quarters did not disappear from this part of the city. After the settlement's division, the Tatars who lived here did not move to the place assigned to them in the suburb, but remained and formed an independent Muslim parish. Tatar estates filled the regular blocks, in one of which a new stone mosque was built in 1798.

In 1818, while petitioning for the construction of another mosque here, Gabida Kitaeva, the Tatar widow of a merchant, called this now officially Russian part of the city an "Old Tatar Sloboda" from the name of the old Tatar settlement, which existed here before the implementation of the regular plan of 1768.[91] The reference to a physically non-existent settlement in a completely transformed urban space is significant. In the minds of the inhabitants, this territory continued to remain the old Tatar settlement, illustrating the conservatism of the mass consciousness both in toponymy issues and in the perception of the living space as a whole. The realization of place, passed down from generation to generation over centuries, was preserved in the collective memory of the population. The persistence of the image of the ancient Muslim cemetery in the memory of the people, where residents recorded the location of the graves of their grandfathers and great-grandfathers, "tying" them to modern buildings, was noted by Shihabeddin Mardzhani in the second half of the nineteenth century.[92]

The sacredness of the place resulted in the purposeful replacement of the Russian population by the Tatars and the spread of the Tatar quarters. As stated above, during the implementation of the regular plan, the eastern side of Sennaia Square was built up with the shops of Tatar merchants while its southern part was occupied by Russian possessions. After a fire in 1859, one of the richest Tatar merchants, Zigansha Usmanov, bought up all the plots belonging to the Russians on the southern side of Sennaia Square and many in the adjacent quarters.[93] They were settled by Tatars, and this allowed a new Muslim parish to be registered in Kazan and the construction of the Usmanovskaia Mosque to begin. Then other merchants followed Usmanov's example. As a result, at the beginning of the twentieth century, Tatars owned almost all possessions on Sennaia Square, except for the northwest corner occupied by Russian Old Believers. Tatars also owned houses in other parts of the city. But it is important that in the area of Sennaia Square, the former Old Tatar settlement was actually reconstructed. The square itself played an important role in the Tatar social movements of the late nineteenth and early twentieth century and became a symbol of the Tatar national revival.

The success of the empire's architectural policies led to the result that the Tatar quarters did not outwardly differ from the Russian part of the city. The Tatar homeowners of Kazan reacted quite positively to the project of the "internal colonization" of the empire, the goal of which was formulated by Catherine II as integration, the creation of a single social space according to common "European" rules. Formed in the course of mutual compromises and projections, a regular space with a European look, interpreted in a peculiar way and adapted to traditions, laid the foundation for the formation of a new urban Tatar-Muslim architectural and urban planning culture. Tatars did not object to the geometric planning of city blocks with the arrangement of the squares near mosques, modeled on the squares in front of churches in European cities. However, they firmly demonstrated their adherence to the tradition and defended the borders of the Tatar settlement. We can say that the European form was adapted to express a specific Tatar content and endowed with its own meanings.

Conclusion

The city of Kazan is particularly suited for analysis through the concept of the imperial city as discussed in the first chapter of this volume. The radical reconstruction of its cityscape since 1768 provided Kazan with an outlook that fully corresponded to the latest urbanistic ideas formulated in the capital. At the same time, the example of Kazan captures the different modes of colonization in overseas empires and inland empires. The architectural and urbanistic processes described in the chapter were embedded in the general doctrine of a cultural development of the Russian province. Tsarist authorities of the eighteenth and nineteenth centuries perceived their activities in the provinces, including the non-Orthodox regions, as civilizational uplifting of a seemingly backward population. As it seemed to them, they were bringing there the basics of European culture and rational organization of life, which were supposed to unite the diverse population on common principles. The coercive nature of implementation by measures of a consistent government policy in architecture and urban planning gives grounds to consider the process through the prism of "internal colonization," inherent in continental empires.[94]

However, the specificity of Kazan as a conquered city with a significant Tatar-Muslim population also gives it the features of external colonization. In both cases of external and internal colonization, the achievements of the allegedly advanced Western civilization were introduced into a different environment. However, with external colonization, such an introduction, even ideally, cannot lead to a complete fusion of the culture of the metropolis with the culture of the colony, while in the case of internal colonization, such an insurmountable barrier between these cultures does not exist. Since the barrier between the culture of the capital on the one hand and the culture of the ethnically Russian provinces on the other hand (which still included various other ethno-confessional groups) has never been impenetrable, and the contact has never been unidirectional, a powerful feedback loop can be observed here. Many features (as, for example, the estate way of life) of the traditional Russian worldview remained valid for the residents of the capital as well. They were not perceived as exotic details of indigenous life; on the contrary, they were considered as important Russian features, as traditional values, in many respects no less significant than, and not contradicting, the European cultural innovations being introduced. The absence of cultural barriers between the metropolis (i.e., the capital, St. Petersburg) and the "colonized" territory (the rest of the Tsarist Empire) turned this process into a series of mutual reflections – i.e., a series of messages from center to periphery and vice versa. The cultural message of the metropolis returns to it from the depths of the provinces in a somewhat transformed form (e.g., as a project of a typical facade adapted to local conditions); here it is again corrected (offering some kind of compromise solution) and returned to the province, etc.

The case of Kazan with its Tatar-Muslim population, which distinguished the city from cities of the culturally homogeneous Russian province, allows these complex dynamics of mutual influence and feedback to be clearly traced. The Tatar population represented a tangible cultural barrier in relation to the St. Petersburg authorities. The cultural identity of the Tatars, which could not always be overcome by administrative means, was fully recognized by the imperial government. Nevertheless, the process of interaction between the provincial townsfolk (both Russian and Tatar) and the St. Petersburg authorities, viewed through the prism of architecture, fits perfectly into the scheme of dialogic relations of internal colonialism. The province also sends a meaningful message to the center, although not as defiantly as the metropolis. In the case of Kazan, this message had a distinctly orientalist character, but it was not about decorative orientalism at the level of external forms, nor was it about Said's orientalism as an attribution by European culture to the imaginary homogeneous "East" of certain common internal qualities, but about deep orientalism associated with civilizational categories.

Notes

1 This chapter was funded by the Program of Fundamental Research of the Ministry of Construction, Housing and Utilities of the Russian Federation and the Russian Academy of Architecture and Construction Sciences 2021–2023.
2 See, for example, Serhii Plokhy, *The Origin of the Slavic Nations. Premodern Identities in Russia, Ukraine, and Belarus* (New York: Cambridge University Press, 2006), 140–41; Robert Geraci, *Window on the East: National and Imperial Identities in Late Tsarist Russia* (Ithaca, NY and London: Cornell University Press, 2001), 3.

3 Mikhail Pinegin, *Kazan' v ee proshlom i nastoiashchem* (Kazan: Globus, 2005; Dubrovin: St. Petersburg, 1890), 323, 325. Citation refers to the Globus publication.

4 Quoted in Pinegin, *Kazan'*, 12, 122–23.

5 Geraci, *Window*, 5–6.

6 See Guzel Ibneeva, "Puteshestvie Ekateriny II po Volge v 1767 godu: uznavanie imperii," *Ab Imperio*, V. 2 (2000): 87–104.

7 Quoted in V.V. Chuiko, ed. *Vol'ter i Ekaterina II*, trans. V.V. Chuiko (St. Petersburg: Novosti, 1882), 20–1.

8 Polnoe sobranie zakonov Rossiiskoi imperii (PSZ RI), collection 1, vol. XVI, 1763, № 11883. The regular principle, as an ideal way of organizing the imperial space, formed the basis of the entire administrative and territorial reorganization of the country, which was divided into provinces and counties with an approximately equal and optimal population from the point of view of power. Its aim was a system of cities at similar distances from each other and with similar populations. Many of them were newly founded from villages by decree, with the aim of streamlining the entire imperial space.

9 The medieval layout of Kazan is recorded on a number of city plans from the eighteenth century; see, for example, Russian State Historical Archive (RGIA), f. 1399, op. 1, d. 409, Plan of Kazan, 1768; Russian State Military Historical Archive (RGVIA), f. 349, op. 17, d. 198; f. 846 (VUA), ed. khr. 21528, Plany gorodov Rossiiskoi imperii, sobrannye po velichaishemu poveleniiu v 1798 g.

10 E.I. Kirichenko, "Imperatorskii Rim v stolitsakh Frantsuzskoi i Rossiiskoi imperi," in *Stil' Ampir. Arkhitektura v istorii russkoi kul'tury* 5, ed. I.A. Bondarenko (Moskow: Rokhos, 2003), 30.

11 Richard Wortman, *Scenarios of Power: Myth and Ceremony in Russian Monarchy, Vol. 1: From Peter the Great to the Death of Nicholas I* (Princeton, NJ: Princeton University Press, 1995).

12 Efimii Malov, *Kazanskii Bogoroditskii Devichii Monastyr'* (Kazan: Kazan University, 1879), 5.

13 Ibid, 6.

14 See, for example, E.I. Kirichenko, "Kazanskii sobor v Peterburge Pavla I," in *Andrei Nikiforovich Voronikhin*, ed. IU.G. Bobrov (St. Petersburg: Kolomenskaya versta, 2010), 52.

15 Sergei Shpilevskii, *Zaboty imperatora Aleksandra I o Kazani. Rech', proiznesennaia ordinarnym professorom S.M. Shpilevskim v torzhestvennom sobranii Imperatorskogo Kazanskogo universiteta 12 dekabria 1877 g. v iubileinyi den' stoletiia rozhdeniia imperatora Aleksandra I* (Kazan: Kazan University, 1877).

16 RGIA, f. 1488, op. 1, d. 1245.

17 State Archive of the Republic of Tatarstan (GART), f. 4, op. 1, d. 5876.

18 GART, f. 2, op. 14, d. 719; RGIA, f. 218, op. 4, d. 1067, l. 15, 106.

19 RGIA, f. 218, op. 4, d. 1067, l. 5.

20 Aleksandr Zeleneckii, *Osviashchenie khrama vo imia Rozhdestva Presviatoi Bogoroditsy i chasovni na meste iavleniia Kazanskoi chudotvornoi ikony Bozh'ei Materi v pamiat' trekhsotletiia tsarstvovaniia Doma Romanovykh* (Kazan: Tsentral'naia tipografia, 1914).

21 GART, f. 1, op. 1, d. 9.

22 Nikolai Zagoskin, *Sputnik po Kazani. Illiustrirovannyi ukazatel' dostoprimechatel'nostei i spravochnaia knizhka goroda* (Kazan: Globus, 2005; Kazan University, 1895), 153.

23 Alexander Kh. Benkendorf, "Zapiski grafa A.Kh. Benkendorfa (1832–1837 gg.)," in *Imperator Nikolai I.: Ego zhizn' i tsarstvovanie: Primechania i dopolnenia ko vtoromu tomu*, ed. N.K. Shil'der (St. Petersburg: A.S. Suvorin, 1903), 734.
24 PSZ RI, collection 2, vol. I, 1825–1826, № 794.
25 GART, f. 1, op. 1, d. 9.
26 Ibid, 7–7ob.
27 GART, f. 2, op. 7, d. 1078; f. 2, op. 7, d. 1590.
28 Benkendorf, "Zapiski," 733.
29 Kazan (Volga region) Federal University Nikolay Lobachevsky Scientific Library, Department of Rare Books and Manuscripts (ORRK), ed. khr. 9599, 9601, 9602, 9603, 9604.
30 GART, f. 409, op. 8, d. 4, l. 1–2, 4–5; ORRK, ed. khr. 9596, 9597, 9598.
31 ORRK, ed. khr. 9500; GART, f. 409, op. 8, d. 4, l. 12–13; RGIA, f. 1488, op. 1, d. 1216, l. 8.
32 RGIA, f. 218, op. 4, d. 7, l. 136–136ob.
33 Ibid, l. 221.
34 E.I. Kirichenko, *Gradostroitel'stvo Rossii serediny XIX – nachala XX veka*, vol. 1, ed. E.I. Kirichenko (Moscow: Progress-Traditsia, 2001), 60.
35 GART, f. 1, op. 2, d. 80, l. 193.
36 ORRK, ed. khr. 3068, 3077.
37 ORRK, ed. khr. 9607, 9608, 9609, 9610, 9611, 9612; RGIA, f. 1488, op. 1, d. 1238.
38 GART, f. 409, op. 1, d. 515, l. 6.
39 Zagoskin, *Sputnik po Kazani*, 141.
40 GART, f. 87, op. 1, d. 10090a.
41 Nikolai Zagoskin, *Istoriia Imperatorskogo Kazanskogo universiteta za pervye sto let ego sushestvovaniia, 1804–1814*, Vol. I (Kazan: Imperial Kazan University Press, 1902), 73.
42 N.A. Evsina, "Progressivnye traditsii v arkhitekture russkikh uchebnykh zavedenii epokhi klassitsizma" (Kand. diss. State Institute for Art Studies, 1967), 278–79.
43 Benkendorf, "Zapiski", 733.
44 GART, f. 977, op. Sovet, d. 1.
45 Kirichenko, *Gradostroitel'stvo Rossii*, 57.
46 GART, f. 2, op. 7, d. 692.
47 Zagoskin, *Sputnik po Kazani*, 238.
48 GART, f. 98, op. 2, d. 2412.
49 Ibid; GART, f. 98, op. 7, d. 182.
50 Ibid.
51 GART, f. 98, op. 2, d. 2412, l. 111.
52 *Sooruzhenie i otkrytie pamiatnika imperatoru Aleksandru II v Kazani: Kratkii istoricheskii ocherk* (Kazan: V.M. Kliuchnikov v Kazani, 1896).
53 Kirichenko, *Gradostroitel'stvo Rossii*, 214–46.
54 PSZ RI, collection 2, vol. IV, 1829, № 2902.
55 RGIA, f. 821, op. 8, d. 646, l. 29 ob.-30; I. K. Zagidullin, *Islamskie instituty v Rossiiskoi imperii. Mecheti v evropeiskoi chasti Rossii i Sibiri* (Kazan: Tatarskoe knizhnoe izdatel'stvo, 2007), 234.
56 RGIA, f. 218, op. 4, d. 37, l. 12.
57 PSZ RI, collection 2, vol. XIX, 1844, № 17539.
58 GART, f. 409, op. 15, d. 2.
59 GART, f. 408, op. 3, d. 53.

60 GART, f. 2, op. 7, d. 702.
61 RGIA, f. 821, op. 8, d. 646, l. 1.
62 PSZ RI, collection 2, vol. XXXVII, 1862, № 39044.
63 For mosque architecture of Kazan, see Niiaz Khalitov, *Arkhitektura mechetei Kazani* (Kazan: Tatarskoe knizhnoe izdatel'stvo, 1991).
64 RGIA, f. 821, op. 8, d. 659, l. 3 ob.
65 Ibid, l. 9.
66 RGIA, f. 821, op. 8, d. 659, l. 10, 16; R.R. Salikhov and R.R. Khairutdinov, *Istoricheskie mecheti Kazani* (Kazan: Tatarskoe knizhnoe izdatel'stvo, 2005), 122.
67 GART, f. 2, op. 7, d. 735.
68 GART, f. 2, op. 7, d. 736.
69 GART, f. 2, op. 2, d. 552; f. 2, op. 7, d. 2121.
70 PSZ RI, collection 2, vol. IVIII, 1868, № 45408.
71 A formal distinction between them was established in 1835 by the government of Nicholas I, introducing the norm that synagogues were allowed to be built once a threshold of 80 "Jewish households" was met; prayer houses could be built at 30 households.
72 GART, f. 2, op. 2, d. 12615, l. 28.
73 Ibid.
74 Ibid, l. 28ob.
75 Ibid, l. 27ob.
76 Ibid, l. 33.
77 Ibid, l. 28, 18.
78 Ibid, l. 42, 45.
79 GART, f. 2, op. 7, d. 1423, l. 38.
80 GART, f. 2, op. 7, d. 2121, l. 19–19ob.
81 Ibid, l. 20.
82 Ibid, l. 10ob.
83 GART, f. 2, op. 7, d. 1423, l. 25.
84 GART, f. 1, op. 4, d. 881, l. 1.
85 Ibid, l. 2.
86 GART, f. 2, op. 7, d. 1423, l. 38.
87 GART, f. 2, op. 7, d. 2121, l. 12ob.–13ob., 40.
88 PSZ RI, collection 2, vol. XVI, 1841, № 15026.
89 G.G. Nugmanova, "Tatarskaia gorodskaia usad'ba Kazani serediny XIX – nachala XX veka" (Kand. diss. State Institute for Art Studies, 2000).
90 G.G. Nugmanova, "Sennaia ploshchad' v Kazani: istoriia formirovaniia, Tatarskie slobody Kazani: ocherki istorii," in *Taraskie slobody Kazani*, ed. R.R. Salikhov and R.R. Khairutdinov (Kazan: Izdatel'stvo Instituta Istorii Academii Nauk Respubliki Tatarstan, 2002), 80–131.
91 GART, f. 2, op. 1, d. 23, l. 653.
92 Shagabutdin Mardzhani, *Mustafadel'-achbar fi achvali Kazan va Bolgar* (Kazan: Kazan, 1989), 206–07. [In Tatar].
93 Nugmanova. "Sennaia ploshchad."
94 Alexander Etkind, *Internal Colonization. Russia's Imperial Experience* (Cambridge: Polity Press, 2011); Aleksandr Etkind, Dirk Uffelman, and Ilia Kukulin, *Tam, vnutri. Praktiki vnutrennei kolonizatsii v kul'turnoi istorii Rossii* (Moscow: Novoe literaturnoe obozrenie, 2012).

Bibliography

Archives

Kazan Federal University Nikolay Lobachevsky Scientific Library, Department of Rare Books and Manuscripts.
Russian State Historical Archive (RGIA)
f. 218: Departament iskusstvennykh del Glavnogo upravlenia putei soobshenia i publichnykh zdanii.
f. 821: Departament dukhovnykh del inostrannykh ispovedanii MVD
f. 1399: Karty, plany I chertazhi Peterburgskogo Senatskogj Archiva
f. 1488: Plany, chertezhy grazhdanskoi architectury
State Archive of the Republic of Tatarstan (GART)
F. 1: Kantseliaria Kazanskogo gubernatora
F. 2: Kazanskoe gubernskoe pravlenie
F. 4: Kazanskaia dukhovnaia konsistoria
F. 87: Pervaya kazanskaya muzhskaya gimnazia
F. 98: Kazanskaia gorodskaia uprava
F. 408: Kazanskaia gubernskaia stroitel'naia i dorozhnaia komissia
F. 409: Kazanskaia gubernskaia stroitel'naia komissia
F. 977: Kazanskii Universitet

Literature

Benkendorf, Alexander. "Zapiski grafa A.Kh. Benkendorfa (1832–1837 gg.)." In *Imperator Nikolai I.: Ego zhizn' i tsarstvovanie: Primechania i dopolnenia ko vtoromu tomu,* edited by N.K. Shil'der, 647–764. St. Petersburg: A.S. Suvorin, 1903.
Chuiko, V.V., ed. *Vol'ter i Ekaterina II.* Translated by V.V. Chuiko. St. Petersburg: Novosti, 1882.
Etkind, Alexander. *Internal Colonization. Russia's Imperial Experience.* Cambridge: Polity Press, 2011.
Etkind, Aleksandr, Dirk Uffel'man, and Ilia Kukulin. *Tam, vnutri. Praktiki vnutrennei kolonizatsii v kul'turnoi istorii Rossii.* Moscow: Novoe literaturnoe obozrenie, 2012.
Evsina, N.A. "Progressivnye traditsii v arkhitekture russkikh uchebnykh zavedenii epokhi klassitsizma." Kand. diss., State Institute for Art Studies, 1967.
Geraci, Robert. *Window on the East: National and Imperial Identities in Late Tsarist Russia.* Ithaca, NY and London: Cornell University Press, 2001.
Ibneeva, Guzel. "Puteshestvie Ekateriny II po Volge v 1767 godu: uznavanie imperii." *Ab Imperio,* V. 2 (2000): 87–104.
Khalitov, Niiaz. *Arkhitektura mechetei Kazani.* Kazan: Tatarskoe knizhnoe izdatel'stvo, 1991.
Kirichenko, E.I. *Gradostroitel'stvo Rossii serediny XIX – nachala XX veka.* Vol. 1, edited by E.I. Kirichenko. Moscow: Progress-Traditsia, 2001.

Kirichenko, E.I. "Imperatorskii Rim v stolitsakh Frantsuzskoi i Rossiiskoi imperi." In *Stil' Ampir*. Architektura v istorii russkoi lul'tury 5, edited by I.A. Bondarenko, 29–35. Moskow: Rokhos, 2003.

Kirichenko, E.I. "Kazanskii sobor v Peterburge Pavla I." In *Andrei Nikiforovich Voronikhin*, edited by IU.G. Bobrov, 49–56. St. Petersburg: Kolomenskaya versta, 2010.

Krylov, M.K. *Plan g. Kazani sostavlen soglasno proekta, utverzhdennogo v 1884 g.* Kazan: V.M. Kluchnikov, 1884.

Malov, Efimii. *Kazanskii Bogoroditskii Devichii monastyr'*. Kazan: Kazan University, 1879.

Mardzhani, Shihabeddin. *Mustafadel'-achbar fi achvali Kazan va Bolgar*. Kazan: Tatarskoe knizhnoe izdatel'stvo, 1989. [In Tatar]

Nugmanova, G.G. "Tatarskaia gorodskaia usad'ba Kazani serediny XIX – nachala XX veka." Kand. diss., State Institute for Art Studies, 2000.

Nugmanova, G.G. "Sennaia ploshchad' v Kazani: istoriia formirovaniia." In *Tatarskie slobody Kazani*, edited by R.R. Salikhov and R.R. Khairutdinov, 80–131. Kazan: Izdatel'stvo Instituta Istorii Academii Nauk Respubliki Tatarstan, 2002.

Pinegin, Mikhail. *Kazan' v ee proshlom i nastoiashchem*. Kazan: Globus, 2005. First published 1890 by Dubrovin (St. Petersburg).

Plokhy, Serhii. *The Origin of the Slavic Nations. Premodern Identities in Russia, Ukraine, and Belarus*. New York: Cambridge University Press, 2006.

Polnoe sobranie zakonov Rossiiskoi imperii, collection 1, vol. XVI, 1763, № 11883.

Polnoe sobranie zakonov Rossiiskoi imperii, collection 2, vol. I, 1825–1826, № 794.

Polnoe sobranie zakonov Rossiiskoi imperii, collection 2, vol. IV, 1829, № 2902.

Polnoe sobranie zakonov Rossiiskoi imperii, collection 2, vol. XVI, 1841, № 15026.

Polnoe sobranie zakonov Rossiiskoi imperii, collection 2, vol. XIX, 1844, № 17539.

Polnoe sobranie zakonov Rossiiskoi imperii, collection 2, vol. XXXVII, 1862, № 39044.

Polnoe sobranie zakonov Rossiiskoi imperii, collection 2, vol. IVIII, 1868, № 45408.

Salikhov, R.R., and R.R. Khairutdinov. *Istoricheskie mecheti Kazani*. Kazan: Tatarskoe knizhnoe izdatel'stvo, 2005.

Shpilevskii, Sergei. *Zaboty imperatora Aleksandra I o Kazani. Rech', proiznesennaia ordinarnym professorom S.M. Shpilevskim v torzhestvennom sobranii Imperatorskogo Kazanskogo universiteta 12 dekabria 1877 g. v iubileinyj den' stoletiia rozhdeniia imperatora Aleksandra I*. Kazan: Kazan University, 1877.

Sooruzhenie i otkrytie pamiatnika imperatoru Aleksandru II v Kazani: Kratkii istoricheskii ocherk. Kazan: V.M. Kliuchnikov v Kazani, 1896.

Wortman, Richard. *Scenarios of Power: Myth and Ceremony in Russian Monarchy. Vol. 1: From Peter the Great to the Death of Nicholas I*. Princeton, NJ: Princeton University Press, 1995.

Zagidullin, I.K. *Islamskie instituty v Rossiiskoi imperii. Mecheti v evropeiskoi chasti Rossii i Sibiri*. Kazan: Tatarskoe knizhnoe izdatel'stvo, 2007.

Zagoskin, Nikolai. *Istoriia Imperatorskogo Kazanskogo universiteta za pervye sto let ego sushestvovaniia 1804–1814*. Vol. 1. Kazan: Imperial Kazan University Press, 1902.

Zagoskin, Nikolai. *Sputnik po Kazani. Illiustrirovannyi ukazatel' dostoprimechatel' nostei i spravochnaia knizhka goroda*. Kazan: Globus, 2005. First published 1895 by Kazan University (Kazan).

Zelenetskii, Aleksandr. *Osviashchenie khrama vo imia Rozhdestva Presviatoi Bogoroditsy i chasovni na meste iavleniia Kazanskoi chudotvornoi ikony Bozh'ei Materi v pamiat' trekhsotletiia tsarstvovaniia Doma Romanovykh*. Kazan: Tsentral'naia tipografia, 1914.

6 Bound by Difference

The Merger of Rostov and Nakhichevan-on-Don into an Imperial Metropolis during the Nineteenth Century

Michel Abesser

Nikolai E. Vrangel, a Baltic noble, businessman, and father to the famous White Army General Piotr N. Vrangel, arrived in Rostov in 1879, eagerly awaiting new challenges. He was involved in the Russian Steam Navigation and Trading Company and was amazed by the opportunities offered by the city's dynamic population growth and the expansion in its trade and industry. For most of his contemporaries in Moscow and St. Petersburg, the city and its surrounding region had remained peripheral terra incognito for most parts of the nineteenth century. In his memoirs, written in German exile and characterized by nostalgia for the vanished Russian Empire, Vrangel describes Rostov:

> This absolutely unique city didn't remind one of the average Russian centers. It arose and grew independently and silently like the cities in free Amerika, but not by the power of bureaucrats that governed Russia, not by the strong nobility, the rich merchants, or the enlightened intelligentsia, but by men, dark people [simple peasants], gathered from all corners of Russia.[1]

While Vrangel later goes on to idealize this stratum of true peasants as the means to resurrect "dead Russia" from Bolshevik rule, the dynamics of demographic growth and city development laid out here by Vrangel seem unusual for an autocratic and estate-based empire.

Rostov developed in the second half of the eighteenth century from a small suburb of the Russian military fortress St. Dmitri Rostovski on the embankment of the Don, 46 kilometers above its estuary where it spilled into the Sea of Azov. Within half a century, the city had transformed into one of the Russian Empire's foremost Black Sea ports and economic centers due to its beneficial geographic location, the unusual migration dynamics described by Vrangel, and a unique proximity to the Armenian colony of Nakhichevan, located a few kilometers east of Rostov on the other side of the military fortress of St. Dmitri. Nakhichevan was founded at the end

DOI: 10.4324/9781003130031-8

of the eighteenth century and flourished due to privileges granted by Empress Catherine II to thousands of Armenian merchants and peasants who left their homeland in Crimea. During the first half of the nineteenth century, the Armenian community of Nakhichevan, bestowed with trade and self-administration privileges, became a vital node in trade and artisanship networks in the Black Sea region. In Vrangel's narrative, which refers to the 1870s, Nakhichevan is mostly absent, likely because both cities had grown by then into one urban area. Nevertheless, Nakhichevan remained an independent city.

From Vrangel's perspective, Nakhichevan appeared as the loser in a century-long quest for modernization. He attributed part of Rostov's success to mistakes made by the Armenian local government – for example, sending energetic and talented settlers away. These would go on to populate Rostov. Similarly, the Armenians of Nakhichevan failed to "get along with the engineers," which would result in the construction of the junction station of the new railroad in Rostov instead.[2] Although historically doubtful in its details, Vrangel's general overview was accurate. From the second half of the nineteenth century, Rostov outranked Nakhichevan in terms of size and demographic and economic growth. In 1914, Rostov ranked among the three fastest-growing urban economies of the empire.

The argument that Nakhichevan paled into insignificance is, however, problematic, both for the difficulties in distinguishing the two cities from one another and their intermingled socioeconomic development from the late eighteenth century. As regional maps from the 1850s on suggest, it was difficult to differentiate the two cities. A geographical survey from 1862 suggests that both would "comprise a coherent territorial whole but not an administrative one."[3] The leading encyclopedia *Brokgauz-Efron* reminded its readers in 1897: "Recently Nakhichevan has expanded towards Rostov so drastically that one needs to look into the old plan of 1811 to rediscover their actual political border."[4] Leaving the administrative division aside for a moment, both cities constituted one urban conglomerate of imperial importance.

To a certain extent, the territorial segregation of its populations resembled that of colonial cities in other parts of the world, but with a genuine "native population" absent. Both displayed features of a settler city based on city plans made of rectangular grid systems subdivided into building blocks.[5] Yet, Russians and Armenians never positioned themselves in a hierarchical relationship typical of European colonialism. While ethnicity played an important role in demarcating administrative order and privileges and as a marker of nationality in the late nineteenth century, class remained an equally important category for framing conflict and cooperation that could at times transgress ethnic boundaries. Both populations embody key features of the Russian imperial experience – namely, ethnic utilization and (the limits of) migration management. From the seventeenth to the early twentieth century, the crown made use, to varying degrees, of Armenian merchants, peasants, and clerics with the aim of positioning the empire within Eurasian trade networks and colonizing the expanding southern periphery. Of the empire's Armenian colonies, Nakhichevan on Don allows for the best long-term micro perspective on how these goals evolved and changed locally through negotiation and conflict.

Rostov's increased pace of development from the 1840s, on the other hand, was fueled by waves of uncontrolled migration from the Russian heartland and the Ukrainian territories. It is precisely this uncontrolled migration that Vrangel idealized in his retrospective view of Rostov. The city's history sheds particular light on the limits of autocratic control over the Russian imperial expanse, both in terms of strategies for urban development and control of the movement of its people. At the same time, Rostov remained noticeably absent from imperial projections until the beginning of the twentieth century. While it became the undisputable economic center of the Don Region, the Russian Empire imagined and administered this area mainly as the heartland of the Don Cossacks according to political premises that prioritized maintaining their military capabilities. Only from the early twentieth century onward did the state adjust its politics to the cities' size and economic importance. Rostov, then the third-largest export hub of the empire, was promoted to the status of a *gradonachal'stvo*, a status reserved for larger or strategically important cities. Making Rostov a main administrative center of the south did late justice to the results of a long-term process of urban development the empire had set in motion by nurturing the Armenian colony of Nakhichevan a century earlier, while not deploying a particular imperial vision and strategy for Rostov's fate during the nineteenth century. Both Rostov and Nakhichevan merged during the nineteenth century and embodied particular characteristics of Russian imperial policy that shaped their socioeconomic as well as urban development significantly. Nakhichevan became an early embodiment of imperial policy toward the Armenians, rendering them "agents and recipients"[6] of Russian imperialism. Rostov testifies to the importance of social and economic forces that had been unleashed but could not entirely be controlled by the Russian autocracy. The discrepancy between its geographical and economic importance and the lack of a coherent political strategy toward its development makes the "Imperial Cities" prism suitable for further exploring inherent tensions of center-periphery relations for urbanization in Eurasian land empires.

Thus, an isolated perspective of one of the two cities based on their administrative division – a division that was only resolved by the Bolsheviks in 1929 – does not do justice to the importance of this dual urban structure for the dynamic of imperial development in the Don region. Residents would develop converging or conflicting local identities through daily interaction, and infrastructural challenges that would require the cooperation of local elites with neighbors would be subjected to very different systems of administration and taxation. Before many of these systems had been homogenized in the course of the Great Reforms of Alexander II that took place from 1856 on, the two adjacent cities resembled an "Empire of Difference," as the Russian Empire has been characterized,[7] in miniature.

The second reason for the argument against Nakhichevan's paling into insignificance is, however, even more important. To understand Rostov's economic success between the foundation of a Russian customs post in 1749 on the Don and the Revolutions of 1917, we have to understand the intermingled dynamics of the Armenian colony and the Russian town. Contrary to Vrangel's interpretation, Rostov's success very much depended on Nakhichevan. Rostov's economic and demographic boom in the second half of the nineteenth century heavily relied on the trade networks, markets, and production that the Armenians had established in the first half of the nineteenth century. Between its foundation and the conquest of the Caucasus in the mid-nineteenth century, Nakhichevan served as a hub linking the Armenians as imperial mediators of diplomatic and economic interests with St. Petersburg, the Ottoman world, and the Caucasus. A gradual succession between Nakhichevan and Rostov as motors of regional development set in from the 1830s onward, a process accompanied by constant conflict and negotiation between the two communities. The resulting regional dynamic of this succession laid the foundation of what enthusiastic historians have referred to as the "Rostov miracle"[8] from the 1860s onward; but perhaps more importantly, it speaks to the unique historical experience of empire-building through cities that characterized the northern Black Sea littoral during the first half of the nineteenth century, before the Great Reforms.

The following chapter argues that four particular features distinguish the conglomerate of Rostov and Nakhichevan from other imperial cities of the late Russian Empire as an imperial center and gateway to the south and the Black Sea. These are (a) a lack of a cohesive imperial design and development plan from St. Petersburg (as Vrangel and other contemporaries already observed), (b) a peculiar succession between the two cities as motors for developing the region and adjacent networks, (c) an intensive interaction between its inhabitants, and (d) the gradual merging of these two towns into one urban conglomerate. A perspective on the entangled history of Rostov and Nakhichevan allows for a debate about the varieties of administrative, economic, and socio-ethnic markers suitable for defining the boundaries between imperial cities and their surrounding regions. Politically defined as a community of taxpayers with very limited opportunities for self-administration, Rostov and Nakhichevan, both part the governorate of Ekaterinoslav, formed an administrative exclave within the Don-Cossack territories of the upper Don River lands and its delta in the southwest. Given the increased economic and demographic entanglement between the exclave and the Don Cossack territory, an argument could be made for an imperial region as well. If we think of the interethnic division of labor as one characteristic of imperial cities in Eurasian empires, a strict delimitation of urban and rural becomes more complicated – all the more so as economic entanglements in the case of Rostov and Nakhichevan subverted the high density of administrative demarcations dividing the local imperial subjects into different legal regimes.

The first section of this chapter focuses on the two cities' emergence, their economic profile, and interaction in the period between the late eighteenth and mid-nineteenth centuries, positioning the two within the southern Russian provinces that experienced a profound social, ethnic, and economic transformation during this period. The chapter addresses in particular the economic dimension of the cities' trade, industry, and markets that allows us to approach the question of succession between the two as well as changes in the ethnic division of labor, characteristic of the empire until the mid-nineteenth century. The second section aims at exploring how during the nineteenth-century local cooperation between the neighboring communities gradually superseded various outstanding conflicts, while still leaving tensions that might occasionally burst into the open. Disputes about the uses of land and the river Don as the lifeline for both cities shed light on conflicting concepts of justice that were projected by these neighboring communities. The final part engages with the loss of political privileges of Nakhichevan during the Great Reforms and the final decades of the Russian Empire in which the increasingly multiethnic society of the imperial metropolis was transformed through rapid socioeconomic modernization, which included both greater prosperity as well as an increase of nationalism.

Dynamic Imperial Periphery of the South – Trade and Urbanization in the Pre-Reform Period

As for the appropriation of New Russia at large, the eighteenth-century history of Rostov and its beginnings reflect the connection between military and economic motives of imperial expansion.[9] In 1749, the Russian government established a customs post where the city would later be located. This was a response to the increased trade between Don Cossacks and Ottoman subjects, most of them either Armenians or Greek who were traveling through the Sea of Azov and the mouth of the Don upstream. After Russia lost its newly conquered possessions on the Sea of Azov to the Ottoman Empire in the Peace of Pruth of 1711, the territorial regulations of the Peace of Belgrade in 1739 made the area the only bottleneck through which limited exchange to the Black Sea world was possible. Rostov's early urban development thus relied on the preexisting transport routes and trade hubs of the Russian-Ottoman borderlands.

The founding of the fortress of St. Dmitri Rostovski in 1761 would play a crucial role in finally subjecting the Don Cossacks to imperial control and also in the military campaigns of the Russian-Ottoman Wars (1768–1774, 1787–1791), including equipping a Don flotilla.[10] The Don and the Zaporozhian Cossacks were the two largest Cossack societies that originated in the autonomous East Slavic nomad warrior communities of the fifteenth-century "wild field" located between the Russian and Ottoman Empire and Polish-Lithuanian Commonwealth. After the Muscovite Empire had relied on Cossacks in its successful campaigns against Poland-Lithuania and the Ottoman Empire in the sixteenth and seventeenth centuries, Russia's gradual expansion into the Black Sea region was accompanied by the Cossack's subjugation to the crown, the end of their political independence, and integration into the empire. The fortresses' patron Dmitri Rostovski (who would later give his name to Rostov) symbolized the particular imperial vision that the crown projected onto this construction. Dmitri, born Daniil Tuptalo of Zaporozhian Cossack origins in 1651, would rise through the clergy as a pious reformer and composer of church music who loyally supported Peter the Great. Canonized in 1757, Dmitri's biography reflected the subjugation of the Cossacks to the Russian crown, positing an idealized mutual relationship between social promotion and loyalty.

Given the enormous distance between the imperial center and this periphery, separated by the steppe (often referred to as an "ocean" by contemporaries), state control over as vast an area as the Don region remained volatile. Its attempts to control migration processes into these new territories constitute a case in point. A constant task the fortress garrisons undertook was to send out expeditions throughout the district to catch runaway serfs, while the crown regularly reminded Cossack atamans to dispatch fugitive peasants back to their masters in the north.[11] As with other areas of the Northern Black Sea coast, the fortress and its beneficial location attracted a growing number of migrants, mainly from Ukrainian territories. The growing suburb east of the fortress would be granted the status of a city in 1802. At the time, the town had approximately 3,000 residents (Figure 6.1).[12]

Nakhichevan and its five surrounding villages were founded in 1779 by Armenians resettled from the Crimean Khanate. The process of resettlement, set into motion by Catherine II, drained the weakened Crimean Khanate of its most important economic actors and became part of the grander scheme of the empress and Count Potemkin of settling non-Russians with

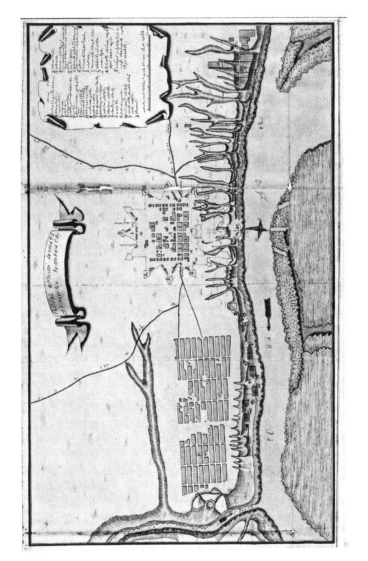

Figure 6.1 Map of Rostov-on-Don from 1768 by Alexander Rigelman.

Source: Vernadsky National Library of Ukraine, Kiev Institute of Handwritings, f. 1, d. 292.
It depicts the St. Dmitri Fortress in the center, a larger suburb west of it that would become Rostov, and a smaller one in the east whose inhabitants would later be resettled, with the Armenians of Nakhichevan taking their place.

beneficial skills and crafts to transform the "wild field" of southern Russia into a prosperous region. The court's constant support for the Armenian settlements was founded on historical experiences of the seventeenth century when the Russian state had started providing Armenian communities with privileges and monopolies over long-distance trade to benefit from their trading networks linking India and Persia with Western Europe.[13] The Archbishop of all Armenians in the Empire Iosif Argutinsky (Ovsep Arlutyan), who was closely associated with the empress and aware of the economic potential of Nakhichevan for the Russian state, became an ardent and influential supporter of the project. He advocated for financial support, a generous assignment of land, and a set of far-reaching privileges.[14] Benefitting from the privileges of self-government, the remission of taxes and services, and generous financial support from Armenian communities in Persia and India, Nakhichevan quickly became a flourishing town of traders and craftsmen with 5,000 residents at the turn of the century.[15] The community of settlers originated from very different social and economic backgrounds in Crimea, ranging from poor peasants of the hinterland to well-connected and prosperous merchants from the trading port of Kaffa/Feodosia. The new economic and political conditions for trade and production in Nakhichevan seem to have offered opportunities for upward mobility to many of them.[16]

While the Russian Empire's acquisition and development of the territories of New Russia can by no means be described as a linear success story, Armenian trade and its networks, in addition to the establishment of various crafts and their influence on the regional economy, add up to a relative success story of enlightened colonialism.[17] Flocks of goats and sheep, many of them imported from Crimea, provided local crafts with the necessary raw materials. Tanneries, soap and candle making, and wool-washing facilities were established on the embankment of the river. Saddle and shoe-making were among the first industries to flourish within the city. Soon more elaborate crafts developed, depending on imported materials from the inland such as iron, copper, silver, and gems, as well as raw silk from the Persian Empire, which Armenian artisans transformed into agricultural tools and weapons, as well as jewelry and more refined silk cloth. By 1825, statistics counted 33 manufactories (among them fish and meat processing, tanning, paper production, and others) in Nakhichevan, while Taganrog, the administrative center 80 kilometers west on the shores of the Sea of Azov, had 26, and Rostov only 12. In 1822, there were 2,940 registered craftsmen (out of a total population of approximately 8,000).[18] The Armenians of Nakhichevan also occupied a superior position compared to the empire's other Armenian communities. Its artisans and merchants contributed more than half of the total guild fees while constituting less than one-third of the empire's Armenian population (Figure 6.2).[19]

Armenian artisan products satisfied the small but growing demand among the Cossack population and the surrounding villages. Extensive networks of Armenian merchants distributed saddles, jewelry, or weapons to the Caucasus; delivered caviar and silk via ship to the Ottoman Empire and the Mediterranean; and transported cattle and horses acquired in the steppes and foothills of the Caucasus to Moscow and Poland, supplying armies and the central European market. Soon after their resettlement, trade networks to the Armenian communities of the Caucasus and in Astrakhan that had been interrupted were renewed and expanded. This allowed access to annual cattle markets in Russian fortresses of the

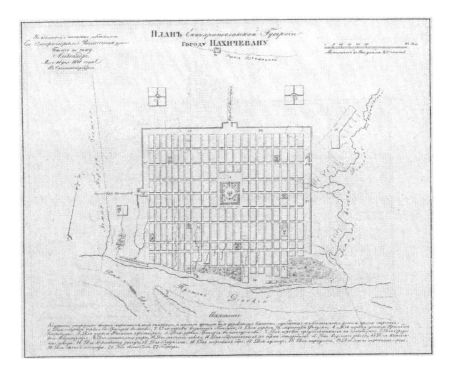

Figure 6.2 Official plan for Nakhichevan from 1811.

Source: Polnoe Sobranie Zakonov Rossiiskoi Imperii (sobranie pervoe), Kniga chertezhei i risunkov (plany gorodov) [Complete Collection of Laws of the Russian Empire (first collection), Book of drawings and illustrations (town plans)], St. Petersburg (Tipografiia II Otdeleniia Sobstvennoi E. I. V. Kantseliarii), 1839.

The Church of Gregory the Illuminator, the main Apostol of the Armenian Church, and the surrounding market rows form the very center of the city whose most prominent feature became the rectangular grid system. Production facilities were mostly located on the Don embankment, while the line in the west demarcates the border to Rostov and the wriggled line in the east the border to the Don Cossack territories.

Caucasian foothills and fostered trade relations with the peoples of Circassia. In 1808, 50 families moved to Stavropol while retaining strong ties to their home colony. Later similar networks were established toward Ekaterinodar (today Krasnodar) and Yeisk in the Azov and Eastern Black Sea region, while Nakhichevanians gradually expanded their ties to Voronezh and the centers of Ukrainian provinces, such as Kharkov (Ukr. Kharkiv) and Kiev (Ukr. Kyiv).[20] These networks transformed the area into an exchange hub between East and West, North and South, but also between the empire and the Black Sea world.[21]

When compared to other new cities of Southern Russia, Rostov provides an interesting case study for an imperial city as it received much less attention and imperial "nourishment" than, for instance, Odessa (Ukr. Odesa) or the capital of the Don Cossack Host Novocherkassk that quickly gained military and strategic importance after its founding.[22] Within this region, which was at some distance even from the regional capital of Ekaterinoslav (today Ukr. Dnipro), Taganrog had been favored and was promoted by St. Petersburg as the administrative center of the area. This was partially due to its historical importance as it was founded by Peter the Great, thus preserving some semblance of continuity after the Russians regained control from the Ottomans in 1776. At the same time, Taganrog's position directly on the Sea of Azov seemed better for trade than Rostov's river location. Taganrog's unfavorable geographical conditions for export by ship came into play only during the course of the nineteenth century, when bigger ships struggled with the shallow waters of its docks. The shoals of the Don river-mouth were equally perilous, yet Rostov's position as a terminal of the Don River ship trade networks and main storage point for various goods from central Russia and the Urals shifted the balance from Taganrog toward Rostov by skipping one additional step of transshipping.

Given the preference St. Petersburg gave to Taganrog during the late nineteenth century, the customs post that had served as a nucleus for the first settlement and the construction of the fortress of St. Dmitri was moved to Taganrog in 1776, seven years after Russian troops had regained control over the city. In 1803, Rostov, Nakhichevan, and Mariupol were subjected to the Taganrog *gradonachal'stvo* "for the benefit of Taganrog trade."[23] The imperial administration excluded important seaports such as Odessa, Nikolaev (today Ukr. Mykolaiv), and Taganrog from the governorates of the New Russian provinces and organized them as territorial units called *gradonachal'stvo*, for better control and more direct promotion of economic and demographic development. A *gradonachal'stvo* was a territorial-administrative unit in the late Russian Empire. It consisted of larger or strategically important cities and their surrounding lands, administered by a *gradonachal'nik*. Excluded from the territory and administration of their respective guberniya, these territorial units were directly subject to a general governor and the Ministry of Interior for more direct control of their development, determined both by status (Moscow, St. Petersburg) and/or strategic location (Sevastopol, Odessa). During the first third of the nineteenth century, Taganrog remained the main port with the customs and quarantine posts, staple right, the trade court, and the first state gymnasium in the region.[24] In 1835, Rostov was separated again from the Taganrog *gradonachal'stvo* and subjected to the Ekaterinoslav governorate administration that resided in the distant provincial capital Ekaterinoslav. The history of Rostov and Nakhichevan in the first half of the nineteenth century illustrates that St. Petersburg overestimated the importance of port cities directly on the Sea of Azov. The location on the river Don provided the city with a decisive geographical advantage, opening up a natural economic hinterland extending to the Urals and the central grain areas in the Russian heartland. Furthermore, Rostov's geographical importance grew over every decade of imperial engagement in the Caucasus, both as an important hub for military deployment and supply and as a port for expanding trade relations with the so-called "mountain people."

Certain interventions by the imperial authorities into Rostov's fate during the first half of the nineteenth century influenced its economic development significantly. The fortress of St. Dmitry had already lost its primary military importance following the peace treaties of Küçük Kaynarca in 1774 and particularly Adrianople in 1829, which had moved the Russian-Ottoman border to the Caucasus and the Danube. Rostov's fortress was consequentially dismantled in 1835, and its space was quickly occupied by new buildings and streets. The imperial authorities in St. Petersburg lacked a coherent vision for the development of the Don region other than its military importance as a privileged area for the Don Cossacks. In this period, a more elaborated regional policy would depend on a more differentiated knowledge of the region's dynamics and an understanding of the city's economic potential. The renewed establishment of a customs post in Rostov in 1836 dramatically transformed the city's importance from military to economic. The closer proximity of Count Mikhail S. Vorontsov, the energetic governor of New Russia (1823–1844) residing in Odessa, resulted in a cohesive strategy for managing migration and developing the economy of the region.[25] Establishing the customs post considerably eased exports, thus boosting Rostov's economic development, and significantly increased the financial scope of its administration, 35 years prior to the reform of the city administration that laid the foundation of an independent, yet limited city budget in the empire's cities. Vorontsov ordered ten percent of the revenue to be allocated to the city's annual budget. Within just ten years, the trade volume in Rostov increased 30 times, surpassing that of the *gradonachal'stvo* of Taganrog. While the total volume of trade in 1823 was under 150,000 silver rubles, the opening of the customs post increased the volume from 342,000 rubles in 1836 to 2.8 million ten years later.[26]

The year 1836 became a watershed for the increasingly interconnected economies of Rostov and Nakhichevan. The export trade in Nakhichevan experienced a "death blow"[27] by the customs post's installation, which led to an outflow of Armenian firms and capital to Rostov. While before, both cities' embankments would be used to store and transship goods on their way to Taganrog, Rostov now directly drew most of the goods dedicated for export. Still, in 1833, Nakhichevan outranked Rostov in terms of population (approx. 14,000/8,500), stone houses (228/22), merchants (191/153), and also shops (647/40; Taganrog: 188).[28] However, the influence of Armenians on Rostov's local economy and its practices since the beginning of the nineteenth century had provided many opportunities for Russian merchants, peasants, and artisans to build upon. Only later would these processes eventually lead to an inversion of the economic relations. While Armenian brick factories provided the very building material needed for Rostov's growth, Armenian windmills, more efficient with their rotating house and windmill sails that could be permanently adapted to changing wind, also processed much of the region's grains until the 1870s. The economic success of Rostov's two annual fairs in the mid-nineteenth century was based on an increased demand from peasants, Cossacks, nomads, and merchants from the region and more distant parts of the empire that Armenian crafts- and tradesmen had created and supplied in the first decades of the century. Nakhichevanean industries such as tanning, candle making, tool manufacture, or wine and liquor production increased the city's attraction for merchants from Odessa and abroad, who settled permanently in Rostov or opened a branch of their own business there. As early as the mid-nineteenth century, Rostov offered not only the chance for merchants to export raw materials but also, increasingly, ways of processing them locally before export. More importantly for merchants from Rostov, their Armenian counterparts would provide credit for more elaborate business operations, which in an age of a chronic capital shortage and lack of banks provided a significant locational advantage. At times, Russian merchants achieved temporary access to Armenian trade networks to purchase rare goods from greater distances.[29] The contact with Armenian and Western merchants influenced (local) Russian economic culture, a culture that in the pre-Reform period was generally dominated by "suspicion and mistrust of the commercial Armenians."[30] Being exposed to the successful business practices of Armenian merchants in close proximity could encourage Russian merchants to adapt.

A prominent characteristic of Armenian business practices was the eagerness to keep revenues and expenses balanced and, if need be, radically cut expenses. Much of the Armenians' reputation among Russian merchants as greedy derived from this economic behavior, today considered rational.[31] Accordingly, merchants would purchase goods at the end of trade fairs around Rostov, when prices would have dropped. Repeatedly, this caused their Russian counterparts to complain to the head of the *gradonachal'stvo* in Taganrog about the Armenians' "unchristian trading practices,"[32] reflecting both Russians' more customary and traditional forms of exchange as well as the deployment of religious differences for "othering" the economic competition vis-à-vis the authorities. However, the practices of Rostov merchants' economic culture did not remain static and gradually changed with the city's burgeoning entanglement with the Black Sea trade. From the 1840s onward, an increasing number of Russian merchants sold their goods at the Rostov trade fair in late summer at prices significantly beyond the value of the goods. Their aim was to quickly accumulate cash money, in chronically short supply within the country, in order to travel to the northern grain-producing provinces to buy grain and linen seeds; these they could sell to Greek and English traders in Rostov with considerable profit margins.[33] This growing flexibility in the Russian merchant's price calculations is indicative of substantial changes in economic practices and mentality set in motion by cooperation and competition with their Armenian counterparts. Rostov's two annual fairs, which experienced continuous growth since the 1820s, provided appropriate stages for these changes and foreshadowed the future economic dominance of Rostov as a hub for long-distance and regional trade. In the late 1840s, the Rozhdestvo-Bogorodniko fair with a total volume of three million rubles constituted the largest fair in the wider region, outranking the fair of the governorate capital Ekaterinoslav (1,000,000 rubles) and Taganrog (1,200,000 rubles).[34]

The gradual succession of Nakhichevan by Rostov as the economic center over the next three decades is evident from changes in trade volume and structure, modes of production, and the ethnic profile of merchants. In 1862, Nakhichevan still exceeded Rostov in its number of manufacturing facilities (25/20), yet Rostov generated six times as much production value (54,000/300,000 rubles).[35] Tanning, one of the foremost Armenian industries, now generated enormous profits for Russian merchants due to mechanized production processes. Wool washing and processing, another traditional segment of Nakhichevan's early economy, experienced similar mechanization and sectoral boom. The resulting demand for workers who would require some training and qualification in the use of machinery made higher wages necessary. These in turn could cause temporary shortages in the labor market, taking Russian office clerks, for example, away from the Armenian self-administrative organ, the magistrate.[36] Both industries illustrate that the rising entrepreneurial class of Rostov was able to accumulate both professional knowledge and skills and the necessary capital for such ventures. The merchants of Nakhichevan, on the other hand, seem to have been neither willing nor able to accumulate the necessary investments.

However, the statistics of the 1850s suggest further underlying changes in the trade structure of both cities. The small joints and booths of the Nakhichevanian bazaars that many Western visitors admired and colorfully described in their Orientalizing testimonies still outmatched those of Rostov in number (368/211). Nevertheless, professional and bigger shops designated for all-year retail trade now prevailed in Rostov and suggested a more constant and demanding variety of customers.[37]

Rostov's economic prospects as perceived by contemporaries encouraged international trading companies to open representations on the spot and also some of their representatives to settle in the town on a permanent basis. The Greek merchant Ivan Skaramanga, a member of one of the most influential Greek family networks in the Black Sea and the Eastern Mediterranean with offices already existing in Odessa, Nikolaev, Mariupol, and Taganrog, settled in Rostov soon after the customs post went into operation.[38] He extended his family's business activities to grain export from the region and stimulated shipbuilding by lending money to Russian merchants and captains. The first civil shipyard opened in 1837. Within this atmosphere of economic awakening, a report from the Ministry of the Interior in 1840 estimated that Rostov could surpass Odessa as the empire's main export port for grain by the end of the century if a feasible long-term strategy could be found for dealing with the shallows at the mouth of the river Don.[39] For the Russian public in the heart of the empire, however, knowledge of Rostov remained rather vague. The first article with an in-depth description of the city was published only in 1850 in one of the so-called "thick journals" of the epoch.[40] And while the economic trajectories of both cities increasingly diverged, their interrelation and connectedness seem to have prevailed for quite some time in the imagination of the regional public. During a debate about the priority of the port of Taganrog over that of Rostov in 1864, the mayor of Taganrog Nikolai T. Dzhurich concluded an intense argument with his Rostovian counterpart, Andrei M. Baikov, with the statement that "Rostov is being founded by the Armenians who have excessive advantages in trade."[41]

The Region as a Stage for Cohabitation and Conflict

While economic indicators provide the necessary perspective on changes in commerce and production and their related effects on both ethnic societies, negotiations, and conflicts over land and the river Don reveals the dynamics of appropriating the prospective shared urban space of the imperial metropolis. Given the sheer size of the empire and its hierarchical and relatively weak and inefficient bureaucracy, some of these contestations would last for decades until resolved or overtaken by later developments. One central issue between the communities was land. When founding the Armenian colony at the end of the eighteenth century, the imperial state partitioned the land for the fortress and its settlements on terms that very much favored the Armenians. Twenty-four thousand hectares were split into 4,000 for the fortress and 20,000 for the Armenian settlement. More land was added after a land survey of the Don-Cossack areas. The fact that the first decree of Catherine II regarding the colony had granted only 12,000 hectares to Nakhichevan in 1779 suggests that delegates of the Armenian community in the capital had been successful in representing their interests at the court through informal channels.[42]

With the population of Rostov growing significantly faster than that of Nakhichevan from the 1850s on, the proportion of land held by each city served as a constant source of conflict. The Armenian magistrate frequently complained about the "wild settlements" erected by runaway peasants from the center of the empire.[43] These very attempts to uphold authority over an ethnically homogeneous settlement would later inspire Vrangel's comments, cited above, on Nakhichevan "sending away energetic and talented settlers who would then populate Rostov."[44]

Thousands of settlers and adventurers, lured by the promise of economic and social improvement and the myth of a secure space in the south ("From the Don, no one gets handed over" – "S Dona vydachi net"),[45] built houses and huts either close to the Don or to the markets, ignoring borders between the two communities. For Armenians, settling outside their own territory in the late eighteenth century could increase the risk of being robbed or murdered by vagabonds or Cossacks.[46] Several cases of such attacks against residents in the five Armenian villages surrounding Nakhichevan in the early period of the two cities (1790–1820) led the local courts and the commander of the fortress to get involved.[47] The Vicegerent of Taganrog as well as the governor in Ekaterinoslav clearly understood the security issues connected to the question of land property as they reviewed and demanded better protection of such property.

However, the greater share of land for the Armenians remained conditional on its agricultural use. Within the context of the leveling of administrative heterogeneity and privileges from the 1850s on, the state demanded statistics for cattle. According to observers, the Armenian community grossly exaggerated these in order to prevent the transformation of the territory into state land.[48] The Armenians seem to have benefited from the recent experience of the Greek community in Mariupol that had understated the number of their cattle for fear of higher taxation and lost significant parts of their communal land to the state as a result.[49] The uneven distribution of land between the two cities, however, remained unchanged. Up until World War I, Nakhichevan could compensate for its smaller trade revenues in comparison to Rostov by renting land to carpenters, traders, and businessmen, thereby significantly increasing its annual budget.[50]

From the foundation of the settlements onward, the river Don, a trading artery and source of fish, was one of the main reasons for conflict between Armenians in Nakhichevan, the mostly Russian citizens of Rostov, and Cossacks. The arrival of the Armenians amplified the preexisting conflict between Russians settled around the fortress and Cossacks regarding fishing rights in the lower Don and its delta. Don Cossacks felt that their monopoly on fishing and customs-free trade granted by the tsars in the sixteenth and seventeenth centuries, a monopoly that provided them with a considerable source of income, had been violated. The court in St. Petersburg was forced to mediate these conflicts throughout the nineteenth century.[51] The distribution of the Don embankment by the state among the communities resulted in an "equally unequal" distribution: The Imperial Senate fixed the partition of the embankment for the first time in 1812. It granted Rostov the western half of the right embankment where its harbor was located and Nakhichevan the eastern half of the right embankment with its main harbor and the whole of the left embankment opposite both cities and the fortress.[52] An additional small Armenian trade harbor toward the Sea of Azov, however, was located at the mouth of the tributary Temernik, west of Rostov within the territory that had been granted to Rostov. The emerging competition between the two cities as export hubs for grain, iron, meat, and fish unfolded from the early nineteenth century on and resulted in concerted efforts to block Nakhichevan's trade port by merchants from Rostov, who claimed their rights to the area. This led to a drastic drop in Armenian exports from that port between 1820 and 1823 (from 2,229 to 326 tons).[53] In reaction to complaints and petitions by the Armenian magistrate to the chancellery of the governorate and St. Petersburg, the senate reaffirmed the division of the embankment in favor of Rostov in 1828, leaving the Armenian part of the right embankment as Nakhichevan's only remaining port.[54] However, the strategic value of this part increased significantly with the construction of a pontoon bridge across the Don prior to 1825. As a result, an increasing flow of goods from the Caucasus and its foothills arrived in Nakhichevan.[55]

With both the Russian and Armenian trade ports on the right side of the river and the two cities gradually expanding, the officially demarcated borders did not always necessarily correspond to the daily trading practices of storing and repacking the goods. After Vorontsov's installation of the customs post and its contribution of ten percent to Rostov's city budget, the members of the Armenian magistrate argued on spatial grounds for a share of that income. They claimed that many goods were actually stored on Nakhichevan's section of the right embankment of the Don before being shipped and that Rostov already possessed two large fairs that provided considerable sources of income.[56] Although the governor denied the claim by pointing out that only five percent of the exported goods actually came from Nakhichevan, the case set statistical evaluations in motion and increased the attention that the governorate authorities accorded to the prosperity of the cities. Given the practice of exporting goods from the countless warehouses on the right embankment, any distinction between the two cities had already become blurred.

With the two cities gradually emerging as economic centers, the river would turn into a locus of contestation in trade. In 1840, Armenians started building shops on the left embankment of the Don, opposite Rostov's port, and bought most of the incoming food from the surrounding areas, food that previously had been sold directly on the market in Rostov to the urban population of the city.[57] The Cossack providers benefitted from the Armenian restructuring of the region's market, as time and effort for selling their goods on the local market could be spared. According to complaints and petitions by Rostov officials, the resale of fish, grain, vegetables, and meat to the residents of Rostov by Armenians led to an increase in market prices and hardship among the poorer strata of the local population. It remains unclear, however, to what extent increased market prices can really be attributed to the Armenian entry into the food trade in Rostov: neither did an Armenian monopoly exist that would prevent others from entering competition, thus reducing prices, nor can we rule out Rostov's population growth as the key factor for this particular price increase. The imperial authorities, however, seem to have adopted the narrative of the Armenians' economic agility threatening the public order. A year later, the governor would give in to a petition and forbid this form of trade.[58]

In order to adapt both cities to administrative, economic, and infrastructural modernization, the river increasingly required technical, administrative, and financial cooperation. Both city councils collaborated in building a new bridge in the 1860s[59] and in accumulating the financial means to rent an expensive dredge able to deepen the river for the passage of larger ships in 1899.[60] Later on, a common horse tramline serviced main streets and squares in both cities. The Delta Committee, founded in 1865, became an institution of merchants, experts, and state administrators of different nationalities that explored the delta, attracted financial support from the state, and realized different projects to deepen the last 20 kilometers of the river between the cities and the Sea of Azov.[61] In 1916, after dredging the Don Delta's main shipping channel back to a depth of ten feet (approx. three meters) during the summer months, the dredge financed by the Delta Committee would remove a newly emerged sandbar blocking the Nakhichevanean port.[62]

City + City = Metropolis? Homogenization, Multi-Ethnicity, and Nationalism as Factors of Urban Development

The economic and political privileges granted to Nakhichevan by Empress Catherine are key to understanding the success of the colony in its first decades. However, they also caused envy among their immediate neighbors and suspicion and critique within the imperial bureaucracy. Armenians within the empire perceived the final abolishment of local self-administrative privileges in the wake of the Great Reforms in the southern periphery negatively. From the viewpoint of a multiethnic empire, however, this caesura in the city's history and the processes leading to it defy easy interpretation. The 1872 abolition of the magistrate and its substitution with an elected city duma as part of the wider municipal reforms occurred during a distinct period in imperial policy toward the former "wild field." Willard Sunderland has termed this "Reformist Colonization."[63] One overall development during this period was the standardization of state rule and administration in the wake of the Great Reforms, a process that led to the reduction of privileges and special administration for various non-Russian communities, be they German settlers, Armenians, Greeks, or Cossacks. At the same time, Ronald Suny convincingly argues that the 1860s and 1870s were the "zenith of Armenio-Russian collaboration"[64] with respect to their engagement in the campaigns against the Ottoman Empire in the Caucasus with the aim of conquering the historically claimed Eastern Armenian territories.

The Armenian privileges granted by Catherine the Great had been contested since the beginning of the short reign of her son Paul. Catherine's decrees had exempted the colonists from the recruit levy, the poll tax, and other payments; they had established a system of local self-administration with an elected magistrate that exercised judicial and financial authority; and they had guaranteed that the land surrounding the town would be accorded to the Armenians as compensation for property left behind in Crimea. The latter point remained a particular object for dispute. With each new ruler on the Romanov throne, these privileges had to be confirmed, so the Armenian magistrate would assemble a delegation of respected citizens to appeal to the court in St. Petersburg for their confirmation, often supported by high-ranking members of the Armenian-Gregorian clergy or nobles residing in the center, such as members of the Lazarev family.[65] These appeals turned out to be particularly successful in the case of Emperor Paul I, who even granted the privileges in perpetuity (that status was later revoked by Alexander I). Over the course of the nineteenth century, however, several of these privileges were abolished or modified, many in relation to changes in the estate structure of the empire with its attempts to unify categories of economic status.[66]

Prior to the Reform era, there had been attempts by the imperial bureaucracy to focus on conflicting aspects of the two legal systems, aiming in particular at a greater degree of transparency. While conducting an audit of the Taganrog *gradonachal'stvo* in 1844, the St. Petersburg senator Mikhail N. Zhemchuzhnikov complained about conflicts between the Armenian self-administration and Russian law, especially the lack of separation between the judicial and police authority of the Armenian magistrate.[67] Because of his review, the Ministry of Justice created the first Russian translation of the local law code, that originated in the Armenian law code from the older Astrakhan community and the medieval Armenian law code Gosh Mitrash. However, the reform was postponed again until the 1848 creation of a new civil code for the empire as a whole.

Gradual shifts in managing the "empire of difference" also provided potent narratives for various opponents of ethnic and religious privileges, narratives that could mix with emerging notions of Russian nationalism. The previously discussed conflicts reveal that the regional and local elites of the Don and the Ekaterinoslav provinces cultivated an ambivalent position vis-à-vis the Armenian colonists of Nakhichevan and its rural surroundings. The mayor of Rostov from 1862 to 1869 and 1884 to 1889, Baikov showed a rather hostile attitude toward his immediate neighbors. In 1866, the provincial assembly of the Ekaterinoslav Governorate appealed to the Senate demanding the abolition of all Armenian privileges and the "adjustment of judicial practices of the Magistrate."[68] After complaining about the constant refusal and protests of the Armenians to even consider the potential advantages of making local administration more efficient, the assembly petitioners asked:

> And can one still speak of privileges now, when there is one wish in all the Russian lands that all the Russian lands will be pure Russian, that they will be united together, that all living on them will be subjected to one law, carry one burden, and that an end will be put to this existing state within a state, so harmful for the economic life of the people?[69]

The urgency for reform of Nakhichevan's self-administration increased with the continuous inflow of Ukrainian and Russian peasants into the area and the consolidation of the two cities. The Great Reforms of Alexander II aimed at the profound modernization of the state, economy, and societal relations and were built upon the premise of a more efficient administrative and legal system and corresponding state institutions. A leveling of differences in the administrative and judicial systems coexisting within the empire was a direct consequence of these reforms, fostered particularly by a new generation of bureaucrats.[70] The Judicial Reform from 1864 and the imperial decree "Rules on the abolition of magistrates and judicial town halls" from 1866 set into motion the process of dismantling Armenian self-administration. The first step occurred in 1868 when police authority was separated from the magistrate and Nakhichevan became part of the Rostov police district administration. Although available statistics for 1866 indicate a crime rate four times lower than for Rostov, tight budgets meant that the magistrate constantly struggled to hire enough policemen.[71] After the extension of the system of city dumas to all the cities of the empire in 1870, a new duma in Nakhichevan was elected in 1872, ending the city's status as an autonomous colony.

The privileges granted by Catherine in the spirit of enlightened absolutism fell victim to an expanding and homogenizing imperial state whose politics of modernization would increasingly overlap with politics directed against non-Russian nationalities in other regions of the empire. Some local elites framed these claims of homogenization as genuine Russian interest, while some non-Russians criticized the abolition of seemingly effective organs of self-administration. Yet a closer look at the magistrate as an urban institution does not lead to a glowing assessment of the local Armenian pre-reform institutions. The position of the Armenian mayor, once in office, remained virtually uncontested and uncontrolled. Office-holders tried to circumvent checks by the so-called "five-head duma," whose election was often influenced by the mayor in order to surround himself with close allies and relatives.[72] Gaps in record keeping indicate a lack of transparency and prolonged inquiries by skeptical imperial authorities. Attentive Western visitors characterized the institution of the mayor as an archaic, patriarchal, and traditional form of authority.[73] The local court systems as well as the police seem to have been increasingly beleaguered with cases deriving from the growing (illegal) inflow of working migrants from the Russian heartland. Here, the intervention of the imperial state also meant more competent personnel and resources. Accordingly, the majority of the city's population reacted rather indifferently to the closure of the magistrate. As Levon V. Batiev has noted, there were no public protests.[74] Even though one of the motives for the reform articulated by regional bureaucrats was the adaptation of local government to the increased influx of Russians into the community of Nakhichevan, the new city duma and its census-based electoral system ensured an Armenian majority for the ensuing decades.

Over the last half-century of the Russian Empire's existence, both cities coalesced into one urban conglomerate with inverted economic roles. From 1809 to 1913, Rostov's population increased from 3,000 to almost 200,000. The abolition of serfdom in 1864 and Rostov's connection to the imperial railway network in the 1870s caused a drastic demographic dynamic during the second half of the nineteenth century: while the population increased by six times during the first 50 years of the nineteenth century, the period between 1860 and 1913 witnessed a 12-fold increase. In comparison, Nakhichevan experienced moderate development both in total numbers and in dynamics of growth following the Great Reforms. In 1779, around 12,600 colonists from Crimea settled at the fortress. From 1857 to 1913, its population grew from 14,500 to 50,000 residents.[75] While both cities increased in ethnic diversity, Nakhichevan became more ethnically heterogeneous. Non-Armenians contributed most of its demographic growth from the second half of the nineteenth century. In 1904, 63 percent of the 32,709 residents were Armenians, 33 percent of Russian or Ukrainian origin, and three percent of other nationalities. Prior to World War I, Rostov's population consisted of 79 percent Russians and Ukrainians, seven percent Jews, and five percent Armenians.[76] With the opening of a stock exchange in 1867 and the modernization of harbor and storage facilities in Rostov, most Armenian trade and businesses moved their headquarters to the center of Rostov. Some merchants generated considerable revenue from renting out houses they owned in Rostov and donated parts of it to various Armenian charities. The wine trader Adzhemov bequeathed two houses in Rostov to the city of Nakhichevan, creating 15,000 rubles of rent, which the city invested in a technical school for Armenian children from poor families.[77] In contrast to the rapidly growing Rostov, Nakhichevan's reputation was less hectic, thus attracting the Russian and foreign business elites eager for weekend houses.[78] Nakhichevan also benefitted from Rostov's rapid population growth, with house owners renting out rooms to a growing number of clerks and workers and their families (Figure 6.3).

Economic divergence accompanied these processes of urban merging and ethnic blending. The traditional Armenian crafts, crucial to Nakhichevan's early economic success, were threatened by increased mechanization by the mid-century and had mostly vanished by around 1900. The teacher, national activist, and member of Nakhichevan's duma Ervand O. Shakhaziz observed that

> the old crafts such as horseshoeing, blacksmithing, manufacturing of arms, felting, hat making, timbering, tailoring, gold- and silver-smithing, tinning, tile manufacturing, baking, saddle-making, and others

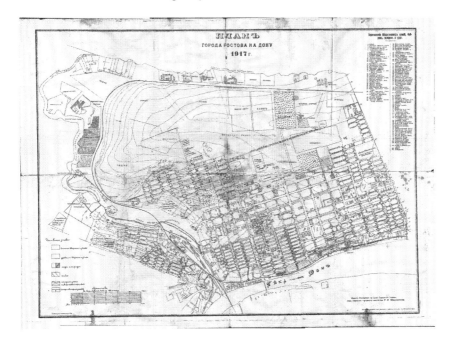

Figure 6.3 Map of Rostov-on-Don 1917, ed. by the City Board of Rostov and its land surveyor Mamontov.

Source: https://commons.wikimedia.org/wiki/File:Plan_of_Rostov-on-Don_1917.jpg

The map depicts the city in a period of rapid demographic and economic growth, partially due to its position as a hub between the different railway networks of the Caucasus region (bridge over the Don), New Russia (south, right embankment), and Central Russia (northeast). Several new factories emerged along the railway tracks entering the city's territory from the east. Within only 20 years' time, new, mostly wooden, living quarters arose west, northwest, and east of the historical center due to massive migration pressure. Tramlines not only linked the main parts of the city with each other but also neighboring Nakhichevan.

have either come to an end or are about to do so, and this allows one to say, in confidence, that at present Nakhichevan has neither crafts nor craftsmen.[79]

Some entrepreneurs from Nakhichevan successfully adapted and transferred classic Armenian trades into the modern era. The trading houses of Magdesiev and Balabanov ran two of the biggest oil-fueled mills in the region, mills that had rendered many Armenian windmills redundant. After the abolishment of the Cossack trade monopoly on coal mining in 1863, merchants developed a strong position in this segment of the market, with some representatives supplying the Black Sea and Caspian fleets with coal.[80] The abundance of land belonging to the city of Nakhichevan allowed lucrative long-term rent contracts for the construction of factories and storage facilities for raw materials and kerosene.

Rostov, on the other hand, transformed from a "small and dirty town without gas lights and mostly roofs made of reed"[81] into a modern metropolis. It surpassed Taganrog in foreign trade volume in 1860, its share of grain exports through the Sea of Azov having risen from one-third to one-half within a decade.[82] Economic growth affected its hinterland as well – parts of the Don Cossack community that traditionally had handled most of the shipping of goods to both cities on the Don managed to monetize their ethnic division of labor and made substantial profits in the transport sector. With 9.4 percent of Rostov's total sales volume in 1902, manufacturing remained insubstantial in comparison to trading. The first industrial installation, a foundry established in the 1850s, profited from the extraction of coal and iron ore in the northern Krivoi Rog region. Emblematic of Russian industrialization, the installation remained dependent on state government orders for years.[83] At the turn of the century, Rostov ranked among the six cities with the most dynamic growth, partly because its trade opportunities attracted capital of various origins. Despite the multiethnic appearance of its elites, 56 percent of the capital invested in joint stock companies came from ethnic Russian investors, while approximately 27 percent came from abroad, 13 percent from Russian Jewish businessmen, and 3.5 percent from Cossack entrepreneurs. Both the absence of significant Armenian capital as well as the "ethnic concentration" of capital in specific sectors speak to the particular circumstances of the region as a commercial center. Ninety-three percent of foreign capital was invested in the trade sector, while Jewish capital led in industry and Cossack capital was almost exclusive to infrastructure.[84]

The lack of imperial engagement in the metropolis's fate remained constant throughout the reform period of Alexander II. There were calls for stricter administration, such as that by Pavel E. Kotsebu, governor-general to New Russia and Bessarabia. Repelled by the cosmopolitan character of Rostov's port and center, he claimed that the city had been taking advantage "of an almost direct communication with foreign lands" that "offers the full freedom for unpunished illegal actions and foreign influence," but his remonstrations remained without consequence.[85] In 1888, however, Rostov and Nakhichevan were excluded from the governorate of Ekaterinoslav and unified with the Province of the Don Cossack Host. Earlier attempts by the duma of Rostov to petition for the creation of a new governorate including Taganrog and Azov, with Rostov at its center, went nowhere.[86] The territorial and administrative reorganization that eventually subjected both cities to the War Ministry fits into the grander scheme of abolishing privileges and gradually homogenizing imperial rule by territorial reorganization.[87] Earlier restrictions related to the lands of the Cossacks were suspended, and non-Cossacks and foreigners received permission to buy land and invest. Uniting these most prosperous cities with the Don Cossack lands clearly aimed at overcoming the economical backwardness of a region that ranked at the bottom of most economic statistics for the Russian regions, despite its abundant resources and fertile lands.[88] This reorganization affected non-Russian groups differently. St. Petersburg transferred Armenian peasants to the category of state peasants and forced them to buy land earlier granted by the privileges for a fixed price over a period of 40 years.[89] Now excluded from the governorate of Ekaterinoslav, Rostov and Nakhichevan no longer constituted the most Eastern part of the "Pale of Settlement," an administrative territory in the western and southern parts of the empire in which the Jewish population was legally allowed to reside. Further in-migration to the regional Jewish community of around 8,000 members was forbidden, and its further demographic growth resulted from reproduction within the existing community. Although a certain improvement in agriculture and trade within some strata of the Cossack society took place, it remains difficult to assess the overall economic and social success of the unification.[90] In 1904, the imperial authorities revoked the unification and excluded Rostov and Nakhichevan from the Don territories once more. They conferred the status of a *gradonachal'stvo* on them, acknowledging Rostov's increased economic importance for the empire.[91]

Despite their growing economic entanglement and the increasing consolidation of the two urban structures into one, Rostov and Nakhichevan remained two separate political entities until the end of the empire. The duma of Nakhichevan repeatedly refused attempts by the Rostov city duma to unite the two cities, as the Armenians would have become a minority in a unified city duma. In the final decades of the empire, the overwhelming majority of Nakhichevan's citizens were Russians. The restrictive electoral law of 1892 constrained the suffrage of the middle class and increased the control of the civil administration of the Don Cossack Host over the city's administration. Yet the strict electoral census system that allowed only a fraction of the residents of one city to vote for representatives in its duma ultimately ensured the political dominance of the Armenian elites, as most of the city's real estate (possession of which granted suffrage) belonged to the Armenians. Thus, a system that in general is associated with the repression of an emerging Russian civil society by the autocratic state became the means to ensure the political power of a minority ethnic elite whose population underwent an unfavorable demographic development. As late as 1913, a local Russian campaign aimed at a re-measurement of landed property in Nakhichevan. By enlarging Russian property at the expense of Armenian, Armenian dominance of its duma would be reduced. The campaign was unsuccessful.[92]

The Armenians' resistance to any attempts at administrative unification resulted from the constant competition with its direct neighbor and the experience of relative loss of economic importance. In an age of increasing nationalism (due both to national movements and imperial policies of Russification), the growth of Rostov combined with the loss of Nakhichevanian privileges might seem to fit a narrative emphasizing polarities separating "Russians" from "Armenians." The increasingly nationalized political discourse under the reign of Alexander III and Nicholas II, as well as the process of transferring both cities to the Province of the Don Cossack Host in 1887–1888, rendered the vague category of Russian nationality a predominant factor within debates on urban consolidation and economic prosperity.[93] The uneven socioeconomic development of the Province of the Don Cossack Host and the related status loss of the Cossack community increased the attraction of nationalistic narratives among certain strata of the Cossack and Russian population.[94] Cossacks felt a growing contrast between their symbolic military role for the Russian state and their declining economic status. The opening of the province to the investment of outsiders increased the popular perception that foreigners, as personified by Jews and Armenians, were catalysts of a capitalist modernization in which the Cossacks felt increasingly left out.[95] Thus, writing in 1912, the local historian Andrei M. Grekov claimed in books and newspaper articles that the Armenians "received land in the interest of developing the region, which they did not do, but rather enriched themselves at the expense of the Russian population."[96]

The numerical predominance of Don Cossacks in the Rostov area and the increasing number of lower-class laborers from central Russia that migrated there changed the popular images of the Armenians as well as the growing Jewish communities of Rostov. Again, socioeconomic transformation influenced the parameters of this broader shift. Rapid economic development drew an ever-greater unskilled workforce from the Russian heartlands to the Don – the share of "peasants" within Rostov's estate structure increased from 45 percent in 1897 to 72 percent in 1907.[97] This fundamental change in the city's social composition not only provided fertile ground for sentiments popular among the newly-urbanized Russian lower classes who were more responsive to nationalist mobilization than townspeople acquainted with multiethnic urban life over long periods of time. This social transformation of the urban society also fueled the emerging political crisis of the empire. State enterprises such as the Southern Caucasian railroad became centers for the mobilization of social democratic workers, heralding the upcoming First Russian Revolution. It was here that one of the first general strikes took place in November 1902, receiving nationwide attention.[98] The most fundamental outburst of radicalized national sentiment and antisemitism occurred between October 18 and 20, 1905, when a pogrom incited by a Russian mob and Cossack units cost the lives of more than 150 Jews, injuring 500 more while destroying shops and warehouses. Prior events in Kishinev (today rom. Chişinău) and Odessa had generated an empire-wide atmosphere of fear among the Jewish population, whose communities warned each other and started establishing self-defense units; in Rostov, these were successful in pushing back some of the attackers.[99]

Among the cosmopolitan-minded economic elites of Rostov, Russian national sentiments do not seem to have been prominent at the turn of the century. Some of the existing Societies for Mutual Credit, which provided local entrepreneurs with capital, began to restrict their activity to Russians only, yet their total share of the credit market remained insignificant.[100] Most of the local political elites seemed to be aware of the correlation between the cities' economic success and disregard for the ethnic and national categories of its dwellers and businessmen. A petition from the Rostov duma to the Ministry of War prevented the expulsion of several thousand Jews from the area in 1887, which the ministry had intended to implement on the grounds that Rostov's Jews no longer resided in the Pale of Settlement following the unification with the Cossack Province.[101] In the last decades of the nineteenth century, with the state as protector of minorities in retreat or even actively engaged in repressing national movements, certain elite individuals became beacons of a multiethnic imperial culture.[102] The Armenian merchant and former mayor of Nakhichevan Karp M. Gairabetov headed the district assembly in the 1870s.[103] Within this imperial metropolis with two centers, the expectations of urban economic and social improvement and healthy competition sufficed to keep these nationalist categories at bay. The opening of a public library in Nakhichevan in 1886 inspired a group in Rostov that led to the founding of a similar institution that same year. Increased investment in the construction of public schools in Rostov was followed by a wave of newly constructed Armenian schools in the 1870s and 1880s.[104] Prior to World War I, both dumas discussed the possibility of founding a single university for both cities.[105]

Conclusion

Nikolai E. Vrangel's reflections on Rostov's origins as a product of ordinary true Russian people confirmed a widespread narrative in the late nineteenth century. A regional folk calendar from 1887 described the 1830s as the true turning point in the city's history: "The 'uninvited' [i.e., fugitive Russian peasants] flocked here from everywhere and with enterprise, energy, and straightforwardness made up the capital and created the force that now needs to be reckoned with."[106] This narrative reflects one attempt by contemporaries to navigate drastic socioeconomic and political changes by idealizing the origins of the city, simplifying the narrative, and sweeping away contradictions. At its core, this narration combined the denial of significant influences of non-Russians on the region's development, an idealization of the simple Russian man as pursued by the Russian intelligentsia, and emphasis on the myth of freedom and the high social mobility in New Russia in contradistinction to the serfdom that characterized the mainland. This trope, popular throughout the political spectrum of the late imperial society, was explored by Grigorii P. Danilevskii in his popular novel *Runaway Peasants in New Russia (Beglye v Novorossii)*.[107]

From the perspective of both the imperial manifestations within cities and their significance for the empire's political, economic, and social fabric, Rostov and Nakhichevan constitute peculiar cases within the urban landscapes of the Russian Empire. The longue durée perspective of this chapter has highlighted the shifting functions both cities fulfilled within the empire at particular times. After losing its importance as a frontier town and fortress to the Ottoman Empire at the end of the eighteenth century, the attention (and imagination) of imperial authorities shifted away from Rostov. With the center now attributing military significance to Novocherkassk as the newly founded capital of the Don Province, Taganrog long found favor as the primary locus of economic growth and imperial administration. For the inhabitants of Rostov, the Armenian colony of Nakhichevan must have appeared as the most visible manifestation of the imperial state until the 1840s. Nakhichevan resembled the protected and administrated "otherness" within the multiethnic empire's south. Differences between Nakhichevan and Rostov derived from the privileged allocation of land to the former, freedoms associated with self-administration, and the oriental appearance of Nakhichevan and its markets. Yet the very proximity between the two communities allowed for participation in the Armenians' economic endeavors, setting cross-cultural influences in motion that would later benefit Russian merchants.

Due to Rostov's double disadvantage when compared to other Black Sea ports – aggravated conditions for ship trade due to the shallow Sea of Azov *and* the challenging delta of the Don – its success remained far from certain at the time. Consequently, the crucial decision to re-establish a customs post in 1836 was based on the assessment of Governor Mikhail Vorontsov. Only in 1888 did the imperial elites apprehend the metropolis' economic potential as an imperial trade hub and its capability for advancing the socioeconomic conditions of the Don Cossacks.

Nakhichevan's history displays similar patterns. With the vanishing of Catherine's enlightened absolutist approach toward ethnic management of the "wild field," no further imperial vision was attached to the Armenian colony.[108] The process of abolishing the Armenian privileges in the 1860s and 1870s is characterized by the hesitation of people in authority at the center and initiatives taken by regional competitors. Rostov and Nakhichevan both constituted imperial cities whose histories clearly reflect key challenges of the Russian imperial experience of the eighteenth and nineteenth centuries, such as the dynamics of migration and economic growth or the adaptation of administrative frameworks within a multiethnic population. Yet both examples indicate that the imperial center was by no means the key protagonist of urban development – just one among different actors.

In a way, the absence of an imperial development strategy and symbols of imperial grandeur and the close and often conflicting relationship between Russians and Armenians (as well as the Greek, Jewish, or German inhabitants of the region) all served as catalysts for increasing prosperity. The Armenian trade networks and craft portfolio of the eighteenth and early nineteenth century helped develop an economic hinterland and market that the empire's supreme Black Sea port, Odessa, would lack.[109] The river Don and trade routes first established by Armenian traders secured a constantly rising inflow of goods long before the railway reached Rostov in 1870. These advantages even outweighed the difficulties of accessing the Sea of Azov and the mouth of the river Don. The urban multiethnic community and its economic networks that emerged after the Great Reforms were a product of the beneficial and conflicting relationship and negotiations between Russian and Armenian merchants and local elites. This constitutes part of the reason for the pre-Reform periods unleashing growth in commerce, population, and urbanization unknown to other parts of the empire. This chapter has shown that a longer historical perspective allows for an evaluation of the importance of interethnic relations for the economy of imperial cities.

The exceptional feature of the case of Rostov and Nakhichevan is that it eludes a clear definition of a distinct city. The study has shown that, depending on the chosen perspective and questions, imperial cities can be conceptualized as more flexible, either by their political-administrative demarcation, their economic embeddedness (e.g., as a hub connecting different networks), or the socio-ethnic markers that define them as (often) multiethnic habitats. These different options to survey and demarcate the imperial urban space not only provide more analytical clarity but can be linked to the experiences of contemporary imperial residents as well, whose differences in gender, faith, class, and estate certainly influenced their conception and experience of urban life.

While Rostov and Nakhichevan became increasingly undistinguishable on the city maps in the 1870s, the proximity between its inhabitants in daily economic, social, and political life provokes associations with other multiethnic cities such as Riga, Odessa, or Baku, which also had neighboring but ethnically homogeneous neighborhoods.[110] The contemporary visitor could distinguish the two parts of the metropolis despite increasing ethnic and economic intermingling through the location of Armenian or Russian Orthodox Churches and through the use of a more pronounced Armenian architectural style described as "northern modern." This style, which combined Russian classicism with Armenian elements, emerged in the 1870s.[111] The administrative division, however, meant the coexistence of different modes of taxation and obligations within a few square miles. At the turn of the century, a resident of Nakhichevan could consider its duma and administration to be a bulwark against the growing presence of Russian residents within "his" city. Yet such a position would also depend on his or her respective class, as neither a rich merchant nor an industrial worker would necessarily comprehend his urban environment exclusively through the lens of nationalism. These city administrations could foster projects that connected their citizens' identities to both the nation and particular aspects of the empire they represented at its periphery. Rostov experienced a long public debate about the erection of a sculpture of Peter the Great prior to World War I, while in 1894, the duma of Nakhichevan planned and financed a monument for Catherine the Great with delay, originally intended to commemorate the 100th anniversary of the city.[112] However, as the infrastructural, architectural, and social results of mutual cooperation between the dumas of both cities have shown, every one of the resulting bridges, tramways, or main streets simultaneously manifested the empire's claim to modernity and prolonged its multiethnic essence in an urban context.

Notes

1 Nikolai Egorovich Vrangel', *Vospominaniia ot krepostnogo prava do bol'shevikov* (Moscow: Novoe literaturnoe obozrenie, 2003), 237.
2 Ibid.
3 *Materialy dlia geografii i statistiki Rossii, sobrannye ofitserami general'nogo shtaba*, ed. V. Pavlovich (St. Petersburg: Tipografiia Departamenta General'nogo shtaba, 1862), 188.
4 "Nakhichevan'-na-Donu" *Entsiklopedicheskii slovar' Brokgauza i Efrona*, vol. 40 (St. Petersburg: Brokgauz/Efron, 1897), 705–6.
5 Thomas R. Metcalf, "Colonial Cities," in *The Oxford Handbook of Cities in World History*, ed. Peter Clark (Oxford: Oxford University Press, 2013), 753–69, 766.
6 Stephen Badalyan Riegg, *Russia's Entangled Embrace. The Tsarist Empire and the Armenians, 1801–1914* (Ithaca, NY: Cornell University Press, 2020), 6.
7 See, for example, Nancy Shields Kollmann, *The Russian Empire, 1450–1801* (Oxford: Oxford University Press, 2017). The term goes back to Karen Barkey's

seminal study on the Ottoman Empire, Karen Barkey, *Empire of Difference: The Ottomans in Comparative Perspective* (Cambridge: Cambridge University Press, 2009).

8 Marianna Abdullayeva, "The Rural Population of Don's Hinterland as a Factor of the Economic Life of Rostov, End of the 19th Century," in *Between Grain and Oil from the Azov to the Caucasus: The Port-Cities of the Eastern Coast of the Black Sea, Late 18th–Early 20th Century*, ed. Gelina Harlaftis et al. (Rethymnon: Centre of Maritime History, 2020), 329–67.

9 Brian Davies, *The Russo-Turkish War, 1768–1774: Catherine II and the Ottoman Empire* (London: Bloomsbury Academic, 2016); John P. LeDonne, *The Russian Empire and the World, 1700–1917: The Geopolitics of Expansion and Containment* (New York: Oxford University Press, 1997), 112–29.

10 *Arkhiv gosudarstvennogo soveta, Vol. 1, 1768–1796, part 1*, "Sovet v tsarstvovanie Imperatritsy Ekateriny II-i" (St. Petersburg: Tipografiia vtorogo otdeleniia sobstvennoi E.I.V. kantseliarii 1868), 333–56.

11 "O poimke beglykh krest'ian" 1791, in: Gosudarstvennyi arkhiv Rostovskoi oblasti (GARO), f. 518, op. 1, d. 68, l. 98ob.

12 Roger Lee Thiede, "Town and Function in Tsarist Russia: A Geographical Analysis of Trade and Industry in the Towns of New Russia, 1860–1910" (PhD diss., University of Washington, 1970), 73–74.

13 Tamara Ganjalyan, *Diaspora und Imperium: Armenier im vorrevolutionären Russland (17. bis 19. Jahrhundert)* (Cologne: Böhlau, 2016); Stefan Troebst, "Isfahan – Moskau – Amsterdam: Zur Entstehungsgeschichte des moskauischen Transitprivilegs für die Armenischen Handelskompanie in Persien (1666–1676)," *Jahrbücher für Geschichte Osteuropas* 41, no. 2 (1993): 180–209.

14 Asmik Ovikovna Amirdzhanian, "Vklad Iosifa Argutiana – glavy armiano-russkoi dukhovnoi eparkhii, v delo osnovaniia i sokhraneniia goroda Novoi Nakhichevani (konets XVIII v.)," in *Armiane iuga Rossii: Istoriia, kul'tura, obshchee budushchee. Materialy III Mezhdunarodnoi nauchnoi konferentsii, Rostov-na-Donu, 30–31 maia 2018 g.*, ed. G.G. Matisov (Rostov-na-Donu: Iuzhnyi nauchnyi tsentr RAN, 2018), 22–25, 25; "Osvobozhdenie grekov i armian Ekaterinoslavskoi oblasti ot nalogov," 22.5.1795 in *Arkhiv gosudarstvennogo soveta, Vol. 1, 1768–1796, part 2* "Sovet v tsarstvovanie Imperatritsy Ekateriny II-i," "Otdelenie iuridicheskoe" (St. Petersburg: Tipografiia vtorogo otdeleniia sobstvennoi E.I.V. kantseliarii 1868), 284.

15 "Vysochaishaia gramota Imperatritsy Ekatariny II-i 1779 goda ob osnovanii g. Nakhichevani-na-Donu i o nadelenii armian zemleiu," in *Zapiski Rostovskogo na Donu Obshchestva istorii, drevnostei i prirody*, vol. 2, ed. A.M. Ilin (Rostov-on-Don: Elektro-tipografiia F. A. Zakroitseva, 1914), 190–92; Sarkis Kazarov, *Nakhichevanskoe kupechestvo, konets XVIII – nachalo XX veka* (Rostov-on-Don: Kovcheg, 2012); Levon Batiev, "Novo-Nakhichevanskii magistrat: proizkhozhdenie, struktura, funktsii," *Bylye Gody* 48, no. 2 (2018): 518–27.

16 Sarkis Kazarov, "Nakhichevan-on-Don: Armenian Merchants and Their Role in the Commercial Development of the Azov-Black Sea Region: Dynamics and Specificities of the Socio-Economic Development," in *Between Grain and Oil From the Azov to the Caucasus: The Port-Cities of the Eastern Coast of the Black Sea, Late 18th–Early 20th Century*, ed. Gelina Harlaftis et al. (Rethymnon: Centre of Maritime History, 2020), 399–427, 403.

17 Marc Raeff, "In the Imperial Manner," in *Catherine the Great: A Profile*, ed. Marc Raeff (New York: Palgrave Macmillan, 1972), 197–246, 198.

18   Kazarov, *Kupechestvo*, 20.

19   "Ob Armianakh, obshchestvami v Rossii vodvorivshikhsia, s pokazaniem chisla zhitelei," in *Sobranie aktov otnosiashchikhsia k obozreniiu istorii armianskogo naroda* (Moscow: Tipografiia Lazarevskogo instituta vostochnykh iazykov, 1833), 1:120–26.

20   Kazarov, "Nakhichevan-on-Don," 420–23.

21   Eyüp Özveren, "A Framework for the Study of the Black Sea World, 1789–1915," *Review (Fernand Braudel Center)* 20, no.1 (1997): 77–113.

22   Irina Savchenkova, "Rostov na Donu," *Mir russkogo slova* 3 (2008): 107.

23   Igor A. Kuznetsov, *Proshloe Rostova: Ocerki po istorii goroda Rostova-na-Donu* (Rostov-on-Don: Tipografiia Donskogo aktsionernogo obshchestva pechatnogo i izdatel'skogo dela, 1897; Rostov-on-Don: NB, 2012), 44.

24   Andrew Robarts, "A Plague on Both Houses? Population Movements and the Spread of Disease across the Ottoman-Russian Black Sea Frontier, 1768–1830" (PhD diss., Georgetown University, 2010), 248.

25   Anthony Rhinelander, *Prince Michael Vorontsov: Viceroy to the Tsar* (Montréal: McGill-Queen's University Press, 1990); John P. LeDonne, "Frontier Governors General 1772–1825 II. The Southern Frontier," *Jahrbücher für Geschichte Osteuropas* 48 (2000): 161–83.

26   Kuznetsov, *Proshloe Rostova*, 73.

27   Kazarov, "Nakhichevan-on-Don," 427.

28   *Obozrenie sostoianiia gorodov rossiiskoi imperii v 1833* (St. Petersburg: Tipografiia Karla Kraia, 1834), 61–62.

29   "Delo o vzyskanii s nakhichevanskogo kuptsa Chekhmakhova 1500 rublei moskovskogo kuptsa Vishnikovskogo na otpushchennoi tovar," June 26, 1851–August 16, 1864, in: GARO, f. 579, op. 1, d. 474.

30   Ronald Grigor Suny, *Looking Toward Ararat: Armenia in Modern History* (Bloomington: Indiana University Press, 1993), 39.

31   See, for example, Robert Geraci, "Capitalist Stereotypes and the Economic Organization of the Russian Empire: The Case of the Tiflis Armenians," in *Defining Self: Essays on Emergent Identities in Russia Seventeenth to Nineteenth Centuries*, ed. Michael Branch (Helsinki: Finnish Literature Society, 2009), 365–81.

32   Kazarov, *Nakhichevanskoe kupechestvo*, 20.

33   *Voennoe-statisticheskoe obozrenie Rossiiskoi imperii 1837–1854, Vol. 11, Novorossiiskaia guberniia, Bessarabskaia oblast' i Zemlia voiska Donskogo 1849–1850* (St. Petersburg: Tipografiia Departamenta General'nogo shtaba, 1849), 142.

34   Ibid, 142.

35   Pavlovich, *Materialy dlia geografii,* 188.

36   Pavel Petrovich Filevskii, "Nakhichevan' i nakhichevantsy: Iz vospominanii o detstve: Byt, obychai, traditsii donskikh armian – 1860-e gody," accessed February 20, 2021, http://www.donvrem.dspl.ru/Files/article/m2/2/art.aspx?art_id=86; Laurence Oliphant, *The Russian Shores of the Black Sea in the Autumn of 1852 with a Voyage Down the Volga, and a Tour through the Country of the Don Cossacks* (Edinburgh, London: William Blackwood and Sons, 1854), 173.

37   Pavlovich, *Materialy*, 216.

38   Natalya Samarina, "Rostov-on-Don in the Second Half of the 19th–Early 20th Century: Dynamics and Specificities of the Socio-Economic Development", in

Between Grain and Oil from the Azov to the Caucasus: The Port-Cities of the Eastern Coast of the Black Sea, Late 18th–Early 20th Century, ed. Gelina Harlaftis et al. (Rethymnon: Centre of Maritime History, 2020), 369–97, 372.

39 Apollon Aleksandrovich Skal'kovskii, *Rostov-na-Donu* (St. Petersburg: Tipografiia ministerstva vnutrennikh del, 1847).

40 "Rostov-na-Donu," *Moskvitianin: Ucheno-literaturnyi zhurnal*, 1850, 3, 91–102.

41 Kazarov, "Nakhichevan-on-Don," 71.

42 *Polnoe sobranie zakonov Rossiiskoi imperii* (PSZ RI), Vol. XX, Art. 14942 (November 24, 1779); Akop Mkrtichevich Bogdanian, *Iz proshlogo (O pereselenii armian Kryma na Don): Kratkii istoricheskii ocherk* (Rostov-on-Don: Rostovskoe knizhnoe izdatel'stvo, 1947).

43 "Perepiska s Nakhichevanskim armianskim magistratom o litsach, samovol'no poselivshichsia na Sambekskoi stepi," 1849–1853, in: GARO, f. 579, op. 1, d. 236.

44 Vrangel', *Vospominaniia*, 237.

45 See, for example, the novel by Grigorii Danilevskii, "Beglye v Novorossii," in *Vremya* 1–2 (1862)/1–3 (1863).

46 "Perepiska s nakhichevanskim armianskim magistratom o litsakh, samovol'no poselivshikhsia na Sambekskoi step," November 16, 1851–March 2, 1857, in: GARO, f. 579, op. 1, d. 236.

47 "Nakhichevanskii gorodskoi magistrat," 1799–1803, in: GARO, f. 790, op. 1, d. 4, l. 28–39ob.

48 Pavlovich, *Materialy*, 188.

49 Ibid; for the Greek colony in Mariupol, see Irina Ponomariova, "Ethnic Processes in Mariupol and Russia's Imperial Migration Policy (19th–Early 20th Century)," in *Between Grain and Oil from the Azov to the Caucasus: The Port-Cities of the Eastern Coast of the Black Sea, Late 18th–Early 20th Century*, ed. Gelina Harlaftis et al. (Rethymnon: Centre of Maritime History, 2020), 235–58.

50 *Smeta dokhodov i raskhodov g. Nakhichevani-na-Donu na 1901* (Rostov-on-Don, 1902).

51 "Pravitel'stvuiushchii senat, pervyi departament: Delo o zapreshchennoi kriuchkovoi lovke ryby v girlakh r. Dona i v Azovskom more, proizvodinnoi zhiteliami Ekat. Gub.," in *Rossiiskii gosudarstvennyi istoricheskii arkhiv* (RGIA), f. 1341, op. 1, d. 330 a, b, v.

52 "Ukaz Senata v Ekaterinoslavskuiu mezhevuiu kontoru" (January 16, 1812), in *Sobranie aktov otnosiashchikhsia k obozreniiu istorii armianskogo naroda* (Moscow: Tipografiia Lazarevskogo instituta vostochnykh iazykov, 1833), 1:50.

53 Vladislav V. Smirnov, *Letopis' Nakhichevani-na-Donu: V istoricheskom, bytopisatel'nom, statisticheskom i illiustrativnom inter'erakh s prilozhenniiami, vkliuchaiushchimi vazhnye, poleznye i interesnye svedeniia* (Rostov-on-Don: Kniga, 2014), 51.

54 Kuznetsov, *Proshloe*, 55.

55 Georgii Bagdykov, *Progulki po Nakhichevani* (Rostov-on-Don: ZAO Kniga, 2011), 4.

56 "Delo o predostavlenie g. Nakhichevani 10% chasti summu tamozhennogo sbora Rostovskoi tamozhennoi zastava s tovarami, otpuskaemuiu za granitsu," January 5, 1848–September 22, 1954, in: GARO, f. 579, op. 1, d. 471, l. 1–7ob.

57　Kuznetsov, *Proshloe Rostova*, 112–13.

58　"Delo o zakrepliaiushchikh ustroistvakh torgovogo zavedeniia na levoi storone Dona," June 16, 1846–February 4, 1867, in: GARO, f. 579, op. 1, d. 465.

59　"Postanovleniia ocherednogo Rostovskogo uezdnogo zemskogo sobraniia: Oktiabr'skoi sessii 1868 goda," (Rostov-on-Don, 1869), 87.

60　*Vedomosti nakhichevanskoi n-D. gorodskoi dumy*, Nr. 1, Ianvar' – Iiun' 1899 (Nakhichevan-on-Don, 1899), 101–4.

61　"Materialy o morskikh portakh Rossii," Folder 2024, Nauchno-spravochnaia biblioteka RGIA; P. E. Beliavskii *Donskie Girla* (St. Petersburg: Tip-litografiia R. Golike, 1888).

62　"Rostovskii-na-Donu torgovyi port: Otchet po Rostovskomu-na-Donu torgovomu portu" (Rostov-on-Don, 1917), 47.

63　Willard Sunderland, *Taming the Wild Field: Colonization and Empire on the Russian Steppe* (Ithaca, NY: Cornell University Press 2016), 137–66.

64　Ronald Grigor Suny, "Eastern Armenians under Tsarist Rule," in *The Armenian People from Ancient to Modern Times, Vol. 2, Foreign Dominion to Statehood: The Fifteenth Century to the Twentieth Century*, ed. Richard G. Hovannisian (Basingstoke: Macmillan, 1997), 109–35, 127.

65　"Vysochaishaia gramota Nakhichevanskomu armianskomu obshchestvu, v podtverzhdenie ikh prav i preimushchestv," in: *Sobranie aktov otnosiashchikhsia k obozreniiu istorii armianskogo naroda* (Moscow: Tipografiia Lazarevskogo instituta vostochnykh iazykov, 1833), 1:49, 248–49.

66　By 1810, fees from various estate cooperation were raised and extended to payments for street construction, public places, and waterways. See "Svedenie ob Armianakh, obshchestvami v Rossii vodvorivshikhsia, s pokazaniem chisla zhitelei porozn' v kazhdom gorode i vsekh voobshche, takzhe ikh povinnostei i podati, v kaznu platimoi," *Sobranie aktov otnosiashchikhsia k obozreniiu istorii armianskogo naroda* (Moscow: Tipografiia Lazarevskogo instituta vostochnykh iazykov, 1838), 2: 120–21.

67　Levon V. Batiev, "Transformatsiia organov samoupravleniia Nakhichevani-na-Donu v 1860-e gody," *Vestnik Rossiiskogo universiteta druzhby narodov* 19, no. 1 (2020): 155–73, https://doi.org/10.22363/2312-8674-2020-19-1-155-173.

68　"Spisok o postanovleniiakh Ekaterinoslavskogo gubernskogo zemskogo sobraniia," December 17, 1866, in: RGIA, f. 1287, op. 5, d. 2209, l. 140–144ob, l. 143ob-144.

69　Ibid, l. 141–155ob, 143.

70　See, for example, Stefan Kirmse, *The Lawful Empire: Legal Change and Cultural Diversity in Late Tsarist Russia* (Cambridge: Cambridge University Press, 2019).

71　Levon Batiev, "Politseiskaia sluzhba v Nakhichevani-na-Donu (konets XVIII-XIX vv.)," *Voprosy armenovedeniia* 3 (2018): 38–51, 42; Edik G. Minasyan, Levon V. Batiev, "'The Name List of … the Cityheads' in Nakhichevan-on-Don and the 'Statement of the Costs of City Revenues and Expenditures' (the End 19th–Mid 20th Century)," *Novoe proshloe* 2 (2019): 218–30. DOI:10.23683/2500-3224-2019-2-218-230.

72　Batiev, "Magistrat."

73　M. Anatole de Demidoff, *Travels in Southern Russia, and the Crimea; through Hungary, Wallachia, & Modavia, during the Year 1837* (London: John Mitchell, 1853).

74　Batiev, "Transformatsiia," 168.

75 Smirnov, *Letopis' Nakhichevani-na-Donu*, 347.
76 *Statisticheskii sbornik po g. Rostovu-na-Donu 1914*, vol. I, January–June (Rostov-on-Don, 1915), 33.
77 Smirnov, *Letopis' Nakhichevani-na-Donu*, 48.
78 Anna Michailovna Ivanova-Il'icheva, Irina Alekseevna Stushniaia, Ol'ga Vladimirnovna Baeva, "Arkhitekturno-gradostroitel'noe razvitie Nakhichevani-na-Donu v kontekste formirovaniia gorodskoi kul'tury," *Istoricheskie, filosofskie, politicheskie i iuridicheskie nauki, kul'turologiia i iskusstvovedenie. Voprosy teorii i praktiki* 10 (2014): 81–83.
79 Ervand Ovakimovich Shakh-Aziz, *Nor Nakhichevan and Residents of New Nakhichevan* (Tiflis, 1903), 141; quote from Kazarov, "Nakhichevan-on-Don," 414.
80 Abdullayeva, "The Rural Population," 357.
81 Mikhail Borisovich Krasnianskii, *Istoricheskii ocherk gg. Rostova i Nakhichevani-n-D.* (Rostov-on-Don: Elektrotipografiia M.I. Guzman, 1911), 32.
82 Samarina, "Rostov-on-Don," 373.
83 Pavlovich, *Materialy*, 204.
84 Samarina, "Rostov-on-Don," 377.
85 Ibid, 397.
86 Kuznetsov, *Proshloe Rostova*, 245–51.
87 Andreas Kappeler, *Russland als Vielvölkerreich: Entstehung, Geschichte, Zerfall* (Munich: Beck, 1992), 203–32.
88 Alexander Maslov and Vyacheslav Volchik, "Institutions and Lagging Development: The Case of the Don Army Region," *Journal of Economic Issues* 48, no. 3 (2014): 727–42. DOI: 10.2753/JEI0021-3624480307.
89 Natalia Samarina, "Nakhichevan'-na-Donu v kontse XIX – nachale XX vv: osobennosti ekonomicheskogo i sotsial'nogo razvitiia," in *Armiane iuga Rossii: Istoriia, kul'tura, obshchee budushchee: Materialy II mezhdunarodnoj nauchnoi konferentsii, Rostov-na-Donu, 26-28 maia 2015 g.*, ed. Gennadii Grigorevich Matishov (Rostov-on-Don: JuNC RAN, 2015), 145–51, 146.
90 Marianna Abdullayeva draws a quite optimistic picture of the Don region's agricultural development since the unification and stresses the success of Armenian agriculture and the increase of productivity in the Cossack territories. Maslov and Volchik, on the other hand, emphasize the minor effects of the opening to foreign capital, agricultural technology, merchants, and peasants. Abdullayeva, "The Rural Population," Maslov, Volchik, "Institutions."
91 "Ob izmenenii ustroistva i shtata upravleniia Rostovskogo-na-Donu gradonachal'stva" v Gosudarstvennoi Dume, MVD, Departament obshchikh del, Otdelenie V, January 9, 1913, Folder 133, Nauchno-spravochnaia biblioteka RGIA.
92 Sarkis Kazarov, "Popytka zakhvata gorodskikh zemel' Nakhichevani-na-Donu v 1913 g.," in *Armiane iuga Rossii: Istoriia, kul'tura, obshchee budushchee: Materialy III mezhdunarodnoi nauchnoi konferentsii, Rostov-na-Donu, 30–31 maia 2018 g*, ed. Gennadii Grigorevich Matishov (Rostov-on-Don: JuNC RAN 2018), 99–102.
93 On Russian nationalism, see Alexei Miller, *The Romanov Empire and Nationalism: Essays in the Methodology of Historical Research* (Budapest: Central European University Press, 2008).
94 Boris S. Kornienko, *Pravyi Don: Kazaki i ideologiia natsionalizma (1909–1914)* (St. Petersburg: Izdat. Evropeiskogo Universiteta, 2013).

95 *Donskoe torgovoe obshchestvo i ego znachenie v zhizni Donskogo kraia*, ed. Ivan S. Koshkin, Ivan I. Zubov (Novocherkassk: Elektro-Tipografiia F. A. Polubatko, 1888), 17–18; Evgraf Petrovich Savel'ev, *Obshchestvo donskich torgovych kazakov 1804–1904* (Novocherkassk: Tipografiia V. I. Babenko, 1904), 37–40.
96 Andrei Mikhailovich Grekov, *Priazov'e i Don: Ocherki obshchestvennoi i ekonomicheskoi zhizni kraia* (St Petersburg: Tipografiia "Obshchestvennaia pol'za", 1912).
97 Samarina, "Rostov-on-Don," 381.
98 Henry Reichmann, "The Rostov General Strike of 1902," *Russian History 9*, no. 1 (1982): 67–85.
99 "Reports of Armed Jewish Self-Defense Groups in Rostov-na-Donu," in *Everyday Jewish Life in Imperial Russia: Selected Documents*, ed. Chaeran Y. Freeze and Jay M. Harris (Waltham, MA: Brandeis University Press, 2013) 555–57; Vladimir Levin, "Preventing Pogroms: Patterns in Jewish Politics in Early Twentieth Century Russia," in *Anti-Jewish Violence: Rethinking Pogrom in East European History*, ed. Jonathan Dekel-Chen (Bloomington: Indiana University Press, 2010), 95–110.
100 *Statisticheskii sbornik*, 143.
101 Kuznetsov, *Proshloe*, 250–51.
102 Kappeler, *Russland*, 263.
103 Vladimir Sidorov, *Entsiklopediia starogo Rostova i Nakhichevani-na-Donu* (Rostov-on-Don: Donskaia gosudarstvennaia biblioteka, 1996), 4:170–74.
104 Ivanova-Il'icheva, "Arkhitekturno-gradostroitel'noe razvitie," 88.
105 Krasnianskii, *Istoricheskii ocherk*, 36.
106 *Donsko-Azovskii Kalendar' na 1887 god*, ed. Ivan Per-Abramian (Rostov-on-Don: Tipo-Litografiia I. A. Per-Abramian, 1886).
107 Danilevskii, *Beglye v Novorossii*.
108 Sunderland, *Taming the Wild Field*, 55–96.
109 Patricia Herlihy, *Odessa: A History, 1794–1914* (Cambridge, MA: Harvard University Press, 1991).
110 Evrydiki Sifneos, *Imperial Odessa: People, Spaces, Identities* (Leiden: Brill, 2018); Ulrike von Hirschhausen, *Die Grenzen der Gemeinsamkeit: Deutsche, Letten, Russen und Juden in Riga, 1860–1914* (Göttingen: Vandenhoeck & Ruprecht, 2006); Ronald Grigor Suny, *The Baku Commune, 1917–1918: Class and Nationality in the Russian Revolution* (Princeton, NJ: Princeton University Press, 1972).
111 Ol'ga Vladimirovna Baeva, "Severnyi modern v zhiloi arkhitekture Nakhichevani-na-Donu," *Khudozhestvennaia kul'tura* 3 (2019): 262–77.
112 Smirnov, *Letopis' Nakhichevani-na-Donu*, 168.

Bibliography

Abdullayeva, Marianna. "The Rural Population of Don's Hinterland as a Factor of the Economic Life of Rostov, End of the 19th Century." In *Between Grain and Oil from the Azov to the Caucasus: The Port-Cities of the Eastern Coast of the Black Sea, Late 18ᵗʰ–Early 20ᵗʰ Century*, edited by Gelina Harlaftis et al., 329–67. Rethymnon: Centre of Maritime History, 2020.
Amirdzhanian, Asmik Ovikovna. "Vklad Iosifa Argutiana – glavy armiano-russkoi dukhovnoi eparchii, v delo osnovaniia i sochraneniia goroda Novoi Nachichevani

(konec XVIII v.)." In *Armiane iuga Rossii: Istoriia, kul'tura, obshchee budush-chee: Materialy III Mezhdunarodnoi nauchnoi konferentsii, Rostov-na-Donu, 30–31 maia 2018 g.*, edited by G. G. Matisov, 22–25. Rostov-on-Don: Iuzhnyi nauchnyi tsentr RAN, 2018.

Baeva, Ol'ga Vladimirovna. "Severnyi modern v zhiloi arkhitekture Nakhichevani-na-Donu." *Khudozhestvennaia kul'tura* 3 (2019): 262–77.

Bagdykov, Georgiy. *Progulki po Nakhichevani.* Rostov-on-Don: ZAO Kniga, 2011.

Barkey, Karen. *Empire of Difference: The Ottomans in Comparative Perspective.* Cambridge: Cambridge University Press, 2009.

Batiev, Levon. "Novo-Nakhichevanskii magistrat: Proiskhozhdenie, struktura, funktsii." *Bylye Gody* 48, no. 2 (2018): 518–27.

Batiev, Levon. "Politseiskaya sluzhba v Nakhichevani-na-donu (konets XVIII-XIX vv.)." *Voprosy armenovedeniia* 3 (2018): 38–51.

Batiev, Levon. "Transformatsiia organov samoupravleniia Nakhichevani-na-Donu v 1860-e gody." *Vestnik Rossiiskogo universiteta druzhby narodov* 19, no. 1 (2020): 155–73.

Beliavskii, Pyotr E. *Donskaia girla.* St. Petersburg: Tip-litografiia R. Golike, 1888.

Bogdanian, Akop Mkrtichevich. *Iz proshlogo (O pereselenii armian Kryma na Don): Kratkii istoricheskii ocherk.* Rostov-on-Don: Rostovskoe knizhnoe izdatel'stvo, 1947.

Danilevskii, Grigorii. "Beglye v Novorossii." *Vremia* 1–2 (1862)/1–3 (1863).

Davies, Brian. *The Russo-Turkish War, 1768–1774: Catherine II and the Ottoman Empire.* London: Bloomsbury Academic, 2016.

Demidoff, M. Anatole de. *Travels in Southern Russia, and the Crimea; through Hungary, Wallachia, & Modavia, during the Year 1837.* London: John Mitchell, 1853.

Filevskii, Pavel Petrovich. "Nakhichevan' i nakhichevantsy: Iz vospominanii o det-stve: Byt, obychai, traditsii donskikh armian – 1860-e gody." Accessed February 20, 2021. http://www.donvrem.dspl.ru/Files/article/m2/2/art.aspx?art_id=86.

Freeze, Chaeran Y., and Jay M. Harris, eds. *Everyday Jewish Life in Imperial Russia: Selected Documents.* Waltham, MA: Brandeis University Press, 2013.

Ganjalyan, Tamara. *Diaspora und Imperium: Armenier im vorrevolutionären Russland (17. bis 19. Jahrhundert).* Cologne: Böhlau, 2016.

Geraci, Robert. "Capitalist Stereotypes and the Economic Organization of the Russian Empire: The Case of the Tiflis Armenians." In *Defining Self: Essays on Emergent Identities in Russia Seventeenth to Nineteenth Centuries*, edited by Michael Branch, 365–81. Helsinki: Finnish Literature Society, 2009.

Grekov, Andrei Mikhailovich. *Priazov'e i Don: Ocherki obshchestvennoi i ekonom-icheskoi zhizni kraia.* St. Petersburg: Tipografiia "Obshchestvennaia pol'za", 1912.

Herlihy, Patricia. *Odessa: A History, 1794–1914.* Cambridge, MA: Harvard University Press, 1991.

Ivanova-Il'icheva, Anna Mikhailovna, Irina Alekseevna Stushnaia, and Ol'ga Vladimirovna Baeva. "Arkhitekturno-gradostroitel'noe razvitie Nakhichevani-na-Donu v kontekste formirovaniia gorodskoi kul'tury." *Istoricheskie, filosofiches-kie, politicheskie i iuridicheskie nauki, kul'turologiia i iskusstvovedenie: Voprosy teorii i praktiki* 10 (2014): 81–83.

Kappeler, Andreas. *Russland als Vielvölkerreich: Entstehung, Geschichte, Zerfall.* Munich: Beck, 1992.

Kazarov, Sarkis. *Nakhichevanskoe kupechestvo, konets XVIII–nachalo XX veka.* Rostov-on-Don: Kovcheg, 2012.

Kazarov, Sarkis. "Popytka zakhvata gorodskikh zemel' Nakhichevani-na-Donu v 1913 g." In *Armiane iuga Rossii. Istoriia, kul'tura, obshchee budushchee: Materialy III mezhdunarodnoi nauchnoi konferentsii, Rostov-na-Donu, 30–31 maia 2018 g,* edited by Gennadii Grigorevich Matishov, 99–102. Rostov-on-Don: IuNTs RAN, 2018.

Kazarov, Sarkis. "Nakhichevan-on-Don: Armenian Merchants and their Role in the Commercial Development of the Azov-Black Sea Region: Dynamics and Specificities of the Socio-Economic Development." In *Between Grain and Oil from the Azov to the Caucasus: The Port-Cities of the Eastern Coast of the Black Sea, Late 18th–Early 20th Century,* edited by Gelina Harlaftis et al., 399–427. Rethymnon: Centre of Maritime History, 2020.

Kirmse, Stefan. *The Lawful Empire: Legal Change and Cultural Diversity in Late Tsarist Russia.* Cambridge: Cambridge University Press, 2019.

Kollmann, Nancy Shields. *The Russian Empire, 1450–1801.* Oxford: Oxford University Press, 2017.

Koshkin, Ivan S. and Ivan Ivanovich Zubov, eds. *Donskoe torgovoe obshchestvo i ego znachenie v zhizni Donskogo kraia.* Novocherkassk: Elektro-Tipografiia F.A. Polubatko, 1888.

Kornienko, Boris S. *Pravyi Don: Kazaki i ideologiia natsionalizma (1909–1914).* St. Petersburg: Izdatel'stvo Evropeiskogo Universiteta, 2013.

Krasnianskii, Mikhail B. *Istoricheskii ocherk gg. Rostova i Nakhichevani n-D.* Rostov-on-Don: Elektrotipografiia M.I. Guzman, 1911.

Kuznetsov, Igor A. *Proshloe Rostova: Ocherki po istorii goroda Rostova-na-Donu.* Rostov-on-Don: Tipografiia Donskogo aktsionernogo obshchestva pechatnogo i izdatel'skogo dela, 1897. Rostov-on-Don: NB, 2012.

LeDonne, John P. *The Russian Empire and the World, 1700–1917: The Geopolitics of Expansion and Containment.* New York: Oxford University Press, 1997.

LeDonne, John P. "Frontier Governors General 1772–1825 II The Southern Frontier." *Jahrbücher für Geschichte Osteuropas* 48 (2000): 161–83.

Levin, Vladimir. "Preventing Pogroms: Patterns in Jewish Politics in Early Twentieth Century Russia." In *Anti-Jewish Violence: Rethinking Pogrom in East European History,* edited by Jonathan Dekel-Chen, 95–110. Bloomington: Indiana University Press, 2010.

Maslov, Alexander, and Vyacheslav Volchik. "Institutions and Lagging Development: The Case of the Don Army Region." *Journal of Economic Issues* 48, no. 3 (2014): 727–42.

Metcalf, Thomas R. "Colonial Cities." In *The Oxford Handbook of Cities in World History,* edited by Peter Clark, 753–69. Oxford: Oxford University Press, 2013.

Miller, Alexei. *The Romanov Empire and Nationalism: Essays in the Methodology of Historical Research.* Budapest: Central European University Press, 2008.

Minasyan, Edik G. and Levon V. Batiev. "'The Name List of … the Cityheads' in Nakhichevan-on-Don and the 'Statement of the Costs of City Revenues and

Expenditures' (the End 19th–Mid 20th century)." *Novoe proshloe* 2 (2019): 218–30. DOI: 10.23683/2500-3224-2019-2-218-230.

Obozrenie sostoianiia gorodov Rossiiskoi imperii v 1833. St. Petersburg: Tipografiia Karla Kraia, 1834.

Oliphant, Laurance. *The Russian Shores of the Black Sea in the Autumn of 1852 with a Voyage down the Volga, and a Tour through the Country of the Don Cossacks.* Edinburgh: William Blackwood and Sons, 1854.

Özveren, Eyüp. "A Framework for the Study of the Black Sea World, 1789–1915." *Review (Fernand Braudel Center)* 20, no. 1 (1997): 77–113.

Pavlovich, V., ed. *Materialy dlia geografii i statistiki Rossii, sobrannye ofitserami general'nogo shtaba.* St. Petersburg: Tipografiia Departamenta general'nogo shtaba, 1862.

Per-Abramiian, Ivan, ed. *Donsko-Azovskii Kalendar' na 1887 god.* Rostov-on-Don: Tipo-Litografiia I.A. Per-Abramiian, 1886.

Ponomariova, Irina. "Ethnic Processes in Mariupol and Russia's Imperial Migration Policy (19th–Early 20th Century)." In *Between Grain and Oil from the Azov to the Caucasus: The Port-Cities of the Eastern Coast of the Black Sea, Late 18th–Early 20th Century*, edited by Gelina Harlaftis et al., 235–58. Rethymnon: Centre of Maritime History, 2020.

Postanovleniia ocherednogo Rostovskogo uezdnogo zemskogo sobraniia: Okt'iabr'skoi sessii 1868 goda. Rostov-on-Don, 1869.

Raeff, Marc. "In the Imperial Manner." In *Catherine the Great: A Profile*, edited by Marc Raeff, 197–246. New York: Palgrave Macmillan, 1972.

Reichmann, Henry. "The Rostov General Strike of 1902." *Russian History* 9, no. 1 (1982): 67–85.

Riegg, Stephen Badalyan. *Russia's Entangled Embrace: The Tsarist Empire and the Armenians, 1801–1914.* Ithaca, NY: Cornell University Press, 2020.

Rhinelander, Anthony. *Prince Michael Vorontsov: Viceroy to the Tsar.* Montreal: McGill-Queen's University Press, 1990.

Robarts, Andrew. "A Plague on Both Houses? Population Movements and the Spread of Disease Across the Ottoman-Russian Black Sea Frontier, 1768–1830." PhD diss., Georgetown University, 2010.

"Rostov-na-Donu." *Moskvitianin: Uchenyi-literaturnyi zhurnal*, 3 (1850): 91–102.

Rostovskii na Donu torgovyi port: Otchet po Rostovskomu-na-Donu torgovomu portu. Rostov-on-Don: Tipografiia N. A. Pastucha, 1917.

Samarina, Natalya. "Rostov-on-Don in the Second Half of the 19th–Early 20th Century: Dynamics and Specificities of the Socio-Economic Development." In *Between Grain and Oil from the Azov to the Caucasus: The Port-Cities of the Eastern Coast of the Black Sea, Late 18th–Early 20th Century*, edited by Gelina Harlaftis et al., 369–97. Rethymnon: Centre of Maritime History, 2020.

Savchenkova, I. "Rostov na Donu." *Mir russkogo slova* 3 (2008): 107.

Savel'ev, Evgraf Petrovich. *Obshchestvo donskikh torgovykh kazakov 1804–1904.* Novocherkassk: Tipografiia V.I. Babenko, 1904.

Sifneos, Evrydiki. *Imperial Odessa: People, Spaces, Identities.* Leiden: Brill, 2018.

Sidorov, Vladimir Sergeevich. *Entsiklopediia starogo Rostova i Nakhichevani-na-Donu.* 6 vols. Rostov-on-Don: Donskaia gosudarstvennaia biblioteka, 1996.

Skal'kovskii, Apollon Aleksandrovich. *Rostov-na-Donu*. St. Petersburg: Tipografiia ministerstva vnutrennikh del, 1847.

Smeta dokhodov i raskhodov g. Nakhichevani na Donu na 1901. Rostov-on-Don, 1902.

Smirnov, Vladislav V. *Letopis' Nakhichevani-na-Donu: V istoricheskom, bytopisatel'nom, statisticheskom i illiustrativnom interesakh s prilozhenniiami, vkliuchaiushchimi vazhnye, poleznye i interesnye svedeniia*. Rostov-on-Don: Kniga, 2014.

Sobranie aktov otnosiashchicksia k obozreniiu istorii armianskogo Naroda. 2 vols. Moscow: Tipografiia Lazarevskogo instituta vostochnykh iazykov, 1833 and 1838.

Statisticheskii sbornik po g. Rostovu-na-Donu 1914. Rostov-on-Don: Pechatnia S. P. Jakovleva, 1915.

Sunderland, Willard. *Taming the Wild Field: Colonization and Empire on the Russian Steppe*. Ithaca, NY: Cornell University Press 2016.

Suny, Ronald Grigor. *The Baku Commune, 1917–1918: Class and Nationality in the Russian Revolution*. Princeton, NJ: Princeton University Press, 1972.

Suny, Ronald Grigor. *Looking toward Ararat: Armenia in Modern History*. Bloomington: Indiana University Press, 1993.

Suny, Ronald Grigor. "Eastern Armenians under Tsarist Rule." In *The Armenian People from Ancient to Modern Times*, Vol. 2, *Foreign Dominion to Statehood: The Fifteenth Century to the Twentieth Century*, edited by Richard G. Hovannisian, 109–35. Basingstoke: Macmillan, 1997.

Thiede, Roger Lee. "Town and Function in Tsarist Russia: A Geographical Analysis of Trade and Industry in the Towns of New Russia, 1860–1910." PhD diss., University of Washington, 1970.

Troebst, Stefan. "Isfahan – Moskau – Amsterdam: Zur Entstehungsgeschichte des moskauischen Transitprivilegs für die Armenischen Handelskompanie in Persien (1666–1676)." *Jahrbücher für Geschichte Osteuropas* 41, no. 2 (1993): 180–209.

Vedomosti nakhichevanskoi n-D. gorodskoi dumy, Nr. 1, Ianvar' – Iiun' 1899. Nakhichevan'-na-Donu, 1899.

Voennoe-statisticheskoe obozrenie Rossiiskoi imperii 1837–1854. Vol. 11, Novorossiiskaia guberniia, Bessarabskaia oblast' i Zemlia voiska Donskogo 1849–1850. St. Petersburg: Tipografiia Departamenta General'nago shtaba, 1849.

von Hirschhausen, Ulrike. *Die Grenzen der Gemeinsamkeit. Deutsche, Letten, Russen und Juden in Riga 1860–1914*. Göttingen: Vandenhoeck & Ruprecht, 2006.

Vrangel', Nikolai Egorovich. *Vospominaniia ot krepostnogo prava do bol'shevikov*. Moscow: Novoe literarturnoe obozrenie, 2003.

Part III

The City as a Palimpsest of Empires

7 Guarding the Imperial Border

The Fortress City of Niš between the Habsburgs and the Ottomans, 1690–1740

Florian Riedler

While in their own self-descriptions, many empires had only loosely defined borders or no limits at all, historians have acknowledged the actual importance of imperial borderlands. For all of the land-based eastern empires in the focus of this volume, border regions had a special role in the way they were established and expanded as well as in the evolution of their politics, military, and culture.[1] Despite the fascination for imperial metropolises, the role of cities in imperial borderlands has also attracted scholarly attention. Especially in relatively sparsely populated steppe or mountain zones, cities acted as anchors and as hubs of infrastructure that guaranteed imperial rule; they were even more important in other areas of inter-imperial competition that were characterized by established urban networks.[2] Such historical constellations deserve more attention, not the least because it has been argued that the way imperial politics shaped cities in borderlands has had an impact on ethnic conflicts in urban environments to this day.[3]

This chapter will use the research perspective proposed in this volume to show how imperial rule characterized Niš in today's Serbia and how especially the border between the Ottoman and the Habsburg Empires was instrumental in that process. Until this border was established at the end of the seventeenth century, Niš (which was also called Niş by the Ottomans and, in a neo-Latin form, Nissa by the Habsburgs) was a small town located in the interior of the Ottoman Balkans. In the sixteenth century, a period for which we have more or less exact figures, it had a population around 300 households with a majority of Muslims and a minority of less than 20 percent Orthodox Christians. Its bridge provided a safe crossing over the river Nišava, on the northern right bank of which the city was located. Consequently, it was as a convenient stop on the route from Istanbul to Belgrade for traveling officials, the Ottoman army, and merchants.[4]

DOI: 10.4324/9781003130031-10

Because of the ongoing Habsburg-Ottoman War at the end of the seventeenth century, Niš gained in importance and attracted the attention of Ottoman imperial politics. As a consequence, the city witnessed a sudden transformation, which was reflected in its material infrastructure and in the structure of its population and urban life. Until the last quarter of the nineteenth century, Niš remained characterized to varying degrees by its role as a city in a border region where Ottoman imperial rule was represented vis-à-vis its neighbor. This situation highlights how different elements of imperial rule play out in the Ottoman context. While mapping the impact of specific *Ottoman* imperial policies on the city, this chapter argues that these policies were always relational – i.e., they have to be conceived as mutual reactions to the imperial competitor beyond the border. As a consequence, imperial border cities were shaped by a high degree of adaptations and transfers from both sides, which were instrumental in defining a common standard among rival empires.

The first section of the chapter will introduce the border region resulting from the conquest of Hungary by the Habsburg Monarchy after 1683. The specific ideological nature of the inter-imperial conflict, the geo-political constellation, and the state of military technology gave strong points and fortresses a high degree of significance in this border region. As a result, not only Niš but also other cities in the region were transformed into fortress cities with this type of military infrastructure becoming the prime manifestation of the empire in the city.

The following two sections will focus more closely on Niš and on its fortress as the dominant architectural feature that defined it as an imperial city. Section two will discuss Niš as an object of Habsburg military strategy and will examine the representation of city and fortress in plans and images that were circulating in Europe. The next section will turn to the Ottoman side and its strategy to develop the fortress not only as the key piece of military infrastructure but also as a theatrical display of imperial power.

As the last section argues, the transformation of Niš into a border city also had far-reaching consequences for its population structure as well as the intercommunal relations between the different religious groups living in the city. Ottoman imperial urban governance combined two approaches: on the one hand, it re-asserted the Muslim character of the city, also in contradistinction to the imperial competitor; on the other hand, it aimed at reestablishing Niš as a city where different religious groups could coexist after the eruption of violence during the wars. While the chapter will focus on the first half of the eighteenth century when the imperial features of Niš were most pronounced, it will close with a survey of the nineteenth century. In addition to the imperial capitals that are usually the center of attention, cities on the periphery can also serve to expose the evolution of forms of imperial power from a long-term perspective.

The Relocation of the Habsburg-Ottoman Border

Niš rather suddenly evolved from a small market town on the overland route from Istanbul to Belgrade to an imperial fortress city when the Habsburg-Ottoman border was relocated from Upper Hungary 500 kilometers to the south-east around the turn of the seventeenth century. In the years after the Ottoman defeat at Vienna in 1683, the whole northern border of the Ottoman Empire from the Adriatic to the Black Sea came under pressure. In a series of wars during the late seventeenth and first half of the eighteenth century, the members of the anti-Ottoman coalition called the Holy League (Venice, the Habsburg Monarchy, the Polish-Lithuanian Commonwealth, and later also Russia) were able to push the Ottoman border to the south. The league, which was brokered by the pope, realized the old project of a common Christian front against the Ottomans as representatives of Islam and therefore emphasized the religious justification for a war that had also imperial goals. The Habsburg Monarchy made the biggest territorial gains by conquering Hungary, Transylvania, Banat, and Slavonia. Between 1718 and 1739, the Habsburgs temporarily ruled Belgrade and its hinterland south of the Danube. While the Habsburg-Ottoman border ran along the Sava and Danube rivers before and after, during this period it came closest to Niš, which became the principal city on the Ottoman side of the border (Map 7.1).[5]

The reversal of the Ottoman Empire's position from a military offensive to the defensive had a fundamental effect on the formation of the new border. Before the wars of the Holy League, the border with the Habsburg Monarchy was conceived in Ottoman imperial ideology in the traditional terms of the "ever-expanding frontier" and was organized as a zone open for raiding. Especially in the 1699 Treaty of Karlowitz (today Sremski Karlovci in Serbia), this approach was abandoned, and the new Habsburg-Ottoman border was demarcated as a line border, by dint of which the Ottoman negotiators hoped to secure its remaining territory from further attacks. The adoption of a line border with the Habsburgs continued a trend that had already started in the border areas to Venice and the Polish-Lithuanian Commonwealth.[6]

Together with transforming the conception and character of the border, the Ottomans' military posture also emphasized the importance of fortresses as defensive military infrastructure. Regarding this aspect, the new border was modeled after the old Habsburg-Ottoman border, which had formed in Upper Hungary after the formal annexation of central Hungary by the Ottomans in 1541. At that time, the militarily weaker Habsburg side had relied on fortresses to check the Ottoman advance. In their propaganda, these fortresses were praised as the expression in stone of the old rhetorical figure of the *antemurale Christianitatis*, the Christian

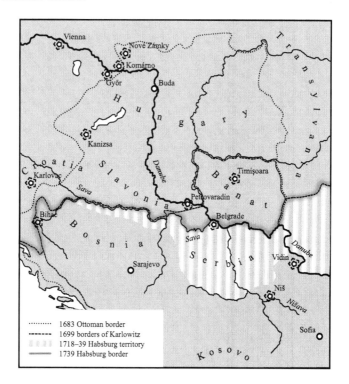

Map 7.1 The relocation of the Habsburg-Ottoman border between 1683 and 1739. Cartography by Florian Riedler, 2022.

bulwark against an external enemy. In the two decades after the first Ottoman siege in 1529, the Habsburgs completely overhauled the medieval fortifications of Vienna; in the second half of the sixteenth century, other cities and smaller border posts in western and northern Hungary as well as in Croatia were likewise modernized or, as in the case of the Croatian Karlovac (Germ. Karlstadt), newly founded. Especially the fortresses closest to Vienna such as Győr (Germ. Raab) and Komárno (Hung. Komárom, Ger. Komorn) on the Danube were essential to block the direct Ottoman advance on the Habsburg heartland.

These fortifications were largely planned by military architects and engineers from Italy who had perfected the design of polygonal, star-shaped fortifications with low-lying, earthen ramparts able to withstand the increasing firepower of artillery. Another new feature was bastions, from which the besieging enemy could be fired upon very effectively. This fortress design, which was adopted and refined all over Europe, was called the *trace italienne* after its inventors.[7]

The towns on the Habsburg-Ottoman border shared the fate of many European cities in contested regions, among them big cities such as Turin, Lille, and Antwerp, which were transformed in radical ways by their fortifications from the fifteenth to the eighteenth centuries. These places were affected by what Martha Pollak calls "military urbanism." Fortresses in such cities were places to represent the military power of the absolutist state vis-à-vis enemies not only from without but also from within. With their ramparts and access ways, they radically intervened in the fabric of organically grown medieval cities and thus gave the state more control over city populations and the traditional leadership. Moreover, the representation of cities also changed, with their citadels becoming major landmarks in plans, city views, and paintings. In many cases, the new military function also affected urban self-representation in processions and festivities.[8]

The Ottoman side did not directly adapt the fortress design described above but continued to use palisade constructions called *palanka* to fortify their border cities in Hungary. However, it quickly became well-acquainted with their adversary's innovation (not only in Central Europe but also in the Mediterranean theatres of war on Crete and Malta, for example) and also found effective ways to deal with the new *trace italienne*. Such fortresses could be overcome with adapted siege tactics and better artillery, as the conquest by the Ottomans of numerous Habsburg and Venetian fortress cities in the late sixteenth and early seventeenth century shows. Some of them such as Győr and Komárno were quickly reconquered by the Habsburgs; others such as Bihać (Germ. Wihitsch, Turk. Bihac) in Bosnia, Kanizsa (Germ. Kanischa, Turk. Kaniye) in western Hungary, and Nové Zámky (Germ. Neuhäusel, Turk. Uyvar) in today's Slovakia remained in Ottoman possession. The Ottomans continued to rely on these fortifications because they appreciated their military value; in a process that will be described below in greater detail, they also began to adopt the polygonal design of these fortresses.[9]

In their offensive after 1683, the Habsburg military had to reconquer these Ottoman border fortresses before they could advance deeper into Ottoman territory, taking Buda in 1686 and Belgrade in 1688. As in other places, immediately after conquering Belgrade, they started modernizing the fortifications they had taken over from the Ottomans. They employed a Venetian or Levantine engineer called Andrea Cornaro who had served in the defense of Candia (today Iraklion) on Crete, which the Ottomans had besieged intermittently from 1647 to 1669. This military engineer, who was by no means an exceptional case, offers an interesting example of the transfer of ideas and acculturation through war. When the Ottomans retook Belgrade in their counter-offensive of 1690, Cornaro switched sides – there are conflicting accounts whether he was forced or did it voluntarily – completed his work in Belgrade, and also fortified Timișoara

(Turk. Temeşvar, Germ. Temeschwar) in the latest style of the French chief military engineer Vauban. Moreover, he trained a number of Greeks and Armenians in the art of modern fortress design, who continued his work.[10] In the religiously charged language of an Ottoman chronicle, the fortified cities on the new border were awarded the honorary title of "Bulwarks of Islam" (*sedd-i sedîd-i İslâmiyye*), which exactly mirrored the expression of *antemurale Christianitatis*.[11]

Instead of Belgrade, Petrovaradin (Germ. Peterwardein), a medieval Hungarian and later Ottoman castle roughly 100 kilometers upstream on the Danube, became the cornerstone of the Habsburg border defense system.[12] The situation changed again when the Habsburgs returned to Belgrade in 1716 and rebuilt it over the next 20 years as their imperial border city. The transformations in Belgrade can serve as a comparative case not only for Habsburg border cities (e.g., Timişoara)[13] but also for Niš and other cities on the Ottoman side. The fortress of Belgrade was modernized in two phases with money raised by the pope for this purpose. The city west to the fortress was enclosed with a fortified line and regularized with a grid of perpendicular streets. Administrative buildings as well as a number of Catholic churches for the new bishop and the main Catholic orders were erected. For practical purposes, but also to show the symbolical subjugation of Islam – all the Muslim inhabitants had already left the city – some of these churches used existing mosque buildings. This part of the town was given to German settlers, who were considered more loyal than the local Christian Orthodox population. Although their bishop was also privileged, the latter had to live in a quarter outside the wall similar to the Jews. The German population formed the elite, but their loyalty was tested by the heavy-handed military administration of the city. The major conflict between the military and civilians centered on the labor duties the latter were supposed to render for the upkeep of the fortress.[14]

Ironically, these fortifications were destroyed by the Habsburgs army itself before it surrendered Belgrade to the Ottomans after the war of 1737–1739. Now the situation was reversed again: Belgrade became the principal Ottoman fortress on this section of the border; the German inhabitants left the city, the Muslims returned, and their mosques were restituted. With the exception of the last Habsburg-Ottoman War of 1787–1791, the border established in 1739 remained intact for the Ottomans until 1867 when they ceded Belgrade to the autonomous Principality of Serbia and for the Habsburgs until 1918.

Similar to Belgrade, other cities were also deeply affected by the new border, which oscillated for a time in the Sava-Danube area before it assumed its final position. The following section will focus on Niš and its transformation into a Habsburg fortress city since it was first conquered by the Habsburg army in 1689.

The Fortress of Niš and Its Representation

In the campaign season of 1689, the Habsburg military decided to continue their advance from Belgrade further south along the road to Istanbul. After smaller encounters in what is today central Serbia, the decisive battle with the main Ottoman army was fought at Niš, 230 kilometers to the south-east of Belgrade. The Habsburg army was able to storm the Ottoman camp and take the city, which had been fortified in the previous year by the Ottoman commander of the Hungarian front with a ring of palisades and a ditch.[15]

After this victory, Niš became the base for further Habsburg military expeditions west into Bosnia, south into Kosovo and Macedonia, north-east to Vidin in today's Bulgaria, and also further along the road to Istanbul. However, the supply lines were overextended so that the few advance units that reached the basin of Sofia were not strong enough to attack the city. In the winter of 1689–1690, the War Council in Vienna considered falling back to Belgrade altogether, but the local commanding general insisted on organizing the defense in the upcoming campaign season from Niš.[16]

As it turned out, this defense was not successful and the Habsburg occupation of Niš ended after roughly one year in September 1690. From an urbanistic perspective, however, the decision to base the Habsburg army there affects Niš to this day. In the spring of 1690, under the supervision of a Habsburg military engineer, soldiers and local peasants built the first version of the fortress that still dominates the northern bank of the river Nišava today. The area was later used by the Yugoslav People's Army as a military base, before it was converted into a park in the 1960s. Built under time constraints and with restricted financial and material resources at hand, this first fortress was no more than a line of earthen ramparts protected by a ditch and a covered way that enveloped the whole city on the north shore of the river. Although the fortress was renovated and upgraded regularly during the eighteenth century when it was in Ottoman possession again, its principal design – i.e., the outline of the bastioned ramparts – did not change significantly and has been preserved to this day. It had a simple but slightly irregular polygonal shape to protect the city and, with the addition of a no-longer-extant fortified bridge-head on the south bank of the Nišava, to provide a secure river crossing. According to the contemporary military doctrine, the purpose of the fortress was to delay the Ottoman advance; a more serious resistance would have required additional fortifications, especially in the surrounding hills, which the Habsburg army could neither build nor man under the given circumstances.[17]

Despite its shortcomings, the fortress forced the Ottoman army to invest four weeks in a siege when it arrived from Sofia at Niš in the summer of 1690. Following common siege tactics, the Ottomans enclosed the city with their own trenches and started to dig perpendicular trenches in the direction of the ramparts to be able to approach under cover. In September, these trenches reached the outer perimeter of the covered way and the ramparts came within range of mining activity or assaults by the janissaries, the core troops of the standing Ottoman army. Consequently, the Habsburg fortress commander negotiated a surrender with the Ottoman side and was allowed to withdraw with his men, their light weapons, and supplies toward Belgrade.[18]

Because of the rather short occupation, Niš was never turned into a full-fledged imperial Habsburg city. Unlike the example of Belgrade discussed above, there was no time to rearrange urban life in the middle of a war. In fact, it seems that very few civilians remained in the city after its Muslim inhabitants had fled. After the reconquest it was the Ottomans' turn to reintegrate the city into their imperial framework. But before we turn in greater detail to this process in the next two sections, let us consider the field of representation where Niš, or rather Nissa as it was called by the Austrians, lingered for a little bit longer in the Habsburg imperial sphere and turned, so to speak, into a virtual Habsburg imperial city.

Like the Habsburg victory at Niš in 1689, which had been celebrated in numerous propaganda publications, the fortress also became part of different media associated with the successful war against the Ottoman Empire. Hand-drawn fortress plans immediately circulated in the Habsburg military; they were possibly copies of the original plans made by the Habsburg military architect Peroni when he designed the fortress in the spring of 1690.[19] Some of them were clearly produced for representational purposes – e.g., a copy inserted into a yearly campaign report bound in red velvet, which was possibly presented to Emperor Leopold I (r. 1658–1705). On this copy of the fortress plans, the seven bastions were named after the emperor himself, his children, and other members of the House of Austria: Elisabeta, Leopold, Carel, Eleonora, Joseph, Theresia, and Antonia. There is hardly a clearer way to integrate the new fortress into the imperial-dynastic project; at the same time, this representation also reveals the virtual nature of the enterprise as it is hardly conceivable that these names had any significance on the ground and were more likely an attempt to flatter the emperor.[20]

To mobilize support for the war, a print of the fortress was made from one of these drawings that aimed at a wider audience. The print's caption claimed to depict the military situation in August 1690 at the moment when the Ottoman army was besieging the city. As a design element, which had already been used in prints illustrating the 1683 siege of Vienna, it showed the Ottoman trenches approaching the fortress walls from the north-west. The engraver was Johann Martin Lerch, who has been characterized as an "unofficial propagandist of the court" and thus clearly connects this print to imperial politics.[21] In an Italian version, the fortress plans were also integrated into a contemporary atlas and collection of famous fortress cities.[22] In this way, Niš – or rather Nissa – became known to the European public first and foremost as a fortress like so many others in Europe. From this rather restricted perspective, it is telling that in all the drawings and prints the space encircled by the ramparts was left blank – apart from its military function the city was not considered interesting.

Due to the geopolitical situation, the Habsburg military kept collecting information on Niš, and wider public interest was rekindled in the subsequent wars during the first half of the eighteenth century. The city was not directly involved in the Habsburg-Ottoman War of 1716–1718, in which the Habsburgs gained the Banat as well as Belgrade and its hinterland, which was now ruled as the Kingdom of Serbia directly by the crown. The new border ran through what is now central Serbia/Šumadija, which made Niš the first major city on Ottoman territory. Because it was the only Ottoman fortress on the road from Belgrade to Istanbul, for a period of 20 years it was one of the most important cities in the Ottoman Balkans. On the occasion of the demarcation of the new border, and possibly again later, a Habsburg military engineer was able to draw a new plan of the fortress, this time also including the settlement that had formed on the opposite (left bank) side of the river. Effectively a spy, he had to draw from observations without being able to employ any land surveying methods or geodetic instruments.[23] Neither this plan nor a detailed account of the visit to Niš by Cornelius Driesch,[24] secretary of the Habsburg ambassador on his way to Istanbul, indicate that they were aware of the fortress's prior Habsburg history. The likely reason was that by this time, following a succession of modernization projects, the fortress was already perceived as an integral part of Ottoman Niš. The next section will deal with this process of Ottomanization and Niš's urban development in greater detail.

Although the 1718 spy map was clearly made for military purposes and initially not accessible to the wider public, it became the basis for several prints, which were published with slight variations during the next decade.[25] They added a street grid to the fortress and the left bank city, details which had been not important for the military maps of 1690. As a consequence, they looked more like ordinary city plans, where Niš was labeled a "Turkish border fortress," with the stress on the border fortress, as I would argue. The way in which this label triggered certain expectations of the prints' audience became apparent when one of them was re-issued in 1737 on the occasion of the second Habsburg occupation of Niš.[26] This print adds to the already known city plan a small vignette depicting the events. In the background, it shows a generic fortress city with ramparts and towers (and steeples?) under siege; in the foreground, four men on their knees offer a set of keys to a group of noble officers emerging from a large tent. While the officers wear knee-long coats and high boots, the inhabitants who obviously present to them the keys of the city in the background wear long, flowing garments. In the whole scene, these clothes, which could be read as oriental, together with what could be a turban lying on the ground at the side of one of the kneeling men, are the only indication that the surrender was not located on one of the many theatres of war in other parts of eighteenth-century Europe. For the artist, the template "surrender of a fortress" apparently seemed more appropriate here than any stereotypical depiction of a victory over the Turkish arch-enemy, which in the eighteenth century often used images connoting antiquity. At the same time, the genre forbade any exoticizing approach as it developed from the late seventeenth century in European arts after the immediate Ottoman threat had already waned.[27]

Lasting just two and a half months, this second Habsburg occupation of Niš was much shorter than the first and this time had only a marginal effect. When the Habsburg army appeared in front of the city, its Ottoman commander negotiated a favorable surrender: the Ottoman garrison with their light arms, together with the Muslim inhabitants, was allowed to leave the city. The Habsburg army even provided the carts for transporting the movable property of the civilian population. During the occupation, the Habsburg army produced a series of more accurate maps of Niš and even devised a plan to totally overhaul the fortifications of the city. However, these plans had to be shelved, because when the Ottoman main army arrived in full strength a couple of months later, the Habsburg commander capitulated under similar terms.[28]

Because Habsburg-Ottoman relations quickly normalized after the peace of 1739, the interest in Niš waned. Moreover, from a geopolitical perspective, Niš was overshadowed by Belgrade, which again became the Ottoman border fortress to the Habsburg Monarchy. Accordingly, there were no further prints, and only the Habsburg military kept collecting information on Niš, which it withheld from the public. Only in the middle of the nineteenth century was the city rediscovered by European travelers as a quintessential Ottoman Balkan city with all the Orientalist stereotyping this implied at the time.

The Ottomanization of the Fortress

The militarization of Niš was kickstarted by the Habsburgs during their short first occupation but was consolidated by the Ottomans over the following decades. When the Ottoman army re-occupied the city after the Habsburg surrender in September 1690, its appearance had changed dramatically from when they had left approximately one year earlier. According to a contemporary chronicler, it had turned from a *palanka* into an "immense earthen fortress."[29] The contemporary Ottoman historian Defterdar Sarı Mehmed Pasha, who was a high financial officer and also had military experience, describes the change even more elaborately:

> By digging long ditches on all four sides of the accursed pagan city and introducing strong and solid bastions and creating and fortifying encircling walls filled with earth, a strong fortress came into being with palisades entirely [around] the space of one arrowshot to the outside of the ditch and a covered way and many similar things [such as] buildings and many tunnels, so that it was surpassing the limits of description.[30]

These fortifications became the main focus of the Ottoman central government's investment in the city. Over several decades, the ramparts were constantly renovated and the space inside, after the houses and mosques had been repaired, was filled with new barracks, army storehouses, powder magazines, and administrative buildings. This construction activity was the most visible side of the process that made Niš an Ottoman imperial city, integrating it into the Ottoman border defense system.

Similar to modern infrastructure projects, early modern fortresses were permanent construction sites. Even if they were not attacked, they had to be constantly repaired and maintained.[31] The first such repair was already ordered by the sultan himself when he visited Niš in 1695.[32] Beyond mere maintenance, the Ottomans also had plans to re-design and extend the fortifications. As already mentioned, Peroni's minimal design clearly reflected the constraints of time, building material, and money the Habsburg army faced. Therefore, shortly after the end of the war in 1699, a general overhaul of the fortress was launched on which the chronicle of Defterdar Sarı Mehmed dwells at length, because of the unfortunate outcome of the project.[33] It started with a feasibility study that revealed how the Ottoman military planned to modernize the fortress:

> Chief miner Mehmed came and inspected the place and found out that 'the necessary things to construct four bastions outside the ditch with the exception of lime, stone and bricks, i.e. only carpenters, workers, carts and the like would altogether cost 361,435 *kuruş.*' And when he arrived there, he presented a plan that he had drawn and on the basis of this plan his building design was approved, because his word was trusted. So a building official was nominated and agents were sent to the districts of the Rumeli province with permission [to recruit] a certain amount of carts, fortress workers and other workers.

By building four outlying bastions, probably in the style of ravelins, the Ottoman military architect wanted to protect the approach to the ramparts. The whole report in the chronicle conveys the routine manner in which the project was initiated. But then things started to go wrong – again, the parallel to modern infrastructure projects is striking:

> So they began to tear down the old walls of the fortress and to dig a wide ditch on the outside and undertook several such things in this manner and with the approaching winter they stopped. According to the design that Mehmed had proposed a shaping [of the ditch] into a long and deep form was necessary. Apart from high costs it would have meant a total injustice and hard labor to the peasants of the district. In contrast, would it have been executed following the old style [i.e. without completely redesigning the fortifications] there would have been enough money. As a consequence, in the new year the fortress was left in the present state to be set down in another manner.

Costs escalated, and there seem to have been complaints by the workers as well as slow progress so that deadlines could not be met. The risks involved in constructing this sort of military infrastructure are immediately apparent, as are the reasons why so many fortresses were in bad shape, even if they were essential from a military standpoint.

Defterdar Sarı Mehmed's explanation for what happened brings us back to the specificities of the Habsburg-Ottoman inter-imperial conflict. The historian's verdict is harsh, charging the architect with treason: "In one word, the so-called Chief miner Mehmed wickedly destroyed the sultan's fortress." Here, the difficulties of infrastructure development are reduced to sabotage, which is ultimately explained by the historian with Mehmed's identity as a European (*Frenk*), who had switched sides and converted to work for the Ottoman military. The episode again reveals the importance of adaptation and acculturation in the border zone and the role of foreign military experts. As in all empires, they were very common in the Ottoman context, but in the still-charged atmosphere of a war, they could also serve as scapegoats.[34]

While this plan for a complete re-design and extension of the fortress failed spectacularly, it shows that the Ottoman military had adopted the polygonal design for one of its most important fortification projects. In other places, such modernization plans were implemented successfully, such as in Kiliia (Turk. Kilya) at the mouth of the Danube and in cities on the Dniestr River, which formed the border to Poland-Lithuania and later to Russia, including Khotyn (Turk. Hotin, Pol. Chocim), Bender, and Bilhorod (Turk. Akkerman). In these places, bastioned fortresses were constructed to strengthen older fortifications at the beginning of the eighteenth century and sometimes extended again in the late eighteenth century.[35]

The next renovation of Niš fortress, ordered in 1716 when a new war with the Habsburg monarchy was imminent, was more successful. Five hundred workers and 200 construction specialists from the surrounding districts were sent to the construction site for which 33,000 trees were cut.[36] This material may have also been used to build the ring of palisades around the left bank part of the city, which can be seen very clearly on the 1718 spy map mentioned above.

When Niš replaced Belgrade as the main Ottoman border city after the peace of 1718, another modernization project was launched to support the new role of the city. Although the huge sum of 390,000 *kuruş* was to be invested over a period of three years, this time the general design of the fortress was not changed. The complexity of such a large project caused some typical problems: the *sipahi*s of the surrounding districts – i.e., the holders of military prebends, who were ordered to assist in the construction work – complained about the workload, just as the other districts in Ottoman Europe did about their financial contributions, and at one stage the governor of Niš was investigated over the embezzlement of funds. However, the government was determined to complete the construction so that the main part of the new fortress could be inaugurated at a ceremony in July 1723 at which the governor and other high-ranking officials were awarded robes of honor.[37]

The result of this modernization concerned not only the fortress as a military object but also as a complex representing Ottoman imperial power at the border. Defining the appearance of the fortress to this day, modernization was the final step in its Ottomanization. Perhaps the largest share of labor and money was invested in the ramparts. All the bastions, together with the curtain walls in between them, were clad in stone, which gave the overall impression of durability and strength. Even more eye-catching were the four new gate houses of the Istanbul Gate, the Belgrade Gate, the Vidin Gate, and the Sofia Gate, which were executed in the same material.

The most important of these gate houses, the merlon-decorated Istanbul Gate, is located immediately at the bridge where the southern tip of the fortress comes close to the river. Similar to other examples, such as the Imperial Gate in Topkapı Palace in Istanbul, there are two niches in a decorated frame to the left and right of the vaulted gateway ending in a simple "honeycomb vault" (*muqarnas*), a common decorative element of Ottoman architecture. Above the gateway, a long Ottoman inscription is placed on a rectangular plate, which gives 1723 (1136 AH) as the date for the completion of the fortress. The body of the heavily Persianized

Ottoman text celebrates the reigning sultan, Ahmed III (r. 1703–1730), who is praised as a victorious conqueror and peacemaker. In line with contemporary court poetry, he is likened to mythical kings like Alexander the Great and Dareios but also depicted as a defender of religion.

> And besides all things [the sultan] created the fortress of Niš and, similar to Alexander, thereby put an iron barrier in the way of the enemy. The fortress had iron gates and Rhodes and Candia envied him because of this city.[38]

Analogous to Alexander, who fortified the Caucasus to keep out the barbarians of the north, Ahmed protects the country with the fortress of Niš. The comparison with Rhodes and Candia on Crete opens the horizon to the Mediterranean frontier of the Ottoman Empire, where the war of 1716–1718 had begun with the Ottoman attack on the Venetian Morea (Figure 7.1).

Belgrade Gate, the second gate which is still extant today but closed, is located only 150 meters from Istanbul Gate at the southern tip of the fortress, but on its south-western flank. It is decorated with two columns at either side of the gateway and a panel above it, which may have been designed to hold an inscription, but today remains empty. It is less splendid than the Istanbul Gate but was probably decorated more richly than the two other gates, which were less frequented and are not preserved in their original form. For foreigners from the north such as merchants or Habsburg ambassadors on their way to Istanbul, the Belgrade Gate must have functioned as an entry not just to the city but to the Ottoman Empire in general. Usually, these travelers used the road coming from Belgrade, which passed the fortress to the west, to reach the bridge.

These gates marked the entry into the fortress as a state space, especially the area at its southern tip accessible through the Istanbul and Belgrade Gates. Here, administrative buildings were concentrated such as a still extant arsenal, a guardhouse, and the seat of the city commander. This new government area added to older forms of imperial presence in the city such as Hünkar (Sultan) Mosque named after Murad I (r. 1359–1389) during whose reign Niš was conquered for the first time by the Ottomans. This mosque, which was rebuilt several times, was located more to the north near the Vidin Gate but is no longer extant. The main part of the fortress consisted of civilian quarters, as we will see in the next section.

Until the end of Ottoman rule in 1878, the fortress basically remained in the state it had taken in 1723. There is constant documentation about repairs in the eighteenth century, but after Belgrade had become Ottoman again in 1739, the Ottoman state understandably felt no urgency to invest

Figure 7.1 Istanbul Gate of Niš Fortress. Photo by Florian Riedler, 2016.

in the military infrastructure of Niš. Only when the Habsburg army captured Belgrade in the last Habsburg-Ottoman War of 1788–1790 did the fortress of Niš became strategically important again for a short time. But because the status quo ante was quickly restored after the peace treaty, a modernization of Niš was not considered necessary afterward.[39]

Imperial Urban Governance

The wars of the late seventeenth and first half of the eighteenth century that resulted in a new border and the fortification of Niš also affected urban life and the city population. The most immediate effect was the garrison of the fortress, which from now on made up a considerable part of the city's population. After 1699, the number of soldiers stationed in the fortress was still relatively small, amounting to just 273 men immediately before the war of 1716–1718. During the war, this number rose to perhaps 15,000 before dropping again to approximately 5,500 in 1727–1728.[40] Still, this was a considerable number for a small town, which according to the census of 1710 comprised fewer than 500 households.[41] The population of Niš later increased, especially after 1718 when many Muslim refugees from Belgrade and the Banat settled in the city. A whole new quarter emerged between the fortress and the river along the road to Belgrade, which was aptly named the Belgrade Quarter, and the refugees also populated the city on the left bank.[42]

Although they were the personnel of the imperial government, the janissary garrisons of eighteenth-century fortress cities were a particular unruly group. In Niš two major mutinies in 1719 and 1721 erupted over outstanding pay, but apparently also because of the government's peace policy.[43] From this milieu a certain Patrona Halil emerged – for a time he was stationed in Niš and in nearby Vidin on the Danube – who incited a janissary revolt in the capital, which in 1730 overthrew Ahmed III.[44] In this way, the militarization of the border had direct repercussions on the imperial center, too.

Besides the fact that there was now a regular garrison in the city, the militarization of the border also affected the local civilian population. It can be argued that the majority of the Muslim male population in the region was involved in the military – some as locally recruited soldiers, others in less direct ways.[45] Together with the many Muslim refugees among the city population, this created a siege mentality, nurturing mistrust and suspicion, especially against the Christian population, which was periodically accused of collaboration with the enemy. It is true that in all the wars the Habsburg military recruited irregulars from among the Christian subjects of the sultan, so the accusation was not entirely unfounded. When Niš was surrendered by the Habsburgs in 1690, members of such irregular Christian militias fell into the hands of the Ottomans and were executed as bandits.[46] When the Ottoman army reconquered areas occupied by the Habsburgs, there were also reprisals against the civilian Christian population, large parts of which fled to Habsburg territory north of the Danube.[47]

The following wars periodically increased the level of distrust toward the local Christian population, sometimes with very tangible effects at the urban level. During the war of 1716–1718, for example, all the Christian inhabitants of the fortress area in Niš were forced to sell their houses and move to other parts of the city; this security measure was later also implemented in Vidin where it was explicitly justified by the "law of the frontier" (*kanun-i serhad*). This shows the direct effect of the geopolitical situation on the emergence of a policy of separation.[48]

In contrast, it was easier for groups that were considered loyal to the Ottoman state to find their place in the city. The Jews are one example: a group of Sephardim had already founded a new synagogue in Niš in 1695. The Jewish community clustered in the heart of the left-bank city immediately on the riverbank, until it was deported and killed in the Second World War. Their synagogue was rebuilt in 1925 in an art deco style and today is a museum.[49] The Roma (Kıptı) constituted another separate group among the inhabitants of Niš. They defied the usual Ottoman state categorization of its subjects according to religion, because among them were Muslims as well as Christians. The 1718 spy map already indicated that they were living in the suburbs of the left-bank city. In 1737, the whole community left Niš together with the Muslims and therefore could easily resettle when the city became Ottoman again.[50]

Ottoman governance of urban diversity sometimes could acquire a political dimension as shown by a drastic intervention that occurred after the short Habsburg occupation in 1737. The loyalty of the Christian community was again at stake, but this time not of its ordinary members but of the Orthodox leadership. While the grand vizier was in the city to prepare the advance on Belgrade, the local Muslim elite accused the bishop of Niš of having collaborated with the Habsburg occupiers. Consequently, the grand vizier confiscated the bishop's church, St. Nicholas, which was situated outside the left-bank city. It was converted to Fethiye, the Conquest Mosque.[51]

This was a late example of a practice that had been more widespread during the fourteenth-century expansion of the Ottoman Empire when many churches in Anatolia and the Balkans had been converted into mosques, some of them bearing this same name, Fethiye. But there were also examples of later church conversions, most prominently the Pammakaristos Church in Istanbul, the main church of the Orthodox Patriarchate, which became Fethiye Mosque in the late sixteenth century (celebrating the conquest of Georgia and not, as was usual, the conquest of the city where the converted church was located).

The conversion of St. Nicholas in Niš mirrored the behavior of the Habsburgs who, apparently on the order of the emperor himself, had turned a mosque into a church during their short occupation.[52] As we have also seen above in the case of Belgrade, such conversion stories were quite common on both sides. They have been interpreted as the expression of dominance of one religious community (or rather the states that identified with them) over another. By alternately appropriating a religious building of the other community, they asserted their own superiority. In the case of Niš, what perhaps triggered imperial intervention into a local issue was a situation where the border of the Muslim religioscape was congruent with the border of the state.[53]

It must be stressed that for the Ottoman authorities such violent interventions never encroached on the general right of non-Muslims to live in
the city. In the case of St. Nicholas, it seems that the grand vizier mainly
targeted the bishop; there is reason to believe that the Orthodox community retained a church inside the left-bank city.[54] In fact, balancing acts of
symbolic subjugation, there was an overall Ottoman policy of reconstruction that aimed at securing the Christian population in the new border
provinces as an important tax base for the state. During the first war, in
1690 and 1691, the authorities resettled prisoners taken from among the
Christian population of the reconquered areas in their former homes and
also allowed them to rebuild their churches instead of selling them off as
slaves to other parts of the empire. As a general policy, the grand vizier
initiated a reform of the poll tax non-Muslims had to pay that would take
into account the economic circumstances of the individual tax payer.[55]

This policy explains the continuous presence of an Orthodox community
in an urban context such as Niš, which developed into the most dynamic
part of the city population despite certain episodes that fostered mistrust.
According to the census of 1710, Christians already accounted for over 20
percent of the total civilian population and grew disproportionally over the
following decades. In the late eighteenth century, a Habsburg spy claimed
that half of the 2,000 households of Niš were Christian.[56] In the nineteenth
century, this balance would tip and Niš became a majority Christian city.

In sum, the border situation also left a deep imprint on the population of
Niš. Imperial policies were instrumental in reviving urban life and governing the relations between the different communities. In order to increase its
tax base, the empire tried to ease tensions and guaranteed a place for all
the groups in the city, though these were arranged in a hierarchical way.

Conclusion: Changing Manifestations of Empire

From the last decade of the seventeenth to the middle of the eighteenth century, the two empires competing in the new border region south of the Danube and the Sava became very present in Niš. They built the fortress, which
stood for a new phase in the history of the city, as the most ostentatious display of imperial military power. While a Habsburg military engineer could
pride himself on the original design, it was the continuous investment of
money and manpower by the sultan that saved the fortress from the wear
of time. The Istanbul Gate in particular came to symbolize Ottoman imperial power very similar to the decorated gatehouses in Baroque fortresses
in Europe. This gate created such a lasting visual impression that it even
became part of the coat of arms of the modern Serbian city of Niš, which
otherwise does everything to gloss over the Ottoman period of its history.

Besides building military infrastructure, the Ottoman state also took measures to reconstruct the urban life and population in the city, which was periodically affected by the imperial wars. Ottoman imperial governance fostered urban diversity: it guaranteed a place for different ethno-religious communities in the city, which in the eyes of the state were important resources, and integrated them into a hierarchical order mirroring the Islamic legitimacy of the empire. As the result of fierce inter-imperial competition, this hierarchy was highly politicized, causing suspicion and tensions from the highest to lowest levels of urban society. This was a particular problem for the local Orthodox Christians who were caught between the imperial fronts.

As much as the border was a cause for war and destruction, it also gave rise to urban growth in Niš. The city's 20 years as the main border fortress (1718–1739) and the following 30 years of peace, which was a period of increasing trade and economic expansion all over Ottoman Europe, were particularly important. The fortress, which had formerly included the civilian city, became part of a larger settlement area in which the opposite left bank became dominant, where most of the population now lived and where economic activity was concentrated. In the second half of the eighteenth century, a local elite formed that steered the city through the period of unrest and crisis in the two decades around 1800 when the imperial center was virtually absent from large parts of the Ottoman Balkans. At that time, Niš was threatened not by the Habsburg army – the Monarchy remained a friendly neighbor except for the short war of 1788–1791 – but by internal Ottoman warlords such as the Pasha of Vidin or the Serbian rebels in the Pashalik of Belgrade.

The constant effort by the imperial government to recentralize the empire began to gain momentum in the 1820s until it peaked in a reform program called the Tanzimat, which was officially adopted in 1839. By modernizing its military, administrative, legal, and educational systems, the Ottomans wanted to stay on par with the European states and be accepted as an equal power. It can count as a diplomatic success that in the Crimean War against Russia (1853–1856), Britain and France sided with the Ottomans while the Austrian Empire observed a benevolent neutrality.

During this war, the fortress of Niš, which was guarding the internal border to the autonomous Principality of Serbia, underwent a long-overdue modernization. Its ramparts were repaired and several new military buildings together with a new governor's palace were erected inside the fortress. Additionally, four forts (*tabya*) were built at some distance from the fortress to secure the approach from the north, finally realizing the strategic considerations from the beginning of the eighteenth century. While these works were supervised by one Captain Şmit and Monsieur Blum from the

Imperial School of Engineering in Istanbul, the labor was provided by Ottoman soldiers as well as by all the citizens of Niš – Muslims, Christians, and Jews.[57] The degree to which the Tanzimat state was dependent on such contributions becomes evident from the fact that they had to be publicly recognized. On a hand-drawn, colored plan of the fortress,[58] the four new forts carry individual names: one was named Mecidiye Fort after Sultan Abdülmecid and one after the Governor of Niš, Ismail Pasha; two were named after the regular army and the reserve, Nizamiye Tabyası and Redif Tabyası; and the last was called Ahali Tabyası, the People's Fort. In this naming practice, we can see in a nutshell one of the new approaches of the Tanzimat – namely, the attempt to broaden the basis of Ottoman imperial rule by democratizing it within the limits of absolutist rule, an approach it shared with its imperial neighbors in Europe.

The fortress was no longer the best means to express the presence of the empire in the city in a modern way. Rather, it was the utilitarian buildings and public infrastructure such as a hospital, an orphanage cum vocational school, many roads, and even the new cathedral that were built under Governor Midhat Pasha (1860–1864) that symbolized the new way of interpreting the imperial city. In the end, the fortress did not even retain its military value. When the Serbian army advanced on Niš during the Ottoman-Russian War of 1877–1878, the heavily outnumbered Ottoman garrison surrendered and left the city together with most of the Muslim inhabitants.

Notes

1 Alfred Rieber, *The Struggle for the Eurasian Borderlands: From the Rise of Early Modern Empires to the End of the First World War* (Cambridge: Cambridge University Press, 2014); Hans-Christian Maner, ed., *Grenzregionen der Habsburgermonarchie im 18. und 19. Jahrhundert: Ihre Bedeutung und Funktion aus der Perspektive Wiens* (Münster: LIT, 2005); Andrew C.S. Peacock, ed., *The Frontiers of the Ottoman World* (Oxford: Oxford University Press, 2009).

2 Serhiy Bilenky, *Imperial Urbanism in the Borderlands: Kyiv, 1800–1905* (Toronto: University of Toronto Press, 2017); Paulus Adelsgruber, Laurie Cohen, and Börries Kuzmany, *Getrennt und doch verbunden: Grenzstädte zwischen Österreich und Russland, 1772–1918* (Wien: Böhlau, 2011).

3 Liam O'Dowd, "Contested States, Frontiers and Cities," in *A Companion to Border Studies*, ed. Thomas M. Wilson and Hastings Donnan (Chichester: John Wiley & Sons, 2012), 158–76.

4 Machiel Kiel, "Niş," in *Türkiye Diyanet Vakfı İslam Ansiklopedisi*, vol. 33, 147–9; Dušanka Bojanić, "Niš do Velikog rata 1683," in *Istorija Niša*, ed. Danica Milić (Niš: Gradina i Prosveta, 1983), 1:107–69.

5 Ivan Parvev, *Habsburgs and Ottomans between Vienna and Belgrade (1683–1739)* (Boulder, CO: East European Monographs, 1995).

6 Rifaat A. Abou-el-Haj, "The Formal Closure of the Ottoman Frontier in Europe, 1699–1703," *Journal of the American Oriental Society* 89, no. 3 (1969): 467–75; Colin Heywood, "The Frontier in Ottoman History: Old Ideas and New Myths," in *Frontiers in Question: Eurasian Borderlands, 700–1700*, ed. Daniel Power and Naomi Standen (Houndmills: Palgrave Macmillan, 1999), 228–50; Dariusz Kolodziejczyk, "Between Universalistic Claims and Reality: Ottoman Frontiers in the Early Modern Period," in *The Ottoman World*, ed. Christine Woodhead (London: Routledge, 2012), 205–19.

7 Tibor Martí, "'Antemurale Christianitatis' en Europa Central: La frontera húngara y croata de la monarquía de los Habsburgo en la época moderna," in *Antemurales de la Fe: Conflictividad confesional en la Monarquía de los Habsburgo, 1516–1714*, ed. Pedro García Martin (Madrid: Universidad Autónoma de Madrid, 2015), 181–95; Géza Pálffy, "The Origins and Development of the Border Defence System against the Ottoman Empire in Hungary (up to the Early Eighteenth Century)," in *Ottomans, Hungarians, and Habsburgs in Central Europe*, ed. Géza Dávid and Pál Fodor (Leiden: Brill, 2000), 39–49; and id., "Die Türkenabwehr der Habsburgermonarchie in Ungarn und Kroatien im 16. Jahrhundert: Verteidigungskonzeption, Grenzfestungssystem, Militärkartographie," in *Türkenangst und Festungsbau: Wirklichkeit und Mythos*, ed. Harald Heppner and Zsuzsa Barbarics-Hermanik (Frankfurt: Peter Lang, 2009).

8 Martha D. Pollak, *Cities at War in Early Modern Europe* (Cambridge: Cambridge University Press, 2010).

9 Klára Hegyi, "The Ottoman Network of Fortresses in Hungary," in *Ottomans, Hungarians, and Habsburgs in Central Europe*, ed. Géza Dávid and Pál Fodor (Leiden: Brill, 2000), 168–69; Mark L. Stein, *Guarding the Frontier: Ottoman Border Forts and Garrisons in Europe* (London: I.B. Tauris, 2007), 36–54.

10 Ömer Gezer, "Kale ve Nefer: Habsburg Sınırında Osmanlı Askerî Gücünün Yeniden Örgütlenmesi (1699–1715)" (PhD diss., Hacettepe Üniversitesi, Ankara, 2016), 116–22; Luigi Fernando Marsigli, *Stato Militare Dell'Imperio Ottomanno: L´état Militaire de l'Empire Ottoman* (The Hague: Gosse, 1732), 2:150. More information on Cornaro and two other captured Habsburg engineers is provided by Radmila Tričković, *Beogradski Pašaluk, 1687–1739* (Belgrade: Službeni Glasnik, 2003), 88–93; I thank Jelena Radovanović for indicating this to me.

11 Defterdar Sarı Mehmed Paşa, *Zübde-i Vekayiât Tahlil ve Metin (1066–1116/1656–1704)*, ed. Abdulkadir Özcan (Ankara: Türk Tarih Kurumu, 1995), 726.

12 Marija Obradović and Slobodan Mišić, "Are Vauban's Geometrical Principles Applied in the Petrovaradin Fortress?," *Nexus Network Journal* 16, no. 3 (2014): 751–76.

13 Cf. Robert Born's chapter in the present volume.

14 H. Langer, "Serbien unter der kaiserlichen Regierung, 1717–1739," *Mitteilungen des Kriegs-Archivs*, NS 3 (1889): 155–247; Theodor Ritter von Stefanovic-Vilovsky, "Belgrad unter der Regierung Kaiser Karls VI. (1717–1739)," *Beiträge zur neueren Geschichte Österreichs* 3 (1908): 2–85; Mirjana Roter Blagojević and Ana Radivojević, "Les espaces publics et la vie publique à Belgrade au XVIIIe et au XIXe siècle et leur transformation au XXe siècle," *Études balkaniques: Cahiers Pierre Belon* 14 (2007): 107–42.

15 Silahdar Fındıklılı Mehmet Ağa, *Nusretname*, ed. İsmet Parmaksızoğlu (Istanbul: Milli Eğitim Basımevi, 1962–63), 2:472, 490.

16 Parvev, *Habsburgs and Ottomans*, 87–98.

17 Federico Veterani, *Feldzüge in Ungarn und den angränzenden Provinzen, vom Jahre 1683 bis 1694* (Dresden: Walter, 1788), 74–6; "Relatio Des Herrn Obristens Conte Marsiglio de dato Nissa den 4. Juli 1690 über den Stand selbiger Festung, der Donaubrücken und selbiger Päß," Austrian State Archive, War Archive, Vienna (herafter KA), AFA 196, VII/6. Veterani was the general who ordered the construction of the fortress; Luigi Ferdinando Marsigli (1658–1730), a scholar, diplomat, and soldier from Bologna, inspected it. He was also involved in the negotiations at Karlowitz that followed and the demarcation and mapping of the new border.

18 Veterani, *Feldzüge*, 101; Defterdar Sarı Mehmed, *Zübde-i Vekayiât*, 107–19.

19 His name was stated on one of these drawn plans: "Abris Von der New Fortification der Stadt Nissa durch den Ingenieur Perony," KA, KPS, Kif, E36-20. Unfortunately, I have no further information about him.

20 "Nissa Anno 1690," KA, AFA 195, XIII/1. Because the general who conquered Niš was Margrave Louis William of Baden-Baden, we find a very similar drawing in his archive; see "Abriss der neuen Fortification der Stadt Nissa," State Archives of Baden-Württemberg, General State Archive Karlsruhe, Hfk Planbände VIII, 6, 1.

21 Johannes Martin Lerch, "Wahrer Grundriß der Vestung Nissa in Servien, Wie selbige anietzo fortificiret, vom 14 Augusti an Anno 1690 durch die türcken in 80 000 Man starck belägert, und dato durch die Kayserl. Waffen Heldenmütig defendiret wird," Vienna 1690, Saxonian State Library, Dresden, http://www. deutschefotothek.de/documents/obj/90048376. On Lerch, cf. Jutta Schumann, *Die andere Sonne: Kaiserbild und Medienstrategien im Zeitalter Leopolds I.* (Berlin: Akademie-Verlag, 2003), 222.

22 Vincenzo Coronelli, "Nissa Città della Servia," 1690, as part of id., *Citta, fortezze, isole, e porti principali dell'Europa, in planta, et in elevatione*, Venice 1689, National Library of France, Paris, http://gallica.bnf.fr/ark:/12148/btv1b55006110j.

23 There are at least three versions of the hand-drawn map by engineer captain C.F. v. Öbschelwiz, which give different dates from 1718 to 1720: "Plan der Türckischen Gräntz Festung Nissa in Servien wie sich solche im Monath Junio Anno 1719 befunden und zwar so gut man dieselbe 1718 im Monath April gegen die Belgrader Seiten von ferne wahrnehmen können...," Riksarkivet, Stockholm, https://sok.riksarkivet.se/bildvisning/K0004799_00001; "Plan von der türck. Gräntz Festung Nissa im Königreich Servien. Wie sich solche im Junio 1719 befunden...," National Széchényi Library, Budapest, TK 533, https://maps.hungaricana.hu/en/OSZKTerkeptar/529/; "Plan von der Türckischen Graenz-Vestung Nissa, und deren Situation in Königreich Servien wie sich solche in Anfang des Monat Junij Anno 1720 befunden," Austrian National Library, Vienna (hereafter ÖNB), AB 465(1), http://data.onb.ac.at/rec/AC03888048.

24 Gerhard Cornelius Driesch, *Historische Nachricht von der Röm. Kayserl. Groß-Botschafft nach Constantinopel* (Nuremberg: Peter Conrad Monath, 1723), 65–6.

25 It is possible that the secret character of the plan was abandoned when the peace proved to be stable. Some of the many extant copies of the prints are: "Plan von der Türckischen Grentz Vestung Nissa und deren Situation im Königreich Servien," ÖNB, ALB Port 247-12; G. Bodenehr, "Plan von der Türckischen Graenz-Vestung Nissa, und deren Situation im Königreich Servien," State

Library Berlin, Kart. X 47145; "Plan der Türckischen Grentz Vestung Nissa in Servien," Riksarkivet, Stockholm, https://sok.riksarkivet.se/bildvisning/K0004798_00001.

26 "Plan von der Türckischen Gräntz-Vestung Nissa, im Königreich Servien wie solche den 28. Julii A. 1737. an die Kaÿserlichen übergeben worden," 1737, Gottfried Wilhelm Leibniz Library, Hanover, Mappe XXXII, B, 2, http://digitale-sammlungen.gwlb.de/resolve?PPN=10064631X.

27 Maximilian Grothaus, "Zum Türkenbild in der Kultur der Habsburgermonarchie zwischen dem 15. und 18. Jahrhundert," in *Habsburgisch-osmanische Beziehungen*, ed. Andreas Tietze (Wien: Verband der wissenschaftlichen Gesellschaften Österreichs, 1985), 67–89.

28 Friedrich Wilhelm Karl Schmettau, *Mémoires secrets de la guerre de Hongrie pendant les campagnes de 1737, 1738 et 1739* (Frankfurt: Compagnie des libraires, 1771), 29–31, 91–101.

29 Silahdar Fındıklılı Mehmet, *Nusretname*, 2:490.

30 Defterdar Sarı Mehmed, *Zübde-i* Vekayiât, 371.

31 Robert Rill, "Die Festung als Baustelle," in *Türkenangst und Festungsbau: Wirklichkeit und Mythos*, ed. Harald Heppner and Zsuzsa Barbarics-Hermanik (Frankfurt: Lang, 2009), 143–74.

32 Silahdar Fındıklılı Mehmet, *Nusretname*, 1:50–51.

33 Defterdar Sarı Mehmed, *Zübde-i Vekayiât*, 726–27.

34 Mehmed's real background remains uncertain. Radmila Tričković, who reconstructed this episode from administrative sources in the Ottoman archive, does not mention a European background of the architect but states that he was from Sofia. See Radmila Tričković, "Urban razvitak Niša u XVIII veku," in *Istorija Niša*, ed. Danica Milić (Niš: Gradina i Prosveta, 1983), 1:243–44. However, Habsburg ambassador Michael Talmann in one of his reports claims that Mehmed was a French renegade. See Ömer Gezer, "Pasarofça Antlaşması'ndan Sonra Habsburg Sınırında Osmanlı Askerî Gücü: Niş Kalesi ve Garnizonu Örneği," in *Harp ve Sulh: 300. Yılında Pasarofça Antlaşması Sempozyumu Bildirileri*, ed. Gültekin Yıldız (Istanbul: Milli Savunma Üniversitesi, 2019), 175.

35 Mariana Şlapac, "Moldavian Bastioned Fortresses: Characteristics," *Historia Urbana* 18 (2021): 231–47.

36 Bekir Gökpinar, "Niş Kalesi'nin Yeniden İnşaatı ve Avusturya Seferlerindeki Rolü (1716–1717)," *History Studies* 11, no. 1 (2019): 22.

37 Tričković, "Urban razvitak," 247–49.

38 The inscription is hard to read not only because of the language but also because it is partly damaged and placed three meters above the readers' heads. The quote is from a nineteenth-century Serbian translation, which seems to correspond to those bits that I was able to decipher from the Ottoman original. See Milan Đ. Miličević, *Kraljevina Srbija: Novi krajevi* (Belgrade: Kr.-Srp. državne štamparije, 1884), 94.

39 Tričkovic, "Urban razvitak," 250–51.

40 Gezer, "Pasarofça Antlaşması'ndan Sonra," 180–81.

41 Tričkovic, "Urban razvitak," 210.

42 Ibid, 258. See also the explanation on Öbschelwitz' 1718 map in the National Széchényi Library, Budapest, TK 533, which states that in the gardens of the left-bank settlement new houses for the refugees from Serbia are being built.

43 Driesch, *Historische Nachricht*, 69–71.

44 M. Münir Aktepe, *Patrona İsyanı (1730)* (Istanbul: İstanbul Üniversitesi Edebiyat Fakültesi Yayınları, 1958), 132.

45 According to the 1710 census, 60 percent of the households in Niš were Muslim. For Vidin, see Rossitsa Gradeva, "Between Hinterland and Frontier: Ottoman Vidin, Fifteenth to Eighteenth Centuries," in *The Frontiers of the Ottoman World*, ed. Andrew C.S. Peacock (Oxford: Oxford University Press, 2009), 331.

46 Silahtar Fındıklılı Mehmet, *Nusretname*, 2:472–74, 518–19.

47 Tatjana Katić, "Viyana Savaşından Sonra Sırbıstan, 1683–1699," in *Türkler*, ed. Hasan Güzel (Ankara: Yeni Türkiye, 2002), 9:766–67.

48 Svetlana Ivanova, "Vidinskiyat varosh i kanun-i serhad," *Istoricheski Pregled* 3–4 (2015): 84–7. I am thankful to Rossitsa Gradeva for pointing out this fact to me.

49 Ženi Lebl, *Do "Konačnog Rešenja": Jevreji u Srbiji* (Belgrade: Čigoja štampa, 2002), 69.

50 Johann Andreas Christoph Kempelen, *Descriptio itineris legatorum Caroli VI. a. 1740 ad Mahmud Turcarum imperatorem missorum*, Ms. p. 47, ÖNB, HAN, Cod. 8640.

51 Constantine Dapontès, *Éphémérides Daces ou chronique de la guerre de quatre ans, 1736–1739*, tr. Émile Legrand (Paris: Leroux, 1880–1888), 2:400.

52 Felix Kanitz, *Donau-Bulgarien und der Balkan: Historisch-geographisch-ethnographische Reisestudien aus den Jahren 1860–1875*, vol. 1 (Leipzig: Fries, 1875), 163.

53 Robert M. Hayden and Timothy D. Walker, "Intersecting Religioscapes: A Comparative Approach to Trajectories of Change, Scale, and Competitive Sharing of Religious Spaces," *Journal of the American Academy of Religion* 81, no. 2 (2013): 399–426. For the whole story of St. Nicholas/Fethiye, which continues into the nineteenth century, see Florian Riedler, "Communal Boundaries and Confessional Policies in Ottoman Niš," *Journal of the Economic and Social History of the Orient* 61, no. 4 (2018): 726–56.

54 This church, about which we have no other information, is shown on a Habsburg map drawn during the occupation of 1737; see "Plan von der Vestung Nissa wie solche Anno 1737 von denen Türcken an die Keÿserliche ist übergeben worden," ÖNB, ALB Port 247-13.

55 Fehmi Yılmaz, "The Life of Köprülüzade Fazıl Mustafa Pasha and His Reforms (1637–1691)," *Osmanlı Araştırmaları* 20 (2000): 165–221.

56 N.N., "Militairische Beschreibung, der Theile Serviens und Bulgariens [...]," in "Vojno-geografski opisi Srbije pred Kočinu krajinu od 1783 i 1784 god.," ed. Dušan Pantelić, *Spomenik SKA 2. Razred* 82 (1936): 36.

57 "Niş kalesinin istihkamat-ı lazimesine ve saireye dair," Prime Ministry's Ottoman Archive (BOA), Istanbul, İ.DH. 303/19233, doc. 2, not dated; the date of the covering letter is 28 L 1270 (24 July 1854).

58 "Niş kale-i hakaniyesi civarında kain [...] mera arazinin bir kıta haritasıdır," BOA, Istanbul, HRT.h 2158, not dated.

Bibliography

Maps

"Abris Von der New Fortification der Stadt Nissa durch den Ingenieur Perony." Austrian State Archive, War Archive, Vienna. KA, KPS, Kif, E36-20.
"Nissa Anno 1690." Austrian State Archive, War Archive, Vienna. KA, AFA 195, XIII/1.

"Abriss der neuen Fortification der Stadt Nissa." State Archives of Baden-Württemberg, General State Archive Karlsruhe. Hfk Planbände VIII, 6, 1.

Lerch, Johannes Martin. "Wahrer Grundriß der Vestung Nissa in Servien, Wie selbige anietzo fortificiret, vom 14 Augusti an Anno 1690 durch die türcken in 80 000 Man starck belägert, und dato durch die Kayserl. Waffen Heldenmütig defendiret wird." Saxonian State Library, Dresden. http://www.deutschefoto-thek.de/documents/obj/90048376.

Coronelli, Vincenzo. "Nissa Città della Servia." 1690. In id. *Citta, fortezze, isole, e porti principali dell'Europa, in planta, et in elevatione.* Venice, 1689. National Library of France, Paris. http://gallica.bnf.fr/ark:/12148/btv1b55006110j.

Öbschelwiz, C.F. v. "Plan der Türckischen Gräntz Festung Nissa in Servien wie sich solche im Monath Junio Anno 1719 befunden und zwar so gut man dieselbe 1718 im Monath April gegen die Belgrader Seiten von ferne wahrnehmen können [...]." Riksarkivet, Stockholm. https://sok.riksarkivet.se/bildvisning/K0004799_00001.

[Öbschelwiz, C.F. v.] "Plan von der türck. Gräntz Festung Nissa im Königreich Ser-vien. Wie sich solche im Junio 1719 befunden [...]." National Széchényi Library, Budapest. TK 533. https://maps.hungaricana.hu/en/OSZKTerkeptar/529/.

Öbschelwiz, O.F.V. "Plan von der Türckischen Graenz-Vestung Nissa, und deren Situation in Königreich Servien wie sich solche in Anfang des Monat Junij Anno 1720 befunden." Austrian National Library, Vienna. AB 465(1). http://data.onb.ac.at/rec/AC03888048.

"Plan von der Türckischen Grentz Vestung Nissa und deren Situation im Königre-ich Servien." Austrian National Library, Vienna. ALB Port 247-12.

Bodenehr, G. "Plan von der Türckischen Graenz-Vestung Nissa, und deren Situa-tion im Königreich Servien." State Library Berlin. Kart. X 47145.

"Plan der Türckischen Grentz Vestung Nissa in Servien." Riksarkivet, Stockholm. https://sok.riksarkivet.se/bildvisning/K0004798_00001.

"Plan von der Türckischen Gräntz-Vestung Nissa, im Königreich Servien wie solche den 28. Julii A. 1737. an die Kaÿserlichen übergeben worden." 1737. Gottfried Wilhelm Leibniz Library, Hanover, Mappe XXXII, B, 2, http://digitale-sammlungen.gwlb.de/resolve?PPN=10064631X.

"Plan von der Vestung Nissa wie solche Anno 1737 von denen Türcken an die Keÿserlichen ist übergeben worden." Austrian National Library, Vienna, ALB Port 247–13.

"Niş kale-i hakaniyesi civarında kain [...] mera arazinin bir kıta haritasıdır." Prime Ministry's Ottoman Archive, Istanbul. HRT.h 2158.

Unpublished sources

Kempelen, Johann Andreas Christoph. *Descriptio itineris legatorum Caroli VI. a. 1740 ad Mahmud Turcarum imperatorem missorum.* Austrian National Library, Vienna. HAN, Cod. 8640.

Marsigli, Luigi Fernando. "Relatio Des Herrn Obristens Conte Marsiglio de dato Nissa den 4. Juli 1690 über den Stand selbiger Festung, der Donaubrücken und selbiger Päß." Austrian State Archive, War Archive, Vienna. KA, AFA 196, VII/6.

"Niş kalesinin istihkamat-ı lazimesine ve saireye dair." Prime Ministry's Ottoman Archive, Istanbul, İ.DH 303/19233.

Published sources

Dapontès, Constantine. *Éphémérides Daces ou chronique de la guerre de quatre ans, 1736–1739*, translated by Émile Legrand. 3 vols. Paris: Leroux, 1880–1888.

Defterdar Sarı Mehmed Paşa. *Zübde-i Vekayiât: Tahlil ve Metin (1066–1116/1656– 1704)*, edited by Abdulkadir Özcan. Ankara: Türk Tarih Kurumu, 1995.

Driesch, Gerhard Cornelius. *Historische Nachricht von der Röm. Kayserl. Groß- Botschafft nach Constantinopel*. Nuremberg: Peter Conrad Monath, 1723.

Marsigli, Luigi Fernando. *Stato Militare Dell'imperio Ottomanno: L´état Militaire De L'empire Ottoman*. The Hague: Gosse, 1732.

Miličević, Milan Đ. *Kraljevina Srbija: Novi krajevi*. Belgrade: Kr.-Srp. državne štamparije, 1884.

N.N. "Militairische Beschreibung, der Theile Serviens und Bulgariens […]." Edition of a Habsburg source in "Vojno-geografski opisi Srbije pred Kočinu krajinu od 1783 i 1784 god.," edited by Dušan Pantelić. *Spomenik SKA 2. Razred 82* (1936): 35–40.

Schmettau, Friedrich Wilhelm Karl. *Mémoires secrets de la guerre de Hongrie pendant les campagnes de 1737, 1738 et 1739*. Frankfurt: Compagnie des libraires, 1771.

Silahdar Fındıklılı Mehmet Ağa. *Nusretname*. Edited by İsmet Parmaksızoğlu. 2 vols. Istanbul: Milli Eğitim Basımevi, 1962–1963.

Veterani, Federico. *Feldzüge in Ungarn und den angränzenden Provinzen, vom Jahre 1683 bis 1694*. Dresden: Walter, 1788.

Literature

Abou-el-Haj, Rifaat A. "The Formal Closure of the Ottoman Frontier in Europe, 1699–1703." *Journal of the American Oriental Society* 89, no. 3 (1969): 467–75.

Adelsgruber, Paulus, Laurie Cohen, and Börries Kuzmany. *Getrennt und doch verbunden: Grenzstädte zwischen Österreich und Russland, 1772–1918*. Wien: Böhlau, 2011.

Aktepe, M. Münir. *Patrona İsyanı (1730)*. Istanbul: İstanbul Üniversitesi Edebiyat Fakültesi Yayınları, 1958.

Bilenky, Serhiy. *Imperial Urbanism in the Borderlands: Kyiv, 1800–1905*. Toronto: University of Toronto Press, 2017.

Bojanić, Dušanka. "Niš do Velikog rata 1683." In *Istorija Niša*, edited by Danica Milić, 1:107–69. Niš: Gradina i Prosveta, 1983.

Gezer, Ömer. "Kale Ve Nefer: Habsburg Sınırında Osmanlı Askerî Gücünün Yeniden Örgütlenmesi (1699–1715)." PhD diss., Hacettepe University, Ankara, 2016.

Gezer, Ömer. "Pasarofça Antlaşması'ndan Sonra Habsburg Sınırında Osmanlı Askerî Gücü: Niş Kalesi ve Garnizonu Örneği." In *Harp ve Sulh: 300. Yılında*

Pasarofça Antlaşması Sempozyumu Bildirileri, edited by Gültekin Yıldız, 171–82. Istanbul: Milli Savunma Üniversitesi, 2019.

Gökpınar, Bekir. "Niş Kalesi'nin Yeniden İnşaatı Ve Avusturya Seferlerindeki Rolü (1716-1717)." *History Studies* 11, no. 1 (2019): 107–28.

Gradeva, Rossitsa. "Between Hinterland and Frontier: Ottoman Vidin, Fifteenth to Eighteenth Centuries." In *The Frontiers of the Ottoman World*, edited by Andrew C.S. Peacock, 331–51. Oxford: Oxford University Press, 2009.

Grothaus, Maximilian. "Zum Türkenbild in der Kultur der Habsburgermonarchie zwischen dem 15. und 18. Jahrhundert." In *Habsburgisch-osmanische Beziehungen*, edited by Andreas Tietze, 67–89. Wien: Verband der wissenschaftlichen Gesellschaften Österreichs, 1985.

Hayden, Robert M., and Timothy D. Walker. "Intersecting Religioscapes: A Comparative Approach to Trajectories of Change, Scale, and Competitive Sharing of Religious Spaces." *Journal of the American Academy of Religion* 81, no. 2 (2013): 399–426.

Hegyi, Klára. "The Ottoman Network of Fortresses in Hungary." In *Ottomans, Hungarians, and Habsburgs in Central Europe*, edited by Géza Dávid and Pál Fodor, 163–94. Leiden: Brill, 2000.

Heywood, Colin. "The Frontier in Ottoman History: Old Ideas and New Myths." In *Frontiers in Question: Eurasian Borderlands, 700–1700*, edited by Daniel Power and Naomi Standen, 228–50. Oxford: Palgrave Macmillan, 1999.

Ivanova, Svetlana. "Vidinskiyat varosh i kanun-i serhad." *Istoricheski Pregled* 3–4 (2015): 83–161.

Kanitz, Felix. *Donau-Bulgarien und der Balkan: Historisch-geographisch-ethnographische Reisestudien aus den Jahren 1860–1875*. Vol. 1. Leipzig: Fries, 1875.

Katić, Tatjana. "Viyana Savaşından Sonra Sırbıstan, 1683–1699." In *Türkler*, edited by Hasan Güzel, 9:765–72. Ankara: Yeni Türkiye Yayınları, 2002.

Kiel, Machiel. "Niş." In *Türkiye Diyanet Vakfı İslam Ansiklopedisi*, vol. 33, 147–49.

Kołodziejczyk, Dariusz. "Between Universalistic Claims and Reality: Ottoman Frontiers in the Early Modern Period." In *The Ottoman World*, edited by Christine Woodhead, 205–19. London: Routledge, 2012.

Langer, H. "Serbien unter der kaiserlichen Regierung, 1717–1739." *Mitteilungen des Kriegs-Archivs*, NS 3 (1889): 155–247.

Lebl, Ženi. *Do "Konačnog Rešenja": Jevreji u Srbiji*. Belgrade: Čigoja štampa, 2002.

Maner, Hans-Christian, ed. *Grenzregionen der Habsburgermonarchie im 18. und 19. Jahrhundert: Ihre Bedeutung und Funktion aus der Perspektive Wiens*. Münster: LIT, 2005.

Martí, Tibor. "'Antemurale Christianitatis' en Europa Central: La frontera húngara y croata de la monarquía de los Habsburgo en la época moderna." In *Antemurales de la Fe: Conflictividad confesional en la Monarquía de los Habsburgo, 1516–1714*, edited by Pedro García Martin, 181–95. Madrid: Universidad Autónoma de Madrid, 2015.

Obradović, Marija, and Slobodan Mišić. "Are Vauban's Geometrical Principles Applied in the Petrovaradin Fortress?" *Nexus Network Journal* 16, no. 3 (2014): 751–76.

O'Dowd, Liam. "Contested States, Frontiers and Cities." In *A Companion to Border Studies*, edited by Thomas M. Wilson and Hastings Donnan, 158–76. Chichester: John Wiley & Sons, 2012.

Pálffy, Géza. "The Origins and Development of the Border Defence System Against the Ottoman Empire in Hungary (up to the Early Eighteenth Century)." In *Ottomans, Hungarians, and Habsburgs in Central Europe*, edited by Géza Dávid and Pál Fodor, 39–49. Leiden: Brill, 2000.

———. "Die Türkenabwehr der Habsburgermonarchie in Ungarn und Kroatien im 16. Jahrhundert: Verteidigungskonzeption, Grenzfestungssystem, Militärkartographie." In *Türkenangst und Festungsbau: Wirklichkeit und Mythos*, edited by Harald Heppner and Zsuzsa Barbarics-Hermanik, 79–108. Frankfurt: Peter Lang, 2009.

Parvev, Ivan. *Habsburgs and Ottomans between Vienna and Belgrade (1683–1739)*. Boulder, CO: East European Monographs, 1995.

Peacock, Andrew C.S., ed. *The Frontiers of the Ottoman World*. Oxford: Oxford University Press, 2009.

Pollak, Martha D. *Cities at War in Early Modern Europe*. Cambridge: Cambridge University Press, 2010.

Rieber, Alfred J. *The Struggle for the Eurasian Borderlands: From the Rise of Early Modern Empires to the End of the First World War*. Cambridge: Cambridge University Press, 2014.

Riedler, Florian. "Communal Boundaries and Confessional Policies in Ottoman Niš." *Journal of the Economic and Social History of the Orient* 61, no. 4 (2018): 726–56.

Rill, Robert. "Die Festung als Baustelle." In *Türkenangst und Festungsbau: Wirklichkeit und Mythos*, edited by Harald Heppner and Zsuzsa Barbarics-Hermanik, 143–74. Frankfurt: Lang, 2009.

Roter Blagojević, Mirjana, and Ana Radivojević. "Les espaces publics et la vie publique à Belgrade au XVIIIe et au XIXe siècle et leur transformation au XXe siècle." *Études balkaniques: Cahiers Pierre Belon* 14 (2007): 107–42.

Schumann, Jutta. *Die andere Sonne: Kaiserbild und Medienstrategien im Zeitalter Leopolds I*. Berlin: Akademie-Verlag, 2003.

Şlapac, Mariana. "Moldavian Bastioned Fortresses: Characteristics." *Historia Urbana* 18 (2021): 231–47.

Stefanovic-Vilovsky, Theodor Ritter von. "Belgrad unter der Regierung Kaiser Karls VI. (1717–1739)." *Beiträge zur neueren Geschichte Österreichs* 3 (1908): 2–85.

Stein, Mark L. *Guarding the Frontier: Ottoman Border Forts and Garrisons in Europe*. London: I.B. Tauris, 2007.

Tričković, Radmila. "Urban razvitak Niša u XVIII veku." In *Istorija Niša*, edited by Danica Milić, 1:243–61. Niš: Gradina i Prosveta, 1983.

———. *Beogradski Pašaluk, 1687–1739*. Belgrade: Službeni Glasnik, 2003.

Yılmaz, Fehmi. "The Life of Köprülüzade Fazıl Mustafa Pasha and His Reforms (1637–1691)." *Osmanlı Araştırmaları* 20 (2000): 165–221.

8 Empire after Empire
Austro-Hungarian Recalibration of the Ottoman Čaršija of Sarajevo

Aida Murtić

When the news from Berlin reached Sarajevo on July 5, 1878, merchants and artisans shut down the shops in Čaršija, the city's commercial center, and streamed to their homes, using a familiar form of urban protest to display a revolt against the decision taken by the Congress of Berlin.[1] Convened to resolve the Eastern Question, the meeting of the Great Powers resulted in border changes: the Congress awarded Austria-Hungary the right to occupy and administer the Ottoman provinces of Bosnia and Herzegovina while nominally preserving the sovereignty of the Sultan over the territories. With a mandate to guarantee peace and order, and to improve the state of affairs that Ottomans supposedly could not handle, Austro-Hungarian troops marched into the provinces and reached the city of Sarajevo on August 19, 1878. Crushing the resistance of local groups, they put an end to four centuries of Ottoman rule.

With the acquisition of Bosnia-Herzegovina, people of divergent identifications, loyalties, and political consciousness joined Austria-Hungary. Groups of South Slavs, with a significant Muslim population for the first time in history, became part of the monarchical mosaic of peoples and cultures. The proclamation to the inhabitants conveyed a clear message, announcing the arrival of a new order and promising that all internal differences would be peacefully negotiated:

> Your laws and institutions should not be arbitrarily overthrown, your customs and practices should be protected. Nothing should be changed by force without careful consideration of what you need [...]
>
> The Emperor-King knows your complaints and wishes for you welfare.
>
> Under his mighty authority, many peoples live next to each other and speak their own language. He rules over the followers of many religions and everyone freely professes its own faith.[2]

DOI: 10.4324/9781003130031-11

The task of administering Bosnia-Herzegovina was given to the Joint Ministry of Finance and the freshly established Provincial Government (*Zemaljska vlada, Landesregierung*). For the next 30 years, Bosnia-Herzegovina was kept in an ambiguous legal position until the moment of annexation on October 7, 1908, when the ideas, fears, and hopes of Ottoman restoration were officially discarded. The satellite province was integrated into the Austro-Hungarian structures as a *Reichsland* belonging to neither part of the Dual Monarchy. The character of this evolving relationship between the imperial core and the new province shaped the attitudes, policies, construction programs, and investment schemes for the city of Sarajevo.

In the process of becoming part of another multicultural empire, Sarajevo joined the network of Austro-Hungarian cities carrying the burden of its Oriental otherness. The city needed to be restructured and expanded – not only to accommodate a growing population, new urban quarters, and public infrastructure but also to represent symbolically the new function as the provincial capital (*Landeshauptstadt*). Already home to an ethnically and religiously diverse population, the city became a destination for military personnel, bureaucrats, and newcomers from different parts of Austria-Hungary. Imagined as a "Bosnian Eldorado,"[3] the physiognomy of rapidly changing Sarajevo often served to narrate the success story of the Austro-Hungarian modernization mission in the land promoted as "the European Orient."[4]

The four decades (1878–1918) of Austro-Hungarian presence in Sarajevo is a well-studied period of the city's history that has received the attention of both local and international scholars who looked at models of urban modernity, architectural styles and building types, architectural professionals, and communities as actors of change.[5] Taking a path less travelled, this chapter uses the case of Čaršija,[6] the craft and trade quarter of the Ottoman-era Sarajevo, to explore the role of inherited urban fabric for the construction of the new urban vision. Looking at the mechanisms of reinscribing the Ottoman past of Čaršija onto the new present, it examines how elements of the earlier urban paradigms not only survived throughout the period discussed in the text but also became ingredients of the new imperial self-conception. Tracing what the people and the city were left with after the Ottomans were gone, the chapter questions how the Austro-Hungarian administrators envisioned being imperial in the world of persisting Ottoman urban legacies. The critical lens focuses on investigating what it meant to accept and work with what is already there in the city, to make it significant for the new political union, and to make the empire manifest in the existing urban structure. A point worth highlighting is that reckoning with the Čaršija lifeworld was embedded in the larger imperial concern of how to rule Muslim subjects and how to approach their spaces, customs, and rituals. Hence, the old commercial center of Sarajevo at the turn of the nineteenth century entered the picture as a terrain of ambivalence, as professionals and authorities tolerated its vernacular peculiarities and enthusiastically embraced imperial additions.

The transformation of Čaršija occurred in tandem with the transformation of disciplinary practices of architecture and urban planning, as well as tools and techniques of understanding urban forms. This chapter draws attention to the diversity of mediums through which ideas about the city quarter were formed and new vocabularies and descriptions were crafted. In addition to textual sources, Čaršija is discussed using a variety of visual genres such as photography, architectural plan, postcard, and painting, additionally seeking to demonstrate how image-making was a constitutive part of the imperial city-making.[7] Čaršija of Sarajevo, therefore, existed not only as a field of intervention but also as an object of discourse and a repository of images and associations.

The Realms of Čaršija

Čaršija was the dominant urban figure of Ottoman Sarajevo, shaped from the fifteenth century onward as a concentrated center with the main market, religious, commercial, and public buildings. Following the clear formula of Ottoman urbanism, the agglomeration of Čaršija in the valley was functionally separated from residential neighborhoods (*mahala*) on the slopes. Being a public arena of the city, Čaršija played a role in bringing together individuals and groups from different social strata and religious and ethnic groups. Catholic, Jewish, Muslim, and Orthodox communities are commonly identified as important collective actors in Sarajevo's urban history. As a locus of religious and intellectual culture, the city quarter accommodated institutions and symbols of all four religions, and its topography was marked by the presence of churches, mosques, synagogues, religious schools, and libraries in close proximity. Developed as a dominantly horizontal entity, Čaršija was composed of a dense network of shopping streets, each serving different craft and trade guilds, and as such, it was a place of knowledge and skills of the city's diverse urban societies. In other words, the realms of sacred, commercial-artisanal, and everyday life coexisted in Čaršija.

Not only the monumental religious and public buildings as bearers of significance but also the fabric of vernacular (minor) architecture shaped Čaršija's character (Figure 8.3). Its basic unit was the *dućan*,[8] a type of artisanal (work)shop, organized as pragmatic space for both production and sale of goods. It was income-producing property, often built to support pious endowments (*vakuf*). As a connective tissue of Čaršija, clusters of shops surrounded commercial buildings such as covered markets (*bezistan*), khans (*han*), and public baths (*hamam*) and integrated them into larger units of urban fabric and systems of urban life.

The greatest in number but the simplest in construction, *dućan*s were persistent creations whose wood-built formats were continually reproduced. Fires, a frequent occurrence, demanded periodic rebuilding of the matrix of shops, and that was often done by replicating what existed before.[9]

Merchants and artisans organized in professional guilds (*esnaf*) and acted as strong social agents in Čaršija, keeping control of spatial organization of production, quality, and prices.[10] Their prestige and dominance collapsed when the Ottoman governor Omer Pasha Latas dissolved the organizations in 1851, seeking to end resistance against institutional reforms (*Tanzimat*). On top of that, the productive apparatus of Čaršija significantly changed when a number of artisans made strategic choices to abandon handwork and became entrepreneurs focused on external trade and import of manufactured goods.[11]

The Austro-Hungarian conquest brought additional waves of changes in Čaršija that dissolved many urban economic networks, disqualifying some of the previously powerful actors and giving rise to new elites. Separation from one empire and inclusion into the other as observed from within the craft and trade quarter appeared not as a radical break but as a reconfiguration of the existing urban system, requiring institutional changes, inventive adaptations, and complex local negotiations.

The Great Fire of 1879

The first encounter of the Austro-Hungarian imperial administration with the landscape of Čaršija was born out of urgency. Just a year after the takeover of Bosnia-Herzegovina, on the night of August 8, 1879, a sudden fire destroyed the greater part of Sarajevo. The fire consumed the area of 36 streets located between the bridges of *Careva ćuprija* and Ćumurija, leaving private houses, shops, and public buildings in ruins, and affecting almost the entire community of Čaršija's merchants and artisans. Among the buildings damaged by this fire were four mosques, the Franciscan church, the Sephardic synagogue, the German consulate, the Hanikah (Sufi lodge), and two khans. The uncontrolled fire that spread from the depot of a merchant named Schwarz in *Latinluk* (Catholic quarter)[12] is considered as one of the defining moments in the urban history of Sarajevo that assists in separating temporal registers and reflections on the form of the Late Ottoman Čaršija (before the fire) and the reconfigured Austro-Hungarian Čaršija (after the fire).

A series of five photographs that Ignaz Funk[13] took in the aftermath of the devastating event provides a glimpse of the affected city fragment. Capturing the collapse of urban space, the photographs were addressed to Emperor Franz Joseph and sent on August 12, 1879, and most likely were not intended for broader audiences.[14] The panoramic view with a

Figure 8.1 Čaršija after the great fire of 1879. The emphasis is on the surviving bridge with the remains of Latinluk and the rest of Čaršija (on the right).

Source: Austrian National Library, PK 904.

focus on the bridge to the *Latinluk* quarter presented here (Figure 8.1) is impressive in its ability to show the vulnerability of the material fabric of the old commercial center and the disappearance of small structures to which Ottoman-era Čaršija owed its very character. Since wood was the predominant building material used for the construction of *dućans*, the fire easily reduced lines of shops to waste together with all the goods and work that merchants and artisans held within. Everyday objects and pieces of furniture were floating in the Miljacka River as ghostly relicts of the lost mundanity. Yet, there are signs of life in this disaster scene. Military personnel and citizens were moving amid the ruins, inspecting the burned-down sites and seeking to salvage whatever they could. Although the city area was largely reduced to skeletal architectural remains, a number of stone structures remained standing, demonstrating an ability to last. The photograph compels the viewer to conceptualize the fire event as a reminder of Čaršija's fragility as well as an indicator of radical possibility. The rubble of Čaršija as recorded here represents a transitional scene determined by things that were no longer there and a new world whose contours were not yet visible.[15]

The self-conviction of being exemplary administrators seemed to crumble as the pages of regional newspapers were filled with the news of the fire in the recently acquired province, describing the event as catastrophic and the city as completely destroyed. Voices from Prague were particularly critical, disapproving the expansionist *Orientpolitik* of the Austro-Hungarian foreign minister Gyula Andrássy and suggesting that the fire of Sarajevo was more than a simple accident. "The future of the Austrian politics in the Balkans hinges on the ruins of the Bosnian capital," wrote *Epoche*, raising the question of who should rebuild the city, for whom, and with what means.[16] "The State? But which state?" the newspaper asked, speculating if the "Man on the Bosporus [the Ottoman Empire]" would use the chance to exercise its functions and intervene in rebuilding Sarajevo, or how Austria and Hungary would eventually arrange to share the costs of reconstruction.[17] Sultan Abdülhamid II did approach the Austro-Hungarian ambassador in Istanbul, but only to express his regrets and sympathy for the city as well as his conviction that the Austro-Hungarian government would do everything to deal with the consequences of this accident.[18] Developing a reconstruction response for Sarajevo, hence, required forging new bonds with the Dual Monarchy as much as settling accounts with the old empire.

As the damage was estimated at 20 million forints, an amount that was almost seven times larger than the annual budget for civil purposes in Bosnia and Herzegovina in 1880, the financially precarious and technically unequipped local government was put to a hard test and needed specialized assistance to rebuild the city.[19] Seeking to prove to Sarajevans that the Monarchy empathized with their misfortune, appeals were sent through press announcements to the Austro-Hungarian population asking for donations that would help alleviate the misery of the city. Members of the imperial family – Emperor Franz Joseph I, Empress Elisabeth, Crown Prince Rudolf – set examples by providing emergency aid for the city and fire victims, which was followed by philanthropic gestures by dignitaries of the empire and key institutions such as the Joint Ministry of Foreign Affairs.[20] Local governments, such as the mayor of Salzburg, also invited their citizens to financially support the recovery of Sarajevo, whose prosperity under the protection of the empire was interrupted by the sudden disaster.[21] In addition, individual and small donations were collected in the Bureau of Bosnian Affairs of the Joint Finance Ministry in Vienna, in the office of *Wiener Zeitung*, and in the offices of the city administration and police headquarters in Prague.

The active involvement of the imperial and provincial networks in developing an emergency response for Sarajevo served to demonstrate that the empire was responsible for the city and that the imperial bonds of solidarity were strong. For the new administrators, it was crucial to replace the image of chaos and arbitrariness in the former Ottoman province with a promise of progress and to see Sarajevo rise from the ruins as soon as possible. Determined to rebuild the city, they propagated the image of Sarajevo as worthy of modern development, investment, and support. Reacting to the news about the devastating fire, companies and suppliers of construction materials from Austria-Hungary started approaching the provincial government, sending telegrams, catalogues, and promotional materials. Directly offering products and expertise, entrepreneurs and enterprises expected to enter a new and yet unexplored regional market.[22] Their opening move was also an invitation to the provincial actors to partake in the imperial circulation of techniques and concepts of architectural intervention.

Local people had their own interpretation of the fire event, speculating that it was an arson attack.[23] They blamed the Austrian newcomers for deliberately razing Čaršija to the ground to justify future clearances and regularizations that otherwise would have been much more difficult to accomplish. For administrators and elites, the devastating fire of 1879, often framed as a natural disaster, indeed appeared as a catalyst of change, giving a patina of legitimacy to the modernization agenda. Out of the rubble of Čaršija, modern planning instruments for Sarajevo and tools of administrative control of its development would be born.

Regulating and Rebuilding Čaršija

Physical transformation of Čaršija after 1879 went hand in hand with reorganizing the disciplinary practices of architecture and urban planning that influenced its urban form. Tracking down the ways in which new approaches to planning and building allied with or disrupted the established ones, hence, appears worthy of scrutiny. In the eyes of Austro-Hungarian commentators, Ottomans were inefficient and incapable of significant infrastructural and organizational achievements. The strategy of devaluing the imperial predecessor's accomplishments was used to help justify and legitimize the self-proclaimed "task of desavagizing and moralizing."[24] By pushing the past away, the Austro-Hungarian administration was selective about the Ottoman policies and structures it was to uphold. Precisely for this reason, the recognition and extension of validity of the Ottoman Street and Buildings Act and its translation into the German language, made soon after taking control of Bosnia-Herzegovina, deserves a special consideration. The law, introduced as a part of a *Tanzimat* reform package in 1863, defined among other things principles for street widening, fire protection procedures, and façade and building height regulations. The translated *Strassen- und Bautengesetz vom 7. Džemaziul-evel 1280 (1863)*,[25] therefore, is not simply a document resulting from the act of changing languages but also a strategic zone of encounter between ideas, value systems, and patterns of thought in different cultural and socio-political contexts that also share a set of assumptions about what a modern, aspirational city should look like and how it should be governed. Published to give guidance to authorities in Bosnia-Herzegovina, the document was a sign of acceptance of the Ottoman ways of doing things until opportunity arose for better solutions. Although applied with varying degrees of rigor, the Street and Buildings Act served as the sole legal guardian of the construction activities until the additional set of detailed building norms for Sarajevo was adopted.

The regulation plan for rebuilding the area of the city affected by fire *(Regulierungsplan)*[26] from 1880 was the first in a line of planning documents that inaugurated novel protocols of seeing and governing Čaršija (Figure 8.2). Palimpsestic in nature, the plan entered into debate with the old street matrix, combining on a single sheet of paper an outlook on the existing urban fabric with a vision for future development.[27] Rendering knowable the city fragment destroyed in the fire of 1879, the *Regulierungsplan* codified and gave a clear indication of old street arteries, plots that

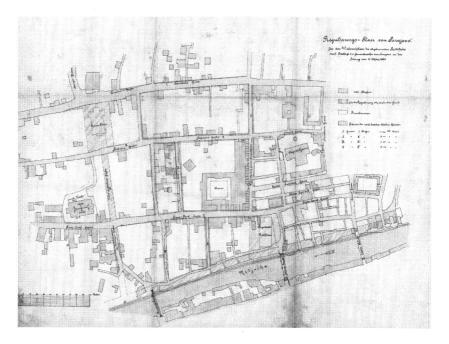

Figure 8.2 Regulation Plan for rebuilding the area of the city affected by fire, adopted on March 11, 1880.

Source: Historical Archives of Sarajevo, ZKP-514.

were subject to new regulations, areas that had been destroyed by fire and considered ruins, and structurally sound individual buildings that could stay standing. The physical boundary of the intervention area was not based on administrative borders or site surveys; it was thought to pragmatically encompass the affected sections of the city. Without marking the lines of division, naming or framing the craft and trade quarter, the contact between the intervention zone and surrounding areas was not addressed at all at the time. Rather than proposing grand architectural schemes for Čaršija, the plan was based on preservation and technical correction of the Ottoman street grid. Providing a sense of order, the plan postulated the idea that the old urban fabric could absorb new building types, proposing plots where a Catholic cathedral with a square and a city hall should be built.[28] Reflecting the key concerns of the new science of city planning at the turn of the century such as public hygiene, sanitation, and circulation, the plan placed great importance on the issue of widening and regularizing streets in Čaršija, introducing four categories of streets and proposing that straight arteries cut through the existing labyrinth-shaped pattern of the city quarter.

In this analysis, the Regulation Plan is considered in tandem with the transcripts of the City Council (*Stadt Magistrat*) meetings. Together they provide an account of struggles to reconcile new urbanism theories with constraints of the existing urban socio-texture and help recast the image of diverse protagonists (locals and administrators, professionals and bureaucrats, and representatives of different ethnic and religious groups) who played roles in shaping choices and implementing urban ideas.[29]

The Government Commissioner Kosta Hörmann opened the meeting about the Regulation Plan on March 8, 1880, asking the council members to comment and approve the version of the plan drafted by the provincial government, acknowledging that it interferes with the interests of some citizens and requires material sacrifices from everyone.[30] The encounter between the members of the two parallel structures in the city council – the elected council appointees from Sarajevo and the bureaucrats from the monarchy representing the provincial government and supervising the work of the council – was characterized by collisions and compromises. With a stake in Čaršija, either as property or business owners, the local council members serviced multiple relationships and addressed their individual or group concerns, while working to ensure orderly urban growth. They were, therefore, not passive recipients of the political and planning imperatives that were foreign to them; indeed, they acquired a political voice, and their collaboration with the imperial civil servants was essential to the process of regulating Čaršija. Voting on the final version of the plan needed to be postponed for three days and was done only after the regulation lines were reconfigured to fit property lines and lived realities. The politics and aesthetics of the new order were negotiated on a scale of individual plots. The City Council of Sarajevo adopted the *Regulierungsplan* at its session on March 11, 1880.[31]

Two months later, the provincial government enacted the Building Code *(Bauordnung)* for the provincial capital Sarajevo, expecting to control all construction activities.[32] The Building Code provided clear regulations and outlined the responsibility for overseeing construction activities. Consequently, builders without formal qualifications were eliminated from the process as the right to supervise construction activities was transferred into the hands of professional engineers and architects. With a ban on non-resistant materials (including wooden structures), the regulatory environment was adapted for use of construction materials and methods projected as modern. Since durability came to be seen as a form of validity, the old commercial center of Sarajevo was discursively shaped in the following years as a problematic and vulnerable site. Using the term "wood-built Sarajevo"[33] to express the distrust of the alien fabric of Čaršija that was highly susceptible to fires, traditional ways of building and working were exposed to the new regimes of valuing and were often dismissed as inferior and outdated. In comparison to the weak structures of Čaršija, the buildings constructed using the "Western" building methods were seen as embodying a powerful permanency due to their architectural styles, mass, and solidity. Thus, the conversion of the built fabric of Čaršija from wood to brick started with assigning a negative valence to the materiality of the existing architecture, legitimizing certain ways of building and planning, and positioning vernacular in opposition to modern architecture.

With the tools for administrative control of urban development in their hands (*Regulierungsplan* and *Bauordnung*), the provincial authorities made a decision to further boost private initiatives and investments, issuing a decree exempting from building tax the buildings in the area destroyed by fire that "get their roofs" – i.e., that are structurally finished – in the following five years.[34] In the absence of a budget for systematic reordering of the city, the authorities did not intervene into projects that their financial resources could not support, but they left the use of land and construction of buildings to the interests of various actors, mostly private property owners. Without resisting change, or proposing forms of preservation, authorities placed trust in ability of developers to navigate the renewal of Čaršija. The chosen model brought a broad register of possible responses – creation, renewal, improvisation – that had transformative effects on both the urban form of Čaršija and the life of its individual structures.

Vernacular and Monumental in Čaršija

As much as the Austro-Hungarian urban program for Sarajevo relied on change, it also relied on continuities. Preserving the urban form of Čaršija was not the direct goal of officials and professionals, but utilitarian and pragmatic reasons drove them to extend the life of the city quarter and give it a place in the modernized urban body. Clearly reluctant to touch the networks of local elites, they dealt carefully with the question of reordering Čaršija, parts of which were under *vakuf* administration, while clusters of shops were owned or used by prominent merchant families. Without systematic knowledge about the principles and techniques that gave form and character to Ottoman Čaršija, and with no clear blueprint on the ways in which to govern the relationship between the individual buildings and the surrounding fabric, authorities learned by trial and error, continuously testing the limits of what was possible, and sometimes improvising in the face of uncertainty.

Resting upon a foundation of orientalist tropes, the space of the craft and trade quarter was initially loaded with a number of negative connotations – backwardness and poor planning and hygiene. When Čaršija's divergence from the prevailing concepts of order and beauty was accepted as something that did not need to be replaced but supervised and gradually reformed, the new palimpsestic version of Čaršija was brought into being. Requiring a continuous alertness to control its difference, the city quarter became subject to new standards of classification, ordering, and documentation. Granting an exception to permit construction in traditional materials, the second version of the Building Code for Sarajevo from 1893 treated Čaršija as a distinctive zone inside the city without formulating it explicitly.[35] More precisely, the building laws allowed the use of wood for the construction in the area of Čaršija if additional fire-resistant materials were used for roof structures.[36] Empire-wide mechanisms of regulatory planning were locally adapted and formulated in specific ways as seen here. Engagement with the "old" order that was allowed to coexist with the "new" and tolerance for the local construction methods was thus a gesture of selective and controlled acceptance of the vernacular (Figure 8.3). In order to succeed, the imperial urban program had to allow diversity of spatial and aesthetic regimes and enable the discursive and symbolical integration of the Muslims of Sarajevo and their symbolic Čaršija spaces into the political framework.

Individual monumental buildings in Čaršija were singled out to function as mnemonic devices remembering the pasts that produced them. Such was the case with the Gazi Husrev-beg Mosque[37] and Kuršumli Madrasa that, together with a type of Muslim residential house, were often selected to

Figure 8.3 Street scene at Čaršija, 1892. People of Čaršija standing in front of a cluster of wood-built shops (dućans). A new type of a multi-story building can be seen on the right.

Source: Austrian National Library, 133.731-D.

represent in a condensed manner the cultural and technological achievements of the Ottomans. Edmund Stix, the head of the provincial building department, included the selected buildings in his authoritative technical-statistical study of the architectural production "before the occupation," making the creations available for analysis and contemplation.[38] Following Stix's summary of the built culture, engineers and architects from Austria-Hungary routinely visited these privileged objects in Čaršija during their study trips to Sarajevo.[39]

The provincial government conferred the status of a valuable object deserving care and maintenance on the Gazi Husrev-beg Mosque soon after the building was damaged in the fire of 1879. The blackened interior decoration was restored in 1885, though not to its earlier state but by removing existing wall paintings and replacing them with a fusion of experimental Orientalizing motifs conceptualized by the architect Hans Niemeczek and implemented by painters from Slavonia.[40] To fit the desirable image, the interior needed to be reshaped based on dominant aesthetic preferences and understandings of Islamic art and architecture. The search for the authentic local was therefore not simply a neutral mapping of past achievements, but was intertwined with the mission of reforming and improving the very same local. In professional discourses, Gazi Husrev-beg Mosque was recognized as the guiding urban landmark in the skyline of Čaršija in 1903 when the city authorities decided to restrict the maximum height of buildings in the proximity of the mosque. Permitting construction of only single-story buildings, the overall goal was to "preserve the oriental character of Čaršija."[41] The size and complex architectural composition of the mosque, as well as its symbiotic relationship with the landscape of Čaršija, granted the mosque the status of an urban icon. "Could it be possible to imagine Athens without Acropolis [...] and *si parva licet componere magnis* [to compare small things with great], Sarajevo without Bey's mosque?"[42] asked Ćiro Truhelka, curator of the provincial museum, putting the final seal of approval on the building in 1912.

Old Urban Fabric and New Landmarks

The contours and physiognomy of Čaršija were greatly determined by the rebuilding choices made after the fire of 1879 as well as the regulation scenario for the Miljacka River after the two floods in 1881 and 1887. The nucleus of Čaršija received its defining contour and southern border when the river was channeled and the Appel Quay was superimposed on the place where buildings used to touch the unregulated riverfront (Figure 8.4). Symbolically rewriting the landscape, the linear boulevard following the riverbank was named after Johann Freiherr von Appel, the head of the provincial government (1882–1903). Already in the years before 1900, two new architectural landmarks flanked the skyline of Čaršija: the Hotel Europe on its western and the City Hall on its eastern edge. The dynamic and sometimes contradictory encounter of the new building types, architectural styles, and functional programs with the existing urban fabric gave a new face to this reformatted city fragment.

One of the first capital interventions in Čaršija after the great fire was the construction of Hotel Europe at its western edge. Wealthy merchant Gligorije Jeftanović, an esteemed member of the local Orthodox elite, funded and finished the hotel in 1882 at the place where Franz Joseph Street met the corner of Čaršija, and where the vitality of a new commercial street and the picturesqueness of a decaying Ottoman khan (Tašlihan) looked straight at each other. The outstanding historicist building was portrayed in the press as exemplary, solid, and modern, expected to pave the way in which new buildings should be built in "wooden Sarajevo."[43] Mentioned in numerous travelogues, Hotel Europe quickly gained popularity as one of the few places in the city that could provide comfort for European visitors.

Figure 8.4 Čaršija of Sarajevo encircled by the Appel Quay from the southern side and flanked by the City Hall sited at its eastern edge. Circulated post-card, Verlag Albert Thier Sarajevo, 1909.

Source: Private collection of the author.

Just a year after its formal opening, the mayor of Sarajevo, Mehmed-beg Kapetanović, requested the City Council to express official appreciation to the hotel's owner Jeftanović, who spared neither effort nor capital to initiate the process of beautifying the city, giving it the touch that other European cities already have.[44]

On the other edge of Čaršija, the City Hall (*Vijećnica*) was conceptualized and constructed between 1891 and 1896, when the imperial project of city building called for manifesting and situating the head and heart of the urban administration of Sarajevo. Staying with the idea that local power stems from the urban networks entangled in the system of Čaršija, a triangular site available for the construction of the seat of the City Council of Sarajevo was found in the old Ottoman commercial center, although all other government buildings were already situated in the new western part of the city in the area shaped as the Austro-Hungarian administrative headquarters. The powerful figure of the provincial governor Benjámin Kállay (1882–1903) controlled and supervised the development of the architectural concept for the City Hall. He was in charge of evaluating the first design plans by architect Karl Pařik and responsible for replacing the proposed Byzantinizing style of the façades with the Orientalizing stylistic repertoire further developed by the architect Aleksandar Wittek. A third architect Ćiril Iveković finalized the project and supervised the construction.[45] With the City Hall, the new regime finally succeeded in the task of monumentalizing its presence at the key site of Ottoman-era Sarajevo. Intended to represent the authority of the local civic government, a new building type and a new political function were added to the sacred and commercial landscape of Čaršija.

When the building was finished – its massing and decoration dwarfing the surroundings – the inferiority of Čaršija became evident as a consequence. Massive in scale, ambiguous in architectural style, and placed in a way to turn its back to the streets of Čaršija, the building did not converse with the shapes, colors, and topography of its surrounding fabric. The picture postcard of Sarajevo included in this analysis (Figure 8.4) bears testimony to the condition where one empire that ceased to lay claims persisted in the urban fabric, while the one replacing it searched for a suitable architectural expression. The postcard as a carrier of messages features the Appel Quay bordering the small structures of the craft and trade quarter and the newly built City Hall dominating the townscape, demonstrating that the visual documentation of Čaršija accompanied its dynamic period of change. The City Hall became a true emblem of the Austro-Hungarian cultural mission, confidently presented and exhibited whenever possible. Its architectural scale model was included in the narrative of construction progress inside the Bosnian pavilions in the Millennium Exhibition in Budapest (1896) and the World Exposition in Paris (1900).

The physiognomy of Čaršija was reconfigured rapidly – not only when authorities and professionals started dealing with its spatial organization but also when property owners and city dwellers reoriented their own priorities and interests, becoming actors of change in the society of competitive capitalism. Since private development practice became the prevailing method of delivering the built environment after the fire of 1879, rebuilding of the shops became a process of negotiating the material qualities of a given structure and aspirations and financial capacities of a user. Focused on demands of the present, individual owners were in favor of upgrading their buildings or replacing existing modest shop formats with multi-story Western-style buildings. Gradual disfigurement of the Čaršija townscape as known from the Ottoman times, therefore, started with the systematic remodeling of its basic unit – the *dućan*.

Experienced and Imagined Čaršija

Although Čaršija lost its accumulated functional centrality due to the shift of the urban core further west to the "European" area of the city – Franz Joseph Street, Rudolf Street, Ferhadija, and Ćemaluša – it continued as a vibrant part of the city and a space for the social experiences of groups and communities. While the new downtown was tailored to fit preferences of city-based elites and newcomers, Čaršija remained a commercial arena where locals from various confessional communities, urban and rural populations, and the rich and poor of Sarajevo interacted, conducted business, and exchanged news and information. The institution and practices of the market appeared to be more durable than the materiality of Čaršija itself. Artisans kept producing certain products, usually for the local market, peasants from the surrounding countryside traveled on market days to sell their products, and visitors to Čaršija had a chance to directly encounter locals and their artifacts in the process of buying and selling. Anthropologist and archaeologist Robert Munro witnessed in 1894 that Čaršija was still a place where "native goods may be seen in the act of being manufactured" and gave an example of the technique of silver inlaid decoration.[46] János de Asbóth, in his depictions of life and customs in Sarajevo, carefully observed the types of craft items produced in Čaršija: pitchers, boxes, bowls, smoking-vessels, coffee-cups, coffeepots, ornamental weapons, knives and scissors, and embroideries, among others.[47] While some branches of local industries could not compete with manufacturers from the Monarchy and lost their relevance, certain types of production were elevated to the status of artisanal traditions and became the focus of a governmental mission to rescue Bosnian crafts. In that way, activities that earlier belonged exclusively to the sphere of Čaršija's urban economy were transferred to government-sponsored ateliers and schools, where production techniques were studied and objects were refined for the urban markets of Austria-Hungary.[48]

The landscape of Čaršija went through a dynamic and conflictual process of interpretation and appropriation that began with the act of naming. Depending upon the audience, it was addressed as the bazaar quarter (*Bazarviertel*), the trade quarter (*Handelsviertel*), or the Turkish quarter (*Türkenviertel*). Before it emerged as an object of historical knowledge and preservation, it existed as an external reality, transposed into images, discourses, and concepts. The theatricality and ornamental richness of the vernacular space offered a palette of new sensations to generations of artists, writers, ethnographers, and explorers, whose imagination and expertise helped shape and organize the representation of Čaršija. Scenes of everyday life were an important part of the repertoire of painters and graphic artists who came to work to Sarajevo, and whose works filled the pages of the magazine *Nada*.[49] Accounts of Bosnia-Herzegovina prepared for European travelers were packed with descriptions of Sarajevo's old craft and trade quarter, promoted as safe, accessible, and nearby but still exotic enough place for an "Oriental holiday."[50] Images of Čaršija moved across imperial borders, circulated in print, and participated in building the visual archive of the empire. In 1901, when the volume of the *Kronprinzenwerk* on Bosnia-Herzegovina was published, the image of Sarajevo's Čaršija was officially integrated into the systems of ethnographic representation of Austria-Hungary.[51] Located at the periphery of the cultural system, the picturesque and outdated city fragment was approached in the positivity of its difference, operating as a part of the imperial whole.

The discourse about the exotic Čaršija had a series of clear consequences. The city quarter emerged as an object belonging to the past that did not share the same time with the rest of the city but offered the ethnological experience of a different urban reality.[52] People of Čaršija became visible as "the good oriental Slavs" residing in the Orient "close to home" (i.e., the imperial center), loyal and responsive to the civilizing mission.[53] Pictorialization of space and time reinforced the paradigm of cultural otherness and incompatibility of the old urban system coexisting with the modern. The essentialized world of Čaršija, whose productive aspect was transformed into an ornamental one, existed in opposition to modern Sarajevo and was seen as having no lessons to offer the future.

Becoming Object of Knowledge and Preservation

The approach to Čaršija slowly began to change after 1910 with the shift from a "progressist" model of planning inspired by a vision of progress to a "culturalist" model organized around a vision of cultural community.[54] The architect Josip Pospišil[55] offered a useful corrective to the existing ideas about the system of Čaršija – questioning, toning down, and discarding some of the orientalist tropes and reductive ideas about it. In texts and public speeches, he approached the devalued other of Čaršija using technical criteria and drawing attention to the city quarter as a coherent ensemble with its own principles that can be classified and studied. Pospišil turned the spotlight on the architecture of an individual *dućan*, recognizing in it a manifestation of creative forces and practical skills of untutored builders, as well as a character-defining element of Čaršija (Figure 8.3). Although the *dućan* did not offer "traces of architecture in a way we usually understand it,"[56] Pospišil acknowledged that it produced an effect and contributed to constituting the order and practices of the community. Converting the old town into an object of knowledge, the architect analyzed Čaršija as a constitutive part of the urban organism. He argued that the dilemma of preserving an individual shop (*Einzeltypus*) cannot be detached from the dilemma of preserving Čaršija as whole (*Gesamtbild*), and that the problem of Čaršija cannot be detached from the problem of regulating the integral city.[57]

By this time, constructions inside the former Ottoman commercial center were subject to widespread criticism. In the rebuilding process after the great fire, Čaršija had lost much of what was seen as its Oriental charm and authenticity. The irreversibility of the destructive process of change became evident with the disappearance of the vernacular forms of shops, street ensembles, and individual structures, as well as the problematic positioning of new historicist buildings inside the existing context, the most striking example being the pseudo-oriental City Hall. Confronted with the actuality of the urban situation, visitors to Sarajevo described the City Hall building as being "alien to the people and the time,"[58] while architectural professionals referred to it as "our youthful delusion."[59] The architect Pospišil called for the imperial-royal Central Commission for the Investigation and Conservation of Architectural Monuments[60] to take co-responsibility, pointing at the ongoing destruction of the physiognomies of Bosnian towns.[61] Witnessing the everyday disfigurement of the townscape of Sarajevo, Pospišil warned in 1909, "Soon there won't be anything else to demolish in Sarajevo."[62]

As the development of planning ideas applied to historic urban environments began to take on a strong culturalist undertone, Čaršija emerged as a resource worthy of care and preservation. The city quarter was not perceived simply in terms of its material otherness – the newly discovered interest in the "Old Town" and discontent with the generic face of the "New Sarajevo" had the effect of turning the spotlight on the qualities of Čaršija's townscape and its vernacular architecture. Encouraged by the development of disciplinary knowledge and the interrelated fields of urban planning (*Städtebau*) and monument preservation (*Denkmalpflege*) in the German-speaking context, local professionals and authorities started reflecting upon the spatial and aesthetic qualities of the old urban cores. Inspired by the ideas of the homeland protection (*Heimatschutz*) movement, they sought to protect traditional forms, promote contextualism, and renew interest in "the authentic" and "the local." The movement expanded the range of objects to be considered worthy of protection, shifting interest from individual objects to the ensemble, the city image (*Stadtbild*), and the entire old town (*Altstadt*).

A careful observer of the Austro-Hungarian administering mission added his voice to the growing chorus of support for the idea of safeguarding Čaršija, pragmatically highlighting the value of its rarity in the existing imperial context:

Here we have a piece of Orient in the middle of a city and in a country where, under the wing of the Austro-Hungarian double-headed eagle, western culture is beginning to gain rapidly a foothold. Would it disappear [the Turkish quarter], it would be hard to bring it back in its original state even with great financial efforts.[63]

Hence, the "pre-modern" urban past, initially seen as an obstacle to development, became valuable only when it became scarce. More precisely, organized protection of the Ottoman urban fabric was not compatible with the goals of the earliest modernization mission that worked to break away from the backward past. Only later did preservation come to be seen as an instrument of good governance and an important ingredient of the imperial project. The impulse to preserve Čaršija as a tradition-bearing urban element through legal instruments and institutions was not simply a gesture towards the heritage of the subject people but also a signal that the imperial project and monarchic trans-nationalism could provide a tent for diverse vernacular forms and practices. Čaršija as a patrimonial project, however, remained unfinished since the outbreak of the First World War prevented the completion of legal and institutional mechanisms that would govern planning and preservation.[64]

Imperial Celebration in Čaršija

The four days that Emperor Franz Joseph I spent in Sarajevo (May 30–June 3, 1910) were remembered and narrated as an outstanding public event that employed a number of city landmarks to perform and articulate imperial authority. The short and sole visit to the provincial capital organized as a part of a greater journey to Bosnia-Herzegovina sought to advance a new social vision in the years after the formal annexation of the provinces in 1908. The emperor's diplomatic *parcours* in Čaršija discussed here represents a legible episode extracted from the longer history of Habsburg imperial celebration.

On the morning of May 31, 1910, in the great hall of the provincial government, Franz Joseph first met the Catholic archbishop, and then the Serbian-Orthodox metropolitan, the Muslim *reis-ul-ulema*, the representatives of Jewish Sephardi and Ashkenazi communities, the Protestant pastor, representatives of provincial and city government, and consular missions, respectively. Responding to the welcome speech of Esad Kulović, the mayor of Sarajevo, Franz Joseph said:

> I am deeply touched and delighted by the many wilful proofs of sincere loyalty and closeness, which were handed to Me during My short stay in My dear capital [...] I assure you that I follow with greatest interest the development of this beautiful city and that I will gladly recall the days I spent here.[65]

Later that day, Franz Joseph met all the confessional leaders in their houses of worship and the city authorities in the City Hall. It took two minutes for the imperial carriage to move between the Sacred Heart Cathedral, the Orthodox Church of the Nativity of the Theotokos, Gazi Husrev-beg Mosque, and the Sephardic synagogue and not more than ten minutes to reach the Protestant church and the Ashkenazi synagogue on the other side of the Miljacka River. From there, an eight-minute ride was needed to take the emperor to the eastern edge of Čaršija to the City Hall where he met the mayor and members of the Sarajevo City Council.[66] The public ceremony was space contingent, as it was choreographed around the network of spaces in and around Čaršija, calling attention to the religious diversity of the city, and desiring allegiance of all confessional groups.

The newspaper *Sarajevski list* ran a series of reports describing the arrival of Franz Joseph in Sarajevo, using a metaphor of a long-expected and warm meeting of a father-figure with his faithful subjects.[67] The newspaper elaborately described how each of the confessional groups worked in a manner of gentle competition to decorate the streets and buildings along the itinerary.[68] Unlike the rest of the year, when each group celebrated its own holy days, the emperor's presence in the city granted everyone "a common holiday."[69] The public ceremony as such aimed to contribute to forging a sense of urban community among Sarajevo's diverse population and facilitate the transformation of affiliations based on ethnicity and religion to a form of composite imperial loyalties. It is worth noting that Čaršija, with its picturesque masses, decorations, and symbolic associations, constituted an excellent *mise-en-scène* for the ceremony. Merchants and artisans made an effort to temporarily cover streets with canopies and tree branches stretched between lines of shops, while *dućan*s were decorated with flags, carpets, images, and lanterns.[70] The emperor's itinerary and interest in attending different rituals gave a local color to the standard ceremonial form.

Some aspects of the journey were particularly memorable and were captured in text and image. The Viennese newspaper *Neue Freie Presse* singled out the favorable Muslim reception, describing in great detail Franz Joseph's visit to the courtyard and interior of the Gazi Husrev-beg Mosque and his meeting with religious dignitaries. The newspaper paid attention to the rumors that circulated in Čaršija suggesting that the local Muslims showed appreciation of the emperor's decision to come to their province. "No sultan has ever visited us," they reportedly stated while reflecting upon four centuries of Ottoman rule.[71] Franz Joseph's encounter with Čaršija left traces in works of art. The painting by Leo Delitz[72] depicts the carriage of Emperor Franz Joseph and Governor Marijan Varešanin in the moment after they left the courtyard of the Gazi Husrev-beg Mosque to greet the colorful crowd in Čaršija (Figure 8.5). Delitz's composition is organized around the triumphal arch in Orientalizing style located in the

Figure 8.5 Leo Delitz, "Der Kaiser verlässt die Begova-Moschee in Sarajevo durch
den offenen Bazar (Carsija)" [The emperor walks out from Bey's Mosque
in Sarajevo to the open bazaar (Čaršija)]. Heliogravure/aquarelle, 1910.

Source: Austrian National Library, Pk 1302, 47.

streets of Čaršija. The arch was one of several temporary structures built
by confessional and entrepreneurial groups to mark the spaces of the city.
Built under the patronage of the *vakuf* administration, it was inscribed
with "Long live Franz Joseph I, the beloved Emperor-King."[73] Delitz's
painting of the festive welcome in the core of Čaršija was included in *Viribus Unitis,* the commemorative collection about the life of the emperor.[74]

The ceremony in Sarajevo illustrates how imperial cultural unity and
local particularity reinforced each other, confirming the scholarly argument that from the center comes "the awareness of the larger political
construct, the consciousness of being part of a broader system, vast and
complex," while the local contributes with "the sense of vitality, myth,

the *elan vital.*"[75] At the end of the engaging day in Sarajevo, Franz Joseph allegedly said to Governor Varešanin, "After what I've seen here, I feel twenty years younger,"[76] putting into words the sense that the experiences of the diverse people and their powerful protector were not separated but mutually entangled. Carefully curated for the ceremonial display, Sarajevo's urban landscape, when experienced in a direct physical encounter, operated as a cumulative site capable of representing the richness of the cultures and their histories without giving exclusivity to any of the constituent groups. The emperor's route carved through Čaršija brought visual, tactile, and aural impulses that served as vitalizing contributions to the Austro-Hungarian imperial project.

Concluding Remarks

On April 7, 1916, Čaršija of Sarajevo traveled to the front page of the Viennese architectural journal *Der Bautechniker.*[77] The author of the article, the architect Josip Pospišil, presented to empire-wide audiences refined arguments about the need to safeguard the city quarter that he had already outlined five years earlier in the local newspaper *Bosnische Post.*[78] The case of Čaršija that entered the picture as the most pressing problem for the Austro-Hungarian imperial reputation upon the takeover of Sarajevo and following the great fire, therefore, remained a topic that could stir debates even in the middle of the First World War.

As discussed earlier, the fire of 1879 that left the old commercial center in ruins eventually shaped the course of urban reforms for Sarajevo. The story of the Austro-Hungarian recalibration of the Ottoman Čaršija is not one of the great planning strategies but of a series of gestures that sought simultaneously to technically correct and improve the city quarter that was evocative of its Ottoman past, as well as to display its picturesque character. Despite some efforts, institutional heritage practices were unable to adopt effective forms of care for the fabric of Čaršija.

Investigating the imperial dimensions of Sarajevo as suggested here required making two intertwined moves. The first one was to trace the marks of empire in its urban structure by questioning new architectural styles and building types, new urban policies, and manners of performing imperial authority. The second move consisted of unpacking how imperial self-conception and self-description were boosted or challenged in Sarajevo by identifying contexts in which the usual way of doing things called for new approaches and definitions. Čaršija of Sarajevo is a rewarding case study that demonstrates what it meant to exist as a field of intervention, object of discourses, and a circulating image that could bring the empire and the city together, always with a new urgency.

Notes

1 The description is found in Joseph Koetschet, *Aus Bosniens letzter Türkenzeit* (Vienna and Leipzig: Hartleben, 1905), 77–9.
2 "Eure Gesetze und Einrichtungen sollen nicht willkürlich umgestossen, Eure Sitten und Gebräuche sollen geschont werden. Nichts soll gewaltsam verändert werden, ohne reifliche Erwägung dessen, was Euch nöththut [...] Der Kaiser und König kennt Eure Beschwerden und wünscht Euer Wohlergeben. Unter seinem mächtigen Scepter wohnen viele Völker beisammen und jedes spricht seine Sprache. Er herrscht über die Anhänger vieler Religionen und Jeder bekennt frei seinen Glauben." "Proclamation an die Bewohner von Bosnien und der Hercegovina," first printed in *Wiener Zeitung*, July 28, 1878, 1, and later included in *Sammlung der für Bosnien und die Hercegovina erlassenen Gesetze, Verordnungen, und Normalweisungen* (Vienna: Kaiserlich-königliche Hof- und Staatsdruckerei, 1880), 3. The publication will henceforth be abbreviated *SGVN*.
3 "bosnische Eldorado" in "Bosnische Eindrücke," *Bosnische Post*, July 16, 1910, 6.
4 "*l'Orient de l'Europe*" in Henri Moser, *Bosnie-Herzegovine: Une oeuvre de colonisation pacifique dans les Balkans* (Paris: Imprimerie V. Goupy, G. Maurin, successeur, 1896), 3.
5 See, for example, Mary Sparks, *The Development of Austro-Hungarian Sarajevo, 1878–1918: An Urban History* (London: Bloomsbury, 2014); Robert J. Donia, "Fin-de-Siècle Sarajevo: The Habsburg Transformation of an Ottoman Town," *Austrian History Yearbook* 33 (2002): 43–75, https://doi.org/10.1017/S0067237800013813; Nedžad Kurto, *Arhitektura Bosne i Hercegovine: Razvoj bosanskoga stila* (Sarajevo: Sarajevo Publishing, 1998); Borislav Spasojević, *Arhitektura stambenih palata austrougarskog perioda u Sarajevu* (Sarajevo: Rabic, 1999).
6 *Čaršija*/Чаршија is a local variation of the Turkish word *çarsu/çarşı* (marketplace), derived from Persian *chahār-sū* (lit. four sides, referring to the intersection of two routes) and designates the commercial center of cities in the Ottoman Balkans. The term as it is used in the Bosnian/Croatian//Montenegrin/Serbian language carries a variety of subtle meanings and can encompass the consideration of urban form, socioeconomic space, and (artisanal) systems of production or can be used as a metaphor for cultural mindsets.
7 My suggestion to add "city" to the existing conversation about intertwined histories of "empire" and "vision" in modernity is based on Martin Jay and Sumathi Ramaswamy, eds., *Empires of Vision: A Reader* (Durham, NC: Duke University Press, 2014).
8 From Turkish *dükkân*.
9 Estimates suggest that more than twenty fires raged in Sarajevo between 1480 and 1879. For a brief history of urban fire in Sarajevo, see Hamdija Kreševljaković, "Požari u Sarajevu do 1879. godine," in *Islamski svijet: Muslimanski književno-publicistički kalendar*, ed. Šahinović-Ekremov (Sarajevo: Štamparija Zadruga 1933), 28–34.
10 The best available analysis of the internal organization of guilds in Sarajevo is found in Hamdija Kreševljaković, "Sarajevska čaršija, njeni esnafi i obrti za osmanlijske uprave," *Narodna starina* 6, no. 14 (1927): 15–58.
11 A treatment of the passage from the regime of guilds to the working classes of the nineteenth century can be found in Iljas Hadžibegović, *Postanak radničke klase u Bosni i Hercegovini i njen razvoj do 1914. godine* (Sarajevo: Svjetlost, 1980).

12 With the arrival of Austro-Hungarian military troops in Bosnia-Herzegovina, there was a growing demand for wine, rum, liquor, and other alcoholic drinks. Merchants who followed the army located their depots and storages in the back streets of *Latinluk*. Surrounded by easily flammable goods (alcohol, petroleum, matches, etc.), they repacked and filled barrels for distribution. (Based on eyewitness accounts, published in the newspaper *Jugoslovenski list* to mark the 50ᵗʰ anniversary of the great fire.) "Veliki požar od 8. augusta 1879," *Jugoslovenski list*, August 8, 1929, 8.

13 Ignaz/Ignác Funk (1835–1886) was born in a Jewish family of Bačka Palanka (Bácspalánka/Plankenburg) and set up a photographic studio in Zrenjanin (Nagybecskerek/Großbetschkerek). Passionate about technology and innovation, he brought the first phonograph to the town and used it for sound recording in his studio. To make a living from photography, he often traveled to Bosnia. A brief biographical information is found in Dragoljub Čolić, "Contribution of the Jews to Banat's Economic Progress", in *Jewish Studies IV: Studies, Archival and Memorial Materials about the Jews in Yugoslavia*, ed. Radovan Samardžić (Belgrade: Federation of Jewish communities in Yugoslavia, 1979), 180.

14 The five photographs framed in white passe-partouts together with a brief note indicating the recipient are kept today in an art folder with a ribbon tie in the Picture Archives of the Austrian National Library. To the best of my knowledge, none of the photographs have even been published before. Der Brand von Serajevo. Austrian National Library, Pk 904.

15 I draw here on the idea of interruption of the course of events creating possibilities for the new to emerge as discussed in Hannah Arendt, *Between Past and Future: Six Exercises in Political Thought* (New York: The Viking Press, 1961), 9.

16 "[A]n den Trümmern der bosnischen Hauptstadt hängt die Zukunft der österreichischen Politik auf der Balkanhalbinsel." In "Die Krankheit des Grafen Andrássy," *Epoche*, August 17, 1879, 2.

17 "Der Staat! Aber welcher Staat? [...] Sarajevo braucht eine Staatssubvention. Wer soll sie ihm aber geben? Oestreich-Ungarn? [...] Und wird man am Bosporus den Moment benützen, um die Rechtskontinuität praktisch zu demonstrieren, wird man sich daselbst entschließen, auf die Wiederherstellung der bosnischen Hauptstadt etwas beizutragen?" In "Das Bosnische Moskau," *Epoche*, August 13, 1879, 2.

18 "Der Sultan und der Brand von Sarajevo," *Prager Abendblatt*, August 13, 1879, 2.

19 Haris Zaimović, *Zapisnici sarajevskog gradskog zastupstva (1878–1881)* (Sarajevo: Historijski arhiv Sarajevo, 2018), 17. Indispensable for any study of the administrative organization of the local government of Sarajevo is the work of Haris Zaimović which includes analytical summaries and inventories of archival records kept in the Historical Archives of Sarajevo.

20 A (partial) list of donors and donated amounts can be made by combining the information from the following archival records: Gradsko poglavarstvo Sarajevo (1879), 3183, 3184, 3268, 3269, Historical Archives of Sarajevo; and Spenden für Brandgeschädigte in Sarajewo (1879), Sarajewo-Sammlung, 1546–1551, HHStA, Austrian State Archives.

21 "Aufruf an die Bewohner der Stadt Salzburg," *Salzburger Chronik*, August 28, 1879, 4.

22 Kommission zum Wiederaufbau der Stadt Sarajevo, Archives of Bosnia and Herzegovina, ZVS₁-15755.

23 Based on the memoires of Julije Makanec published retrospectively in *Jugoslovenski list*: "Veliki požar Sarajeva g. 1879," *Jugoslovenski list*, July 4, 1929, 3.

24 Joseph Alexander Helfert, "[E]ine Aufgabe der Entwilderung und Gesittung," in Joseph Alexander Helfert, *Bosnisches* (Vienna: Manz'sche k.k. Hof-Verlags- und Universitäts-Buchhandlung, 1879), 157.

25 "Strassen- und Bautengesetz vom 7. Džemaziul-evel 1280 (1863)," in *SGVN*, 180.

26 Regulierungs-Plan von Sarajevo für den Wiederaufbau des abgebrannten Stadttheiles nach Beschluß des Gemeinderathes von Sarajevo von Sarajevo in der Sitzung von 11. März 1880. Historical Archives of Sarajevo, ZKP-514. For generous assistance in finding materials and navigating the collection of maps and city plans in the Historical Archives of Sarajevo, I am extremely grateful to Saša Beltram.

27 Originally referring to a manuscript on which earlier writing has been erased so that it could be reinscribed with a new text, the term "palimpsest" is used here to suggest that traces of multiple (re)making episodes remain recorded in the physical and cartographic space of Čaršija.

28 Elements of the plan were reassessed several times in the years to come. The location for the city hall was changed and moved several blocks to the east of the plot proposed here. The case of the city hall will be discussed in detail in what follows.

29 Following the principles from the Ottoman era, Sarajevo Council members were elected based on their confessional affiliation. According to the provisional statute (1878–1884), council seats were reserved for six Orthodox, five Muslim, three Catholic, and four Jewish representatives. The permanent city statute enacted in 1884 preserved the principle of religious quota. "Provisorisches Statut für die Errichtung einer Gemeindevertretung in der Stadt Sarajevo vom 22. August 1878," in *SGVN*, 585.

30 "Viesti Sarajevske," *Bosanskohercegovačke novine*, March 28, 1880, 2.

31 Ibid.

32 "Bau-Ordnung für Sarajevo und jene Städte und Märkte in Bosnien und der Hercegovina, welche dieser Vorschrift durch eine Verordnung der Landesregierung ausdrücklich unterworfen werden (Genehmigt mit Allerhöchster Entschliessung vom 14. Mai 1880)," in *SGVN*, 249–71.

33 "Požarna služba u Sarajevu," *Sarajevski list*, October 3, 1883, 2; "Gospodska kuća u Sarajevu," *Sarajevski list*, January 16, 1883, 2.

34 "Verordnung, betreffend die für Neu- und Umbauten auf den Brandstätten von Sarajevo zu gewährenden Begünstigungen (Genehmigt mit Allerhöchster Entschliessung vom 18. Mai 1880)," in *SGVN*, 271–2.

35 Clause 36 of the Building Code. "Bau-Ordnung für die Landeshauptstadt Sarajevo (Genehmigt mit Allerhöchster Entschliessung vom 23. Juli 1893 und publicirt mit Verordnung der Landesregierung für Bosnien und die Hercegovina vom 5. August 1893, Zahl 76.174.)," in *Gesetz- und Verordnungsblatt für Bosnien und die Hercegovina* (Sarajevo: Druck der Landesdruckerei, 1893), 422.

36 Ibid.

37 Gazi Husrev-beg Mosque (*Begova džamija*) is a complex-spaced, multi-domed mosque finished in 1531. It is the central object of the building complex, the endowment of the Ottoman governor Husrev-beg, which also included the Kuršumli Madrasa, Quranic school, library, soup kitchen, public bath, khan, covered market, shops, etc.

38 Edmund Stix, *Das Bauwesen in Bosnien und Hercegovina vom Beginn der Occupation durch die österr.-ung. Monarchie bis in das Jahr 1887* (Vienna: Landesregierung für Bosnien und die Hercegovina, 1887).

39 See, for example, P. Kortz, "Bericht über die Studienreise im Mai 1888," *Wochenschrift des Österr. Ingenieur- und Architekten-Vereines* 13, no. 36 (1888): 325.

40 A comprehensive treatment of the biography of the mosque building is given in Nihad Čengić, *Begova džamija kao djelo umjetnosti* (Sarajevo: Sarajevo Publishing, 2008).

41 "Aus den Gemeinderathe," *Bosnische Post*, May 12, 1903, 1.

42 Ćiro Truhelka, "Gazi Husref-beg, njegov život i njegovo doba," *Glasnik Zemaljskog muzeja* 24 (1912): 91.

43 "Gospodska kuća u Sarajevu," *Sarajevski list*, January 16, 1883, 2.

44 "Iz sarajevske gradske općine," *Sarajevski list*, February 24, 1883, 2.

45 The authorship and pseudo-oriental architecture of the City Hall have received significant scholarly attention and continue to give rise to new interpretations. A number of commentators have considered in detail the motives of professionals and administrators for employing Mamluk and Moorish references in Bosnia-Herzegovina, interpreting the act either as a gesture to a large Muslim population in Bosnia or as a variant of romantic historicism tendencies in the nineteenth-century Europe. For more details, see: Nedžad Kurto, *Arhitektura Bosne i Hercegovine: Razvoj bosanskoga stila* (Sarajevo: Sarajevo Publishing, 1998); Alexander Zäh, "Die orientalisierende Architektur als ein stilistischer Ausdruck des offiziellen Bauprogramms der k. u. k. Bosnisch-Herzegowinischen Landesregierung 1878–1918'," *Südost-Forschungen* 72 (2013): 63–97; Maximilian Hartmuth, "K.(u.)k. Colonial? Contextualizing Architecture and Urbanism in Bosnia-Herzegovina, 1878–1918," in *WechselWirkungen: Austria-Hungary, Bosnia-Herzegovina, and the Western Balkans, 1878–1918*, ed. Clemens Ruthner et al. (New York: Peter Lang, 2015), 155–84.

46 Robert Munro, *Rambles and Studies in Bosnia-Herzegovina and Dalmatia with an Account of the Proceedings of the Congress of Archaeologists and Anthropologists Held at Sarajevo, August 1894* (Edinburgh: William Blackwood, 1900), 13.

47 János de Asbóth, *An Official Tour through Bosnia and Herzegovina: With an Account of the History, Antiquities, Agrarian Conditions, Religion, Ethnology, Folk Lore, and Social Life of the People* (London: Swan Sonnenschein, 1890), 180.

48 For a more detailed discussion of craft reform and protection of artistic traditions as part of the Austro-Hungarian civilizing mission, see Diana Reynolds-Cordileone, "Displaying Bosnia: Imperialism, Orientalism, and Exhibitionary Cultures in Vienna and Beyond, 1878–1914," *Austrian History Yearbook* 46 (2015): 29–50, https://doi.org/10.1017/S0067237814000083.

49 *Nada* (1895–1903) was a lavishly illustrated magazine for education, entertainment, and art, edited by Kosta Hörmann. As an imperially sponsored project, *Nada* significantly defined the canon of representation of Bosnia-Herzegovina. Contributing artists Ewald and Leo Arndt, Max Liebenwein, and Ivana Kobilica formed "The Sarajevo Painter's Club" in 1900.

50 Henri Moser, *An Oriental Holiday: Bosnia and Herzegovina: A Handbook for the Tourist* (London: Eustace Curzon, 1895).

51 *Die Österreichisch-ungarische Monarchie in Wort und Bild* (*The Austro-Hungarian Monarchy in Word and Image*), usually referred to as the *Kronprinzenwerk*, was an illustrated historical and ethnographic encyclopedia of Austria-Hungary organized by territory in 24 volumes. It appeared between 1889 and 1902 in a German and a Hungarian version. *Die*

Österreichisch-Ungarische Monarchie in Wort und Bild: Bosnien und Herce-govina (Vienna: Druck und Verlag der kaiserlich-königlichen Hof- und Staats-druckerei, 1901).

52 My observation about Čaršija of Sarajevo being located far from the modern in terms of both time and space is based on Johannes Fabian, *Time and the Other: How Anthropology Makes Its Objects* (New York: Columbia University Press, 2014).

53 For the variants of the Habsburg orientalist discourses, and the distinction be-tween the "distant" Orient represented by the Ottoman Empire and Turks, and the Orient "close to home" epitomized by Bosnia-Herzegovina and South-Slav people, see Johann Heiss and Johannes Feichtinger, "Distant Neighbors: Uses of Orientalism in the Late Nineteenth-Century Austro-Hungarian Empire," in *Deploying Orientalism in Culture and History: From Germany to Central and Eastern Europe*, ed. James Hodkinson et al. (Rochester: Camden House, 2013), 149.

54 I draw here on terminology developed by Françoise Choay, *The Modern City: Planning in the 19th Century* (New York: George Braziller, 1969), 31.

55 Josip Pospišil (1867–1918) was born in Moravia, attended the school of crafts in Brno, and studied at the Academy of Fine Arts in Vienna. He worked in architectural ateliers in Vienna, Zürich, Zagreb, and Prague before moving to Sarajevo in 1908. He was a pioneering voice and advocate of preserving urban ensembles and old towns. For Pospišil's built and written opus, see Me-hmed Hrasnica, *Arhitekt Josip Pospišil: Život i djelo* (Sarajevo: Arhitektonski fakultet, 2003).

56 "Es ist keine Spur von Architektur nach unserer gewohnten Auffassung [...]." In Josip Pospišil, "Die Čaršija und die Wege zur Erhaltung ihres Charakters," *Bosnische Post*, March 22, 1913, 11.

57 Ibid, 10.

58 "*volksfremd und zeitfremd*" in Adolf Vetter, *Bericht über eine Studienreise nach Bosnien und der Herzegowina (September–Oktober 1910)*. Unpublished report (copy). Volkskundemuseum Wien, Sig. 2324 N:10, 23.

59 Josip Pospišil, "Für Sarajevoes Schönheit," *Sarajevoer Tagblatt*, April 21, 1909, 1.

60 The institution of the *k.k. Central-Kommission zur Erforschung und Erhaltung der Baudenkmale* was established by imperial decree on December 31, 1850, with the task to document, register, and protect monuments within the empire. Unlike in other provinces, the structure for governing monument protection with the Central Commission in the center and appointed conservators for dif-ferent regions and districts was not formalized in Bosnia-Hercegovina.

61 Josef Pospišil, "Bosnische Städte," *Der Städtebau* 8, no. 1 (1911): 9.

62 Josip Pospišil, "Für Sarajevos Schönheit," *Sarajevoer Tagblatt*, April 21, 1909, 1.

63 "Denn wir haben hier ein Stück des Orients mitten in einer Stadt und in einem Lande vor uns, wo unter den Fittichen des österreichisch-ungarischen Dop-pelaars die abendländische Kultur immer rascher und mächtiger Fuß zu fassen beginnt. Würde dasselbe verschwinden [Türkenviertel], so könnte es selbst mit den größten finanziellen Opfern in dieser seiner Ursprünglichkeit kaum wieder hervorgezaubert werden." In Ferdinand Schmid, *Bosnien und die Herzegovina unter der Verwaltung Österreich-Ungarns* (Leipzig: Veit, 1914), 746.

64 Provincial monument protection laws that would regulate the legislative pro-tection and practical preservation of monuments were drafted but not enacted.

Aspects of the General Regulation Plan for Sarajevo and the new Building Code containing clauses about the protection of characteristic city elements were discussed in 1911, but were not enacted until the formal end of Austro-Hungarian rule in 1918.

65 "Od srca dirnut i obradovan sa mnogih svojevoljnih dokaza iskrene vjernosti i privrženosti, koji su Mi za kratko vrijeme Mojega boravka u Mojem dragom glavnom gradu pruženi... uvjeravam Vas, da razvitak ovoga lijepoga grada pratim najtoplijim interesom i da ću se rado sjećati na ove provedene dane." In "Njeg. Veličanstvo car i kralj u Sarajevu," *Večernji sarajevski list*, June 1, 1910, 2.

66 Newspapers informed the public of the emperor's full schedule and the strictly regulated program for the entire journey Bosanski Brod–Sarajevo–Mostar–Bosanski Brod. See "Raspored puta Njeg. c. i kr. Apostolskog Veličanstva," *Večernji sarajevski list*, May 30, 1910, 4.

67 "Dobro nam došao," *Sarajevski list*, May 30, 1910, 2.

68 "Pripreme za doček Njeg. Veličanstva u Sarajevu," *Sarajevski list*, May 28, 1910, 2.

69 "*zajednički praznik*" in "Sličice s ulice," *Sarajevski list*, June 2, 1910, 3.

70 "Svečano iskićenje Sarajeva," *Sarajevski list*, May 31, 1910, 5.

71 "Es sind jetzt schon mehr als vierhundert Jahre, daß die Türken Bosnien erobert haben, und seit dieser Zeit hat uns kein Sultan besucht. Kaiser Franz Josef aber kommt sofort, nachdem dieses Land unter sein Szepter gelangt ist, um uns zu besuchen und alles selbst zu sehen. Wir müssen ihm dafür danken und ihm einen festlichen Empfang bereiten." In "Der Besuch der Begovamoschee," *Neue Freie Presse*, June 1, 1910, 7.

72 Leo Delitz (1882–1966) was an Austrian painter and graphic artist. He graduated from the Academy of Fine Arts Vienna in 1904, was a member of *Hagenbund* artistic group from 1905 until 1910, and joined the *Künstlerhaus* in Vienna in 1914. He spent the First World War as a war painter on the Eastern Front.

73 An Ottoman Turkish greeting was written in Arabic script. *Sarajevski list* offered a clumsy transliteration in Latin script for its readers: "Čok jaša ševket Impertator emir mirindži Franc Žosaf hezlert leri." In "Pripreme za doček Njeg. Veličanstva u Sarajevu," *Sarajevski list*, May 28, 1910, 3.

74 Zweite Folge zu Viribus Unitis. Das Buch vom Kaiser. Franz Joseph I., 80 neue Bilder aus dem Leben unseres Kaisers, Herausgegeben von Max Herzig, 1910. Konvolut, Austrian National Library, Pk 1302, 47.

The collection also includes visual depictions of several other sequences from Franz Joseph's visit to Bosnia-Herzegovina in 1910: the meeting with Archbishop Stadler at the door of the Sarajevo Cathedral (by Max von Poosch) and the visit to the Old Bridge in Mostar together with Mayor Mujaga Komadina (by Sigmund Ajdukiewicz).

75 Charles Maier, "City, Empire, and Imperial Aftermath: Contending Contexts for the Urban Vision," in *Shaping the Great City: Modern Architecture in Central Europe, 1890–1937*, ed. Eve Blau and Monika Platzer (Munich: Prestel, 1999), 30.

76 "Ich versichere Sie, daß Ich Mich nach dem, was Ich hier gesehen habe, um zwanzig Jahre jünger fühle." In "Ein Wort des Kaisers," *Neue Freie Presse*, June 1, 1910, 7.

77 Josip Pospišil, "Die Caršija von Sarajevo," *Der Bautechniker* 36, no. 14 (1916): 105–6.

78 Pospišil, "Die Čaršija und die Wege zur Erhaltung ihres Charakters," 10–11.

Bibliography

Arendt, Hannah. *Between Past and Future: Six Exercises in Political Thought.* New York: Viking Press, 1961.

Asbóth, János de. *An Official Tour through Bosnia and Herzegovina: With an Account of the History, Antiquities, Agrarian Conditions, Religion, Ethnology, Folk Lore, and Social Life of the People.* London: Swan Sonnenschein, 1890.

"Bau-Ordnung für die Landeshauptstadt Sarajevo (Genehmigt mit Allerhöchster Entschliessung vom 23. Juli 1893 und publicirt mit Verordnung der Landesregierung für Bosnien und die Hercegovina vom 5. August 1893, Zahl 76.174.)," in *Gesetz- und Verordnungsblatt für Bosnien und die Hercegovina* (Sarajevo: Druck der Landesdruckerei, 1893), 410–435.

Kortz, P. "Bericht über die Studienreise im Mai 1888." *Wochenschrift des Österr. Ingenieur- und Architekten-Vereines* 13, no. 36 (1888): 321–6.

Bosansko-hercegovačke novine. "Viesti Sarajevske." March 28, 1880.

Bosnische Post. "Aus dem Gemeinderathe." May 12, 1903.

Bosnische Post. "Bosnische Eindrücke." July 16, 1910.

Čengić, Nihad. *Begova džamija kao djelo umjetnosti.* Sarajevo: Sarajevo Publishing, 2008.

Choay, Françoise. *The Modern City: Planning in the 19th Century.* New York: George Braziller, 1969.

Čolić, Dragoljub. "Contribution of the Jews to Banat's Economic Progress." In *Jewish Studies IV: Studies, Archival and Memorial Materials about the Jews in Yugoslavia,* edited by Radovan Samardžić, 111–91. Belgrade: Federation of Jewish Communities in Yugoslavia, 1979.

Die Österreichisch-Ungarische Monarchie in Wort und Bild: Bosnien und Hercegovina. Vienna: Druck und Verlag der kaiserlich-königlichen Hof- und Staatsdruckerei, 1901.

Donia, Robert J. "Fin-de-Siècle Sarajevo: The Habsburg Transformation of an Ottoman Town." *Austrian History Yearbook* 33 (2002): 43–75. https://doi.org/10.1017/S0067237800013813.

Epoche. "Das Bosnische Moskau." August 13, 1879.

Epoche. "Die Krankheit des Grafen Andrássy." August 17, 1879.

Fabian, Johannes. *Time and the Other: How Anthropology Makes Its Objects.* New York: Columbia University Press, 2014.

Hadžibegović, Iljas. *Postanak radničke klase u Bosni i Hercegovini i njen razvoj do 1914. godine.* Sarajevo: Svjetlost, 1980.

Hartmuth, Maximilian. "K.(u.)k. Colonial? Contextualizing Architecture and Urbanism in Bosnia-Herzegovina, 1878–1918." In *WechselWirkungen: Austria-Hungary, Bosnia-Herzegovina, and the Western Balkans, 1878–1918,* edited by Clemens Ruthner, Diana Reynolds Cordileone, Ursula Reber, and Raymond Detrez, 155–84. New York: Peter Lang, 2015.

Heiss, Johann, and Johannes Feichtinger. "Distant Neighbors: Uses of Orientalism in the Late Nineteenth-Century Austro-Hungarian Empire." In *Deploying Orientalism in Culture and History: From Germany to Central and Eastern Europe,* edited by James Hodkinson, John Walker, Shaswati Mazumdar, and Johannes Feichtinger, 148–65. Rochester: Camden House, 2013.

Helfert, Joseph Alexander. *Bosnisches.* Vienna: Manz'sche k.k. Hof-Verlags- und Universitäts-Buchhandlung, 1879.

Hrasnica, Mehmed. *Arhitekt Josip Pospišil: Život i djelo.* Sarajevo: Arhitektonski fakultet, 2003.

Jay, Martin, and Sumathi Ramaswamy, eds. *Empires of Vision: A Reader.* Durham, London: Duke University Press, 2014.

Jugoslovenski list. "Veliki požar Sarajeva g. 1879." July 4, 1929.

Jugoslovenski list. "Veliki požar od 8. augusta 1879." August 8, 1929.

Koetschet, Joseph. *Aus Bosniens letzter Türkenzeit.* Vienna and Leipzig: Hartleben, 1905.

Kreševljaković, Hamdija. "Sarajevska čaršija, njeni esnafi i obrti za osmanlijske uprave." *Narodna starina* 6, no. 14 (1927): 15–58.

Kreševljaković, Hamdija. "Požari u Sarajevu do 1879. godine." In *Islamski svijet: Muslimanski književno-publicistički kalendar,* edited by Šahinović-Ekremov, 28–34. Sarajevo: Štamparija Zadruga, 1933.

Kurto, Nedžad. *Arhitektura Bosne i Hercegovine: Razvoj Bosanskoga Stila.* Sarajevo: Sarajevo Publishing, 1998.

Maier, Charles. "City, Empire, and Imperial Aftermath: Contending Contexts for the Urban Vision." In *Shaping the Great City: Modern Architecture in Central Europe, 1890–1937,* edited by Eve Blau and Monika Platzer, 25–41. Munich: Prestel, 1999.

Moser, Henri. *An Oriental Holiday: Bosnia and Herzegovina. A Handbook for the Tourist.* London: Eustace Curzon, 1895.

Moser, Henri. *Bosnie-Herzegovine: Une oeuvre de colonisation pacifique dans les Balkans.* Paris: Imprimerie V. Goupy, G. Maurin, successeur, 1896.

Munro, Robert. *Rambles and Studies in Bosnia-Herzegovina and Dalmatia with an Account of the Proceedings of the Congress of Archaeologists and Anthropologists Held at Sarajevo, August 1894.* Edinburgh and London: William Blackwood, 1900.

Neue Freie Presse. "Ein Wort des Kaisers." June 1, 1910.

Pospišil, Josef. 'Bosnische Städte'. *Der Städtebau* 8, no. 1 (1911): 6–9.

Pospišil, Josip. "Für Sarajevos Schönheit." *Sarajevoer Tagblatt,* April 21, 1909.

Pospišil, Josip. "Die Čaršija und die Wege zur Erhaltung ihres Charakters." *Bosnische Post,* March 22, 1913.

Pospišil, Josip. 'Die Caršija von Sarajevo'. *Der Bautechniker* XXXVI, no. 14 (1916): 105–6.

Prager Abendblatt. "Der Sultan und der Brand von Sarajevo." August 13, 1879.

Prager Abendblatt. "Hilfe für Sarajevo." August 20, 1879.

Reynolds-Cordileone, Diana. "Displaying Bosnia: Imperialism, Orientalism, and Exhibitionary Cultures in Vienna and Beyond, 1878–1914." *Austrian History Yearbook* 46 (2015): 29–50. https://doi.org/10.1017/S0067237814000083.

Salzburger Chronik. "Aufruf an die Bewohner der Stadt Salzburg." August 28, 1879.

Sammlung der für Bosnien und die Hercegovina erlassenen Gesetze, Verordnungen, und Normalweisungen (SGVN). Vienna: Kaiserlich-königliche Hof- und Staatsdruckerei, 1880.

Sarajevski list. "Gospodska kuća u Sarajevu." January 16, 1883.
Sarajevski list. "Iz sarajevske gradske općine." February 24, 1883.
Sarajevski list. "Požarna služba u Sarajevu." October 3, 1883.
Sarajevski list. "Pripreme za doček Njeg. Veličanstva u Sarajevu." May 28, 1910.
Sarajevski list. "Dobro nam došao." May 30, 1910.
Sarajevski list. "Svečano iskićenje Sarajeva." May 31, 1910.
Sarajevski list. "Sličice s ulice." June 2, 1910.
Sarajevski list. "Tri dana u Sarajevu." June 3, 1910.
Schmid, Ferdinand. *Bosnien und die Herzegovina unter der Verwaltung Österreich-Ungarns.* Leipzig: Veit, 1914.
Sparks, Mary. *The Development of Austro-Hungarian Sarajevo, 1878–1918: An Urban History.* London: Bloomsbury, 2014.
Spasojević, Borislav. *Arhitektura stambenih palata austrougarskog perioda u Sarajevu.* Sarajevo: Rabic, 1999.
Stix, Edmund. *Das Bauwesen in Bosnien und Hercegovina vom Beginn der Occupation durch die Österr.-Ung. Monarchie bis in das Jahr 1887.* Vienna: Landesregierung für Bosnien und die Hercegovina, 1887.
Truhelka, Ćiro. "Gazi Husref-beg, njegov život i njegovo doba." *Glasnik Zemaljskog muzeja,* 24 (1912): 91–233.
Večernji sarajevski list. "Njeg. Veličanstvo car i kralj u Sarajevu." June 1, 1910.
Vetter, Adolf. *Bericht über eine Studienreise nach Bosnien und der Herzegowina (September–Oktober 1910).* Unpublished report (copy). 1911. Volkskundemuseum Wien, 2324 N:10.
Zäh, Alexander. "Die orientalisierende Architektur als ein stilistischer Ausdruck des offiziellen Bauprogramms der k. u. k. Bosnisch-Herzegowinischen Landesregierung 1878–1918." *Südost-Forschungen* 72 (2013): 63–97.
Zaimović, Haris. *Zapisnici sarajevskog gradskog zastupstva (1878–1881).* Sarajevo: Historijski arhiv Sarajevo, 2018.

9   Lemberg or L'vov

The Symbolic Significance of a City at the Crossroads of the Austrian and the Russian Empires

Elisabeth Haid-Lener

Today's city of Lviv in western Ukraine has had a checkered history. The city has been located in a disputed border region under changing rule since the Middle Ages, and in the twentieth century, the region became a shatter zone once again. The frequent changes of rule are also reflected in the many names by which the city is known – as L'viv in Ukrainian, Lwów in Polish, Lemberg in German, or L'vov in Russian. In the late eighteenth century, in the course of the partition of the Polish-Lithuanian Common-wealth between Russia, Prussia, and Austria, the region was incorporated into the Austrian Empire, and Lviv became the Austrian city Lemberg for 140 years – until Austrian rule in the region was challenged by the Russian Empire in World War I. However, in the nineteenth and early twentieth centuries, Lviv was a city where imperial and national interests crossed.

The research perspective on Lviv as an imperial city reveals on the one hand how the empire manifested itself in the capital of a border region, which had been incorporated into the Habsburg Monarchy relatively recently compared to other parts of the empire, and how its urban structure was shaped by institutions of the imperial state as well as by its ethnoculturally mixed population. On the other hand, it examines the significance of the city for the empire. Lviv, the center of a peripheral province, had less economic but rather political and representative significance and mirrored Austrian ideological ambitions – the more so as it was a potential part of the sphere of influence of the neighboring Russian Empire.

This chapter outlines the symbolic significance of the city for local national movements as well as for imperial rule in the region: Lviv was perceived as a regional political and cultural center and as an outpost of the Austrian and Russian Empires. The focus of the article will be on Austrian and Russian discourses on Lemberg/L'vov during World War I, when imperial as well as national conflicts over the city culminated. How was Lviv conceptualized as an Austrian or Russian city? Which concepts of imperial rule underly these discourses? To what extent does a transfer of concepts

DOI: 10.4324/9781003130031-12

between the two empires become apparent? This will be analyzed on the basis of wartime reporting in Austrian and Russian newspapers.

This chapter first gives an overview of the integration of the region into the Austrian Empire and highlights Lviv's role as a capital of the new Austrian province Galicia and as a starting point for reforms. Moreover, the effects of Austrian rule on the development of the city are shown. Furthermore, the article outlines the role of the multiethnic city as a site of national formation of the different population groups in the region. Thereafter, it shows the growing interest of the Russian Empire in neighboring Galicia and its capital from the late nineteenth century against the backdrop of the growing political tensions between the Austrian and Russian Empires which culminated in World War I and the impact of Russian national concepts and local national movements. The analysis of Austrian and Russian wartime reporting highlights the propagandistic claims to Lviv as an outpost of Western culture in the East or as the most westward outpost of the Russian people and reveals differences in the underlying concepts of imperial rule in the region, which emphasized the multinational character of the Austrian Empire or postulated a Russian character of the Russian Empire. Finally, the chapter juxtaposes these propagandistic concepts with the politics of the changing Austrian and Russian wartime regimes in Lviv.

The Galician Capital

When the new crownland Galicia and Lodomeria was incorporated into the Austrian Empire in the late eighteenth century, Lviv became the capital of this new province that was (apart from Hungary) the largest and easternmost in the Habsburg Monarchy. Thus, Lviv maintained its role as the center of a border region, a region where the borders changed again and again.[1] In the thirteenth century, the city had developed into the center of the Principality of Galicia-Volhynia, which was the western part and one of the successors of the Kievan Rus'. In the fourteenth century, the region became a part of the Kingdom of Poland and was now known as Ruthenian Voivodeship (referring to the region's former affiliation with the Rus'). While the rural population was henceforth ruled by Polish or polonized nobility, Lviv was granted Magdeburg city rights. The city was a major trading center at that time, inhabited by a variety of population groups, including Armenians and Germans. Over time, Poles became the dominant group in the city, and Jews the second. Thus, the urban population significantly differed from the rural surroundings, where the population majority was Ruthenian (later known as Ukrainian). Religious divisions between the different population groups played a major role and mostly coincided with social and linguistic divisions. While the majority of Poles belonged to the Roman Catholic Church, the Ruthenian population belonged at first to the Orthodox and later to the Greek Catholic Church. The latter dates back to the Union of Brest 1596, when most of the Ruthenian Orthodox Church eparchies in the Polish-Lithuanian Commonwealth placed themselves under the authority of the Pope but maintained the eastern rite. In the Galician territories, it took longer for the Union to prevail than in many other regions of the Polish-Lithuanian Commonwealth. Around 1700, however, the Eparchy of Lviv joined the Greek Catholic Church. Also, the predominantly Yiddish-speaking Jewish population differed not only in their religion but also linguistically from other population groups. Jews were therefore often conceived as a national group in Galicia, while in Austria they were considered a religious group.

When Lviv became the center of the new Austrian administration in 1772, the city gained in significance compared to other cities in the region and its population grew steadily. Indeed, Lviv had lost some of its importance as a commercial center to Brody, which was located directly on the new border with the Russian Empire.[2] However, it gained political relevance. The new Austrian crownland comprised not only parts of the former Principality of Galicia-Volhynia or Ruthenian Voivodeship but also other parts of the Lesser Poland Province in the west. As the capital of the Austrian crownland, Lviv became a serious competitor to Krakow, the hitherto undisputed center of Lesser Poland. Although the city of Krakow was temporarily granted the status of a Free City in 1815, it was finally incorporated into Galicia in 1846. Moreover, in the late eighteenth century, Lviv became the starting point for the reforms of the Austrian Emperor Joseph II in the region. Galicia, which was perceived as the most backward area of the Habsburg Monarchy, served as an experimental ground for Joseph's ideals of an enlightened state.[3] The emperor's efforts for centralization, however, met with resistance from the local Polish nobility. Not only in Austria, but even more so in neighboring Russia and Prussia, the Polish elites' intentions to restore an independent Polish state caused unrest and repeatedly led to Polish uprisings. Like other border regions, Galicia played an important role as a seismograph for the course of domestic politics as well as foreign policy.[4] Since Galicia was bordering two major powers, the region was, not least, of military importance. While the Austrian government initially perceived Prussia as the major threat, in the late nineteenth century the increasing political tensions with Russia came to the fore.[5] The military significance of the region is also evident in Lviv's position as an important garrison city. However, the Galician capital lost its role as the main fortress to the city of Przemyśl. Lviv's fortifications were pulled down and boulevards took their place.[6]

The Austrian rule also had at least a temporary impact on Lviv's population structure. Austrian German-speaking officials first came to the city to administer the province. However, this changed in the 1860s. As a result of the Austro-Hungarian Compromise of 1867, Galicia became part of the Austrian half of the empire. The Austrian government now made major concessions to the Polish elites in Galicia, who were willing to cooperate after the failed uprisings and became important supporters of the government in the Austrian parliament. Galicia was granted self-government and Polish was introduced as the administrative language. Poles thus started to play an important role in Galician politics and administration, which also encouraged the assimilation of German speakers into the Polish language and culture. At the same time, Lviv became a statutory city and had self-government rights of its own. Thus, the Galician capital was not only the seat of the governor (the representative of the imperial central power) and the Galician self-government (including the Galician Diet) but also a self-assured municipal government. From the 1860s, all these institutions were dominated by the local Polish elites.[7] Although political reforms in the Habsburg Monarchy had expanded opportunities for participation since the 1860s, the electoral rules at the regional and local levels continued to privilege the upper class.

The city's political and administrative functions were an important factor in its dynamic population growth, especially in the late nineteenth and early twentieth centuries, when it developed into the fifth largest city in Austria-Hungary.[8] Lviv experienced a moderate economic upswing at that time. It was an important sales and consumer market and a service and administrative center, but it was not an important industrial location. Overall, the level of industrialization was relatively low in Galicia, which earned the province the reputation of backwardness.[9] Hence, Lviv exemplifies the concept of "emerging cities," a city at the imperial periphery that showed that modernization did not necessarily have to be interconnected with high industrialization. Its assumed backwardness became an important resource for an ambitious urban development policy that was at the same time nationally charged.[10] The Polish city administration pushed for construction activity and investment in infrastructure, including the first electric tramway of the Habsburg monarchy.[11] Thus, the Galician capital positioned itself as a "metropolis," as a modernization engine of the region, and as a modern Polish center, competing with Krakow, the more traditional, historic center of the region. At the same time, it claimed the status of a "substitute capital" of divided Poland since Polish culture was able to develop more freely in Austrian Galicia than in Russian-ruled Warsaw.[12]

However, these Polish aspirations did not challenge Austrian rule in the region or the loyalty of locals to the Habsburg Monarchy. The Polish political actors knew that Lviv had taken over the function of a Polish political center due to the favorable political conditions of Habsburg rule.[13]

The role of Lviv as a Polish or an Austrian provincial capital was not mutually exclusive: Lviv was perceived as an Austrian *and* Polish city.[14] In this sense, the imperial as well as the Galician provincial government underlined their contribution to the prosperity of the city – the latter arguing that Lviv flourished only under the conditions of gained autonomy. At the same time, Polish claims to the multiethnic city were increasingly challenged by its Ruthenian/Ukrainian counterpart at the local level, while at the imperial level, neighboring Russia laid claim to the region.

A Multiple National Center

Lviv owed its symbolic significance for local as well as imperial actors not only to its role as a political and administrative capital but also to its increasing role as a cultural center within the region. Besides administrative institutions, educational and cultural institutions played a major role in the flourishing of the city and were a major concern of first the imperial and later the municipal government and local national movements.

The reform policies of Emperor Joseph II had laid the foundation for Lviv's revival as a cultural center in the late eighteenth century. Besides initiatives of the imperial authorities, the fact that more and more members of the Polish nobility took up residence in the city played a role. In 1784, Joseph II established a new university in Lviv. Five years later, the city's first public theater was established, where a German company and a Polish company performed alternately. The repertoires of both companies were quite similar. The Polish theater was quick to incorporate new cultural trends from Vienna and intended to show that the Poles were on the same cultural level as the Germans. The German theater lost its prestige over the course of the nineteenth century. By the end, the audience of the German theater was de facto limited to the soldiers and officers garrisoned in Lviv.[15]

The Jewish population also played an essential role as a bearer of German culture in Lviv. From the late eighteenth century, Austrian politics and access to education had led to the Germanization of Jewish elites in the city, while the majority of Jews were Yiddish-speaking.[16] In the first half of the nineteenth century, Lviv was an important center of the Haskalah (Jewish Enlightenment). In the late nineteenth century, however, the outstanding role of German language and culture was gradually replaced by assimilation into the Polish ones. The Polish education system played a crucial role in this process.[17]

In the second half of the nineteenth century, Galician autonomy and municipal self-government contributed to the strengthening of Polish cultural and educational institutions in Lviv. At that time, however, the main competitor of Polish culture in Lviv was the local national movements rather than imperial German culture. The city became a magnet for the intelligentsia of *all* religious and national groups in Galicia.

While in the first half of the nineteenth century, the small Ruthenian elite and urban population in Lviv still tended to assimilate into Polish culture, they began to distance themselves from the Poles and to develop a distinct national consciousness in the mid-nineteenth century. The Greek Catholic clergy played an important role in this process. However, united in their resentments against Polish domination, the national activists were disunited on the matter of their national orientation. Some of the activists were inspired by Ukrainian activists in the Russian Empire, who had begun to distinguish themselves from the Russians a few decades earlier. An important factor was that literary Ukrainian, as it was first formulated by the writers of the Ukrainian movement in Russia, was almost perfectly intelligible to Galician Ruthenians. Thus, some activists saw Galician Ruthenians as part of a Ukrainian nation and distanced themselves from Russians and Poles alike. Other activists, however, who became known as Russophiles, tended toward the Russian culture. Inspired by Russian pan-Slavists, they saw Galician Ruthenians as part of an all-Russian nation. While the Russophile orientation initially prevailed in Galicia, the Ukrainophile orientation won out in the 1880s. Russophiles continued to play a role in cultural and political life, but the Ukrainian national movement now took the lead.[18] Thus, the term "Ukrainians" for the Ruthenian population in Galicia became more and more widespread. However, "Ruthenians" remained the official term in the Habsburg Monarchy. Moreover, the term "Ruthenians" reflects that still in the early twentieth century not all of them identified as Ukrainians.

Lviv was the most important location for both Russophile and Ukrainophile institutions in Galicia. In addition to rather elitist cultural institutions controlled by Russophiles such as the Ruthenian "National House" and the Stauropegion Institute, Ukrainophile organizations in Lviv in particular gave a great deal of attention to the mobilization of peasants, and thus they had a strong influence on the rural areas of Eastern Galicia.[19] However, the attraction of Lviv reached even beyond Galicia. Though the Ruthenian/Ukrainian population was a minority in the city, Lviv finally became the undisputed center of the Ukrainian national movement – not only in the Habsburg Monarchy, but in general. The Ukrainian national movement had its origins in the Russian Empire. However, the Russian imperial authorities soon took repressive measures against the Ukrainian national movement. They denied the existence of a Ukrainian language and banned the printing of Ukrainian books. Ukrainians (or Little Russians as they were called in the Russian Empire) were considered part of the Russian nation. The Russian authorities thus regarded the Ukrainian national movement as a threat to the unity of the Russian nation. In Austria, the conditions for the Ukrainian national movement were significantly better, even though Galician politics and administration were Polish-dominated. Ruthenians were recognized as a distinct nationality and their national rights were protected by the Austrian Constitution of 1867.[20] Thus, the Ukrainian national movement increasingly challenged the local Polish elites in Lviv.

The Polish-dominated city administration, which discursively constructed Lviv as a purely Polish city, responded to the challenge posed by the Ukrainian national movement with increased efforts to "secure Lwów's Polish character." The city administration actively supported the founding and expansion of *Polish* museums, theaters, and other cultural institutions; schools and educational institutions were of particular importance.[21] Whereas in the first decades of Austrian rule in Galicia German was the dominant language of education, it was largely replaced by Polish in the second half of the nineteenth century. But Ukrainian also gained in presence. At the turn of the century, there were five gymnasia in Lviv: three with Polish, one with German, and one with Ukrainian language of instruction. Nevertheless, German remained an important educational language and was also taught in the non-German secondary schools.[22] As a seat of several secondary schools (including the first Ukrainian gymnasium in Galicia) and higher education institutions – including one of two universities in Galicia (beside Krakow) and a higher polytechnical school – the city provided access to education and positions, and thus was a gate to social mobility and a window to the wider world, especially to Vienna, the center of the empire.[23]

The University of Lviv in particular was a main attraction as well as a site of national formation. Academic life increasingly adhered to the national idea. The educational languages Latin and German were gradually replaced by Polish in the course of the nineteenth century; Ukrainian played a secondary role.[24] While Polish professors promoted the expansion of the use of Polish as the only language of instruction and administration at the University of Lviv, Ukrainian aspirations for a separate Ukrainian university in the Galician capital increased at the turn of the century, and the university became a major site of Polish-Ukrainian conflicts in Galicia.[25] The symbolic significance of Lviv as a cultural center becomes evident in debates on the location of a Ukrainian university, the foundation of which was finally approved by the Polish-dominated Galician government on the eve of World War I. While the Ukrainian representatives insisted on Lviv as the location for "their" university, the Lviv City Council vehemently rejected this request, as a Ukrainian university posed a threat to the "Polish character" of the city.[26]

Though the Polish-Ukrainian competition was at the foreground of political debates, Lviv was also one of the largest and most important centers
of Jewish population in the Habsburg Monarchy, and Jews made an important contribution to the cultural life of the city. Besides the progressive
assimilation into the Polish language and culture, Zionism and the concept
of an independent Jewish nation gained more and more influence. By the
end of the nineteenth century, Lviv had become one of the first strongholds
of Zionist organizations. However, large parts of the Jewish population
remained bound to the Orthodox tradition.[27] Thus, Lviv was a center of
Zionist as well as Orthodox and Hasidic associations.[28]

Overall, Lviv represented a site of national formation for Poles, Ukrainians, and Jews which was reflected in the numerous Polish, Ruthenian/
Ukrainian, and Jewish political parties, educational and academic societies, newspapers, welfare organizations, and cultural institutions.[29] In
addition to the Polish and German theaters, for example, there was a
Ukrainian theater company[30] as well as a Yiddish one.[31] Lviv's symbolic
significance for the local population groups was reflected in the perceptions of the city as a "Polish bastion" amid the Ukrainian rural surroundings, as a "Ukrainian Piedmont," or "Mother of Israel."[32] Thus, the city's
public space became a battlefield for representation on behalf of its ethnic
groups, in particular Poles and Ukrainians.

These national aspirations were also reflected in building activities. Polish efforts to shape the public space had great support in the provincial and
municipal administrations. This is exemplified by the building of Lviv's
new theater, which was designed by a Polish architect from the Lviv Polytechnical School and opened in 1900. The project was inspired by the
Czech national theater in Prague. However, while the Czech theater had
been financed by private donations, the Lviv theater was financed by the
provincial and municipal administrations and thus was an expression of
the Polish elite's control of the province. The building was a typical late
nineteenth-century opera house, with an iconographic program aiming to
integrate Polish culture into the cultural canon of European civilization.
Soon after, the idea of building a Ukrainian national theater in Lviv was
born, which aimed at demonstrating the Ukrainians' cultural equality with
the Poles. A Ukrainian modernist architect drafted a design combining folk
motifs and elements of Greek Catholic church architecture with the decorative styles associated with the Secessionists, emphasizing the uniqueness
of Ukrainian culture while linking it to modernity. However, the project
lacked financing and was never realized.[33]

Despite the efforts of Poles and Ukrainians to express their national ambitions in architecture, it was to a large extent the Austrian Empire that left
its stamp on the local environment. In urban planning and in architectural

fashion, Lviv was strongly shaped by Vienna throughout the nineteenth century and was frequently called "little Vienna of the East" for its architectural tradition.[34] Although the German language gradually lost its importance in the course of the nineteenth century, imperial buildings continued to bear witness to Lviv's affiliation with the Habsburg monarchy. And there were also other cultural phenomena which testified to Lviv's connections to Vienna. One example is coffee house culture.[35] Hence, Lviv was not only the administrative center of Austrian rule in Galicia but was also perceived as a stronghold of Austrian culture in this remote province.

A City at the Crossroads of the Austrian and the Russian Empires

Due to its political, cultural, and symbolic significance, Lviv was a contested city, and it was not only local population groups, especially Poles and Ukrainians, that competed for the city and its public space – Galicia and its capital had increasingly become the subject of tensions between the Austrian and the Russian Empires.[36] Galicia's location at the border between the two empires drew the attention of the imperial governments to the region when, in the late nineteenth and early twentieth centuries, the foreign relations of Austria-Hungary and Russia deteriorated due to their competition in the Balkans. In addition, the agency of national activists in Russia and Galicia, as well as the two empires' different treatment of local national movements, caused considerable resentment.

In the first decades after the partition of the Polish-Lithuanian Commonwealth, the partitioning powers had been mainly concerned about Polish insurrections aimed at restoring the Polish state. The Austrian and the Russian Empires therefore, had a common interest in countering these Polish aspirations. However, Austrian and Russian politics gradually diverged. While Russia took increasingly repressive measures, Austria eventually made far-reaching concessions to the Polish elites in Galicia. Moreover, from the mid-nineteenth century, Galician Ruthenians/Ukrainians increasingly became the focus of attention.

Russian pan-Slavists made contacts with Russophile activists in Galicia with whom they shared the view of the Galician Ruthenians as part of the Russian nation. These were mostly private contacts among intellectuals. However, to some extent, Russian government funds were spent through the activities of the "Slavic Benevolent Committee." They supported Russophile newspapers in Galicia, which gradually lost popularity among the Galician readership, and cultural institutions such as the Ruthenian "National House" in Lviv. Contacts intensified at the beginning of the twentieth century, when a radical faction developed among the Galician

Russophiles that was oriented not only culturally but also politically toward Russia. The most important organ of the radical Russophiles was the Russian-language newspaper *Prikarpatskaia Rus'* published in Lviv. At the same time, Russian nationalists devoted themselves more to Galicia and promoted a Russian commitment to the "compatriots" in Eastern Galicia, which were suppressed by the Polish provincial authorities and "German" central bureaucrats. These contacts were especially centered around the "Galician-Russian Benevolent Society" in St. Petersburg, which consisted of Galician émigrés and Russian nationalists and enjoyed support, particularly among the Russian provincial elites in the western periphery of the Russian Empire. Also, some high-ranking clerics of the Russian Orthodox Church called for increased engagement in Galicia and were sympathetic to the efforts of individual Galician rural parishes to convert to Orthodoxy. The Austrian government was greatly concerned about these contacts of Galician Russophiles with Russian nationalist and pan-Slav activists and tried to counteract these activities. In 1882 and 1914, several Galician Russophiles went on trial in Lviv for treason. However, the Austrian authorities overestimated the political importance of the Russophiles and the Russian government's involvement in Galicia.[37] It was only on the eve of World War I that the Russian government was increasingly willing to support action groups who claimed Eastern Galicia for the Russian Empire.[38]

Overall, the Russian presence in Lviv was relatively modest and was mainly limited to supporting cultural institutions of local actors, who identified with Russian culture. Russia was officially represented by a consulate in Lviv, but there was no major Russian diaspora in the city. The only Orthodox church in Lviv was under the jurisdiction of the Austrian metropolitan archdiocese of Bukovina and was built for Orthodox soldiers from Bukovina serving in the Lviv garrison.[39] Indeed, the most important group of Russian citizens in Lviv were Ukrainian intellectuals.

Due to the severe restrictions of the Ukrainian national movement in the Russian Empire, several Ukrainian intellectuals from Russia found a cultural-political field of activity in Galicia. The University of Lviv was a main attraction. Though the language of instruction was in general Polish, there were several Ukrainian chairs and Ukrainian courses, which would have been unthinkable in Russia at that time. One of the most prominent Ukrainian immigrants was the historian and political activist Mykhailo Hrushevs'kyi who held the chair of Eastern European history at the University of Lviv from 1894. Hrushevs'kyi took an active part in the Ukrainian national movement in Galicia and was particularly committed to the establishment of a Ukrainian university in Lviv.[40] In this respect, the plans to establish a Ukrainian university in Lviv were a thorn in the side of both the Polish city administration and the Russian government, as the university would attract Ukrainian activists at both sides of the border.[41] The Russian government was concerned about the Ukrainian national activists' contacts across the borders and their anti-Russian attitudes. It suspected that Austria was deliberately promoting the Ukrainian movement in order to use it as a weapon against Russia. Moreover, the fact that the Austrian authorities tolerated Polish paramilitary organizations in Galicia which engaged in anti-Russian agitation further worsened Russian-Austrian relations.[42]

Austrian-Russian conflicts culminated during the war. Large parts of Galicia became a war zone in August 1914, when Russian troops advanced far into the province. Hence, the war offered the opportunity for geopolitical change, and the annexation of Eastern Galicia became an official war aim of the Russian government.[43] The Galician capital was the focus of attention from both sides at that time. The "Battle of Lemberg," as it was called in the Austrian press, lasted for about two weeks,[44] and the capture of the city in early September was a major triumph for the Russian army. Lviv remained under Russian occupation for several months. In a joint offensive, the Central Powers recaptured most of Galicia and the Galician capital in June 1915. During the major Russian offensive of summer 1916 (known as the Brusilov offensive), the Russian army advanced again in Galicia but this time did not reach Lviv.[45] Overall, the Galician capital received a great deal of attention in the Austrian and the Russian press during the war. Lviv was a contested city – not only on the battlefield but also in wartime propaganda.[46]

An "Outpost of Western Culture"

An analysis of press reporting during World War I provides an insight into the strategies which were used by the various actors to justify their claim to Lviv. Pre-war Polish-Ukrainian competition in Galicia continued in wartime mobilization. Indeed, a vast majority of Galicia's Polish, Ukrainian, and Jewish activists declared their loyalty to the Habsburg Monarchy – but they did so almost always separately.[47] In fact, they highlighted the role of their own nation in the fight against Russia. The common enemy thus hardly represented a unifying element. Nevertheless, the varying Austrian, Polish, and Ukrainian narratives about Lviv and its role in the war had a common determinator: the Galician capital was an "outpost of Western culture" that had to brave the assailing "Russian-Asiatic barbarism."

The sense of belonging to European, western culture was usually based on historical arguments. Hence, outlines of the history of Lviv figured prominently in war reporting. Moreover, Polish as well as Ukrainian activists published numerous brochures to win a wider Austrian and international audience for their cause.[48] However, Polish and Ukrainian historical arguments differed significantly. Ukrainian authors referred to the foundation of the city by King Danylo in the thirteenth century and highlighted the close relations of the Galician-Volhynian prince to the "European West." In contrast to Russian concepts of the Kievan Rus' as a proto-Russian state, they considered the Rus' as a Ukrainian state and highlighted in particular the role of the Galician-Volhynian principality, its dynastic ties to European rulers, and finally, the royal crown offered to Danylo by the pope.[49] Regarding Lviv's European culture, Ukrainian authors were often willing to acknowledge German-Austrian influences on the "Ukrainian city" Lviv, but they notedly downplayed Polish contributions to the development of the city.[50] From a Polish perspective, in contrast, Lviv's European culture dated back to its incorporation into the Kingdom of Poland in the fourteenth century. Polish authors, on the one hand, pointed to the city's flourishing under Polish rule. On the other hand, they emphasized Lviv's mission as a bulwark against the East, as a defender of Polishness and of European civilization over the centuries. This narrative, which picked up the widely accepted myth of Poland as *Antemurale Christianitatis*, had been used to legitimize the Polish dominance in the city in the context of Polish-Ukrainian conflicts in the pre-war years. However, in light of the war against Russia, the interpretation of Lviv as a bulwark gained additional significance.[51] From a Viennese perspective, Lviv's "German character" was added to the set of interpretations. German nationalists usually reduced the flourishing of the city to the positive influence by German settlers who had allegedly brought "trade, commerce, and culture" to the Polish-ruled city in the Middle Ages: "With the decline of Germanness, of course, the decline of the city went hand in hand." But after a period of decline, the "Austrian administration, full of German spirit," had revived the city, as the German nationalist newspaper *Ostdeutsche Rundschau* put it.[52] Viennese liberals also often linked Lviv's "intimate" affiliation with the Habsburg monarchy and the "indissoluble bond that connects us to it" with the presence of German culture in the city,[53] and referred to an Austrian or German civilizing mission at the eastern outpost of the empire. The assumed civilizing activities of the Austrian state and its institutions ranged from the enlightened reforms in the eighteenth century to improvements in Galicia's infrastructure by the army during the war.[54] However, except for German nationalist newspapers preoccupied with Germanness, Viennese reporters were usually willing to integrate Polish and Ukrainian narratives on their contribution to the defense of western culture against "eastern barbarism" into an Austrian imperial narrative.[55] Concepts of an Austrian mission to defend and develop European culture at the empire's eastern periphery did not exclude the idea of Lviv's mission as a shield for the Austrian Empire and European civilization. Some authors compiled different, even contradictory historical arguments, which ranged from claims to the region as an "ancestral Germanic territory," and dynastic rights of the Hungarian crown dating back to the Middle Ages, to anti-Russian Polish narratives,[56] provided that they were compatible with Galicia's affiliation with the Austrian Empire and served to distinguish Galicia from Russia. Lviv's "western culture" was a key argument.

The "Russian City L'vov"

The advance of the Russian army in Eastern Galicia was also accompanied by an appropriation of the region in Russian press reporting. The goal was not only a military occupation but the permanent integration of this "Russian region" into the Russian Empire. Particular attention was paid to the Galician capital. Russian newspapers as well as brochures popularized the image of the "Russian city of L'vov." In contrast to the idea of Lviv as a bulwark of Polish or Western culture, from a Russian perspective the city seemed to be the most westward outpost of Russian culture, which had to be reconnected to its motherland.[57]

Russian representations of Lviv were also often based on historical arguments.[58] They usually located not only the foundation but also the heyday of the city in the time of the Kievan Rus'. As in Russian discourse the Rus' (contrary to Ukrainian views) was generally recognized as a Russian state, these representations emphasized the "Russian character" of the city. Some authors went even further, equating the capture of the city by the Polish king Casimir III in the fourteenth century with the beginning of the city's decline. This narrative obscured the economic prosperity and expansion of the city under Casimir and his successors, as well as the significant boom from the late nineteenth century, and regarded both the Polish and Austrian periods as "foreign domination" that entailed a decline of the Russian character of the city.[59]

Galician Russophiles who had emigrated or fled to the Russian Empire at the beginning of the war played an important role in popularizing the image of the "Russian city L'vov."[60] Indeed, the Galician-Russian Benevolent Society had promoted the unification of the "subjugated Russian territories" in the Austrian Empire with Russia for several years.[61] However, they only reached a wider Russian audience during World War I, when an annexation of Eastern Galicia became realistic. In September 1914, the conquest of Lviv, the "heart" of this "Russian fiefdom which had been detached from Russia 600 years ago," was praised by Russian nationalists as the completion of the "reunification of the Russian territories."[62] Moreover, Russian nationalists sometimes based their claims on religious arguments, presenting the Russian Tsar as "anointed by God to guide the whole, united from now on and forever indissolubly Orthodox Russian people."[63] They considered Greek Catholics to be in fact Orthodox and regarded the Greek Catholic Church as imposed by Catholic Poles and Austrians as a tool for violently separating Galician Ruthenians from the Orthodox community,[64] referring to the relatively late acceptance of the church union in Lviv.

This interpretation of Lviv's history, which clearly dominated in Russian press reporting, was partly reflected in descriptions of the contemporary city as well. Some of the Russian reports on Lviv highlighted "Russian elements" in Lviv's cityscape, focusing on a few buildings and thus omitting all the other architectural traditions that would disturb the image of the "ancient Russian city of L'vov." They ignored the fact that virtually no monuments from the time of the Kievan Rus' were preserved in Lviv. One article referred, for example, to the St. Paraskeva Church as "one of the oldest Russian churches in L'vov, built by Prince Lev Daniilovič."[65] The newspaper did not mention that the ancient church had been destroyed by fire and rebuilt in the seventeenth century nor that it currently belonged to the Greek Catholic Church.[66]

Other authors, on the contrary, emphasized "foreign" architectural influences and criticized them as a symbol of centuries of foreign rule. One of these articles pointed to the numerous churches and synagogues in Lviv, arguing that even the Ruthenian – that is, Greek Catholic – churches hardly differed in their appearance from the Roman Catholic ones.[67] Besides the city's architecture, the Russian nationalists were also bothered by the presence of Orthodox Jews and their exotic appearance with sidelocks and long black coats[68] as well as by the presence of the Polish language – the "Polish talk all-around"[69] – which marked the foreign domination over the Russian city.[70]

Though these nationalist discourses were widespread in the Russian press, there were other approaches that showed the newly conquered city in a positive light. In particular, the liberal newspaper *Rech'* took a position counter to Russian nationalist narratives, characterizing Lviv on the one hand as an "unquestionable Polish city"[71] and appreciating, on the other hand, the diversity of the cityscape with its various influences, which had imposed a "strong local stamp" on Galician architecture.[72] The newspaper thus defended the historically developed multicultural character of the city and the region. This perspective was rather an exception in Russian public discourse. More common were depictions of Lviv which kept aloof from these political debates. Many war correspondents and reports of Russian soldiers who invaded Lviv in the autumn of 1914 were less concerned with whether it was a Russian, Polish, or Austrian city. Rather, they were impressed by the beauty of the city, the wonderful architecture of the stone rows of houses, and the wide belt of parks and avenues.[73] Only Kiev could compare with this magnificent city, as several Russian correspondents argued.[74] A highlight in Lviv's cityscape was the railway station with its unforgettable, majestic architecture,[75] which appeared as a symbol of the city's progressiveness.[76] In contrast to the historical narratives of a decline of Lviv under Polish and Austrian rule, these reports valued the conquered city as an enrichment of the Russian Empire.

Concepts of Imperial Rule

Austrian and Russian war reporting on Lviv and Galicia in general aimed to legitimate Austrian or Russian rule in the region.[77] To this end, the reports transmitted different concepts of the city and of imperial rule in the region. One important aspect of these concepts was the handling of the multiethnic character of the city. Neither Austrian nor Russian discourses were uniform in this respect. However, there was a dominant concept in each of the two states. Austrian wartime propaganda was inspired by the concept of the Habsburg Monarchy as a multi-ethnic state or *Nationalitätenstaat*. This was also reflected in the image of Lviv as a multi-ethnic city. Indeed, several reports in Viennese newspapers claimed a kind of German cultural hegemony in the city that tied it to the Austrian Empire. At the same time, Polish and Ukrainian authors often laid exclusive claims to Lviv as a Polish or Ukrainian city. However, Austrian propaganda aimed to integrate all these contradictory nationalist narratives into the image of "unity in diversity" and transmitted the ideal of the cooperation of all peoples of Austria-Hungary in the fight against the external enemy. Thus, Viennese newspapers referred to the activities and declarations of Polish, Ukrainian, and Jewish organizations; their loyalty to the Habsburg Monarchy; and their contribution to the war against Russia.[78] Overall, the Austrian Empire presented itself as a guarantor of nationality rights and as a beloved multinational monarchy standing united against the Russian threat.[79]

Apart from varying historical arguments and different national goals,[80] Polish and Ukrainian national activists usually shared the view that the Austrian Empire provided significantly better conditions for Lviv's thriving than the Russian Empire, as it granted freedom to the development of national cultures. Thus, various national organizations in Lviv cooperated with the imperial government in the effort to mobilize for war and presented the war against Russia as a war against Russian oppression. The latter argument was of particular importance to Lviv's Jewish population to whom the anti-Jewish violence of the Russian army posed an immediate threat. However, by no means did the external threat lead to a settlement of internal conflicts. On the contrary, conflicts and mutual mistrust between Poles, Ukrainians, and Jews significantly increased during the war. Russian occupation politics contributed to these conflicts, as did the Austro-Hungarian army's spy hunt. Austrian politics were less and less in line with its claim to guarantee the rule of law and the equality of nationalities.

With the beginning of the war against Russia, the Austrian authorities' fears of Russian espionage in Galicia increased dramatically. They especially suspected alleged Ruthenian Russophiles. Russophile institutions were closed as soon as war was declared. Some activists fled to Russia, while those who remained were arrested on charges of high treason. However, these measures were not confined to Russophile activists. The Austro-Hungarian military administration, which wielded administrative power in Galicia due to the province's status as a war zone, suspected the Ruthenian/Ukrainian population, in general, to be sympathetic to Russia. Military defeats encouraged this hysteria about possible treason at the local level. Thousands of Ruthenians/Ukrainians were deported from the war zone and interned in camps in the monarchy's interior; summary executions were regular occurrences. Suspicions were often based on the nationality of the accused, and not on evidence. The actions of the military authorities thus stood in stark contrast to the propagated unity and cooperation of all peoples of Austria-Hungary in the fight against the external enemy.[81] Rather, they seemed to share the Russian assessment that the local Ruthenian/Ukrainian population longed for unification with Russia. Russian newspapers reported extensively on the Austro-Hungarian army's acts of violence, which confirmed their allegations about Austrian oppression of the "Russian people" in Galicia and legitimated Russia's mission in the region.[82]

In Russian discourse, concepts on the Russian character of the Russian Empire clearly prevailed, although Russia was undoubtedly a multi-ethnic state as well. However, Russian nationalist discourses dominated, especially with regard to Galicia and its capital L'vov, which was considered to be a Russian national territory and thus part of the heartland of the Russian Empire.[83] While the Ruthenian/Ukrainian population was regarded as part of the Russian people,[84] the presence of Poles and Jews in the city as well as the activities of Ukrainian national activists disturbed the image of Russian L'vov. Thus, Ukrainian activists as well as Jews and Poles were frequently perceived as Austrian agents who helped to consolidate Austrian rule in the region and to suppress the "Russian" majority in Galicia. Accordingly, Russian nationalists demanded that measures be taken to strengthen the "Russian character" of the Galician capital.

These ideas were widespread in Russia but not without controversy. The leader of the liberal Constitutional Democratic Party Pavel Miliukov, for example, opposed this Russian nationalist concept and explicitly referred to the concept of the Austrian *Nationalitätenstaat*. He argued that the freedom of development of their national cultures would strengthen the loyalty of the local population to the state, and he pointed to the widespread Austrian patriotism among the local population. By no means did Miliukov reject Lviv's incorporation into the Russian Empire. He highlighted the fact that the actions of the Austro-Hungarian military administration in Galicia during the war were far from the principles of the Austrian constitution and thus had undermined the loyalty of the local population to the Habsburg Monarchy; and even before the war, the principle of equality of nationalities hardly corresponded to reality. In fact, the Galician autonomy at the provincial level established a Polish dominance in politics and administration. This dominance was even more pronounced at the municipal level in Lviv. However, Miliukov questioned the widely held assessment in Russia that the vast majority of the Ukrainian population in Lviv felt Russian and was seeking unification with "Mother Russia." Instead, he proposed recognizing Ukrainians as a nationality in order to win their loyalty. Overall, Miliukov advocated rethinking the concept of Russian rule in the region and regarded the Austrian *Nationalitätenstaat* as a role model.[85]

Realities of Wartime Regimes

These debates took place in the context of the Russian occupation in Galicia which gave rise to the Austrian propaganda about Russia's "barbaric oppression" of the local national cultures, in contrast to the Habsburg Monarchy as a guarantor of nationality rights.[86] After the Russian victory at Lviv, the temporary military General Government of Galicia and Bukovina was established in September 1914 with Lviv as its administrative center. Besides ensuring stability in the hinterland of the Russian army, an important aim of the Russian occupying regime was to prepare Galicia for "reunification" with Russia. Hence, the policies of the Russian military governor in Lviv were heavily influenced by the demands of Russian nationalist circles to promote the "Russian character" of the city and the region. Accordingly, the Russian occupation regime introduced the Russian language in schools and administration. On the one hand, these measures were directed against Polish dominance in the city, as the Russian authorities regarded Poles as "foreign elements" in a "Russian national territory." On the other hand, Russification efforts targeted the Ukrainian language, which the Russian authorities did not recognize as a language, but rather considered a Russian dialect. Ukrainian cultural institutions were regarded as anti-Russian separatist organizations and thus closed. Many Ukrainian political activists were accused of Austrian sympathies, arrested, and deported to Russia. At the same time, the Russian spy-hunt was directed especially against the Jewish population. Jews were regular victims of physical violence in Russian-occupied Galicia. One of the most violent wartime pogroms occurred in Lviv at the end of September 1914. However, even though the Russian policy in Galicia was clearly aimed at Russianizing the region, the occupying regime had to make some concessions in order not to jeopardize stability in the hinterland of the Russian front. For example, plans for missionary work by the Russian Orthodox Church among Greek-Catholics were postponed to the post-war period. Though the Russian authorities intended in the long term to ban Polish from the Galician administration and schools, they made interim compromises with the local Polish elites and decided for practical reasons to keep most of the Polish civil servants in office during occupation. In this respect, the Russian occupation regime disappointed the Galician Russophile activists, who had hoped for leading positions in the local Russian administration.[87]

When the Russian army had to withdraw from Lviv in the summer of 1915, criticism of the failed occupation regime soon became loud in Russia. Although most critics did not question the objective of Galicia's Russification in principle, the russifying policy of the occupying regime was considered premature. In the event of a new occupation of Galicia by the Russian Empire (which was hardly in doubt for most observers), the military interests should therefore be given priority.[88] In Austria there also were some doubts about the commensurability of the violent measures of the Austro-Hungarian army at the beginning of the war. However, when the Austro-Hungarian army re-entered Lviv in 1915, they again cracked down on alleged collaborators. While at the beginning of the war, it was mainly the Ruthenian/Ukrainian population that suffered from the Austrian spy hunt, in 1915 accusations of collaboration were often directed against the local Polish elites. Instead of restoring constitutional order and local self-government, the Austrian authorities once again established a military regime in Galicia. The appointment of a "neutral" German-speaking general as Galician governor could not appease the growing national conflicts among the local population and was met with criticism, especially among the Polish population. Large numbers of the Polish and Ukrainian elites lost their loyalty to the Habsburgs and began to work for national independence.[89] The discrepancy between the promised liberation from the "Russian yoke" and the reality of Austrian military rule was an important factor that undermined confidence in the Austrian Empire. After all, Austrian as well as Russian political practices during the war had little in common with the propagated concepts of rule and were often inspired by military considerations.

Conclusion

Lviv, the capital of the Austrian province Galicia and one of the largest cities in Austria-Hungary, was of decisive symbolic significance – not only for the local population groups but also for Austrian imperial rule. Though it was not a principal economic center, it was the uncontested political and cultural center of the region. Thus, the city represented a site of national formation for Poles, Ukrainians, and Jews, as well as a stronghold of Austrian imperial culture, in this remote eastern province. At the same time, Lviv was of crucial importance for Russian interests in the region. On the one hand, the role of the city as a Ukrainian cultural center thwarting the suppression of the Ukrainian movement in Russia was a thorn in the Russian government's side. On the other hand, as the historical "Russian city L'vov," it was crucial for Russian claims to the region.

Yet the symbolic significance of the city at the crossroads of the Austrian and Russian Empires increased even more during World War I, when Galicia became a theater of war between the two. The needs of war time propaganda reinforced efforts to exalt Lviv as an outpost of the Austro-Hungarian Empire and of Western culture in the East or as the most westward outpost of the Russian people. Moreover, the shifting front lines and the changing rule in the city allowed an immediate comparison between the policies of the two empires, which both sides sought to use for their own interests. The Russianizing policy of the Russian occupation regime in Lviv, for example, was picked up by Austrian propagandists to underline Russia's "barbaric oppression" of the local national cultures in contrast to the ideal of the Habsburg Monarchy as a multi-ethnic state and guarantor of nationality rights. And Russian propaganda referred to the persecution of Russophiles in Galicia by the Austrian army to underline the Austrian oppression of the "Russian people" in Galicia and legitimate Russia's mission in the region. Both sides paid a great deal of attention to the other empire's actions. However, open efforts to adopt the other's concept of rule – that is, for example, the Austrian *Nationalitätenstaat* as a role model for Russian rule in the region – were relatively rare. Rather, both sides sought to distinguish their own policies from those of the enemy, even though the actions of the Austrian and Russian military regimes in the region did not differ much as both sides relied on repressive measures toward certain population groups. Despite the promises to liberate Lviv from the oppression of the enemy, the situation of the local population deteriorated during the war under both Russian and Austrian rule and increasingly alienated the local population from the Austrian Empire. At the same time, national conflicts between the local population groups increased.

World War I marked a climax of Lviv's symbolic significance for the Austrian and the Russian Empires. At the same time, the war led to the deterioration of imperial rule and to the rise of a new political order in the region. However, the city did not lose its symbolic significance for the local population with the dissolution of the empires – on the contrary. Polish-Ukrainian competition for the city, which dated back to the mid-nineteenth century, took on a new dimension. Both Poles and Ukrainians insistently claimed Lviv for their nation-states coming into being, and the competition for the city ended in a Polish-Ukrainian war.

Notes

1 For an overview of the city's history, see Yaroslav Hrytsak, "Lviv: A Multicultural History through the Centuries," in *Lviv: A City in the Crosscurrents of Culture*, ed. John Czaplicka (Cambridge, MA: Ukrainian Research Inst., Harvard Univ., 2005), 47–73.

2 Börries Kuzmany, *Brody. Eine galizische Grenzstadt im langen 19. Jahrhundert* (Wien: Böhlau, 2011), 39–71.

3 On Austrian politics in Galicia, see in detail Hans-Christian Maner, *Galizien. Eine Grenzregion im Kalkül der Donaumonarchie im 18. und 19. Jahrhundert* (Munich: IKGS-Verl., 2007); on the reforms of the late eighteenth century, see especially 28–53.

4 Hans-Christian Maner, "Zentrum und Grenzregionen in der Habsburgermonarchie im 18. und 19. Jahrhundert. Eine Einführung," in *Grenzregionen der Habsburgermonarchie im 18. und 19. Jahrhundert. Ihre Bedeutung und Funktion aus der Perspektive Wiens*, ed. Hans-Christian Maner (Münster: Lit Verlag, 2005), 10.

5 Maner, *Galizien*, 168–97.

6 Hrytsak, "Lviv," 54.

7 On Galician Autonomy, see Józef Buszko, *Galicja 1859–1914. Polski Piemont?* (Kraków: Krajowa Agencja Wydawnicza, 1989); on Lemberg's municipal government, see Heidi Hein-Kircher, *Lembergs "polnischen Charakter" sichern. Kommunalpolitik in einer multiethnischen Stadt der Habsburgermonarchie zwischen 1861/62 und 1914* (Stuttgart: Franz Steiner Verlag, 2020).

8 John Czaplicka, ed. *Lviv: A City in the Crosscurrents of Culture* (Cambridge, MA: Ukrainian Research Inst., Harvard Univ., 2005), 36.

9 Christoph Mick, "Nationalismus und Modernisierung in Lemberg 1867–1914," in *Städte im östlichen Europa. Zur Problematik von Modernisierung und Raum vom Spätmittelalter bis zum 20. Jahrhundert*, ed. Carsten Goehrke and Bianka Pietrow-Ennker (Zürich: Chronos, 2006), 181.

10 Hein-Kircher, *Lembergs "polnischen Charakter" sichern*, 16; on the concept of "emerging cities," see also Eszter Gantner, Heidi Hein-Kircher, and Oliver Hochadel, "Introduction: Backward and Peripheral? Emerging Cities in Eastern Europe," *Zeitschrift für Ostmitteleuropa-Forschung* 67, no. 4 (2018), 479–82.

11 Mick, "Nationalismus."

12 Heidi Hein-Kircher, "Securitizing the Polish Bulwark. The Mission of Lviv in Polish Travel Guides during the Late Nineteenth and Early Twentieth Centuries," in *Rampart Nations: Bulwark Myths of East European Multiconfessional Societies in the Age of Nationalism*, ed. Lilija Berežnaja and Heidi Hein-Kircher (New York, Oxford: Berghahn, 2019).

13 Hein-Kircher, *Lembergs "polnischen Charakter" sichern*, 330–31.

14 Hein-Kircher, "Securitizing the Polish Bulwark."

15 Hugo Lane, "The Ukrainian Theater and the Polish Opera: Cultural Hegemony and National Culture," in *Lviv: A City in the Crosscurrents of Culture*, ed. John Czaplicka (Cambridge, MA: Ukrainian Research Inst., Harvard Univ., 2005), 153–54.

16 Yiddish, however, was not recognized by the Austrian administration as an independent language but classified as a German dialect. Yiddish speakers were therefore classified as German speakers in the censuses.

17 Wacław Wierzbieniec, "The Process of Jewish Emancipation and Assimilation in the Multiethnic City of Lviv during the Nineteenth and Twentieth Centuries," in *Lviv: A City in the Crosscurrents of Culture*, ed. John Czaplicka (Cambridge, MA: Ukrainian Research Inst., Harvard Univ., 2005), 226–36.

18 John-Paul Himka, "The Construction of Nationality in Galician Rus': Icarian Flights in Almost All Directions," in *Intellectuals and the Articulation of the Nation*, ed. Ronald Grigor Suny and Michael D. Kennedy (Ann Arbor: The University of Michigan Press, 1999), 111–45; Anna Veronika Wendland, *Die Russophilen in Galizien: ukrainische Konservative zwischen Österreich und Rußland, 1848–1915* (Vienna: Verl. d. Österr. Akad. d. Wiss., 2001).

19 John-Paul Himka, *Galician Villagers and the Ukrainian National Movement in the Nineteenth Century* (Basingstoke: Macmillan, 1988); Wendland, *Die Russophilen in Galizien*, 82–87.

20 Andreas Kappeler, "Die ukrainische Nationalbewegung im Russischen Reich und in Galizien: Ein Vergleich," in *Entwicklung der Nationalbewegungen in Europa 1850–1914*, ed. Heiner Timmermann (Berlin: Duncker & Humblot 1998), 179–85. On the Russian Empire, see also Alexei Miller, *The Ukrainian Question. The Russian Empire and Nationalism in the Nineteenth Century* (New York: Central European Univ. Press, 2003).

21 Hein-Kircher, *Lembergs "polnischen Charakter" sichern*, 214–66.

22 Stefaniya Ptashnyk, "Deutsch im alten Österreich: Zur Mehrsprachigkeit und Sprachvariation im habsburgischen Bildungswesen in der 2. Hälfte des 19. Jahrhunderts am Beispiel der Stadt Lemberg," in *Dimensionen des Deutschen in Österreich: Variation und Varietäten im sozialen Kontext*, ed. Alexandra N. Lenz (Frankfurt am Main: Lang, 2015), 383–87.

23 Czaplicka, *Lviv*, 36–40.

24 Stefaniya Ptashnyk, "Sprachengebrauch und Sprachenwechsel an der Lemberger Universität im ausgehenden 18. und in der ersten Hälfte des 19. Jahrhunderts," in *Vernakuläre Wissenschaftskommunikation: Beiträge zur Entstehung und Frühgeschichte der modernen deutschen Wissenschaftssprachen*, ed. Michael Prinz and Jürgen Schiewe (Berlin: De Gruyter, 2018), 341–55.

25 Jan Surman, "Figurationen der Akademia. Galizische Universitäten zwischen Imperialismus und multiplem Nationalismus," in *Galizien – Fragmente eines diskursiven Raums*, ed. Doktoratskolleg Galizien (Innsbruck: StudienVerl., 2009), 20–28.

26 Harald Binder, *Der nationale Konflikt um die Universität Lemberg* (Praha: Výzkumné Centrum pro Dějiny Vědy, 2003), 201–2; 211–12.

27 Wierzbieniec, "Process"; Hrytsak, "Lviv," 56.

28 Mick, "Nationalismus."

29 Czaplicka, *Lviv*, 36–40.

30 Lane, "Theater," 157.

31 Delphine Bechtel, "Le théâtre yiddish Gimpel de Lemberg: une Odyssée oubliée," *Yod* 16 (2011), 83–98.

32 Yaroslav Hrytsak and Victor Susak, "Constructing a National City: The Case of L'viv," in *Composing Urban History and the Constitution of Civic Identities*, ed. John Czaplicka (Washington, DC: Woodrow Wilson Center Press, 2003), 142–5.

33 Lane, "Theater," 154–61.

34 On Lemberg's architecture and its symbolic significance, see Markian Prokopovych, "Lemberg (Lwów, L'viv) Architecture, 1772–1918: If Not the Little

Vienna of the East, or the National Bastion, What Else?," *East Central Europe* 36 (2009), 100–24.

35 Even today, Lviv advertises its Viennese cafés. Delphine Bechtel, "Von Lemberg nach L'viv. Gedächtniskonflikte in einer Stadt an der Grenze," *Osteuropa 58*, no. 6 (2008): 221.

36 Klaus Bachmann, *"Ein Herd der Feindschaft gegen Rußland." Galizien als Krisenherd in den Beziehungen der Donaumonarchie mit Rußland (1907–1914)* (Vienna: Verl. für Geschichte u. Politik, 2001).

37 Wendland, *Die Russophilen in Galizien*, 468–72; 514–39.

38 M.E. Klopova, "Vneshniaia politika Rossii i problemy Galitsii nakanune pervoi mirovoi voiny (K postanovke voprosa)," *Vestnik Moskovskogo Universiteta, Seriia 8: Istoriia*, no. 3 (1999), 39–47.

39 Wendland, *Die Russophilen in Galizien*, 479–80.

40 Surman, *Figurationen*, 25–28.

41 Bachmann, *Herd der Feindschaft*, 194–95; Armin Mitter, "Galizien – Krisenherd in den Beziehungen zwischen Österreich-Ungarn und Rußland (1910–1914)," *Jahrbuch für die Geschichte der sozialistischen Länder Europas* 28 (1984): 223.

42 Bachmann, *Herd der Feindschaft*, 65–127.

43 Aleksandra Iu. Bakhturina, *Politika Rossiiskoi Imperii v Vostochnoi Galitsii v gody Pervoi mirovoi voiny* (Moskva: Airo-XX, 2000), 57–60.

44 The first phase of the battle lasted from August 26 to 30. As a result, the Austro-Hungarian army withdrew from the city on September 2. In the second phase from September 6 to 11, Austro-Hungarian troops made an unsuccessful attempt to recapture Lemberg.

45 Mark von Hagen, *War in a European Borderland. Occupations and Occupation Plans in Galicia and Ukraine, 1914–1918* (Seattle: Univ. of Washington Press, 2007).

46 Elisabeth Haid, *Im Blickfeld zweier Imperien. Galizien in der österreichischen und russischen Presseberichterstattung während des Ersten Weltkriegs (1914–1917)* (Marburg: Verlag Herder-Institut, 2019).

47 Maciej Górny, "Identity under Scrutiny. The First World War in Local Communities," in *Imaginations and Configurations of Polish Society. From the Middle Ages through the Twentieth Century*, ed. Yvonne Kleinmann, et al. (Göttingen: Wallstein Verlag, 2017), 264.

48 Ukrainian activists focused on a German-speaking audience in particular to win the support of the Central Powers. On their publication activities, see Rudolf A. Mark, "Zur ukrainischen Frage im Ersten Weltkrieg: Flugschriften des 'Bundes zur Befreiung der Ukraine' und ihm nahestehender Publizisten, 1914–1916," *Zeitschrift für Ostforschung* 33, no. 2 (1984), 197–222.

49 Burkhard Wöller, *"Europa" als historisches Argument. Nationsbildungsstrategien polnischer und ukrainischer Historiker im habsburgischen Galizien* (Bochum: Winkler, 2014), 335–42; Stephan Tomaschiwskyi, *Die weltpolitische Bedeutung Galiziens*, vol. 1 (München 1915), 20–21. "Bilder aus der Geschichte Galiziens. I.," *Reichspost*, June 20, 1915, supplement *Der Sonntag*, 24–25.

50 See, in particular, Eugen Lewicky, *Galizien. Informativer Ueberblick über nationale, wirtschaftliche, soziale und kulturelle Zustände des Landes* (Vienna: Verlag des Bundes zur Befreiung der Ukraina, 1916), 17–18.

51 Alois Woldan, "Lemberg als *Antemurale christianitatis* zur Zeit des Ersten Weltkriegs," *Studi Slavistici* IX (2012), 56–59; Hein-Kircher, "Securitizing the Polish Bulwark."

52 Zöckler, "Aus Lembergs deutscher Vergangenheit," *Ostdeutsche Rundschau*, June 12, 1915, 2–3.

53 "Die Räumung Lembergs durch unsere Truppen. Ein Wort der Sympathie für diese Stadt," *Neue Freie Presse*, September 8, 1914, morning ed., 3.

54 Alice Schalek, "Bilder von der russischen Front. I.," *Neue Freie Presse*, July 6, 1917, morning ed., 2. On the "civilizing activity" of the Austro-Hungarian army, see also "Die Armee im Dienste der Kultur," *Reichspost*, October 26, 1915, morning ed., 4.

55 See "Kaiserworte über Galizien. Der Empfang der galizischen Adelsvertreter in Schönbrunn," *Reichspost*, January 10, 1915, morning ed., 2; "Eine Kundgebung der vereinigten polnischen Parteien," *Reichspost*, May 4, 1916, evening ed., 3; "Die Kundgebung der Polen in Krakau," *Neue Freie Presse*, May 3, 1916, morning ed., 5; "Die Ukrainer gegen den Zarismus. Ein Aufruf an Europa," *Reichspost*, September 10, 1914, morning ed., 2.

56 See, for example, "Zur Geschichte Galiziens," *Reichspost*, June 06, 1915, supplement *Der Sonntag*, 26.

57 Woldan, "Lemberg," 60.

58 See, for example, "Obzor voennykh deistvii," *Novoe Vremia*, August 21, 1914, 2; "Gorod L'vov", *Rech'*, August 21, 1914, 2. All Russian newspaper articles are cited according to the Julian calendar. According to the Gregorian calendar, the two above-mentioned articles appeared on September 3 – that is, in the context of the capture of Lemberg by the Russian army.

59 Dm. Vergun, "Slavianskiia zametki," *Novoe Vremia*, August 15, 1914, 4; "Na russko-avstriiskom fronte," *Russkoe Znamia*, August 24, 1914, 1–2.

60 For example, the Galician Russophile Dmitrii Vergun, the vice-chairman of the Galician-Russian Benevolent Society, played an important role. Apart from publishing Russian-language pamphlets on Galicia, Vergun had been a journalist of *Novoe Vremia* – one of Russia's most influential newspapers – since his emigration to St. Petersburg in 1907. Moreover, the Russian-language newspaper *Prikarpatskaia Rus'* – the paper of radical Russophiles in Lviv – served as an important source of information for Russian reporters. When the paper was banned by the Austrian authorities at the beginning of the war, it was published in Kiev. After the capture of the Galician capital by the Russian troops, the *Prikarpatskaia Rus'* returned to Lviv.

61 Wendland, *Die Russophilen in Galizien*, 468–78.

62 M. Men'shikov, "Dolzhny pobedit'," *Novoe Vremia*, August 23, 1914, 3–4, and August 18, 1914, 2–3.

63 "Petrograd, 11 aprelja 1914 g.," *Russkoe Znamja*, April 11, 1915, 1.

64 "Reč archiepiskopa char'kovskago Antonii posle molebna o darovanii pobedy russkomu oružiju," *Russkoe Znamja*, September 4, 1914, 1–2.

65 *Novoe Vremia*, August 30, 1914, supplement, 7.

66 A Russian book on Lviv's history and architecture, in contrast, described the Baroque architecture of the St. Paraskeva church. The author also mentioned that it was a Uniate church. He emphasized, however, that divine service here was closer to the Russian rite than in other Uniate parishes. V. A. Vereshchagin, *Staryi L'vov* (Petrograd: Tipografiia Sirius, 1915), 62–63.

67 R. I., "Na voine," *Russkoe Znamia*, November 6, 1914, 3.

68 I. K-iarov, "Na voine," *Novoe Vremia*, September 19, 1914, 4.
69 R. I., "Na voine," 3.
70 Vergun, "Slavianskiia zametki."
71 "Vo L'vove," *Rech'*, September 13, 1914, 3.
72 A. Rostislavov, "Starinnaia arkhitektura Galitsii v ocherkakh i risunkakh," *Rech'*, June 1, 1915, 4.
73 K-iarov, "Na voine," 4.
74 V. Bauder, "S letuchim otriadom," *Rech'*, April 18, 1915, 2; "Avstriiskaia Lemberg – snova drevnii russkii L'vov," *Ogonok*, August 31, 1914, 1–2.
75 K-iarov, "Na voine," 4; S. Bel'skii, "Po L'vovskoi gubernii," *Novoe Vremia*, October 11, 1914, 3.
76 On the Lviv railway station and its function as a prestigious building, see Nadja Weck, "Ein neuer Bahnhof für Lemberg (Lwów, L'viv) – Die symbolische Bedeutung der Eisenbahn für das Selbstbewusstsein einer modernen Stadt," in *Galizien. Peripherie der Moderne – Moderne der Peripherie?*, ed. Elisabeth Haid, Stephanie Weismann, and Burkhard Wöller (Marburg: Verl. Herder-Inst., 2013), 31–43.
77 Haid, *Im Blickfeld zweier Imperien.*
78 See, for example, "Ein Aufruf des Polenklubs an das polnische Volk," *Neue Freie Presse*, August 18, 1914, morning ed., 6; "Die polnischen Legionäre," *Reichspost*, September 7, 1914, midday ed., 2; "Aufruf des ukrainischen Nationalrates," *Neue Freie Presse*, August 18, 1914, morning ed., 6; Roda Roda, "Das Volk und der Krieg," *Neue Freie Presse*, August 23, 1914, morning ed., 4.
79 Elisabeth Haid, "Galicia: A Bulwark against Russia? Propaganda and Violence in a Border Region during the First World War," *European Review of History: Revue européenne d'histoire* 24, no. 2 (2017): 203–5.
80 Although the political parties of the Galician Poles and Ruthenians swore loyalty to the Habsburg Monarchy, an important purpose of their wartime organizations was to represent own national interests, and both appealed to the national enthusiasm of their people. While Polish politicians pursued the goal of expanded Galician autonomy and various concepts of a united Poland, Ukrainian politicians called for the province of Galicia to be divided into Polish and Ukrainian provinces. Both claimed Lviv for their national goals.
81 Elisabeth Haid, "Nationalitätenpolitik und Kriegspropaganda. Die galizischen Ruthenen aus der Perspektive Österreich-Ungarns und Russlands," in *Frontwechsel. Österreich-Ungarns „Großer Krieg" im Vergleich*, ed. Wolfram Dornik, Julia Walleczek-Fritz, and Stefan Wedrac (Wien: Böhlau, 2014), 17–23; Hagen, *War in a European Borderland*, 10–6; Christoph Mick, *Lemberg, Lwów, L'viv, 1914–1947: Violence and Ethnicity in a Contested city* (West Lafayette, IN: Purdue University Press, 2016).
82 See, for example, Galičanin, "Pered vzjatiem L'vova," *Novoe Vremja*, September 10, 1914, 2; "V L'vovskoj tjur'me," *Novoe Vremja*, September 20, 1914, 15.
83 Alexei Miller, *The Romanov Empire and Nationalism. Essays in the Methodology of Historical Research* (Budapest: Central European Univ. Press, 2008), 161–79.
84 See Miller, *Ukrainian Question.*
85 P. Miliukov, "Soedinennye shtaty Avstrii," *Rech'*, September 4, 1914, 2–3; P. Miliukov, "Poliaki v Avstrii," *Rech'*, September 7, 1914, 2; P. Miliukov, "Pol'skij P'emont," *Rech'*, September 15, 1914, 2; "Petrograd, 4 sentiabria," *Rech'*, September 4, 1914, 1.

86 See, for example, "Die Polen und die Russifizierung Galiziens," *Reichspost*, March 13, 1915, morning ed., 3; "Russische Freundschaft für die Ruthenen," *Reichspost*, October 31, 1914, morning ed., 2–3.
87 On the Russian occupation of Lemberg, see Mick, *Lemberg, Lwów, L'viv*, 23–62. On the policies of the Russian occupation regime in Galicia, see also Bakhturina, *Politika Rossiiskoi Imperii*.
88 Bakhturina, *Politika Rossiiskoi Imperii*, 214–22.
89 Mick, *Lemberg, Lwów, L'viv*, 62–96.

Bibliography

"Aufruf des ukrainischen Nationalrates." *Neue Freie Presse*, August 18, 1914.
"Avstriiskaia Lemberg - snova drevnii russkii L'vov." *Ogonok*, August 31, 1914.
Bachmann, Klaus. *"Ein Herd der Feindschaft gegen Rußland." Galizien als Krisenherd in den Beziehungen der Donaumonarchie mit Rußland (1907–1914)*. Vienna: Verl. für Geschichte u. Politik, 2001.
Bakhturina, Aleksandra Iu. *Politika Rossiiskoi Imperii v Vostochnoi Galitsii v gody Pervoi mirovoi voiny*. Moskva: Airo-XX, 2000.
Bauder, V. "S letuchim otriadom." *Rech'*, April 18, 1915.
Bechtel, Delphine. "Von Lemberg nach L'viv. Gedächtniskonflikte in einer Stadt an der Grenze." *Osteuropa* 58, no. 6 (2008): 211–27.
———. "Le théâtre yiddish Gimpel de Lemberg: une Odyssée oubliée." *Yod* 16 (2011): 83–98.
Bel'skii, S. "Po L'vovskoi gubernii." *Novoe Vremia*, October 11, 1914.
"Bilder aus der Geschichte Galiziens. I." *Reichspost*, June 20, 1915.
Binder, Harald. *Der nationale Konflikt um die Universität Lemberg*. Praha: Výzkumné Centrum pro Dějiny Vědy, 2003.
Buszko, Józef. *Galicja 1859–1914. Polski Piemont?* Kraków: Krajowa Agencja Wydawnicza, 1989.
Czaplicka, John, ed. *Lviv: A City in the Crosscurrents of Culture*. Cambridge, MA: Ukrainian Research Inst., Harvard Univ., 2005.
"Die Armee im Dienste der Kultur." *Reichspost*, October 26, 1915.
"Die Kundgebung der Polen in Krakau." *Neue Freie Presse*, May 3, 1916.
"Die Polen und die Russifizierung Galiziens." *Reichspost*, March 13, 1915.
"Die polnischen Legionäre." *Reichspost*, September 7, 1914.
"Die Räumung Lembergs durch unsere Truppen. Ein Wort der Sympathie für diese Stadt." *Neue Freie Presse*, September 8, 1914.
"Die Ukrainer gegen den Zarismus. Ein Aufruf an Europa." *Reichspost*, September 10, 1914.
"Ein Aufruf des Polenklubs an das polnische Volk." *Neue Freie Presse*, August 18, 1914.
"Eine Kundgebung der vereinigten polnischen Parteien." *Reichspost* May 4, 1916.
Galičanin. "Pered vzjatiem L'vova." *Novoe Vremja*, September 10, 1914.
Gantner, Eszter, Heidi Hein-Kircher, and Oliver Hochadel. "Introduction: Backward and Peripheral? Emerging Cities in Eastern Europe." *Zeitschrift für Ostmitteleuropa-Forschung* 67, no. 4 (2018): 475–84.

Górny, Maciej. "Identity under Scrutiny. The First World War in Local Communities." In *Imaginations and Configurations of Polish Society. From the Middle Ages through the Twentieth Century*, edited by Yvonne Kleinmann, Jürgen Heyde, Dietlind Hüchtker, Dobrochna Kałwa, Joanna Nalewajko-Kulikov, Katrin Steffen, and Tomasz Wiślicz, 261–77. Göttingen: Wallstein Verlag, 2017.

"Gorod L'vov." *Rech'*, August 21, 1914.

Haid, Elisabeth. "Nationalitätenpolitik und Kriegspropaganda. Die galizischen Ruthenen aus der Perspektive Österreich-Ungarns und Russlands." In *Frontwechsel. Österreich-Ungarns "Großer Krieg" im Vergleich*, edited by Wolfram Dornik, Julia Walleczek-Fritz, and Stefan Wedrac, 259–82. Vienna: Böhlau, 2014.

———. "Galicia: A Bulwark against Russia? Propaganda and Violence in a Border Region during the First World War." *European Review of History: Revue européenne d'histoire* 24, no. 2 (2017): 200–13.

———. *Im Blickfeld zweier Imperien. Galizien in der österreichischen und russischen Presseberichterstattung während des Ersten Weltkriegs (1914–1917)*. Marburg: Verlag Herder-Institut, 2019.

Hein-Kircher, Heidi. "Securitizing the Polish Bulwark. The Mission of Lviv in Polish Travel Guides during the Late Nineteenth and Early Twentieth Centuries." In *Rampart Nations: Bulwark Myths of East European Multiconfessional Societies in the Age of Nationalism*, edited by Lilija Berežnaja and Heidi Hein-Kircher. New York: Berghahn, 2019.

———. *Lembergs "polnischen Charakter" sichern. Kommunalpolitik in einer multiethnischen Stadt der Habsburgermonarchie zwischen 1861/62 und 1914*. Stuttgart: Franz Steiner Verlag, 2020.

Himka, John-Paul. *Galician Villagers and the Ukrainian National Movement in the Nineteenth Century*. Basingstoke: Macmillan, 1988.

———. "The Construction of Nationality in Galician Rus': Icarian Flights in Almost All Directions." In *Intellectuals and the Articulation of the Nation*, edited by Ronald Grigor Suny and Michael D. Kennedy, 109–64. Ann Arbor: The University of Michigan Press, 1999.

Hrytsak, Yaroslav. "Lviv: A Multicultural History through the Centuries." In *Lviv: A City in the Crosscurrents of Culture*, edited by John Czaplicka, 47–73. Cambridge, MA: Ukrainian Research Inst., Harvard Univ., 2005.

Hrytsak, Yaroslav, and Victor Susak. "Constructing a National City: The Case of L'viv." In *Composing Urban History and the Constitution of Civic Identities*, edited by John Czaplicka, 140–64. Washington, DC: Woodrow Wilson Center Press, 2003.

I., R. "Na voine." *Russkoe Znamia*, November 6, 1914.

"Kaiserworte über Galizien. Der Empfang der galizischen Adelsvertreter in Schönbrunn." *Reichspost*, January 10, 1915.

Kappeler, Andreas. "Die ukrainische Nationalbewegung im Russischen Reich und in Galizien: Ein Vergleich." In *Entwicklung der Nationalbewegungen in Europa 1850–1914*, edited by Heiner Timmermann, 175–96. Berlin: Duncker & Humblot, 1998.

K-iarov, I. "Na voine." *Novoe Vremia*, September 19, 1914.

Klopova, M.E. "Vneshniaia politika Rossii i problemy Galitsii nakanune pervoi mirovoi voiny (K postanovke voprosa)." *Vestnik Moskovskogo Universiteta, Seriia 8: Istoriia*, no. 3 (1999): 36–47.

Kuzmany, Börries. *Brody. Eine galizische Grenzstadt im langen 19. Jahrhundert.* Vienna: Böhlau, 2011.

Lane, Hugo. "The Ukrainian Theater and the Polish Opera: Cultural Hegemony and National Culture." In *Lviv: A City in the Crosscurrents of Culture*, edited by John Czaplicka, 149–70. Cambridge, MA: Ukrainian Research Inst., Harvard Univ., 2005.

Lewicky, Eugen. *Galizien. Informativer Ueberblick über nationale, wirtschaftliche, soziale und kulturelle Zustände des Landes.* Vienna: Verlag des Bundes zur Befreiung der Ukraina, 1916.

Maner, Hans-Christian. "Zentrum und Grenzregionen in der Habsburgermonarchie im 18. und 19. Jahrhundert. Eine Einführung." In *Grenzregionen der Habsburgermonarchie im 18. und 19. Jahrhundert. Ihre Bedeutung und Funktion aus der Perspektive Wiens*, edited by Hans-Christian Maner, 9–24. Münster: Lit Verlag, 2005.

——. *Galizien. Eine Grenzregion im Kalkül der Donaumonarchie im 18. und 19. Jahrhundert.* Munich: IKGS-Verl., 2007.

Mark, Rudolf A. "Zur ukrainischen Frage im Ersten Weltkrieg: Flugschriften des 'Bundes zur Befreiung der Ukraine' und ihm nahestehender Publizisten, 1914–1916." *Zeitschrift für Ostforschung* 33, no. 2 (1984): 196–226.

Men'shikov, M. "Dolzhny pobedit'." *Novoe Vremia*, August 18 and 23, 1914.

Mick, Christoph. "Nationalismus und Modernisierung in Lemberg 1867–1914." In *Städte im östlichen Europa. Zur Problematik von Modernisierung und Raum vom Spätmittelalter bis zum 20. Jahrhundert*, edited by Carsten Goehrke and Bianka Pietrow-Ennker, 171–213. Zürich: Chronos, 2006.

——. *Lemberg, Lwów, L'viv, 1914–1947: Violence and Ethnicity in a Contested City.* West Lafayette, IN: Purdue University Press, 2016.

Miliukov, P. "Soedinennye shtaty Avstrii." *Rech'*, September 4, 1914.

——. "Poliaki v Avstrii." *Rech'*, September 7, 1914.

——. "Pol'skii P'emont.", *Rech'*, September 15, 1914.

Miller, Alexei. *The Ukrainian Question. The Russian Empire and Nationalism in the Nineteenth Century.* New York: Central European Univ. Press, 2003.

——. *The Romanov Empire and Nationalism. Essays in the Methodology of Historical Research.* Budapest: Central European Univ. Press, 2008.

Mitter, Armin. "Galizien – Krisenherd in den Beziehungen zwischen Österreich-Ungarn und Rußland (1910–1914)." *Jahrbuch für die Geschichte der sozialistischen Länder Europas* 28 (1984): 207–33.

"Na russko-avstriiskom fronte." *Russkoe Znamia*, August 24, 1914.

"Obzor voennykh deistvii." *Novoe Vremia*, August 21, 1914.

"Petrograd, 11 aprelja 1914 g." *Russkoe Znamja*, April 11, 1915.

"Petrograd, 4 sentiabria." *Rech'*, September 4, 1914.

Prokopovych, Markian. "Lemberg (Lwów, L'viv) Architecture, 1772–1918: If Not the Little Vienna of the East, or the National Bastion, What Else?" *East Central Europe* 36 (2009): 100–29.

Ptashnyk, Stefaniya. "Deutsch im alten Österreich: Zur Mehrsprachigkeit und Sprachvariation im habsburgischen Bildungswesen in der 2. Hälfte des 19. Jahrhunderts am Beispiel der Stadt Lemberg." In *Dimensionen des Deutschen in*

Österreich: Variation und Varietäten im sozialen Kontext, edited by Alexandra N. Lenz, 377–92. Frankfurt am Main: Lang, 2015.

———. "Sprachengebrauch und Sprachenwechsel an der Lemberger Universität im ausgehenden 18. und in der ersten Hälfte des 19. Jahrhunderts." In *Vernakuläre Wissenschaftskommunikation: Beiträge zur Entstehung und Frühgeschichte der modernen deutschen Wissenschaftssprachen*, edited by Michael Prinz and Jürgen Schiewe, 335–59. Berlin: De Gruyter, 2018.

"Reč' archiepiskopa char'kovskago Antonii posle molebna o darovanii pobedy russkomu oružiju." *Russkoe Znamja*, September 4, 1914

Roda Roda. "Das Volk und der Krieg." *Neue Freie Presse*, August 23, 1914.

Rostislavov, A. "Starinnaia arkhitektura Galitsii v ocherkakh i risunkakh." *Rech'*, June 1, 1915.

"Russische Freundschaft für die Ruthenen." *Reichspost*, October 31, 1914.

Schalek, Alice. "Bilder von der russischen Front. I." *Neue Freie Presse*, July 6, 1917.

Surman, Jan. "Figurationen der Akademia. Galizische Universitäten zwischen Imperialismus und multiplem Nationalismus." In *Galizien – Fragmente eines diskursiven Raums*, edited by Doktoratskolleg Galizien, 15–35. Innsbruck: StudienVerl., 2009.

Tomaschiwskyi, Stephan. *Die weltpolitische Bedeutung Galiziens*. Vol. 1. München, 1915.

"V L'vovskoj tjur'me." *Novoe Vremja*, September 20, 1914.

Vereshchagin, V. A. *Staryi L'vov*. Petrograd: Tipografiia Sirius, 1915.

Vergun, Dm. "Slavianskiia zametki." *Novoe Vremia*, August 15, 1914.

"Vo L'vove." *Rech'*, September 13, 1914.

von Hagen, Mark. *War in a European Borderland. Occupations and Occupation Plans in Galicia and Ukraine, 1914–1918*. Seattle: Univ. of Washington Press, 2007.

Weck, Nadja. "Ein neuer Bahnhof für Lemberg (Lwów, L'viv) – Die symbolische Bedeutung der Eisenbahn für das Selbstbewusstsein einer modernen Stadt." In *Galizien. Peripherie der Moderne – Moderne der Peripherie?*, edited by Elisabeth Haid, Stephanie Weismann, and Burkhard Wöller, 31–43. Marburg: Verl. Herder- Inst., 2013.

Wendland, Anna Veronika. *Die Russophilen in Galizien: ukrainische Konservative zwischen Österreich und Rußland, 1848–1915*. Vienna: Verl. d. Österr. Akad. d. Wiss., 2001.

Wierzbieniec, Wacław. "The Process of Jewish Emancipation and Assimilation in the Multiethnic City of Lviv during the Nineteenth and Twentieth Centuries." In *Lviv: A City in the Crosscurrents of Culture*, edited by John Czaplicka, 223–50. Cambridge, MA: Ukrainian Research Inst., Harvard Univ., 2005.

Woldan, Alois. "Lemberg als *Antemurale christianitatis* zur Zeit des Ersten Weltkriegs." *Studi Slavistici* IX (2012): 53–69.

Wöller, Burkhard. *"Europa" als historisches Argument. Nationsbildungsstrategien polnischer und ukrainischer Historiker im habsburgischen Galizien*. Bochum: Winkler, 2014.

Zöckler. "Aus Lembergs deutscher Vergangenheit." *Ostdeutsche Rundschau*, June 12, 1915.

"Zur Geschichte Galiziens." *Reichspost*, June 6, 1915.

10 Kars

Bridgehead of Empires

Elke Hartmann

Since ancient times, the abundance of snow and the anxiety that the snow masses cause among locals and travelers alike have determined every description of the city of Kars.[1] Only at second glance do other dimensions become visible. This is, for example, how Ka, the narrator in Orhan Pamuk's novel *Snow*, arrives in Kars:

> Once caked with snow, the road signs were impossible to read. When the snowstorm began to rage in earnest, the driver turned off his brights and dimmed the lights inside the bus, hoping to conjure up the road out of the semidarkness. The passengers fell into a fearful silence with their eyes on the scene outside: the snow-covered streets of destitute villages, the dimly lit, ramshackle one-story houses, the roads to farther villages that were already closed, and the ravines barely visible beyond the street-lamps. If they spoke, it was in whispers.[2]

With only a few hints, the Turkish writer and Nobel Prize winner Orhan Pamuk draws his picture of Kars – not a description of the city, but a sketch of what Kars means to him for his novel. The town of Kars, located in the far east of today's Turkey on the border with Armenia, entered the consciousness of an international reading public with Pamuk's novel *Snow*. The author admittedly moved the remote border town to the center of the international (literary educated) field of vision. With his portrait, however, he simultaneously pushed it into the distance. The choice of Kars as the setting is certainly partly due to a play on words and names – "Ka" is the name of the novel's protagonist – and associations with Kafka and Brecht suggest themselves. "Kar" is the Turkish word for the snow that provides the title and cuts the city off from the world in winter. It runs through the novel as a symbol for the remoteness and inaccessibility of the place, also referring to the descriptions of the place since antiquity. Finally, by adding a letter, the name of the town is derived from "kar." On the other hand, Kars was undoubtedly chosen as the setting for the novel – which is

DOI: 10.4324/9781003130031-13

as much a social analysis of Turkey as it is literary fiction – because of the city's geographical location and its history.

In the cityscape of Kars, Ka sees evidence of the city's checkered past, the most salient feature of which was the multiple massive population shifts. Like other eastern Anatolian cities, the cityscape with its mosques and baths first reflects Muslim-Ottoman history. The imposing fortress also testifies to the garrison town's martial past since the Middle Ages. Unlike most Anatolian cities, where Armenian cultural monuments have been almost completely destroyed, the former presence of this population group, which was so important until the First World War, is still visible in Kars, especially in the form of the large and exposed Church of the Holy Apostles (Surp Arakelots), built in the tenth century at the foot of the citadel (Figure 10.1).

Above all, however, the cityscape of Kars is marked by the architectural legacy of the period of Russian rule between 1878 and 1918, which

Figure 10.1 "Russian" residential building on Gazi Ahmet Muhtar Paşa Caddesi in Kars. The building served as Soviet consulate after 1930. Photo by Elke Hartmann, 2005.

distinguishes this city from all other Turkish cities. The hotel – named "Snow Palace Hotel" – where Ka stays is "one of those elegant Baltic buildings," a two-story building with tall and narrow windows and a high gateway for horse-drawn vehicles.[3] "The Kars police headquarters" was "a long three-story building" with "high ornate ceilings," and "this forty-room mansion was first home to a rich Armenian and later a Russian hospital." The same street on which this building stands, Faik Bey Street, is lined with other "old stone buildings that had once belonged to wealthy Russians and Armenians [and] now housed mostly government offices."[4]

However, the multifaceted past appears here only in its remnants, its empty traces, no longer as the wealth of the present or the promise and starting point for a new departure, but as a witness and memorial of loss, a blank space in Turkish history. Kalealtı, the neighborhood below the castle complex is now "the poorest part of Kars," a slum, and as Ka takes a walk through the streets, he sees "the old decrepit Russian buildings with stovepipes sticking out of every window, the thousand-year-old Armenian church towering over the wood depots and the electric generators, the pack of dogs barking at every passerby from a five-hundred-year-old stone bridge" over the river Kars – the Ottoman stone bridge built in 1725, so not quite 500 years old after all.[5] The whole scenery is deserted. The Russians are gone, the Armenians are gone. In particular, the disappearance of the Armenians from Kars and from today's Turkey was explicated by Orhan Pamuk in an interview in connection with his novel *Snow* as one of the most problematic blanks in Turkish history – at the price of death threats and trials for "denigrating Turkishness" (Figure 10.2).[6]

Unlike the Armenian population, the Russian officials, military personnel, and settlers were newcomers when the Tsarist Empire took over the administration of the city in 1878. With their authorities, "Russian" buildings, and various practices of everyday culture, the immigrants from the Tsarist Empire brought a visible piece of Europe to, of all places, the easternmost, supposedly most backward, and barely controlled edge of the country. In the midst of the debate about modernization and Europeanization that pervaded the entire Ottoman nineteenth century, which continues to this day and essentially determines Turkish politics, the eastern periphery became the bridgehead of Westernization. Russia may have been perceived in Western Europe as a symbol of the distant and backward, but from the Ottoman-Turkish point of view, Russia – not only in Kars – was part of Europe and "Western modernity." Ka, the hero of Orhan Pamuk's novel, who, like his author, comes from the Westernized milieu of Istanbul's educated elite, actually only feels a little bit comfortable in Kars in view of the European-modernist element embodied by the Russian buildings.[7]

Figure 10.2 Historical postcard of Kars, showing the district below the citadel, Taşköprü (Ottoman bridge), and the Surp Arakelots Armenian Church. To the left of the medieval Armenian church is, the bell tower added during Russian rule and demolished after 1918; to the right of the church are two minarets from the Ottoman period.

Source: Houshamadyan Collection.

The Russian buildings remind us that Kars has always flourished when the borders were open and the city became a hub of cultural and commodity exchange between East, West, North, and South – and their mere presence makes all attempts to conceal this plurality come to nothing. Russian rule in Kars was undoubtedly a period of revival and new impetus, and for the time being the last. The Russian buildings, not only in their decaying splendor, but above all in their obvious otherness, give us a glimpse, or even a wistful dream, of the potential this city would have had – and indeed once had – under different political conditions.

Population Shifts and Economic Structural Change since the Middle Ages

Kars experienced its heyday in the tenth and early eleventh centuries. During this period, it was the capital of an Armenian kingdom and a hub of trade along the Silk Road. Kars was a political, economic, and cultural center and open to all directions, a contact zone of cultures engaged in fruitful exchange. Since the crushing of the Armenian kingdoms by the Byzantines and Seljuks in the mid-eleventh century, however, Kars became a contested border town on the extreme edge of competing great empires. For centuries, the city and its environs suffered from the devastation and depopulation caused by the wars, as well as from the neglect and isolation that came with its peripheral location.

On several occasions, conquests or long wars triggered profound demographic and structural changes in the Armenian highlands, which also affected Kars.[8] The history of the thirteenth century – as in the Russian principalities – was also marked in Armenia by the Mongol move to the west. Kars was destroyed in 1236.[9] A good century and a half later, Kars succumbed to Timur Lenk (Tamerlan) in 1394. Timur's devastation caused a severe famine in Asia Minor, a significant decrease in population, and the decline of cities in the Caucasus and the Armenian highlands. Further contributing to the impoverishment of Northeast Armenia was the fact that around the middle of the fourteenth century, trade routes also shifted further south from the northern hubs of Kars and Ani.[10]

In 1501, the Persian Safavids conquered Kars. Their westward expansion and the religious conflict between the Sunni Ottomans and the Shiite Safavids soon led to the first Safavid-Ottoman clashes, which lasted with interruptions throughout the sixteenth and the first half of the seventeenth centuries.[11] The most devastating of the Ottoman-Persian wars was undoubtedly the campaign of the Persian Shah Abbas. As part of his scorched earth warfare, he ordered the depopulation of the eastern Armenian provinces and the resettlement of their inhabitants in Iran. Fields and settlements were burnt down, and only a small fraction of the Armenians deported in the winter of 1604–1605 survived. Kars was one of the depopulated cities. Only the peace treaty of 1639 ended a century and a half of war. The western part of the Armenian highlands, including Kars, fell to the Ottoman Empire and remained Ottoman until the nineteenth century.

Kurdish and Turkmen nomadic tribes moved into the deserted regions where they could use the fallow land for pasture, while many of the Armenian craftsmen and merchants who had escaped deportation followed their compatriots to Iran because the economy had ground to a halt in their devastated homeland. Ottoman policy supported the influx of nomadic Kurds because of their Sunni religion, even at the price of further decline in agriculture.[12]

The devastation was not entirely man-made. Since Kars – and the Armenian highlands as a whole – is not only located at an intersection of different cultures but also at the boundary of tectonic plates, the frequent earthquakes played their considerable part in the periodic destruction of the city.

Kars in the Focus of the Russian Empire's Southern Expansion

In the nineteenth century, Kars was once again caught between the front lines. As an opponent of the Ottoman Empire in the east, Iran was now displaced by the Russian Empire, which continued its southern expansion in Transcaucasia at the beginning of the nineteenth century. A first attempt to conquer Kars failed in 1807. In 1828 and 1855, the Tsar's armies conquered Kars, only to surrender the city both times in the subsequent peace negotiations in exchange for concessions elsewhere. In relation to Russian interests in the Balkans and the Straits of the Bosporus and Dardanelles, Kars (and eastern Anatolia as a whole) were secondary. Only after the third conquest in the Russo-Ottoman War of 1877–1878, when the Tsarist army had crushed the Ottoman forces and were able to dictate their peace to the Sultan at the gates of Istanbul, did the Kars region, together with the territories of Ardahan and Batum (Georg. Batumi), come under Russian administration.[13] For forty years, from 1878 to 1918, Kars remained part of the Tsarist Empire.

With the incorporation of the previously Ottoman province of Kars into the Russian Empire in 1878, the city gained new importance as the seat of a Russian garrison and experienced a boom. The city became not only the bridgehead of the Tsarist Empire on its Transcaucasian border but also a Russian laboratory in the Ottoman world. With the Russian soldiers and administrators came immigrants from different parts of the Russian Empire. Kars became the new home for Russian minorities, refugees, and exiles. The city's upswing owed much to this new diversity of its population with its dynamism and connections in all directions.

From a national Turkish perspective, Russian rule was interpreted as oppressive foreign rule.[14] Tsarist rule certainly came at the expense of the local Muslim elites and religious scholars, who feared for the continuation of their privileges. Many Muslims followed their teachings and the promises of the Ottoman government and resettled in the provinces that remained Ottoman after the Russian conquest.[15] For the Muslim population remaining in Kars province, however, the Tsarist administration did not mean hardship, but de facto an improvement in their standard of living, a lower tax burden, and better infrastructure than in the Ottoman Empire.[16]

Flight, Expulsion, Genocide: Population Politics of Modernity

Each of the conquests and reconquests of Kars in the nineteenth and twentieth centuries entailed massive population shifts. Even more than in the pre-modern eras, the demographic upheavals in the "long" nineteenth century determined the history of the city of Kars and its surrounding area. This is also reflected in the historiography. The rather sparse research on Kars has dealt with this topic in particular, while most other fields, from economic development to the social differentiation of the population to aspects of the history of ideas and cultural life, have so far remained largely unaddressed.

The withdrawal of Russian troops from Kars, Ardahan, Bayazit (Turk. Doğubayazıt), and Erzurum (Arm. Garin) after the Treaty of Adrianople in 1829 triggered a wave of Armenian refugees to Georgia and the Eastern Armenian territories ceded to Russia by Iran only the previous year. There were two reasons for the eastward migration of around 100,000 Armenians. First, the Tsarist government encouraged the immigration of Armenians from Iran and the Ottoman Empire in the first half of the nineteenth century. After the victory over Iran in 1828, the government in St. Petersburg negotiated with the Shah of Persia the release of Armenians from northern Iran who were willing to emigrate. The Treaty of Adrianople in 1829 enshrined a similar passage that allowed Ottoman Armenians to emigrate to Russia after an eighteen-month restriction period.[17]

The second reason was more important. Under Muslim rule, Christian Armenians were recognized as a minority but discriminated against in important political, economic, and cultural areas. During the Russo-Persian War of 1826–1828, for the first time in centuries, the possibility arose of coming under Christian rule and thus shedding the structural inequality imposed by Islamic law. In this situation, religious attachment in parts of Armenian society expressed itself in a "spontaneous and naïve Russophilia."[18] How widespread pro-Russian attitudes were among the Armenian population on both sides of the Russo-Ottoman border; which parts of the Armenian spiritual, political, economic, and cultural elites held Russophile or Turkophile positions; and with what arguments and through what experiences these changed, if any, would be a worthwhile set of questions for further research. For the time being, a review of individual highlights must suffice.

In 1827, the Armenian prelate of Tbilisi (which had been part of the Tsarist Empire since 1801), and later Catholicos Nerses Ashtaraketsi, called on his compatriots to support the Russian campaign. Several hundred Armenian volunteers from Georgia, the Persian parts of Armenia, and the Armenian provinces of the Ottoman Empire then gathered in Tbilisi. When the Russian army advanced to Kars in 1828, General Ivan F. Paskevich and his troops were received with jubilation by the Armenian population. In his *Journey to Arzrum*, which also took him through Kars, the Russian national poet Alexander S. Pushkin describes the hopeful reception of the

Russian troops when they entered Erzurum.[19] After the return of Kars and the other conquered territories to the Ottoman Empire, the Armenians who stayed behind feared retaliation by the Muslims and followed the departing Russian troops, just as the Ottoman Armenian spiritual and secular elites, together with the Ottoman government, tried to prevent them from fleeing.[20] The place of the Armenians who fled was taken by Kurds, Karapapakhs, and other Muslim groups.[21]

The initial Russophilia among the Ottoman Armenians quickly gave way to disappointment at the lack of help. As a result of the Ottoman policy of centralization since the 1840s, the settlement of Muslim immigrants from the Caucasus, and the settling of Kurdish tribes, violence and insecurity in the Armenian provinces of the Ottoman Empire increased sharply from the middle of the nineteenth century.[22] Especially during the war of 1877–1878, atrocities by Ottoman regular and irregular troops (primarily Kurdish tribal regiments) against Armenians in the border regions increased. Therefore, the Russian army was also welcomed by many as a liberator in 1877, and the annexed territories of Kars, Ardahan, and Batum filled up with thousands and thousands of Armenian refugees from the Ottoman provinces, although the Russian authorities meanwhile tried to prevent the influx of Armenians by all means.[23]

In 1895–1896, nationwide massacres of Armenians took place in the Ottoman Empire in response to the demands of the major European powers to improve the situation of the Armenians in the eastern provinces. As a result, the number of Armenian refugees and migrant workers in Kars jumped, equaling or even exceeding the population of the city as a whole, despite the Russian administration's rigid ban on settlement. At the same time, Armenians also migrated from Russian Transcaucasia.[24]

For the Armenians, Kars had become a safe refuge under Russian administration. For the Muslims, on the other hand, the Russian conquest was cause for flight. Since the middle of the eighteenth century, Russian southern expansion, first in the Crimea and later in the Caucasus, was accompanied by massive waves of emigration and expulsions of Muslims. Especially in the Caucasus, the Russian conquerors proceeded with particular brutality.[25] The Ottoman Empire advocated the flight of Muslims from the regions that had fallen under non-Muslim rule for religious-ideological as well as reasons of population policy and granted tax and exemption privileges for their immigration.[26] The Russian occupiers also encouraged the mass and permanent departure of Muslims from Kars. Even before the San Stefano peace treaty, the governor of Kars issued an order in January 1878 that forced every Muslim family leaving the region to sign a written declaration that they would never return. Around 11,000 Muslims left the city of Kars by the mid-1880s, and 65,000 Muslim emigrants are estimated to have left the Kars province as a whole.[27]

The large movements of refugees – the expulsion of Muslims as well as efforts to restrict the influx of Armenians – were countered by an active Russian settlement policy. Since Kars was developed as an important garrison after 1878, the Russian soldiers stationed there consistently made up a considerable contingent of the city's population. On a larger scale, Cossacks, Orthodox Russians, or Greeks, as well as Molokans and Dukhobortses (heterodox Russian communities that had split off from the Russian Orthodox Church in the seventeenth and eighteenth centuries, respectively, with popular Protestant teachings and practices) were also deliberately settled as peasants in the Kars province, along with German and Baltic settlers.[28] The population structure of Kars became more diverse than it had probably ever been in the history of the city. The city also changed again from a majority of Sunni Muslims to a Christian-dominated settlement.[29] However, Kars only became "Russian" to a very limited extent. By the end, the number of soldiers and civil servants stationed in Kars clearly outweighed the city's Russian resident population. Even at the end of Tsarist rule (according to Russian census data from 1912), the proportion of Russian immigrants in the province of Kars was less than ten percent, and in the entire Kars region in 1911 only a good five percent.[30] The defining element of the Kars population during the Russian period was not the Russian immigrants but the Armenians. In the local area as well as in Kars province, they made up just under a third of the population in 1911–1912. In the regional capital Kars, on the other hand, an absolute majority of almost 85 percent were Armenians in 1911, compared to 5.6 percent Russians, a little over 4.5 percent Greeks, and three percent Turks (various smaller communities accounted for the remaining less than two percent).[31]

The relationship between Christians and Muslims was once again reversed after the First World War by the Armenian genocide, this time with unprecedented radicalism. By the middle of the twentieth century, the Russian Molokans had also left the region. In place of the Armenians, many of the Azeris or Tatars who had been expelled from the Ararat Plain and the region around Lake Sevan in the course of the creation of the Armenian nation-state in 1919 settled in Kars, so that today the population of Kars consists almost entirely of Muslims – Turks, Kurds, Azeris, Karapapakhs, Turkmens, and others.[32]

The Russian Heritage

Kars as the end of its own world; Kars as the gateway to Transcaucasia, as a strategically central outpost; Kars as a strong fortress and last bastion;

Kars as a hub for the exchange of goods and culture; and, finally, Kars as a new home for settlers, refugees, and exiles – everything that has characterized Kars in the course of its long history is also reflected in the city's Russian heritage.

The first thing that is visible is the city's built structure. The citadel, the nucleus of the city, known in ancient Armenia as "Karuts Berd" (Stone Fortress), was rebuilt again and again by its Armenian and Georgian medieval kings. The Ottomans fortified the site repeatedly, with the help of British in the nineteenth century, and later Prussian advisors. In this long line, the Russian military was the last to rebuild and again extend the site.[33]

After 1878, however, the Russians did not only rebuild Kars Fortress. They rebuilt the entire city as a garrison town, with a new ground plan based on a chessboard-shaped street network, along which the Russian-Baltic style houses described by Orhan Pamuk in his novel *Snow* were lined up in perimeter block structure. None of these urban planning and architectural elements were common to the traditional cities of the region described as "oriental."[34] However, they were all regarded by the Ottoman reformers of the nineteenth century as models of modernization, which were modeled on the examples of Vienna and Paris, among others, and realized at selected points in the capital Istanbul.[35] Last but not least, the rather inconspicuous fountains in the public spaces of Kars are part of the "Russian" cityscape, but because of their sculptures of women, they are not to be found in any other city in Islamic Turkey (Figure 10.3).

The former Russian presence in Kars has also left traces in other fields. One of these is language. The historians Candan Badem and Rohat Alakom list a whole series of words of Russian origin that are used in today's Kars dialect.[36] One can probably assume that these linguistic influences go back more to the Russian administration and military and less to the Russian settlers. Their lasting legacy in Kars is cheese-making. Swiss cheesemakers who settled in the Kars region after the Russian conquest introduced the production of semi-hard cheese (*kaşar*) and hard cheese (*gravyer*: Gruyère) in the Kars region.[37] Today, these cheeses represent a particular specialty of Kars and are among the important export products of the region. The list of local cheese dairies – referred to by the Russian word for production facilities in general, *zavod*, which is still stamped as a trademark on Kars cheeses today – shows that the actual production of cheese was mainly in the hands of Armenians, in addition to the Swiss. However, the Molokans and Dukhobortses had specialized in breeding dairy cows and also produced a robust breed of horse that was particularly valued in the military.[38]

With the Russian conquest and the rebuilding of the garrison town, the Kars region experienced an economic and demographic boom. After Kars lost most of its pre-war population of around 9,000 due to the war and

Figure 10.3 One of the Russian fountains in Kars. Photo by Elke Hartmann, 2005.

the flight of Muslims after 1878, the Russian census of 1881 showed only 3,665 inhabitants for the city of Kars. By the eve of the First World War, this number had quadrupled, although the many thousands of Armenian refugees and migrant workers without immigration permits were not included in the statistically recorded population. In the region as a whole, the population increased in similar proportions, and numerous new settlements were founded.[39]

The economy retained its predominantly agrarian character. Kars did not experience any significant industrialization. However, the rapid upswing in agricultural production after the Russian annexation of the province is remarkable. Between 1883 and 1915, grain yields in the Kars region increased almost sixfold. Besides the rapid population growth in the same period, improved cultivation methods and the introduction of modern agricultural machinery brought by the Russian settlers were mainly responsible for this. The livestock population also multiplied. Compared to the situation immediately before the Russo-Ottoman War, the number of cows kept in the Kars region had increased more than sevenfold in 1912. By crossing with Swiss dairy cattle, the settlers also bred a more productive breed.[40] The processing of agricultural products also developed with a slight time lag. In addition to the dairies and cheese dairies, the hundreds of water mills that went into operation are particularly noteworthy – in Ottoman times there were only five of them in the entire Kars region.[41]

Essential for the rapid development of agriculture was the expansion of the infrastructure, the connection of the Kars region to Transcaucasia and the Russian imperial territory as a whole. In the province, which in Ottoman times was marginal and poorly connected even to the neighboring Ottoman provinces, transregional trade links to the Transcaucasian sales markets developed in addition to local trade as a result of the elimination of the border and above all because of the new transport routes. With the opening of the railway line that connected Kars with Tbilisi via Alexandropol (today Giumri in Armenia) from 1899, trade experienced a further boom. Between 1902 and 1912, the volume of sales doubled. Kars also became a hub of transit trade for Russian goods to the Ottoman provinces.[42] Wholesale and long-distance trade as well as small and local trade were almost entirely in Armenian hands. Almost all trades in the city were also Armenian-dominated. In his study of the Kars and Ardahan region, the historian Georg Kobro provides a list of all the industrial and commercial enterprises registered in Kars in 1914. The 154 names listed here are almost without exception Armenian.[43]

For the Armenians in particular, who made up the majority of the population, political security and economic prosperity also brought a cultural blossoming. They benefited from founding of Russian schools, which they later sought to replace with their own schools – especially after the Russian 1903 decree confiscating Armenian church property – and also used the Russian newspaper *Kars* as an intellectual forum.[44] Today, no traces of this legacy are visible in Kars. In Armenian literature, it is echoed in the novel *Yergir Nairi* by Yeghishe Tcharents, who was born in Kars in 1897 and murdered in 1937. Tcharents is one of the most important Armenian authors of modern times, and his work is a lament for a lost homeland, in which Kars stands as a symbol for Armenia as a whole (the "land of Nairi").[45]

In the roughly 2,000-year history of the city of Kars, the period of Russian presence, which lasted a good 40 years, is only a brief episode. And Kars is hardly more than a marginal note in the history of Russia. The Tsarist intermezzo, on the other hand, was of great importance, especially for the Armenians. For them – farmers and craftsmen as well as the new elite of traders and entrepreneurs – the Russian period meant an era of security and opportunities for development that had not existed for a millennium since the time of the Armenian kingdom of the Bagratids. Russian rule made the city less a Russian place than an Armenian one, and the boom that the city and the region experienced during this period was above all an Armenian awakening.

The First World War abruptly ended this development. After the founding of the republic in 1923, the new Turkey turned away from the past for decades. In Kars, the Armenian and Russian heritage were equally rejected. Armenian and Russian churches were partly destroyed, partly converted into mosques. Of the Russian administrative buildings, some continued to be used for administration and housing the gendarmerie, but many Russian buildings also stood empty and decayed into ruins. Even the Russian dairy cows died because the expertise to keep them was lacking after the Molokans left.[46] However, the Ottoman heritage was hardly treated more carefully; it too was left to decay.

To Orhan Pamuk's novel hero Ka, Kars seems deserted, "desolate," "forgotten," and hopeless.[47] But it is not the topos of backwardness that Pamuk invokes here, but that of the end of time and space and the loss that this end signifies. It is not only the snow that closes off the city of Kars, but above all the border. After the Second World War, Kars found itself between the blocs of the Cold War. For decades, the almost hermetically sealed border between the Soviet Republic of Armenia and its NATO partner Turkey ran behind Kars. A wide border strip was a restricted military area. The region became desolate.

In addition to being geographically cut off, the city and region also suffered from a temporal capping. The official Turkish policy of denial, suppression, and reinterpretation, especially of the Armenian Genocide during the First World War, but also of the massacre of the Alevi Kurds of Dersim (today Tunceli) in 1937–1938, robs the former Kurdish-Armenian provinces of their past and thus also of their perspectives for the present and future.

Kars is still struggling with its Armenian past. The Russian heritage, on the other hand, became for a short time at the beginning of the twenty-first century a symbol of hope for political opening, tourism, and economic development. In those years, some local Kars politicians and entrepreneurs also revived the memory of the Russian period as an era in which a spirit of optimism, openness, and cross-border exchange had brought prosperity to their city and region. They called for reflection on a specific regional identity and history, including the four decades of Russian rule. A local newspaper called for the preservation and reconstruction of the Ottoman buildings as well as the Russian houses and solicited volunteers.[48] Local politicians also got involved in the reconstruction. Thus, some architectural monuments were renovated.[49]

The reference to the Russian heritage is also a way of promoting reconciliation with one's own history as well as with the Russian and even more so the Armenian neighbors and thus striving for an opening of the borders and good neighborly relations, but not explicitly mentioning Armenia and the Armenians. This is because the interest in open borders and normalized relations with Armenia at the local level does not resonate at the Turkish national level – on the contrary. Since 1993, Turkey has participated in the blockade of land routes imposed by Azerbaijan on Armenia in the conflict over Nagorno-Karabakh.[50] Turkish politicians, academics, and school textbooks, as well as films, TV series, and other mass media, continue to stir up prejudice and hostility against the Armenians.[51] As existential as a new opening to the East with exchange relations to Armenia is on the local and regional levels, they are not politically communicable in such an atmosphere – especially since part of the current population of Kars is descended from Azeris who were expelled from what is now the Republic of Armenia after 1918.

It is no coincidence that Orhan Pamuk also wrote his Kars novel *Snow* in the same period – the early years of the twenty-first century – when there was a certain intellectual freedom for debates on which political direction to take. In *Snow*, Pamuk condenses the political debate about the character and future direction of his country. This includes, in a very prominent place, the treatment of the Armenian Genocide, from which is also derived the attitude to cultural and linguistic diversity today and, in particular, the treatment of the Kurds. Ultimately, this great social debate also includes the question of the relationship with Russia and how to deal with the long, intertwined Turkish-Russian history, which is nowhere more visible in Turkey than in Kars. There may always be strategic rapprochements between Presidents Erdoğan and Putin. In Turkey's domestic political space, on the other hand, the window for political debates about the diversity of its own historical heritage and its significance for shaping the present has closed again, especially since the failed coup attempt of 2016. The massive curtailment of academic, journalistic, and political freedoms has a direct impact on the city of Kars, for which the prospect of opening the border has once again receded into the distant future.

In contrast to the Turkish city of Kars, where the Russian heritage has its place in the cityscape, in local historical consciousness, and in political thinking, Kars as a Russian place has largely disappeared from Russian consciousness. This reflects not least the selectively limited and overall rather marginal importance of the city and its region for the Tsarist Empire. So insignificant was Kars for the Russian intellectual world and politics that none of the Russian authors who wrote about the Caucasus and Transcaucasia paid any significant attention to the city of Kars in their works. As long as the Tsarist Empire was engaged in the ever-flaring conflict with the Ottoman Empire, Kars was of strategic importance as a military base. In modern times, the fortress has long since lost its defensive significance. It did, however, have value as a bridgehead to Anatolia, and this background probably ultimately explains the Russian annexation of the three provinces of Kars, Ardahan, and Batum after the Russo-Ottoman War in 1878. Kars and its surrounding area served to consolidate Russian rule in the Caucasus and Transcaucasia. However, the conquest of the provinces of Kars, Batum, and Ardahan never had the same urgency for Russian expansionist policy that the Crimea or the Caucasus had. As late as 1856, after the Crimean War, Kars was exchanged for the withdrawal of British and French troops from Crimea, who had fought there as allies of the Ottoman Empire against Russia. Accordingly, argues Candan Badem, who has penned the most important research contributions on the Russian history of Kars, the Tsarist government also failed to colonize Kars and to incorporate it into the Russian Empire in a similarly lasting way as Crimea, or even to hold on to the area with the same unconditional commitment as it did to the Caucasus.[52]

Kars as an Imperial City?

In his introductory chapter to the present volume, Ulrich Hofmeister offers a conceptual framework for the discussion of "imperial cities." Whereas the field of urban history looks at the structure and functions of the city, the field of imperial history focuses on the functioning of empires. Hofmeister proposes bringing together the two aspects of empire and city to contribute from a fresh perspective to both fields of study. Assuming that the structure of empires becomes most manifest in the cities, a closer look at the city as an imperial city would allow a better understanding of empire. Equally, under the assumption that cities in empires are largely shaped by the conditions of empire, the analysis of a city as imperial would broaden our understanding of the characteristics of cities.[53]

Imperial cities would serve as administrative centers, as centers of education and learning, centers of trades and commerce, or sites of imperial representation. An important sign of imperial presence could also be the stationing of soldiers and the erection of barracks. It is astonishing, however, how little attention is paid in research literature to the aspect of the military in regard to imperial cities, despite the fact that quite a number of cities are visibly dominated by the presence of the military, by barracks, or, even more, by impressive citadels and fortresses. One reason for this neglect could be a long-lasting tendency to isolate military matters from general historiography.[54] Another, more important reason could be the specific characteristics of the military element in shaping a city in contrast to other features like imperial administration, culture, and learning or economy. Yet it is worth including the military in the discussions of imperial cities to complete the picture. The example of Kars can contribute to this aspect.

The troubled history of Kars shows the city as important fortress and garrison town over long periods of time. In ancient times, throughout the Middle Ages, and until the eve of modern history, the massive fortress undoubtedly had an important military significance, which it gradually lost in modern times as military techniques and warfare changed and the role of fortifications diminished. However, the fortress overlooking and dominating the city also had significance as a powerful symbol of imperial presence. A strong fortress like the one in Kars, visible from a distance and controlling the surroundings, marked imperial domination of the borderlands even in times when it had mostly lost its military function. In the nineteenth century, when the reign around Kars shifted from the Ottomans to the Romanovs and back, restoring and maintaining the fortress meant setting up an imperial bridgehead in a contested borderland, thus also establishing and symbolizing modern imperial territoriality. For the Ottoman Empire, the symbolic value was enough, which explains the halfhearted refortification of the Kars fortress when the military strategic center of the region shifted to Erzurum, leaving Kars in its wake. For the Russian Empire, however, Kars was the imperial bridgehead to the west, which lead the tsars to leave their mark not only and not primarily in the renovation of the fortress but even more in the architectural, economical, and cultural reshaping of the city.

A strong military presence may well be interpreted as one feature of imperial manifestation in the city. However, I would argue that a fortified imperial bridgehead like Kars differs from other types of imperial cities that are characterized by imperial representation, administration, or function as economic or cultural centers of an empire or one of its regions. The military presence shapes the city, and the permanent presence of a larger number of soldiers in a garrison has its impact on the city's economy as well.[55] But the military stays outside the society of the city; it is not integrated into, connected to, and interwoven with the other segments of the population as all other groups are. Second, while all other functional groups of an imperial city are rooted in or bound to the city and contribute to the city's development and flourishing, the military is not a productive element, and its presence may, in cases of mutiny, even bring upheaval to the city.

In addition, the history of Kars as an imperial bridgehead also demonstrates the special case of imperial cities in the borderlands. At times, they are influenced by their vicinity to the border in terms of transimperial exchange and play a specific role as intermediaries bridging boundaries within these transimperial entanglements. But in contrast to imperial cities in the center, an imperial bridgehead city like Kars is much more often affected by the repeated clashes between the empires, resulting in the devastations of war, in massive violence, and radical changes in the population structure. The more empires became territorialized, the more the imperial bridgehead cities became a special type of imperial city where the shifting empires manifested themselves in a fundamental re-structuring and re-population of the city. The specificities of imperial borderland cities, the role gradually fixed borders and border cities played for the functioning of the empire, and the manifestations of plurality under the conditions of a precarious border existence may well deserve additional research.

Notes

1 Strabo, *Geographika*, book XI, chapter 14, 528; in English translation: *The Geography of Strabo*, trans. Horace Leonard Jones (Cambridge, MA: Harvard University Press, 1928), 323. An earlier version of this chapter will be published in Helena Holzberger, Andreas Renner, and Sören Urbansky, eds., *Russlands Orte in Asien* (forthcoming).
2 Orhan Pamuk, *Snow*, trans. Maureen Freely (New York: Vintage International, 2005), 5.
3 Pamuk, *Snow*, 7–8.
4 Pamuk, *Snow*, 11.
5 Pamuk, *Snow*, 9.
6 Jürgen Gottschlich, "Dafür hassen sie mich," *taz*, June 23, 2005; Thomas Seibert, "Orhan Pamuk soll für Armenien-Äußerungen zahlen," *Tagesspiegel*, October 8, 2009; Michael Thumann, "Meinungsfreiheit nur auf dem Papier," *Zeit Online*, March 31, 2011; Murat İri and H. Esra Arcan, "The Orhan Pamuk Case: How Mainstream Turkish Media Framed His Freedom of Speech," *Sosyal Bilimler Dergisi* 18 (2007): 17–24; Anett Biernath, *Die Meinungs- und Pressefreiheit in der Türkei im Spiegel der EMRK* (Münster: Lit, 2013), 302.
7 Pamuk, *Snow*, 7.
8 Nina Garsoian, "The Byzantine Annexation of the Armenian Kingdoms in the Eleventh Century," in *The Armenian People from Ancient to Modern Times*, Vol. 1, ed. Richard G. Hovannisian (New York: St. Martin's, 1997), 192–97; Robert Bedrosian, "Armenia during the Seljuk and Mongol Periods," in *The Armenian People from Ancient to Modern Times,* Vol. 1, ed. Richard G. Hovannisian (New York: St. Martin's, 1997), 247–48, 263.
9 Bedrosian, "Armenia," 256–63.
10 Bedrosian, "Armenia," 267–69. See also the contemporary account of the Timurid wars by Grigor Khlatetsi Tserents, "Report on the Timurid Wars," in *Colophons of Armenian Manuscripts, 1301–1480: A Source for Middle Eastern*

History, ed. Avedis K. Sanjian (Cambridge, MA: Harvard University Press, 1969), 150–63; Akov A. Manandian, *The Trade and Cities of Armenia in Relation to Ancient World Trade* (Lisbon: Livrania Bertrand, 1965), 173–202.

11 For a good overview from the Ottoman perspective, see Ebru Boyar, "Ottoman Expansion in the East," in *The Cambridge History of Turkey, Vol. 2: The Ottoman Empire as a World Power, 1453–1603*, ed. Suraiya N. Faroqhi and Kate Fleet (Cambridge: Cambridge University Press, 2013), 74–140; for the Iranian perspective, see also H. R. Roemer, "The Safavid Period," in *The Cambridge History of Iran, Vol. 6: The Timurid and Safavid Periods*, ed. Peter Jackson and Laurence Lockhart (Cambridge: Cambridge University Press, 1986), 189–350; Roger Savory, *Iran under the Safavids* (Cambridge: Cambridge University Press, 1980). On the destruction (1555) and rebuilding (1584) of the fortress of Kars in the course of these wars, see Dickran Kouymjian, "Armenia from 1375 to 1604," in *The Armenian People from Ancient to Modern Times*, Vol. 2, ed. Richard G. Hovannisian (New York: St. Martin's, 1997), 18, 24.

12 Kouymjian, "Armenia," 20–24; Arakel Tavrijetsi, *Badmoutiun* (Vagharshabad, 1896), 16–92; Ghevon Alishan, *Sisagan* (Venice, 1893), 414–18.

13 To this day, one of the most cited accounts of the Russian-Ottoman wars of the nineteenth century remains W.E.D. Allen and Paul Muratoff, *Caucasian Battlefields* (Cambridge: Cambridge University Press, 1953).

14 Fahrettin Kırzıoğlu, *Kars Tarihi* (Istanbul: Işıl Matbaası, 1953); Fahrettin Kırzıoğlu, *Edebiyatımızda Kars* (Istanbul: Işıl Matbaası, 1958).

15 Candan Badem, "'Forty Years of Black Days'? The Russian Administration of Kars, Ardahan, and Batum, 1878–1918," in *Russian-Ottoman Borderlands: The Eastern Question Reconsidered*, ed. Lucien J. Frary and Mara Kozelsky (Madison: University of Wisconsin Press, 2014), 222, 228.

16 Ibid, 226, 244–45.

17 Anahide Ter Minassian, "L'Arménie et l'éveil des nationalités (1800–1914)," in *Histoire du peuple arménien*, ed. Gérard Dédéyan (Toulouse: Éd. Privat, 2007), 483–84.

18 Ibid, 484.

19 Aleksandr Sergeevich Pushkin, *A Journey to Arzrum*, trans. Birgitta Ingemanson (Ann Arbor, MI: Ardis, 1974).

20 Ter-Minassian, "L'Arménie," 484.

21 Ashot A. Melkonyan, "The Kars Oblast', 1878–1918," in *Armenian Kars and Ani*, ed. Richard G. Hovannisian (Costa Mesa: Mazda Publishers, 2011), 228.

22 See in more detail Elke Hartmann, "The Central State in the Borderlands: Ottoman Eastern Anatolia in the Late 19th Century," in *Shatterzone of Empires: Coexistence and Violence in the German, Habsburg, Russian, and Ottoman Borderlands*, ed. Omer Bartov and Eric D. Weitz (Bloomington: Indiana University Press, 2013), 172–90.

23 Christopher J. Walker, "Kars in the Russo-Turkish Wars of the Nineteenth Century," in *Armenian Kars and Ani*, ed. Richard G. Hovannisian (Costa Mesa: Mazda Publishers, 2011), 218–19; Ter-Minassian, "L'Arménie," 494–500.

24 Melkonyan, "Kars Oblast'," 232–33.

25 More and more authors now speak of genocide in this context; see, for example, Walter Richmond, *The Circassian Genocide* (New Brunswick: Rutgers University Press, 2013).

26 Paul Dumont, "La période des Tanzîmât (1839–1878)," in *Histoire de l'Empire ottoman*, ed. Robert Mantran (Paris: Fayard, 1989), 488–89; François Georgeon, "Le dernier sursaut (1878–1908)," in *Histoire de l'Empire ottoman*, ed.

Robert Mantran (Paris: Fayard, 1989), 544–46; Elke Hartmann, *Die Reichweite des Staates: Wehrpflicht und moderne Staatlichkeit im Osmanischen Reich 1869–1910* (Paderborn: Schöningh, 2016), 302–9.

27 Melkonyan, "Kars Oblast'," 229.

28 Candan Badem, *Çarlık Rusyası Yönetiminde Kars Vilayeti* (Istanbul: Birzamanlar Yayıncılık, 2010), 45–126; cf. Melkonyan, "Kars Oblast'," 232.

29 Badem, *Kars Vilayeti*, 304–61 provides detailed demographic listings for the years 1886–1906 in the appendix of his profound study; the Russian census of 1897 for Kars is also available online: Pervaya vseobshchaya perepis' naseleniya Rossiyskoy Imperii 1897 g., *Demoskop weekly*, No. 963–964, November 1–21, 2022, accessed November 21, 2022, http://demoscope.ru/weekly/ssp/emp_lan_97_uezd.php?reg=403.

30 Georg Kobro, *Das Gebiet von Kars und Ardahan: Historisch-landeskundliche Studie zu einer Grenzregion in Ostanatolien/Transkaukasien* (München: Neimanis, 1989), 110–11.

31 Ibid, 111, 113.

32 Peter Alford Andrews, ed., *Ethnic Groups in the Republic of Turkey* (Wiesbaden: Reichert, 2002).

33 Walker, "Kars," 220.

34 Eugen Wirth, "Die orientalische Stadt: Ein Überblick aufgrund jüngerer Forschungen zur materiellen Kultur," *Saeculum* 26 (1975).

35 Zeynep Celik, *The Remaking of Istanbul: Portrait of an Ottoman City in the Nineteenth Century* (Seattle: University of Washington Press, 1986).

36 Badem, *Kars Vilayeti*, 302–3; Rohat Alakom, *Kars Kürtleri* (Istanbul: Avesta, 2009), 156–57.

37 Candan Badem, "Rus Yönetiminde Kars ve Kars'ta Peynir Üretimi (1878–1918)," in *Alplerden Kafkaslara: Kars Peynirciliğinin 150 yıllık Tarihi* (Istanbul: Boğatepe Çevre ve Yaşam Derneği, 2014, exhibition catalogue).

38 Ibid, 57.

39 Badem, *Kars Vilayeti*, chapter 3 and the tabular overview on 48–49; Melkonyan, "Kars Oblast'," 226–33.

40 Kobro, *Gebiet*, 81–83.

41 Ibid, 83–84.

42 Sonya Mirzoyan and Candan Badem, *The Construction of the Tiflis-Alexandropol-Kars Railway (1895–1899)* (The Hague: IHJR, 2013); Badem, *Kars Vilayeti*, 169–95; Kobro, *Gebiet*, 85–86, 90–91.

43 Kobro, *Gebiet*, 86–90.

44 Onur Önol, *The Tsar's Armenians: A Minority in Late Imperial Russia* (London: I.B. Tauris, 2017), 17–26; Melkonyan, "Kars Oblast'," 234–35.

45 Vartan Matiossian, "Charents: Mourning the Loss of Kars," in *Armenian Kars and Ani,* ed. Richard G. Hovannisian (Costa Mesa: Mazda, 2011); Marc Nichanian, *Writers of Disaster: The National Revolution* (Princeton, NJ: Gomidas Institute, 2002), 44–51.

46 İlber Ortaylı, "Çarlık Rusyası Yönetiminde Kars," *Tarih Enstitüsü Dergisi* 9 (1978), 410.

47 Pamuk, *Snow*, 7, 9, 10.

48 Kars Haber, May 25, 2012. http://www.karsmanset.com/print.php?type=1&id=12457 (Accessed July 24, 2017); Kars Haber, August 2, 2015. http://www.karsmanset.com/haber/gamp-konagi-yardim-eli-bekliyor-28904.htm (Accessed July 24, 2017).

49 Kars Haber, September 29, 2015. http://www.radikal.com.tr/kars-haber/gazi-ahmet-muhtar-pasa-konagi-restore-ediliyor-1442187/ (Accessed July 24, 2017).
50 See, for example, Gayane Novikova, "Blockade à trois: Das Beziehungsdreieck Armenien-Aserbaidschan-Türkei," *Osteuropa* 65, no. 7–10 (2015): 427–41; Petra Morsbach, "Das türkische Sibirien," *Spiegel Spezial* 6 (2008).
51 See, for example, the history school textbook for the tenth grades: Vicdan Turan et al., *Tarih 10* ([Ankara], 2014), 187–89, 210–17.
52 Badem, "Forty Years," 245–46.
53 See chapter one of this volume.
54 Thomas Kühne and Benjamin Ziemann, eds., *Was ist Militärgeschichte?* (Paderborn: Ferdinand Schöningh, 2000); Jutta Nowosadtko, *Krieg, Gewalt und Ordnung: Einführung in die Militärgeschichte* (Tübingen: edition diskord, 2002).
55 One example of such interaction and economic entanglement is demonstrated by Yaşar Tolga Cora, "Why Was Pastırmacı Khatchatur Efendi Killed? The Life of an Ottoman-Armenian Elite in Mid-19th-Century Erzurum/Karin," in *Ottoman Armenians: Life, Culture, Society*, ed. Vahe Tachjian (Berlin: Houshamadyan, 2014), 65–87.

Bibliography

Alakom, Rohat. *Kars Kürtleri*. Istanbul: Avesta, 2009.

Alishan, Ghevond. *Sisagan*. Venice, 1893.

Allen, W.E.D., and Paul Muratoff. *Caucasian Battlefields*. Cambridge: Cambridge University Press, 1953.

Andrews, Peter Alford, ed. *Ethnic Groups in the Republic of Turkey*. Wiesbaden: Reichert, 2002.

Badem, Candan. *Çarlık Rusyası Yönetiminde Kars Vilayeti*. Istanbul: Birzamanlar Yayıncılık, 2010.

Badem, Candan. "'Forty Years of Black Days'? The Russian Administration of Kars, Ardahan, and Batum, 1878–1918." In *Russian-Ottoman Borderlands: The Eastern Question Reconsidered*, edited by Lucien J. Frary and Mara Kozelsky, 221–50. Madison: University of Wisconsin Press, 2014.

Badem, Candan. "Rus Yönetiminde Kars ve Kars'ta Peynir Üretimi (1878–1918)." In *Alplerden Kafkaslara: Kars Peynirciliğinin 150 yıllık Tarihi*, 44–71. Istanbul: Boğatepe Çevre ve Yaşam Derneği, 2014 (exhibition catalogue).

Bedrosian, Robert. "Armenia during the Seljuk and Mongol Periods." In *The Armenian People from Ancient to Modern Times*, Vol. 1, edited by Richard G. Hovannisian, 241–71. New York: St. Martin's Press, 1997.

Biernath, Annett. *Die Meinungs- und Pressefreiheit in der Türkei im Spiegel der EMRK*. Münster: Lit, 2013.

Boyar, Ebru. "Ottoman Expansion in the East." In *The Cambridge History of Turkey, Vol. 2: The Ottoman Empire as a World Power, 1453–1603*, edited by Suraiya N. Faroqhi and Kate Fleet, 74–140. Cambridge: Cambridge University Press, 2013.

Celik, Zeynep. *The Remaking of Istanbul: Portrait of an Ottoman City in the Nineteenth Century*. Seattle: University of Washington Press, 1986.

Cora, Yaşar Tolga. "Why Was Pastırmacı Khatchatur Efendi Killed? The Life of an Ottoman-Armenian Elite in Mid-19th-Century Erzurum/Karin." In *Ottoman*

Armenians: Life, Culture, Society, edited by Vahe Tachjian, 65–87. Berlin: Houshamadyan, 2014.

Dumont, Paul. "La période des Tanzîmât (1839–1878)." In *Histoire de l'Empire ottoman,* edited by Robert Mantran, 459–522. Paris: Fayard, 1989.

Garsoian, Nina. "The Byzantine Annexation of the Armenian Kingdoms in the Eleventh Century." In *The Armenian People from Ancient to Modern Times,* Vol. 1, edited by Richard G. Hovannisian, 187–98. New York: St. Martin's Press, 1997.

Georgeon, François. "Le dernier sursaut (1878–1908)." In *Histoire de l'Empire ottoman,* edited by Robert Mantran, 523–76. Paris: Fayard, 1989.

Gottschlich, Jürgen. "Dafür hassen sie mich." *taz,* June 23, 2005.

Hartmann, Elke. *Die Reichweite des Staates: Wehrpflicht und moderne Staatlichkeit im Osmanischen Reich 1869–1910.* Paderborn: Schöningh, 2016.

Hartmann, Elke. "The Central State in the Borderlands: Ottoman Eastern Anatolia in the Late 19th Century." In *Shatterzone of Empires: Coexistence and Violence in the German, Habsburg, Russian, and Ottoman Borderlands,* edited by Omer Bartov and Eric D. Weitz, 172–90. Bloomington: Indiana University Press, 2013.

İri, Murat, and H. Esra Arcan. "The Orhan Pamuk Case: How Mainstream Turkish Media Framed His Freedom of Speech." *Sosyal Bilimler Dergisi* 18 (2007): 17–24.

Kars Haber. May 25, 2012. Accessed July 24, 2017. http://www.karsmanset.com/print.php?type=1&id=12457.

Kars Haber. August 2, 2015. Accessed July 24, 2017. http://www.karsmanset.com/haber/gamp-konagi-yardim-eli-bekliyor-28904.htm.

Kars Haber. September 29, 2015. Accessed July 24, 2017. http://www.radikal.com.tr/kars-haber/gazi-ahmet-muhtar-pasa-konagi-restore-ediliyor-1442187/.

Khlatetsi Tserents, Grigor. "Report on the Timurid Wars." In *Colophons of Armenian Manuscripts, 1301–1480: A Source for Middle Eastern History,* edited by Avedis K. Sanjian, 150–63. Cambridge, MA: Harvard University Press, 1969.

Kırzıoğlu, Fahrettin. *Kars Tarihi.* Istanbul: Işıl Matbaası, 1953.

Kırzıoğlu, Fahrettin. *Edebiyatımızda Kars.* Istanbul: Işıl Matbaası, 1958.

Kobro, Georg. *Das Gebiet von Kars und Ardahan: Historisch-landeskundliche Studie zu einer Grenzregion in Ostanatolien/Transkaukasien.* München: Neimanis, 1989.

Kouymjian, Dickran. "Armenia from 1375 to 1604." In *The Armenian People from Ancient to Modern Times,* Vol. 2, edited by Richard G. Hovannisian, 1–50. New York: St. Martin's Press, 1997.

Kühne, Thomas, and Benjamin Ziemann, eds. *Was ist Militärgeschichte?* Paderborn: Ferdinand Schöningh, 2000.

Manandian, Akov A. *The Trade and Cities of Armenia in Relation to Ancient World Trade.* Lisbon: Livrania Bertrand, 1965.

Matiossian, Vartan. "Charents: Mourning the Loss of Kars." In *Armenian Kars and Ani,* edited by Richard G. Hovannisian, 319–48. Costa Mesa: Mazda Publishers, 2011.

Melkonyan, Ashot A. "The Kars Oblast', 1878–1918." In *Armenian Kars and Ani,* edited by Richard G. Hovannisian, 223–44. Costa Mesa: Mazda Publishers, 2011.

Mirzoyan, Sonya, and Candan Badem. *The Construction of the Tiflis-Alexandropol-Kars Railway (1895–1899)*. The Hague: IHJR, 2013.

Morsbach, Petra. "Das türkische Sibirien." *Spiegel Spezial* 6 (2008): 71–73.

Nichanian, Marc. *Writers of Disaster: The National Revolution*. Princeton, NJ: Gomidas Institute, 2002.

Novikova, Gayane. "Blockade à trois: Das Beziehungsdreieck Armenien-Aserbaidschan-Türkei." *Osteuropa* 65, no. 7–10 (2015): 427–41.

Nowosadtko, Jutta. *Krieg, Gewalt und Ordnung: Einführung in die Militärgeschichte*. Tübingen: edition diskord, 2002.

Önol, Onur. *The Tsar's Armenians. A Minority in Late Imperial Russia*. London: I.B. Tauris, 2017.

Ortaylı, İlber. "Çarlık Rusyası Yönetiminde Kars." *Tarih Enstitüsü Dergisi* 9 (1978): 343–62.

Pamuk, Orhan. *Snow*. Translated by Maureen Freely. New York: Vintage International, 2005.

Pervaya vseobshchaya perepis' naseleniya Rossiyskoy Imperii 1897 g., *Demoskop weekly*, nos. 963–964, November 1–21, 2022. Accessed November 21, 2022. http://demoscope.ru/weekly/ssp/emp_lan_97_uezd.php?reg=403.

Pushkin, Aleksandr S. *A Journey to Arzrum*. Translated by Birgitta Ingemanson. Ann Arbor, MI: Ardis, 1974.

Richmond, Walter. *The Circassian Genocide*. New Brunswick: Rutgers University Press, 2013.

Roemer, H. R. "The Safavid Period." In *The Cambridge History of Iran, Vol. 6: The Timurid and Safavid Periods*, edited by Peter Jackson and Laurence Lockhart, 189–350. Cambridge: Cambridge University Press, 1986.

Savory, Roger. *Iran under the Safavids*. Cambridge: Cambridge University Press, 1980.

Seibert, Thomas. "Orhan Pamuk soll für Armenien-Äußerungen zahlen." *Tagesspiegel*, October 8, 2009.

Strabo. *Geographika [The Geography of Strabo]*. Translated by Horace Leonard Jones. Cambridge, MA: Harvard University Press, 1928.

Tavrijetsi, Arakel. *Badmoutiun*. Vagharshabad, 1896.

Ter Minassian, Anahide. "L'Arménie et l'éveil des nationalités (1800–1914)." In *Histoire du peuple arménien*, edited by Gérard Dédéyan, 475–521. Toulouse: Éd. Privat, 2007.

Thumann, Michael. "Meinungsfreiheit nur auf dem Papier." *Zeit online*, March 31, 2011.

Turan, Vicdan et al. *Tarih 10*. Ankara, 2014.

Walker, Christopher J. "Kars in the Russo-Turkish Wars of the Nineteenth Century." In *Armenian Kars and Ani*, edited by Richard G. Hovannisian, 207–22. Costa Mesa: Mazda, 2011.

Wirth, Eugen. "Die orientalische Stadt: Ein Überblick aufgrund jüngerer Forschungen zur materiellen Kultur." *Saeculum* 26 (1975): 45–94.

11 (De)constructing Imperial Heritage

Moscow Zaryadye in Times of Transition

Olga Zabalueva

Even though Moscow lost its status as Russia's capital in 1712 to St. Petersburg and regained it only in 1918, this city combines an abundance of imperial trajectories in its cityscape. From the grand historical projects of the nineteenth century aiming to legitimize the connection with the pre-Petrine Russian state to Stalin's plan of urban reconstruction, Moscow's city center can be conceived as a *palimpsest* containing different ages and (hi)stories. What I propose in this chapter is a kind of imaginary archaeology, where I suggest carefully unfolding the layers of time and political narratives in one specific locality of the city's historical center to investigate what kind of ways of producing meanings and agendas are contained there and how the empire(s) manifest(s) itself/themselves through them.[1]

This chapter aims to analyze discourses that emerged in a certain urban area of Moscow in times of transition when the imperial heritage was becoming of special interest in the state's cultural and national policies. Moscow as an imperial city is a complex example due to its role as a capital, a colonial metropolitan city of the continental empire, a place of national history formation and inscription into the urban heritage and its performances. One example of such (attempts at) inscriptions is the neighborhood that this chapter focuses on.

The *Zaryadye* neighborhood is located near the Kremlin in the ancient quarter of *Kitai-gorod* – a trading district that was surrounded by fortifications from the mid-sixteenth century.[2] I will start my narration from the end, from the *status quo* of the locality, the park "Zaryadye" (opened in 2017), which was coined by its creators as a "park of the present future."[3] However, as cultural geographer Doreen Massey points out, places are always already hybrid,[4] containing both spatial and temporal dimensions, and it is impossible to talk about a "present future" without looking at the "past," which is "present in places in a variety of ways."[5] The second milestone bearing the mark of imperial discourses that I plan to analyze is the Soviet period and the never implemented plan of constructing a highrise building in the area. The third layer of imperial representations in

DOI: 10.4324/9781003130031-14

this chapter belongs to the Russian Empire and the "invented tradition"[6] of the old Muscovite Tsardom as the source of the sovereign's power – namely, the historical reconstruction of the Chambers of the Romanov Boyars, the alleged birthplace of the first tsar of the Romanov dynasty. I am not moving any deeper into the multi-layered history of the place as this chapter focuses on the empire(s) – the Russian Empire, the Soviet Union, and an aspiring successor of both, Putin's Russia – that tried to employ this place (and its history) in their narratives. Richard Wortman identifies a "European myth" and a "National myth" as the two opposing narrative templates of the Russian Empire in the eighteenth and nineteenth centuries, and Moscow and its heritage have an important place in the "National myth."[7]

In this chapter, I am taking on three steps or stages of the imperial discourses performed in Zaryadye in reverse – contemporary, Soviet, and Tsarist – following my explorative metaphorical archeology of place, but in the section about each of the stages I will narrate the story chronologically for the sake of coherence. There is a substantial body of research on each of the Zaryadye projects, especially in Russian, and an equally considerable number of popular publications on the history of the place. However, not much is being written on the continuity of all three stages that I am investigating in this chapter, and especially on how the empire(s) tried to employ this area as a space of representation.

As I argue in the conclusion, despite being a site for the performance of imperial heritage in various ways, the subject place – the Zaryadye district – remained somewhat resilient to the imported changes. The attempts to turn it into a public space (or rather into a "non-place" in Marc Augé's sense,[8] a non-inhabited spatiality where human beings remain anonymous and transient passers-by, as in parks, shopping malls, or the fairs) eventually ended in demolition and new construction. These demolitions and (re)constructions eroded the initial relationality of the place, making space for new representations and performances.

What I suggest here is that since the nineteenth century, Zaryadye has been an immanent site of the construction of national identity with an ingrained imperial discourse – and often quite literally a construction site, as the park's webpage puts it: "Zaryadye had remained a featureless wasteland, fenced off like a construction-site."[9] What is so remarkable about this specific locality that it has attracted the attention of the state at times when visual representations of imperial ideologies were needed?

The historical district of Zaryadye in Moscow is located on the left bank of the Moskva River at the eastern side of the Kremlin, in close proximity to Red Square and St. Basil's Cathedral. The name of the district means that the place was situated *za ryadami* – "behind the rows" – that is, the trade rows in front of Red Square. In the sixteenth and seventeenth centuries, this district housed the residences of boyars (noblemen) and foreign embassies alongside the mint court, craftsmen, and court servants. The latter, however, gradually moved to the new capital St. Petersburg in the eighteenth century. New earthwork fortifications added to the ancient Kitai-gorod wall in 1708–1709 cut off the Zaryadye district from the water supply of the Neglinka River, so that for a long time it became a dormant (and, due to drainage problems, even unhealthy and unsafe) small town in the heart of Moscow. In a way, the district was a "periphery of the center," functioning as a residential and trade area until the mid-twentieth century. One of the "borders" of the district, Varvarka Street, features a unique array of architectural monuments from the sixteenth to the eighteenth century, both religious and secular buildings, which partly survived through consecutive renovations and reconstructions of the architectural landscape. Most of them were "reopened" as monuments in the 1960s when the neighborhood lost its residential status. Now they are included in the landscape of Zaryadye Park.

Park "Zaryadye" and the Identity of the (New) New Moscow

Zaryadye Park was opened on September 9, 2017, and inaugurated by Russian President Vladimir Putin. The park had been designed by the New York-based Diller Scofidio + Renfro studio, one of the world's leading design studios which is famous for the High Line Park in Manhattan, New York, among other projects. They had won an international competition of urban designers for the Zaryadye area with their proposal to turn it into a "park, urban plaza, social space, cultural amenity, and recreational armature"[10] all at once. Zaryadye Park now includes artificial "natural" landscapes that recreate different natural zones found in Russia, including steppe, forest, and wetlands, which – according to the park designers – are "overlaid on top of constructed environments, creating a series of elemental face-offs between the natural and the artificial, urban and rural, interior and exterior."[11] This open green public space in the center of Moscow, filled with a combination of recreational and entertainment venues, signified the ambition of the Russian capital to be a modern city that adapts its public spaces to its citizens and supports a green, healthy, and innovative way of life. The organization of the park's attractions suggests leisure and cultural activities: there are several viewpoints such as the "soaring bridge" that looks out on Moskva River and the Kremlin, interactive media complexes, the underground museum, the food court, the Ice Cave, several botanical installations (such as a florarium with a collection of rare exotic plants), and the Concert Hall. The park won the 2018 Building of the Year award in *Public Architecture* and is promoted as one of the central tourist attractions in the city.

From July to August 2018, the exhibition *Portal Zaryadye,* curated by Michał Murawski and Daria Kravchuk, opened at the Shchusev State Architecture Museum, Moscow. As the exhibition booklet states, "Zaryadye Park is a flagship of the current Mayoralty's ongoing campaign to erase troublesome legacies of the Soviet era and the era of 'wild capitalist' reign [...] from its urban fabric. This campaign, it has been proposed, constitutes nothing less than the most grandiose attempt to engineer the aesthetics and substance of the Russian capital – and its citizens – since the Stalinist General Plan of 1935."[12] Zaryadye Park was planned and performed as the core for the "New Moscow"[13] (which also resembles the name of the Soviet plans of renovation) centripetal discourse, programmed by the consulting company Strelka KB.[14] One of the main "ideologists" of Strelka, Grigory Revzin, the author of the research initiative "How to Build a New Moscow" put it as follows: "We are the General Staff of colonial armed forces that aim to conquer Russia."[15] He also emphasized a "Western democratic" influence behind the urban development of Moscow in the late 2010s.[16] Along with the international nature of the Zaryadye design competition, this assertion of borrowing and adapting "foreign" values of people-centered urban design[17] showcases the ambition of the new "New Moscow" to redefine its imaginary, renounce the past, and focus on the "present future." In 2018, *Time* magazine included Zaryadye Park in the list of the 100 best places in the world – the only object from Russia – which might indicate the success of this strategy, alongside the rising numbers of domestic and international visitors to the park.

The idea of the "internal coloniality"[18] of such a project, alongside the "devices of identification with foreign sources of power,"[19] shifts Zaryadye Park from a national to an imperial narrative, merging together the "European myth" (which in the twenty-first century can be coined as a "Global North" or "Western" myth instead) and the "National myth" and placing the Russian capital in the global power discourses as a "civilized" and international city. The district's heritage and history are claimed (as it was in previous periods as we shall see further) to be outdated and underdeveloped – thus only fragments of them are included in the park structure, as the contemporary "Western myth" includes the focus on historical landscapes and heritage preservation in the old city centers. On the other hand, the elements that might be perceived as contested in a capital (imperial) city of the Global North (such as, for example, the vegetation of the Crimean Peninsula) are not included.[20]

The park aims to be a modern and innovative urban landscape in the city center – but what becomes of it eventually, as the Zaryadye district itself seems to deconstruct any ambitious narrative implanted into it? Viktoriia Kudriavtseva from the design institute Strelka, who studied Zaryadye's urban potential in 2011, had framed it as an "emptiness that haunts this place."[21] From the first days of public access, Zaryadye Park was criticized in the press and social media for, among other things, the insufficient vegetation that was trampled down or even torn out and stolen by visitors – Michał Murawski called the public on this occasion "ungrateful gift recipients."[22] The other form of the ambiguity in this "open public space" was the presence of security controls at the entrances to the park after the inauguration (which was later lifted). The construction work never left the place either: it was partly fenced off in April 2018 when the *Imperial Cities* conference took place in Moscow, as, for instance, the Concert Hall was still under construction – it was opened a year later than the park itself. Later, due to constant construction and reconstruction work in the center of Moscow, the crane towers and scaffolding still haunted the area's vistas, and at the time of writing, there is still a construction site for the "multifunctional hotel complex" *Zaryadye Gardens* in the park itself behind the Concert Hall. The exhibition *Portal Zaryadye* from 2018 addressed among, other things, the construction worker's daily life in the documentary film *On the Other Side of the Wall* by Egor Isaev.[23] Ethnographic material from the "slum-like workers' settlement opposite the main entrance to Zaryadye Park" was also mentioned in Murawski's article *Zaryadyology*, where the immigrant workers' meals were described in contrast to the "multinational traditional meals" served in the park's cafés.[24]

Margarita Chubukova suggests the term "landscape nationalism,"[25] following Russian anthropologist Sergey Shtyrkov who wrote on "patriotic landscapes." The vegetation and climate zones chosen for the park reflect the natural heritage of the country in a generalized sense (starting with such a well-known symbol of Russia as the birch trees that now frame the view to St. Basil's Cathedral and Red Square from the park's side) (Figure 11.1).

The initial invitation for the design competition contained such conditions as

> amplifying the identity of the territory considering its importance for the city and the country. [...] As the main park of Moscow and Russia, it is supposed to become a world-class public space with local specifics. [...] The Park project must contain branding elements and identify with Russia without direct indications.[26]

At the very stage of the inception of the project, it was supposed to signify Russian (and Moscow's) identity via different means, being, therefore, a "national" project. What is interesting here is the reference to the "identity of territory," considering that, unlike the neighboring monumental complexes of the Kremlin and Red Square, the Zaryadye territory, as I argue in this chapter, didn't have any specific "identity" apart from that of a liminal

Figure 11.1 The view of Kremlin and St. Basil's Cathedral from Zaryadye Park. Photo by Galina El'tsova, 2020.

space of transition. It can refer, however, to the sacred role of the Kremlin as the political center of power.[27] The "imperial" self-representation, though, seeps through this "National myth" with the landscapes as the echoes of imperial expansion, with the notion of "colonizing" the space, and with international ideas of what is regarded to be of value for the global citizen today – closeness to nature in the heart of the metropolis, sustainability, ecology, and edutainment. The park itself signals how city authorities want to see Moscow's citizens engage in leisure: strolling through the "wilderness," which is carefully organized for them; this kind of flânerie resembles strolls performed at open-air museums or ethnographical exhibitions of the great empires at the turn of the twentieth century.

Zaryadye Park was clearly a top-down, authoritarian initiative (like any other state construction initiative at the place in the past, as we shall see); however, it implies public engagement and appreciation as all the visual attractions need visitors. Zaryadye Park also bears all the taxonomical features of a *fair* – with its *vistas* and spaces designed specifically for taking pictures (for example, the "soaring bridge" that is not connected to the other bank of the Moskva River), artificial collections of vegetation that represent the "whole Russia," and multimedia attractions, such as

the "Time Machine" where the history of the Zaryadye district is sub-
stituted by a more generic historical timeline of Moscow and Russia.[28]
Murawski mentions another *fair* structure – the VDNKh (Exhibition of
Achievements of National Economy) exhibition park in the northern part
of Moscow, which was constructed in the 1930s and served as the "center
and ideal symbolic performance of the Soviet cosmos"[29] and which was
also organized to represent all the nationalities of the Soviet Union and
their "achievements" alongside Soviet industries in modernist pavilions. In
Zaryadye, the nationalities are reduced to the exotic cuisines in the food
court, and the main focus is laid on the natural diversity of the Russian
landscape – the aesthetic of "Eco Nationalism" and "urban wilderness"[30]
and, at the same time, the formation of a new urban identity with an emphasis on pedestrians, safety, ecology, and high tech.[31] The park becomes a
popular tourist spot, a possibility to "pack" the unpackable geographical
wideness into one concentrated experience, and a part of the international
presentation of the capital of the Russian Federation as a visible political
power of the global contemporary.[32]

The Soviet Period: Grand Projects of the Red Capital

What was happening in Zaryadye before? A waste – and the most
expensive – land in the center of Moscow stayed barren for several years
until it was decided to turn it into an urban park. Behind the row of historical buildings on Varvarka Street, a huge deconstruction site was slowly
decaying, debris left after the demolition of what was once the largest hotel
in Europe, the *Rossiia* hotel, built in the 1960s, closed in 2006, and demolished between 2006 and 2010.

The Soviet period in Zaryadye, however, was not primarily about the
hotel. Grand projects that were supposed to celebrate the modern socialist
"empire" were developing and disappearing in the area, cross-pollinating
one another. Since Moscow became the capital again in 1918, the city was
perceived as a "showcase" of the young Soviet state (and, consequently,
the Communist International), and it was to be transformed into a "model
capital of the model socialist state."[33] Plans for urban reconstruction had
been developed since the 1920s with titles such as "New Moscow" (1918–
1923) or "Greater Moscow" (1921–1925). All these plans included recreational ecological zones incorporated into the city as "green wedges"
coming from the periphery to the center, following the idea of the socialist
"Garden-City"[34]; however, none of them considered the Zaryadye district
as a possible place for a park. In a closed (non-public) international competition for the reconstruction and development of Moscow in 1932, most
of the projects gave Zaryadye political, administrative, economic, and
cultural functions.[35] The General Plan for the reconstruction of Moscow

(which was also sometimes called the "New Moscow" plan),[36] discussed since 1931 and published in 1935, adopted some of these ideas; however, its main focus was on the radical modernization of the city's infrastructure.[37] Moscow's rapid urbanization and rising population rate demanded modern drainage and water supply systems, new means of transportations, the broadening and re-planning of the main roads and squares, and construction of new residential quarters. At the same time, the socialist city's architectural façade was being formed through several symbolic projects, the most ambitious of which was the Palace of Soviets, planned to be constructed on the western side of Kremlin, at the site of the Cathedral of Christ the Savior, which was built from 1837 to 1860 and demolished in 1931. A lot has been written on the political symbolism of these two buildings: the largest cathedral in Moscow – "the personification of tsarist authority" and for many a sacred space – was to be replaced by the temple of the revolution. Being among the most significant "imperial marks" in Moscow's cityscape (especially since the reconstruction of the Christ the Savior Cathedral in 1994–1999), they attract much more academic interest than Zaryadye, partly due to the scale of the international competition for the Palace of Soviets project with participation of leading avant-garde architects of the time (including Le Corbusier, Walter Gropius, and the Vesnin brothers) and partly because of the prominence of these projects for the development of Stalinist architecture.[38] Located on the opposite side of the Kremlin on the same bank of Moskva River as Zaryadye, but higher up on the hill, the Cathedral's site attracted the attention of architects, researchers, and the general public – the bright and big church building signified the tsarist epoch that was demolished in the framework of Soviet anti-clerical policies. Zaryadye, on the contrary, entered the Soviet period as a quiet residential neighborhood where the churches and significant buildings from the period of the Russian Empire were rebuilt, repurposed, and hidden from the view.

A part of the Zaryadye housing district, which by that time had already become slums right outside the Kremlin, was demolished in the 1930s when the Bolshoi Moskvoretskii Bridge was built (1936–1938) and Zaryadye was supposed to be used as a construction site for the NKTP (People's Commissariat [Ministry] of Heavy Industry) building.

The NKTP building was designed to frame the expansion of Red Square and to emphasize the view of St. Basil Cathedral as part of the unique architectural heritage of the capital.[39] The construction of the NKTP building in close proximity to the Kremlin was supposed to signify the importance of heavy industry in the process of Soviet modernization.[40] The first project competition in 1934 did not include Zaryadye specifically as a possible site of the building's construction, but most of the competing architects suggested their own ideas for the area's urban development in connection with the new building and in one way or another expanded the NKTP complex to Zaryadye. The General Plan for the reconstruction of Moscow of 1935 called for the total demolition of the Zaryadye district and suggested placing several People's Commissariats (ministries) there. The second competition for the NKTP building (1936) specifically moved the future construction site there. However, the colossal project (the NKTP building would be matched only by the Palace of Soviets) was never realized, partly because of the decline and dissolution of the People's Commissariat of Heavy Industry at the end of the 1930s. Zaryadye was, nevertheless, still a desirable spot for symbolic architecture: in 1940 a new competition, this time for the "Second Building for the Council of People's Commissars," was announced. As Tkachenko points out, by this time Soviet architects were increasingly interested in the high-rise buildings in North America, as they were considered the most progressive architectural style and, at the same time, they allowed a monumental approach to urban development.[41] The project that won the 1940 competition implied demolishing the whole Zaryadye district and moving some of its architectural monuments (including the sixteenth-century church of St. Anna, the "Romanov Chambers," and parts of the Kitai-gorod fortifications) into an open-air museum in the south of Moscow. The construction work had barely started and was halted in 1941 with the German invasion of the Soviet Union (construction work on the Palace of Soviets was stopped at the same time), with only one-third of the foundation laid down. Parts of the residential area, however, still existed near the giant construction site. In 2008, Pavel Kupriianov and Ludmila Sadovnikova did an ethnographic study of the memories and perception of space of Zaryadye's inhabitants from 1930 until the 1960s, and some of their informants remembered playing among the abandoned foundations and in the construction pit, which naturally turned into a pond, as children.[42]

The post-war period was characterized by a renewed interest in high-rise buildings. The most ambitious undertaking was "Stalin's favorite project"[43]: eight skyscrapers that were designed to represent the skyline of the victorious socialist capital. The designs for these new high-rise buildings bear much resemblance to the Palace of Soviets, which was, however, not part of them. The Palace of Soviets had not been officially dismissed, but the scale of the project was constantly reduced until 1956, and construction work never resumed.[44] Building activity now concentrated on the new project of eight skyscrapers in central Moscow that were intended to glorify the Soviet capital vis-à-vis its Western allies. One of them was planned in Zaryadye, at the site where the high-rise building's foundations had already been laid, and it was – again – supposed to be the highest one of all. The Palace of Soviets was never built, and neither was the Zaryadye high-rise building – the so-called Eighth Sister. The other Seven Sisters, or

"Stalin's skyscrapers," were built in Moscow between 1947 and 1953[45] in what would later be called "Stalinist style" (or even "Stalin's empire style" in Russian) – a combination of gothic and neo-classic architecture. These skyscrapers were supposed to emphasize the new architectural landscape of the capital with vertical accents. This type of architecture was condemned as "excessive" after Stalin's death, but in the post-war period, it played an important role both in the reconstruction of the city centers of destroyed republican capitals (such as Minsk and Kyiv) and in planting "imperial marks" in the Soviet satellite states in Eastern Europe, such as the Palace of Culture and Science in Warsaw, the House of the Free Press in Bucharest, the *International* hotel in Prague, and the Academy of Sciences building in Riga.

The foundations for Moscow's eight high-rise buildings were laid simultaneously on September 12, 1947, the day when the 800th anniversary of Moscow was celebrated.[46] Hence, even though attempts to appropriate Zaryadye's space by a new imperial discourse had been made since the 1930s, it was the anniversary of the ancient Russian capital that culminated these attempts and opened space for reclaiming it by a new architectural narrative (Figure 11.2).

Zaryadye's high-rise administrative building was conceived as the most important one among the Sisters due – again – to its proximity to the

Figure 11.2 A view of Zaryadye Park, the "soaring bridge," and the Kotel'nicheskaia Embankment high-rise building. Photo by Olga Kuznetsova, 2021.

Kremlin. This new project was supposed to become a part of a governmental administrative complex that would complement the urban landscape that, as Soviet architect Iakov Kornfel'd wrote in 1953,

> embodies in the Kremlin towers, the Belfry of Ivan the Great, and St. Basil's Cathedral the might and glory of the Russian people and commemorates its victories. It [the Zaryadye administrative building] will rise adjacent to them as a symbol of a new socialist state [...]. Together with the Palace of Soviets and the other high-rise buildings, which are being constructed along the Moskva river banks, the administrative building will define a new panorama of Moscow, which will reflect the magnificence of the socialist epoch.[47]

For the construction of this complex, the remains of the Zaryadye residential area were torn down, and a new space, a "clean slate" for the possible Eighth Sister, emerged (the final demolition of the Zaryadye residential district happened in the 1950s–1960s in the course of the construction of the Rossiia Hotel).

Simultaneously, the Soviet modernization of the city, which is often associated with the blind demolition of cultural heritage,[48] brought "to the surface" some ancient buildings hidden within the cityscape, or even within other buildings, such as the Old English Embassy from the 1550s, which was discovered and restored by the architect Petr Baranovskii in the late 1960s. Just as Le Corbusier's *Plan Voisin* was supposed to save both the future and the past of Paris from the "dangerous forces of modernity,"[49] the Soviet grand projects were also continuing the heritage narrative in "cleansing the monuments of all accretions."[50] The existing cityscape was perceived as "an architectural natural environment"[51] where a new skyscraper was to be inserted to preserve and highlight the ancient buildings (made visible by tearing down the slum-like old houses) and, at the same time, to dominate them. As the ancient buildings had been hidden in later constructions or deprived of their specific functions, such as churches that had been turned into warehouses, offices, and residential units, some of Kupriianov and Sadovnikova's informants insisted in 2008 that the ancient buildings and churches that they could see at the time of the study were reconstructed from scratch as they could not remember these buildings in the residential space.[52]

The high-rise building project, however, was cancelled after the construction of its ground level in 1953 – it became the only Sister that was never built, as progress was slower than at the other construction sites, and the gargantuan program of "Stalin's skyscrapers" was called off after Stalin's death. It is worth pointing out that in non-specialist literature and media, the pre-war and post-war projects are sometimes mixed and merged together, but for tracing the imperial discourses it is important to separate them. The NKTP building of 1934–1936, which remained a draft, was part of the struggles of domestic politics. It is most likely no coincidence that the project was called off after the Minister of Heavy Industry, Sergo Ordzhonikidze, fell from grace and the NKTP itself was gradually dissolved. In a way, these projects were more part of an internal political discourse of the USSR, alongside the Palace of Soviets as the ultimate representation of the socialist state. The Seven Sisters, however, came to signify the victorious Soviet Empire on an international stage. Dmitrii Khmel'nitskii points out that the plans of the eight high-rise buildings remained secret and under the supervision of the Soviet Ministry of Internal Affairs and Lavrentii Beriia himself, who was also overseeing the Soviet atomic bomb project.[53] Therefore, "Stalin's skyscrapers" became part of the Cold War imperial discourse, implying the power, glory, and superiority of the Soviet state on a global scale.

The Eighth Sister in Zaryadye, even though it was never finished, had an author – architect Dmitrii Chechulin, the head architect of Moscow from 1945 to 1949 and one of the main supervisors for the Seven Sisters project. After the plans for the Zaryadye high-rise building were abandoned in 1953, Chechulin used the already-built stylobate to design the construction of a lesser-scale project, a hotel complex for international guests. The first drafts of the Rossiia Hotel project (then called the "Zaryadye" hotel) were made in 1958.[54] The hotel, designed by Chechulin in 1964–1967 in the functionalist International Style, defined the appearance of the city center for the late twentieth century and became a place to stay for foreign guests and diplomatic missions. Demolished in 2006–2010 due to its outdatedness, the hotel was initially planned to be rebuilt as part of a newly erected city quarter that would recall the streets of "Old Moscow"; but even before its demolition, in the 1990s, urban development projects had suggested building the Parliamentary Center of the Russian Federation in Zaryadye.[55] All these projects were postponed until it was decided (allegedly by President Putin himself) to prioritize the green zone idea in 2012.[56]

The foundation for the Zaryadye high-rise building was used during the construction of the Rossiia Hotel, but despite the size of the hotel, it never rose as high as Stalin's skyscraper would have. Even though its modernist silhouette dominated the landscape, Zaryadye was still perceived as a kind of open-air museum due to the historical importance of the quarter and especially of Varvarka Street (during the Soviet period called Razin Street),[57] which became a kind of gallery – a *fair* – of churches and palaces due to the work of the architects and restorers, with the monumental façade of the hotel building behind them setting a theatre-like stage.[58] One of the historical buildings on this street is the next stop in our journey: the museum of the Boyar everyday life, or the Chambers of Romanov Boyars.

Chambers of Romanov: The Legacy of the Dynasty

The first time when Zaryadye came into the spotlight of imperial history-making was in the middle of the nineteenth century, long before "Stalin's skyscrapers," when it became a venue for one of the first national historical projects of the Russian Empire.

On August 26, 1856, on the day of the coronation of Alexander II, an imperial decree on the "renewal" of one of Zaryadye's ancient buildings, the Chambers of the Romanov Boyars,[59] was announced. It was a symbolic act that implied the idea of continuity of power in the Russian Empire – from the Grand Princes and Tsars of Muscovy to the nineteenth century (in contrast to Peter the Great's imperial legacy of a "westernized" St. Petersburg). The Chambers formed part of a large city mansion of the Boyar Nikita Romanovich Iur'ev and had already been marked on one of the first known maps of Moscow (1597). Researchers assume that this large urban estate dates back to the end of the fifteenth century. According to legend, on July 12, 1596, Mikhail Fedorovich Romanov, the founder of the new Romanov dynasty, was born here. After being elected to the Russian throne, Mikhail Fedorovich settled in the Kremlin, and the Zaryadye estate was called the "Old Tsar's Court." In 1631, after the death of his mother, the nun Marta Ivanovna, Mikhail Fedorovich founded in Zaryadye the Znamenskii Monastery and granted it some of the royal family's estates and lands, including the Chambers (the "Old Tsar's Court"), which became a part of the monastery.

The recognition of the Chambers in the mid-nineteenth century as a relic embodying the dynasty was inseparably linked with the memory of the coronation.[60] The "monument" to the first tsar of the Romanov dynasty became simultaneously a monument to the current emperor: "Let the centuries preserve [...] the monument of Mikhail, which should henceforth be a monument to Alexander II,"[61] as Metropolitan Filaret said on August 3, 1858, during the ceremony of laying the foundation stone for the renovated Chambers. Following a thorough restoration, the Chambers were supposed to not only demonstrate the history of the House of Romanov but also mark the reigning dynasty as supporters and preservers of the national heritage.

The emergence of the national historical narrative was intertwined with the evolution of the notion of heritage, which in turn "crucially participated in the shaping of modernity."[62] The "heritage boom" of the nineteenth century produced new architectural projects, monumental reconstructions, and publications in Russia.[63] A significant figure in this area was one of the leading Russian specialists in archaeology, the artist, architect, and historian Fedor Solntsev, whose fundamental work *Antiquities of the Russian State* was published in 1849–1853.[64] In addition to the scientific text, it consisted of several albums with more than 500 sheets of color chromo-lithographs with images of material objects of ancient Russian culture. Contemporaries highly praised Solntsev's work:

> In his accurate and elegant drawings [...] our Russian antiquities, the remains of the legacy of past centuries, all the evidence of our ancient church architecture and monuments of artistic and religious technique of our ancestors' disappeared life will forever remain untouched,

wrote the journal of the Imperial Russian Archaeological Society.[65] The development of Russian archaeology in the 1830s received support and funding from the state (for example, the decree "On the delivery of information about the remains of ancient buildings and the prohibition to destroy them" in 1826, which for a long time determined how ancient monuments in Russia would be protected), outlining the transition to a broader and more systematic protection of heritage.

Historians of architectural restoration often mark two discourses in nineteenth-century Western Europe which deal with the authenticity of historical monuments: the antiquarian approach taken by John Ruskin and the reconstruction school that suggested unity of style, introduced by Eugène Viollet-le-Duc.[66] As Thordis Arrhenius puts it, in the process of Viollet-le-Duc's restoration, "the significance of the monument shifted from commemorating the local society into commemorating France at large."[67] John Ruskin, on the other hand, advocated the conservation of ancient monuments and called the "restoration" propagated by Viollet-le-Duc "the most total destruction which a building can suffer: a destruction out of which no remnants can be gathered: a destruction accompanied with false description of the thing destroyed."[68]

Even though the European history of architectural restoration did not have a significant direct impact on pre-revolutionary Russian theory and practice,[69] the parallels in documenting, mapping, and organizing national history via monuments are very clear. Russian architects and conservators working on the Romanov Chambers' renovations were mostly inspired by the German memorial buildings devoted to national history and the ancestors of the dynasties. In 1843, German architect Leo von Klenze built the Valhalla Memorial (also known as the Glory Gallery), dedicated to German history, located near the city of Regensburg. It was commissioned by the king of Bavaria, Ludwig I. At the same time, the restoration of castles belonging to the Hohenzollern dynasty was carried out under the patronage of the Prussian king Friedrich Wilhelm IV. The reconstruction of the royal dynasty's heritage as a project of national history, therefore, was not something invented in Russia. The German examples of monumental nation-building relied on the French restoration approach: the "folk spirit," seen by Viollet-le-Duc in medieval architecture, became a state program for the glorification of the ruling dynasty and deeply impacted the architecture, archeology, conservation, and restoration of monuments.

Prince M.A. Obolensky, chairman of the Academic Commission for the Renovation of the Chamber of the Romanov Boyars, wrote to the President of the Moscow Palace Office N.I. Trubetskoi:

> Your Excellency knows that in all enlightened European states, when the ancient monuments are renewed, they proceed as follows: first [...] they arrange appropriate galleries and staircases convenient for the nearest and full overview of the surviving parts of the monument, such as they appear in their ancient form before renovation; they allow everyone who wants to observe these curious remnants of antiquity, they publish accurate drawings and plans of them and listen to the voice of the public opinion. And only after this they are establishing a draft competition [...] for projects [...]; the best [...] is approved and, according to it, the renewal is being accomplished.[70]

In other words, Russian (architectural) conservation of the nineteenth century adopted the Western practice for the historical narrative of an emerging nation-state which was articulating its non-Western origin.[71]

A specific group of monuments, for which the desire to restore them "in their ancient form" prevailed, consisted of memorial buildings associated with the reigning dynasty. Emperor Nicholas I paid special attention to the glorification of his royal ancestor – the first tsar of the Romanov dynasty, Mikhail Fedorovich. An especially prominent project in this context was the restoration of the Ipat'evskii Monastery in the city of Kostroma in 1833–1840. The monastery was the place where Mikhail Romanov had received the call from the "Muscovy people" to become their newly elected tsar in 1613 and was thus regarded as the "place of birth" for the Romanov dynasty. The restoration project of the 1830s was drafted by the leading Russian architect Konstantin A. Ton. In this project, special attention was paid to revealing and emphasizing the historical significance of the monastery – for example, above the outer entrance to the chambers of Mikhail Fedorovich in the monastery complex, planners wanted "to put up a royal coat of arms of that time; and to make it clear that it was not made in 1613, the inscriptions of the year in which the coat of arms is placed should be made around it."[72] Thus, the restoration program included not only renovation or repairs of the building but also commemoration of the *fact of the restoration*, emphasizing the memorial significance of the monastery for the current Russian emperor. The restored building thus became not only a monument of a historical epoch but also a monument to the one who decided to restore it. Another project of architectural restoration was implemented in the Moscow Kremlin in 1836–1849 by a commission chaired by Solntsev: the reconstruction of the Terem Palace, the "home palace" of the second tsar from the Romanov dynasty, Alexei Mikhailovich, where, again, the focus was on "ancient Russian," non-Western architecture.

The Romanov Chambers in Zaryadye followed the Terem Palace's example of establishing a special connection between the Russian emperors and the city of Moscow. The reconstruction of the Chambers had to contribute to the national program of glorifying the heritage of Muscovy and the first tsars of the dynasty. The task was to recreate the chambers as the "habitation" of Mikhail Fedorovich and his family. The focus was on the visual imaginary of the boyar house, and some of the previously reconstructed "antiquities" were used as analogs: the Terem Palace of the Moscow Kremlin and the chambers of the Kostroma Ipat'evskii Monastery, which were also called "the chambers of Tsar Mikhail Fedorovich." After its restoration by Solntsev, Terem Palace was considered a relevant source for the palace architecture of the first Romanov era. In the contract records of the Chambers, one can read: "To decorate the entrance [...] use the lion gracefully holding the shield, like the lions on the Terem's gates."[73] The question of authenticity, therefore, was not as important in the reconstruction process as the "spirit of the ancient life," which was given priority by architects and commissioners; in a way, the Chamber's historical interior and façade are a multilayered mix of the research conducted by architects and archaeologists and the "invented tradition" in Eric Hobsbawm's sense.

Both the Terem Palace of the Moscow Kremlin and the Chambers of Romanov Boyars in Zaryadye became part of the state program of representation for relics associated with the ruling dynasty; but if in the first case, the function of the reconstructed buildings was politically-utilitarian, the case of Zaryadye was about making a public space out of the "sacred" dynastic monument, recently reconstructed by the force of an imperial decree. The renovated Chambers of the Romanov Boyars were opened in 1859 as one of the first public historical museums, where the staff had to have "ancient Russian names and wear ancient Russian dress" to maintain the spirit of the place.[74] As the founder of the Imperial Historical Museum in Moscow and Russian historian Ivan Zabelin put it, a museum should "visually and continuously promote the development of self-reflection and Russian identity in people and society"[75] – in the case of the Romanov's Chambers, this identity clearly meant the identity of the imperial dynasty.

In 1913, the Chambers were one of the venues for the grand celebrations of the House of Romanov's 300th anniversary (Ipat'evskii Monastery in Kostroma was another venue of these celebrations, but the main part was held in Moscow), thus putting the symbolic performance of sovereign power into the very place where the dynasty was allegedly born (Figure 11.3).

Nevertheless, the housing area of Zaryadye behind the Chambers was not deeply affected by the renovations and the imperial discourse inherent in them. Hidden behind the façades of the churches and classicist buildings embossing Varvarka Street, surrounded by the walls of Kitai-gorod,

Figure 11.3 Emperor Nicholas II in front of the Romanov Chambers, during the celebrations of the 300th anniversary of the House of Romanov, May 25, 1913. Unknown photographer. Collodion photography.

Source: State Historical Museum, Moscow, #82964/2666 И VI 40462, State Catalogue #7599402.

Zaryadye was maintaining its existence as a residential, trade, and crafts district. Since 1826, Glebovskoe Podvor'e, one of the inns in Zaryadye, was a hub of Moscow's Jewish community, which turned the locality into a sort of Jewish quarter until the end of the nineteenth century. From the 1890s on, when more than 30,000 Jews were banished from Moscow by the Governor-General's order,[76] the district stagnated but was still a place for small businesses, cheap rental housing, and the garment industry. In Kupriianov and Sadovnikova's ethnographical study, the informants described their housing district as "gray," "shabby," and "run-down."[77] This was, however, the outcome of later developments: after the revolutions of 1917, the closure and secularization of the religious buildings, and the rapid urbanization and industrialization of the country, all possible buildings were overcrowded by residents or used as warehouses and administrative buildings; some of the district's inhabitants even made their quarters in the belfries of former churches.[78]

The first imperial impulse of Zaryadye thus was focused on only one specific location within the Zaryadye quarter – the Romanov Chambers. It was Stalin's plan of reconstruction that shifted the focus from one particular group of buildings to the whole district (but it implied that there would be *one* meaningful building here).

Zaryadye as a Liminal Space

From these milestones of the district's history and development, one can argue that Zaryadye came into the political limelight when the demand for showcasing both a national and an imperial narrative was high (and the wasteness (or vastness) of the place so close to the Kremlin became unbearable for the current regime) and that the discourses that emerged in this place are inherent to each period of history, be it the glorification of the royal ancestors and the construction of a national historical narrative, the socialistic modernization that fused nostalgia and utopia in the unreachable dream of the future, or the "urban wilderness" of the postmodern age which intends to create a livable environment in the middle of an overcrowded megapolis. The personal input from the respective current Russian ruler was also necessary for a project to get started.[79] The Romanovs' heritage was specifically marked by the emperor's personal promise to restore the Chambers.[80] Stalin's personal interest and influence on the General Plan of Moscow's reconstruction from 1935 and the construction of the Seven Sisters is sometimes discussed by researchers,[81] but the involvement of the highest Soviet authorities in the planning of Moscow's city center remains undisputed, as well as the significance of a "personality cult" during Stalin's reign. The concept of Zaryadye Park as a gift from President Putin and Moscow Mayor Sobianin to the citizens is well-covered in media.[82]

In each case, however, these projects (which were aimed at identity construction) ultimately adapted and translated Western practices and/ or were intended to impress global communities and represent the power and the glory of the state in consecutive imperial narratives. The inherent "original Russianness" and orientation toward an "ancient tradition" of the nineteenth-century project was the same effort to civilize the populace and teach it the "right way" of using heritage as the one of the "colonial troops" of the twenty-first century that aim to bring a "sustainable city" model to the capital of the Russian Federation. In a way, all three cases are different modernities trying to take form in this specific place and embed both national and imperial narratives.

The other layer of Zaryadye as palimpsest is its myth-making capacity. Since for long periods of its history, the district was walled-off or closed from one side (first by the Kitai-gorod fortifications that started to decay in the beginning of the twentieth century, then by the construction sites), it provided fertile ground for urban legends of hidden passages and constructions. Thus, the former inhabitants of the residential area tell stories of mysterious and dangerous underground trails,[83] the users of a portal of old Moscow photographs discuss if on a photo from the late 1940s one can see the construction site for a "secret governmental underground station,"[84] and some employees of Zaryadye Park think that in "ancient times" there was also a park in this place, where "boyars could take promenades."[85]

Doreen Massey points out that "debates over how to think the relationship between past, present and future can help us to reinvigorate the way in which we conceptualize geographical places."[86] My suggestion is not only reading Zaryadye as a palimpsest that contains the layers of such a relationship but also addressing it as a specific liminal place for imperial urban statements in Moscow. Through the different periods of its history, Zaryadye was often a stage for architectural and heritage performances in processes of transition (or "rites of passage"[87]); however, all previous efforts to create a significant place-making construction in it either failed or only partly succeeded. Indeed, the Chambers exist as a historical building and a museum, but the Russian Empire, the imperial narrative of which was placed in them in the form of glorification of the ruling dynasty, is long gone. Moreover, the celebration of the 300th anniversary of the tsardom of Mikhail Fedorovich in 1913 is often called "the last great celebration of the Romanovs." The high-rise building – the construction of which was called off after the death of Josef Stalin – also signifies the changes in the imperial representations of the Soviet Russia.

The notion of liminality as an "interstitial position between fixed identifications"[88] can help to explain this natural resilience of the place to the discourses planted in it; as Murawski and Kravchuk put it in their 2018 exhibition, Zaryadye can be read as a portal, as a place of transition with its endless construction, reconstruction, and deconstruction sites. Marc Augé writes: "a space which cannot be defined as relational, or historical or concerned with identity will be a non-place."[89] Zaryadye stopped being a lived place – a human habitat – in the 1960s and achieved the status of a "place of memory,"[90] but in a sense any attempt to construct an identity of this place moves it further into non-place territory; the construction of new sights that were supposed to contribute to the imperial form of the city led to the simultaneous deconstruction of the imperial narrative. As Augé states, "empire, considered as a 'totalitarian' universe, is never a non-place,"[91] it rewrites history by removing the individual reference from ideology and projecting it outside the imperial frontiers – the imperial ambitions that were put into Zaryadye projects to stabilize and imbue this place with a certain identity came (and are coming) across the fluidity and ambivalence of non-place conditions, of the wasteland behind the fences and construction sites, of the heritage displayed and yet hidden from view.[92] Architect and local historian Aleksandr Mozhaev calls out this ambivalence in his piece on confrontation between the city and urban developers:

> It is telling how little interest there is for this topic, which is rather new to the city [the open-air archaeological exhibits]: at the unique site where it is possible to organize a one-of-a-kind museum, to show vividly a slice of the nine ages of Moscow history, the scenario of steppe, tundra and swamp is being performed. The displaying of the literal depth of historical memory is not among the priorities for this new symbol of Russia.[93]

As I was trying to show in this chapter, the imperial manifestations in Zaryadye, though ambitious and grand as projects, often did not succeed as planned – they definitely did not bring together imperial subjects and did not become "a spatialized expression of authority,"[94] be it for reasons of drastic historical change (i.e., Russian revolutions and the fall of the Romanov Empire) or because of ambiguous messages and public reception, as it seems to be happening with the park.[95]

Zaryadye Park continues this line and creates a mythological narrative which is "patchworked" from diverse discourses that have nothing in common apart from belonging to "Russian history" or "Russia." The images and meanings of a "new Russia" are communicated through

> the vegetation from the different regions of the country, fragments of historical facts, the bionic architecture as a symbol of connectedness with the global practices, 'wow-effects' which basically continue the

Soviet tradition of presenting the astonishing and hyperbolized figures; all these elements are neither in a contradiction, nor in a correlation to each other.[96]

One cannot predict what will happen to this latest effort to reconceptualize Zaryadye, the "park of the present future," which has become an acclaimed tourist spot in central Moscow. However, it was turned (once again, or – this time – definitively) into an open public place where the national identity is narrated in a manner relevant to current state policies. But what lies underneath the surface – who knows?

Notes

1 A range of theoretical frameworks can be used in addressing the topic, from Henri Lefebvre's *Production of Space* to Pierre Nora's *Lieux des Memoires* (or, as we shall see, rather the *sites of forgetting*). In my analysis, following the archaeological metaphor, I suggest using the Foucauldian *discursive formation* as a key concept in the sense of discourses "as practices that systematically form the objects of which they speak" (Michel Foucault, *The Archaeology of Knowledge* [London and New York: Routledge, 2002], 54). Another important concept for this text is *narrative*, which is understood as a consecutive story consisting of several discourses, as in, for example, the (national) historical narrative or the imperial narrative. James Wertsch uses the term "narrative template" to devise the connection between historical narratives and collective memory (James V. Wertsch, "Collective Memory and Narrative Templates," *Social Research* 75, no. 1 [2008]: 133–56). Both concepts draw on the notions of power and ideology, which, as I argue, became the key notions for the transformations and ambitious projects described in this chapter.

2 The name *Kitai-gorod* was already found on city maps from the end of the sixteenth century, with the Zaryadye area marked as the center for trade and public life (*Pamiatniki arkhitektury Moskvy: Kreml', Kitai-gorod, tsentral'nye ploshchadi*, ed. Alexei Komech and Vladimir Pluzhnikov [Moscow: Iskusstvo, 1982], 50–59); the Zaryadye district as an inhabited part of Moscow dates back to the twelfth century (Aleksandr Mozhaev, "Moskovskoe Zariad'e : zatianuvsheesia protivostoianie goroda i gradostroitelei," *Revue des études slaves* 86, no. 1–2 [2015]: 3).

3 "Park nastoiashchego budushchego," which can be also translated as "park of the real future"; see the official website: https://www.zaryadyepark.ru (Accessed January 10, 2021). All translations from Russian to English in the following text are made by the author.

4 Doreen Massey, "Places and Their Pasts," *History Workshop Journal* 39 (1995): 183.

5 Ibid, 186.

6 See Eric Hobsbawm and Terence Ranger, *The Invention of Tradition* (Cambridge: Cambridge University Press, 2012).

7 See Richard S. Wortman, *Scenarios of Power: Myth and Ceremony in Russian Monarchy from Peter the Great to the Abdication of Nicholas II* (Princeton, NJ: Princeton University Press, 2006). Wortman, however, suggests that the "national" narrative was introduced in the late nineteenth century after the

assassination of Alexander II. As I will argue further in the section on the Romanovs' Chambers, this introduction happened earlier with the growing interest in national heritage and the development of the *Slavophiles'* rhetoric among the educated society and during the search for a new ideological paradigm in the time of Nicholas I's reign.

8 Marc Augé, *Non-Places: An Introduction to Anthropology of Supermodernity* (London: Verso, 1995). One can argue that these efforts became successful in the 1960s, when the last remnants of the residential area were torn down, turning Zaryadye from an inhabited neighborhood into a transient non-place. However, my point here is that the universalized imperial narrative that was implanted into Zaryadye contradicted the actual features of "place" or "anthropological place" as Augé describes it – "relational, historical and concerned with identity" (ibid, 77).

9 "About Zaryadye Park," *Zaryadye*, https://www.zaryadyepark.ru/en/about/ (Accessed January 10, 2021).

10 "Zaryadye Park, Moscow, Russia," *Diller Scofidio+Renfro* (website), https://dsrny.com/project/zaryadye-park (Accessed January 10, 2021).

11 Ibid.

12 Michał Murawski, "Portal Zaryadye," 2018, *Communist Spectres Haunting Capitalist Cities*, https://www.michalmurawski.net/portal-zaryadye-eng (Accessed December 20, 2020).

13 "New Moscow" in the 2010s can refer to the new residential and urban areas included in Moscow City in 2012. Despite being promoted as a step toward "polycentric" urban development that will break up the traditional structure of the city growing in concentric rings, the area's growth in the first five years was lower than was expected, and the focus of the "New Moscow" policies in a more general sense (as the capital's urban development plan) is still being directed to objects and facilities in "Old Moscow," which resembles the relationship between the center and periphery in the colonial setting.

14 Founded by the Strelka Institute for Media, Architecture and Design in Moscow, the company's "central aim is to effect a qualitative change in the Russian urban landscape and create a comfortable and modern environment in our cities. Russia's cities should be adapted for life in the era of the knowledge economy. Their inhabitants should have opportunities for development, creativity, the education of their children, opening businesses and coming up with new products." ("Strelka KB", https://strelka-kb.com/en [Accessed February 23, 2021]).

15 Michał Murawski, "Zaryad'elogiia," *Urban Studies and Practices* 2, no. 4 (2017): 74.

16 Ibid.

17 See, for example, Jan Gehl, *Cities for People* (Washington, DC: Island Press, 2010).

18 Coloniality, as distinct from colonialism, is an ongoing condition of the modern world, which describes the social, cultural, and epistemic impacts of colonialism. This concept is linked to the Latin American school of thought and such scholars as Aníbal Quijano and Walter Mignolo, among others; see Walter Mignolo, "Delinking: The Rhetoric of Modernity, the Logic of Coloniality and the Grammar of De-coloniality," *Cultural Studies* 21, no. 2 (2007): 449–514.

19 Wortman, *Scenarios of Power,* 2.

20 One can argue that much is determined by the touristic value of the park and the demand to look "respectable" in the eyes of international guests, whereas in

central Moscow museums and exhibitions, the modern annexation of Crimea is more blatantly described as a "homecoming," as I write elsewhere; see Olga Zabalueva, "Multimedia Historical Parks and the Heritage-Based 'Regime of Truth' in Russia," *Culture Unbound – Journal of Current Cultural Research,* 14, no. 2 (2022): 83–106.

21 Mariia Troshina, "Moskovskii Downtown," *Moskovskoe Nasledie* 19 (2012): 5.

22 Murawski, "Zaryad'elogiia," 75.

23 Murawski, "Portal Zaryadye," 22.

24 Murawski, "Zaryad'elogiia," 74.

25 Margarita Chubukova, "Sarkophag gostinitsy 'Rossiia': k voprosu o vospriiatii gorozhanami prostranstva 'Zariad'ia'," *Urban Studies and Practices* 2, no. 4 (2017): 82.

26 Ibid, 80.

27 See Clementine Cecil, "Fortress City: The Hegemony of the Moscow Kremlin and the Consequences and Challenges of Developing a Modern City around a Medieval Walled Fortress," in *Re-Centering the City: Global Mutations of Socialist Modernity,* ed. Michal Murawski and Jonathan Bach (London: UCL Press, 2020), 37–43.

28 Daria Volkova, "Mifologiia 'Zariad'ia'," *Urban Studies and Practices* 2, no. 4 (2017): 89.

29 Murawski, "Zaryad'elogiia," 72.

30 Alex Ulam, "In Putin's Moscow, an Urban Wilderness Emerges," *Bloombergs CityLab,* May 17, 2017, https://www.bloomberg.com/news/articles/2017-05-17/liz-diller-and-charles-renfro-talk-about-zaryadye-park (Accessed December 13, 2020).

31 Daria Paramonova, "Mutant Centralities: Moscow Architecture in the Post-Soviet Era," in *Re-Centering the City: Global Mutations of Socialist Modernity,* ed. Michal Murawski and Jonathan Bach (London: UCL Press, 2020), 73–76.

32 One may recall another grand project of Putin's Russia, the reconstruction of Sochi for the Winter Olympic Games 2014.

33 Sergej Kuznetsov, "Rol' Stalina v organizatsii konkursa na proektirovanie Dvortsa Sovetov (1931–1932 gg.)," *Architecture and Modern Information Technologies* 3, no. 48 (2013): 29.

34 Sergej Tkachenko, "Moskva – neosushchestvlennyi gorod-sad v plane 'Novoi Moskvy'," *Architecture and Modern Information Technologies* 2, no. 47 (2019): 232–50.

35 Sergej Tkachenko, "Kontseptsii zastroiki Zariad'ia s 1918 do 1991 goda," *Izvestiia Vuzov. Investitsii. Stroitel'stvo. Nedvizhimost'* 8, no 4. (2018): 253.

36 As, for example, in the movie *New Moscow* by Aleksandr Medvedkin (1938; see "Novaia Moskva," *IMDb,* https://www.imdb.com/title/tt0174990/ [Accessed March 23, 2021]).

37 Sergei Kuznetsov, "Vlast' i general'nyi plan rekonstruktsii Moskvy (1931 – nachalo 1950-kh gg.)," *Architecture and Modern Information Technologies* 4, no. 49 (2019): 28–46.

38 Sona Stephan Hoisington, "'Ever Higher': The Evolution of the Project for the Palace of Soviets," *Slavic Review* 62, no. 1 (2003): 41–68; Kuznetsov, "Rol' Stalina," 51–60.

39 There is a popular belief that the cathedral was also supposed to be demolished, but by good fortune, it was spared and preserved as a museum – allegedly due to the commitment of the architect Petr Baranovskii or by the decision of Josef Stalin himself.

40 Tkachenko, "Kontseptsii zastroiki Zariad'ia s 1918 do 1991 goda," 253.

41 Ibid, 259.

42 Pavel Kupriianov and Ludmila Sadovnikova, "Mesto pamiati v pamiati mest-nykh: Kul'turnye Smysly Gorodskogo Prostranstva (Po Materialam interv'iu zhitelei Moskovskogo Zariad'ia)," *Antropologicheskii forum* 11 (2008): 387.

43 According to popular belief, the high-rise buildings in Moscow were planned by Josef Stalin himself and are still called *Stalinskie vysotki* (Stalin's skyscrapers) in Russian.

44 Dmitrii Khmel'nitskii, "Stalin i arkhitektura," *archi.ru* 2004, https://web.archive.org/web/20070317113506/http://www.archi.ru/publications/virtual/hmelnitsky.htm (Accessed January 20, 2021).

45 The "Seven Sisters" are Moscow State University, Hotel Ukraina, the Kudrinskaia Square Building, the Ministry of Foreign Affairs, Leningradskaia Hotel, the Red Gates Administrative Building, and the Kotel'nicheskaia Embankment Building.

46 The foundation for the monument of Iurii Dolgorukii, a medieval prince and the legendary founder of Moscow, was laid on the same day, and both events were highlighted in newspapers with the following comments: "the whole soul of the Soviet state goes before our eyes: the ancient history of Rus', an equestrian warrior in helmet and chainmail, who points with his hand down: 'Here will be Moscow,' and gigantic high-rise buildings, built with the use of the latest technology for the people of a socialist society, for the builders of communism, for the new people" (Natal'ia Shashkova, "O moskovskom vysotnom stroitel'stve v 40–50-e gody XX veka: idei, tseli, rezul'taty i znachenie", *Tsennosti i smysly* 3, no. 25 [2013]: 143).

47 Iakov Kornfel'd, *Laureaty Stalinskikh premii v arkhitekture 1941–1950* (Moscow: Gosudarstvennoe izdatelstvo literatury po stroitel'stvu i arkhitekture, 1953): 124.

48 Aleksandr Mozhaev and Konstantin Mikhailov, "Poteriannyi mir. Zariad'e i Moskvoretskaia ulitsa," *Moskovskoe nasledie* 3 (2007): 79–92.

49 Thordis Arrhenius, *The Fragile Monument: On Conservation and Modernity* (London: Artifice, 2012): 115.

50 Ibid, 121.

51 Nikolaj Kruzhkov, *Vysotnye zdanija v Moskve: Fakty iz istorii proektirovaniia i stroitel'stva, 1947–1956* (Moscow: Izdatel'skii dom "Agni", 2007).

52 Kupriianov and Sadovnikova, "Mesto pamiati v pamiati mestnykh," 377.

53 Khmel'nitskii, "Stalin i arkhitektura."

54 Sergej Tkachenko, "Kontseptsii zastroiki Zariad'ia: ot gostinitsy do parka," *Izvestiia Vuzov. Investitsii. Stroitel'stvo. Nedvizhimost'* 9, no. 1 (2019): 198.

55 Ibid, 201.

56 Ibid.

57 Kupriianov and Sadovnikova, "Mesto pamiati v pamiati mestnykh," 374. Architects and historians today refer to the whole range of buildings demolished during the Soviet time, which were a unique part of Zaryadye's architectural heritage (see Mozhaev and Mikhailov, "Poteriannyi mir"), from the seventeenth-century St. Nicholas church to the apartment block with arches and galleries from the end of the nineteenth century, filmed by Sergei Eisenstein in *Strike* (1925).

58 Tkachenko, "Kontseptsii zastroiki Zariad'ia: ot gostinitsy do parka," 198.

59 *Chambers* is a traditional translation of the Russian *Palaty*, which means "palace," usually the main part of a larger estate complex. *Boyar* refers to the highest rank of Russian nobility from the tenth to the seventeenth century.

60　Traditionally, even though the imperial capital was in St. Petersburg, the coronations of the Russian emperors and empresses took place in the Moscow Kremlin. For more on the symbolical performances, see Wortman, *Scenarios of Power.*

61　Alexei Shchenkov, *Pamiatniki arkhitektury v dorevoliutsionnoi Rossii. Ocherki istorii arkhitekturnoi restavratsii* (Moscow: Terra, 2002), 230.

62　Arrhenius, *The Fragile Monument.*

63　Marta Polyakova, "Podkhody k izucheniiu kul'turnogo naslediia Rossii v XVIII – nachale XX v.", *Vestnik RGGU: Literaturovedenie. Iazykoznanie. Kul'turologiia* 10 (2008): 257–66. The architectural-historical monuments were considered archaeological undertakings at the time, hence most of the research was done by diverse archaeological commissions and societies, such as the Moscow Archaeological Society (founded in 1864, it has been called the Emperor's Moscow Archaeological Society since 1881). A strong focus was on documentation and preservation of the "traces of the past."

64　Fedor Solntsev, *Drevnosti Rossiiskogo Gosudarstva.*

65　Fedor Solntsev, "Moia zhizn' i khudozhestvenno-arkheologicheskie trudy," *Russkaia Starina* 15, no. 1 (1876): 109.

66　See Arrhenius, *The Fragile Monument,* 94, 125.

67　Arrhenius, *The Fragile Monument,* 98.

68　John Ruskin, *The Seven Lamps of Architecture* (New York: J. Wiley, 1849): 258–59.

69　Shchenkov, *Pamiatniki arkhitektury v dorevoliutsionnoi Rossii,* 489.

70　Shchenkov, *Pamiatniki arkhitektury v dorevoliutsionnoi Rossii,* 231.

71　As a result of the contradiction between the "European" and the "National" myths, two national policies came into being in nineteenth-century Russia: the so-called Official Nationality agenda in 1833 (or "Orthodoxy, Autocracy, and Nationality," where the "Nationality" part implied that the Russian people, being deeply religious and devoted to the emperor, should preserve national traditions and fight any foreign influences) and emphasis on the importance of the national and religious unity of the Russian people, threatened by (external and internal) liberal social movements, declared in the Manifesto on Unshakable Autocracy during the reign of Alexander III (1881).

72　Shchenkov, *Pamiatniki arkhitektury v dorevoliutsionnoi Rossii,* 100.

73　Ibid, 245.

74　Shchenkov, *Pamiatniki arkhitektury v dorevoliutsionnoi Rossii,* 236.

75　Ivan Zabelin, *Rech' ob obshhestvennom znachenii uchenykh trudov Grafa Alekseia Sergeevicha Uvarova* (Moscow, 1885), 15.

76　Troshina, "Moskovskii Downtown."

77　Kupriianov and Sadovnikova, "Mesto pamiati v pamiati mestnykh."

78　Ibid, 382.

79　Cecil, "Fortress City," 42.

80　During the restoration of the Chambers of Romanov Boyars, special "larger bricks were ordered, to distinguish them from the ancient ones by a special stamp" (Shchenkov, *Pamiatniki arkhitektury v dorevoliutsionnoi Rossii,* 231). The year that was put on the stamp, 1856, was not the year of the bricks' creation, as they were ordered in 1858, but the year of the decree on the "renewal" and the coronation of Alexander II.

81　Cf. Kuznetsov, "Vlast' i general'nyi plan"; Kuznetsov, "Rol' Stalina"; Khmel'nitskii, "Stalin i arkhitektura"; Shashkova, "O moskovskom vysotnom stroitel'stve."

82 "'Zariad'e' — glavnyi podarok Putina Moskve," *The Village*, September 11, 2017, https://www.the-village.ru/city/photo-reportage/282650-zaryadie-opened (Accessed February 23, 2021).

83 Kupriianov and Sadovnikova, "Mesto pamiati v pamiati mestnykh," 384.

84 Iskander Haliullin, "Zariad'e s reki" [Zaryadye from the riverside], 1948–1950, Retro View of Mankind's Habitat, https://pastvu.com/p/104573 (Accessed February 23, 2021).

85 Volkova, "Mifologiia 'Zariad'ia'," 86.

86 Massey, "Places and Their Pasts," 186.

87 See Arnold van Gennep, *The Rites of Passage* (Chicago, IL: University of Chicago Press, 1960).

88 Bjørn Thomassen, "Revisiting Liminality: The Danger of Empty Spaces," in *Liminal Landscapes: Travel, Experience and Spaces In-Between*, ed. Hazel Andrews and Les Roberts (London: Routledge, 2012), 27.

89 Augé, *Non-Places*, 78.

90 Kupriianov and Sadovnikova, "Mesto pamiati v pamiati mestnykh"; the title of the article is translated literally as "A place of memory in the memory of locals."

91 Augé, *Non-Places*, 114.

92 One of the examples of such a "superficial" approach to heritage can be seen in the "Time Machine" attraction (https://vimeo.com/245385245), which represents the generalized historical narrative of Moscow, the Muscovy state, and Russia, even though it starts with the introductory words, "Where did the history of Zaryadye begin" (Volkova, "Mifologiia 'Zariad'ia'," 90). Instead of emphasizing the *locality* of the place, the multimedia installation falls into the trap of the "narrative template" (Wertsch, "Collective Memory and Narrative Templates") of glorious Russian history.

93 Mozhaev, "Moskovskoe Zariad'e," 12.

94 Augé, *Non-Places*, 113.

95 One can also argue that the top-down changes in the Russian historical "narrative template" are coming too fast for the actual place to be stabilized in one of them.

96 Volkova, "Mifologiia 'Zariad'ia'," 91.

Bibliography

"About Zaryadye Park." *Zaryadye*. Accessed January 10, 2021. https://www.zaryadyepark.ru/en/about/.

Arrhenius, Thordis. *The Fragile Monument: On Conservation and Modernity*. London: Artifice, 2012.

Augé, Marc. *Non-Places: An Introduction to Anthropology of Supermodernity*. London: Verso, 1995.

Cecil, Clementine. "Fortress City: The Hegemony of the Moscow Kremlin and the Consequences and Challenges of Developing a Modern City around a Medieval Walled Fortress." In *Re-Centering the City: Global Mutations of Socialist Modernity*, edited by Michal Murawski and Jonathan Bach, 37–43. London: UCL Press, 2020.

Chubukova, Margarita. "Sarkophag gostinitsy 'Rossiia'": k voprosu o vospriiatii gorozhanami prostranstva 'Zariad'ia'" ['The sarcophagus of Hotel Rossiya':

Citizens' perceptions of Zaryadye Park]. *Urban Studies and Practices* 2, no. 4 (2017): 78–84.

Foucault, Michel. *The Archaeology of Knowledge*. London: Routledge, 2002.

Gehl, Jan. *Cities for People*. Washington, DC: Island Press, 2010.

Haliullin, Iskander. "Zariad'e s reki" [Zaryadye from the riverside], 1948–1950. *Retro View of Mankind's Habitat*. Accessed February 23, 2021. https://pastvu.com/p/104573.

Hobsbawm, Eric, and Terence Ranger. *The Invention of Tradition*. Cambridge: Cambridge University Press, 2012.

Hoisington, Sona Stephan. "'Ever Higher': The Evolution of the Project for the Palace of Soviets." *Slavic Review* 62, no. 1 (2003): 41–68.

Khmel'nitskii, Dmitrii. "Stalin i arkhitektura." *archi.ru*, 2004. Accessed January 20, 2021. https://web.archive.org/web/20070317113506/http://www.archi.ru/publications/virtual/hmelnitsky.htm.

Komech, Alexei, and Vladimir Pluzhnikov, eds. *Pamiatniki arkhitektury Moskvy: Kreml', Kitai-gorod, tsentral'nye ploshchadi*. Moscow: Iskusstvo, 1982.

Kornfel'd, Iakov. *Laureaty Stalinskikh premii v arkhitekture 1941–1950*. Moscow: Gosudarstvennoe izdatelstvo literatury po stroitel'stvu i arkhitekture, 1953.

Kruzhkov, Nikolai. *Vysotnye zdaniia v Moskve: Fakty iz istorii proektirovaniia i stroitel'stva, 1947–1956*. Moscow: Izdatel'skii dom "Agni," 2007.

Kupriianov, Pavel, and Ludmila Sadovnikova. "Mesto pamiati v pamiati mestnykh: Kul'turnye smysly gorodskogo prostranstva (Po materialam interv'iu zhitelei Moskovskogo Zariad'ia)." *Antropologicheskii forum* 11 (2008): 370–407.

Kuznetsov, Sergej. "Rol' Stalina v organizatsii konkursa na proektirovanie Dvortsa Sovetov (1931–1932 gg.)" [Stalin and the first stages of the competition for the design of the Palace of Soviets (1931–1932)]. *Architecture and Modern Information Technologies* 3, no. 48 (2013): 51–60.

Kuznetsov, Sergej. "Vlast' i general'nyi plan rekonstruktsii Moskvy (1931–nachalo 1950-kh gg.)" [Soviet political leadership and the general plan for the reconstruction of Moscow (1931–early 1950s)]. *Architecture and Modern Information Technologies* 4, no. 49 (2019): 28–46.

Massey, Doreen. "Places and Their Pasts." *History Workshop Journal* 39 (1995): 182–92.

Mignolo, Walter. "Delinking: The Rhetoric of Modernity, the Logic of Coloniality and the Grammar of De-Coloniality." *Cultural Studies* 21, no. 2 (2007): 449–514.

Mozhaev, Aleksandr. "Moskovskoe Zariad'e: zatianuvsheesia protivostoianie goroda i gradostroitelei." [Le quartier du Zarjad'e à Moscou : Un conflit entre la ville et les architects qui s'éternise]. *Revue Des Études Slaves* 86, no. 1–2 (2015): 1–16.

Mozhaev, Aleksandr, and Konstantin Mikhailov. "Poteriannyi mir: Zarjad'e i Moskvoreckaia ulitsa." *Moskovskoe Nasledie* 3 (2007): 79–92.

Murawski, Michal. "Zaryad'elogiia" [Zaryadyology]. *Urban Studies and Practices* 2, no. 4 (2017): 71–77.

Murawski, Michał. "Portal Zaryadye." *Communist Spectres Haunting Capitalist Cities*, 2018. Accessed December 20, 2020. https://www.michalmurawski.net/portal-zaryadye-eng.

"Novaya Moskva." *IMDb*. Accessed March 23, 2021. https://www.imdb.com/title/tt0174990/.

Paramonova, Daria. "Mutant Centralities: Moscow Architecture in the Post-Soviet Era." In *Re-Centering the City: Global Mutations of Socialist Modernity*, edited by Michal Murawski and Jonathan Bach, 73–76. London: UCL Press, 2020.

Polyakova, Marta. "Podkhody k izucheniiu kul'turnogo naslediia Rossii v XVIII–nachale XX v." [The approaches to study of a cultural heritage of Russia from the eighteenth to the beginning of the twentieth century]. *Vestnik RGGU: Literaturovedenie. Iazykoznanie. Kul'turologiia* 10 (2008): 257–66.

Ruskin, John. *The Seven Lamps of Architecture*. New York: J. Wiley, 1849.

Shashkova, Natal'ia. "O moskovskom vysotnom stroitel'stve v 40–50-e gody XX veka: idei, tseli, rezul'taty i znachenie." *Tsennosti i smysly* 3, no. 25 (2013): 142–57.

Shchenkov, Alexei, ed. *Pamiatniki arkhitektury v dorevoliutsionnoi Rossii. Ocherki istorii arkhitekturnoi restavratsii*. Moscow: Terra, 2002.

Solntsev, Fedor. "Moia zhizn' i khudozhestvenno-arkheologicheskie trudy." *Russkaia starina* 15, no. 1 (1876): 109–28.

"Strelka KB." Accessed February 23, 2021. https://strelka-kb.com/en.

Thomassen, Bjørn. "Revisiting Liminality: The Danger of Empty Spaces." In *Liminal Landscapes: Travel, Experience and Spaces In-Between*, edited by Hazel Andrews and Les Roberts, 21–35. London: Routledge, 2012.

Tkachenko, Sergej. "Kontseptsii zastroiki Zariad'ia s 1918 do 1991 goda" [Concept of Zaryadye development from 1918 to 1991]. *Izvestiya Vuzov: Investitsiyi, Stroyitelstvo, Nedvizhimost* 8, no. 4 (2018): 246–66.

Tkachenko, Sergej. "Moskva – neosushchestvlennyi gorod-sad v plane 'Novoi Moskvy'" [Moscow – unrealised Garden-City in 'New Moscow' plan]. *Architecture and Modern Information Technologies* 2, no. 47 (2019): 232–50.

Tkachenko, Sergej. "Kontseptsii zastroiki Zariad'ia: ot gostinitsy do parka" [Zaryadye development concept: From hotel to park]. *Izvestiia Vuzov: Investitsii, Stroitel'stvo, Nedvizhimost'* 9, no. 1 (2019): 196–213.

Troshina, Mariia. "Moskovskii Downtown." *Moskovskoe nasledie* 19 (2012): 2–5.

Ulam, Alex. "In Putin's Moscow, an Urban Wilderness Emerges." *Bloombergs CityLab*, 17 May 2017. Accessed December 13, 2020. https://www.bloomberg.com/news/articles/2017-05-17/liz-diller-and-charles-renfro-talk-about-zaryadye-park.

van Gennep, Arnold. *The Rites of Passage*. Chicago, IL: University of Chicago Press, 1960.

Volkova, Daria. "Mifologiia 'Zariad'ia'" [The mythology of Zaryadye]. *Urban Studies and Practices* 2, no. 4 (2017): 85–92.

Wertsch, James V. "Collective Memory and Narrative Templates." *Social Research* 75, no. 1 (2008): 133–56.

Wortman, Richard S. *Scenarios of Power: Myth and Ceremony in Russian Monarchy from Peter the Great to the abdication of Nicholas II*. Princeton, NJ: Princeton University Press, 2006.

Zabalueva, Olga. "Multimedia Historical Parks and the Heritage-Based 'Regime of Truth' in Russia." *Culture Unbound - Journal of Current Cultural Research* 14, no. 2 (2022): 83–106.

Zabelin, Ivan. *Rech' ob obshhestvennom znachenii uchenykh trudov Grafa Alekseia Sergeevicha Uvarova.* Moscow: Imperatorskoe obshchestvo istorii i drevnostei rossiiskikh pri Moskovskom universitete, 1885.

"'Zariad'e' – glavnyi podarok Putina Moskve." *The Village,* September 11, 2017. Accessed February 23, 2021. https://www.the-village.ru/city/photo-reportage/282650-zaryadie-opened.

"Zaryadye Park, Moscow, Russia." *Diller Scofidio+Renfro* (website). Accessed January 10, 2021. https://dsrny.com/project/zaryadye-park.

Part IV

Conclusion

12 Imperial Cities and Recent Research Trends

Nostalgia, Water Infrastructure, and Segregation

Julia Obertreis

The main idea of this volume as outlined by Ulrich Hofmeister in his conceptual chapter is very appealing: to combine two productive research fields, imperial history and urban history. The "imperial city" is not, as Hofmeister explains, understood as a certain type of city, such as a harbor city or industrial city, but rather as a research approach that opens up opportunities for studying the imperial in cities, be it in an administrative sense, in representation, in the composition of a given city's population, or in the city's importance for imperial politics.

The contributions to this volume show how great the potential is at the intersection of these two established research fields for the continental empires at stake – i.e., the Russian, Habsburg, and Ottoman Empires. The following is not an attempt to comment on the individual contributions to this volume. Instead, departing from these contributions, the following reflections aim at opening up additional research fields for integration into the study of imperial cities in the future. Three areas for further research are considered here: first, the ambivalence of imperial pasts and presents; second, the mastering of nature on the example of river transformations and water infrastructure; and third, new views on segregation.

Ambivalent Pasts and Presents

Imperial history, including colonial history, is present in today's societies in many ways. Remembering the imperial and colonial (grandeur, status, territory, and diverse populations but also submissive force, violence, exploitation, etc.) can take very different forms and serve different purposes. "Imperial pasts continue to inspire nostalgia, identification, pride, anxiety, skepticism, and disdain in the present. Material remnants of empire, both monumental and mundane, are cues and canvasses for reflection and refraction."[1] In the case of imperial cities, the intersection of the material heritage and discourses about the past becomes very concrete, small-scale, spatially grounded, and controversial. The naming of streets or the keeping

DOI: 10.4324/9781003130031-16

or removing of monuments, for example, can be highly contested. If we take into account that imperial powers in the past appropriated historical pasts to their own ends, as is shown in the contribution to this volume by Gulchachak Nugmanova on Kazan and the Russian Empire's appropriation of both the Russian and Tatar pasts, the picture becomes even more complicated.

Many of the imperial cities in the continental empires underwent at least two profound transformations in the twentieth century as regards their attitudes toward the imperial and their dealing with imperial heritage: one at the formal end of the empires' existence (1917–1922) and another one after the collapse of the state-socialist governments when Soviet or People's Republics gained state independence or independence from Moscow, respectively (1989–1991). The trajectories of individual cities are very different, but we can see patterns and waves of (re-)appropriation, code-switching, re-naming, re-planning, and even destruction of different kinds of buildings, places, and streets.[2]

The renaming of settlements and cities on political grounds was very common in the Soviet Union, and in a first anti-tsarist wave from 1917, many Aleksandrovsks and Nikolaevsks were given new names even if they hadn't been originally named after the respective tsars. Efforts to overcome the tsarist past in non-Russian regions had their own peculiarities. Elizavetpol', for example, today the third largest city of Azerbaijan, returned to its previous non-Russian name Ganja in the early Soviet years.[3] Buildings representing rule and power were appropriated and re-coded by new rulers as in the famous example of the Red Stars on the Kremlin, which replaced the Tsar's two-headed eagles. Religious buildings like churches and mosques were destroyed or appropriated for other purposes by the Bolsheviks after 1917, and many of them were re-established in their original function after 1991. Streets were renamed and re-renamed, which was sometimes opposed by the local population who continued to use old names.[4] After 1991 we also see a nationalization of city squares and spaces.[5] Imperial pasts, whether real or imagined, could play a role in that. Under the label "Skopje 2014," Macedonia's ruling, nationalist party VMRO–DPMNE (Internal Macedonian Revolutionary Organization – Democratic Party for Macedonian National Unity) and especially Prime Minister Nikola Gruevski began in 2010 to cover the city center with giant monuments and bronze lion statues. An oversized monument to Alexander the Great on the city's central square testified to the government's attempt to reclaim him as the father of the Macedonian nation by what is known as the "antiquization" (*antikvizacija*) policy. This policy was one of the reasons for heightened tensions with Greece and other Balkan states. In the eyes of critics, Skopje was transformed into a "pseudo-ancient Disneyland."[6]

After 1991, the imperial and the national formed different amalgamations in city festivities. Istanbul is a case in point. The 1980s and 1990s witnessed a general rise of political Islam in Turkey. Against this background, Islamist circles and political parties celebrated the "Conquest of Istanbul Day" in honor of the city's conquest by Sultan Mehmed II in 1453. In doing so they established "an alternative national time," challenging the official secular one that took the foundation of the Turkish Republic in 1923 as a starting point. They integrated the long imperial Ottoman period into national memory.[7]

Besides individual buildings, street names, and the coding and usage of squares, memorials were and are also contested. Heated debates tend to come up in some cases over the question whether to remove or keep a memorial, and the meanings ascribed to it can be wide-ranging and conflictual. One of the well-known examples is the memorial to Empress Catherine II in Odesa (Russ. Odessa), which was one of the city's main sites.[8] Inaugurated in 1900, it had been removed by the Bolsheviks in 1920 and was re-erected in 2007 in the context of re-establishing the historical square named in the empress' honor, Ekaterininskaya Square. Against the background of Russia's full-scale war against Ukraine since February 24, 2022, the monument was dismantled again in late December 2022. This happened after an online vote by Odesa residents and a decision by the local authorities in November, both in favor of removal. The city council announced that the monument would be transferred to the Odesa Fine Arts Museum.[9] The many questions this single example raises show how complex and varied a monument's history can be.

The waves of transformation of cities and the public memory expressed in them do not obey fixed chronological patterns and can be quite different, as, again, the example of Ukraine shows with its seemingly belated "Leninopad" (the "fall" of Lenin and other Communist-Soviet monuments) since 2014, followed by a "Pushkinopad" since spring 2022.[10] In the words of the Ukrainian historian Georgyi Kasianov, the "Lenin Fall" turned into a "Leninocide" in February 2014, at the peak of its second wave during the Euromaidan. Prior to 2022, Lenin and Stepan Bandera were the main protagonists of the "war of the monuments" in Ukraine.[11]

For the imperial city, this means that several layers of the imperial past itself and how it is approached can be unfolded. Different historical empires can be involved as is shown in the contributions to this volume by Aida Murtić on Sarajevo, Florian Riedler on Niš, Elke Hartmann on Kars, and Robert Born on Temeswar, who refer not only to the empires of the period they focus on but also to the predecessor empires. Several imperial histories intertwine in this way.

In studying historical layers of empires, one finds that there is not simply the imperial and the post-imperial. Recent research on imperial nostalgia and imperial cities has highlighted aspects of longevity and duration as opposed to this simple binary. Ann Stoler, whose work on "imperial formations" has greatly influenced the historiography of imperial and colonial contexts, maintains that the manifold relations between past and present do not come down to memory alone.[12] Her concept of *imperial duress* "undoes the very distinctions between imperial and post-imperial, colonial and post-colonial, past and present."[13] Jeremy F. Walton, who elaborates on these and other concepts, speaks of "modes of continuity, moments of duress, and ongoing effects of empire throughout former Habsburg and Ottoman lands,"[14] and this characterization is true for the territories of the former Russian Empire as well. In searching for new concepts to be used to study the crossroads of pasts and presents, Walton proposes the concept of "textured historicity." The textures, such as smooth, rough, or gritty, he explains, emerge at the "distinctive, embodied encounter between the subject in the present and the objects that convey the past in the present," thus highlighting the material and located nature of this encounter.[15]

Taking up these theoretical reflections, a recent strand of scholarship focuses on empire and nostalgia.[16] In the following paragraphs, I will elaborate on how to regard the imperial cities' past(s) and present(s) with attention to ambivalences, ambiguity, and nostalgia. Nothing seems to be unequivocal; instead, many imperial markers contain mixed messages. In this volume, Nilay Özlü shows this using the example of the imperial palaces, which after the collapse of the respective empires "conveyed ambiguous messages of history and patrimony" (p. 75).

The former Habsburg territories serve as a relatively well-studied example of the interrelations between nostalgia and urban imperial history. In some cases, the multi-ethnic past is being assessed and evaluated very positively, especially in cities with a (former) Jewish quarter like Lviv. Historians and expats/exiles can be important actors in this trend toward idealization.[17] The latter contrasts with the actual historical conflicts between Polish, Ukrainian, and Jewish population groups and the mutual observation and rivalry between the Russian Empire and the Habsburg Empire in the early twentieth century, as Elisabeth Haid-Lener shows in this volume.

City governments, marketing divisions, and businesspeople try to attract outside/foreign investment and tourists by referring to the (allegedly) peaceful and colorful diversity of ethnic and religious belongings. But imperial nostalgia in itself can be very ambivalent. Aspects of power relations and dependence are negotiated in seemingly harmless ways. This is vividly shown by Giulia Carabelli using the example of Trieste's city marketing strategies and coffeehouses.[18] Popular representations of Trieste as a nostalgic city which longs for the empire are widespread. In municipal activities like the staging of a "Kaiserfest" on the occasion of the centennial of Franz Joseph's death in November 2016, the nostalgia not only of Trieste citizens but also of Austrian tourists is used for commercial ends. (Austrian tourists make up the biggest part of tourism in the city.) At the same time, in such a staging and the accompanying statements, the former dependence of Trieste on Vienna is downplayed. Instead, the two cities are presented as partners or "sisters." The coffee houses represent an imperial narrative that is contradictory in itself: aesthetically, the Viennoise and Habsburg imperial style dominates while discursive representations stick to the Italian irredentism narrative.[19] The tension between imperial supranational and nationalist discourses and marketing strategies is surely typical for many imperial cities. In the case of Trieste, a central European perspective with the city as a commercial and trade hub is present, too.

Using the example of the Kaiserforum in Vienna, Miloš Jovanović directs our view to the nostalgic imperial framing of spatial assemblages.[20] In what he proposes calling "whitewashed empire," taking inspiration from studies on (post)colonialism and race, he examines "the redeployment of imperial structures through the preservation, renovation, and assemblage of material heritage." The author positions the "whitewashed empire" at the intersection of material and discursive constructions and highlights the need to approach imperial history and historicity critically. Reflecting the selected narratives and (exploitative) economic relations of the past, imperial nostalgia "extends the work of Habsburg spatial production into the present."[21] The Vienna Kaiserforum consists of the Neue Burg, Heldenplatz, Maria-Theresienplatz, the museums of Art History and Natural History, two equestrian statues, and the Museumsquartier. It is not unique in its imperial nostalgic character but in the multiplicity of its meanings. Tracing the history of the individual buildings' construction and usage, Jovanović shows how aristocratic dominance, displays of military prowess and might, bourgeois advancement, colonial exhibits, and colonial knowledge have merged to form the forum, a mixture enriched by modern architecture. In his reading, which can be seen as a counterpoint to superficial celebrations of imperial grandeur and multi-culturality, the inequalities of the past are preserved in the imperial assemblage. Today's visitors' gazes are directed to certain perspectives and views that reproduce imperial visions from the past – e.g., on the website of the Museumsquartier.[22] Through a certain visual language, the legacy of the empire is continued. It is the interplay of aesthetical-visual, discursive, and material aspects that makes Jovanović's research inspiring.

Both examples – the Trieste coffeehouses and marketing strategies and the "whitewashed" Vienna Kaiserforum – offer stimulating insights into the interaction between material heritage and discursive constructions; the tensions between the national, city specifics, and the imperial; and today's reproduction and upholding of imperial visions. It is these and other aspects that could be used productively in future research on imperial cities.

The Mastery of Nature and Infrastructure Perspectives

In some of the chapters in this volume, the mastering of nature, the usage of natural resources, and the existence or construction of urban infrastructure play a prominent role. In Born's piece on Temeswar, the transformation of landscapes and bodies of water is addressed, including the melioration of swamp areas and the regulation of the river Bega for transporting goods and supplying water. Nilay Özlü examines the imperial politics related to access to gardens and parks by the imperial families only and the public. And Olga Zabalueva delivers the fascinating example of the contemporary Zaryadye Park in Moscow that represents different "Russian" landscapes as a form of survey and exploitation of natural environments. As she explains, the "national myth" also contains imperial self-representation by referring to imperial expansion and the "colonizing" of space.

Lately, quite a lot of research has been done on environmental aspects of imperial expansion and colonial power relations, as in the case of cotton as a global commodity. The triangle of empires – environment – knowledge has received much attention.[23] But cities aren't necessarily the focus of this research. The imperial cities of the Eastern land-bound empires in particular have so far been studied little from environmental and infrastructure perspectives. This is a research gap as nature politics can tell us much about imperial legitimization and delegitimization, representation and the construction of grandeur, or very concrete urban needs and connections.

A notable exception is the history of St. Petersburg and Vienna and their rivers.[24] Interestingly, both cities and both rivers have been studied to some extent in the context of environmental history research; however, as Verena Winiwarter observes, "city-river interaction has received little attention."[25] As her research and an innovative and interdisciplinary project on the Danube and Vienna have shown, it can be fruitful to not only regard the river itself but water resources more broadly and the whole floodplain area. Destructive floods were a real threat to citizens and an important issue of city and state politics. Among the biggest flooding events were those in St. Petersburg in 1824 (and then again a hundred years later, in 1924) and in Vienna in 1830. These floods have been depicted in impressive poems and paintings and remain stable elements of the cities' collective memory.[26] Most prominently, Alexander Pushkin addressed the 1824 flood in his poem "The Bronze Horseman" (*Mednyi vsadnik*) written in 1830.

St. Petersburg's history is in any event a history of mastering "nature." Projected and planned as the new capital of the Russian Empire, its founder, Peter I, had to conquer the terrain very literally and transform mud into stable ground for construction. Many workers lost their lives in this ruthless effort. From the start, struggling against a nature perceived as hostile or reluctant was part of St. Petersburg's identity. Mastering nature contributed greatly to its imperial grandeur and signified the empire's performance.

At the city's center at first was not the emperor's palace but the Admiralty Building, the headquarters of the Admiralty Board and the Imperial Russian Navy. In the 1730s, the building was erected as a stone construction. In its center, a slim tower was erected with a gilded spire and a figure of a ship on its top. The tower with the ship has remained one of the iconic emblems of the city to this day. The Admiralty symbolized the might of the Navy and Russia's dominance over several seas. The admiralty shipyard was interesting in terms of water infrastructure as under its arches a network of canals existed which served to deliver all kinds of goods to the Admiralty. The importance of the Neva and other bodies of water for the establishment and existence of St. Petersburg can hardly be overestimated. The Neva and smaller rivers and canals became "something like the skeleton of the city's urban structure."[27]

The eighteenth and nineteenth centuries saw an intense and effortful transformation of St. Petersburg's water bodies. Among them were, for example, the conversion of the river Krivusha into the Ekaterininskii Canal, today Griboedov Canal, in the second half of the eighteenth century or the gradual construction of a network of bridges, first made of wood and later of steel and granite. A canal system served flood prevention. The hydrological engineering was by no means a purely Russian or inner-imperial enterprise. On invitation of the government, engineers from the Netherlands and Venice, and later many German and French ones, took part in the work. By the early twentieth century, technical institutes had been established in St. Petersburg and hydrological technologies could be exported abroad.[28] The modern face of St. Petersburg is characterized not least by its famous granite embankments that followed wooden piers during the nineteenth century. With their cool, stone monumentality they provided much nourishment for the "Petersburg text," the cultural universe of this imperial city.[29]

The history of the Danube and Vienna is very different. The imperial aspects of the city-river relationship, it seems, have been neglected so far, which is surprising given the fact that one of the empire's names was the "Danubian Monarchy." This said, it is not easy to talk of *the* river as Vienna today has four watercourses which are called the "Danube." In the past, the riverine landscape stretched out more than six kilometers wide. The "Old Danube" (*Alte Donau*) was the main channel until the 1870s but was situated some distance from the city itself. The "Danube Canal" (*Donaukanal*) was the main shipping route and essential for the city's food supplies. Until the late nineteenth century at least, fruit and vegetables were sold on the riversides directly from boats.[30] It was the main river arm until the early modern period, but the whole river system shifted northwards due to natural processes. The Danube Canal remained "the town's main and most vibrant river arm" until the great regulation was carried out between 1870 and 1875. The regulation created a new straight riverbed, which was a forceful intervention into existing ecosystems. Shipping and landing places were transferred to the new riverbed. The lands gained from securing territories from floods became an important factor in the fast growth and industrialization of Vienna.[31]

The interventions into the Danube in Vienna and immediate surroundings have been much more thoroughly studied than those on other stretches of the river. An Imperial Navigation Directorate was established in the early 1770s by Maria Theresa for the purpose of improving waterway transport and navigability. It was responsible for a stretch of the Danube about 1000 km long, between Engelhartszell, which was the border between Austria and Bavaria at that time, and Semlin/Zemun, the then Habsburg outpost on the border with the Ottoman Empire. Another specialized Habsburg authority, the Danube Regulation Commission, consisting of experts and stakeholders, undertook a systematic regulation of the river beginning in the 1820s, including the "correction" of channels, the cutting off of meanders, and the erection of flood protection dykes.[32] Austrian transformations of the river course reached into the Ottoman territories and represented an important arena of inter-imperial cooperation. The Ottoman Empire had its own logic of infrastructure policies which affected several cities, such as Ruse or Varna.[33]

This example of rivers and water infrastructure shows the potential of environmental and infrastructure history perspectives. Rivers were crucial for the delivery and disposal systems of the cities (food, wastewater) and for the trade of goods with other countries or regions. They were connectors within the empire between different regions. Rivers and other water bodies were arenas for international, including inter-imperial, conflict and cooperation, as is shown by inspiring works on Germany.[34] The mastery of nature in the shape of the rivers, which had long been perceived as uncontrolled, wild, and potentially dangerous (even if nurturing at the same time), was put in the context of imperial power and capability by contemporary elites. For legitimizing imperial power, the mastery of nature was an important element.

Segregation and Urban Spaces

Segregation and, more generally, socio-spatial differentiation in cities is a very broad phenomenon. Generally, it can be observed in any city at any historical time. The contributions to this volume do relate to socio-spatial differentiation, especially its ethnic and religious components. But there is some potential for further elaboration on this subject.

Ethnic, religious, and social segregation certainly was the standard in the continental empires' cities, and the ways this has played out needs both closer examination and broader generalizations. Inspiration for this can be taken from the spatial turn that has affected the urban history of Eastern Europe as well as from the theory and research on intersectionality. The aim is to show how imperial cities dealt with diversity in a spatial sense and how their inhabitants and authorities marked certain territories as "wealthy," "Muslim," etc. Diversity is not to be understood simply as a colorful, positively evaluated variety of forms, as it is often referred to nowadays by companies or universities. Instead, the study of historical diversity is and must be aware of the fact that diversity always implies not only inclusion but also exclusion.[35] It is one of the main challenges of empires to manage diversity and difference, and urban history can contribute greatly to studying which complex processes of participation and exclusion were at work.

Existing research on the Russian, Habsburg, and Ottoman Empires deals, on the one hand, with ethnic difference, estate and class, and (to a much lesser extent) gender. Studies on social, ethnic, and gender difference, however, are often not related to urban history, even if their empiric materials mostly stems from urban contexts. On the other hand, there is a strand of literature that nicely characterizes different urban spaces, but the results are more often than not confined to the individual city. Outspoken research on segregation – for example, in Vienna or Istanbul – is usually related to the last decades of the twentieth and the early twenty-first centuries only.[36] In the future, these three research trends should be connected more strongly.

Cities were (and still are) sites of segregation but also of encounters and mingling. In certain types of urban places, the representatives of different ethnic groups, confessions, and social strata met each other. In the bigger yards of apartment houses and on the city squares of St. Petersburg, for example, the ethnic and regional diversity of the imperial city became very apparent. Street traders selling their goods on the streets, in the yards, and at doors were a phenomenon that city politics have dealt with and tried (mostly unsuccessful) to combat since the city's foundation. A yard in Kolomna district, for example, was a "microcosm of the empire" for the working poor where street traders sold their goods – e.g., secondhand clothes offered by Tatar traders from Kazan.[37] Markets and bazaars were sites of intermingling in Ottoman cities as well. Markets were also socially coded. The self-identification of being part of the "poor people" in

St. Petersburg was, for example, spatially connected to the rather well-researched Hay Market (*Sennaia ploshchad'*).[38]

The interleaving of different categories of difference has to be seen as historically changing, especially during the nineteenth century with its profound and rapid economic and social changes partly induced or channeled by the big reform programs of the era. Influences from "Europe" or the West and the emergence of new kinds of public spheres were also important. Regarding the example of the Ottoman cities, Florian Riedler states that in newly-emerged urban spaces influenced by European culture such as parks or cafés, the religious borders became more porous while social status was important. At the same time, new kinds of communities and public spheres emerged, such as charity or education associations, which were based on religious and language differences. In the given political system, they tended to function as national minorities.[39] The synopsis of larger historical processes such as industrialization or migration with specific urban spaces can be very productive.

Inspiration for the study of segregation and stratification can also be taken from global history. A global history of segregation by Carl H. Nightingale concentrates on the USA and South Africa. The high time of the "segregation mania" he describes was in the first decades of the twentieth century.[40] Russia and the Soviet Union as well as the Habsburg and the Ottoman Empires are hardly mentioned in this book. And indeed, the strict segregation according to "race" realized in Johannesburg or Chicago does not seem to have played a major role in the continental empires' cities, although Tashkent's division into a "Russian" and an "Asian" part, for example, bears traits of it.[41] The canal Ankhor in Tashkent marked the dividing line. Typically, besides walls, fences, and gates, local natural features such as rivers or canals served as barriers between segregated city territories. But the dividing line in Tashkent was far from as strict as, for example, in Baltimore, where the simple crossing of the "color line" by black citizens could lead to harsh punishments.

While there might have been no "color lines" in the continental empires, one of the harshest and most well-known forms of segregation, the ghetto, was widespread in Central and Eastern Europe from the medieval and early modern periods. A ghetto can be defined as "the enforced spatial segregation of part of a population into a closed, demarcated space for habitation, work, and life."[42] It can also be characterized succinctly by three words: "compulsory, segregated, and enclosed."[43]

The ghetto as a concept and reality has served to maintain different kinds of hierarchies in cities and societies, including religious, social, and racial hierarchies. In the early modern period in Europe, the Jewish ghetto was not only a product of a Christian or Catholic struggle to maintain power or to aim for the Jews' conversion but can be seen as a response to rapid economic and demographic change as well as shifts in the real estate market, as demonstrated by Bernard Dov Cooperman in relation to the case of the early modern city of Kraków.[44] Existing research takes different perspectives, though, and differs greatly on some points, such as the question to what extent the ghetto allowed the strengthening of Jewish institutions.[45] Throughout the eighteenth and nineteenth centuries, the ghetto spread in Europe, including in the Habsburg Empire, but it never existed in the Ottoman Empire. The largest ghettos were in Frankfurt, Venice, Prague, and Trieste. Around 1900, in the wake of the Jewish struggle for enfranchisement, the Jewish ghetto became obsolete for a short period (but persisted as a self-reference and widespread notion for segregated spaces) before returning in different forms in the inter-war period of the twentieth century and, of course, in the National-Socialist dictatorship and occupation. The study of Jewish ghettos shows that, more often than not, several factors have to be taken into account, among them social, economic, racial, and religious.[46]

Among the economic factors, housing and related markets are crucial for urban segregation.[47] Early forms of gentrification took place around 1900, as Hans-Christian Petersen has observed in a comparison of St. Petersburg with Vienna and London. In St. Petersburg, housing prices exceeded even those of Berlin and other Central and Western European cities. Less affluent citizens moved from the very center – e.g., from Admiralteiskii District – to adjacent or less expensive districts like the Vasilievskii Island. Vienna, though very different in structure and history, also experienced gentrification at this time: the historical center developed into a city characterized by the provision of services where only high nobility and wealthy industrialists lived. Poor segments of the population were driven out of the city center and tended to live near the factories in the peripheral districts.[48]

The importance of real estate and land markets can also be confirmed when looking at the history of Chinese inhabitants in cities outside of China across the Pacific Rim. Be it in San Francisco, Singapore, or Vladivostok, the Chinese lived in central and very densely populated quarters at the beginning of the twentieth century, as in the case of the "Millionka" in Vladivostok, the biggest city in the Far East of the Russian Empire. Next to apartments, small rooms without windows were rented out; one house had 500 names on the entrance for 94 apartments. House owners, which in the case of Vladivostok were usually Europeans, earned a fortune with very high rents and by applying the principle of re-densification. City administrations condemned the lack of hygiene in the Chinese quarters but at the same time structurally neglected them and didn't integrate the Chinese population into urban health care systems.[49] It doesn't make much sense to hold "capitalism" in general responsible for segregation since it took very different forms in different countries and historical contexts. Instead, a promising question for further research is to what extent the general aversion by Russian governments and elites to "capitalism," which is often mixed with antisemitic stereotypes, has influenced the real estate business and city politics. In any case, the ongoing research on the Chinese quarters by Sören Urbansky shows how class and gender played out to define race in the context of anti-Chinese attitudes and stereotypes. The Chinese quarters' history sheds light on how the empire dealt with graded privileges for individual population groups in practice in an urban context, the global comparability of these phenomena, and the interactions between ethnic population groups across the empire's borders.

Next to class/social status, ethnic, and religious criteria, segregation by gender is important as gender is one of the main categories of difference both for cities' populations and for empires at large. Urban spaces and mechanisms of segregation often reflect general trends. By way of background, it should be noted that both fields – urban history and gender history – are not sufficiently interrelated in general, and especially not in the case of imperial cities. Nazan Maksudyan laments that "serious urban histories of the empire still suffer from the [...] male bias and usually remain silent about the female members of urban communities."[50] While she refers to the Ottoman Empire, this is generally true for the Russian and the Habsburg Empires as well.

Segregation by gender was not considered in relation to whole districts even though military institutions and workers' settlements and barracks in the early phase of industrialization were almost exclusively male territories. Gender-specific spaces were also smaller in scale. The female workers in St. Petersburg, for example, were not allowed to enter taverns (*traktiry*). Instead, they sat outside on the stairs and listened to the music coming from inside.[51] They were excluded from these spots of socialization so important for males, a case that clearly shows the reinforcement of two categories of discrimination – class and gender – in an intersectional sense.

In sum, the results of studies on segregation and housing should be more systematically related to ethnic and religious belongings, regional descent, gender, and age. The attention to small-scale stratification and specific urban spaces as yards or squares, as well as to different crossings and overlaps of categories of inequality and difference, can be used to study complex segregation processes. Even more attention should be paid to economic realities, especially the complex conditions and effects of the real estate and land markets. In the end, imperial cities offered spaces of encounters and approximation but also manifold mechanisms of segregation and exclusion. These urban constellations reflect the complex fabric of the empire that was subject to constant change.

Notes

1 Jeremy F. Walton, "Introduction: Textured Historicity and the Ambivalence of Imperial Legacies," *History and Anthropology* 30, no. 4 (2019), 353.

2 A pioneering work for the Russian-Soviet context is Orlando Figes and Boris Kolonickii, *Interpreting the Russian Revolution: The Language and Symbols of 1917* (New Haven, CT: Yale University Press, 1999).

3 G.R.F. Bursa, "Political Changes of Names of Soviet Towns," *The Slavonic and East European Review* 63, no. 2 (1985): 161–93.

4 An example of Soviet street names that were never in use by the local population is St. Petersburg's Gorokhovaya ulitsa, which was renamed Komissarovskaya ulitsa in 1918 and ulitsa Dzerzhinskogo in honor of Feliks Dzerzhinskii, founder of the Soviet secret police Tcheka, in 1927. The street was re-renamed Gorokhovaya ulitsa in 1991. In Kyiv, one of the most hotly debated street renamings was the renaming of Moscow Avenue (*Moskovs'kyj prospekt*) into Stepan Bandera Avenue (*prospekt Stepana Bandery*) in 2016. Gibfried Schenk, *Zwischen Sowjetnostalgie und "Entkommunisierung": Postsowjetische Geschichtspolitik und Erinnerungskultur in der Ukraine* (Erlangen: FAU University Press, 2020), 235–36.

5 In Tashkent, the capital of Uzbekistan, in the 1990s this was very much a top-down process characterized by the "halting search by the Uzbek political elite for new symbols of legitimacy." James Bell, "Redefining National Identity in Uzbekistan: Symbolic Tensions in Tashkent's Official Public Landscape," *Ecumene* 6, no. 2 (1999), 184.

6 Florian Hassel, "Hinter neuen Fassaden," *Süddeutsche Zeitung*, December 27, 2016, https://www.sueddeutsche.de/politik/mazedonien-hinter-neuen-fassaden-1.3311464.

7 Alev Çinar, "National History as a Contested Site: The Conquest of Istanbul and Islamist Negotiations of the Nation," *Comparative Studies in Society and History* 43, no. 2 (2001): 364–91, especially 388–89.

8 https://contestedhistories.org/resources/case-studies/catherine-the-great-monument-in-odessa/.

9 https://kyivindependent.com/news-feed/odesa-begins-dismantling-monument-to-russian-empress.

10 Wikipedia article "Demolition of monuments to Alexander Pushkin in Ukraine". https://en.wikipedia.org/wiki/Demolition_of_monuments_to_Alexander_Pushkin_in_Ukraine.

11 Heorhyi Kas'yanov [Georgiy Kasianov], *Past Continuous: Istorychna Polityka 1980-kh - 2000-kh: Ukrayina ta Susidy* (Kyiv: Laurus, 2018), 261. Georgiy Kasianov, "How a War for the Past Becomes a War in the Present," *Kritika: Explorations in Russian and Eurasian History* 16, no. 1 (2015), 154.

12 Ann L. Stoler, *Duress: Imperial Durabilities in Our Times* (Durham, NC: Duke University Press, 2016).

13 Walton, "Introduction: Textured Historicity," 3.

14 Ibid, 8.

15 Ibid, 5.

16 See earlier important contributions: Renato Rosaldo, "Imperialist Nostalgia," *Representations* 26 (1989); Svetlana Boym, *The Future of Nostalgia* (New York: Basic Books, 2001); Berny Sèbe and Matthew G. Stanard, eds., *Decolonising Europe? Popular Responses to the End of Empire, Empires and the Making of the Modern World, 1650–2000* (London: Routledge, 2020).

17 See Delphine Bechtel, "Von Lemberg Nach L'viv: Gedächtniskonflikte in einer Stadt an der Grenze," *Osteuropa* 58, no. 6 (2008): 211–27.

18 Giulia Carabelli, "Habsburg Coffeehouses in the Shadow of the Empire: Revisiting Nostalgia in Trieste," *History and Anthropology* 30, no. 4 (2019): 382–92.

19 See the telling history of the Café San Marco, ibid, 385.

20 Miloš Jovanović, "Whitewashed Empire: Historical Narrative and Place Marketing in Vienna," *History and Anthropology* 30, no. 4 (2019): 460–76.

21 Ibid, 460.

22 Ibid, 461, 467.

23 For an overview, see Jonas van der Straeten and Ute Hasenöhrl, "Connecting the Empire: New Research Perspectives on Infrastructures and the Environment in the (Post)Colonial World," *NTM Zeitschrift für Geschichte der Wissenschaften, Technik und Medizin* 24 (2016): 355–91.

24 Regarding Istanbul, the Bosporus would be interesting to analyze in comparison.

25 Verena Winiwarter, Martin Schmid, and Gert Dressel, "Looking at Half a Millennium of Co-Existence: The Danube in Vienna as a Socio-Natural Site," *Water History*, no. 5 (2013): 104.

26 See the visuals in the online exhibition "'Commanding, Sovereign Stream': The Neva and the Viennese Danube in the History of Imperial Metropolitan Centers" by Gertrud Haidvogl, Alexei Kraikovski, and Julia Lajus on the "Environment & Society Portal" of the Rachel Carson Center, Virtual Exhibitions 1/2019, https://www.environmentandsociety.org/exhibitions/neva-and-danube-rivers/rivers-and-cities-brief-introduction.

27 Ibid.

28 Ibid.

29 Just two examples of studies on the Petersburg text: Iurii M. Lotman, "Simvolika Peterburga i problemy semiotiki goroda," in *Izbrannye stat'i v trekh tomakh: Stat'i po istorii russkoi literatury XVIII – pervoi poloviny XIX veka*, vol. 2 (Tallinn: Aleksandra, 1992), 9–21. Grigorii Z. Kaganov, *Images of Space: St. Petersburg in the Visual and Verbal Arts* (Stanford, CA: Stanford University Press, 1997).

30 https://www.environmentandsociety.org/exhibitions/neva-and-danube-rivers/rivers-and-cities-brief-introduction.

31 Ibid; Verena Winiwarter et al., "The Environmental History of the Danube River Basin as an Issue of Long-Term Socio-Ecological Research," in *Long Term Socio-Ecological Research: Studies in Society-Nature Interactions Across Spatial and Temporal Scales*, ed. S. Singh et al. (Dordrecht: Springer, 2013), 103–22.

32 Winiwarter, "The Environmental History of the Danube," 114.

33 Florian Riedler, "Integrating the Danube into Modern Networks of Infrastructure: The Ottoman Contribution," *Journal of Balkan and Black Sea Studies* 3, no. 5 (2020): 97–120; Constantin Iordachi, "Global Networks, Regional Hegemony, and Seaport Modernization on the Lower Danube," in *Cities of the Mediterranean: From the Ottomans to the Present Day*, ed. Biray Kolluoğlu and Meltem Toksöz, (London: I.B. Tauris, 2010), 157–82.

34 David Blackbourn, *The Conquest of Nature: Water, Landscape and the Making of Modern Germany* (London: Cape, 2006); Christoph Bernhardt, *Im*

Spiegel des Wassers: Eine transnationale Umweltgeschichte des Oberrheins (1800–2000) (Cologne: Böhlau, 2016).

35 See Moritz Florin, Victoria Gutsche, and Natalie Krentz, eds., *Diversität historisch: Repräsentationen und Praktiken gesellschaftlicher Differenzierung im Wandel* (Bielefeld: transcript, 2018).

36 As examples: Melih M. Pinarcioğlu and Oğuz Işik, "Segregation in Istanbul: Patterns and Processes," *Tijdschrift voor Economische en Sociale Geografie* 100, no. 4 (2009); Ela Ataç, "Segregation in Istanbul: Measuring Segregation in an Ever-Changing City," *Social Space* 9, no. 1 (2015); Gerhard Hatz, Josef Kohlbacher, and Ursula Reeger, "Socio-Economic Segregation in Vienna: A Social-Oriented Approach to Urban Planning and Housing," in *Socio-Economic Segregation in European Capital Cities: East Meets West*, ed. Tiit Tammaru et al. (London: Routledge, 2016), 80–109.

37 Hans-Christian Petersen, *An den Rändern der Stadt? Soziale Räume der Armen in St. Petersburg (1850–1914)* (Vienna: Böhlau, 2019), 316–17; quotation 97.

38 Ibid, 352; Hubertus F. Jahn, "Der St. Petersburger Heumarkt im 19. Jahrhundert: Metamorphosen eines Stadtviertels," *Jahrbücher für Geschichte Osteuropas* 44, no. 2 (1996): 162–77.

39 Florian Riedler, "Segregation oder Gemeinschaftliches Zusammenleben? Vom Umgang mit Vielfalt in der Osmanischen Stadt," *Moderne Stadtgeschichte*, no. 1 (2018), 51–52.

40 Carl H. Nightingale, *Segregation: A Global History of Divided Cities*, Historical Studies of Urban America (Chicago, IL: University of Chicago Press, 2012), 3.

41 Jeff Sahadeo, *Russian Colonial Society in Tashkent, 1865–1923* (Bloomington: Indiana University Press, 2007).

42 Wendy Z. Goldman and Joe W. Trotter, "Introduction: The Ghetto Made and Remade," in *The Ghetto in Global History, 1500 to the Present*, ed. Wendy Z. Goldman and Joe W. Trotter (New York: Routledge, 2018), 1.

43 Referring to Benjamin Ravid, ibid, 2.

44 Bernard D. Cooperman, "The Early Modern Ghetto: A Study in Urban Real Estate," in *The Ghetto in Global History, 1500 to the Present*, ed. Wendy Z. Goldman and Joe W. Trotter (New York: Routledge, 2018), 57–73.

45 Goldman and Trotter, "Introduction," 12–13.

46 See ibid, 4.

47 Nightingale addresses "the modern capitalist real estate industry" as one of three sets of institutions crucial for urban segregation, next to governments and intellectual networks; Nightingale, *Segregation*, 5.

48 Hans-Christian Petersen, "Gentrifizierung in historischer Perspektive? Aufwertung und Verdrängung in St. Petersburg, Wien und London (1850–1914)," in *Arm und Reich: Zur gesellschaftlichen und wirtschaftlichen Ungleichheit in der Geschichte*, ed. Günther Schulz (Stuttgart: Steiner, 2015), 188–89, 197–98.

49 The initial research results were presented by Sören Urbansky at the global history colloquium at FAU Erlangen-Nürnberg on February 2, 2021.

50 Nazan Maksudyan, "Feminist Perspectives on Ottoman Urban History," *Moderne Stadtgeschichte*, no. 1 (2018): 30.

51 Petersen, *An den Rändern*, 78–79.

Bibliography

Ataç, Ela. "Segregation in Istanbul: Measuring Segregation in an Ever-Changing City." *Social Space* 9, no. 1 (2015): 1–28.

Bechtel, Delphine. "Von Lemberg Nach L'viv: Gedächtniskonflikte in einer Stadt an der Grenze." *Osteuropa* 58, no. 6 (2008): 211–27.

Bell, James. "Redefining National Identity in Uzbekistan: Symbolic Tensions in Tashkent's Official Public Landscape." *Ecumene* 6, no. 2 (1999): 183–13.

Bernhardt, Christoph. *Im Spiegel des Wassers: Eine transnationale Umweltgeschichte des Oberrheins (1800–2000)*. Cologne: Böhlau, 2016.

Blackbourn, David. *The Conquest of Nature: Water, Landscape and the Making of Modern Germany*. London: Cape, 2006.

Boym, Svetlana. *The Future of Nostalgia*. New York: Basic Books, 2001.

Bursa, G.R.F. "Political Changes of Names of Soviet Towns." *The Slavonic and East European Review* 63, no. 2 (1985): 161–93.

Carabelli, Giulia. "Habsburg Coffeehouses in the Shadow of the Empire: Revisiting Nostalgia in Trieste." *History and Anthropology* 30, no. 4 (2019): 382–92.

Çinar, Alev. "National History as a Contested Site: The Conquest of Istanbul and Islamist Negotiations of the Nation." *Comparative Studies in Society and History* 43, no. 2 (2001): 364–91.

Cooperman, Bernard D. "The Early Modern Ghetto: A Study in Urban Real Estate." In *The Ghetto in Global History, 1500 to the Present*, edited by Wendy Z. Goldman and Joe W. Trotter, 57–73. New York: Routledge, 2018.

Figes, Orlando, and Boris Kolonickii. *Interpreting the Russian Revolution: The Language and Symbols of 1917*. New Haven, CT: Yale University Press, 1999.

Florin, Moritz, Victoria Gutsche, and Natalie Krentz, eds. *Diversität historisch: Repräsentationen und Praktiken gesellschaftlicher Differenzierung im Wandel*. Bielefeld: transcript, 2018.

Goldman, Wendy Z., and Joe W. Trotter. "Introduction: The Ghetto Made and Remade." In *The Ghetto in Global History, 1500 to the Present*, edited by Wendy Z. Goldman and Joe William Trotter, 1–20. New York: Routledge, 2018.

Hatz, Gerhard, Josef Kohlbacher, and Ursula Reeger. "Socio-Economic Segregation in Vienna: A Social-Oriented Approach to Urban Planning and Housing." In *Socio-Economic Segregation in European Capital Cities: East Meets West*, edited by Tiit Tammaru et al., 80–109. London: Routledge, 2016.

Iordachi, Constantin. "Global Networks, Regional Hegemony, and Seaport Modernization on the Lower Danube." In *Cities of the Mediterranean: From the Ottomans to the Present Day*, edited by Biray Kolluoğlu and Meltem Toksöz, 157–82. London: I.B. Tauris, 2010.

Jahn, Hubertus F. "Der St. Petersburger Heumarkt im 19. Jahrhundert: Metamorphosen eines Stadtviertels." *Jahrbücher für Geschichte Osteuropas* 44, no. 2 (1996): 162–77.

Jovanović, Miloš. "Whitewashed Empire: Historical Narrative and Place Marketing in Vienna." *History and Anthropology* 30, no. 4 (2019): 460–76.

Kaganov, Grigorii Z.: *Images of Space: St. Petersburg in the Visual and Verbal Arts*. Stanford, CA: Stanford University Press, 1997.

Kasianov, Georgiy [Kas'yanov, Heorhyi]. "How a War for the Past Becomes a War in the Present." *Kritika: Explorations in Russian and Eurasian History* 16, no. 1 (2015): 149–55.

Kas'yanov, Heorhyi [Kasianov, Georgyi], *Past Continuous: Istorychna Polityka 1980-kh -2000-kh: Ukrayina ta Susidy*. Kyiv: Laurus, 2018.

Kolluoğlu, Biray, and Meltem Toksöz, eds. *Cities of the Mediterranean: From the Ottomans to the Present Day*. London: I.B. Tauris, 2010.

Lotman, Iurii M. "Simvolika Peterburga i problemy semiotiki goroda." In *Iz-brannye stat'i v trekh tomakh: Stat'i po istorii russkoi literatury XVIII – pervoi poloviny XIX veka*, vol. 2, 9–21. Tallinn: Aleksandra, 1992.

Maksudyan, Nazan. "Feminist Perspectives on Ottoman Urban History." *Moderne Stadtgeschichte*, no. 1 (2018): 26–38.

Nightingale, Carl H. *Segregation: A Global History of Divided Cities*. Historical Studies of Urban America. Chicago, IL: University of Chicago Press, 2012.

Petersen, Hans-Christian. "Gentrifizierung in historischer Perspektive? Aufwertung und Verdrängung in St. Petersburg, Wien und London (1850–1914)." In *Arm und Reich: Zur gesellschaftlichen und wirtschaftlichen Ungleichheit in der Geschichte*, edited by Günther Schulz, 177–206. Stuttgart: Steiner, 2015.

———. *An den Rändern der Stadt? Soziale Räume der Armen in St. Petersburg (1850–1914)*. Vienna: Böhlau, 2019.

Pinarcioğlu, Melih M., and Oğuz Işik. "Segregation in Istanbul: Patterns and Processes." *Tijdschrift voor Economische en Sociale Geografie* 100, no. 4 (2009): 469–84.

Riedler, Florian. "Segregation oder gemeinschaftliches Zusammenleben? Vom Umgang mit Vielfalt in der osmanischen Stadt." *Moderne Stadtgeschichte*, no. 1 (2018): 39–52.

———. "Integrating the Danube into Modern Networks of Infrastructure: The Ottoman Contribution." *Journal of Balkan and Black Sea Studies* 3, no. 5 (2020): 97–120.

Rosaldo, Renato. "Imperialist Nostalgia." *Representations* 26 (1989): 107–22.

Sahadeo, Jeff. *Russian Colonial Society in Tashkent, 1865–1923*. Bloomington: Indiana University Press, 2007.

Schenk, Gibfried. *Zwischen Sowjetnostalgie und 'Entkommunisierung': Postsowjetische Geschichtspolitik und Erinnerungskultur in der Ukraine*. PhD diss., Erlangen: FAU University Press, 2020.

Schulz, Günther, ed. *Arm und Reich: Zur gesellschaftlichen und wirtschaftlichen Ungleichheit in der Geschichte*. Stuttgart: Steiner, 2015.

Sèbe, Berny, and Matthew G. Stanard, eds. *Decolonising Europe? Popular Responses to the End of Empire*. London: Routledge, 2020.

Singh, Simron Jit, ed. *Long Term Socio-Ecological Research. Studies in Society-Nature Interactions Across Spatial and Temporal Scales*. Human-Environment Interactions. Dordrecht: Springer, 2013.

Stoler, Ann L. *Duress: Imperial Durabilities in Our Times*. Durham, NC: Duke University Press, 2016.

Tammaru, Tiit, Szymon Marcinczak, Marten van Ham, and Sako Musterd, eds. *Socio-Economic Segregation in European Capital Cities: East Meets West*. London: Routledge, 2016.

van der Straeten, Jonas, and Ute Hasenöhrl. "Connecting the Empire: New Research Perspectives on Infrastructures and the Environment in the (Post)Colonial World." *NTM Zeitschrift für Geschichte der Wissenschaften, Technik und Medizin* 24 (2016): 355–91.

Walton, Jeremy F. "Introduction: Textured Historicity and the Ambivalence of Imperial Legacies." *History and Anthropology* 30, no. 4 (2019): 353–65.

Winiwarter, Verena, Martin Schmid, and Gert Dressel. "Looking at Half a Millennium of Co-Existence: The Danube in Vienna as a Socio-Natural Site." *Water History*, no. 5 (2013): 101–19.

Winiwarter, Verena, Martin Schmid, Severin Hohensinner, and Gertrud Haidvogl. "The Environmental History of the Danube River Basin as an Issue of Long-Term Socio-Ecological Research." In *Long Term Socio-Ecological Research. Studies in Society-Nature Interactions Across Spatial and Temporal Scales*, ed. by Simron Jit Singh, 103–22. Dordrecht: Springer, 2013.

Name Index

Place Name Index

Note: *Italic* page numbers refer to figures and page numbers followed by "n" denote endnotes.

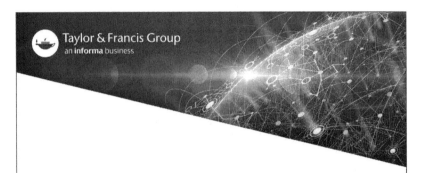

Printed in Great Britain
by Amazon

54722024R00220